INTRODUCTION TO COUNSELING

Integration of Faith, Professional Identity, and Clinical Practice

Robyn Trippany Simmons, Ed.D. • Stacey Custer Lilley, Ph.D. • Anita Knight Kuhnley, Ph.D.

Kendall Hunt
publishing company

This book is not intended as a substitute for the medical advice of physicians or other clinicians. The reader should regularly consult a physician or clinician in matters relating to his/her health or the health of another; and particularly with respect to any symptoms that may require diagnosis or medical/clinical attention.

Kendall Hunt
publishing company

www.kendallhunt.com
Send all inquiries to:
4050 Westmark Drive
Dubuque, IA 52004-1840

Copyright © 2020 by Robyn Simmons, Stacey Lilley, and Anita Kuhnley

ISBN 978-1-5249-9697-0

Published in the United States of America

CONTENTS

Foundations of Professional Identity: Counseling in Practice

Foundations of Professional Identity: Looking to the Future

EDITOR BIOGRAPHIES

Robyn Trippany Simmons, Ed.D., LPC-S (AL), NCC, RPT-S is Professor of Counseling in the CACREP accredited Clinical Mental Health Counseling program at Liberty University. Dr. Simmons received her Ed.D. in Counselor Education from the University of Alabama in 2001 and has been a practicing counselor since 1996. Her research and clinical interests include sexual trauma, vicarious trauma, play therapy, and professional identity issues. Dr. Simmons publishes and presents locally, regionally, nationally, and internationally on play therapy, creative approaches to therapy and clinical supervision, counselor education, and trauma counseling.

© Brett Hartley

Stacey Lilley, Ph.D., LPC-S (VA) is Assistant Professor and Program Director of a CACREP accredited, M.A. Clinical Mental Health Counseling program at Liberty University. Dr. Lilley earned her undergraduate from Longwood University and her graduate degrees from Virginia Tech; she began her career as a school counselor. After 8 years she transitioned to Director of Counseling and wellness at a medical college. Dr. Lilley was able to pursue her research interests in effective teams and wellness. She enjoys presenting at conferences, supervision, growing counselor identity, and team research. Dr. Lilley sees a few clients weekly to remain active in the field; her individual practice focuses on improving mental health issues, individual wellness, and family unity.

© Brett Hartley

Anita Knight Kuhnley, Ph.D. is a licensed professional counselor (LPC) in the state of Virginia and an Associate Professor of Counseling in Regent University's School of Psychology and Counseling. Kuhnley earned her doctorate in Counselor Education and Supervision from Regent University. Kuhnley is certified as a highly reliable coder of the Adult Attachment Interview (AAI) through Mary Main and Eric Hesse's UC Berkeley AAI coder certification program and is the co-author of several books including *Redeeming Attachment* and *Research Based Counseling Skills*. Her most recent book is *The Mister Rogers Effect*, which unpacks the psychological secrets Mister Rogers used to reach his television neighbors. You can find out more about her via her website: https://dranitakuhnley.com/books/

© Brett Hartley

AUTHOR BIOGRAPHIES

Dr. Andrea Barbian earned her Ph.D. in Counselor Education and Supervision from University of the Cumberlands and her M.A. in Professional Counseling from Liberty University. She is a Licensed Professional Counselor in North Carolina and a National Certified Counselor (NCC). Dr. Barbian has research interests related to counselor education and supervision, eating disorders, and first responders and is a member of many professional organizations and associations.

© Andrea Barbian

Dr. Capri Brooks is a professor of Counselor Education at Liberty University. Prior to becoming a counselor educator in 2014, Brooks spent time working in both clinical counseling and school counseling where she specialized in children and adolescents. Dr. Brooks serves as the head of the women's ministry at her church and serves as volunteer counselor at a local school. Dr. Brooks is a National Certified Counselor and a National Certified School Counselor, a Licensed Professional Counselor-Supervisor, and a Licensed School Counselor in Mississippi.

© Tate Tullier

David R. Brown, PhD, LPCC-S, LCDC-III, NCC, ACS is a professor in the Department of Counselor Education & Family Studies at Liberty University. Professionally active in several regional and national counseling organizations and currently serving on the Board of Directors for the Greater Cincinnati Counseling Association, he presents regularly at state, regional, and national conferences. His research interests include the assessment of spirituality and religiosity, counseling pedagogy, and the use of technology in counseling.

© Dustin Clark

© Brandi Chamberlin

Dr. Brandi Chamberlin is a Department Chair for Counselor Education and Family Studies department at Liberty University. She received her Ph.D. in Counselor Education and Supervision from Liberty University and received a Masters of Arts in Counseling from Cincinnati Christian University. She has worked in many clinical settings including intensive in-home therapy, drug and alcohol rehabilitation, and psychiatric inpatient. Her primary research interests are counselor identity, attachment, multicultural issues, and trauma. She currently serves on the board of the Virginia Association of Counselor Education and Supervision.

© April Crable

April R. Crable specializes in teletherapy, crisis and trauma and counseling, substance abuse, ethics, and sex offender treatment. She has been a distance educator for ten years. Dr. Crable is currently a professor at Liberty University in the Counselor Education and Family Studies Department. Dr. Crable is also the President and CEO of Fruition Counseling and Consulting Services, LLC. The practice specializes in providing teletherapy services. Dr. Crable has worked in the mental health field for over a decade providing services to various populations. She is a Licensed Professional Counselor in the states of Arizona, Florida, Virginia, Texas, and New York. Additionally, she is both a Certified Substance Abuse Counselor and Sex Offender Treatment Provider in the state of Virginia. Her research and teaching interests include field experience, ethics, crisis and trauma, and distance counseling and supervision.

© Randall Davis

Jama Davis, PhD, LMHC (IN), LPC (NC), NCC is an Associate Professor and Core Faculty member in the Center for Counselor Education and Family Studies at Liberty University. She has been actively involved in the counseling profession as a counselor, supervisor and professor for over 30 years. Her work has led her to counsel and teach internationally, most recently training lay counselors and attorneys in Rwanda. She has made numerous conference presentations and published for professional associations.

© Mark Myers

Dr. Mary Deacon has specialized in counseling research and career counseling. Dr. Deacon was also part of a research team focusing on middle and high school career development and presented research findings at national conferences. Her teaching and research interests include the areas of girls' and women's career development, gender equity, and multicultural competency.

Nivischi N. Edwards, PhD, LMHC, LPC, NCC, BC-TMH, is a Core Faculty member of the Department of Counselor Education and Family Studies at Liberty University. She researches and presents on Black female faculty success; race and mental health including the impact of microaggression on persons of color. Her teaching and research interests include marriage and family therapy and healthy relationships – including relationships with self and others.

© Adam Dean

Dr. Kristy Ford is a Licensed Mental Health Counselor specializing in clinical supervision and counseling research. Her clinical experience includes private practice, pastoral counseling, managed care, and community based care. Her research has focused on the use of spiritual interventions in counseling and multicultural issues related to religious accommodation of mindfulness practice in treatment, and she has presented research findings at national conferences. Her continued research and teaching interests include the integration of spirituality and effective counseling practice, mindfulness practice, attachment-based treatments, and neuroscience.

© Jake Ford

Dr. Patricia Hinkley is a professor in the Department of Counselor Education & Family Studies at Liberty University. In addition, she has been actively involved in various administrative roles for Liberty including Executive Director of LU's Distance Program, Associate Dean, and Department Chair. Dr. Hinkley is also a Licensed Professional Counselor, a Licensed Marriage and Family Therapist, and a Nationally Certified Counselor. She practiced as a professional counselor for 19 years with Light Counseling Associates in Lynchburg, Virginia.

© Tom Hinkley

Vasti P. Holstun, Ph.D., LPC, NCC, NCSC, is an assistant professor in the Counselor Education and Family Studies department at Liberty University. She has conducted research and written on supervision in counseling, specifically on providing positive and corrective feedback. She has also written and published on school counseling topics, advocating for supporting mental health in school settings. Prior to becoming a counselor educator, Dr. Holstun was a school counselor for 16 years. She continues to provide counseling to children, adolescents, and adults in private practice. Dr. Holstun presents at state and national conferences on spirituality in counseling, mental health in schools, and counseling supervision.

© Vasti Holstun

© Kevin Hull

Dr. Kevin Hull is an Assistant Professor of Counseling with Liberty University and owns and operates Hull and Associates, P.A. a private practice in Lakeland, Florida. Dr. Hull is a licensed counselor who has worked with children and adolescents and their families on the Autism spectrum since 2001. He conducts weekly individual and group therapy sessions with children, adolescents, young adults, and families. Dr. Hull has written multiple books book chapters on counseling neuro-atypical children and using technology in counseling. Dr. Hull specializes in using electronic devices in play therapy, specifically the use of video/computer games as a play therapy tool with children with emotional difficulties.

© John King

Dr. John A. King serves as Assistant Professor of Counseling at Liberty University. He is a 2013 PhD graduate of Regent University, as well as a Licensed Professional Counselor in Pennsylvania. He resides in Mechanicsburg, Pennsylvania where he is also an ordained pastor (part-time) at Mechanicsburg Brethren in Christ Church. As the father of nine children, he and his wife, Cindy are strong orphan care advocates and are co-directors of Victorious Hope Adoption Consulting, LLC.

© Sabrina Walsh

Summer Perhay Kuba, Ph.D., Ed.S., MSW, is an assistant professor at Liberty University. She has written on school counseling topics including assessments, the MTSS process, and student mindsets. She has diverse counseling experience working with children/students ranging from toddlerhood to the college level. In addition, Dr. Kuba served as the Chair of the Board of Directors for the Florida School Counselor Association in 2016 and continues to serve as their advocacy chair. Dr. Kuba actively presents at state and national conferences and continues to seek out opportunities to advocate for students, school counselors, and the profession

© Brett Hartley

Edward John Kuhnley, MD is an Adjunct Clinical Assistant Professor of Psychiatry at the Liberty University College of Osteopathic Medicine, Department of Primary Care in Lynchburg, VA. He is in active practice of child, adolescent, and adult psychiatry. Dr. Kuhnley completed medical school at the University of Virginia School of Medicine in Charlottesville, VA, followed by a general psychiatry residency at the Eastern Virginia Graduate School of Medicine and a child psychiatry fellowship at the Yale University Child Study Center in New Haven, CT. He is board certified in adult as well as child and adolescent psychiatry. He has published articles and given presentations throughout the US and in the UK.

Arleezah Marrah Ph.D., is a Core Faculty member of the Department of Counselor Education and Family Studies at Liberty University. She specializes in counseling and trauma. Dr. Marrah has presented research on racial trauma and research mentorship for Black women in doctoral programs. Her teaching and research interests include the areas of racial trauma, racial minorities experiences in higher education, standardized testing, academic self-efficacy, and play therapy.

© Michael Owens

Jill Schwirzer, MA, LPC, is currently pursuing a doctorate in Counselor Education and Supervision (CES) from Liberty University, a professional counselor, author, world-traveled speaker and director of Abide Counseling Network, a faith-based counseling group, and Project Safe Church, a faith-based abuse prevention and response initiative. Jennifer has trained scores of counselors and coaches in biblical mental health principles.

© Adam Dean

Gary A. Sibcy II, Ph.D. is a professor of Counselor Education and Supervision and has educated, trained, and supervised counselors for over 15 years. Dr. Sibcy has a broad range of research and clinical interests, including the assessment and treatment of childhood disorders, anxiety and trauma disorders, and personality disorders. He also has an interest in the integration of religious beliefs in clinical practice. His current research interests focus on developing and disseminating empirically supported treatments for both children and adults. Dr. Sibcy writes, speaks, and consults nationally and internationally.

© Wolf Creek Photography

Dr. Yulanda Tyre received her PhD in Counselor Education from Auburn University. She currently serves Liberty University as a Professor in Counselor Education and Family Studies. She is a Nationally Board Certified and State Licensed Counselor and Supervisor. She is Past-President for the Alabama Association for Counselor Educators and Supervisors, Past-President of the Alabama College Counseling Association, the current Chair of Current Issues and Trends for the Alabama Counseling Association Board. She has extensive experience in student affairs, has served as Assistant Vice Chancellor Student Affairs for over 10 years. Dr. Tyre has presented at the local, state and international level on Counselor Wellness and Counselor Resilience.

© Felix Tyre

© Amanda Farrell

Dr. Kevin Van Wynsberg Ph.D., is an associate professor at Liberty University, where he has served in a variety of capacities since 2007, including as associate dean of the Department of Counselor Education and Supervision. He has clinical experience working as an in-home counseling, a Christian outpatient counselor, as well as a counselor in an outpatient hospital setting. He has taught a variety of courses in biblical counseling, undergraduate psychology, and graduate professional counseling. His research interests include online education and retention as well as the integration of counseling and Christianity.

© Toni Arauza

Christina Villarreal-Davis, Ph.D., is a Licensed Professional Counselor and Supervisor (LPC-S), Registered Play Therapist and Supervisor (RPT-S), and National Certified Counselor (NCC). She served as an Assistant Professor in the Department of Counselor Education and Family Studies at Liberty University. She specializes in Child-Centered Play Therapy, expressive arts therapies, Cognitive Behavioral Therapy, and incorporating neuroscience-informed approaches in working with clients who have experienced trauma. has published on play therapy, expressive arts therapies, and helping women overcome perinatal loss.

© Steven Yeoh

Jerry Vuncannon, Jr., PhD, LPC (NC), NCC is Assistant Professor of Graduate Counseling in the Department of Counselor Education and Family Studies with Liberty University. He has worked in counselor education since 2006 with the last 7 years in full-time capacity and often presents at conferences. His counseling interests in multicultural work, international counseling, spiritual integration, attachment theory, and group work. His involvement in international counseling includes counseling-related endeavors in Singapore, Malaysia, Cambodia, South Africa, Mexico, and China. He lives in Singapore full-time with his beautiful wife Stephanie.

PREFACE

One day, in a meeting with several faculty, I (Robyn) made the comment that it would be great if there was a textbook that had both an introduction to the profession and faith integration. One of my colleagues (Stacey) indicated that she would like to write this textbook with me. Another colleague (Anita), who has published several books, also indicated a desire to work on this textbook idea. We were **not** trying to create something that was BETTER than other textbooks. There are some ***really*** great introduction to counseling textbooks in circulation. What we were looking to create is something that would help students understand how to be and think like an *ethically responsible Counselor who is also a Christian* and sought an education which included a Christian worldview. Because not all students who seek a Christian education desire to practice counseling in a Christian setting, this textbook is not focused on training Christian counselors. Rather, it is focused on training future Professional Counselors who want to understand how to be true to their faith without imposing values on clients.

In this textbook, we want to introduce you to what it means to be a professional counselor, the roles and functions included in being a professional counselor, as well as the historical antecedents, current trends, and future outlook of the profession. When you complete this text you should have a clear idea of how your role is complementary and distinct from other professionals, what you uniquely bring to the counseling profession, and an understanding of how to integrate your identity as a Christian into the profession.

We see your development of becoming a counselor as akin to being on a journey. You will walk with others on this journey. Initially, you will start out walking with your professors who will pour into you, helping you develop counseling identity, skills, and knowledge. You will then walk with supervisors and colleagues as you also walk alongside clients on their journey to find mental health. On this scenic route to becoming a counselor, we may realize we need to do some of our own work, and sometimes see that our clients want to take a circuitous route. However, the efforts will lead you to the final destination of helping others.

It is our prayer that, in reading this textbook, you will be energized and inspired about your own development and professional identity as a future counselor.

"God said, "My presence will go with you. I'll see the journey to the end."
Exodus 33:14 The Message (MSG)

ORIENTATION TO THE TEXTBOOK

When we decided to pursue writing this textbook, we were not sure if we wanted to write each chapter collectively or if we wanted to create an edited textbook, drawing from the expertise and passions of our colleagues. As we discussed the pros and cons of either choice, we realized that the voices of our colleagues could provide a depth that would be missing if only the three of us wrote each word. Thus, we prayed over the selection of potential authors for whom we would ask to write specific chapters. What resulted is a text that pulls from the professional wisdom and rich resources of beloved colleagues.

This 14 chapter book is designed to address CACREP standards related to Professional Identity. We conceptualize the chapters falling into 4 main categories of foundational information about professional identity: Who We Are and What We Do, Spiritual and Ethical Cornerstones, Counseling in Practice, and Looking to the Future. Chapters 1-3 fall discuss who we are and what we do. In Chapter 1, we cover the historical roots and current happenings in the profession. Chapter 2 introduces you to the elements that make up professional identity. In Chapter 3, we look at the various settings, roles, and specializations for which counselors can work. In Chapters 4-7, you will learn more about spiritual and ethical cornerstones of the ethical and integrated professional identity. Chapter 4 introduces you to a Christian integration model, which is based in ethical practices. In Chapter 5, you will learn about foundational values of respect for diversity, cultural humility, and being and advocate. Chapter 6 focuses on ethics and legal considerations in counseling. Chapter 7 introduces you to counselor impairment and counselor wellness. In considering the practical applications of counseling, you will encounter Chapters 8–12. Chapter 8 focuses on the counseling relationship. In Chapter 9, you will learn about Counseling Skills. Chapter 10, you will explore the theoretical models in counseling. Chapter 11 introduces you to the concept of assessment and diagnosis. Chapter 12 focuses on helping counselors understand and apply research. Chapters 13 and 14 comprise the final category, which involves looking to the future of our profession. In Chapter 13, you will learn about neuro-informed counseling. Chapter 14 provides a glimpse into the future of counseling.

ACKNOWLEDGMENTS

We would like to thank our graduate student, Victoria Gravatt, for her keen eye and attention to detail. Victoria has been a wonderful formatting editor. We would also like to thank our dear friend and colleague, Dr. Kristy Ford, for her dedication to editing for voice and content. We owe a special debt of gratitude for our colleagues who joined us in creating the additional video segments which accompany the textbook, Drs. Brandi Chamberlin, Nivischi Edwards, Ron Hawkins, Kevin Hull, Trish Kimball, Arleezah Marrah, Mike Takacs, Christina Villarreal-Davis, and Mr. Wayne Powell. Additionally, we want to thank all of our professional colleagues and students who contributed to the textbook either through written content or in the video segments. We would also like to thank Curtis and Noelle, our KH representatives, who have been a constant source of support.

Finally, we wish to collectively thank our family and friends for their support, encouragement, and never-ending patience.

CHAPTER 1
Historical Overview and Current Trends

Jama Davis, Ph.D. & Jerry Vuncannon, Jr., Ph.D.

> "A people without the knowledge of their past history, origin and culture is like a tree without roots."
> - Marcus Garvey

Following Christ: Grace for Our Work

Jesus was teaching the Sermon on the Mount in Matthew 5 when he said, "You are the salt of the earth...(v. 13a, New International Version). You are the light of the world. A town built on a hill cannot be hidden. Neither do people light a lamp and put it under a bowl. Instead they put it on its stand, and it gives light to everyone in the house. In the same way, let your light so shine before others, that they may see your good deeds and glorify your Father in heaven" (v. 14 – 16). Continuing on, John 16:13a tells us "But when he, the Spirit of truth, comes, he will guide you into all the truth."

© EvgeniiAnd/Shutterstock.com

1

You may be asking yourself what these verses have to do with the history of counseling and current trends. Well, the first three verses speak to the idea of influence and how far reaching it can be, and the fourth verse speaks to the idea of knowing truth. Within this chapter, we provide an overview of the key aspects of counseling in its progression, some key information and figures in that evolvement, and how the history continues to impact counseling. In essence, today's counseling is influenced by many key individuals and concepts that are inherent to the field and that continue to contribute to its progress. Our hope in this chapter is that the Holy Spirit will guide you as you begin reading foundational aspects of the counseling profession to increase your knowledge about how the profession started and what concepts are prominent today.

CHAPTER OBJECTIVES

After reading this chapter, you will understand more about:
- The historical perspective of the counseling profession
- The philosophy of counseling
- The influential 'waves' of counseling
- The key distinctions between other mental health disciplines and counseling

The following CACREP standards are addressed in this chapter:
Professional Counseling Orientation and Ethical Practice:
- History and philosophy of the counseling profession and its specialty areas (CACREP, 2016, Standard 2.F.1.a.)

In this chapter, the history of counseling along with current and evolving trends in professional counseling will be explored. Knowledge of the historical perspective is important in understanding the foundation and progress in the counseling profession. Counselors who understand the history of the counseling profession develop a stronger professional identity and make noteworthy contributions to the profession (Gladding, 2018). See this historical look at counseling as a part of your professional identity development, and take your time as you read through this chapter, noticing the many changes that have occurred along with the number of people involved in the progression of the profession

People around the world are familiar with the word *counselor*. For some, the meaning of the word is similar, and for others, it brings different images and thoughts. Most consider a counselor to be someone who offers help to others. People find themselves in need of help at different times in their lives. The situation before a person most often determines who a person seeks during the time of need.

WHAT WOULD BE SOME REASONS PEOPLE SEEK COUNSELING?

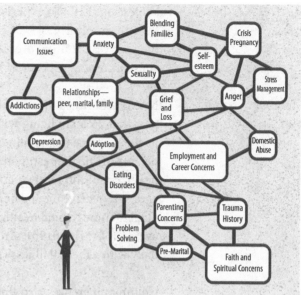

Modified from © Nattapol_Sritongcom/Shutterstock.com

What might be some other reasons not mentioned?
Ask yourself: Have I ever pursued counseling? What was that experience like? Did the experience influence my decision to pursue a degree in counseling?

If we were to ask people what they think of when they hear the word *counselor*, most likely we would hear different answers. Pastors, mentors, and friends are examples of people we may go to for direction. These individuals can offer support to others, often stemming from a previously established relationship with the person seeking help. They would be considered people-helpers but not professional counselors.

Professional counselors are those individuals who have earned a master's or doctorate degree, passed counseling licensure exams, and met all licensing requirements for the state in which they practice. These professionals are not involved with their clients outside of the professional relationship and adhere to ethical codes of professional organizations.

You might also hear two terms used interchangeably – *psychotherapy/therapy* and *counseling*. Both psychotherapy and counseling have been referred to as *talk therapy* and are used to address emotional and behavioral problems. Psychologists and psychiatrists working from a medical model often prefer the term *psychotherapy*, with the emphasis on testing, diagnosis and treatment planning, while professional counselors most often use the term *counseling*, with a goal of improved overall functioning and well-being utilizing a wellness perspective. The National Alliance on Mental Illness (NAMI, 2019a) provides a clear indication of an ever- growing need for professional counselors. Nearly 1 in 5 adults in the U.S. (18.5%) experience mental illness in any given year. It is estimated that 1 in 5 adolescents (21.4%) experience a severe mental disorder at some point in their lives. Nearly 20% of U.S. adults experienced an anxiety disorder in the past year. Of the over 20 million adults in the U.S. with a substance abuse disorder, just over 50% of those have a co-occurring mental illness.

NAMI (2019a) estimates, within the homeless population staying in shelters, that 26% are living with a serious mental illness, with 46% of those having a severe mental illness co-occurring with/or a substance use disorder. NAMI further estimates that only 41% of adults living with a mental health condition receive services in a given year. Just over half of children ages 8-15 receive mental health care. It is important to recognize that 50% of all lifetime mental health conditions begin by age 14 and 75% begin by age 24 (NAMI, 2019b). An estimated 60 million people in the U.S. live daily with a mental illness (NAMI, 2019b).

Cultural differences also impact how mental health care is perceived and sought. NAMI (2019a) reports Hispanic Americans and African Americans using mental health services at nearly one-half the rate of Caucasian Americans with Asian Americans utilizing at nearly one-third the rate of Caucasian Americans. It is imperative to understand the cultural considerations that are necessary in order to effectively counsel. Each person is a unique individual created by God (Genesis 1:27), and professional counselors have an ethical responsibility to develop their multicultural competencies.

WHAT IS THE HISTORY OF THE COUNSELING PROFESSION?

If we glimpse at the history of counseling, we find it has been in process since the 1800s with many individuals involved. Ginter (2002), who was at one time the editor of the *Journal of Counseling and Development*, reminds counselors that the true identity of the profession of counseling has adapted over time while remaining consistent with necessary features that have been connected over the decades. This identity has provided an effective and meaningful guide to the professional actions of those within the counseling profession. Next you will read how the counseling profession evolved, and we hope that you will see how understanding this developmental process is important both in counselor identity development as well as in understanding the profession of counseling as a whole.

Late 1800's

It is hard to imagine counseling extending back to the late 1800s, yet we find the influence of psychology on the field in this early time period. In 1879, Germany was the setting where Wilhelm Wundt worked in the first experimental research laboratory, focusing his study on the human mind (Guindon, 2010). Wundt is known as the "Father of Psychology" (Belkin, 1988). During this same time period, Sigmund Freud's influence grew, and he is credited with influencing others in their research and development of various theoretical approaches. Carl Jung and Alfred Adler began their professional work as Freudian psychoanalysts and then expanded their approach to include theories and techniques they each developed. Jung and Adler found talking to be of value when working with others to address emotional concerns.

Interestingly, G. Stanley Hall, identified as the "Father of American Psychology" (Belkin, 1988), began his training at Williams College, graduating in 1867 and enrolling at Union Theological Seminary the same year. With his theological education complete in 1870, he became a pastor at a church where he ministered for 10 weeks before making a decision to step away from this role (Parry, 2006). His work then led him to teaching and research. In 1878, Harvard University awarded G. Stanley Hall the first doctorate in psychology in the United States. He founded a psychology laboratory at Johns Hopkins University in 1883. Hall went on to become one of the early organizers of the American Psychological Association (APA) in 1892 (Parry, 2006).

Early 1900's

Frank Parsons founded the Boston Vocational Bureau in 1908 after collaborating with Mrs. Quincy A. Shaw regarding his plans for the organization (Parsons, 1909). He entered counseling as a profession after serving as an attorney, engineer, social worker and professor (Gladding, 2018) and became known as the "Father of Vocational Guidance" (Guindon, 2010, p. 38). Parsons was influential in naming the profession of counseling. His law background gave him an appreciation for the English term, counsellor, used for attorneys. Notably this was spelled with two L's, so one of the L's was removed and we became known as counselors (Duggan & Kaplan,

2015). Parsons' work to establish the Boston Vocational Bureau was a major step in the field of counseling, with the bureau focusing on career counseling. During these early years, Parsons worked to establish ways for clients to develop increased personal insight and expand their understanding of the employment marketplace.

In the first few months of operation, men and women ranging in age from 15 to 72 came for what was referred to as "consultation." All but two of these individuals reported receiving insight and help, and some stated the time with the counselor "was the most important hour of their lives" (Parsons, 1909, p. 91). From this effort, the Young Men's Christian Association (YMCA) established a branch of the vocational department, and the counseling services continued to expand.

Parsons' work and its impact was recognized and Boston took the first step to create the first counselor certification program which was adopted by Harvard University (Hollis & Dodson, 1999). Boston School Superintendent named 100 counselors in the school system as vocational counselors. In 1910, the progressive actions occurring in Boston moved across the country with 35 counties adopting vocational counselors. In the year 1911, the first vocational guidance program was started in schools in Cincinnati, Ohio. Vocational guidance positions were the primary place of employment for counselors as counseling was gaining recognition as a positive influence (Hollis & Dodson, 1999). The U.S. Federal Government passed the Smith-Hughes Act of 1917, which provided mandated funding for public schools to provide vocational education. This focus further fueled the movement to expand counseling in schools.

Parsons' work leads well beyond the early 1900s as he set in motion the counseling movement. In this early time period, Parsons (1909) identified important counselor characteristics that remain true for today's counselors which include excellent character, mature judgment, a personality that invites respect and confidence, a "working knowledge of the fundamental principles and methods of modern psychology" (p. 94), and the ability to be "sympathetic, earnest, searching, candid and helpful" (p. 95). In comparison, Ginter (2002) identified "effective counselor traits" (p. 23) as empathy, objectivity, sensitivity, observational ability, self-awareness, awareness and acceptance of diverse worldviews, open-mindedness, integrity, problem-solving creativity, personal energy, competence, and good mental health. In his early work, Parsons demonstrated foresight and understanding of some of the core qualities professional counselors need to manifest.

In 1913, the counseling career profession was formalized with the founding of the National Vocational Guidance Association (NVGA; Gladding, 2018). This organization was later renamed The National Career Development Association, a division of the American Counseling Association (ACA). The National Association of Deans of Women also began in 1913 and was then renamed the National Association of Women Deans and Counselors in 1914 (Hollis & Dodson, 1999). The NVGA published a counseling bulletin in 1915 which grew to be the *National Vocational Guidance Bulletin* in 1921. This publication provided information for those with an interest in vocational counseling and brought those individuals together with a unified interest (Gladding, 2018). Over the years the publication evolved and changed names several times, including: *National Vocational Guidance Magazine* (1924–1933), *Occupations: The Vocational Guidance Magazine* (1933–1944), *Occupations: The Vocational Guidance Journal* (1944–1952), *Personnel and Guidance Journal* (1952–1984), and now what is known as the flagship journal of the American Counseling Association, the *Journal of Counseling and Development* (1984–present).

World War I occurred during the decade of 1910–1920, bringing the need for counseling to the forefront. Hollis and Dodson (1999) note the military began using testing to assist with the placement of military personnel and in Veterans' Administration positions. This eventually led to greater engagement of counselors with the military.

1920's

In this decade, the program offered by Harvard University became more focused on vocational guidance which further strengthened the counseling movement. The federal government increased the employment of counselors working with war veterans. Other developments included an important psychological instrument, Strong's Vocational Interest Inventory (SVII), which was developed in 1927. Coupled with Parsons (1909) model for matching individuals with careers, this inventory opened the pathway for counseling assessment development and use (Donnay, 1997). An updated version of Strong Interest Inventory remains in use and has the longest history of currently used psychological assessments.

During this decade, G. Stanley Hall (who was discussed for his work in the late 1800s) retired but continued to contribute to the field by writing on the subject of aging adults. His work was considered visionary as he focused on what he called a "crisis of aging" that would occur in the 20th century (Parry, 2006, p. 1161). Hall believed the lifespan would increase and aging adults would become more isolated as they were removed from the workforce. Further, this crisis would also include the loss of valuable contributions and wisdom of aging adults. In these early years of the 20th century, Hall was calling for the importance of expanding understanding of aging adults. The value of this insight is evident today with the growing field of gerontology and counseling focused on this population.

1930's

During the 1930s, the Great Depression impacted counseling as the emphasis to create strategies and approaches to counseling for those in need of employment grew. New in development was the trait-factor theory or Minnesota Point of View developed by E.G. Williamson (1947). This theory provided a way to define behavior by various traits and determine what would lead to effective and successful individuals. This theory was used extensively in the 1930's and 1940's with World War II military personnel. U.S. Congress approved the George-Deen Act in 1936. This resulted in the Vocational Education Division in the U.S. Department of Education. From this act, state supervisors of guidance were added in individual state departments of education and school counseling became more widespread. With the focus on the guidance area, there were some who realized the focus was narrow and there were more opportunities for counseling to be utilized.

World War II brought a time when psychologists and counselors were employed to help with the selection and training of military specialists and also those who would better serve as industrial specialists. You may recall we discussed earlier how counselors were utilized during World War I. The engagement of counselors with the military developed stronger connections as the value of counseling for active military personnel and veterans became more understood.

As a departure from vocational counseling, an interest in individual counseling advanced in the 1940s with greater theoretical development. Carl Rogers wrote *Counseling and Psychotherapy*, which detailed his Client-Centered approach and became a key contributor in this decade. Rogers challenged the more directive approach of Williamson (1930s) and instead focused on individuals being responsible for their own growth. Rogers embraced the approach that viewed counselors as more reflective and accepting rather than directive. As a result, Rogers was labeled as a "steamroller" due to the most profound impact on changing the development of the counseling movement (Aubrey, 1977, p. 292). With the influence of Rogers, counseling began to change dramatically with greater emphasis on the counseling relationship, techniques, and research (Aubrey, 1977). Training of future counselors became increasingly important along with identifying clear goals and objectives in counseling. The focus on guidance began to lessen as research moved to a greater concentration on counseling.

Post World War II, the George Barden Act of 1946 was passed which provided funding for counselor training programs and the supervisors of those who were in training (Barrett, 1948). As a result of this Act, the U.S. Department of Veterans' Affairs (VA) began offering scholarships and grants along with internships for graduate students. With these efforts the opportunities to expand the counseling field multiplied.

With growing awareness of mental health needs in

America, May was identified as Mental Health Awareness month in 1949 (Mental Health America, 2019a). Since its inception, organizations have joined together offering mental health screenings and local events in an effort to increase awareness and ultimately encourage people to seek mental health support and care. The impact of this focus on mental health is still strong. In recent years, Mental Health America (2019b) reported that during Mental Health Awareness month, over four million people have taken one of their eight available mental health screenings with over 3,000 completed daily. Reportedly, many people who complete the screenings do ask for more information about mental health, referrals, or request a phone number for more immediate support.

1950's

The 1950s brought expanded theoretical contributions in developmental psychology, sociology and learning theory from Erikson, Piaget, and others (Aubrey, 1977). From this, additional theoretical approaches were formed along with marriage and family counseling theories. Before the 1950s, the main theoretical approaches were psychoanalysis (Freud), Trait-Factor Theories (Williamson), Client-Centered (Rogers) and Behavioral (B.F. Skinner).

The Association for Spiritual, Ethical, and Religious Values in Counseling (ASERVIC, 2019) has a heritage dating back to 1951 when a Catholic Guidance Council was formed in New York to provide support for counseling in schools within the diocese. In 1955, a group of Catholics met in Chicago to explore expanding the support found in New York across the country and the development of a national Catholic guidance organization. This group identified as "Catholic Counselors in APGA", meeting annually at the APGA convention (ASERVIC, 2019). The organization now has over 4,000 members from various faith traditions, and the organization's role is viewed as important to increase the presence of spiritual, ethical and religious values in counselor education and practice.

As a way to expand the voice of counseling, several counseling-related organizations met in Los Angeles, CA in 1952. Organizations such as The National Vocational Guidance Association, National Association of Guidance and Counselor Trainers, Student Personnel Association for Teacher Education and the American College Personnel Association formed the

American Personnel and Guidance Association (APGA), the predecessor to today's American Counseling Association. (American Counseling Association [ACA], 2019). Other organizations formed counseling divisions such as The American Psychological Association (APA) adding Division 17, the Division of Counseling Psychology. In addition, the American School Counseling Association (ASCA) was founded and a year later became a division of APGA. Aubrey (1977) referred to this decade as having the "most profound impact on counselors" (p. 292) with the coming together of these groups and the first APGA (now ACA) professional conference of this magnitude occurring. An annual conference has been held each year since this time (ACA, 2019).

The Christian mental health movement has its roots in the 1950s as Fritz Kunkel, in 1956, used the term "integration" to describe what he believed to be an interdisciplinary activity between theology and psychology. In Kunkel's discussion of integration, he referred to "a holistic process of self-development which simultaneously touches on psychological, spiritual and emotional components of experience" (Haynes, 2016, p. 5). Kunkel's approach was called *We-Psychology* in order to place emphasis on the relationship of individuals with other people and God.

A small group of Christians working in the mental health field founded the Christian Association for Psychological Studies (CAPS) in 1956. CAPS currently has over 1200 members in the U.S., Canada, and over 25 countries. To date, CAPS remains a member-supported, non-profit organization and publishes the peer-reviewed *Journal of Psychology and Christianity*. Annual conferences (national, regional and local) are held in various locations in the U.S. (CAPS International, 2019).

1960's

The Community Mental Health Act was signed by President John F. Kennedy on October 31, 1963 (National Council for Behavioral Health, 2019). This drastically changed how mental health services were delivered and many felt a sense of optimism for the future of mental healthcare. Community-based mental healthcare become more accessible to those with mental illness as there was a growing realization that many people with mental health issues could be well-served in a community setting rather than what had been the traditional psychiatric hospital. This movement resulted in people who were previously in psychiatric hospitals moving back into their communities to receive care, opening the door for increased personal support from friends and family. Currently, community mental health facilities are run by a variety of government, county, for-profit and private non-profit organizations.

The first code of ethics was published by APGA in 1961, and this raised the professionalism in the field through guidelines for ethical practice. In the present day, professional counseling organizations and state licensing boards align with ethical codes that counselors are required to follow as part of their professionalism in practice.

APGA which later became the American Counseling Association (ACA) last updated its code of ethics in 2014. In the 1960s, an increasing number of professional conferences were being developed to bring counselors together for additional training and collaboration.

David Capuzzi, Ph.D.
Walden University

I began my career as a counselor in the summer of 1965 after completing my master's in counseling at Florida State University. Initially, I had planned to seek employment as a counselor in a community college in Florida but changed my plans at the last minute and applied for and was accepted as a doctoral student in Counselor Education, also at Florida State University. A deciding factor in the decision to pursue a doctoral degree was the fact that, in January of 1965,

I was hired by Florida State's university counseling center on a quarter time basis to plan early orientation for incoming students and their parents. I enjoyed and did well in that role and the counseling center decided to employ me half time as I started my doctoral studies to continue doing the planning for early orientation and to serve as a counselor for students who were undecided about their university major and its relation to possible careers; this was later changed to a three quarter time position.

The master's degree I completed in the spring of 1965 was a one year 40 semester credit degree program which was, at that time, much more specific to the role of a counselor than what existed at many universities at which a degree in education with as few as 12 or 15 credits in counseling courses served as preparation for a position as a counselor. There was no entity, like the Council for the Accreditation of Counseling and Related Educational Programs, that specified what universities needed to provide to an individual seeking employment and licensure as a counselor. (Licensure did not exist at the time and neither did certifications such as those offered by the National Board for Certified Counselors since NBCC was also non-existent). There were no personal computers available for use during the process of writing a dissertation (the dissertation had to be keyboarded onto stencils which were mimeographed for use by the student and the student's committee members. If a committee member suggested changes that could not be contained on a single page, everything past that page had to be rekeyboarded). There were no cell phones, only three major television stations, and the concept of living in a location other than the location of your employer was unheard of since it was not possible to work remotely from a home office. I don't think people even imagined the possibility of earning a master's or doctoral degree via an on-line degree program.

As I think about the dramatic changes that have occurred over time, I remember wondering if I would be able to "survive" in my chosen career as a counselor and a counselor educator. Taking my licensure exam and becoming licensed, earning an NCC designation, learning to use a computer at the age of 55, etc., were all experiences that were not part of my frame of reference in 1965! I have enjoyed my role as a counselor educator, with periodic opportunities to engage in private practice, since 1968. I have been employed at seven universities with my longest tenure at Portland State University (26 years with one year in absentia as I served as president of ACA). Even during the years I spent at Portland State, I could not have predicted that I would later be hired by Johns Hopkins University, Penn State University, and currently, Walden University without needing to leave our home in Oregon. (My current half-time position at Walden University, by the way, is a position I accepted because I had never done on-line counselor education. I have been happily rewarded by experiencing a quality program amidst a network of productive and affirming colleagues). Change and transition are a constant and meeting the challenges that are inherent in transitions are necessary components of all career fields--- the counseling profession is no exception.

Contributed by David Capuzzi. © Kendall Hunt Publishing Company.

Counseling grew significantly in the 1970's, including the development of counselor licensure. The Commonwealth of Virginia provided the first opportunity for counselors to be licensed in 1976. Arkansas and Alabama followed closely behind with counselor licensure offered in 1979; however, it was not until California offered licensure in 2010 that all states had counselor licensure requirements. With these licensure efforts, employment opportunities for counselors continued to expand as counselors found employment at mental health centers and community agencies. Title IX, a comprehensive law prohibiting sex-discrimination in federally funded programs and activities, opened opportunities for women, minorities and individuals with disabilities. With increased financial assistance available, this enactment along with affirmative action laws and anti-discrimination legislation involving those with disabilities began to open the doors for more women to be involved in the counseling profession.

Title IX of the Education Amendments of 1972

No person in the United States shall, on the basis of sex, be excluded from participation in, be denied the benefits of, or be subjected to discrimination under any education program or activity receiving federal financial assistance.

Early in the 1970s, standards for counselor training programs were proposed. Robert Stripling, while serving as a professor at the University of Florida, led the effort to standardize counselor training programs utilizing standards proposed by the Association of Counselor Educators and Supervisors (ACES), a division of APGA. In 1977, ACES approved the first guidelines for counselor preparation doctoral programs (Stripling, 1978). The strength of APGA was growing and they relocated their headquarters to their current location of Alexandria, Virginia.

In addition, the integration movement that started in the 1950s continued. John Carter and Bruce Narramore (1979) wrote *Integration of Psychology and Theology* in 1979. In this writing, the authors discussed barriers of integration as well as four integrative models, including what they believed to be the process of integration from within each of these views. Since this time, several (Entwistle, 2015; Jones & Butman, 2011; McMinn, 2011; Tan, 2011; & McMinn & Campbell, 2007, among others) have also written on the subject of integration from a Christian perspective. The importance of understanding integration continues to be affirmed through the work of ASERVIC and counselors worldwide who are committed to ethical integration.

1980's

The awareness of the counseling profession grew substantially in this decade. People began to talk more openly than in the past about counseling, and graduate degree programs began to increase in number. The Council for Accreditation of Counseling and Related Educational Programs (CACREP), a partner of APGA, was established. CACREP added clarity to the APGA standards of the 1970s with the first CACREP accredited programs moving from application in 1980 to accreditation in 1981 (CACREP, 2019; Duggan & Kaplan, 2015). Since its inception, CACREP has led to the standardization of master's and doctoral programs in clinical, school, and marriage and family studies with over 630 programs currently accredited (CACREP, 2019).

The National Board for Certified Counselors (NBCC) was established in 1982 with the goal of certifying counselors on a national level. With counselor licensure in the early stages, this allowed for counselors to take a standardized test covering the eight knowledge areas that CACREP requires in their accredited programs. These areas include: (1) human growth and development, (2) social and cultural diversity, (3) counseling and helping relationships, (4) group counseling and group work, (5) career counseling, (6) assessment and testing, (7) research and program evaluation and (8) professional counseling orientation and ethical practice (NBCC, 2019). The National Board for Certified Counselors administers the National Counselor Examination (NCE) and the National Clinical Mental Health Counseling Examination (NCMHCE).

These exams are used by the majority of states to meet counseling licensure requirements. In 1983 the American Personnel and Guidance Association (APGA) changed its name to the American Association of Counseling and Development (AACD) which later became the American Counseling Association on July 1, 1992 (ACA, 2019). This name change to AACD more closely represented the membership of the organization during this time of change in the counseling profession. Various divisions continued to be added to encourage counselors to engage in specialty areas within the profession.

Chi Sigma Iota (CSI, 2018), a counseling academic and professional honor society, was formed in 1985 at Ohio University. Currently, CSI has over 125,000 members who portray academic and professional excellence in counseling while developing a strong counselor identity (CSI, 2018).

> Read about **Chi Sigma Iota** and their mission here:
> https://www.csi-net.org/

The decade of the 1980s brought many changes, including the development of the American Association of State Counseling Boards (AASCB, n.d.) with Ted Remley being named the Founding President in 1986. This organization seeks to encourage communication among state licensing boards while promoting "regulatory excellence in the counseling profession by providing leadership, education, and service" to Member Boards (AASCB, n.d.). AASCB has held an annual conference each year since 1987.

Ted Remley, Ph.D., J.D.
University of Holy Cross

I became a counselor in 1971 after completing a two-year 60-credit master's degree program at the University of Florida. After graduating, I was a high school counselor for one year, was on active duty as an Army Officer for three months (followed by six years in the reserves), and was a full-time counselor in a community college after that. I earned my JD in law at Catholic University in Washington, DC, in May, 1980 and my PhD in counselor education and supervision at the University of Florida in December, 1980. I taught graduate courses in counseling part-time from 1980 to 1983 then

© Ted Remley

became a full-time counselor educator in 1983. Except for the years when I was the Executive Director of the American Counseling Association (1990-1994), I have been a full-time counselor educator at five universities.

During my master's degree program in counseling from 1969-1971, my impression from the instruction I received was that counseling was secular and that counselors should not engage in discussions with clients regarding the clients' spirituality or religion. At that time, if a client had brought up his or her religious beliefs in a counseling session, I was under the impression counselors should tell the client that such issues should be addressed with a minister or priest because counseling was not the place to discuss religion. I believe most counselor educators today would agree that a client's spirituality or religion is an important part of a person's life and certainly should be addressed in counseling if clients want to talk about their beliefs. As I think about the how this position in the counseling profession shifted so profoundly over the span of my career, I wonder how those of us who are counselor educators came to adopt the position we have today. I think contemporary counselor educators have embraced the concept that counselors must accept and embrace all of the dimensions of a client's life if we are to be helpful. Holistic approaches to counseling demand that counselors be able to assist clients in their self-exploration without imposing our own values. Today, I am comfortable teaching beginning counselors that we must be open to clients talking about their religious beliefs without imposing our own, which means that, as counselors, we must know ourselves and our own beliefs well so that we can refrain from imposing them.

Another huge change I have observed during my career as a counselor educator is the acceptance of counselor educators and practicing counselors of both distance or online instruction of counselors and distance or online delivery of counseling services. When the two concepts were first introduced, there was almost universal resistance by counselor educators and practicing counselors. Those who were against such practices argued that the process of counseling, which involves human encounters that are verbal and visual, could not be taught or delivered if professors and students or counselors and clients were not in the same room at the same time. Over the years, however, university counseling preparation programs have demonstrated that counselors can be ethically prepared through online and distance education. And counselors who deliver counseling services online or through distance means have proven that such services can be delivered ethically. Online counselor preparation programs and the delivery of counseling services through online or distance means have become almost universally accepted by society and by those in the counseling profession.

Contributed by Ted Remley. © Kendall Hunt Publishing Company.

As a movement towards a greater Christian counseling presence, the American Association of Christian Counselors (AACC) was founded in late 1986. This organization seeks to equip licensed professional counselors, pastors, pastoral counselors and lay counselors (those with little to no formal training; AACC, 2019). AACC identifies as the largest organization of Christian mental health providers in the world. The organization holds a World Conference every two years with other training options available annually.

Prior to the 1980s, there was limited consideration given to multicultural counseling, and as a result, there were unmet needs among counselees. As mentioned earlier NBCC (2019) and CACREP (2019) included requirements of social and cultural diversity. This led to increased attention being given to multicultural competencies in graduate programs. This is an area of continued emphasis and growth as research has grown tremendously. It is important for counselors in training to understand the importance of and their ethical responsibility in developing competencies in social and cultural diversity as well as the broad spectrum this represents.

1990's

Within the 1990s counseling began to form a more established identity and recognition. For example, the changing of names from American Association of Counseling and Development (AACD) to the American Counseling Association (ACA) occurred in July 1, 1992. This organization continued to grow in an effort to provide services and support to professional counselors in the United States as well as 50 other countries with a total of 18 divisions and 56 branches. In addition, Counseling Awareness Month was celebrated for the first time in 1994 (ACA, 2019). During this month, ACA focuses on increasing awareness about counseling professionals and expanding the knowledge of others concerning the benefits of counseling. The promotions for Counseling Awareness Month involve all areas of counseling: mental health, school and college, substance abuse, and career.

In 1996, "ACA filed an amicus brief to the U.S. Supreme Court which was cited along with the ACA Code of Ethics and Standards of Practice in the Court's 7-2 ruling in Jaffee vs. Redmond stating that clients have the right to expect confidentiality. The Court ruled that communications between psychotherapists and their clients are privileged and protected from forced disclosure" (ACA, 2019)

Just as the ACA became more established as the flagship counseling organization, the Christian counseling movement experienced significant growth. Gary Collins (n.d.) became the Executive Director and then President of the American Association of Christian Counselors in 1991, leading this organization through a time of growth from approximately 700 members to over 15,000 members until he resigned in 1998. From AACC, Dr. Collins transitioned his efforts to the worldwide development of Christian counseling and Christian coaching. Following Gary Collins as president of AACC was Tim Clinton, who remains the president as of this writing.

21st Century

As a push for counseling to have a more established identity distinct from the other mental health professions, the American Counseling Association (2019c) led a movement known as 20/20: A Vision for the Future of Counseling beginning in 2005. This is often referred to as an abbreviated 20/20. Thirty-one counseling associations were involved in developing an easy to understand, concise definition of counseling that professional counselors and counseling organizations could use with the general public

American Association of State Counseling Boards
American Collage Counseling Association
American Counseling Association (ACA)
ACA Midwest Region
ACA North Atlantic Region
ACA Southern Region
ACA Western Region
American Mental Health Counselors Association

Association for Multicultural Counseling and Development
Association for Specialists in Group Work
Association for Spiritual, Ethical, and Religious Values in Counseling Chi Sigma Iota
Commission on Rehabilitation Counselor Certification
Council for Accreditation of Counseling and Related Educational Programs Council on Rehabilitation Education

20/20: A Vision for the Future of Counseling

Organizations and Divisions Endorsing the Definition of Counseling

American Rehabilitation Counseling Association
Association for Adult Development and Aging
Association for Assessment in Counseling and Education
Association for Counselor Education and Supervision
Association for Counselors and Educators in Government
Association for Creativity in Counseling
Association for Lesbian, Gay, Bisexual and Transgender Issues in Counseling

Counseling Association for Humanistic Education and Development, now the Association for Humanistic Counseling
International Association of Addictions and Offender Counselors
International Association of Marriage and Family Counselors
National Board for Certified Counselors
National Career Development Association
National Employment Counseling Association
National Rehabilitation Counseling Association

Courtesy of Robyn Simmons

(Kaplan, Tarvydas, & Gladding, 2014). Twenty-nine of the 31 counseling associations came to a consensus for this concise definition of counseling. The American School Counseling Association and Counselors for Social Justice declined endorsement as each believed there were shortcomings (Kaplan et al., 2014).

20/20 Definition of Counseling
Counseling is a professional relationship that empowers diverse individuals, families, and groups to accomplish mental health, wellness, education, and career goals.

The American School Counselor Association (ASCA) was one of the organizations that chose not to support the 20/20. On April 1, 2018, ASCA moved from being a division of ACA and became a separate and independent organization. ASCA and ACA continue to collaborate as appropriate to serve the needs of school counselors. Examples of collaboration surround advocacy issues that support children and adolescents and strengthen school counselors and their work (ACA, 2019b). Counselors bring skills and expertise to situations that require them to be active in advocacy. For example, both ACA and AMHCA advocated for mental health parity laws for work with veterans.

The Veterans Benefits, Healthcare and Information Act increased access of veterans to mental health counselors. Included was Public Law 109-461, enacted in December 2006 placed mental health counselors on parity with social workers in the U.S. Department of Veterans Affairs. The Affordable Health Care for America Act was signed into law in 2010 and included a provision for licensed professional counselors and licensed marriage and family counselors to provide Medicare coverage (ACA, 2019). The increased ability for counselors to receive insurance reimbursement has made services more accessible. It is important for counselors to be aware that even with increased accessibility, many people still have stigmas connected with participation in counseling. Culture can impact personal views about seeking counseling, and this can result in a hesitancy to engage in counseling or in questions about whether or not counseling is beneficial.

Along with the history already presented, there are some important distinctions, perspectives, and trends to consider that have shaped the counseling profession. Counseling, social work, psychology, psychiatry, and marriage and family therapy all bring something different to the helping professions. Several "waves" throughout the development of the counseling field distinguish the perspectives that have shaped the profession as we know it today. More recently, trends in technological advances have impacted how services can be provided.

WHAT ARE THE DISTINCTIONS BETWEEN COUNSELING, SOCIAL WORK, PSYCHOLOGY, AND PSYCHIATRY?

Space will not allow to fully share the scope of each mental health discipline; however, it is prudent to discuss an overview of the distinctions between the professions of counseling, social work, psychology, psychiatry, and marriage and family therapy. Each of these falls under the larger umbrella of the field of mental health, using similar approaches when it comes to helping people, but with unique differences among them. Specific details about the counseling profession itself will be shared in Chapter 2; however, we will offer introductory information here as well as for the other helping professions.

The Mental Health Sisters: Helping Students Conceptualize the Distinctions among the Mental Health Disciplines

Beginning counseling students may be confused about professional identity and have difficulty distinguishing the field of counseling from other mental health disciplines. The metaphor of a family allows students a context in which to understand and conceptualize the distinctions that exist (Rush-Wilson & Trippany Simmons, 2009). Following is an introduction to the mental health sisters:

- Psychiatry, the oldest sister, has a medical degree. She understands and prescribes medications, may not do much talk therapy, but has the proper credentials to do so.
- Psychology, the second sister, is distinct from her older sister but acknowledges general similarities in values. Usually, she is REQUIRED to have a doctorate. She has many subspecialties (e.g., industrial/organizational, clinical, school, developmental, cognitive, sports, media, and counseling psychology).
- The fraternal twins, Counseling and Social Work (SW), are interested in helping people identify strengths and secure resources. The twins are especially aligned with the wellness philosophy. Many people know SW because of her work helping those in need, protecting children and securing safety for elder persons. Counseling, while having a long history, is becoming more well-known among the general population. Both SW and Counseling learn clinical skills, but Counseling specializes in the theory and practice of individual and group counseling, while SW specializes in securing resources. While a doctorate can be obtained in Counseling or SW, both allow direct clinicians to practice at the Master's level.
- The fifth sister, Marriage and Family Therapy (MFT), is interested in interpersonal and family systems. She considers the experiences of the individual, how they fit into their system, the impact they have on that system, and its influence on the person (Rush-Wilson & Trippany Simmons, 2009).

It is important to note that the sisters are a family; with each member bringing something of value to the family. In fact, outcome studies on the client satisfaction do not favor one degree or discipline over another. It is the working alliance that seems to be the most salient predictor of therapeutic success As with any other family, "sibling rivalry" can occur when the scope of practice of one profession begins to encroach on the scope of practice historically held by another profession

(Rush-Wilson & Trippany Simmons, 2009). Examples would include legislative initiatives extending the scope of practice to render diagnoses initially excluded counselors (Pennsylvania, 2018) or attempting to eliminate licensure altogether in Arizona (MacConomy, 2018). This is why we need to have a strong professional identity and advocate for our profession in a respectful manner. This will allow us to build bridges and facilitate the cohesion that will allow us to come together, capitalize on our strengths, and defend one another if an outsider attacks.

Counseling

Each helping profession has its own defining distinction, and for counseling this key distinction is that of a wellness and strengths-based model. In essence, it is about the positive assets or experiences that one has or what can be called 'the good stuff of life.' In other words, its primary tenet is on building existing strengths and not fixed on weaknesses (Key, 2010). For clients who face the ups and downs of life or one negative life event after another, they may feel distressed and overwhelmed. There can be so much distress that they may focus more on the downs of life rather than their positive experiences. Counseling does not deny the downs of life; however, for clients who experience negative life events, focusing on their strengths and positive assets can bring hope and offer an avenue for healing. Since counseling is viewed as a participatory and educational process, clients can experience healthy growth as they refocus on their strengths (Key, 2010).

Licensure is available in all 50 states, and credential titles vary and can include one of the following: Licensed Professional Counselor (LPC), Licensed Clinical Mental Health Counselor (LCMHC), Clinical Mental Health Counselor (CMHC), Licensed Clinical Professional Counselor (LCPC), Licensed Professional Clinical Counselor (LPCC), Licensed Professional Counselor of Mental Health (LPCMH), Licensed Professional Counselor – Mental Health (LPC-MH), or Licensed Professional Counselor-Mental Health Service Provider (LPC/MHSP). To become licensed in the counseling profession, one must earn a master's degree (MA or MS) in counseling. Many counseling programs have either a 48- or 60-hour degree program (varies by program and state requirements); however, programs are beginning to shift to a 60-hour degree program to offer a counseling degree accredited by the Council for Accreditation and Related

Educational Programs (CACREP). In addition, counselors may have degrees that focus on one of the following speciality areas: school, mental health, marriage and family, rehabilitation, or college student counseling (Granello & Young, 2019). Further, there are requirements regarding post-master's supervised clinical experience and licensure examinations which will be discussed in Chapter 2.

Social Work

Social work is the most versatile of the mental health disciplines in that it is a highly regarded degree and one of the most recognized in the helping professions. Although counseling is gaining more professional recognition, social workers have been prioritized over other mental health professions as a result of their long-standing historical recognition.

A social worker can earn a degree in social work with a Bachelor of Social Work (BSW), Master of Social Work (MSW), or the less common Doctor of Social Work (DSW). For all 50 states, professional licensure is available for all who hold the MSW degree, and licensure titles include one of the following (depending on state regulations): Licensed Clinical Social Worker (LCSW), Certified Independent Practice Social Worker (CIPSW), Independent Social Worker (ISW), Licensed Advanced Practice Social Worker (LAPSW), Licensed Independent Social Worker – Advanced Practice (LISW-AP), and Licensed Master Social Worker – Advanced Practice (LMSW-AP), just to name a few. Along with the MSW level licensures noted here, some states allow for preliminary licensing on the bachelor level and an associate licensure after graduating with an MSW. Obtaining these licensures are the first steps towards full clinical licensure within the given state. A master's degree program will be about 60 semester hours in total, and depending in the social work program, 30 hours from a BSW can count towards the MSW thus finishing the degree in one year (Granello & Young, 2019).

One key distinction between the social work and counseling fields is that social workers take a more community-based focus in addressing client problems. A social worker's training is more extensive in "utilizing and understanding the environment, social, and economic forces on clients" (Granello & Young, 2019, p. 9), and they are often client advocates pointing them to available community resources for aid. While counselors can utilize existing community resources for their clients, they may need to refer to social workers who may be more knowledgeable about available resources. In addition, counselors are more prepared in the area of the helping relationship (i.e., counselor-client dynamics, with skills, knowledge associated with individual and group therapy; Granello & Young, 2019).

Psychology

Psychologists are mental health practitioners who hold a doctoral degree in psychology. There are three primary avenues for practitioner-related doctorates in psychology, including Clinical Psychologist (PhD), Doctor of Psychology (PsyD), or a Counseling Psychologist (PhD or EdD). While the term psychologist is used for each of these options, there are distinctions among them. The clinical psychologist (PhD) is based in a scientist/practitioner model which emphasizes research, testing, and clinical internship. The PsyD emerged as a "pure therapist doctorate" (Granello & Young, 2019, p. 10), and many PsyD programs are an American Psychological Association (APA) approved program which are focused more on the practitioner role, including clinicians and supervisors. Counseling psychologists have a degree in counseling psychology, and while this degree is practitioner-focused, it can have a research emphasis as well. Many APA psychology programs are five-year programs wherein students earn not only a master's degree in psychology but also their doctorate.

As with the other mental health professions, psychologists are licensed practitioners but are licensed at the doctoral level with one of the following possible titles (varies by state): Licensed Clinical Psychologist (LCP), Licensed Psychologist (LP), or Health Service Provider in Psychology (HSPP). Some states have what is called a master's degree psychologist licensure with some having associate or assistant as part of the licensure name which helps distinguish between the master's level and doctoral level licensure.

What makes psychology distinctive from counseling is that it may address more serious mental illnesses such as schizophrenia or personality disorders due to its medical model emphasis on treating symptoms. In addition, psychologists may have a more specialized scope of practice and focus on assessment testing along with writing psychological reports. In contrast, counseling based on a wellness model may address more general mental health concerns (Key, 2010) as it takes a strengths-based approach with focusing on more positive assets in an individual's life. What is interesting to note about counseling is that it evolved from the psychology field, specifically, counseling psychology, to become its own mental health profession.

Psychiatry

Psychiatry is one of the more distinctive mental health professions in that there is less confusion between this profession and counseling compared to other helping professions (Granello & Young, 2019). Psychiatrists are medical doctors (MDs) who become psychiatric residents after medical school training (which can last up to 5 years). The training emphasizes psychological/biological theories of behavior, psychopathology, diagnosis, and psychopharmacology. In addition, psychiatrists can lead interdisciplinary teams to discuss patient matters, prescribe medications, treat several mental illnesses, and determine diagnoses. Also, they may receive referrals from other mental health professions including counselors, social workers, and psychologists (Granello & Young, 2019).

In addition to the above, the psychiatric profession through the American Psychiatric Association (along with representatives from other mental health professions), publishes the *Diagnostic and Statistical Manual of Mental Disorders* (DSM) which can be considered the diagnostic and conceptualization bible of mental health professionals. The DSM includes information about a number of mental health disorders, symptoms associated with these disorders, prevalence information, development and course information, and culture-related diagnostic considerations (American Psychiatric Association, 2013).

Marriage and Family Therapy

Just as with the other major mental health professions, marriage and family therapy (MFT) has its own distinction. While MFT can overlap with the other professions, its major emphasis is on a systems perspective for individuals, couples, and families that are impacted by family dynamics. In essence, it is the healthiness or unhealthiness of the family system that impacts a person's mental health and functioning from this perspective. MFT addresses system dynamics and processes that become part of treatment procedures. The hope is that addressing and changing an unhealthy family dynamic will impact the family system and those within that system in a positive way.

In contrast to other mental health professions, the licensure title for MFT workers is rather straightforward. Most, if not all, states use the acronym LMFT which can mean either Licensed *Marital* and Family Therapist or Licensed *Marriage* and Family Therapist; however, there are exceptions such as Ohio which uses Licensed Independent Marriage and Family Therapist as their top-tiered MFT-related licensure. In addition, Maryland has what is called the Licensed Clinical Marriage and Family Therapist. To become licensed, students can attend an MFT program that is accredited by the Commission on Accreditation of Marriage and Family Therapy Education (COAMFTE; think of COAMFTE as the MFT version of CACREP). And as part of the MFT community, their main professional association is known as the American Association for Marriage and Family Therapy (AAMFT).

Counseling and MFT are similar in that practitioners work with individuals, couples, and families and that both conduct marriage and family counseling. However, what makes MFT unique are the educational and field experience requirements. Generally speaking, MFT qualifications include more marriage and family focused academic courses as compared to what is offered in counseling programs. In addition, field experiences (internship and licensure processes) require more contact time (clinical hours) with clients who are either couples or families. MFT practitioners do still work with individuals; however, the primary focus of their work is with couples and families.

WHAT ARE THE WAVES OF COUNSELING?

In this section, we introduce to you several counseling perspectives that have influenced and shaped counseling as a profession today. Historically speaking, the counseling and psychology professions have experienced several shifts. These shifts, also known as forces or waves, include the following: 1) psychoanalytic, 2) cognitive-behavioral, 3) existential-humanistic,

4) multicultural, and 5) social justice advocacy. Each wave "was developed to address perceived limitations in existing understandings, and how each transcended explanations of human development and changed the rules of how psychology is approached" (Ratts & Pedersen, 2014, p. 17). In addition, each shift sheds light on the limitations of previous waves and also on the controversies surrounding one shift to another. Despite the reasons for the shifts and the challenges emerging from them, each wave has deepened the understanding of human development and has contributed to the profession as it exists today, especially as new counseling theories and perspectives emerged. The profession has evolved in a different understanding of human nature, in knowing a counselor's role and function in counseling, and in understanding the dynamics between counselor and client (c.f., Corey, 2017). Along with great influence, each new wave brought a paradigm shift to counseling and psychology. Each historical wave will be discussed below, along with a possible sixth wave of counseling that has emerged within the last decade.

1st Wave—The Psychodynamic Wave

Sigmund Freud, known as the father of modern psychotherapy, developed what is known today as the psychoanalytic approach (See Figure 1.1). Freud's approach to helping others changed the face of psychotherapy by giving it a new look (Corey, 2017). Although there are views that Freud's work is outdated (c.f., Ratts & Pedersen, 2014), "Freud's theory is a benchmark against which many other theories are measured" (Corey, 2017, p. 58). In addition, Corey noted other theories were developed that furthered the psychoanalytic model, that modified psychoanalytic concepts and processes, and that emerged as a reaction against this approach (p. 58). In fact, aspects of psychodynamic theory have not only influenced today's counseling but have also become part of the cultural mainstream. Have you ever seen media images of a person lying on a couch with a therapist sitting behind? Have you ever heard the phrase "Freudian slip?" These are examples of the influence of the psychoanalytic approach on culture.

Freud's psychoanalytic approach allowed for a new way of understanding abnormal behavior with a distinct view of structural personality with the id, ego, and superego. He also introduced other concepts such as addressing conscious and unconscious motivations and ego defense mechanisms (Corey, 2017). Despite the outdated view of psychoanalysis (c.f., Ratts &

Pedersen, 2014), there are modern approaches that are based on psycho-analytic principles for today's profession. These approaches, also known as contemporary psychoanalysis, include ego psychology, object-relations theory, self-psychology approaches, and relational model of psychoanalysis (or relational approaches). These modern approaches retain focus on unconscious processes, transference and countertransference, ego defenses, and internal conflicts, all which were part of Freud's original psychoanalytic approach (McWilliams, 2016). One of the lasting impressions of the psychoanalytic approach is how the past shapes and informs the present (Ratts & Pedersen, 2014).

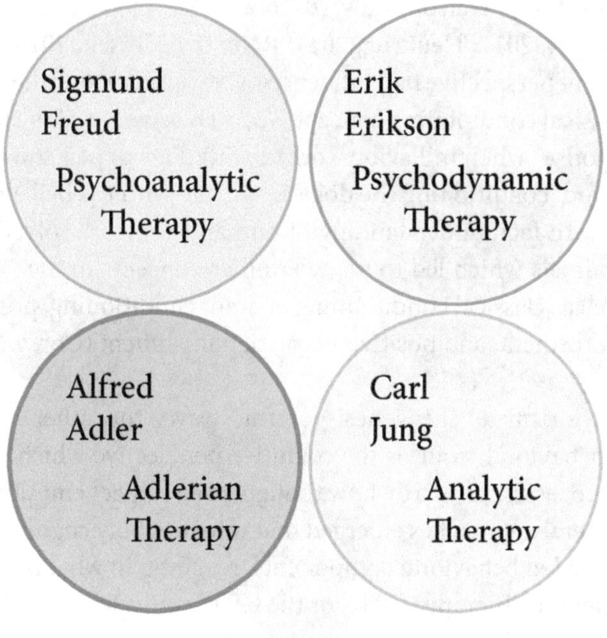

FIGURE 1.1

Prominent Figures in the Psychodynamic Wave

Sigmund Freud

Psychoanalytic Therapy

Erik Erikson

Psychodynamic Therapy

Alfred Adler

Adlerian Therapy

Carl Jung

Analytic Therapy

Courtesy of Robyn Simmons

2nd Wave—The Cognitive-Behavioral Wave

The cognitive-behavioral wave is one of the more well-known waves, or more accurately theories, that has emerged since the "dawn of counseling." We will not discuss the theoretical tenets of this wave in significant detail as these will be described in Chapter 10; however, what is worth noting is its prevalence and its applied use across many types of settings such as schools, college/university counseling centers, private practices, community agencies, and hospitals. In addition, it is a preferred evidence-based approach due not only to its efficacy but also to its cost-effectiveness (Ikic et al., 2017; Myhr & Payne, 2006). In fact, many counseling students during their field experience courses (i.e., Practicum and Internship) either choose this approach for their primary counseling orientation or utilize it as the approach of choice by their field experience site.

The cognitive-behavioral wave emerged from two views which include the behavioral perspective and the cognitive perspective. The behavioral perspective, also known as behaviorism, was the "dominant school of thought" (Ratts & Pedersen, 2014, p. 21) during the 1950s with the influences of John B. Watson, Edward Thorndike, Clark L. Hull, and B. F. Skinner (Corey, 2017; Neukrug, 2011; Ratts & Pedersen, 2014); however, the behavioral perspective had influences as early as 1906 with Ivan Pavlov and his classical conditioning concept. You may have heard the term "Pavlovian response" wherein Pavlov worked with dogs to pair the sound of a bell with food, conditioning the dogs to salivate with the bell alone (Neukrug, 2011). In fact, understanding of human behavior evolved from the study of animals which led to many familiar concepts in the "behavioral family" such as classical conditioning, operant conditioning, positive/negative reinforcement, and positive/negative punishment (Corey, 2017).

With behaviorism as the genesis of this wave, the other side of the cognitive-behavioral "coin" is the cognitive perspective which focuses on cognitive processes, primarily how thoughts can impact emotions and behaviors. Several approaches emerged that were not only cognitive-focused but also included behavioral components, resulting in what is called Cognitive-Behavioral Therapy (CBT), or the CBT family, which includes Cognitive Therapy (CT), Rational-Emotive Behavior Therapy (REBT), and Cognitive-Behavior Modification (CBM). In working with clients with depression, Aaron Beck developed CT as an evidence-based approach to change negative thinking patterns (Corey, 2017). Around the same time and independently from Beck, Corey noted that Albert Ellis developed Rational-Emotive Behavior Therapy (REBT) which assumes that psychological distresses and symptoms are affected by beliefs about a specific event. In other words, it is how one perceives an event that impacts feelings and thoughts about the event. The key difference between CT and REBT is that

REBT is highly directive and confrontational with the therapist functioning in a teacher role while CT is less directive. The CT therapist supports clients to become their own teacher, helping them arrive to conclusions about their cognitive distortions. One last approach that takes a more behavioral focus is called Cognitive-Behavioral Modification (CBM) by Donald Meichenbaum. As CT and REBT focus on changing thinking processes, "Meichenbaum suggests that it may be easier and more effective to change our behavior rather than our thinking" (Corey, 2017, p. 293).

No matter the approach within the CBT family, each one shares the same assumptions and characteristics. Beck and Weishaar (as cited in Corey, 2017) noted the following:

> Although the approaches are quite diverse, they do share these attributes: (1) a collaborative relationship between client and therapist; (2) the premise that psychological distress is often maintained by cognitive processes; (3) a focus on changing cognitions to produce desired changes in affect and behavior; (4) a present-centered, time limited focus; (5) an active and directive stance by the therapist; (6) an educational treatment focusing on specific and structured target problems. (p. 270)

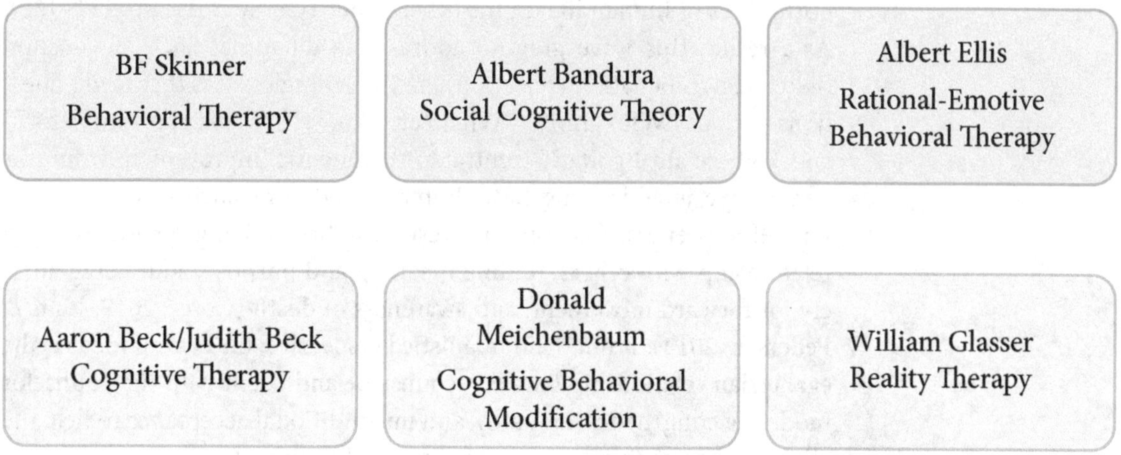

BF Skinner Behavioral Therapy	Albert Bandura Social Cognitive Theory	Albert Ellis Rational-Emotive Behavioral Therapy
Aaron Beck/Judith Beck Cognitive Therapy	Donald Meichenbaum Cognitive Behavioral Modification	William Glasser Reality Therapy

Courtesy of Robyn Simmons

FIGURE 1.2

The Prominent Figures in the Cognitive Behavioral Wave

The existential-humanistic wave emerged as a reaction against the limited views of both psychodynamic and cognitive-behavioral approaches (See Figure 1.3). More specifically, this third wave evolved with a more holistic view of persons in mind. Comparatively, psychodynamic theorists viewed persons with a structural perspective, with a focus on the id, ego, and superego, while the cognitive-behavioral approaches primarily viewed others through a cognitive and behavioral lens. The theorists behind this new wave "saw limitations in viewing fragmented parts of a client's personality and in examining only client cognitions, and they questioned the validity of using experiments conducted on animals to explain human behavior" (Ratts & Pedersen, 2014, p. 23). In essence, this shift represented a transition from a myopic view of people, focusing on fragmented parts of the self, to a more holistic view that encompassed all of their human experience. In addition, this wave was best described as a more philosophical approach rather than a defined model (Corey, 2017).

Just as the cognitive-behavioral wave merged from two schools of thought, this third wave emerged from the existential and humanistic perspectives in psychology. In the existential perspective, individual psychological processes seek "a balance between recognizing the limits and tragic dimensions of human existence on one hand and the possibilities and opportunities of human life on the other hand" (Corey, 2017, pp. 137–138). As a result, this wave grew to address life dilemmas such as isolation (loneliness), alienation (rejection), and meaninglessness that bring questions such as "Who am I?", "What can I know?", "What can I hope for?", and "Where am I going?" Central to therapeutic improvement from this perspective is addressing basic human conditions such as the capacity for self-awareness, freedom and responsibility, striving for identity and relationship with others, finding meaning and purpose, addressing anxiety for forward movement, and awareness of death (Corey, 2017; Ratts & Pedersen, 2014). From the humanistic perspective, the central focus is the egalitarian relationship between counselor and client with the counselor modeling congruence, empathy, and unconditional acceptance to help the client achieve their potential and find self-fulfillment.

Carl Rogers, one of the more well-known names associated with the humanistic side of this movement and the developer of person-centered therapy (PCT), believed in the potential of people, that they are trustworthy, that they are capable of self-directed growth, and that they can resolve personal problems due to understanding themselves (Corey, 2017; Ratts & Pedersen, 2014). In other words, it is about the belief of one's own experience that can help to resolve problems and concerns. In fact, Rogers (1961) valued so much the whole of human experience, he stated the following:

> Experience is, for me, the highest authority. The touchstone of validity is my own experience. No other person's ideas, and none of my own ideas, are as *authoritative as my experience* (emphasis added). It is to experience that I must return again and again, to discover a closer approximation to truth as it is in the process of becoming in me. Neither the Bible nor the prophets—neither Freud nor research—neither the revelations of God nor man—can take precedence over my own direct experience. My experience is not authoritative because it is infallible. It is the basis of authority because it can always be checked in new primary ways. In this way its frequent error or fallibility is always open to correction. (pp. 23–24)

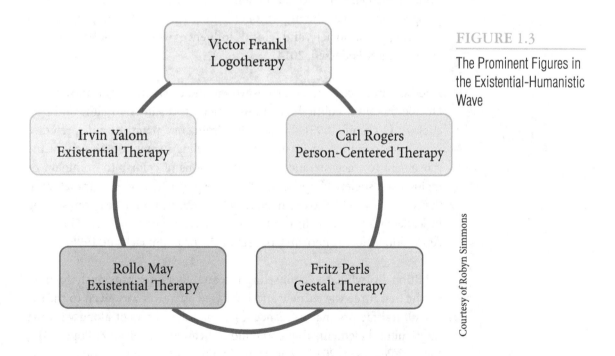

FIGURE 1.3

The Prominent Figures in the Existential-Humanistic Wave

Although this movement has been around for quite some time, Corey (2017) noted that Rogers hoped this theory would evolve and become a set of principles related to therapy processes. In fact, Rogers three core conditions of congruence, unconditional positive regard, and empathy are part of several counseling approaches and are considered central for an optimal counselor-client relationship no matter a counselor's theoretical orientation.

4th Wave—The Multicultural Wave

The multicultural wave emerged as a reaction to the limitations of counseling approaches within the first three waves and became just as influential as the previous ones (Pedersen & Pope, 2016). This wave takes a more holistic and ecosystemic approach in that it looks at individuals from both internal factors, such as biological and psychological elements, and external factors, such as the cultural context, in addressing a person's mental health (Ratts & Pedersen, 1995). In contrast, Jackson (1995) noted that the use of theories and techniques, historically speaking, were "at odds with the cultural background" of clients (p. 6) and did not account for cultural influences. With the first three waves, counseling was viewed with what some would call a "monocultural lens" without taking into account larger perspectives such as the impact of changing American demographics, an emerging global society, and "glocal" influences where the global becomes local (Ratts & Pedersen, 2014).

Another influence on the fourth wave was the 1950s civil rights movement. During this time, cultural factors were not a focus in counseling and psychology (Jackson, 1995). In fact, discriminatory practices and prejudice were more common in professional counseling in spite of the goal of the movement to integrate and assimilate persons of color into dominant or mainstream society (Copeland, 1983). The prevalence of discrimination in the counseling field also excluded racial and ethnic minorities from serving in leadership positions in the former American Personnel and Guidance Association (now American Counseling Association; Jackson, 1995).

Additionally, while the counseling research literature previously focused on the first three waves, new and increased attention was given to the sociocultural factors that influence a person's development along with the multicultural elements that could aid in healing (Pedersen & Pope, 2016; Ratts & Pedersen, 2014). For example, textbooks began including information on utilizing indigenous healing practices, using inclusive cultural empathy, increasing one's cultural awareness, and understanding cultural meanings of culturally different persons (Pedersen & Pope, 2016). Furthermore, the professional counseling literature began to address how existing counseling approaches could be modified or adapted to be more effective with culturally different persons (c.f., Draguns, 2016). Even counseling language regarding culturally different (non-Caucasian) persons was beginning to change. The term "minority counseling" was used in the 1960s but then changed to cross-cultural counseling and multicultural counseling in the 1970s (Key, 1995). In addition, wherein once the term "minority" was used, it transitioned to the term "person of color."

As noted previously, the multicultural focus emerged with the need to view clients from the context of their culture and environment (Sue & Sue, 2015). Along with this need to view clients within the context of their culture, there was also a need to explore counselor-client dynamics in a new way (Ratts & Pedersen, 2014). What emerged from this was the development of multicultural counseling competencies which focused on beliefs and attitudes, knowledge, and skills (this will be discussed in greater detail in Chapter 5). Within multicultural counseling practice, these competencies can be framed as counselors encompassing the following: becoming aware of one's own assumptions, biases, and attitudes towards those who are culturally different; understanding the worldview of culturally different persons; and utilizing culturally sensitive interventions, strategies, and techniques (c.f., Sue, Arrendondo, & McDavis, 1992; Sue & Sue, 2015).

It is clear that this wave has had and continues to have significant influence, advancing the counseling profession through a better understanding of the more dynamic aspects of clients. From this wave, another focus emerged, leading to a fifth wave known as the social justice wave.

5th Wave—The Social Justice Advocacy Wave

As the counseling profession advanced with the emergence of each wave, a new understanding in addressing mental health concerns arose. The advent of the social justice advocacy wave was no different, emphasizing advocacy not only in the process of individual counseling but also in what is known as systems-level advocacy (c.f., Ratts, 2009; Ratts & Pedersen, 2014). Prior views from previous waves focused on inherent aspects of individuals and ways to address difficulties; however, this new wave looked at the external factors that impact these internal factors. Ratts and Pedersen noted that this "approach is based on the belief that toxic environmental conditions influence human development issues" (p. 28). Addressing these conditions means addressing social issues enshrined in policy and laws which can negatively influence personal development. For example, social justice advocacy might look like challenging the discriminatory practices within a company's policies and leading a campaign to implement fair policy.

Addressing these conditions is dependent on the domain in which these conditions are enshrined; however, the American Counseling Association has adopted this fifth wave as a new competency expectation for counselors and created several domains wherein advocacy may be addressed: Client/Student Empowerment, Client/Student Advocacy, Community Collaboration, Systems Advocacy, Public Information, and Social/Political Advocacy (Lewis, Arnold, House, & Toporek, 2003). With this new emergence, social justice advocacy has become an expected practice among today's professional counselors (Dixon, Tucker, & Clark, 2010) and counseling programs are tasked to train future professional counselors to be social justice advocates (Shin, 2008). However, the actual look of this advocacy role has been historically ambiguous, without clear direction on how to put advocacy concepts into practice (Ratts & Hutchins, 2009; Roysircar, 2009). Even with increased publications focusing on social justice advocacy, these publications have emphasized philosophical and theoretical approaches rather than integrative or pragmatic approaches (c.f., Motulsky, Gere, Saleem, & Trantham, 2014).

Recent research has shown that social advocacy training can influence increased advocacy competence (Decker, 2013) and publications on the application of social justice competency concepts have increased (c.f., Arthur, 2018; Motulsky et al., 2014). With the noted research on advocacies and competencies, counselor education programs are able to more effectively incorporate these competencies in the training of future counselors.

Is there a 6ᵗʰ Wave? The Neuroscience Wave

While the literature has not identified advances in neuroscience as an official 6th wave, its emergence in recent years has had a significant influence on the counseling profession. In its basic definition, neuroscience focuses on the study of the structure and function of the brain and the nervous system (Neuroscience, n.d.). While the neurosciences field has been around for quite some time, its application to counseling has become increasingly apparent over the last decade. In an ACA *Counseling Today* article titled "Counseling and neuroscience: The cutting edge of the coming decade," Ivey and colleagues (2009) noted how "neuroscience and neuroimaging have found that measurable structural changes occur in client brains as a result of cognitive and interpersonal therapy" (para. 3). In other words, research findings show that common therapeutic practices have an impact on rewiring the brain with new neurons and new neural networks. The significance of neuroscience is also reflected in the 2016 Council for Accreditation of Counseling and Related Educational Programs education standards.

2016 CACREP Standards includes the
following language related to neuroscience:
Section 5.C.1.d. – neurobiological and medical foundation and
etiology of addiction and co-occurring disorders
Section 5.C.2.e. – potential for substance use disorders to
mimic and/or co-occur with a variety of neurological, medical,
and psychological disorders
Section 5.C.2.g. – impact of biological and neurological
mechanisms on mental health

To share the application of neuroscience to counseling, Ivey et al. (2009) focused on the following five basic concepts: 1) neuroplasticity – the idea that the brain is not fixed and that it can change through various counseling approaches; 2) neurogenesis – the idea that new neurons can develop with new learning or even exercise such as the application of counseling techniques; 3) importance of attention and focus – basic counseling skills such as attending behavior arouses the client's brain resulting in increased attention due to the counselor's positive communication and interest in client; 4) clarifying understanding of emotions – different areas of the brain are connected with different emotions: sad, mad, and fear are associated with the amygdala while positive emotions are associated with the prefrontal cortex; and 5) focusing on wellness and the positives – in line with the wellness perspective of counseling, focusing on a person's positive assets and strengths can help one to overcome the negative such as negative thinking patterns which then impacts the brain's neural processes.

Not only do counseling approaches impact brain development and re-wiring as previously noted, some studies have shown that counseling can impact brain function for those suffering from depression, anxiety, and borderline personality disorder (c.f., Goss, 2016). While the immediate application to counseling is limited, the increased understanding of brain function can inform the counselor of the impact of their work. For example, the brain can adapt to new changes throughout a person's life, dispelling the myth that an older person cannot learn anything new. Also, the brain changes to new stimuli such as new learning experiences, and the brain can impact emotions through specific neural processes. In application with clients, using brain scans of specific diagnoses such as PTSD helps to normalize the experience as having a "normal response to an abnormal situation." In addition, sharing physiological explanations can reduce the stigma and shame of mental health concerns and make it more tangible (Bray, 2018). Chapter 13 of this textbook is dedicated to a thorough explanation of neuroscience and how it can be applied to counseling.

> For more information on the helpful aspects of neuroscience and counseling, read the following *Counseling Today* article published by the American Counseling Association:
> https://ct.counseling.org/2018/03/why-neurocounseling/

As you can see, the counseling profession has experienced several major paradigm shifts influenced by significant researchers in the field. Each wave emerged as a reaction to or as an outgrowth of prior waves. No matter the reason for each wave's emergence, each one has impacted the counseling profession in that it created a new way of understanding and helping people. In addition, the tenets of each wave still influence today's profession with updates and variations of fundamental theories as well as new ways of helping people based on those theories.

Linda Martin
Master's of Counseling Student
Liberty University

© Linda Martin

When I first started working towards my Masters in Professional Counseling, I expected to learn every right answer that my future clients would possibly need to know. I had this image of the professional I would become; there was this huge gap between what I envisioned as a professional counselor and what I saw when I looked in the mirror, and that was scary! I was incredibly overwhelmed trying to figure out what kind of therapy I wanted to do and what type of clients I wanted to work with, while my peers seemed to already have those answers in stone. I suffered from a major case of "Imposter's Syndrome."

That first semester of graduate school, I un-learned everything I thought I knew about counseling and made room for the knowledge paid for by my tuition. At each leg in the journey, the educational process worked to open my eyes to experiences that helped widen my world view. The further the journey went, the clearer my perception of who I am, what my passions are, and what my purpose could be as a counselor became. My story, my background, and my influences have come together with my education to help clarify my professional direction. I have learned that even if the opportunity in front of me seems daunting, if I stay true to who I know I am, my authenticity connects with the client's vulnerability and progress is made. Amusingly, therapists seem to usually be portrayed on T.V. as this know-it-all lone wolves that have all the client's answers. Thankfully, real life is not like television and it is not supposed to be! I take comfort in the reality that our profession was intentionally designed as a team sport! As students, we can reach up to our professors; as Masters-level therapists, we can reach out to our supervisors; and as professional counselors we will be able to collaborate with the professional support network we create during the journey.

As I let go of all of the fear from that first semester of having to carry the weight of my client's burdens and relaxed into the process of becoming the counselor I was meant to be, the image of the counselor in the mirror started to take shape. The professional I see when I look into the mirror now is me, exactly as I am, and I am not alone. Standing around me are all the professors, peers, and supervisors that I have already crossed paths with and there is still room for more! Trust the process—it works!

Contributed by Linda Martin. © Kendall Hunt Publishing Company.

WHAT ARE CURRENT TRENDS IN COUNSELING?

Technology and Counseling

Before ending this chapter on the history and current trends of counseling, it is important to address an increasingly important focus in today's counseling profession: technological influences in counseling. As technology is ever-changing, this is both a current trend and a future direction (you will read more about this in Chapter 14). The traditional practice of counseling may conjure an image of a client and counselor sitting together, using talk therapy as a way for the counselor to offer help and the client to receive help. While this still presents as true, this traditional practice is quickly evolving, with more versatile ways of helping clients becoming available. While not directly related to technology, one example of this versatility is the concept of in-home counseling or home-based therapy. This allows convenience for clients who have limited mobility and a more comfortable setting for counseling to be conducted. Although some have expressed initial concerns about this model, it has become more commonplace and accepted as standard practice. Another emerging modality for counseling practice is telemental health or online counseling. This offers even more convenience, with opportunities for counselors to offer help to clients in places of accessibility and security.

One other notable mention regarding technology and counseling is the influence of social media and smartphone counseling-related apps. The far-reaching impact of social media is obvious in today's world, and this is no less true for the counseling profession. Social media allows for ease of connection through Facebook, Instagram, Twitter and the like; however, it also can blur professional boundaries between counselor and client. In understanding its extensive influence, even the ACA Code of Ethics was modified to include information about social media relationships. In addition, counseling-related apps can offer a beneficial way for clients to be their own counselors, with techniques and homework assignments that provide structure for self-awareness and improvement. These apps can also be utilized in the counselor-client relationship for homework between sessions or a post-counseling framework to continue with individual efforts toward wellness.

SUMMARY

The profession of counseling has come a long way, due to the contributions of prominent persons who have been instrumental in shaping the field by recognizing the value of counseling. With their efforts, they partnered together to organize a number of counseling-related organizations, eventually forming today's counseling flagship organization, the American Counseling Association. In this chapter, we reviewed the history of counseling with influences from as early as the late 1800s to current trends impacting today's profession. You were introduced to historical developments by decade, showing how the profession advanced, as well as to paradigm shifts that changed our broad understandings about people as the profession evolved. The information presented can deepen personal insights into the counseling profession, distinguishing it from other mental health professions including social work, psychology, psychiatry, and marriage and family therapy.

FOR THE ROAD AHEAD

Check out the Chapter 1 video at this link:

https://www.khpcontent.com/

Reflections on the Journey

As you begin to understand more about the development of the counseling profession and some of the waves that have influenced the profession, it is important to consider how you plan to engage with the profession to continue your learning. What areas of counseling are you specifically interested in at this time? Keep in mind that your focus may change over the course of your studies, and that changes in interest are common. Reading scholarly material, listening to podcasts and webinars, and attending professional conferences are all ways to expand your learning that are very accessible in the 21st century.

For Further Exploration

Bray, B. (2018, March). Why neurocounseling? *Counseling Today.* Retrieved from https://ct.counseling.org/2018/03/why-neurocounseling/

Ivey, A., Ivey, M. B., Zalaquett, C., & Quirk, K. (2009, December). Counseling and neuroscience: The cutting edge of the coming decade. *Counseling Today.* Retrieved from https://ct.counseling.org/2009/12/

reader-viewpoint-counseling-and-neuroscience-the-utting-edge-of-the-coming-decade/

Langberg, D. (n.d.) Lessons Learned in the Therapist's Chair [Audio]. Retrieved from http://www.dianelangberg.com/2018/01/lessons-learned-from-the-therapists-chair/

Ratts, M. (2012). *Five forces of counseling and psychotherapy* (Microtraining Associates) [Video] Retrieved from https://search.alexanderstreet.com

Shook, M. (Producer). (2017, February 8). What Makes a Counselor a Counselor? Professional Identity and Other Musings with Carl Sheperis [Audio podcast]. *The Thoughtful Counselor*. Retrieved from http://wp.me/p7R6fn-8u

Check your school or local library database for following video series entitled *Five Forces of Counseling and Psychotherapy* on the Alexander Street database. It also may be under ProQuest as Alexander Street is a ProQuest Company.

REFERENCES

American Association of Christian Counselors [AACC, 2019]. About: Mission. Retrieved from https://www.aacc.net/about/

American Association of State Counseling Boards [AASCB] (n.d.). About. Retrieved from http://www.aascb.org/aws/AASCB/pt/sp/about

American Counseling Association (2019a). ACA Conference Locations, Dates and Themes. Retrieved from https://www.counseling.org/about-us/about-aca/our-history/past-conference-dates-and-locations

American Counseling Association (2019b). News: American Counseling Association and the American School Counselor Association Announce New Collaborative Relationship. Retrieved from https://www.counseling.org/news/updates/2018/03/21/american-Counseling-association-and-the-american-school-counselor-association-announce-new-collaborative-relationship

American Counseling Association (2019c). 2020: A Vision for the Future of Counseling. Retrieved from https://www.counseling.org/about-us/about-aca/20-20-a-vision-for-the-future-of- counseling

American Psychiatric Association. (2013). *Diagnostic and statistical manual of mental disorders* (5th ed.). Arlington, VA: Author.

Arthur, N (Ed.). (2018). *Counselling in cultural contexts: Identities and social justice*. Switzerland: Springer Publishing.

Association for Spiritual, Ethical, and Religious Values in Counseling [ASERVIC] (2019). About: History. Retrieved from http://www.aservic.org/about-2/history/

Aubrey, R. F. (1977). Historical development of guidance and counseling and implications for the future. *Personnel and Guidance Journal, 55*(6), 288-295.

Barrett, E. S. (1948). Vocational Guidance and the George-Barden Act. *The High School Journal, 31*(1), 1-3. Retrieved from https://www.jstor.org/stable/40367635

Belkin, G. S. (1988). *Introduction to counseling* (3rd ed.). Dubuque, IA: Wm. C. Brown.

Bray, B. (2018, March). Why neurocounseling? *Counseling Today.* Retrieved from https://ct.counseling. org/2018/03/why-neurocounseling/

CAPS International (2019). Christian Association for Psychological Studies: About us. Retrieved from https:// caps.net/about/

Chi Sigma Iota (2018). About CSI: History of CSI. Retrieved from https://www.csi-net.org/

Collins, G. R. (n.d) Meet Gary Collins. Retrieved from https://www.garycollins.org/new-page

Copeland, E. J. (1983). Cross-cultural counseling and psychotherapy: A historical perspective, implications for research and training. *The Personnel and Guidance Journal, 62*(1), 10-15.

Corey, G. (2017) *Theory and practice of counseling and psychotherapy* (10th ed.). Boston, MA: Cengage Learning.

Council for Accreditation of Counseling and Related Educational Programs [CACREP] (2016). 2016 standards for accreditation. Alexandria, VA: Author.

Council for Accreditation of Counseling and Related Educational Programs [CACREP] (2019). For students: Finding a CACREP program. Retrieved from https://www.cacrep.org/directory

Decker, K. M. (2013). *A study of relationships between counselor education, social justice advocacy competence, and likelihood to advocate* (Doctoral dissertation). Retrieved from ProQuest Dissertations & Theses Global. (3602466)

Dixon, A. L., Tucker, C., & Clark, M. A. (2010). Integrating social justice advocacy with national standard of practice: Implications for school counselor education, *Counselor Education & Supervision, 50,* 103-118.

Donnay, D. A. C. (1997). E. K. Strong's legacy and beyond: 70 years of the strong interest inventory. *The Career Development Quarterly, 46*(1), 2-22.

Draguns, J. G. (2016). *Counseling encounters in multicultural contexts.* In P. B. Pedersen, W. J. Lonner, J. G. Draguns, J. E. Trimble, & M. R. Scharron-del Rio *Counseling across cultures* (7th ed., pp. 31-49). Thousand Oaks, CA: Sage Publications.

Duggan, J. H. & Kaplan, D. (2015). *ACA podcast: Accreditation and licensure policies* [Audio podcast]. Retrieved from https://www.counseling.org/docs/default-source/library-archives/podcast-transcripts/special-topic---accreditation-and-licensure-policies.pdf?svrsn=2555442c_12

Entwistle, D. N. (2015). *Integrative approaches to psychology and Christianity* (3rd ed.). Eugene, OR: Cascade.

Ginter, E. J. (2002). Journal of Counseling & Development (JCD) and counseling's interwoven nature: Achieving a more complete understanding of the present through "historization" (Musings of an Exiting Editor–An Editorial Postscript). *Journal of Counseling & Development, 80,* 219-222.

Gladding, S. T. (2018). *Counseling: A comprehensive profession* (8th ed.). New York, NY: Pearson.

Goss, D. (2016). Integrating neuroscience into counseling psychology: A systematic review of current literature. *The Counseling Psychologist, 44*(6), 895-920.

Granello, D. H., & Young, M. E. (2019). *Counseling today: Foundations of professional identity* (2nd ed). Boston, MA: Pearson.

Guindon, M. H. (2010). *A counseling primer: An introduction to the profession.* New York, NY: Routledge.

Haynes, C. (2016). Identity, transcendence and the true self: Insights from psychology and contemplative spirituality. *HTS Teologeise Studies/Theological Studies, 72*(4) a3455.

Hollis, J. W. & Dodson, T. A. (1999). *Counselor preparation 1999-2001: Programs, faculty, trends.* Philadelphia, PA: Taylor & Francis.

Jones, S. L. & Butman, R. E. (2011). *Modern Psychotherapies: A comprehensive Christian appraisal* (2nd ed.). Downers Grove, IL: InterVarsity.

Ikic, V., Bélanger, C., Bouchard, S., Gosselin, P., Langlois, F., Labrecque, J., . . . Marchand, A. (2017). Reduction in costs after treating comorbid panic disorder with agoraphobia and generalized anxiety disorder. *Journal of Mental Health Policy and Economics, 20*(1), 11-20.

Ivey, A., Ivey, M. B., Zalaquett, C., & Quirk, K. (2009, December). Counseling and neuroscience: The cutting edge of the coming decade. *Counseling Today*. Retrieved from https://ct.counseling.org/2009/12/reader-viewpoint-counseling-and-neuroscience-the-cutting-edge-of-the-coming-decade/

Jackson, M. L. (1995). Multicultural counseling: Historical perspectives. In J. G. Ponterotto, J. M. Casas, L. Suzuki, & C. M. Alexander (Eds.), *Handbook of Multicultural Counseling* (pp. 3-16). Thousand Oaks, CA: Sage Publications.

Kaplan, D. M., Tarvydas, V. M., & Gladding, S. T. (2014). 20/20: A vision for the future of counseling: The new consensus definition of counseling. *Journal of Counseling & Development, 92*, 366-372. doi:10.1002/j.1556-6676.2014.00164.x

Key, K. (2010, November). How the evolution of psychology gave birth to counseling. *Psychology Today*. Retrieved from https://www.psychologytoday.com/us/blog/counseling-keys/201011/how-the-evolution-psychology-gave-birth-counseling

Lewis, J., Arnold, M. S., House, R., & Toporek, R. (2003). *Advocacy Competencies*. Alexandria, VA: American Counseling Association.

MacConomy, S. (2018 Jan). *ACA takes action against state-based legislation threatening licensure for counselors.* ACA Government Affairs News Blog. Retrieved from https://www.counseling.org/news/aca-blogs/aca-government-affairs-blog/aca-government-affairs-blog/2018/01/29/aca-takes-action-to-block-bill-that-could-eliminate-licensure-for-counselors-in-arizona

Mental Health America (2019a). Programs: Mental Health Month. Retrieved from http://www.mentalhealthamerica.net/may

Mental Health America (2019b). Programs: Screening to Supports (S2S). Retrieved from http://www.mentalhealthamerica.net/screening-supports-s2s

McMinn, M. R. (2011). *Psychology, theology and spirituality in Christian counseling* (Rev. ed.). Carol Stream, IL: Tyndale.

McMinn, M. R. & Campbell, C. D. (2007) *Integrative psychotherapy: Toward a comprehensive Christian approach.* Downer's Grove, IL: Intervarsity Press.

McWilliams, M. (2016). Psychoanalysis. In I. Marini & M. A. Stebnicki (Eds.), *The professional counselor's desk reference* (2nd ed., pp. 183-190). New York, NY: Springer.

Motulsky, S. L., Gere, S. H., Saleem, R., & Trantham, S. M. (2014). Teaching social justice in counseling psychology. *The Counseling Psychologist, 42*(8), 1058-1053.

Myhr, G., & Payne, K. (2006). Cost-effectiveness of cognitive-behavioural therapy for mental disorders: Implications for public health care funding policy in Canada. *Canadian Journal of Psychiatry, 51*(10),662-670.

National Alliance for Mental Illness (2019a). Learn more: Mental health by the numbers. Retrieved from https://www.nami.org/Learn-More/Mental-Health-By-the Numbers

National Alliance for Mental Illness (2019b). There is a virus spreading across the country. It's stigma. Do you have it? Retrieved from https://www.nami.org/Press-Media/Press-Releases/2018/There-is-a-virus-spreading-across-the-country-It

National Board for Certified Counselors (2019). Board certification. Retrieved from https://www.nbcc.org/Certification

The National Council (2019). Community Mental Health Act. Retrieved from https://www.thenationalcouncil.org/about/national-mental-health-association/overview/community-mental-health-act/

Neukrug, E. S. (2011). *Counseling theory and practice.* Belmont, CA: Brooks/Cole.

Neuroscience. (n.d.) In *English Oxford living dictionaries.* Retrieved from https://en.oxforddictionaries.com/definition/neuroscience

Parsons, F. (1909). *Choosing a vocation.* Boston, MA: Houghton Mifflin.

Parry, M. (2006). G. stanley hall: Psychologist and early gerontologist, *American Journal of Public Health, 96*(7), 1161.

Pedersen, P. B., & Pope, M. (2016). *Towards effectiveness through empathy.* In P. B. Pedersen, W. J. Lonner, J. G. Draguns, J. E. Trimble, & M. R. Scharron-del Rio (Eds.), *Counseling across cultures* (7th ed., pp. 13-30). Thousand Oaks, CA: Sage Publications.

Pennsylvania General Assembly (2018) *Act 76: Social Workers, Marriage And Family Therapists and Professional Counselors Act - Omnibus Amendments.* Retrieved from https://www.legis.state.pa.us/cfdocs/legis/li/uconsCheck.cfm?yr=2018&sessInd=0&act=76.

Ratts, M. J. (2009). Social justice counseling: Toward the development of a "fifth force" among counseling paradigms. *Journal of Humanistic Counseling, Education, and Development, 48,* 160-172.

Ratts, M. J., & Hutchins, A.M. (2009). ACA advocacy competencies: Social justice advocacy at the client/student level. *Journal of Counseling & Development, 87*(3), 269-275.

Ratts, M. J., & Pedersen, P. B. (2014). *Counseling for multiculturalism and social justice: Integration, theory, and application* (4th ed.). Alexandria, VA: American Counseling Association.

Rogers, C. R. (1961). *On becoming a person: A therapist's view of psychotherapy.* New York, NY: Houghton Mifflin Company.

Roysircar, G. (2009). The big picture of advocacy: Counselor, heal society and thyself. *Journal of Counseling & Development, 87*(3), 288-294.

Rush-Wilson & Trippany Simmons, R. (2009). The mental health sisters: Helping students conceptualize the distinctions among the mental health disciplines. *SACES Newsletter, 5(3),* p. 7.

Shin, R. Q. (2008). Advocating for social justice in academia through recruitment, retention, admissions, and professional survival. *Journal of Multicultural Counseling and Development, 36*(3), 180-191.

Stripling, R. O. (1978). Standards and accreditation in counselor education: A proposal. *Personnel and Guidance Journal, 56*(10), 608-612.

Sue, D. W., Arrendondo, P., & McDavis, R. J. (1992). Multicultural counseling competencies and standards: A call to the profession. *Journal of Multicultural Counseling and Development, 20,* 64-89.

Sue, D. W., & Sue, D. (2015). *Counseling the culturally diverse: Theory and practice* (7th ed.). New York, NY: John Wiley and Sons.

Tan, S.-Y. (2011). *Counseling and psychotherapy: A Christian perspective.* Grand Rapids, MI: Baker.

United States Department of Labor (2017). Occupational Employment Statistics. Retrieved from https://www.bls.gov/oes/2016/may/oes211014.htm

Williamson, E. G. (1947). Counseling and the Minnesota point of view. *Educational and psychological measurement, 7,* 141-155.

CHAPTER 2

Professional Identity: Associations, Credentials, and Licenses

Mary Deacon, Ph.D., Kevin Van Wynsberg, Ph.D., Robyn Simmons, Ed.D., & Brandi Chamberlin, Ph.D.

"In the social jungle of human existence, there is no feeling of being alive without a sense of identity."
-Erik Erikson

Following Christ: Grace for Our Work

As future professional counselors, consider how you can embrace your professional identity whole-heartedly. Ecclesiastes 9:10 (International Standard Version) says, "Whatever the activity in which you engage, do it with all your ability, because there is no work, no planning, no learning, and no wisdom in the next world where you're going".

This verse encourages development of your professional identity in that it means actively seeking to be the best you can be in your work, and even to pour into the profession as opposed to simply receiving from it. This involves a shift from being a consumer in the profession to being a producer. The motivation to love

After reading this chapter, you will understand more about:

- The importance of developing and maintaining counselor professional identity.
- The American Counseling Association, and it's branches and divisions, as well as specialty counseling organizations and honor societies.
- Counselor credentialing, including licensure and certification.
- The Council for Accreditation of Counseling and Related Educational Programs (CACREP) and the benefits and standards associated with accreditation.

The following CACREP standards are addressed in this chapter:

Professional Counseling Orientation and Ethical Practice:

- Professional counseling organizations, including membership benefits, activities, services to members, and current issues (CACREP, 2016, Standard 2.F.1.f.)
- Professional counseling credentialing, including certification, licensure, and accreditation practices and standards, and the effects of public policy on these issues (CACREP, 2016, Standard 2.F.1.g.)

God and love others should be readily apparent in the words and actions of the counselor. In all actions, God calls us to "leave it better than we found it." Consider how you might make a positive and God-honoring mark through your work. You might do this through continually sharpening your clinical skills, through advocating for counseling-related causes, or through developing the profession of counseling in your involvement or leadership in counseling organizations.

2 Thessalonians 1:11-12 says:

> With this in mind, we always pray for you, asking that our God might make you worthy of his calling and that through his power he might help you accomplish every good desire and faithful action. That way the name of our Lord Jesus will be glorified by you, and you by him, according to the grace of our God and Lord, Jesus, the Messiah.

Building a strong, clear counselor identity accomplishes this purpose. Pursuing licensure, certifications, and being active in professional counseling organizations are ways to engage in your work with all of your ability. These activities demonstrate a commitment to being a professional and being in a profession. And as well see from the scriptures, these activities also demonstrate a commitment to God when we carry them out with a motivation to answer his call.

Understanding the development of the profession is a critical first step in the development of a professional identity. In Chapter 1, you were introduced to the counseling profession's historical and philosophical antecedents. In this chapter, you will encounter the practical elements of the profession of counseling, including how to develop and integrate your professional identity into your personal identity.

When considering professional identity, it is important to start with exploring what constitutes a profession. Put simply, a profession has a professional identity, and this identity is developed as you incorporate the attitudes, values, and activities of the profession into who you are as a person (Lile, 2017). This identity is also reflected in the unifying bodies and practice standards of the profession. Professional associations (e.g., the American Counseling Association), regulation of the profession (i.e., licensure, certification), and standardization of core values (e.g., Codes of Ethics, Standards of Practice) and training (i.e., accreditation, certifications) all allow for a clear definition and unification of a professional identity (Myers & Sweeney, 2001).

© Kheng Guan Toh/Shutterstock.com

Perhaps you are wondering why professional identity is so important. Developing a unified professional identity allows for a sense of belonging, enhances allegiance, fosters competency, and provides a schematic framework for the profession and professional community (Dong, Campbell & Vance, 2017). As a future counselor, or a counselor-in-training (CIT), you will want to begin embracing your new identity by becoming knowledgeable about and involved in the professional activities associated with the field. It is important to note, however, that there is more to developing this sense of professional identity than simply engaging in the behaviors of a counselor. "Being a counselor is not just what you do, it is who you are" (R. Comas, personal communication, August 25, 1994). This chapter is focused on helping you to understand the foundations of professional identity as well as the associations, credentials, and training standards that come together to form this unified identity.

THE MENTAL HEALTH FIELD

When establishing your professional identity as a counselor, you first need to understand the unique role that counseling has in the field of mental health. One way to do this is to think about a baseball game. In a baseball

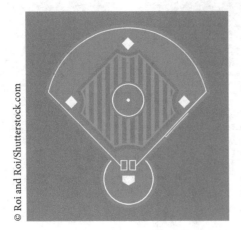

game, there is a field on which the game is played. The players on the field have different foci and different roles, some of which include pitcher, catcher, 1st baseman, 2nd baseman, shortstop, 3rd baseman, and outfielders. Each player is vital to the team; however, each has a specific role and purpose (See Figure 2.1 below).

Similarly, mental health is a field. As you learned in Chapter 1, there are 5 professions in the field (See Figure 2.1; The Five Professions in the Mental Health Field). These include Psychiatry, Psychology, Social Work, Counseling, and Marriage and Family Therapy. It is important to understand your role as a counselor and embrace that professional identity. This will allow you to not only learn about your unique "position" on the team, but it will also help you to educate others on the unique skills that counselors bring to the field. This knowledge of how you fit into the big picture of mental health services is one way that you can advocate for your professional identity as a counselor. This will allow you to have an answer when well-intended family, friends, and others ask the question, "What exactly do you do as a counselor?"

FIGURE 2.1

The Five Professions in the Mental Health Field

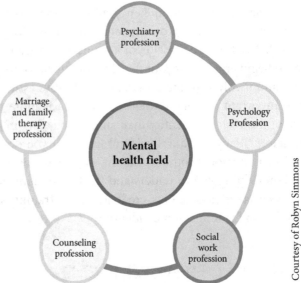

Securing a strong professional identity as a counselor, as well as engaging in professional advocacy, are important activities for you as a future counseling professional. One of your first tasks in developing a professional identity is to learn how to define the term *counseling*, as it is often used to describe activities that are not a part of the identity of the counseling profession. In 2010, the American Counseling Association's (ACA) 20/20 Task Force revised ACA's definition for the profession as follows: "Counseling is a professional relationship that empowers diverse individuals, families, and groups to accomplish mental health, wellness, education, and career goals" (ACA, 2010, para. 2). This definition paints a broad stroke explanation for how counselors assist clients. Keywords that identify values of our profession include empowers, diverse, and accomplish. These words represent our belief in our clients' ability to actualize their respective resources such that wellness is achievable. Professional identity as a counselor begins, then, with a belief system that clients have internal resources and are able to be empowered to find success in counseling (Kaplan, Tarvydas, & Gladding, 2014).

Chart 2.1 highlights the identified principles for improving and promoting a sense of professional identity, as identified by the 20/20 Task Force (Kaplan & Gladding, 2011, p. 371).

CHART 2.1

Principles of Professional Identity

Sharing a common professional identity is critical for counselors.	Presenting ourselves as a unified profession has multiple benefits.	Working together to improve the public perception of counseling and to advocate for professional issues will strengthen the profession.	Creating a portability system for licensure will benefit counselors and strengthen the counseling profession.
	Expanding and promoting our research base is essential to the efficacy of professional counselors and to the public perception of the profession.	Focusing on students and prospective students is necessary to ensure the ongoing health of the counseling profession.	Promoting client welfare and advocating for the populations we serve is a primary focus of the counseling profession.

Courtesy of Robyn Simmons

Guided by these principles, counselor educators (i.e., counseling professors in graduate school) are committed to helping you develop a strong sense of professional identity. This will ensure that you are equipped to educate the public, advocate for the profession, advance the counseling field through research and scholarly activity (e.g., presentations to colleagues locally, regionally, and/or nationally), promote client welfare, and advocate for the populations that counselors serve.

© Mike Shook

The Thoughtful Counselor Podcast, Mike Shook, Producer

The genesis of The Thoughtful Counselor is quite simple – a combination of wanting a resource like it but none existing, a desire to be connected to others in the counseling profession, a general love of ideas, and the boredom of working in isolation moved me to start the podcast. I learned very quickly that if this thing was to succeed over time and showcase the diversity of people and ideas in the counseling profession, I would need a team of contributors from different backgrounds with different interests and approaches to counseling. While I may have started the podcast, our team of interviewers/counselors/counselor educators sustain it. Allison Kramer, Raissa Miller, Megan Speciale, Aaron Smith, Priscilla Wilson, and Stephen Dickson deserve as much credit as anyone as without them the podcast would have died years ago.

I am very grateful for the numerous counselors and counselor educators who have responded to my "cold-call" emails regarding an interview with a "yes." I am still surprised and thankful when people want to participate. I'm nearly 100 conversations in and a few things that I have learned about the counseling profession and my personal professional identity include:

- The counseling profession is young. We are still hashing out what it really means to be a counselor (vs. clinical social work, marriage and family therapist, psychologist, etc.) and there are a variety of ideas, opinions, and positions on what direction the counseling profession should take moving forward. This has helped me both appreciate and respect those who have worked so hard to get the profession to where it is, while also contributing my own thoughts and ideas to the ongoing development of the profession.
- The counseling profession is diverse. Not only in the traditional categories of race, gender, sexual orientation, religious identities which are so deeply important, but also ideas. Sometimes it easy to think *everyone* in the counseling profession endorses things such as the ACA code of ethics or the profession's embrace of the DSM, yet there are many voices from inside the profession that offer important critiques and alternatives. I believe this strengthens the profession and we do our best to showcase this with The Thoughtful Counselor.
- The counseling profession is important (but not everything). I have found that it has been extremely useful to be housed within the counseling profession as a starting point for my professional formation, yet I have also seen the limits of a profession. Whether it be counseling or any other profession, there

are always certain ideas that are elevated or "in vogue" while other ideas are hidden or dismissed. This has been true in the past and will be true as the counseling profession moves forward. Having our identities firmly rooted outside the counseling profession, in our most intimate relationships and communities, gives each of us the ability to offer thoughtful and critical reflections that are enriching for the profession as a whole.

Contributed by Mike Shook. © Kendall Hunt Publishing Company.

WHAT ARE THE HALLMARKS OF PROFESSIONAL IDENTITY?

As mentioned earlier in the chapter, our professional identity as counselors is reflected in the counseling professional associations, the requirements for profession licensure and certification, our standards of practice and codes of ethics, and our educational training standards. Without these entities, we would lack a cohesive counselor identity. Professional organizations for counselors and counselor educators provide the setting where counselors define professional identity,

what professional roles, and application of professional roles in practice. It is also through counseling-related professional organizations where counselors establish codes of ethics and professional competencies that define competent ethical practices for the counseling specializations. Licensure and certifications define the academic, clinical, examination, and supervision requirements counselors must meet to practice, as well as define the scope of practice and the legal regulations and ethical codes counselors must follow. Finally, counselors' educational training standards are designed to ensure that all graduates of a counseling program have the knowledge, skills, and dispositions required to practice ethically when serving pluralistic and culturally rich and diverse populations.

Challenges to Identifying a Professional Identity

The challenges to identifying a professional identity are found by closely examining the current status of the entities that define a counselor identity: professional associations, the requirements for professional licensure and certification, our standards of practice and codes of ethics, and our educational training standards. Unlike other mental health professions, the field of counseling does not have a singular entity that defines each of these areas. Rather, the field of counseling is still in the process of becoming unified. The principle professional organization, the American Counseling Association (ACA), is expanding their sphere of influence in defining and advocating for the profession. In addition, as you read through the following sections, you will see that among the states, there are variations in our profession licensure and certification requirements as well as our standards of practice and codes of ethics. Finally, there is not a singular educational training standard for the field of counseling. Thus, the challenge that the counseling field faces as a profession is to recognize the need to advocate for a strong unified professional identity as reflected in these four entities that define counseling as a profession.

Perhaps as a result of this lack of uniformity in educational standards and licensure regulations, the general public seems to be unaware of what it means to be a counselor. Complicating this further is the common non-clinical use of the term *counseling*, such as lay counseling, pastoral counseling, financial counseling, etc. Thus, to differentiate that a clinical mental health counselor is practicing at a licensure-level practice, many practicing licensed counselors do not colloquially refer to what they do as counseling. When professional counselors describe their work, 54 percent of independently licensed counselors never used the words counselor or counseling when talking to others about their occupational role (Burns & Cruikshanks, 2017). Instead, these counselors identify as therapist or psychotherapist. In a qualitative study investigating the impact of mindfulness on the development of professional identity, Dong et al. (2017) found that mindfulness (i.e., readings, reflections, and meditations) assisted in the development of a more sophisticated understanding of professional identity for counseling internship students. What this means for you, as a future counselor, is that you will need to be intentionally reflective as you learn more about what it means to be a counselor, including how you explain your professional goals to be a professional counselor rather than a therapist (Doyle, 2016).

Rather than solely focusing on practical elements of counselor identity (e.g., licensure, etc...), counselor education programs also need to promote the unique values, attitudes and behaviors related to, as well as a sense of pride in, counselor identity (Burns & Cruikshanks, 2018). Burns and Cruikshanks (2018) noted that these values were shared across the mental health disciplines, however the attitude and behaviors related to the values differ across professional orientation:

> . . . the five hallmarks of the counseling profession (normal development, prevention, wellness, advocacy, and empowerment) are not exclusively valued by counselors but differ in focus from other mental health professions. For example, in the profession of counseling, counselors use empowerment by encouraging client autonomy, self-advocacy, self-validation, and self-determination. In comparison, social workers encourage clients' socially responsible self-determination to balance the needs of clients and society. In psychology, empowerment occurs when the psychologist respects cultural differences, safeguards client welfare, and allows the client to make their own decisions. (p. 33)

Ultimately, stabilizing professional identity among counselors will provide multiple benefits. Not only will it address the challenges noted here, it will also likely speak to the discussion on licensure portability in Chapter 14. Further, stronger professional identity inevitably results in greater recognition from governmental policies (e.g., Medicare) and third party payers (i.e., insurance companies). Additionally, as noted by Burns and Cruikshanks (2018), this recognition will carry more weight at counselors advocate for their clients.

Building a Counselor Identity
Maria Morton

Last year I had a mid-life crisis (not so much a crisis, but a crossroads), particularly vocationally. After 25 years of raising funds for nonprofits, I felt like that season had ended – there was just no more life in that work for me. I then went on a journey to discover what's next, which was scary, given I am in my mid-50s. After spending months with mentors and counselors, and much time in self-reflection, I discovered that counseling

is what I was created to do. When I told my friends that I made a decision to pursue a professional counseling career, they said "You are doing that already!"

Reflecting back on my 50+ years, I realized there were signs along the way, pointing me to the calling as a counselor. I served a number of years as a lay counselor in various ministerial settings. I have a lot of life experiences that developed me into not just a survivor, but a thriver, on the other side of trauma. God provided so much comfort in my troubles over the years, so now I can comfort those in any trouble with the comfort I received from God (based on 2 Corinthians 1:3-4, The Passion Translation). Humbly, I must admit, I thought I already had what it took to be a counselor — compassion, lay experience, my own experience as a counseling client for years, resourcefulness, and a listening ear. I just needed a license and then I could get paid for what I was already doing. I could pass on my wealth of knowledge and make everyone's lives better.

Once I started professional courses at Liberty, I discovered developing a counselor identity is not what I expected at all. In my very first class, I realized just how much I would have to unlearn and relearn to excel as a counselor. I had to put down my biased ideas and start with a fresh, teachable slate.

One of the first things I learned is that counseling excellence comes from the counselor's character and how they relate with people. It is mostly about building trusting relationships with clients, so they feel safe to bravely explore and pursue the changes they want to make in their lives. It is not about giving direction or advice but listening and helping clients discover their own answers — answers they already have deep within themselves. It is certainly not "dragging" someone down the same healing paths I traveled but helping them to discover their own path. It is about putting my own worldviews and religious beliefs aside and accepting (and loving) people right where they are (especially when their choices do not match my values), with the recognition they too were created in the image of God and are extremely valuable to Him.

I discovered counselors must work extremely hard to "know thyself," so a counselor does not allow his or her preferences and values to interfere with client care, potentially causing them harm and thwarting their journey to wellness. This self-awareness is critically important for those of us from majority populations, who do not experience overt and covert discrimination and oppression as do others from multicultural backgrounds.

I learned the importance of championing the counseling profession. My identity as a counselor will involve ongoing advocacy, at local, state, and national levels, to support my peers and the profession as a whole to be seen as effective and necessary for empowering people to achieve health and wellness, not just make problems right or divert a crisis.

I so much appreciate the educators I have worked with thus far, who continue to encourage CITs by reminding us to expect cycles of feeling insecure and then courage, self-doubt and then confidence, failure and then higher learning, and anxiety and then satisfaction in watching a client develop into his or her best self. It is because of this satisfaction of seeing clients become their true selves that will make this roller-coaster of a journey well worth it.

Contributed by Maria Morton. © Kendall Hunt Publishing Company.

WHAT ARE COUNSELING ORGANIZATIONS?

Building a strong professional identity is a large part of being a counselor. One of the most practical ways to build and maintain that professional identity as well as advance the field is through membership in professional counseling associations. These associations are made up of professionals in the field, educators, students, and individuals interested in the profession. Associations help to organize the members to advocate for the profession, to facilitate opportunities for networking, to provide ongoing training, and to advance the body of knowledge by the dissemination of information essential to the field. Many licensed counselors attend conference workshops and seminars to obtain the Continued Education Units (CEUs) required to maintain their licenses and/or certifications. Association membership provides a wonderful path for counseling students to develop their professional identity. Professional organizations usually offer students discounted rates for membership and conference registrations as well as special membership benefits for students, such as liability insurance for practicum and internship at a reduced rate or free of change.

Most associations have regular conferences that include workshops, trainings, and networking opportunities. They often produce guidance documents to the profession, such as ethical codes and standards of practice. These organizations provide a great way to be involved in advocating for the profession, to stay competent by getting the latest training, and to stay connected to other individuals and organizations in counseling. Members also can contribute to these organizations through the dissemination of research and training, through serving in leadership roles (such as association president or treasurer), through involvement in subcommittees and workgroups, and through advocacy activities.

Below, some of the main counseling organizations are listed. Keep in mind that while this chapter will cover some of the main associations, there are many more organizations that exist at the national, regional, state, and even local levels.

USEFUL ACRONYMS

ACA -American Counseling Association. This is the flagship professional organization for counselors. There are 19 specialty divisions of the ACA and each has its own acronym, as well.

AMHCA – American Mental Health Counselors Association. This is a professional organization whose focus is solely on mental health counseling. It was once a division of ACA.

CACREP – Council for Accreditation of Counseling and Related Educational Programs. This is the accrediting body for counseling programs.

CCMHC – Certified Clinical Mental Health Counselor. This is the national certification for mental health counselors.

CPCE – Counselor Preparation Competency Exam. This is the comprehensive examination many counseling programs use for their students. It is administered by the same credentialing body that writes the NCE and the NCMHCE.

CSI – Chi Sigma Iota. This is the International Counseling Honor Society.

NBCC – National Board for Certified Counselors. This is the credentialing body that regulates the NCC and NCMHCE credentials, the NCE, and CPCE.

NCC – National Certified Counselor. This is the national certification for counselors.

NCE – National Counselor Examination. This is the examination used by many state counseling licensure boards for their licensure examination. This is also the exam used in conjunction with academic and clinical preparation that enables counselors to become NCC's.

NCMHCE – National Clinical Mental Health Counselor Examination. This is the examination used by several state counseling licensure boards for their licensure examination. This is also the exam used in conjunction with academic and clinical preparation that enables counselors to become CCMHC's.

American Counseling Association (ACA)

In 1952, the American Personnel and Guidance Association (APGA) was formed through the merger of The National Vocational Guidance Association (NVGA), the National Association of Guidance and Counselor Trainers (NAGCT), the Student Personnel Association for Teacher Education (SPATE), and the American College Personnel Association (ACPA). This merger was formation of the APGA was to provide a national voice to the guidance and counselor profession. In 1983, the organization was renamed the American Association of Counseling and Development (AACD) and less than ten years later, in 1992, the name American Counseling Association was given to this organization. The organization now boasts more than 50,000 members and is a major voice in representing the counseling profession.

There are 56 state and regional branches of ACA, including affiliate branches in most states in the United States (US) and US territories, as well as a European Branch and a Philippine Branch. Further, there are four regions: North Atlantic, Western, MidWest, and Southern.

The ACA publishes a quarterly journal which contains practice-oriented, theoretical, and research-based articles. This publication, the Journal of Counseling and Development (JCD) and other counseling journals, shape the profession of counseling through informing practicing counselors, counselors-in-training, and professors. Additionally, ACA publishes a monthly magazine, Counseling Today.

© Matej Kastelic/Shutterstock.com

The ACA hosts a yearly convention every spring. Members of the ACA receive a discount on the registration fee. The conference is easily the largest counseling conference, with an attendance of nearly 5,000 people. It boasts nearly 500 sessions organized into different "tracks" by major subject area.

The ACA stands as one of the major unifying voices in the counseling profession, providing guidance to the field through its *Code of Ethics*, support to its members through development and training, and direct advocacy for counseling such as lobbying for Medicare reimbursement for treatment by licensed counselors.

As much as involvement in the ACA benefits students, professionals, and educators, the relationship between the ACA (as well as other professional organizations) is mutually beneficial. Members of the ACA have the opportunity both to serve and to be served by the organization. For example, since the ACA provides a voice to the profession through legislative lobbying efforts, members can and should be a part of these efforts to make a strong case to legislatures by showing strong support from the profession, both in sheer numbers as well as through consensus. Additionally, the members of the ACA inform one another on their research and best practices. Members make up the association's governance and divisions; the ACA serves to represent its members and its essence is its members.

MEDICARE, COUNSELORS, AND THE ACA

One of the ACA's top advocacy priorities is to obtain Medicare reimbursement to licensed professional counselors. Medicare is federal health insurance provided to the elderly (age 65 and older) and certain populations of individuals with disabilities. While Medicare allows reimbursement to psychiatrists, psychologists, mental health clinical nurse specialists, and clinical social workers, it currently does not provide coverage for treatment from LPCs. The ACA is currently working to lobby for this coverage, arguing that LPCs have training and education in mental health treatment equal to or greater than those professionals already covered by Medicare. Additionally, the ACA sees this as a client advocacy issue, as many Medicare recipients may only have immediate access to LPCs to obtain mental health services. As the situation currently stands, those in such positions may be required to travel long distances or be placed on a waiting list prior to obtaining care. The ACA provides a platform to advocate for a change in Medicare's reimbursement. It has met with members of Congress to provide rationale, explanation, and personal accounts. It also encourages members to call and write their members of Congress, providing direction for a unified effort in obtaining reimbursement for LPCs. This change would allow for greater opportunities for work for licensed professional counselors as well as greater mental health access for a large population of Americans.

In addition to general membership, ACA members can join one of the ACA's 18 special interest divisions, including:

Association for Adult Development and Aging (AADA). Recognizing that development occurs throughout the entirety of the lifespan, the AADA seeks to improve standards of professional services to adults of all ages. The AADA's mission states that it seeks to achieve this by 1) improving the skills and competence of ACA members, 2), expanding professional work opportunities in adult development and aging, 3) promoting the life-long development and well-being of adults, and 4) promoting standards for professional preparation for counselors of adults across the lifespan. The association publishes the journal *Adultspan* twice per year and offers a yearly conference.

Association for Assessment and Research in Counseling (AARC). Formerly the Association for Assessment in Counseling and Education (AACE) was formed in 1965, AARC's vision is to advance the counseling profession by promoting best practices in assessment, research, and evaluation in counseling, fulfilling six purposes: 1) professional development, 2) professionalization, 3) research and knowledge, 4) human development, 5) public awareness, and 6) collaboration. The AARC also provides guiding documents such as the *Code of Fair Testing Practices in Education* (Joint Committee on Testing Practices, 2004) on their website. Their journal, *Measurement and Evaluation in Counseling and Development,* is published quarterly and the division also publishes *Counseling Outcome Research and Evaluation* biannually. The AARC holds an annual conference.

Association for Child and Adolescent Counseling (ACAC). The ACAC is an organization committed to advocating for and developing counseling practice with children and adolescence. Its goals demonstrate a commitment to such actions as promoting awareness, the support of counseling, consultation, and education of parents, children, and professionals, and dissemination of professional materials. These goals are fulfilled in part through the *Journal of Child and Adolescent Counseling.* The association held its inaugural conference in 2017. The association was an organizational affiliate of the ACA until becoming an official division in 2013.

Association for Creativity in Counseling (ACC). This division of the ACA was formed in 2004, with a focus on exploring and developing creative, diverse, and relational approaches to counseling. The creation of the

ACC was chronicled in an article in its journal, the *Journal of Creativity in Mental Health* (Duffey & Kerl-McClain, 2007). The association also holds an annual conference. ACC also maintains a database of creative interventions called the ACA-ACC Creative Interventions and Activities Clearinghouse. It is available to all ACA members and features activities in 5 practice areas: 1) Mental Health Agency/Private Practice Counseling, 2) Rehabilitation Counseling, 3) School Counseling, 4) College Counseling, and 5) Counselor Education and Supervision.

American College Counseling Association (ACCA). "The mission of the American College Counseling Association is to be the interdisciplinary and inclusive professional home that supports emerging and state of the art knowledge and resources for counseling professionals in higher education" (ACCA Bylaws, Revised 2018, Article I, Section 2) The ACCA's website houses a job board for postings such as college counselors, college counseling center directors, and even high administrative positions related to student wellness and counseling services. Other resources such as webinars, a listserv, and information on advocacy and awareness are available. As with many counseling organizations, the ACCA hosts an annual conference.

Association for Counselor Education and Supervision (ACES). ACES focuses on both formal education of counselors as well as the ongoing training and supervision of counselors that is an integral part of the profession. ACES was founded in 1952 and has a great impact on counselor education in supervision. In fact, its efforts led to the creation of the Council for Accreditation of Counseling and Related Programs (CACREP), the primary accreditor of counseling training programs (https://www.cacrep.org/about-cacrep/). Additionally, ACES provides the ACA-ACES Syllabus Clearinghouse on the ACA website, providing counselor educators. ACES holds their conference on odd numbered years and publishes their own journal, *Counselor Education and Supervision*.

Association for Humanistic Counseling (AHC). One of the founding divisions of the ACA, the Association for Humanistic Counseling (AHC) values human dignity, personal choice and responsibility, and advocacy for the greater good of humanity. An overview of its website reveals verbiage and principles consistent with a humanistic approach to counseling. As with many of the divisions, the AHC has a newsletter, an annual conference, and a journal, the *Journal of Humanistic Counseling*. The aim of the association is well-defined by its vision statement, which includes three areas: 1) promote the growing body of theoretical, empirical, and applied knowledge about human development and potential; 2) encourage philosophical reflection on counseling practices and outcomes; and 3) advocate for counseling, supervisory, and educational policies and practices that benefit individuals within their communities, environments, and cultures.

Association for Lesbian, Gay, Bisexual, and Transgender Issues in Counseling (ALGBTIC). ALGBTIC exists to promote awareness and provide information related to the specific needs of LGBT clients in counseling (www.afhc.camp9.org/). ALGBTIC strives to provide training resources to counselors to ensure a high quality of care. Members have access to the division's *Journal of LGBT Issues in Counseling*, an extensive bibliography of resources for counselors working with LGBT populations, and a therapy resource directory. ALGBTIC holds an annual conference.

Association for Multicultural Counseling and Development (AMCD). Originally founded as the Association for Non-White Concerns (ANWC) in Personnel and Guidance in 1972. The AMCD works to represent diverse populations in counseling through advocacy, the elimination of barriers to marginalized populations, the creation of awareness of such populations and their needs, and through publishing materials that address and educate counselors in multicultural issues (https://multiculturalcounselingdevelopment.org/). The association offers resources such as webinar series and an annual summit, and its journal, the *Journal of Multicultural Development*.

American Rehabilitation Counseling Association (ARCA). ARCA exists to serve students, educators, and counseling practitioners concerned with the needs and treatment of individuals with disabilities. The mission of ARCA is "to enhance the development of people with disabilities throughout their life span and to promote excellence in the rehabilitation counseling profession" (Welcome to ARCA, para. 2). To this end, ARCA provides guidance on the scope of practice and best practices in rehabilitation counseling. ARCA publishes a newsletter, hosts an annual conference, and publishes the *Rehabilitation Counseling Bulletin* (RCB) in association with the Hammill Institute on Disabilities. More information on the RCB can be found at https://journals.sagepub.com/home/rcb.

Association for Spiritual, Ethical, and Religious Values in Counseling (ASERVIC). Out of its roots in the Catholic church, ASERVIC was first charted in 1974 under the National Catholic Guidance Conference (http://www.aservic.org/). As the division developed over time, its focus widened, and ASERVIC is now comprised of professionals of various faiths and value systems. ASERVIC recognizes the importance of spirituality in human development, as well as the unique place of spirituality in counseling. ASERVIC has published spiritual and religious competencies for human development professionals and publishes the *Counseling and Values Journal* as well as a regular newsletter. Additionally, ASERVIC has developed spiritual competencies for counselors to provide guidance for the intersectionality of counseling and spirituality (Cashwell & Watts, 2010). ASERVIC hosts a yearly national conference.

Association for Specialists in Group Work (ASGW). ASGW was founded to guide research, practice, and advocacy related to group work in counseling. ASGW publishes the *Journal for Specialists in Group Work* as a resource for practitioners, educators, and individuals interested in group work. Additionally, the division endorses the *ASGW Best Practices Guidelines*, the *ASGW Professional Standards for Training Group Workers*, and the *Multicultural and Social Justice: Competence Principles for Group Workers* documents, which provide guidance for practitioners in ethical and competent group practice, research, and education. The ASGW Conference meets biannually.

Counselors for Social Justice (CSJ). CSJ seeks to promote social justice in counseling practice as well as within the systems and contexts that affect clients. CSJ seeks to accomplish this by 1) increasing awareness of social justice concerns; 2) enhancing the ability of counselors to engage in social justice issues; and 3) building a community of social justice nationally and internationally. The *Journal for Social Action in Counseling and Psychology* supports the association's mission by providing a voice for the association in its advocacy for social justice in counseling. The organization's website provides a resource library for members and non-members alike, including links to social justice competency documents, such as those provided by ASERVIC and ALGBTIC. CSJ organizes CSJ-specific events during the annual ACA Conference.

International Association of Addictions and Offender Counselors (IAAOC). The mission of IAAOC is to provide leadership in the advancement of the fields of addictions and offender counseling. The organization considers itself a home to counselors and other professionals working in these counseling areas, providing guidance, research, training, and advocacy in these areas. IAAOC was formed in 1972 initially as the Public Offender Counselor Association (POCA) and granted division status in 1974 with the ACA (APGA at the time). The IAAOC produces a monthly newsletter, the *Journal of Addictions & Offender Counseling*, and has held IAAOC-specific events within the ACA Conference as well as other conferences.

International Association of Marriage and Family Counselors (IAMFC). The IAMFC is dedicated to quality research, training, and practice in marriage, couple, and family counseling. Its goals include promoting research and knowledge, networking within and outside of the association, and advocating to reduce hindrances to healthy relationships within marriage, family, and couples counseling. IAMFC has produced ethical guidelines for marriage and family counselors (International Association of Marriage and Family Counselors, 2017). The association's newsletter is entitled *The Family Digest*, and its journal is called *The Family Journal*. The association holds an international conference annually.

Military and Government Counseling Association (MGCA) formerly ACEG. MGCA has undergone name changes over time, being known first as the Military Educators and Counselors Association (MECA), then the Association for Counselors and Educators in Government (ACEG), and finally to the Military and Government Counseling Association (MGCA) in 2015, expanding its reach to professionals in a wide range of military, government, and related settings. The association seeks to "serve those who have served" by advocating for sound training, practice, and education in these settings. The *Journal of Military and Government Counseling* (JMGC) is an official publication of the MGCA. The MGCA holds an annual professional development institute during the ACA's annual conference.

National Career Development Association (NCDA). The mission of the National Career Development Association (NCDA) is to provide professional development, publications, standards, and advocacy to practitioners and educators who inspire and empower individuals to achieve their career and life goals. Founded in 1913 as the National Vocational Guidance Association and later renamed NCDA, the association is the oldest career development association in the world. The division provides ethical standards related to career development as well as the *Career Counselor*

Assessment and Evaluation Competencies document, available on the association website. The official journal of the NCDA, *Career Development Quarterly*, is available to members, while the *Career Convergence* web magazine is freely available on the website.

National Employment Counseling Association (NECA). NECA is another division of ACA. NECA exists to support individuals' employability and long-term employment through resources, through the support of career-development professionals such as counselors, and through community advocacy. NECA holds a professional development institute yearly at the ACA Conference and publishes the *Journal of Employment Counseling*.

To get a practical idea of why membership in professional organizations are important, consider the case of Carol. Carol is a newly enrolled student in a clinical mental health program and is interested in joining ACA after hearing about ACA in her orientation. She likes the idea of networking with other students and professionals. Carol first goes to the ACA's website to take a look at what benefits are offered. She already knew of the ACA's conference and planned to attend, but she was surprised to see what other benefits the ACA offers to its members. Carol was appreciative of the discounted rate for students since finances can be tight for students. In exploring the website Carol also notices that the ACA has special-interest divisions such as ASERVIC, Association for Spiritual, Ethical, and Religious Values in Counseling (ASERVIC). She can see that both the ACA and its divisions will be great sources of information to her as she studies more about the profession and the current, critical issues related to the field. For example, she notices that the Government Affairs blog on the website names a current bill related to mental health that is soon to go before the House of Representatives. The website summarizes the bill and provides steps for members to help. Carol reflects on the fact that her textbooks certainly refer to advocacy efforts, but they often do not contain up-to-date information on specific pieces of legislation. Carol takes a moment to write her representative right from the ACA website.

Carol decides to join the ACA as well as some of its member divisions. She notices that her membership includes an ACA region of her division as well, which will provide her with connection opportunities and information more specific to her geographic location. She also begins to receive Counseling Today in print as well as the ACA's electronic newsletter. Right away she can see how these publications help to keep her informed and connected. ACA's newsletter reminds her that May is Mental Health Month. She decides to share the suggested hashtag on social media to help increase awareness, and shares one of her favorite articles from the website, providing positive support to her social media circle while also increasing awareness of the counseling profession.

As Carol continues along in her program she gets the opportunity to carry out a research study with one of her faculty members. Carol asks whether the professor might be interested in presenting the research at the ACA. The faculty member accepts, and the two respond to ACA's call for proposals for the upcoming annual conference. Later, Carol is excited to learn that their presentation has been accepted as a poster presentation.

The time comes for the annual ACA conference. Carol is excited to meet fellow students from other universities, to attend workshops covering the latest research in some of her interest areas, and of course to present her own work. Carol notices that the conference has a welcome reception, and is able to meet fellow ACA members from around the country. She enjoys presenting her poster at the conference, and meets other students interested in the same subject of research. They exchange contact information and later connect to conduct further research together.

Throughout her program, Carol enjoys the benefits of her membership, regularly reading her publications, attending events, and staying informed on the latest trends and issues in the field. When Carol is ready for practicum, she takes advantage of discounted liability insurance made available through her membership.

Finally, Carol graduates from the program and continues into the field as a resident. She decides to stay in her school's state to become licensed, but has noticed that the licensure requirements of her home state vary from those of her school's state. Here, she is appreciative of the ACA's efforts for licensure portability.

Carol eventually becomes licensed and continues to practice as a professional. Her state requires her to obtain continuing education units (CEUs) each year to maintain her license. She easily meets these requirements by utilizing the ACA's online CEUs and also through attending CE-approved workshops at ACA conferences. She also maintains connections with contacts she has made through networking in the ACA, and even continues to present at conferences from time to time. Her clinical work is supported through her use of the ACA's online mental health resources, not to mention the knowledge she gains from CEUs and workshop attendance.

Of course, Carol, like many other clinicians, sometimes faces difficult or confusing situations in her work. Carol finds herself concerned when working with a minority client who appears to be facing discrimination in the workplace. Carol wants to ensure that she is fulfilling her ethical duties and also fully appreciating all of the ethical considerations of the case. She is grateful that her membership allows her to consult with the ACA's Ethics Department, and she emails ethics@counseling.org to set up an appointment.

Carol continues to enjoy her work as a counselor, but notices that she can not seem to shake her love of research. She has also since become a licensed clinical supervisor, and loves to work with students who are developing in the profession. Carol decides that she would like to enroll in a Ph.D. in Counselor Education and Supervision program, with the hopes of becoming a professor in a counseling program. Throughout her program, she continues to take advantage of the ACA as she did when she first began to study counseling.

Fast forward a few years later, and Carol is getting ready to defend her dissertation. The dissertation itself has been built on top of much of the research she had produced with colleagues in the ACA. At this year's ACA conference, Carol attends the ACA's Career Center, where she schedules face-to-face interviews for faculty positions in counseling programs. She is able to share that she is presenting during the conference, and invites her interviewers to attend her presentation. Ultimately, Carol's experience in advocacy, professional practice, her history of research and scholarship, along with her strongly-demonstrated counselor identity, make her an ideal candidate for a faculty role, and she is offered a position.

As Carol gets ready to teach her first classes, she consults the ACA-Association for Counselor Education and Supervision (ACES) Syllabus Clearinghouse to help her prepare to teach the next generation of counselors. She continues to maintain her membership with the ACA, both benefiting from the ACA and contributing meaningfully to it as well.

While not all counseling students will follow Carol's path, this case demonstrates many of the ways a counseling student, a clinician, and even a counselor educator can benefit from what ACA has to offer. Counseling organizations like the ACA provide connection, education, and support to their members. Consider which benefits you have read about that appeal to you most, and what steps you might take now to get involved in counseling organizations.

Other Professional Associations

While the ACA is perhaps the most recognized counseling association, you may find yourself interested in other associations related to counseling, mental health, or related fields. There are many other valuable professional associations in addition to the ACA, some of which were previously divisions of the ACA that have gone on to develop their own sense of identity apart from the ACA. Other organizations may have a particular focus, purpose, or identity that is distinct from that of the ACA.

Chi Sigma Iota (CSI). As the international honor society for counselors, counselor educators, and students, Chi Sigma Iota (CSI) is particularly applicable to students in a counselor educator program and to counseling professionals. CSI was formed in 1985 at Ohio University to recognize academic achievement, leadership, and service in counseling program, as well as advancing excellence and leadership of counseling professionals and promoting professional advocacy in the field of counseling.

CSI believes its primary means of achieving its goals is through localized action, so many schools have their own CSI chapter, allowing students to become involved in the international counseling organization at the local level. Typically, these chapters are student-led with at least two doctoral-level program faculty serving as chapter advisors. Chapters serve the mission of CSI through advocacy, professional development, local service projects, and networking.

Schools must be nationally accredited (CACREP or CORE) in order to have a chapter. Ask faculty members to see if your school has a chapter. Because it is an honor's society, students become members of CSI by invitation only, which can be extended once they have completed a full semester of study in the program and have achieved at least a 3.5 GPA on a 4.0 scale.

American Mental Health Counselors Association(AMHCA). A former division of ACA, AMHCA separated from the ACA to advocate for mental health counselors in broader settings, including school counseling, rehabilitation counselors, and employment counselors. While now distinct organizations, ACA and AMHCA have both expressed a desire to continue working closely with one another. AMHCA publishes the *Journal* *of Mental Health Counseling* quarterly as well as its magazine, *The Advocate*. Like many other associations, AMHCA holds an annual conference. AMHCA also often provides advocacy programs in the nation's capitol. They provide transportation and training to help counselors communicate and advocate with representatives in Washington.

American School Counselor Association(ASCA). Like AMHCA, ASCA was also once a division of the ACA. ASCA focuses on support school counselors specifically by supporting their efforts in developing programs, providing counsel, and meeting student needs in a variety of ways. ASCA's professional journal, the *Professional School Counseling Journal*, is provided to members at no charge, as is the bi-monthly magazine, the *ASCA School Counselor Magazine*. ASCA provides its members with liability insurance and holds an annual conference.

Other Professional Organizations

In addition to organizations specifically for counselors and aligned with a counselor identity, counselors also join other professional organizations that may not be counseling specific. Some examples include but are not limited to: the Association for Play Therapy (www.a4pt.org), The Association for Traumatic Stress Specialists (www.atss.info), the Christian Association for Psychological Studies (CAPS), and The Society for Emotion and Attachment Studies (SEAS), who sponsors the International Attachment Conference.

National Association for Alcoholism and Drug Abuse Counselors (NAADAC). NAADAC, the Association for Addiction Professionals, was initially founded in 1972 as the National Association of Alcoholism Counselors and Trainers (NAACT). Through subsequent name changes the organization further developed its identity to encompass a variety of different types of addiction-related professionals, including counselors, administrators, social workers. It is open to all professionals related to the field of addiction and recovery. NAADAC holds an annual conference, publishes *Advances in Treatment and Recovery*, and provides certification in addiction-related areas, including National Certified Addiction Counselor, Nicotine Dependence Specialist and Masters Addiction Counselor.

American Association for Marriage and Family Therapists (AAMFT).
The goal of AAMFT is to promote healthy families and couples through the education, training, development, and support of marriage and family therapists. Marriage and family therapists have begun to develop an identity distinct from mental health counselors, with a systemic focus and often separate licenses in states (e.g., LPC licensure versus LMFT licensure). AAMFT serves this population as its primary goal, but also works in conjunction with other organizations such as the ACA and AMHCA to advocate for counseling and therapy as a whole. The organization hosts an annual conference, publishes *Family Therapy Magazine* as well as three journals, the *Journal of Family Therapy,* the *Australian and New Zealand Journal of Family Therapy,* and the *Journal of Marital and Family Therapy.* AAMFT also provides members with various tools online such as access to webinars and online continuing education courses.

American Association of Christian Counselors (AACC). The AACC is an association founded to support Christians who work in a variety of counseling and pastoral settings, from church lay counseling to professional clinical work. The AACC alternates between a national and world conference every other year. These conferences provide networking opportunities, CEUs, and trainings. The AACC also produces online courses and resources. Additionally, AACC's code of ethics is published on its website and is discussed in detail in Chapter 4. These codes can provide guidance for Christians who are professional counselors. It is important to note that licensed and certified counseling professionals must adhere to the code of ethics established by their state board, which is the *ACA Code of Ethics.*

Getting Involved in Organizations

With so many different counseling organizations available, how can a person choose which organization, or even how many to be a part of? To begin with, students might find it helpful to start with an organization that has a broader focus, such as the ACA or AMHCA. From there, attending a conference or even just reviewing a conference's past or present program guide or schedule can provide a window into the type of research interests and connections that a conference and its association can provide. Another great place to get involved is in your state and/or local ACA-affiliated organizations. State-level conferences tend to be held in various locations across the state, making it easier to attend. As mentioned earlier, professional organizations offer students discounted rates for membership and conference registrations as well as special membership benefits for students. Many organizations also offer volunteer opportunities for graduate students that allow them to attend the conferences for free as well as grant funding to support student professional development activities. If you are not able to attend a national conference as a student, you should try to take advantage of opportunities that are much closer to home.

If you are eligible, it would be beneficial to consider joining your school's chapter of CSI. This can help you to experience the benefits of joining a professional organization, provide a richer educational experience in your program as you connect with other students and faculty who are a part of CSI, and provide opportunities to develop your leadership and advocacy skills. Finally, you may find it helpful to simply speak to faculty members and other students in your program to explore the possibilities and benefits associated with other counseling associations.

Keaghlan Macon, MA in Clinical Mental Health Counseling Student

© Ketluimar Vallecillo-Samot

Developing my professional identity as a counselor is a task I began during my first year in my master's program at Liberty University. After presenting a group project for my Human Growth and Development class, my professor encouraged my group to consider presenting at the Virginia Association for Counselor Education and Supervision Graduate Student Conference (VACES). My team had our first crash course introduction to the world of counseling organization acronyms during our second semester as we presented at the VACES Graduate Student Conference, and I decided to join the Virginia Counselors Association (VCA). We eased into presentations with a poster session, and then decided to present an educational session at VCA's Annual Convention later that year. Many of my co-presenters were accepted as Emerging Leaders to VCA's Leadership Academy that summer to learn the value of joining professional organizations and getting involved at the state and local level. There we made meaningful connections with leaders in the field of counseling and were encouraged to continue researching and staying involved. As a member of VCA, I began receiving the *Virginia Counselors Journal*, in which I would later publish my first professional publication.

During this first year in my education, I began joining more organizations because of the support and community I received from VCA. I joined the American Counseling Association (ACA), American Association of Christian Counselors (AACC), and the Southern Association of Counselor Education and Supervision (SACES). At the various conferences for each of the organizations I joined, I was given opportunities to present, network, listen to experts in the field, and gain access to new research and tools to later use with my clients during practicum and internship.

During my second year in my counseling program, I became President of Liberty University's Rho Eta Chapter of Chi Sigma Iota International Honors Society (CSI) and was given the opportunity to use my leadership role to encourage students to get involved on the local and state level. We partnered with local universities to host events for our students to offer resources and challenge our students to become leaders in the field. Through CSI, we also participated in VCA's annual Legislative Day to advocate for the counseling profession through conversations with state legislators.

During my last year in my program, I took on a leadership role on the state level as VCA's Treasurer for the Association of Spiritual, Ethical, and Religious Values in Counseling (ASERVIC). All of these organizations have shaped my professional identity by helping me to be aware of key issues affecting counselors and how, even as a student, I can advocate for our profession. As I prepare for entering into the counseling field and future doctoral coursework, the invaluable experiences I have gained through presenting research at each of these conferences provides me with the skills and confidence needed to succeed wherever my education may take me.

Contributed by Keaghlan Macon. © Kendall Hunt Publishing Company.

WHAT ARE COUNSELOR CREDENTIALS?

Counselor Licensure

The purpose of counselor licensure is to govern the practice of counseling. Licensure requirements and ethical codes become part of the state legislation, which then regulates the practice of counseling. Licensure establishes the level of training and supervised experiences that counselors must possess before they are allowed to independently practice in the field. In this way, licensure protects both the public and the professional (Spurgeon, 2012).

The laws for licensure are unique to each state, as well as the designation of the license title. All 50 states, the District of Columbia, and two United States territories (Guam and Puerto Rico) have counselor licensure laws, however 35 years passed between when the first state adopted a counselor licensure law (Virginia in 1976) and the last state (California in 2009). There are two types of laws which govern counselor licensure: title and practice laws. Title laws are in place to regulate using the title for that state's adopted licensure term. Practice laws work to regulate the independent practice of counseling. Further, practice laws identify the eligible service provision and scope of practice for counselors. The majority of states have both practice and title laws, while roughly 20% have only practice law and a little more than 10% have only title law.

LICENSURE

Academic Training

Post-Master's Supervised Clinical Experience

Examination

Stool © BEPictured/Shutterstock.com

Licensure requirements can be conceptualized as the legs on a three-legged table. These three "legs" of licensure include academic training, examination, and post-master's supervised experience. As you read about the three "legs" of licensure, keep in mind that while there are some differences from state to state, the function of the "table" itself remains the same and represents an important part of counseling's professional identity.

In order to become licensed, you must graduate from a counselor training program that meets the minimum academic training standards as identified by the state in which you are seeking licensure. Some states require 48 semester hour degrees while others require 90. Some states require that you graduated from a CACREP accredited program while other states require CACREP equivalent coursework. States also may require that you take a course that is not required by the other states. You want to make sure that your degree meets your state's requirements.

States also differ with regard to which examination is required for licensure. All states require either (or both) the National Counselor Examination (NCE) or the National Clinical Mental Health Counselor Examination (NCMHCE). Eighteen states and one territory require the NCE, 10 states require the NCMHCE, nine states require both exams as part of a tiered licensure process, and 14 states and one district allow either exam. Additionally, some states also require a state law and ethics or jurisprudence examination.

There are differences among the states in the required amount and type of post-master's supervised clinical experience. Most states require between 2000-4000 clinical hours under supervision between the time you graduate and the time you earn your license. States also differ in the regulations governing the types of activities that can apply towards supervised hours and the qualifications of the supervisors. These differences in academic, examination, and post-master's supervision requirements from state-to-state highlight the importance of knowing what your state requires for licensure at the start of your program and continuing to monitor for changes that may be adopted by your state legislature. You can check state licensure laws for your state by visiting the American Association of State Counseling Boards at www.aascb.org.

Lastly, once you are licensed, you will find that the differences in state's licensure regulations extend to the title used to designate a counselor as a licensed professional. Nine different counselor licensure titles exist for the states and territories. Review the following chart to see these differences, as well as to identify the nomenclature used in your state.

TABLE 2.1

Titles Used to Identify
Professional Counselors

Jurisdiction	License
Utah	Clinical mental health counselor (CMHC)
New Hampshire, Rhode Island	Licensed clinical mental health counselor (LCMHC)
Idaho, Illinois, Iowa, Kansas, Maine, Maryland, Montana, Nevada	Licensed clinical professional counselor (LCPC)
Florida, Guam, Hawaii, Indiana, Massachusetts, New York, Washington	Licensed mental health counselor (LMCH)
California, Kentucky, Minnesota, New Mexico, North Dakota, Ohio	Licensed professional clinical counselor (LPCC)
Alabama, Alaska, Arizona, Arkansas, Colorado, Connecticut, District of Columbia, Georgia, Louisiana, Michigan, Mississippi, Missouri, Nebraska, New Jersey, North Carolina, Oklahoma, Oregon, Pennsylvania, Puerto Rico, South Carolina, Texas, Virginia, West Virginia, Wisconsin, Wyoming	Licensed professional counselor (LPC)
South Dakota	Licensed professional counselor-mental health (LPC-MH)
Tennessee	Licensed professional counselor-mental health service provider (LPC/MHSP)
Delaware	Licensed professional counselor of mental health (LPCMH)

Source: Henrikson, Henderson, Liang, Watts, & Marks, 2019, p. 164

© Gayvoronskaya_Yana/Shutterstock.com

Licensure portability. These differences in licensure requirements create a challenge for licensure portability, which is the ability to obtain a license in a new state on the basis of being licensed in another state. To date, there is no national counselor license, so counselors who move from one state to another are not granted reciprocity for their existing license. As a result, counselors are required to apply for licensure, and adhere to the varied licensing requirements for that state. If you have been a practicing licensed counselor for twenty years in one state and move to another, you may find that you have to take additional coursework or accrue additional supervised clinical hours to be eligible for the new state's license. The lack of standardization of counselor licensure requirements has been and still is a concern in the profession. As our principle professional organization, ACA has developed a proposal for licensure portability. More about licensure portability is discussed in Chapter 14.

Licensure regulation. State licensure boards, as noted above, serve the purpose of regulating the profession. In this way, the boards serve the purpose of reviewing licensure applicants, making decisions about approving those applications, managing counselor licensure renewals, reviewing and investigating ethical complaints, and making decisions about disciplinary actions against licensed counselors who have breached an ethical standard. Carnahan and Jungers (2015) identified forms of discipline which may occur as a result of a founded ethical complaint: written formal warning, suspension of license, and revocation of license. As a result of warnings and suspensions, the disciplined counselor will often have sanctions for which they must comply. Licensure boards also serve as enforcers of those sanctions. According to Wilkinson, Smith, and Wimberly (2019), data from 49 states regarding the most frequently occurring ethical violations between 2010 and 2014 indicated that the top three ethical infractions included: (1) failure to acquire the required number of continuing education units (16.8%); (2) dual relationships (12.5%); and (3) sexual relationships with clients (9%). In a four-year study investigating ethical infractions and regulatory actions across 28 states, Ahia and Boccone (2017) identified 29 categories of disciplinary actions, with fines being the most common (53.96%) and mandatory continuing education being the second most common (44.84%). Some less common actions include required counseling, practice restrictions, and professional or jurisprudence examination requirements.

Certification

Certification is the recognition that you met a set of standards determined by a professional body, often for a specialty area in the profession. Certification is primarily granted at a national level, although some states have their own certification for substance abuse counselors, school counselors, and other specializations. At the national level, certification crosses state boundaries. While counselor licensure provides the title and/or practice of counseling in a state, certification does not offer those privileges. Certification can demonstrate that you obtained additional training and have a certain level of expertise. However, for most certifications, the practice is still regulated at the licensure level and not by the certifying agency. Certification does not grant state practice or title rights.

The National Board of Certified Counselors (NBCC) is the primary credentialing organization for the certification of counselors. Candidates can become National Certified Counselors (NCC), Certified Clinical Mental Health Counselors (CCMHC), National Certified School Counselors (NCSC), and Master Addictions Counselors (MAC) through the NBCC. To be eligible for NCC certification, you must have graduated with a master's degree in counseling that includes coursework in eight designated content areas as well as supervised field experience, you must pass the respective examination (NCE or NCMHCE), and you must meet post-master's clinical experience requirements. If you graduate from a program accredited by the Council for Accreditation of Counseling and Related Educational Programs (CACREP), you may be eligible to take the respective exam while in your internship. If you pass this exam, the NBCC will waive the post-master's supervised clinical experience requirement, allowing you to become certified upon graduation and after paying the certification fee. Visit NBCC's website (www.nbcc.org) to find out more information about certification and the specific requirements involved.

There are other certifications which cross mental health disciplines. For these, psychiatrists, psychologists, social workers, counselors, and marriage and family therapists are all eligible for the certification. As an example, a mental health practitioner is eligible to become a Registered Play Therapist regardless of discipline, as long as the necessary requirements are met (see https://www.a4pt.org/page/CredentialsHomepage). Other popular certifications include Eye Movement Desensitization and Reprocessing (EMDR), Dialectical Behavior Therapy (DBT), and Myers Briggs Type Indicator (MBTI) Certification, among others. It would be wise for you to research the certification you are interested in to determine the quality of training as well as whether it provides a meaningful professional credential.

WHAT IS ACCREDITATION AND HOW DOES IT IMPACT THE COUNSELING PROFESSION?

Accreditation is a way to verify that an academic institution or program met or exceeded all required standards for academic quality, improvement, and accountability standards set by an accrediting organization. As a student, accreditation allows you to verify that an organization from outside of the institution and/or program of study found that it meets or exceeds a minimum standard of quality. The accreditation status of your school and/or program is important to know because students who plan to be licensed or certified as counselors must meet the institutional and/or pro-

© Castleski/Shutterstock.com

gram accreditation requirements set by the state. For counseling students, this may involve two distinct accreditation processes: institutional and programmatic accreditation.

In the United States, institutes of higher education are accredited through one of six regional accreditation bodies recognized by the Council for Higher Education Accreditation (CHEA, 2019), with each of these regional organizations responsible for specific states. Regional accreditation is important because it verifies the quality of the institution that conferred your degree. However, in addition to institutional accreditation, CHEA recognizes programmatic accrediting organizations. For counseling programs, this is the Council for Accreditation of Counseling and Related Educational Programs (CACREP). You can find out more about accreditation at the CHEA website https://www.chea.org/chea-recognized-organizations.

The process of accreditation is important across educational settings and programs, including elementary, secondary, tertiary, and higher education. Most settings depend upon accreditation for federal funding and legitimacy. Within higher education, more nuanced accreditation bodies are found. This is especially true for specialty areas such as nursing, education, medicine, and of course counseling. There are varying levels of accreditation for higher education with regional accreditors and the specialized accrediting bodies mentioned previously. CACREP is one of the specialized accrediting bodies recognized by the Council for Higher Education Accreditation (CHEA). CACREP has been accrediting counseling programs for over three decades. Urofsky (2013) discussed CACREP accreditation and the challenges experienced over the years with accrediting counseling programs, including the varying requirements by states for counseling licensure and programmatic concerns raised by agencies such as the VA. Urofsky (2013) emphasized the need to become more unified as a profession citing several changes made to the 2009 CACREP standards that seek to do this, including establishing the Counselor Education and Supervision doctorate as the terminal degree in the counseling profession. More recently, CACREP adopted the 2016 CACREP standards which seek to further clarify and unify counselor identity and address the concerns of assessing student outcomes.

CACREP. As you read through the licensure section, perhaps you noticed that the acronym CACREP appeared several times. This is because the Council for Accreditation of Counseling and Related Educational Programs (CACREP) is the sole CHEA recognized credentialing agency for counseling programs. CACREP provides counseling programs with the professional practice and educational standards that guide how counselor educators train competent and ethical counselors. Because the counseling field is constantly evolving and growing, CACREP reviews and updates their standards every seven years. This ensures that accreditation standards reflect the current knowledge, skills, and dispositions that all counselors need in order to practice competently. You can find more information about CACREP, including a copy of the most recent standards, at https://www.cacrep.org.

Research shows programs accredited through the CACREP have higher National Counselor Exam pass rates, retain students to graduation, and provide greater job opportunities for graduates (Adams, 2006). Further, professionals who graduate from a CACREP accredited program are less likely to have ethical violations, are able to work in more settings, and achieve greater licensure portability than those who graduate from non-CACREP programs. Clearly, CACREP accreditation is an important factor for programs, students, faculty, and the field of counseling. However, research into the CACREP accreditation process is limited, with a primary focus on faculty experiences and the evaluation of the CACREP standards.

Nonetheless, there are many schools who have chosen not to seek CACREP accreditation for their counseling programs. This does not imply that these schools are not regionally accredited nor does it mean that they are not excellent counseling programs. This is a choice that they make based on what they feel is best for their programs and their institution. But whether a program is CACREP accredited or not, most counseling programs will use the CACREP standards as a guide when designing their academic courses and clinical experiences for their counseling students.

CACREP accredits seven different entry-level (i.e., master's-level) specialty areas: Addiction Counseling, Career Counseling, Clinical Mental Health Counseling, Clinical Rehabilitation Counseling, College Counseling and Student Affairs, Marriage, Couple, and Family Counseling, and School Counseling, as well as doctoral programs in Counselor Education and Supervision. For each entry-level program, CACREP has three distinct sets of training standards that schools must meet for accreditation: Professional Counseling Identity, Entry-Level Specialty Areas, and Professional Practice. As you read about each of these areas, you will see how each of these training standards help to shape your professional identity as a counselor.

CACREP Spotlight
J. Kelly Coker, Ph.D., LPC
Associate Professor, Palo Alto University

© J. Kelly Coker

When I was a doctoral student in my CACREP accredited Counselor Education and Supervision program, I remember there being a lot of energy around our upcoming reaccreditation self-study and site visit. If you are a masters or doctoral student in a counseling program that is either seeking a first CACREP accreditation or reaccreditation, you may wonder what all the fuss is about? Why do your faculty, who otherwise seem always calm, cool, and collected, before a CACREP site visit, act like nervous teenagers on a first date? What is the deal with all of those CACREP standards and student learning outcomes in your course syllabi and attached to your assignments? And finally, what does being CACREP accredited actually mean to you as a future counselor or counselor educator?

Since that first site visit in my doctoral program, I have been a part of CACREP accreditation for all of my professional life. I have served as the CACREP liaison for several counseling programs. I have conducted CACREP site visits as a CACREP team leader. I have also recently served on the CACREP board of directors as a member, the vice chair, and then the chair of the CACREP board. I have also been involved in several CACREP accreditation and re-accreditation efforts as a faculty member and academic administrator, including writing my fair share of CACREP self-studies, so I feel that I have some pretty good insight into what this whole CACREP thing is about!

CACREP stands for the Council on Accreditation of Counseling and Related Educational Programs. It was established in 1981 by the American Personnel and Guidance Association (APGA), which was a precursor to the American Counseling Association (ACA; CACREP, n.d.). Quite simply, CACREP was developed to promote excellence in counselor preparation through the development of standards for accredited programs. From its humble beginnings, CACREP has grown to be the one accrediting body recognized by the Council for Higher Education Accreditation (CHEA) and it currently accredits over 860 masters and doctoral programs in counseling (CACREP, n.d.). In addition, more and more counseling programs are seeking accreditation, including private and public universities and colleges, distance education and on-ground programs, and small and large programs.

As a student, there are several reasons that being in a CACREP accredited program is to your benefit. The first benefit is quality. If you are in a CACREP accredited program, then you can feel confident that your curriculum, learning experiences, caliber of faculty, and quality of practicum and internship have met rigorous external standards.

The second benefit is licensure. Most masters-level students of counseling programs have the goal of being licensed and practicing in the field of counseling once they graduate. The majority of states in the United States recognize CACREP accredited as meeting educational requirements including curriculum and practicum and internship for licensure. While you will need to check with your own state licensure board for specific requirements, more and more states are moving towards adopting CACREP accreditation as the standard for evaluating the quality of counselor training programs.

The third benefit is related to a few Federal Regulations. If you have an interest in working with active-duty military or veterans once you are a practicing counselor, graduating from a CACREP accredited program will serve you well! The Veterans Administration (VA) has adopted qualification standards that indicate licensed mental health counselors who have graduated from CACREP accredited programs can serve as mental health specialists for the VA (Veterans Administration, 2018). In addition, the Department of Defense (DOD) now requires licensed counselors to have graduated from a CACREP accredited counseling program in order to receive reimbursement as an independent provider from TRICARE, the insurance offered to service members and families (Department of Defense, 2014).

If you are a doctoral student in a CACREP accredited Counselor Education and Supervision program, there is an added benefit of marketability after graduation. According to the 2016 CACREP standards, "Core counselor education program faculty have earned doctoral degrees in counselor education, preferably from a CACREP-accredited program, or have related doctoral degrees and have been employed as full-time faculty members in a counselor education program for a minimum of one full academic year before July 1, 2013" (CACREP, 2015, Standard 1.W.). This means that once you graduate from a CACREP accredited Counselor Education Doctoral Program, you will be sought by other counseling programs who are either CACREP accredited or seeking CACREP accreditation since your preparation program meets the criteria for eligible full time faculty.

So the next time you are asked to participate in a CACREP accreditation process as a student, remember that achieving this accreditation represents the highest mark of excellence, stability, quality, and opportunity. If you have the good fortune to participate in such an endeavor, this will likely be in the form of meeting with a visiting on-site team during a CACREP site visit. Keep in mind that these visitors are usually also faculty in counseling programs, so they approach this task of helping your program achieve accreditation with respect, support, and collegiality. Be honest with them about your experiences in your program. Highlight strengths that you feel are noteworthy. Offer suggestions for improvements. Speak to your experiences as students and the ways in which you feel your counseling program is preparing you for your role as a counselor or counselor educator. Site teams love to use the comments of students in their team reports which are read by the program faculty, university leadership, and CACREP board of directors. You play a pivotal role in the process! So when your program is accredited for the first time or reaccredited, you can say with pride, "I helped to achieve that!"

Contributed by J. Kelly Coker. © Kendall Hunt Publishing Company.

The CACREP standards are rigorous and have received some criticism because of the resources necessary to achieve and maintain accreditation. However, as mentioned previously, the standards are beneficial in many ways. The standards can best be understood as categories which need to be addressed in a process known as a self-study. In a self-study, the program applying for accreditation laboriously assesses their program in order to ensure they meet the standards and then provides evidence of how they are meeting these standards. All of this information is provided to CACREP where a team will begin to review the documents. The standards are in relation to the following: faculty, clinical, curricula, assessment and evaluation, structure, support and resources, and perhaps most notably identity.

CACREP Common Core

© fizkes/Shutterstock.com

All master's-level counseling programs must include the eight common core areas defined in the CACREP Professional Counseling Identity standards. As the name suggests, CACREP's common core curricular standards form the foundation for the professional identity of all counselors. In fact, they encompass the foundational knowledge and skills required of *all* master-level counselor education graduates (CACREP, 2016, Standard 2.F.). Therefore, regardless of the specialty area, all counseling programs must include learning experiences in each of the following eight common core curricular areas:

- Professional counseling orientation and ethical practice (2.F.1.);
- Social and cultural diversity (2.F.2.);
- Human growth and development (2.F.3.);
- Career development (2.F.4.);
- Counseling and helping relationships (2.F.5.);
- Group counseling and group work (2.F.6.);
- Assessment and testing (2.F.7.);
- Research and program evaluation (2.F.8.)

PUTTING THE PUZZLE PIECES TOGETHER: THE EIGHT CACREP CONTENT AREAS

The eight identified CACREP content areas work together to form a whole. Ultimately, each content area fits together like pieces of a puzzle. To know what we do, we first need to understand who we are and how we practice. To this end, it is necessary to understand the history of the profession, the philosophy and values of the profession, and the elements that make counseling unique from other other mental health disciplines. Further, we must understand the boundaries of the practice of counseling. Together, these inform the criteria that fall under the professional counseling orientation and ethical practice standards.

Building on this foundational knowledge of who counselors are, what counselors do, and what counselors value, we also need to develop an awareness of who we are and how we function in the world so that we can then value the same in others. Coursework in social and cultural diversity allows us to become more aware of the impact of culture on each individual. We also need to have a strong understanding of human growth and development. This information helps us to understand how their developmental stage informs physical, emotional, cognitive, and language development. From this understanding, we can help clients successfully navigate the various developmental stages, including those experiences that do not fit in a typical developmental trajectory.

Coursework in career development prepares us to help clients gain a greater understanding of their identity and calling, so they can make decisions regarding career exploration, choice, and satisfaction, all of which can have an impact on emotional health. Coursework in assessment prepares us to select, comprehend, and utilize assessments which will further our conceptualization of client cases. Research and program evaluation allows us to assess whether programs are effective and read and understand research findings which inform counseling practice.

Skill-related coursework prepares counselors to understand theory by practicing the individual and group counseling skills used with clients. Together, these eight foundational areas prepare students for the culminating experience of the specialization courses and the professional practice (practicum and internship) courses. So remember that every course impacts what we eventually do and how we understand our work as counselors.

Because the focus of this text is on counseling within the mental health field, it is easy to view the term *Professional Counseling Identity* as one and the same as the licensure and/or certification of an individual as a *Professional Counselor*, which is commonly associated with clinical mental health counseling. However, these are two different processes (CACREP, 2019). The curricular standards that CACREP classifies under Professional Counseling Identity (Section 2.F) refer to the *professional preparation standards* that *all* counseling programs must meet to be accredited. So whether you are training to be a school counselor, marriage and family counselor, clinical mental health counselor, or any of the other specialty areas, the professional identity curricular standards help to ensure that programs provide a common foundation for your professional identity as a counselor.

CACREP Entry-Level Specialty Areas. In addition to the common core courses, you will take courses that prepare you to work in one of the seven entry-level specialty areas, such as Clinical Mental Health Counseling, Marriage, Couple, and Family Counseling, and School Counseling. Because each of the *Entry-Level Specialty Areas* (CACREP, 2016, Standards 5.A.-G.) is unique, CACREP requires that programs meet the specialization-specific *professional preparation standards* that represent the knowledge and skills necessary to address the wide range of issues you will encounter when practicing in that area. In simple terms, Clinical Mental Health Counseling programs must meet the Clinical Mental Health Counseling standards, Marriage, Couple, and Family Counseling programs must meet the Marriage, Couple, and Family Counseling standards, School Counseling programs must meet the School Counseling standards, and so on for the other specialization areas. As you take the coursework that will prepare you to specialize in your particular area of counseling, you will expand your professional counseling identity to include the professional identity unique to your chosen specialty area.

CACREP Professional Practice Standards. In addition to coursework, the *Professional Practice* standards (CACREP, 2016, Standard 3.) provide the *professional preparation standards* for programs' counseling field experiences, including the practicum (Section 3.F-I) and internship (Section 3.J-M). Counseling field experiences provide you with the opportunity to become familiar with a variety of professional activities suitable to your specialty area, including counseling clients. During this time, you learn how to apply what you have learned in practice and how to develop your counseling skills at a site under the supervision of a licensed/certified counseling professional (Section 3.N-R) as well as by your program faculty (Section 3.S-V). By the time you complete these field experiences, you will have developed the third layer to your professional identity, that of a counseling professional practicing in a specialty area under the supervision and mentorship of both your site and faculty supervisors.

During your practicum, you will obtain a minimum of 100 hours of supervised experiences over a full academic term of at least 10 weeks. As a practicum student, you will experience a minimum of 40 hours of direct service with actual clients, average one hour per week of individual and/or triadic supervision with your site supervisor, and participate in an average of 1½ hours per week of group supervision provided by a member of the counselor education program faculty.

Your internship is where you will obtain 600 hours of supervised experiences that focus on the professional counseling roles and settings *relevant to your specialty area*. As a counseling intern, you will experience a minimum to 240 hours of direct service with actual clients, average one hour per week of individual and/or triadic supervision with your site supervisor, and participate in an average of 1½ hours per week of group supervision under the mentorship of your program's faculty.

WHAT DOES IT MEAN TO ADVOCATE FOR THE PROFESSION?

The *ACA Code of Ethics* defines advocacy as the "promotion of the well-being of individuals, groups, and the counseling profession within systems and organizations" (2014, p. 20). Advocacy in counseling can be broadly divided into two aspects: advocating for the counseling profession and being an advocate for marginal populations, and client welfare (Lawson, Trepal, Lee, & Kress, 2016). For the purposes of this section, the primary focus here is advocating for the counseling profession.

As discussed, one of the major issues facing counseling is a lack of a unified identity across the profession (CESNET, 2018; Davis & Gressard, 2011; Reiner, Dobmeier, & Hernandez, 2013). Understanding how to assist future counselors in developing a professional identity is an important factor for educational programs and clinicians (Gale & Austin, 2003; McLaughlin & Boettcher, 2009; Myers, Sweeney, & White, 2002) and is an ethical mandate. Additionally, advocacy works to further professional recognition. Past efforts have resulted in federal recognition of professional counselors, resulting in expanded opportunities for counselors to serve the military populations (Spurgeon, 2012).

The *2016 CACREP Standards* address the concern in the counseling field related to a united professional identity, with a tremendous impact on the continued growth of the counseling profession. As discussed earlier in this chapter, research shows programs accredited through the Council for Accreditation of Counseling and Related Educational Programs (CACREP) have a number of advantages including higher National Counselor Exam pass rates, better student retention, and wider job opportunities (Mascari & Webber, 2013; Urofsky, 2013; West & Moore, 2015). Furthermore, graduates from CACREP accredited programs are less likely to have ethical violations, are able to work in more diverse settings, and are granted greater licensure portability than those who graduate from non-CACREP programs (Mascari & Webber, 2013; Urofsky, 2013; West & Moore, 2015). Clearly CACREP has had a positive impact on the unification efforts for counselors. However, there is additional work needed to continue to strive toward the 20/20 vision (Kaplan et al., 2014).

Organizations such as ACA, NBCC, and CSI have advocacy opportunities available to members. Involvement in these organizations provides practical and simple ways to advocate for the counseling profession. The American Counseling Association (ACA) regularly alerts members of legislative action through "Action Alerts". Members of ACA are able to stay abreast of current issues in the field and take action. Additionally, ACA provides members with a toolkit for government relations. This can be found on their website counseling.org. https://www.counseling.org/docs/default-source/government-affairs/advocacytips.pdf?sfvrsn=6dcf532c_2

In a similar way, Chi Sigma Iota (CSI) offers members insight into how to advocate for the profession through a resource with advocacy tips: https://cdn.ymaws.com/www.csi-net.org/resource/resmgr/professional_advocacy/professional-advocacy-tips.pdf.

The National Board of Certified Counselors (NBCC) also provides guidance for advocacy efforts by counselors. The NBCC divides these efforts into six broad categories: facilitating licensure portability, supporting counselor ethics, growing counseling around the world, promoting educational standards, fighting for counselor rights, and strengthening diversity in communities (nbcc.org/advocacy). Involvement in these important professional organizations is an essential part of advocacy efforts.

SUMMARY

In this chapter, we focused on helping you to understand the foundations of professional identity. You learned that the counseling profession has a distinct professional identity, which is developed as you incorporate the attitudes, values, and activities of the profession. This professional identity is also reflected in our professional counseling associations, the state and national requirements for professional licensure and certification, our standards of practice and codes of ethics, and our educational training standards. Together, these unifying bodies provide a clear definition of a cohesive counselor professional identity.

FOR THE ROAD AHEAD

Check out the Chapter 2 video at this link: https://www.khpcontent.com/

We also discussed why professional identity is so important. Developing a unified professional identity allows you to gain a sense of belonging, fosters competency, and provides a framework for the professional practice and professional community. As a future counselor, you need to be intentionally reflective as you begin developing your new identity. It is far deeper than gaining book knowledge; it is about professional and personal growth as you learn more about what it means to be a counselor. This includes becoming aware of and actively participating in the entities that shape a counseling professional identity: professional counseling associations, the requirements for professional licensure and certification, our standards of practice and codes of ethics, and our educational training standards.

Finally, unlike other mental health professions, the field of counseling does not have a singular entity that defines each of the areas that form a professional identity. Rather, as a relatively young profession, we are still in the process of developing a cohesive identity. Therefore, it is important to understand the current status of our unifying bodies and where we are heading as a profession so you can advocate for a strong unified professional identity. By your participation in professional organizations, such as those affiliated with the American Counseling Association, you can influence and advocate for the profession. Through these associations, you can also help work towards national professional licensure and certification requirements, common standards of practice and codes of ethics, and a singular educational training standard for the field of counseling. As a new member of this profession, as you develop and embrace your professional identity, you will both establish the cohesive professional identity within yourself and advance the process of developing that same cohesive identity in the field.

Reflect on your current understanding of Counselor identity. Personally, how do you understand this differently now compared to when you first decided to pursue this degree? Where do you feel there is room for growth?

Imagine a friend introduces you to another person and adds this detail, ". . . and this is my psychologist friend." How could you take this moment to engage in professional advocacy?

Which ACA division can you see yourself joining? Can you imagine yourself participating in a leadership role in a counseling organization?

Visit the American Association of State Counseling Boards (www.aascb.org) and look up the Board of Counseling for your state. How do they name the license? What are the coursework requirements? What do they require for your field experiences (practicum and internships)? Are there special requirements for supervision? What are the post-graduation supervised practice requirements? What exam do they require for licensure?

Go to the National Board of Certified Counselors (www.NBCC.org). What are some of the certifications that you would consider obtaining? What are the requirements for these certifications?

Review the courses that you will take in your program. Can you pick out the courses that meet the eight professional identity curriculum standards? Can you pick out the courses that will train you specifically for your specialization?

Go to the ACA, NBCC, and CSI websites provided in the Advocacy section. What are some of the current issues in the field of counseling? Are there any current legislative initiatives that impact counselors/counseling? Are there ways that you can become involved in working towards a solution? What are some other ways that you can advocate for the profession?

For Further Exploration

ACA Student Membership Video: https://www.youtube.com/watch?v=bLh-JavHrrwU

Duggan, J. (Producer). (2015, November). Accreditation and Licensure Policies with David Kaplan [Audio Podcast]. *American Counseling Association*. Retrieved from https://www.counseling.org/knowledge-center/podcasts/docs/default-source/aca-podcasts/special-topic---accreditation-and-licensure-policies

Gladding, S. (2018). *The counseling dictionary* (4th ed.). Alexandria, VA: American Counseling Association.

Rosenthal, H. (2008). *Encyclopedia of counseling: Master review and tutorial for the National Counselor Examination, state counseling exams, and the Counselor Preparation Comprehensive Examination* (3rd ed.). New York: Routledge.

Shook, M. (Producer). (2019, February 28). Taking the NCMHCE- A Crash Course in (Nearly) All You Need to Know with Alyson Carr [Audio podcast]. *The Thoughtful Counselor*. Retrieved from https://wp.me/p7R6fn-EF.

Shook, M. (Producer). (2017, February 8). What Makes a Counselor a Counselor? Professional Identity and Other Musings with Carl Sheperis [Audio podcast]. *The Thoughtful Counselor*. Retrieved from http://wp.me/p7R6fn-8u

Shook, M. (Producer). (2018, May 3). CACREP – Part 1: Origins, History, and Purpose with Kelly Coker and Tyler Kimbel [Audio podcast]. *The Thoughtful Counselor*. Retrieved from https://wp.me/p7R6fn-ow.

Shook, M. (Producer). (2018, May 9). CACREP – Part 2: Advocacy, Barriers, and the Road Ahead with Kelly Coker and Tyler Kimbel [Audio podcast]. *The Thoughtful Counselor*. Retrieved from https://wp.me/p7R6fn-oZ.

REFERENCES

Adams, S. A. (2006). Does CACREP accreditation make a difference? A look at NCE results and answers. *Journal of Professional Counseling, Practice, Theory, & Research, 34*(1), 60-76.

Ahia, C. E. & Boccone, P. J. (2017). Licensure board actions against professional counselors: Implications for counselor training. *VISTAS*. Retrieved from https://www.counseling.org/knowledge-center/vistas.

American College Counseling Association. (2019) *AACC by-laws*. Retrieved from http://www.collegecounseling.org/ACCA-By-Laws

American Counseling Association. (2010). Consensus definition of counseling. Retrieved from http://www.counseling.org/20-20/ definition.aspx

Burns, S., & Cruikshanks, D. R. (2017). Evaluating independently licensed counselors' articulation of professional identity using structural coding. *The Professional Counselor, 7*, 185–207.

Burns, S., & Cruikshanks, D. R. (2018). Independently licensed counselors' connection to CACREP and state professional identity requirements. *The Professional Counselor, 8*, 29-43.

Carnahan, B. & Jungers, C. (November 10, 2015). Understanding how counselors are regulated. *Counseling Today*. Retrieved from https://ct.counseling.org/2015/11/understanding-how-counselors-are-regulated/

Cashwell, C. & Watts, R. (2010). The new ASERVIC competencies for addressing spiritual and religious issues in counseling. *Counseling and Values, 55*, 2-5. doi: 10.1002/j.2161-007X.2010.tb00018.x.

Joint Committee on Testing Practices. (2004). *Code of Fair Testing Practices in Education*. Washington, DC: American Psychological Association.

Davis, T. & Gressard, R. (2011). Professional identity and the 2009 CACREP standards. *Counseling Today*, 46-47.

Dong, S., Campbell, A., & Vance, S. (2017). Examining the facilitating role of mindfulness on professional identity development among counselors-in-training: A qualitative approach. *The Professional Counselor, 7*, 305-317.

Doyle, K. (2016 April). Don't use the 't' word and five other tips for counselor advocacy. *Counseling Today*. American Counseling Association. Retrieved from http://ct.counseling.org/2016/03/dont-use-the-t-word-and-five-other-tips-for-counselor-advocacy

Duffey, T. & Kerl-McClain, S. (2007). History of the association for creativity in counseling: The evolution of a conference, division, and journal. *Journal of Creativity in Mental Health, 2*(3), 61-70. doi:10.1300/J456v02n03_06 61

Gale, A. U., & Austin, D. B. (2003). Professionalisms' challenges to counselors' collective identity. *Journal of Counseling & Development, 81*, 3–10. doi:10.1002/j.15566678.2003.tb00219.x

Henriksen, R. C., Henderson, S. E., Liang, Y., Watts, R. E., & Marks, D. F. (2019) Counselor supervision: A comparison across states and jurisdictions. *Journal of Counseling & Development, 97*, 160-170.

International Association of Marriage and Family Counselors. (2017). *IAMFC Code of Ethics*. Alexandria, VA. Author.

Kaplan, D. M., & Gladding, S. T. (2011). A vision for the future of counseling: The 20/20 principles for unifying and strengthening the profession. *Journal of Counseling & Development, 89*(3), 367-372.

Kaplan, D. M., Tarvydas, V. M. & Gladding, S. T. (2014). 20/20: A vision for the future of counseling: The new consensus definition of counseling. *Journal of Counseling & Development, 92*, 366-372. doi: 10.1002/j.1556-6676.2014.00164.x

Lawson, G, Trepal, H.C., Lee, R.W., & Kress, V. (2016). Advocating for educational standards in counselor licensure laws. *Counselor Education & Supervision, 56, 162-176*.

Lile, J. J. (2017). Forming a professional counselor identity: The Impact of identity processing style. *The Journal of Counselor Preparation and Supervision*, 9(2), doi:10.7729/92.1163

Mascari, J. B, & Webber, J. (2013). CACREP Accreditation: A solution to license portability and counselor identity problems. *Journal of Counseling & Development, 91*, 15-25.

Mascari, J. B., & Webber, J. M. (2006). Salting the slippery slope: What licensing violations tell us about preventing dangerous ethical situations. In G. R. Walz, J. C. Bleuer, & R. K. Yep (Eds.), *Vistas: Compelling perspectives on counseling 2006* (pp. 165–172). Alexandria, VA: American Counseling Association.

McLaughlin, J. E., & Boettcher, K. (2009). Counselor identity: Conformity or distinction? *Journal of Humanistic Counseling, Education, and Development, 48,* 132–143. doi:10.1002/j.2161-1939.2009.tb00074.x

Myers, J. E. & Sweeney, T. J. (2001). Specialties in counseling. In D.C. Locke, J.E. Myers, and E.L. Herr (Eds.), *The Handbook of Counseling* (pp. 43-54). Thousand Oaks, CA: Sage Publications.

Myers, J. E., Sweeney, T. J., & White, V. E. (2002). Advocacy for counseling and counselors: A professional imperative. *Journal of Counseling & Development, 80,* 394–402. doi:10.1002/j.1556-6678.2002.tb00205.x

Reiner, S. M, Dobmeier, R. A., & Hernandez, T. J. (2013). Perceived impact of professional counselor identity: An exploratory study. *Journal of Counseling & Development, 91,* 174-183.

Spurgeon, S. L. (2012). Counselor identity: A national imperative. *Journal of Professional Counseling: Practice, Theory, and Research, 39,* 3-16.

Urofsky, R. I. (2013). The council for accreditation of counseling and related educational programs: Promoting quality in counselor education. *Journal of Counseling & Development, 91,* 6-14.

West, S. C., & Moore, J. L. (2015). Council for accreditation of counseling and related educational programs (CACREP) at historically black colleges and universities. *The Journal of Negro Education, 84*(1), 56-65.

Wilkinson, T., Smith, D., & Wimberly, R. (2019). Trends in ethical complaints leading to professional counseling licensing boards disciplinary actions. *Journal of Counseling and Development, 97,* 98-104.

CHAPTER 3
Professional Counselor Roles and Practice Settings

ROBYN SIMMONS, ED.D., STACEY LILLEY, PH.D., & ANITA KUHNLEY, PH.D.

"The purpose of life is not to be happy. It is to be useful, to be honorable, to be compassionate, to have it make some difference that you have lived and lived well."

–Ralph Waldo Emerson

Following Christ: Grace for Our Work

© maradon 333/Shutterstock.com

Consider the words of the Apostle Paul to the Church in Corinth, "Now there are varieties of gifts, but the same Spirit; and there are varieties of service, but the same Lord; and there are varieties of activities, but it is the same God who empowers them all in everyone. To each is given the manifestation of the Spirit for the common good. For to one is given through the Spirit the utterance of wisdom, and to another the utterance of knowledge according to the same Spirit, to another faith by the same Spirit, to another gifts of healing by the one Spirit, to another the working of miracles, to another prophecy, to another the ability to distinguish between spirits, to another various kinds of tongues, to another the interpretation of tongues. All

- The various settings for which counselors can practice, including outpatient, inpatient, private practice, telemental health, college counseling centers, among others.
- The foundational philosophy of prevention and intervention with clients with practice settings.
- The specialty areas for which counselors can gain expertise, including marriage and family, substance abuse, crisis and trauma, addictions, among others.
- The professional roles and functions of counselors, including administrative, consultative, and supervisory roles.
- The roles and responsibilities of counselors in work with treatment and interdisciplinary response teams.

The following CACREP standards are addressed in this chapter:
Professional Counseling Orientation and Ethical Practice:

- The multiple professional roles and functions of counselors across specialty areas, and their relationships with human service and integrated behavioral health care systems, including interagency and interorganizational collaboration and consultation (CACREP, 2016, Standard 2.F.1.b.)
- Counselors' roles and responsibilities as members of interdisciplinary community outreach and emergency management response teams (CACREP, 2016, Standard 2.F.1.c.)
- The role of counseling supervision in the profession (CACREP, 2016, Standard 2.F.1.m.)

these are empowered by one and the same Spirit, who apportions to each one individually as he wills. For just as the body is one and has many members, and all the members of the body, though many, are one body, so it is with Christ" (1 Corinthians 12:4-12, English Standard Version).

Paul's words are also fitting for counselors. We are all part of the same profession, but we will have different practice settings and different populations with whom we work. God gifts each of us with passions and desires for certain client populations, allowing us to meet the variety of client needs which exist.

There are many different settings and contexts in which counselors may find themselves working, and all make important contributions to the mental health profession. One is not more significant than the other. Imagine if a cardiologist were to say to a neurologist, "Well, the heart is the most important organ, after all, it is the heart of the matter." Or, imagine if a pulmonologist were to say, 'No, no, it is the lungs, they are the most important organ, after all, they are the breath of life" (Sibcy & Knight, 2018). This would not make sense! Just as all of the organs play a significant role in the body's proper functioning, the spiritual gifts are important in the church's functioning, and the various roles and context that counselors work in are significant to the ministry of the clinical mental health field.

As counselor educators review applications for admission to their counseling programs, it happens, at times, that in the statement of purpose potential students indicate that they would like to work as a psychologist or have professional goals that are more traditionally aligned for social workers (e.g., Child Protective Services). The challenge is that counseling programs train students to do the therapeutic work of counseling, which, as you learned in previous chapters, is distinct from other mental health disciplines. This means that, at times, potential students are

referred to a program that is in alignment
with their professional goals; other times,
potential students are provided educational materials on the differences and
commonalities between the helping professions. In this chapter, you will be introduced to what it means to be a counselor
in a professional practice setting, what
those settings can be, and what roles you
will play as a counselor.

© Lisa F. Young/Shutterstock.com

WHERE DO COUNSELORS WORK?

The grassroots of clinical mental health counseling (formerly called community counseling) focused on issues relevant to the community using
outreach and prevention focused interventions to help individuals deal
with those issues. This integration of a mental health approach as an addition to the career and school-based counseling origins of the profession
began during the late 1960s. The focus of intervention needs shifted during
this time of overseas war, civil and women's rights activism, the sexual revolution, and the decreased stigma of substance abuse. Mental health care
was no longer solely focused on the seriously mentally ill. Counseling became an opportunity to not only help clients individually but to intervene
with the entire community through advocacy efforts. Further, counselors
needed to consider the ecological development of client problems and aid
clients by providing services such that the ecosystem as a whole would
benefit from minimizing or ameliorating the problems that occur individually. As a result, and along with changes in governmental policy, mental
health centers were created within the community.

Counselors and other mental health workers in mental health centers
provide preventive services. There are three types of prevention: primary,
secondary, and tertiary (Caplan, 1964). In primary prevention, you may
work to develop programs that reach healthy individuals and their communities. This is a proactive approach that focuses on the total population,
provides education, and equips individuals with skills to preclude a mental health crisis. An example of primary prevention is a stress management

program instituted for employees. Secondary prevention involves the early identification and treatment of problems. An example of this type of prevention is working with an at-risk youth population to help prevent suicide, substance abuse, and a variety of other concerns. Even though research supports that most mental health problems are preventable at the primary and secondary level (Furber et al., 2015), much of your work as a counselor will likely be focused on tertiary prevention. Tertiary prevention attempts to decrease the long-term effects of problems. For example, working with combat war veterans to help minimize the impact of post traumatic stress disorder or working with children to increase coping skills for attention deficit hyperactivity disorder would be tertiary prevention. It is important to note that the work of Furber et al. (2015) indicated that adult mental illness is often an extension of childhood issues. Thus, the authors argue, some adult mental illness could be prevented by engaging in greater efforts to target interventions toward children and adolescents. This prevention and intervention process could involve direct application of therapy with youth who are at risk for adult mental illness as a result of conduct issues and adverse experiences (to be discussed more later in the chapter) as well as indirectly intervening through programs directed toward parents and other caregivers.

Miller (2014) identified the following actions that counselors can take as prevention efforts:

- Promoting a data-driven, strategic prevention framework that includes multiple community sectors, including education, business, justice, housing, and health care to support prevention efforts and promote social and emotional health.
- Encouraging an integrated model of care that incorporates mental health, substance abuse, and physical health care services into coordinated care systems.
- Partnering with state officials and other stakeholders to design and implement primary, secondary, and tertiary mental health-focused awareness campaigns.
- Working to define and implement universal and evidence-based screening for mental health and substance use conditions within medical health homes, safety net programs, and school-based clinics.

- Collaborating with public and private sector stakeholders to utilize evidence-based prevention interventions with a focus on children and youth.
- Communicating with primary care professional organizations, state medical boards, and medical schools to promote universal adoption of standardized screening and assessment for mental health and substance use conditions.
- Preventing and reducing the consequences of the following: underage drinking and adult problem drinking and prescription drug use; suicide and attempted suicides among populations at high risk, particularly for service members, veterans and their families; preventing and ameliorating the effects of bullying for LGBTQ youth.
- Working in partnership with key stakeholders to eliminate tobacco use among youth and prevent and reduce tobacco use among persons with behavioral health disorders.
- Recognizing that the efficient and effective implementation of a coordinated and comprehensive approach to mental health will involve many challenges, including a reallocation of resources, a retooling of the workforce, and a broader conceptualization of mental health promotion that includes healthy functioning (cognitive, social, and physical) across multiple domains and settings (home, school, work). (pp. 2-4)

Counselors engage with clients through direct or indirect service. Direct services include programs or individual counseling that provides direct assistance to clients. Essentially, direct services are anything you do *with* a client to prevent (primary and secondary prevention), treat, or help improve (tertiary prevention) mental health problems. Indirect services can include training, supervision, consultation and advocacy for systemic change and influencing public policy. Indirect services are anything you do *for* a client to prevent (primary and secondary prevention), treat, or help improve (tertiary prevention) mental health problems.

There are a variety of settings in which you may work. Next, we will provide a general overview of the types of agencies and organizations for which counselors can be employed.

NOT-FOR-PROFIT, NON-PROFIT, FOR-PROFIT

Most organizations which offer mental health care will fall under three categories: for-profit, not-for-profit, and non-profit. Generally speaking, for-profit organizations intend to make a profit on the work that is provided. Private practices are for profit as the profits not only support the infrastructure of the practice but also pay the salary of the practitioner. Being for-profit does not necessarily equate with the profit margins of many large corporations. Rather, it is related to how the additional monies are utilized. Not-for-profit organizations will charge for services, but all of the monies are folded back into the organization for growth and infrastructure. Many of these agencies rely on insurance reimbursement and private pay clients to allow for services to continue and to possibly create other ways to serve. These agencies can be public or government funded. Non-profit organizations are almost always grant-funded and/or have fund-raising efforts, allowing clients access to services at no cost. Examples of these include child advocacy centers, relationship violence agencies, agencies that serve individuals with HIV/AIDS, and the like.

For-profit settings are primarily private, including private residential programs, private hospitals, private agencies, and private practices. Non-profit settings are often state, federal, grant-funded, public service agencies. Examples of public agencies include state-funded community mental health facilities, mental health services from the Department of Veterans Affairs, and sexual assault crisis centers. Not-for-profit settings can be both private and public agencies.

Community Agencies

Generally speaking, clinicians in outpatient settings may develop specialty areas. Some clinicians are well-matched for general outpatient counseling which, very often, includes working with clients who experience depression, anxiety, and other more common diagnoses. Some clinicians will focus on more specialized work, such as substance abuse, the seriously mentally ill (SMI) population (i.e., clients with schizophrenia or other psychotic disorders), children and adolescents, crisis and trauma, or couples and families. Many counselors will have a few specialty areas to be able to work with a variety of client issues.

Private Practice

Those wanting to set their own schedule may choose to work with individuals, families, or groups in a *private practice* setting. New counselors seeking licensure may need to work in a group setting to obtain the state requirements to sit for their exam. Most counselors still working toward licensure will see private pay and Medicaid clients, because most insurances will not cover the cost of counseling provided by someone working towards licensure. Supervision is a factor that should be explored when working with a group, and the best case scenario is if supervision is offered free as a perk in working with that group.

A key factor in the decision is whether or not the person would like to work solo or with a group; there are benefits and concerns with both settings. In an individual setting, one will be able to decide on the location, decor, and operating details. While being the only counselor you incur all the costs, however, you will also receive all the profits. An additional consideration is there may be group practices (i.e. paperwork) that are required by that organization but not necessarily mandated by the licensure board. Both groups must adhere to the state and licensure guidelines for ethical and practical procedures. One advantage of a group is that usually, in addition to your own malpractice insurance, the protection of the group's insurance/legal team may also be accessed should legal concerns arise. You also split the cost incurred from rental space, supplies, administrative help, etc. It is typical for a group to offer a payout split from the billable amount, for example 70% reimbursement from what insurance pays out. Group practices may also differ in whether they pay the counselor when insurance is billed or after they are reimbursed. Regardless of your private location, whether you are in a solo practice or a group, it is important to consult colleagues when needed.

Short-Term and Long-Term Care

In the preceding section, the settings in which counselors work in an outpatient environment, delivering individual, couple, or family services, were described. However, the level of care is a consideration most counselors must make for clients. Is outpatient all that is needed? In cases where it is not, counselors must consider if short-term or long-term intensive care is more appropriate. Sometimes these decisions are made by other entities, including court or legal systems.

The deciding factor is associated with the severity of the symptoms or behaviors associated with the primary problem. For example, an adult who has repeatedly been arrested for driving under the influence (DUI), in addition to the legal consequences, may be sentenced to an intensive outpatient program (IOP) for a month or perhaps to inpatient hospitalization for detox.

A Tough Call: Private or Public?

Maranda is a mental health counselor who has worked in a community agency since completing her master's degree almost three years ago. She is less than twenty clinical hours away from meeting her state's licensure requirements. She is trying to decide if she would like to stay in community agency work or join a practice group. She has really appreciated the work she has done over the last few years in her agency's day treatment, or partial psychiatric hospitalization, program. She recently shared with her supervisor that her favorite part of her work is helping clients get the level of care they need. For some, this means graduating from the day treatment program to general outpatient care. For others, it means determining if they need to be admitted to inpatient care or if long-term residential care is needed. Maranda remarked that this skill set is not something she learned during her graduate school training, rather it was on the job training as she interacted with each individual client and understood their specific symptomatic representation of the ascribed mental disorder. For Maranda, a counselor who is a Christian, she believes her work in the day treatment center has responded to God's command in 1 John 3:17-18, "But if anyone has the world's goods and sees his brother in need, yet closes his heart against him, how does God's love abide in him? Little children, let us not love in word or talk but in deed and in truth."

Residential Care

Residential care is a context of care where clients come to a facility and receive treatment on a temporary basis (e.g., substance abuse treatment facility, eating disorders facility, etc.). There are a variety of different residential programs where counselors may find employment opportunity. Consider an example of a facility that is designed specifically for the treatment of depression.

© tommaso79/Shutterstock.com

According to Locke et al (2017), depression is one of the primary causes of disability and is forecasted to be the number two highest predictor of global health burden (World Health Organization, 2008). Of patients suffering from a first depressive episode, approximately 50% will experience a recurrence (Eaton et al., 2008). "About one-third of episodes of major depression take a persistent form in which symptoms persist for at least 2 years without remission" (Locke et al, 2017, p. 595). Given both the overwhelming prevalence and persistence of depression, we will introduce you to a residential facility in order for you to understand what working in a setting such as this would be like.

Nedley's Residential Treatment for Depression. Dr. Neil Nedley offers residential programs to treat depression in several states across the United States, currently including both Georgia and California. This residential program is a ten-day treatment for individuals who have symptoms of depression. When residents enroll in treatment, they are provided a plant-based diet (based in part on research Dr. Nedley and colleagues have gathered which indicates that animal products may impact mood). This intensive residential treatment program includes a holistic model that has components focusing on hydrotherapy, nutrition, circadian rhythm, and spirituality. In addition to addressing these areas, the program also offers counseling.

© wavebreakmedia/Shutterstock.com

A counselor working in a residential facility like this may use an integrative approach, having the opportunity to consult with the patient's physician, nutritionist, and spiritual counselor as well. The counselors use cognitive behavioral therapy as a treatment approach. Elma Marie Heldzinger, one of the program directors who serves in the Georgia program, shared that when individuals come to the residential program, their treatment team collaborates in a "professionals meeting", working together to develop a treatment plan.

You may be wondering how a physician (an internist, rather than a psychiatrist) develops credibility to specialize in the treatment of depression. Dr. Nedley, a physician of internal medicine, noticed that one of the most common presenting issues his patients discussed was depression. As a result, he spent much time investigating depression symptoms. Some of his studies include an article published in the journal of *Drug Metabolism and Pharmacokinetics* called, "Effect of High Mercury Fish Consumption on Emotional Intelligence"(Nedley & Ramirez, 2018). In this article, he discussed how all fish contains mercury and that seafood intake has been associated with not only depression but also suicidality.

A Portrait of a Residential Counselor: Paul Coneff

© Rebekah Fisher

Paul Coneff is a Licensed Marriage and Family Therapist in the state of Washington, and provides Counseling services at Dr. Nedley's inpatient program called, "Depression The Way Out." Paul Coneff is the co-author of the forthcoming book entitled, *Brutally Honest: Discovering a God Who Can Heal our Deepest Wounds and Darkest Desires*. It is a modern day parable about Psalm 109.

What is a day in the life of Paul's work at the Nedley Depression Recovery program like? Paul shared that he begins his day by providing a presentation that highlights what scriptures have to say about important topics such as shame, abuse, betrayal, and rejection. After his morning presentation is complete, he begins meeting with the guests for individual sessions. He spends time listening to their stories. As a counselor who is Christian and practicing in a faith-based setting, he also interjects conversation about Jesus. He shares that Jesus was not a Savior unfamiliar with our sorrow, but one who experienced feelings of being overwhelmed to the point of death as he prayed in the garden of Gethsemane. This is inspired by the words the disciple Matthew wrote, "Then he said to them, 'My soul is overwhelmed with sorrow to the point of death. Stay here and keep watch with me' (Matthew 26:38, New International Version)."

Paul also reminds his clients how Jesus experienced much of the pain that we do, including praying the "loneliest prayer in human history" on the cross, while he still maintained his connection with his father (Coneff, 2019, personal communication).

Paul also integrates Cognitive Behavioral Therapy (CBT) strategies into his sessions. He uses an approach that integrates faith and biblical principles with CBT strategies and solution-focused strategies to help his clients make sense of their stories in a more adaptive way. He ends his day the same way he began his day, by sharing presentations that illustrate the power and relevance of biblical principles in his clients' spiritual journeys.

One of Paul's favorite aspects of working with the Nedley program is being part of a team. He enjoys collaborating with doctors, nurses, and massage therapists. He enjoys seeing the power of the holistic approach and noticing how exercise, hydrotherapy, and healthy food helps to increase blood flow to the frontal part of the brain. He enjoys seeing how CBT, spiritual counseling, and group sessions all work together synergistically to "shine hope into hearts who have lived with anxiety, depression, hopelessness (and for many) suicidal ideation" (Coneff, 2019, personal communication). Paul also appreciates what an integrated care approach provides and notes that his clients have access to more resources with the team of medical professionals working together at the residential facility than they would have if he were working with them in private practice. Paul acknowledges a personal journey of becoming the person he is today by addressing his own struggles. He encourages clients that treatment is not a one-time session or fix, but a journey of becoming. For more information and work by Paul Coneff, see the additional reading list at the close of the chapter.

Inpatient Hospitalization

Most hospitals will have a ward specifically for patients who need to have around-the-clock care. These patients are admitted if they need to have medical management to regulate mood, are a danger to themselves or others, or are in need of detoxing from drugs and/or alcohol. Counselors will work with a treatment team of other mental health professionals (psychologists, psychiatrists, social workers, psychiatric nurses, recreational therapists, etc…) to assist patients in stabilizing the problems for which they were admitted. Because this type of program offers around-the-clock care, counselors may not work a traditional 8:00am to 5:00pm work week.

State Mental Hospitals

State mental hospitals provide around-the-clock care for individuals who are seriously mentally ill (SMI). In 2017, it was reported that there are only 14 beds per 100,000 individuals in the United States (Raphelson, 2017). This is a rate of .014%; however, the rate of occurrence for a serious mental illness, such as schizophrenia which often requires hospitalization, is 1.2% (American Psychiatric Association, 2013). Further, the symptom exacerbation of other diagnoses may result in the need for hospitalization, thus creating competition for limited beds in psychiatric units.

Historically, state mental hospitals (previously known as asylums) were institutions in which those with severe and chronic mental illnesses were placed. These hospitals often contained hundreds of patients with very few staff. Patients were often medicated and corralled in general areas, without regard to individual needs. The 1971 landmark case of Wyatt vs. Stickney resulted in a federal court determining that involuntarily committed individuals have a right to fair and humane treatment that will ultimately prepare them to reenter society (Stickney, 1974). Out of this court decision, Bryce Hospital in Tuscaloosa, AL was ordered to decrease the number of patients institutionalized, increase the number of staff, provide individualized treatment plans, institute activities and work therapies, develop advocacy efforts for patients, and operate within the least restrictive environments. This court ruling led to the nationwide reformation of psychiatric inpatient care.

Prior to Wyatt vs. Stickney, the federal government worked toward reducing the number of individuals committed to state mental hospitals. As you read in Chapter 1, in 1963, former President John F. Kennedy signed into legislation the Community Mental Health Centers Act (CMHCA). The purpose of this act was to remove people from long term, sometimes a lifetime, commitment to state hospitals and allow them to live in and seek services within their communities through the development of community mental health centers. The process of moving patients from state hospitals into community agencies is called deinstitutionalization. Many factors informed the deinstitutionalization movement. Less than ten years prior to the CMHCA, the first antipsychotic medication was released (Stubbs, 1998). Additionally, the 1960s were a time of social movements that focused on the rights of individuals (Goodwin, 2005). Along with the rights of women and African Americans, the rights of those held in institutions came to the forefront of society.

Deinstitutionalization was the catalyst for the growth of the professional counseling field. Because the need arose for mental health professionals to staff these community agencies, graduate programs training mental health counselors increased. While deinstitutionalization allowed for the protection of individual rights and freedoms, it also created new problems for those who were in need of the more intensive level of services which were now limited. Thus, many of those who were released from institutions became homeless, were discriminated against, died, and/or were imprisoned (Kliewer, McNally, & Trippany, 2009).

At present, there are a limited beds compared to the number of individuals who need them. Counselors who work in community mental health often have large caseloads which may not accommodate weekly sessions with their SMI clients. This deficit has resulted in greater collaboration and a multidisciplinary team approach (Kliewer et al., 2009). Additionally, counselors have recognized the need for greater advocacy efforts to assist with procuring needed services for the SMI population. Organizations like the National Alliance on Mental Illness (NAMI) and the National Campaign for Mental Health Reform continue to educate, decrease stigma, and fight for needed funding to assist those who are impacted by mental illness.

Partial Psychiatric Hospitalization/Intensive Outpatient

In response to the paucity of inpatient psychiatric beds for clients who are in need of more intense mental health care, Partial Psychiatric Hospitalization Programs (PPHP) and Intensive Outpatient Programs (IOP) were developed.

PPHPs and IOPs are often a step-down program from inpatient care; however, they may also serve as a step-up from outpatient services. In a PPHP, clients will spend roughly 30 hours a week in both intensive group and individual counseling for up to 21 days. Clients return home when they are not in the treatment setting. While there, they are often monitored by psychiatric nurses and a psychiatrist. In an IOP, the set up is similar, but with a reduced number of hours of roughly 20 per week.

This intensive treatment provides clients with significantly more than one hour per week of counseling. while allowing the client to practice skills learned in the program in real time as they are in their own homes and with their families during non-program hours.

TeleMental Health

© Aaron Amat/Shutterstock.com

Fifteen million Americans seek some form of mental health care, and the ratio of mental health professionals to those seeking services is roughly one for every 800 individuals (American Telemedicine Association, 2013). These staggering numbers speak to the need for innovation in providing those needed services. Telemental health is the use of technology- or internet-based methods of providing mental health services to clients (Ostrowski & Collins, 2016). Telemental health may involve telephone counseling, online counseling via chat, online counseling via video platform, and/or texting.

Research has supported the efficacy of telemental health in decreasing symptoms of postnatal depression (O'Mahen et al., 2013), decreasing symptoms of mood and anxiety disorders (Andrews & Titov, 2007), and decreasing the need for inpatient hospitalization (Godleski, Darkins, & Peters, 2009), among other concerns. However, there has been concern over the protection of client material when technology is used. Some states regulate online practices, requiring that the client physically lives in the same state as the state for which the clinician is licensed. Further, not being able to be in the physical presence of the client can pose challenges when the client is in crisis. Thus, training requirements and ethical standards regarding the practice of telemental health are being developed. Other concerns are related to the lack of standardization in terminology and state regulation. Ostrowski and Collins (2016) examined the licensing board for various mental health disciplines across all 50 states and found that 14 states did not include regulations for the practice of telemental health. Across the licensure boards which did regulate, there were 19 different terms for telemental health, including: "distance counseling, distance therapy, electronic-assisted counseling, electronic means, electronic practice, electronic telepractice, electronic transmission, Internet counseling, Internet practice, online counseling, online psychotherapy, remotely, technology-assisted, teleconferencing, telehealth, telemental health, telepractice, telepsychology and teletherapy" (p. 391). For counseling and social work, the most commonly used term was electronic counseling or therapy, and for psychology, the most commonly used term was telehealth. Standardization of terminology and adoption of standardized practice regulation would assist with the ability to research telemental health, develop competencies, and enhance training (Ostrowski & Collins, 2016).

> Counselors who wish to practice telemental health can seek specialty certification. The National Board for Certified Counselors (NBCC) offers A Board-Certified Telemental Health Provider credential (BC-TMH). The requirements include already holding a state counseling license, training in HIPAA compliance, best practices, crisis planning, orienting clients, and client care coordination, among other topics, and an examination. For more information, see https://www.cce-global.org/Credentialing/BCTMH/Requirements.

Dr. Timothy and April Crable

As owners of a clinical mental health service for over a decade, we have been privileged with front row seats to the evolutionary changes both in terms of service delivery and client needs. In 2007, we opened the doors to our practice with a single office, no secretary or billing service, in the small town of Franklin, Virginia. At that time, our clients wanted traditional face-to-face counseling within a comfortable, professional grade in-office setting. We are now headquartered in Scottsdale, AZ and serve a clientele open to the incorporation of technology into their counseling sessions.

© April Crable

Dr. Timothy Crable and Dr. April R. Crable, Owners of Fruition Counseling and Consulting Services, Scottsdale, Arizona.

Therapists made time to see clients in scheduled sessions between other commitments within the practice when we started. Furthermore, clients made honest efforts to make mental health appointments while balancing work and family obligations. Our private practice has provided services to clients for 11 years, the last three of which were via teletherapy. As a result, incorporating teletherapy to our services, we have licensed therapists serving clients in five states.

Our therapists now appreciate the flexibility that teletherapy offers. They can provide services from their secured-home office. We require that our therapists maintain home offices free of background distraction. It has decreased their need to drive back and forth to and from the office. They can offer earlier and later hours to clients. The therapists have also enjoyed collaborating and receiving supervision from an online platform. Clients have reported that they feel more comfortable and secure receiving services from their home. They also shared that there are times when they did not have the strength to drive to their sessions, and they would cancel. The practice has experienced minimal cancellations. When we do, it is easier to reschedule the appointment because the client and therapist do not need to travel to the office.

Teletherapy is not for every client or therapist. Assessing clients for their appropriateness for teletherapy is vital. For example, we considered clients who are actively experiencing psychosis not to be appropriate for teletherapy. Likewise, therapists who are not comfortable with managing the technical requirements necessary for facilitating a teletherapy session are not a good fit. As owners, we had to do the same with our therapists. If you are interested in providing teletherapy, it is imperative that you research the cost and benefits of this model of therapy. We suggest you reach out to other clinicians who are proving teletherapy, as well as learn your state and federal regulations and guidelines and best practices to decide if teletherapy is right for you. We are enjoying this journey and are looking forward to growing as the field of teletherapy grows.

WHAT ARE COUNSELING SPECIALIZATIONS?

As noted at the beginning of the chapter, you may have a passion for some, but not all, populations that are in need of counseling services. As a result, you will likely target reading books and journal articles about, developing skills related to, seeking continuing education workshops for, pursuing employment opportunities with, and perhaps even conducting research on those populations for which you feel most passionate. These activities result in developing specialty areas. Below, we will discuss some common specialty areas.

Community College and University Counseling Centers

Community College/University Counseling Centers would likely fall under not-for-profit settings. Amherst College was credited with developing the first student health center in 1861 and later, in 1920, Princeton hired a psychologist to assess students' personality development (Kraft, 2011). However, it was not until the 1950s that college campuses began to employ multi-disciplinary mental health staff to provide direct care for students and proactive treatment (Kraft, 2011).

Today, college campuses offer counseling, support groups, wellness programs, health centers for medical treatment, and religious support through individuals or collective entities. This area of counseling continues to grow as more students are not only faced with stressors, but also experience mental health needs during this time. The increasing prevalence of mental health issues among college students is supported by multiple research groups. The Winter 2018 publication of the National Association of Student Personnel Administrators (NASPA) noted a few reports depicting mental health concerns on college campuses:

- The 2018 Healthy Minds Study reported 23% of college students are taking psychiatric medication.
- The same study found that 37% of college students report symptoms of moderate or major depression.
- The American College Health Association National College Health Assessment (ACHA-NCHA), the longest-running study of college student health, supports the increase in the prevalence of mental health issues.

Additionally, the Center for Collegiate Mental Health (Penn State Student Affairs, 2004-2019) produced by Penn State found significant growth in students seeking counseling services (up 29.6%) which was more than 5 times the rate of institutional enrollment (+5.6%). There was also a growth in counseling center appointments (+38.4), more than 7 times the rate of institutional enrollment growth.

According to the most current statistics in a report from the Association for University and College Counseling Directors (2018), services have a positive impact on retention, as measured by student self-report: 65.2% of clients stated that counseling services helped them stay in school and 66.8% of clients stated that counseling services helped with their academic performance. For individual concerns, anxiety continues to be the most frequent concern among college students (48.2%), followed by stress (39.1%), depression (34.5%), suicidal ideation (25.2%), specific relationship concerns (22.9%), and family concerns (21.2%). College students also reported dealing with interpersonal functioning problems (18.8%), sleep problems (15.8%), and loneliness/social isolation (15.5%; Levines, Bershad, & Gorman, 2017).

A Community College Growth Group: The Case of Jo

It was a warm June day in Virginia Beach. A group of students and two counselors were seated in a circle in a musty smelling classroom with a green chalkboard and a room full of chairs and desks. As was their habit, the group together in unison recited the following poem (Wintle, 1905):

> If you think you are beaten, you are
> If you think you dare not, you don't,
> If you like to win, but you think you can't
> It is almost certain you won't.
>
> If you think you'll lose, you're lost
> For out of the world we find,
> Success begins with a fellow's will
> It's all in the state of mind.
>
> If you think you are outclassed, you are
> You've got to think high to rise,
> You've got to be sure of yourself before
> You can ever win a prize.
>
> Life's battles don't always go
> To the stronger or faster man,
> But soon or late the man who wins
> Is the man who thinks he can!

Next, the counselor, in a soft-spoken voice asked, "Now, that we have reminded ourselves of the adaptive attitude for overcoming math anxiety, let's take a moment to check in with everyone in the group by doing a round. On a scale of 1-10, where 10 is perfect peace related to your math goals, and 1 represents high math anxiety, where are you on this scale?" A young woman named Jo with a round face and an anxious smile said, "This week has been so stressful! My husband was away at drill. I had my kids alone. I had a test in three classes including my math class. We are talking about algebraic formulas combining letters and numbers, and I would just like to slap the person that thought it was a good idea to combine letters and numbers!"

The counseling supervisor leaned in and stated, "Jo, I can feel your anxiety, it sounds intense, let's do a relaxation breathing exercise with some visualization called grounding confidence." In a low soothing voice, she continued, "If you feel comfortable let's close our eyes and take some deep breaths, let the air fill your abdomen, pause and then slowly exhale. As you continue breathing slowly and deeply imagine filling your abdomen with air and then slowly exhale. Now, let your mind go back to a time in your life when you felt very confident and at peace, envision the sights and sounds of the occasion in your mind's eye. Continue breathing slowly and deeply. When you have fully recreated the experience in your mind, then snap your fingers. " The sighs of relief were audible, and smiles spread across group members faces. One of the counselors asked, "What did it feel like to do this exercise?"Jo exclaimed, "WHEW! I feel like I just smoked a cigarette! What a relief!"

The group laughed and began to make another round, going around the circle each sharing how they experienced some relief from their anxiety doing this activity. The counselor added, "If you continue to visualize and snap or do some sort of motion, the same motion, each time, you can eventually ground that feeling of confidence into the motion and before you know it. With a tap of the foot or the snap of the fingers, you will feel confident calm cool and collected!"

This was the first half of a Math Anxiety Group Counseling session in a community college setting. Jo was a client who was being seen for both group and individual counseling sessions at the community college. This is just one case example: students attending community college have many needs and may come into counseling for not only academic struggles but other life struggles as well. We found that students who struggled with math anxiety also tended to sometimes struggle with generalized anxiety.

Recently, researchers encourage counselors and counselor educators to increase their focus on community counseling (Schwitzer, Pribesh, Ellis-O'Quinn, Huber, & Wilmer, 2016) and what practices are most effective in the community college setting. Schwitzer and colleagues make the case that more research in this area is needed, especially due to the prevalent choice of community college for many young adults. They call for more research and focus on community college student adjustment asserting, "in fact, historically, whereas community colleges educate about 44% of undergraduate students in the United States (American Association of Community Colleges, 2009), only 5% of educational research focuses on student adjustment" (p. 76).

Community college counselors do important work, and given that nearly half of undergraduate students pursue community college at some point in their academic career, this will be an important area for further study in the counseling literature. In order to get a sense of what a day in the life of a community college counselor is like, read the counselor profile for Amy Beldon below.

© Amy Beldon

Amy Beldon, LPC served as the Head Counselor at a Women's Center at a Community College in Eastern Virginia.

Amy worked as a college counselor from 1995 until she retired in 2004. She enjoyed conducting weekly topical growth groups, doing individual counseling sessions, and mentoring and supervising rising counselors and supervised approximately 2-5 interns per year. Amy's favorite thing about her work as a college counselor was helping women overcome challenges and thrive. She was loved by the interns she supervised, and they learned a great deal from her experience and her helpful supervision sessions. Some of her interns shared that their favorite experiences working with Amy involved being a part of the community she created within the office that made going to work fun.

School Counselors

School counselors have been instrumental in assisting students since 1890 with the social reform movement. However, the name and focus have greatly changed throughout the last two centuries. Initially, guidance counselors were used to direct career paths, but in the 1980s and 1990s, school counselors began to realize the need to create a professional school counselor (PSC) identity in order to advocate for their profession (Lambie & Williamson, 2004). There has also been a need to increase research for school counselors to improve accountability and outcome of their services (Sabella, 2006). With this movement came not only the need to advocate for their roles, but also to standardize their practices (Lambie & Williamson, 2004). Out of this restructuring, the American School Counseling Association (ASCA) national model was developed and has since gone through multiple revisions. The current ASCA model (ASCA, 2019) details the standards for counselors and the materials that can be distributed to help the PSC advocate for their program. On their national website, they have provided resources for the PSC ranging from curriculum planning to setting up SMART goals for program evaluation (see Chapter 7 for an explanation of SMART goals).

States vary with regard to training and licensure requirements; however, all require some graduate level education with the majority requiring a master's degree and a minimum number of hours interning within a school system. Some counseling programs require that students have multiple internships that include clinical experiences alongside their school experiences. Historically, teaching experience was a prerequisite to becoming a school counselor; however, some states have discontinued this requirement as the required field experience in school counselor training is increasingly considered full preparation for future school counselors. Some states also include testing as part of the school licensure, while others use the master's degree to meet this competency.

In addition to training and practice standards set forth by ACA, ASCA, and CACREP, school counselors also have different responsibilities based on the grade level and school district leadership. At the elementary level, school counselors will work with students individually and in groups and/or in classrooms. It is typical for an elementary counselor to be familiar and have contact with all students in their school. Some school counselors may teach weekly classroom lessons, while others do group guidance as needed. It is also common for counselors to work with students to minimize unwanted behaviors and participate in parent/teacher meetings. Counselors may participate in standardized testing and/or individual assessments based on the school's needs. The school counselor may also have duties that are not job-related, but that fulfill needs in the school such as monitoring the cafeteria and bus duty. At the middle and high school level, similar responsibilities are being met in addition to a career counseling component and managing student class schedules. The variety of student counseling issues change with an emphasis on personal, academic, social, and career issues. The secondary school counselor will assess the severity of the issue to determine if the student's needs can be handled at the school or if a referral to a professional counselor needs to occur.

Variances between state legislations will dictate the emphasis placed on school counseling. School districts are responsible for allocating funds and people based on their needs. Many states have standardized the number of trained counseling professionals per student as a minimum standard. ASCA recommends the counselor to student ratio 250:1. However, this is not met in many situations. According to the latest ASCA 2015/16 report, Arizona (903:1) and Michigan (744:1) are ranked among the highest in student to counselor ratio, while Vermont (197:1) and New Hampshire (220:1) are ranked the lowest. The full school listing can be viewed at https://www.schoolcounselor.org/asca/media/asca/home/Ratios15-16-LowesttoHighest.pdf.

While many schools systems have work to do to minimize their ratio numbers. Some states have increased their counselor ratio and are working to work towards ASCA standard recommendations (https://www.schoolcounselor.org/asca/media/asca/Publications/ratioreport.pdf). One issue that affects the ratio is the allocation of funding decided by individual schools. The school system may hire additional professionals whether that be a counselor, a reading specialist, or even a testing coordinator to best suit their school's specific needs. It is common practice to have multiple professional counselors at the middle and high school level with a coordinator at each site. School systems also usually have a representative at the central office level to help offer guidance and advocacy to counselors in the district.

In some states, school systems will contract with local mental health agencies to provide school-based *mental health counselors* in addition to school counselors in the schools. For children and adolescents who need more intensive treatment than a school counselor can provide, a school-based therapist offers the same services on-site that can be received at a mental health agency. This assists in helping these clients receive needed care while supporting parents who do not have time and/or ability to take kids to see a clinician during the school day. Additionally, school-based counselors have more access to real-time assessment and/or crisis intervention as a result of placement directly in the school.

Crisis and Trauma Counseling

While it is being called out as a specialty area, crisis and trauma counseling covers a variety of client needs. It is important to offer a few definitions in order to discuss the focus on crisis and trauma counseling. First, a critical incident is the activating event. A crisis, however, is the emotional response to a critical incident. Trauma refers to the overall experience of a critical incident. Not all critical incidents result in crisis and/or traumatization. However, a critical incident(s) is the source of a crisis or trauma. For example, you have a car wreck (critical incident), and you feel afraid (crisis), and then you avoid driving because you don't want to experience another wreck (traumatization). The car wreck is not synonymous with traumatization; rather the traumatization resulted from the wreck.

Critical incidents can be conceptualized as "Big T" or "little t" traumas (Barbash, 2017). Barbash (2017) defined Big T traumas as significant, resulting in feelings of powerlessness and loss of control, and little t traumas as less significant, but still able to cause a disruption in emotional processing and ability to cope. It is important to note that the emotional response to a critical incident is specific to the individual experiencing it and the extent of the trauma. Looking back at the car wreck, a fender bender would be a little t trauma and a more severe wreck would be a Big T trauma. However, a 16-year-old who just received her driver's license may be significantly shaken by a fender bender whereas a more seasoned driver may be frustrated but not shaken. Big T trauma often includes natural and human-made disasters, criminal victimization, war, childhood abuse, rape, mass killings; however, they can also include a health-related diagnosis, divorce, and the loss of a loved one, among other life events.

Regardless of the type of critical incident, the level of emotional response can be informed by the resilience of the individual experiencing it. Ego resiliency is the ability of an individual to psychologically adapt to the continuous changes in his or her world (Block & Kremen, 1996). More recently, the term psychological flexibility has been introduced to encompass the notion of resiliency (Kashdan & Rottenberg, 2010). An individual who is psychologically flexible "(1) adapts to fluctuating situational demands; (2) reconfigures mental resources; (3) shifts perspective; and (4) balances competing desires, needs, and life domains" (Kashdan & Rottenberg, 2010, p. 866). Psychological flexibility/resilience allows for post-traumatic growth to occur in the aftermath of tragedy. Post-traumatic growth is the experience of positive change as a result of traumatization (Cohen & Collins, 2013). For example, an individual who survived a sexual assault may find great intrinsic reward in being a crisis counselor for those who have been sexually assaulted or in leading governmental legislation to abolish the statute of limitations for felony sex crimes.

Counselors who specialize in crisis and trauma can work in any setting. There are some agencies which focus specifically on crisis and trauma. The Veterans Affairs, a federal agency which provides resources and physical and mental health care works solely with military veterans, many of whom are diagnosed with post traumatic stress disorder (PTSD). In fact, a study which investigated the mental health treatment seeking behaviors of army soldiers revealed that they have the greatest trust in both clinical psychologists and licensed professional counselors, as compared to social workers, psychiatrists, and other mental health disciplines (Hartman, Schuermann, & Kenny, 2018). Further, their trust level correlated with their decision of whether to seek treatment or not. Thus, counselors have a prime opportunity to assist army soldiers as they navigate mental health concerns. Rape crisis centers, child advocacy centers, and domestic violence shelters provide services solely to individuals who have experienced sexual trauma or relationship violence. Further, volunteer opportunities abound. For example, you can donate your time and expertise at a suicide prevention call center, join a disaster mental health team with the American Red Cross, or participate in a critical incident stress debriefing team with other non-governmental organizations (NGOs). Additionally, counselors can pursue certifications which include coursework requirements for understanding crisis/trauma and appropriate interventions. Some examples include Crisis Intervention Counseling Certification through the American Institute of Health Care Professionals (https://aihcp.net/crisis-intervention-counseling-certification/), Certified Clinical Trauma Professional through the International Association of Trauma Professionals (https://www.traumapro.net/evgcert/cctp), and other crisis and trauma counseling certifications offered through universities.

Working with Clients Who are at Risk for Suicide
by Dr. Mary Bartlett

It is not a question of *if* a counselor will work with suicide, but a matter of *when*. The rate of suicides across the United States continues to increase and is a national public health issue. While a counselor will screen to determine if a client is suicidal at initial intake, there is no telling if/when a client might present as having suicidal ideation or intent, therefore, counselors need to stay educated about suicide risk and how to assess and treat a client who may be having thoughts about dying by suicide.

© Mary Bartlett

In order to provide good prevention, intervention, and postvention, the first thing a counselor will need to understand is how a person becomes suicidal. Thomas Joiner, one of America's leading Suicidologists, and his Interpersonal Theory of Suicide (IPTS) explains suicide intent most foundationally. Joiner contends that when a person has a sense of burdensomeness, a lack of connection (or thwarted belongingness), and has acquired the capacity to enact lethal self-injury he or she is at a higher risk for suicide. However, according to the theory, not only must a person have the capability to die, he or she must also have the desire to die. Burdensomeness, a lack of connection, acquired capacity, and the desire to die put a person at highest risk for suicide.

Most people who have risk factors do not kill themselves, but the risk for suicide remains complex. The main risk factors for suicide include a prior suicide attempt, exposure to others' suicide, having guns and other firearms in the home, depression and other mental health disorders, severe psychological pain, family history of suicide, the presence of a plan, hopelessness, constricted thinking, substance abuse, medical illness, being in prison or jail, struggling with sexual identity, and being between the ages of 15 and 24 years or over the age of 60. According to the Centers for Disease Control and Prevention (CDC) men are more likely to die by suicide, and women are more likely to attempt, and there has been a significant increase in the suicide rate among youth ages 10 to 14. In fact, suicide ranks as the second leading cause of death for this age group. In addition to risk factors, it is equally important for counselors to consider what a person's protective factors are, in other words, what is keeping them alive and what are their reasons for living. Protective factors may include having children, faith, pets, restricted access to means, family cohesion, access to care, connection to communities, and futuristic thinking. When a client presents with a series of risk factors, or warning signs which include recent changes in behavior or personality, recent family changes, recent losses, suicide statements, feeling no sense of purpose or reason for living, feeling trapped, or a preoccupation with death, a counselor should assess for suicidal desire and ideation.

The most effective treatments for those at risk of suicide include Interpersonal Therapy, Cognitive-behavioral Therapy, Problem-solving Therapy, and medications. The use of a Safety Plan can help to prevent acting on suicidal feelings, having access to means removed from the home, and being empathic to the suicidal desire in order to understand the thoughts of a person at risk are crucial. Exploring the person's religious and spiritual stance on suicide can also amplify your understanding of the person's suicide risk, as studies have linked greater degrees of religious involvement to lower rates of suicide. For more information go to www.faith-hope-love.org an initiative of the National Action Alliance for Suicide Prevention. No matter how much experience a counselor may have, counselors should not work in isolation when assessing suicide and should consult with a colleague before breaching confidentiality (having already told a client the limitations of confidentiality). If a client is at imminent risk (if the counselor believes the person will kill him or herself if left alone) an immediate referral for hospitalization is required.

Contributed by Mary Bartlett. © Kendall Hunt Publishing Company.

Counseling Children and Adolescents

In a longitudinal study of mental health diagnoses, Kim-Cohen et al. (2003) found that roughly 80% of adult diagnoses stemmed from issues that were present in juveniles. Additionally, Ruther, Kim-Cohen, and Maughan (2006) found that depression and anxiety in childhood and adolescence are significant predictors for similar diagnoses in adulthood. The findings also indicated that conduct issues in adolescence were predictive of substance abuse in adulthood. Navalta, McGee, and Underwood (2018) indicated stressors early in life are positively correlated to mood and anxiety concerns later on. Further, the 1998 Adverse Childhood Experiences (ACE) study (Felitti et al., 1998) indicated that 50% of children experienced at least one, and 25% of children experienced two or more stressors, or ACEs (i.e., abuse, neglect, parental drug abuse, domestic violence, and/or criminal activity). For children who experienced four or more ACEs, the risk for substance abuse, depression, risky sexual behavior, and suicidality increased significantly (Navalta et al., 2018). The study of neuroscience informs us that there is a negative neurobiological impact from

ACEs. Navalta, Tomoda, and Teicher (2008, as cited in Navalta, McGee, & Underwood, 2018) identified the following model to explain this impact:

(1) The brain goes through one or more sensitive periods in postnatal life when exposure to high levels of stress hormones selects for an alternative pathway of neurodevelopment; (2) the ensuing developmental trajectory is an adaptive one; (3) exposure to corticosteroids is a keystone element in organizing the brain to develop in this manner; and (4) disparate brain systems are affected by different types of ACEs, particularly the primary and secondary sensory systems that may be especially involved in perceiving or recalling the adversities. (p. 267)

As you will learn in Chapter 13, the brain is capable of neurogenesis and creating new neural pathways. Neurocounseling interventions, such as trauma-focused cognitive behavioral therapy (TF-CBT), have empirical support at a secondary prevention level. Additionally, child-centered play therapy is noted to be an effective intervention (Navalta et al., 2018).

Play Therapy is a specialty area in which mental health professionals use play media as part of the therapeutic process. Landreth (2012) indicated "toys are used like children's words and play is their language" (p. 156). In play therapy, trained clinicians use select toys to help children process through their experiences. Play therapy can be non-directive (i.e., the clinician allows the child to lead the session) or directive (i.e., the clinician utilizes prescriptive interventions with the child). To become a Registered Play Therapist, you must receive 150 clock hours of play therapy specific training, be supervised by a Registered Play Therapist-Supervisor, accrue 350 hours of direct contact utilizing play therapy and 35 hours of supervision. Additionally, you must hold your state's license for your mental health discipline (i.e., counselor, social worker, psychologist, etc...). For more information, go to www.a4pt.org.

Marriage and Family Counseling

For counselors wanting to work with families or relationships, there are many venues and degrees that will lead to marriage and family counseling. Counselors may choose to specialize in this area by obtaining an LPC or seeking a degree/certification and/or special training in marriage and family counseling. This is not to be confused with the Marriage and Family Therapy degree discussed in the previous chapter.

For counselors who wish to work with this population, specialty agencies, community agencies, and private practices are all options for pursuing this type of counseling. Dr. Sam Gladding, a counselor educator and practicing marriage and family counselor, stated in an interview, "I'm usually fairly excited when I'm working with couples and families, but it is exhausting. You've got to keep track of everything and remain focused. It's kind of like running a marathon. It's exhausting in one way but exhilarating in another. You're really glad when you've crossed the finish line and can see where you've been" (Donovan & Weigel, 2015, p. 206).

In a private practice setting, it is common that the family comes to work on communication or perhaps to deal with the stress of a traumatic event. A counselor may have the entire family at intake, or sometimes one or both parents will attend in hopes of scoping out the situation. The counselor may also be working with one family member, and it is decided that an issue would be best worked through if the entire family received counseling services. It is important, whether the counselor is working with the whole family each session or parts of the family, to discuss boundaries and roles especially pertaining to confidentiality. The family will be privy to information when the entire family is present. However, if parts of the family unit are seen separately, this information should be kept confidential and not shared by the counselor with other family members to maintain confidentiality among members. As a result of these open discussions, the family counselor may decide that it is in the best interest of the client(s) to have a secondary counselor to work with other aspects. This would be true if family members feel uncomfortable "sharing" the counselor among the group or if presenting issues work towards a counselor's specialty area. For example, if a counselor is working with the family on communication issues and it becomes apparent in the process that one of the children need to work on tools to deal with their ADHD, it may be advantageous for this child to see their own counselor familiar with this issue. Another example would be if in the family session, it is discussed and decided that the parents need a separate counselor to work on their marital issues. They may decide as a group that the counselor could serve both needs or that a second counselor would need to address the marriage issues. If working with young children, the counselor may also want to have "adults only" sessions to discuss parenting strategies or issues not needing to be discussed in front of the children.

Considerations for Offender Counseling:
Kristin Hauswirth

For approximately five years, I worked in various criminal justice institutions. During most of that time, I was a "Psychology Associate" (mental health counselor) on a licensed mental health unit in a men's prison in Virginia. My day started with a quarter mile outdoor walk to my office combined with walking through approximately 16 gates—doors that I did not have control over; I had to wait for a correctional officer to "pop" the door open from a central control room. In the rain or snow, it was challenging just to get to the office to begin my day!

© Kristin Hauswirth

This mental health unit was called a "residential treatment unit" and was designed for offenders who experienced serious mental illnesses and co-occurring disorders. My caseload primarily consisted of offenders who were diagnosed with schizophrenia, schizoaffective disorder, or bipolar disorder. Our unit was designed to be a "step-down" from more restrictive mental health units and a place where offenders could stabilize their mental health before moving or returning to the general population. However, some individuals were housed there for the duration of their incarceration, their mental health remaining so unstable that they were not safe to the general population, or even if relatively mentally stable, they were too vulnerable and easily victimized in general population.

One of my main tasks as a counselor was to meet with every offender on my caseload at least once per month (at a minimum) and my caseload was typically between 20-25 individuals. We also held quarterly treatment team meetings with the offender, counselor, other counselors on the unit, nurse, director, assistant director, and occasionally, the staff psychiatrist. Some examples of our treatment goals included medication compliance, symptom management, and social skills development. Yet no two goals were the same, as each offender had a different presentation even if they had the same diagnosis. For example, two offenders who were both diagnosed with schizophrenia had very different goals: one's goal was regarding self-care (i.e., taking three showers per week), while another's goal was coping with the "radio frequencies" that were interfering with his thoughts.

This job was especially rewarding because of the rapport that I was able to develop with my clients, as some clients I worked with for almost three years. Some clients were incarcerated for long-term or even life sentences and had "burned bridges" with family and friends over the years. I believe these offenders, in particular, appreciated having someone to talk to on a regular basis. Hearing the words "thank you" is rare in a prison setting, so when I heard it, I believed I made a positive impact in that individual's life, even if just a small one.

If you are flexible, open-minded, empathetic, and have a passion for helping underserved populations, then this type of counseling might be a good fit for you! As Matthew 9:12 (New International Version) says, "On hearing this, Jesus said, 'It is not the healthy who need a doctor, but the sick.'" This verse has guided me in working with difficult populations who may be considered society's "outcasts." It helps me to remember that underneath a tough exterior, my offender clients have experienced hurt, pain, and trauma that can be addressed in counseling.

Addictions Counseling

In a 2011 Harvard Mental Health Letter published by the Harvard Medical School, it was discussed that the word *addiction* is actually derived from a Latin word, meaning enslaved by or bound to. From a spiritual perspective, we may identify the bondage as a form of idolatry, where the substance of the addiction becomes one's central focus, rather than God Himself.

Addictions counseling can include treatment for substance addictions such as drugs or alcohol and other addictions such as pornography, sex and shopping. Dr. Patrick J. Carnes is an author, speaker, and counselor educator who has authored texts on the topic of sexual addiction. In his 1992 book, *Out of the Shadows: Understanding Sexual Addiction*, he outlines the addictive cycle and the recovery cycle. See Figure 3.1 adapted from Carnes (1992).

Carnes (1992) indicated that within this addictive system (See Figure 3.1 below), the sexual compulsivity becomes the primary reason for existence. The sexual experience meets the person's need for nurturing, and they move toward the addictive practice rather than true connection or relationship. Thus the sexual experience (or perhaps the shopping spree, indulgence in alcohol, sugar binge, or pornography viewing/masturbation), becomes the primary focus of the individual's energy and resources. In some ways, a faulty belief develops that the addiction is the panacea. It is the center of the solar system of the addict's life, and other experiences revolve around the addictive experience. In the example of a sexual addiction to pornography, the pornography becomes the antidote to pain and anxiety, the reward for success, and the source for stimulation and excitement. This faulty belief system might include thoughts that the addict is not worthy of love, or if others knew him or her they would not love him or her. Faulty belief systems lead to impaired thinking (e.g., sex is love itself, rather than sex serving as one of a variety of expressions of care and connection within a loving relationship). As the addiction then becomes a way to cope with the pain of other unmet needs or faulty beliefs, the unmanageability of life becomes overwhelming and the addiction becomes a welcome escape. As it's role increases in the addict's life, the addiction eventually takes center stage and is associated with preoccupation. Rituals are developed, compulsive behaviors occur, and then subsequent despair, hopelessness, and powerlessness to stop the addiction results. In addition, Carnes reports that alcoholism, cocaine addiction, and other addictions are often comorbid with sexual addictions. The dual addictions may be associated with increases in shame and distress (Carnes, 1992).

FIGURE 3.1

The Addictive System

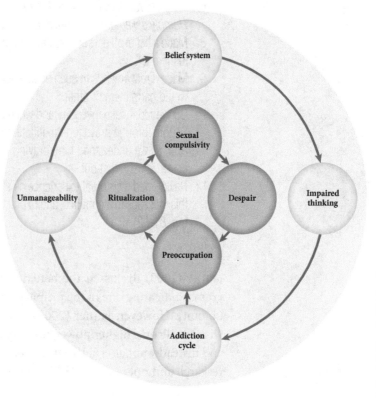

© Kendall Hunt Publishing Company

Addictive struggles have wreaked more havoc with the onset of the opioid epidemic. Classic treatments of addictive behaviors have included 12 step programs, beginning with Alcoholics Anonymous (Alcoholic Anonymous, 2014). The original publication date of their program was in 1939. Alcoholics Anonymous starts with the first step of acknowledging powerlessness, and the confession that there is one that is all powerful, God.

The Twelve Steps (W.B., 1953)

1. *We admitted that we are powerless over alcohol- that our lives had become unmanageable.*
2. *Came to believe that a Power greater than ourselves could restore us to sanity.*
3. *Made a decision to turn our will and our lives to the care of God as we understood Him.*
4. *Made a fearless and moral inventory of ourselves.*
5. *Admitted to God, to ourselves, and to another human being the exact nature of our wrongs.*
6. *Were entirely ready to have God remove all these defects of character.*
7. *Humbly asked him to remove our shortcomings.*
8. Made a list of all persons we had harmed and became willing to make amends to them all.
9. Made direct amends to such people wherever possible, except when doing so would harm them or others.
10 Continued to take inventory and when we were wrong promptly admit it.
11. Sought through prayer and meditation to improve our conscious contact with God, as we understood him, praying for knowledge of his will for us and the power to carry that out.
12. Having had a spiritual experience as a result of these steps, we tried to carry this message to alcoholics, and to practice these principles in all of our affairs. (pp. 81-82)

Janner (2009) discussed the benefits and the limitations of 12 step programs, indicating one of the primary strengths of 12 step programs is their ubiquity. However, Janner (2009) reported that some individuals do not wish to rely on a higher power, identify as addicts, or identify as powerless, and instead want alternative treatment that is grounded in evidence based research and not tied to a 1930's philosophy and culture.

Clinical mental health counselors working in residential treatment facilities or in outpatient facilities may provide treatment that complements 12 step program involvement or as an alternative to that involvement. According to Astramovich and Hoskins (2013), approximately 9% of the population meets the criteria for substance abuse or dependence and the need for substance abuse counselors is expected to rise. There are now master's programs that specialize in training counselors specifically for addictions counseling. Addictions counselors are encouraged to conduct program evaluation on counseling effectiveness, which you will learn more about in Chapter 12.

© Photographee.eu/Shutterstock.com

In practice, counselors working in addictions may use interventions such as psychoeducation on neuroscience, dopamine, and the brain's reward system. Counselors are most likely to work with clients struggling with alcohol or drug addiction to opioid pain reliever, marijuana, and cocaine, since these are the top three most addictive drugs (Harvard Medical School, 2011). For further exploration of neuroscience concepts of addiction, see Chapter 13.

Brief Motivational Interventions, Motivational Interviewing, and Behavioral Interventions for Addictions. Brief behavioral interventions also involve psychoeducation, targeted at helping clients struggling with addictions to understand the addictive cycle and long term implications, appealing to motivation for longer term rewards. Regions of the brain implicated in this process include the prefrontal cortex associated with executive functions such as planning and goal oriented decisions (Potenza, Sofuoglu, Caroll, & Rounsaville, 2011). Individuals struggling with addictive behaviors may tend to prioritize short term rewards over long-term rewards due to what is known as temporal discounting. Thus, counselors may identify interventions that assist with this. Note that counselors treating clients with co-morbid depression and addiction may find behavioral activation strategies such as activity scheduling (which may involve rating the enjoyment of various activities) helpful. Lewinsohn (1974) and Lewinsohn, Biglan, and

Zeiss (1976) were among the first researchers to integrate activity scheduling into the behavioral activation treatment that they created to treat depression (Martell, Dmidjian, & Herman-Dunn, 2010). This intervention allowed them to measure the frequency with which clients engaged in pleasurable activities and the intensity of the pleasure associated with each activity. This intervention involves having a schedule divided into hourly increments. The behavioral counselor then encourages clients to engage in executive function activities involving the prefrontal cortex, which is the area of the brain associated with planning and goal oriented behaviors. Clients are then encouraged to schedule pleasurable activities into each of their days. Perhaps these naturally rewarding activities could trigger the natural release of dopamine and, combined with psychoeducational interventions, provide an alternative to addictive dopamine shortcuts, thus positioning clients to find healthy coping mechanisms. Often, there is a certain degree of ambivalence related to change, and a client may feel the desire to continue to receive the short term rewards of behavior rather than the long term rewards of change. Miller and Rollnick (2013) indicated a method of intervening with clients to help them move past ambivalence and increase motivation to change. They stated, "No one is unmotivated. Motivation for change is a continual companion in life. At times it is as simple as finding the next meal or getting some sleep" (Miller & Rollnick, 2013, p. 74). You will learn more about MI in your addictions courses.

Faith-Based Counseling

A counselor using a faith-based approach would seek to use their counseling skills in conjunction with theology and spiritual beliefs. This topic will be fully explored in Chapter 4, but a general explanation is provided here. A counselor who is advertising a faith-based approach will make it a focus of the counseling session to explore and understand how the client's faith frames their thoughts, feelings, and actions. The counselor will focus on treating the whole person, making sure the spiritual and faith-based belief system is intertwined in all aspects. As in other areas, the counselor should be licensed and following their legal and ethical codes first and foremost. As part of the informed consent, it will be the counselor's job to discuss how their faith-based program/practice differs from other groups that could also offer to counsel the client. Being at a faith-based setting does not mean that the counselor practices Christianity but that they are open to exploring the spiritual lenses from which the client operates. In a study investigating the effects of spiritual discourse in counseling sessions on resilience, the results suggested that client freedom to process through their belief system led to a statistically significant level of resiliency (Brelsford & Ciarrocchi, 2013). This does not mean that a counselor can impose his or her own values on a client (you will explore more about this in Chapter 6), but allows the client to define his or her own spiritual identity. Conversely, to not attend to a client's spiritual beliefs is also imposing your own values (Balkin,

Watts, & Ali, 2014). In either scenario, Balkin, Watts, and Ali (2014) indicated that it is "unethical and immoral to invoke the scope of competence principle as a smokescreen for discriminatory behaviors" (p. 192). This foundation should not be judged, but used to aid the client in their holistic healing. Some clients may seek out a faith-based counselor if they have had positive experiences in the past or want to participate in family counseling in which the spiritual beliefs are equally shared.

When a counselor is deciding whether to work in a faith-based group, they must decide if this would be a good fit for them based on the typical clients seen and their training/experiences. It would even be advisable to have different experiences through practicum and internship for the counselor in training to have comparisons to base their decision. The counselor may also want to speak with veteran counselors regarding their experiences to gain additional insight.

HOW DO COUNSELORS WORK WITH OTHER PROFESSIONALS?

In your work as a professional counselor, you will have many occasions to work with other mental health professionals. Historically, terms such as *treatment teams* or *wrap-around care* have been used to denote this interrelationship. Currently, the term *integrated care* is most commonly used. Both common chronic medical conditions and common conditions in behavioral health are benefited by a treatment team approach, also known

as an integrated behavioral health approach (Christian, Krall, Hulkower, & Stigleman, 2018). For the purposes of this text, _integrated care_ is defined as a team-based approach that includes both behavioral health providers (BHP's) and primary care providers (PCP's) working collaboratively to provide counseling services and traditional medical services. The treatment team may be employed within the same organization and can meet as part of the work day, or the integrative team may be employed with different organizations and schedule meetings off-site or through video conferencing with those involved in client care. Some providers have found that a "one-stop shop" approach where the behavioral health and traditional health providers are located at the same facility may be associated with increases in both patient and provider levels of satisfaction. In these contexts, "hallway" conversations take place related to cases between providers as physical proximity within the same location makes it possible and probable. Researchers have not only compared integrated care to traditional care with adults, but the phenomenon has also been investigated with respect to children and adolescents and was found to increase benefits (Asarnow, Rozenman, Wiblin, & Zeltzer, 2015).

Supervision, Consultation, and Administration

Not only do counselors provide counseling services to clients, but counselors can also serve in roles as a supervisor, consultant, and administrator. Below, you will find a discussion of each of these roles. It is important to note that you will need experience as a clinician before you are adequately prepared to serve in these roles.

Supervision. In an apprenticeship, a more experienced person in the field oversees the work of someone who is in training to develop the skills of the field. In this way, the purpose and process of supervision for counselors-in-training and licensure seeking counselors is similar to an apprenticeship. When you are moving toward the end of your counselor preparation program, you will be engaged in field work, called Practicum and Internship, where you work in a counseling setting under the supervision of a more experienced clinician. Additionally, you will have supervision from a faculty member at your university. Before you begin your practicum, you will have taken the majority of your coursework. These courses provide an understanding of human behavior and theories of personality development and change, an understanding and sensitivity toward cultural awareness, opportunity for the application of counseling skills in both individual and group settings, practice in conceptualizing and assessing client needs and issues, and practice in developing a treatment plan to respond to those issues. However, you likely will not have had the opportunity to work with real clients. Having an on-site supervisor to support, instruct, and guide you through this work with clients is critical to your continued skill development. While some of the mechanics may work differently in varying counselor preparation programs, in general, you will accrue between 700 to 1000 total supervised hours between both Practicum and Internship.

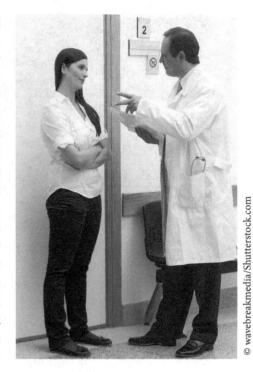

© wavebreakmedia/Shutterstock.com

When you complete your master's training, you will still need supervision; however, this process is somewhat different between the various U.S. states and territories. The requirements for licensure can vary, but in general, you will need to work between 1-3 years under supervision. In most states, a board-approved supervisor must supervise you. It is possible that this supervisory relationship occurs on the job and the provision of licensure supervision is a benefit that is included in your hiring package. It is possible that you will need to procure your own supervision outside of your employment and at your own expense. It is possible that you can negotiate to have your agency pay for your licensure supervision if there is not a board-approved supervisor available to you in your job setting. After you have gained experience in the field, including a minimum number of years post-licensure along with supervisory training in most states, you can become a supervisor for graduate students in their practicum and internship and/or a licensure supervisor.

Consultation. Scott, Royal, and Kissinger (2015) defined consultation as ". . . a mental health professional (consultant) helping facilitate change in a person or organization (consultee) of an identified issue that would benefit the person, organization or both" (p. 5). As such, the consultation process

involves a triadic relationship between a consultant, counselor, and client or client system. Because of the benefit of the third party (client or client system), consultation is considered an indirect service. It can be formal or informal, and it may be a one-time event or occur over several sessions.

In your career as a counselor, you might act as a consultant, providing assistance or guidance to solve a concern regarding a client system. You might also be the consultee, or the one seeking the assistance. The client may be an individual, group, family, or couple, or perhaps the client may be a population, program, agency, or organization.

Unlike supervision, consultation is not hierarchical, nor does it contain an evaluative function (Carney & Jefferson, 2014). Rather, it is to empower the consultee. In this way, it is more similar to a mentoring process while still maintaining a professional, working relationship. The benefits of consultation include improvements in client care, clinician effectiveness, ethical practices, and advocacy efforts (Carney & Jefferson, 2014).

Caplan (1970) developed a model of consultation that has been adopted by the counseling profession. In his model, he included the following:

- Client-Centered Case Consultation - This type of consultation occurs when a consultant helps the consultee identify services for a client.
  - Example: If you are not certain whether you should recommend a residential treatment program for a client rather than continuing to see the client individually. Or, perhaps, you are the one contacted for the consultation.
- Consultee-Centered Case Consultation - In this form of consultation, the consultant assists in helping the consultee develop new skills for working with clinical issues for a client or client population.
  - Example: If you have been seeing an influx of clients presenting with a disorder for which you have had limited experience and want to gain knowledge to be able to assist them. Or, if you have expertise with a certain client population, you may be asked to consult with and provide training for a clinician or an agency.

- Program-Centered Administrative Consultation - With this mode of consultation, a consultee receives help with program development or program administration needs.
  - Example: You may be the administrator of an agency and decide to hire a consultant to help develop a program that reaches a new population. You may have started a new program and then serve as a consultant to other agencies who are wanting to develop a similar program.
- Consultee-Centered Case Consultation - This category of consultation is focused on directly helping the consultee improve the effectiveness of the team and/or organization.
  - Example: You may hire a consultant to come in and train you to be a more effective leader for your program. Or, if you have expertise in using the Myers-Briggs or another personality type system, you may be hired to consult with an agency for team building.

When the consultee identifies a need, the consultee will seek the guidance of the consultant, who is in a position of greater expertise or specialization. The consultant provides guidance, education, and support as it relates to the consultee needs (Scott, Royal, & Kissinger, 2015).

Carney and Jefferson (2014) proposed that consultation services can center around the foci of process, education, ethical issues, clinical decisions, client resources, and/or advocacy. The authors developed the following chart (p. 314) to provide suggestions for consultation needs and what the outcomes may look like:

Situation	Types of Consultation	Outcome Goals
Stress/burnout support	Process, education	Increased awareness and Identification of resources
Ethical issues	Expert	Alternative perspectives Informed decision-making
Clinical decisions	Expert	Client/treatment understanding Informed decision-making
Lack of client resources	Advocacy	Improved client resources/support
Business management knowledge	Education	Increased business

TABLE 3.1

Consultation Needs and Outcomes

© fizkes/Shutterstock.com

Organizational administration. Counselors can also be employed in an administrative capacity within an agency or organization. A *Clinical Director* is usually in charge of planning, developing and coordinating the mental health services provided at a particular organization. Part of managing the clinical program may include developing and managing a fiscal budget and improving the performance of the clinicians. This individual would work to maintain medical records and other case-related documentation. If it is a small group, the director may also be in charge of maintaining personal files and information on the clinicians.

The title of *Executive Director* would be reserved for a next level counselor who is in charge of the entire organization. They may wear many hats as they are called upon to be leaders as well as managers. Smaller organizations would not have an executive director that is a counselor and may oversee a few offices within the organization. They would be aware of staff, budget issues and company resources to help the organization be as profitable and high profile as possible. For non-profit organizations, this individual may be actively fundraising to obtain additional resources for the group.

The *Program Director* would include an individual or group of individuals primarily in charge of specific programs within the larger organization. This person(s) would not only know the specific areas of the program and be the contact person, but they would also manage those day to day responsibilities of those clinicians working in their program.

SUMMARY

The focus of this chapter was structured to introduce you to the counseling world. It provided a snapshot of populations counselors may choose to serve, exploring various locations, client groups, and specialties. As a counseling student, it is important to gain as many experiences as possible as you rule in or rule out where and with whom you would like to work. This is a time for exploration and it is exciting to see where your journey will take you. Begin thinking now about potential sites for which you would be interested in doing your Practicum and/or Internship. If you have the opportunity, perhaps through the local chapter of your state counseling organization, connect with counselors who are already in the field and find out more about their roles, settings, and specializations. Remember, most paths are not straight, and the most important part is to focus on moving from point A to point B.

FOR THE ROAD AHEAD

Check out the Chapter 3 video at this link:

https://www.khpcontent.com/

Reflections on the Journey

- As you begin to understand more about the profession and the roles, settings, and specialties that inform how counselors work, how do you envision your personal roadmap? Where will you be in 5, 10, 15, 25 years?
- What population do you feel most passionate about? What population do you feel least passionate about?
- What setting or population was neglected in the chapter discussion? How would you advocate for this to garner more attention?

For Further Exploration

Kelly, K. & Lees-Oakes, R. (Producer). (2018, September 15). Working with Suicidal Clients [Audio podcast]. *The Counseling Tutor*. Retrieved from https://player.fm/series/counselling-tutor-1717611/ep-086-working-with-suicidal-clients-in-counselling

Shallcross, L. (May 1, 2012). Specialist, generalist, or niche provider. *Counseling Today*. Retrieved from: https://ct.counseling.org/2012/05/specialist-generalist-or-niche-provider/

Shook, M. (Producer). (2017, January 4). Suicide Prevention, Risk, and Assessment – Part 1: Risk Factors, Warning Signs, and Protective Factors with Julia Whisenhunt [Audio podcast]. *The Thoughtful Counselor*. Retrieved from http://wp.me/p7R6fn-7G.

Shook, M. (Producer). (2017, January 11). Suicide Prevention, Risk, and Assessment – Part 2: Assessment Tools, Interventions, and Documentation with Julia Whisenhunt [Audio podcast]. *The Thoughtful Counselor*. Retrieved from http://wp.me/p7R6fn-7I

Shook, M. (Producer). (2017, November 24). Online Counseling and Telemental Health: A Conversation with Telehealth Certification Institute's Ray Barrett [Audio podcast]. *The Thoughtful Counselor*. Retrieved from https://wp.me/p7R6fn-hS

Shook, M. (Producer). (2017, August 22). Integrated Care – Part 1: Foundations, Effectiveness, and Predictions for the Future with Russ Curtis [Audio podcast]. *The Thoughtful Counselor*. Retrieved from http://wp.me/p7R6fn-dy

Shook, M. (Producer). (2017, August 30). Integrated Care – Part 2: Models, Ethics, and Spirituality with Russ Curtis [Audio podcast]. *The Thoughtful Counselor*. Retrieved from http://wp.me/p7R6fn-dQ

REFERENCES

American School Counselor Association (2019). *ASCA School Counselor Professional Standards & Competencies*. Alexandria, VA: Author.

American Psychiatric Association. (2013). *Diagnostic and statistical manual of mental disorders* (5th ed.). Arlington, VA: Author

American Telemedicine Association. (2013). Practice guidelines for video-based online mental health services. Washington, DC, USA. Retrieved from https://www.integration.samhsa.gov/operations-administration/practice-guidelines-for-video-based-online-mental-health-services_ATA_5_29_13.pdf

Andrews, G., & Titov, N. (2007). Changing the face of mental health care through needs-based planning. *Australian Health Review, 31*(1-1), S122+. Retrieved from http://link.galegroup.com.ezproxy.liberty.edu/apps/doc/A166935276/HRCA?u=vic_liberty&sid=HRCA&xid=b3263b75

Asarnow, J. R., Rozenman, M., Wiblin, J. & Zeltzer, L. (2015). Integrated medical-behavioral care vs usual primary care for child and adolescent behavioral health: A meta-analysis. *Journal of American Medical Association Pediatrics, 169*, 929-937.

Astramovich, R. L., & Hoskins, W. J. (2013). Evaluating addictions counseling programs: promoting best practices, accountability, and advocacy. *Journal of Addictions & Offender Counseling, 34*(2), 114+. Retrieved from http://link.galegroup.com.ezproxy.liberty.edu/apps/doc/A348215799/AONE?u=vic_liberty&sid=AONE&xid=3842b753

Balkin, R. S., Watts, R. E., & Ali, S. R. (2014). A conversation about the intersection of faith, sexual orientation and gender: Jewish, Christian, and Muslim Perspectives. *Journal of Counseling and Development, 92,* 187-193.

Barbash, E. (March 13, 2017). Different types of trauma: Small 't' versus large 'T.' *Psychology Today.* Retrieved from:https://www.psychologytoday.com/us/blog/trauma-and-hope/201703/different-types-trauma-small-t-versus-large-t

Block, J., & Kremen, A. M. (1996). IQ and ego-resiliency: Conceptual and empirical connections and separateness. *Journal of Personality and Social Psychology, 70,* 349-361.

Brelsford, G. M. & Ciarrocchi, J. (2013). Spiritual disclosure and ego resiliency: Validating spiritual competencies. *Counseling and Values, 58,* 130-141.

Caplan G. (1964). *Principles of prevention psychiatry.* Oxford, England: Basic Books; 1964.

Caplan, G. (1970). *The theory and practice of mental health counseling.* New York, NY: Basic Books.

Carnes, P. (1992). *Out of the shadows: Understanding sexual addiction.* Center City, Minnesota: Hazelden, Publishing.

Carney, J. M. & Jefferson, J. F. (2014). Consultation for mental health counselors: Opportunities and guidelines for private practice. *Journal of Mental Health Counseling, 36,* 302-314.

Christian, E., Krall. V., Hulkower, S., & Stigleman, S. R. (2018). Primary care behavioral health integration: Promoting the quadruple aim. *North Carolina Medical Journal, 79,* 250-255.

Cohen, K., & Collens, P. (2013). The impact of trauma work on trauma workers. A metasynthesis on vicarious trauma and vicarious posttraumatic growth. *Psychological Trauma: Theory, Research, Practice, and Policy, 5,* 570-580.

Donovan, K. A., & Weigel, D. J. (2015). Samuel T. Gladding: A consistent and creative voice in the field of marriage, couple, and family counseling. *The Family Journal, 23*(2), 201–208.

Eaton, W. W., Shao, H., Nestadt, G., Lee, B. H., Bienvenu, O.J., & Zandi, P. (2008). Population-based study of first onset and chronicity in major depressive disorder. *Arch Gen Psychiatry, 65*(5), 513-520. doi:10.1001/archps

Felitti, V. J., Anda, R. F., Nordenberg, D., Williamson, D. F., Spitz, A. M., Edwards, V., & Marks, J. S. (1998). Relationship of childhood abuse and household dysfunction to many of the leading causes of death in adults: The adverse childhood experiences (ACE) study. *American Journal of Preventive Medicine, 14*(4), 245-258.

Furber, G., Segal, L., Leach, M., Turnbull, C., Procter, N., Diamond, M., ... McGorry, P. (2015). Preventing mental illness: closing the evidence-practice gap through workforce and services planning. *BMC Health Services Research, 15*(1). Retrieved from http://link.galegroup.com.ezproxy.liberty.edu/apps/doc/A541448652/HRCA?u=vic_liberty&sid=HRCA&xid=50387b70

Godleski, L., Darkins, A., & Peters, J. (2009). Outcomes of 98,609 u.s. department of veterans affairs patients enrolled in telemental health services, 2006–2010. *Psychiatric Services, 60.* Retrieved From https://ps.psychiatryonline.org/doi/full/10.1176/appi.ps.201100206.

Goodwin, S. (2005). American Cultural History, 1960-1969. *The Kingwood College Library*, Kingwood, TX. Retrieved on January 12, 2007, from http://kclibrary.nhmccd.edu/decade60.html

Hartman, A., Schuermann, H., & Kenney, J. (2018). U.S. army soldiers trust and confidence in mental health professionals. *The Professional Counselor, 8,* 213-225.

Harvard Medical School Mental Health Letter (July 2011). How addiction hijacks the brain. Retrieved from: https://www.health.harvard.edu/newsletter_article/how-addiction-hijacks-the-brain

Janner, M. (2009). 12-step programmes - several steps too far? *Advances in Dual Diagnosis, 2*(3), 8-10. doi:10.1108/17570972200900018

Kashdan, T. B., & Rottenberg, J. (2010). Psychological flexibility as a fundamental aspect of health. *Clinical Psychology Review, 30,* 865-878.

Kim-Cohen, J., Caspi, A., Moffitt, T. E., Harrington, H., Milne, B. J., & Poulton, R. (2003). Prior juvenile diagnoses in adults with mental disorder: Developmental follow-back of a prospective-longitudinal cohort. *Archives of General Psychiatry, 60,* 709–17.

Kliewer, S., McNally, M. & Trippany, R. (2009). Deinstitutionalization: Its impact on community mental health centers and the seriously mentally ill. *The Alabama Counseling Association Journal, 35,* 40-45.

Kraft, D. P. (2011). One hundred years of college mental health, *Journal of American College Health, 59*(6), 477-481, doi:10.1080/07448481.2011.569964

Knight, A. & Sibcy, G. (2019). Challenging skills and immediacy. In R. Hawkins, A. Knight, G. Sibcy, & S. Warren (Eds.), *Research based counseling skills: The art and science of therapeutic empathy.* Dubuque, IA: Kendall Hunt.

Landreth, G. L. (2012). *Play therapy: The art of the relationship* (2nd ed.) New York: Brunner-Routledge.

Lambie, G., & Williamson, L. (2004). The challenge to change from guidance counseling to professional school counseling: A historical proposition, *Professional School Counseling, 8*(2), 124-131.

Levines, P., Bershad, C. & Gorman, K. (2017). The Association for University and College Counseling Center Directors Annual Survey. Retrieved from https://www.aucccd.org/assets/2017%20aucccd%20survey-public-apr17.pdf

Locke, K. D., Sayegh, L., Penberthy, J. K., Weber, C., Haentjens, K. & Turecki, G. (2017). Interpersonal circumplex profiles of persistent depression: Goals, self-efficacy, problems, and effects of group therapy. *Journal of Clinical Psychology, 73,* 595–611.

Lewinsohn, P. M. (1974). A behavioral approach to depression. In R. M. Friedman & M. M. Katz (Eds.), *The psychology of depression: Contemporary theory and research.* (pp. 157-185) New York, New York, Wiley.

Lewinsohn, P. M., Biglan, A., & Zeiss, A. S. (1976). Behavioral treatment of depression. In P. O. Davidson (Ed.), *The behavioral management of anxiety depression, and pain* (pp. 91-146). New York, New York: Brunner-Mazel.

Martell, C. R., Dmidjian, S., & Herman-Dunn, R. (2010). *Behavioral activation for depression: A clinician's guide.* New York: New York: Guilford Press.

Miller, J. E. (2014). *Mental illness prevention.* Alexandria, VA: American Mental Health Counselors Association.

Miller, W. R. & Rollnick, S. (2013). *Motivational interviewing: Helping people change.* New York: New York: The Guilford Press.

Navalta, C. P., McGee, L., & Underwood, J. (2018). Adverse childhood experiences, brain development, and mental health: A call for neurocounseling. *Journal of Mental Health Counseling, 40,* 266-278.

Nedley, N., & Ramirez, F. E. (2016). Nedley depression hit hypothesis: Identifying depression and its causes. *American Journal of Lifestyle Medicine, 10*(6), 422–428. Retrieved from https://doi.org/10.1177/1559827614550779.

Nedley, N. (n.d.). Depression Recovery Residential Treatment. Retrieved from: https://nedleyhealthsolutions.com/index.php/programs/residential-depression-recovery.ht

O'Mahen, H. A., Woodford, J., McGinley, J., Warren, F. C., Richards, D.A., Lynch, T. R., & Taylor, R. S. (2013). Internet-based behavioral activation—Treatment for postnatal depression (Netmums): A randomized controlled trial. *Journal of Affective Disorders, 150,* 814-822.

Ostrowski, J. & Collins, T. (2016). A comparison of telemental health terminology used across mental health state licensure boards. *The Professional Counselor, 6,* 387-396

Potenza, M., Sofuoglu, M., Carroll, K., & Rounsaville, B. (2011). Neuroscience of behavioral and pharmacological treatments for addictions. *Neuron, 69*(4), 695-712. doi:10.1016/j.neuron.2011.02.009

Penn State Student Affairs. (2004-2019). Counseling and psychological services center for collegiate mental health. Retrieved from https://ccmh.psu.edu/

Raphelson, S. (2017, November 30). How the loss of U.S. psychiatric hospitals led to a mental health crisis. Retrieved from https://www.npr.org/2017/11/30/567477160/how-the-loss-of-u-s-psychiatric-hospitals-led-to-a-mental-health-crisis

Ruther, M., Kim-Cohen, J., & Maughan, B. (2006). Continuities and discontinuities in psychopathology between childhood and adult life. *Journal of Child Psychiatry and Psychology, 47*, 276-295.

Sabella, R. (2006). The ASCA national school counseling research center: A brief history and agenda. *Professional School Counseling, 9*(4), 412-415.

Scott, D. A., Royal, D. B., & Kissinger, C. W. (2015). *Counselor as consultant.* Los Angeles: Sage.

Sibcy, G. & Knight, A. (2018). *CBASP treatment and attachment.* Nashville, TN: American Association of Christian Counselors World Conference.

Schwitzer, A. M., Pribesh, S., Ellis-O'Quinn, A., Huber, P. B., & Wilmer, E. C. (2016). Community college counseling: Why are research outcomes so elusive? *Journal of College Counseling, 19(1)*, 76+. Retrieved from http://link.galegroup.com/apps/doc/A450695470/AONE?u=vic_liberty&sid=AONE&xid=97a92f27

Stickney, S. (1974). Wyatt vs stickney: The right to treatment. *Psychiatric Annals, 4*(8), 32-45.

Stubbs, P. M. (1998). Broken Promises: The Story of Deinstitutionalization Perspectives, *3*(4). Retrieved July 5, 2007, from http://www.mental help.net/poc/view_doc.php?type=doc&id=368

W., B. (1953). *Twelve steps and twelve traditions.* (1st ed.). [New York]: Alcoholics Anonymous Publishing, Inc.

Wintle, W. (1927) Poem: "Thinking." in: *The World's Best-loved Poems.* by James Gilchrist Harper & Brothers. Retrieved from https://books.google.com/books?id=2UxAAAAAIAAJ&focus=searchwithinvolume&q=Thinking

World Health Organization. (2008). WHO global burden of disease (2008): 2004 update. Retrieved from http://www.who.int/healthinfo/global_burden_disease/GBD_report_2004update_full.pdf World Health Organization

CHAPTER 4
Counseling: Integrating a Christian Worldview

JOHN KING, PH.D. & STACEY LILLEY, PH.D.

> "I believe in Christianity as I believe that the sun has risen: not only because I see it, but because by it I see everything else."
> —C.S. Lewis

Following Christ: Grace for Our Work

Following his baptism by John and 40 days of temptation in the wilderness, Jesus set out to begin his public ministry. Luke Chapter 4 describes how he entered his hometown synagogue on the Sabbath, and he read from the book of Isaiah to the congregation gathered there:

He went to Nazareth, where he had been brought up, and on the Sabbath day, he went into the synagogue, as was his custom. He stood up to read, and the scroll of the prophet Isaiah was handed to him. Unrolling it, he found the place where it is written [what we commonly refer to as Isaiah 61]:

CHAPTER OBJECTIVES

After reading this chapter, you will understand more about:

- The difference between various Christian counseling roles
- How credentialing, work setting and ethics can affect the Christian Counselor
- As a Christian and a counselor, working with those who have differing beliefs/values
- Integrating faith through counseling conversations and putting clients needs first

The following CACREP standards are addressed in this chapter:

Professional Counseling Orientation and Ethical Practice:

- The multiple professional roles and functions of counselors across specialty areas, and their relationships with human service and integrated behavioral health (CACREP, 2016, Standard 2.F.1.b.)
- The role and process of the professional counselor advocating on behalf of the profession (CACREP, 2016, Standard 2.F.1.d.)

Social and Cultural Diversity:

- The impact of heritage, attitudes, beliefs, understandings, and acculturative experiences on an individual's views of others (CACREP, 2016, Standard 2.F.2.d.)
- The impact of spiritual beliefs on clients' and counselors' worldviews (CACREP, 2016, Standard 2.F.2.g.)

The Spirit of the Lord is on me,
because he has anointed me
to proclaim good news to the poor.
He has sent me to proclaim freedom for the prisoners
and recovery of sight for the blind,
to set the oppressed free,
to proclaim the year of the Lord's favor.

Then he rolled up the scroll, gave it back to the attendant and sat down. The eyes of everyone in the synagogue were fastened on him. He began by saying to them, "Today this scripture is fulfilled in your hearing." (Luke 4:16-20, New International Version)

Although written more than 600 years earlier, this passage from the book of Isaiah was well known to the Jews. The words that Jesus chose to read are the very first public words that Jesus is recorded to have said as he started his public ministry. Throughout the rest of Luke's gospel, we find Jesus proclaiming good news to the poor and freedom for the prisoners, giving sight to the blind, and setting the oppressed free.

As those who seek to follow Jesus, we also take our cues from Jesus to do the things that he did. Especially as counselors who are Christian, we can see some of the principles from Luke 4/ Isaiah 61 and how they can relate very well to our profession. As Christian counselors, we are to be both distinctively Christian and thoroughly professional (Hawkins & Clinton, 2015). We help people who are in relational, emotional and spiritual bondage to find freedom. We help people who are "blind" finally receive their sight. We find people who are emotionally, spiritually and relationally poor and bring good news for their lives.

Our role as counselors who are Christian is to represent Jesus Christ well in our profession. Diane Langberg writes, "I believe that trauma is a tremendous mission field and that the church worldwide needs to be trained to understand it and respond in healing ways" (Langberg, 2011, para. 4). If this is true, then as counselors we have the honor and privilege of being on the front line of seeing God's Kingdom grow in the hearts and lives of people - people experiencing brokenness. As you study to learn and grow as a professional counselor, I encourage you to pray and ask God what seeing captive people set free might look like for you in your own setting.

Counselors who are Christian may ask, "How do I counsel individuals whose beliefs and values do not align with my own?" This concern is vitally important to understanding and responding to the professional and ethical responsibilities of counselors, particularly in an age of heightened multicultural considerations. In this chapter, you will be introduced to concepts and terminology associated with the integration of faith in counseling. Further, this chapter will help you understand and articulate the nuances between roles and practice settings as you navigate the practice of counseling as a Christian and responding to the challenges which may arise in an increasingly pluralistic culture that does not support Christian values. As we begin this chapter, consider this quote from Mother Teresa, widely known in her lifetime for her selfless care for lepers and the poor of Calcutta, India.

Stay where you are. Find your own Calcutta. Find the sick, the suffering, and the lonely right there where you are - in your own homes and in your own families, in your workplace and in your school. You can find Calcutta all over the world, if you have eyes to see. Everywhere, wherever you go, you find people who are unwanted, unloved, uncared for, just rejected by society - completely forgotten, completely left alone.

–St. Teresa of Calcutta (Glover, 2018).

© mark reinstein/Shutterstock.com

Self-exploration is necessary to help you understand your values, your biases, and how to make ethical decisions with clients. In the process of gaining this self-awareness, you must first consider your beliefs and values and how these interface with your role as a future counselor. Understandably, for a Christian with a spiritual foundation, you may view a problem differently than other professionals. Nevertheless, the first consideration as a counselor is to uphold the ethics code of the American Counseling Association (ACA, 2014), particularly focused in Section A, where the code addresses the counseling relationship and the need for multicultural sensitivity.

During intake, the client and counselor are typically assessing any ethical considerations and considering if the counseling setting will provide the best help for the client and their needs. During this time, clients should also be given the opportunity to decide whether they want to address spiritual concerns within their counseling treatment. It may take a few sessions to come to this determination. (Chapter 11 will provide additional information on the intake process.)

WHAT DOES THE BIBLE SAY ABOUT COUNSELING?

In 2010, the delegates at the American Counseling Association (ACA) met in Pittsburgh, Pennsylvania and settled on a definition of counseling: "Counseling is a professional relationship that empowers diverse individuals, families, and groups to accomplish mental health, wellness, education, and career goals" (ACA, 2019, para. 1). To responsibly and ethically integrate faith in counseling, it is important to critically consider this definition of counseling and how it compares to Scripture. It is important to note that Scripture should always be approached with a proper understanding of how it was written and how to read it. The Bible was written by a number of different writers over a number of centuries, and inspired by the Holy Spirit (2 Timothy 3:16). There are a number of different literary forms that certain books of the Bible take: historical accounts, wisdom literature, poetry, prophetic literature, and one-way conversation through the epistles of the Apostle Paul, among others. Attempting to see the book of Genesis as a science textbook, for example, is not in line with the intent of the original story that was passed down through generations of followers of God. In other words, when reading the Bible, it is important to consider the context of where specific books of the Bible were written, under what circumstances they were written, and to whom they were written. Context is an important consideration both when applying scripture and when considering the application of counseling skills and concepts. Dr. Ron Hawkins, also emphasizes the importance of context in counseling. A counselor working in a state school setting may interact with clients differently than a counselor in a Christian private practice or a counselor in a prison system (Hawkins, Knight, Sibcy, & Warren, 2019).

As you look more closely at the ACA definition of counseling in the sections to follow, consider the context to which you aspire to work as a professional counselor, and consider your personal theological views of God and Scripture. As a Christian, where are the places where Christian theology may overlap in the classic ACA definition of counseling, and how might you ethically operate as a professional counselor from a Christian worldview?

Counseling Is a Professional Relationship

Much like the fields of medicine, social work, engineering, and even plumbing and carpentry, the field of counseling has been impacted by the development of specialty areas, licensure, accreditation standards, and organizational (i.e. ACA) structure. Regardless of the influences that continually shape the profession, the one constant is that *relationship* is the most critical aspect of counseling (Wampold, 2015). Similarly, the Bible stresses the importance of relationship. In Genesis 1 and 2, for example, we read that God created the world in six days, and throughout the creation process, He paused at times and said that it was *good* (Genesis 1:31). But in Genesis 2:18 (NIV), God indicated *"It is not good for the man to be alone. I will make a helper suitable for him."* God's answer to what was not good was to create another human being, and as He did, we catch a glimpse of the need for human beings to be in relationship with one another. Human beings, made in the image of God (Genesis 1:27) are created to be relational. As Christians, we are declaring ourselves to be Trinitarian. Christians believe that God Himself is relational: Father, Son, and Holy Spirit, in perfect unity and relationship. As you study to be a counselor, it is very important to understand that you are in the relationship business. Your tools are highly relational, and this is a "very good" thing. The relationships that you impact, the people you come into contact with, and the care that you provide is eternal in nature. Think about it: when all is said and done on this earth, what will last? What is eternal? The short answer is *relationships*. Christians believe that God Himself is relational: Father, Son, and Holy Spirit, in perfect unity and relationship.

As counselors, our professional relationship is unique to our clients. After termination, we may or may not see our clients again. However, our work with them can have an enduring impact and can propel them to make a significant life change that will impact their children, grandchildren, great-grandchildren, and beyond. As a counselor-in-training, you are gaining tools that will help broken people be made whole. Because counselors see both clients' brokenness and the potential for healing, this eternal work in the lives and hearts of people is worth doing, despite the potentially long and hard work that it may take.

Counseling Empowers Diverse Individuals, Families, and Groups

In John Chapter 5, Jesus went to the Pool of Bethesda, where a great number of disabled people would spend their day. Jesus noticed a man who had been an invalid for 38 years. "When Jesus saw him lying there and learned that he had been in this condition for a long time, he asked him, 'Do you want to get well?'" (John 5:6, NIV).

This question is essential for counselors because we may encounter people who really *do not* want to get well. It is interesting that the man never really answered Jesus' initial question: "Do you want to get well?" He did not know what 'well' looked like. *His identity was rooted in his disability or his disease.*

Our role as counselors is to *empower* others, and by giving people the right tools, they can make decisions for themselves. Counselors do not enable, control, or give advice. Webster's Dictionary defines the word *empower* as "to give official authority or legal power to," and it also means "to promote the self-actualization or influence of." When we encounter people who are struggling, we should empower them to set good and healthy boundaries for their lives, to define or redefine their identities, and to be empowered to regain control of their lives.

© Thomas Andre Fure/Shutterstock.com

Counselors also empower *diverse* individuals, groups and families. The Bible is very clear about this as Christians, and centuries of Christian thought have pointed to the fact that the Church exists for all people (Galatians 3:26-29). This emphasis on appreciating diversity parallels the thinking of ACA's definition of diversity. According to Hawkins and Clinton (2015), our professional field has demonstrated a faith gap between those who needed counseling and those who were providing counseling. Previously, faith would not be discussed in therapeutic settings, and often a sense of insignificance placed on the client's faith. Currently, faith is increasingly viewed as an effective tool in counseling. This positive relationship between faith and mental health is so great that many have begun calling it the *fifth force*, placing it's value alongside the other forces psychotherapy: psychodynamic, behavioral, humanistic, and multicultural influences (Garzon, 2011). Knowing your clients' needs, particularly the importance they place on their faith, will support you in working with diverse populations.

Counseling Accomplishes Mental Health, Wellness, Education, and Life Goals

Both mental health and holistic wellness are very important concepts in the counseling profession. As you learned in Chapter 1, the counseling profession is much more focused on mental health, wellness, education, and life goals as opposed to only mental illness and dysfunction. Counselors tend to focus on a more holistic perspective of the client's life situation.

In looking back to the definition of counseling from the ACA (2019), it is apparent that counselors who operate from a Christian worldview have a lot in common with the values and principles of the counseling profession.

While many Christian groups and professional counseling groups alike would be quick to point out the differences between historically orthodox Christian theology and the *ACA Code of Ethics* (2014), there are many commonalities. For example, Section A.1.a of the Code says, "The primary responsibility of counselors is to respect the dignity and promote the welfare of clients." Scriptures that speak to treating others with dignity and promoting their welfare include Matthew 7:12, Luke 6:31, and Ephesians 4:29. Section B of the Code speaks to the establishment of trust, a relationship value that is found throughout the Bible and that comes alongside acting in respect of the rights of others, a theme also found throughout the Bible. In the introduction of Section C, the Code says, "Counselors aspire to open, honest, and accurate communication in dealing with the public and other professionals" (ACA, 2014, p. 8). This theme is highlighted throughout Scripture. Even Jesus admonished his followers to simply let their "yes" be "yes", which means that all of our communication with others should be truthful and forthright (Matthew 5:33-37). Section D of the Code also offers the following insight in the introduction: "Counselors develop positive working relationships and systems of communication with colleagues to enhance services to clients" (ACA, 2014, p. 10). Again, the idea of positive and respectful relationships has much Scriptural foundation.

HOW DO SPIRITUALITY AND RELIGION RELATE TO COUNSELING?

Effective counseling addresses clients from a holistic perspective, to include mind, body, and spirit. While the counseling community has been slow to make this connection (Corey, n.d.; Walker, Gorsuch, & Tan, 2011), it is important that the counselor asks how spirituality and religion affect the client in order to not only address the issue but provide value to this area. For many counselors, this kind of training was lacking in their counseling education, and many counselors also do not actively engage in religious practice themselves (Walker et al., 2011). For some clients, spirituality may be part of the presenting issue that brings them to counseling, and the client may not see a spiritual connection regarding their presenting issue. Spiritual beliefs provide a foundation for the client, providing hope, security, and a sense of peace as they work through their problems (Corey, n.d.), and giving the client a greater sense of optimism that their problems will be worked out. Conversely, spiritual or religious experiences may add a layer of guilt as the client is sorting through how to handle their situation. Regardless, the counselor must meet the client where they are and focus on the issues that the client is bringing to the counseling session, which may or may not focus on spiritual aspects.

Counselors must be self-aware of their personal opinions or biases regarding the helpfulness of spirituality in order to be able to have this open exploration and discussion with their client. They must assess how important this is to the client and whether the client is able and willing to connect spirituality to their presenting issues. For a counselor with Christian beliefs, it is important to first be able to define the differences between religion and spirituality. These terms are used interchangeably at times, and not only are the definitions very different, but your client may also view these two terms differently.

Religion. Merriam-Webster's Dictionary (2017) defines religion as *"commitment or devotion to religious faith or observance… a personalized set or institutionalized system of religious attitudes, beliefs, and practices."* Geertz (1973) defined religion as:

> (1) a system of symbols which acts to (2) establish powerful, pervasive, and long-lasting moods and motivations in men by (3) formulating conceptions of a general order of existence and (4) clothing these conceptions with such an aura of factuality that (5) the moods and motivations seem uniquely realistic. (p. 90)

For clients, religion can be both institutionalized, meaning that it is communal in nature, or it can also be personal, meaning that people have their own personal set of beliefs, values, and practices that are distinct from others' viewpoints. Religion can also be tribal, meaning that there are groups or sub-groups of people who gather together under a set of values, beliefs, and practices. Bauman (2019) says that religion becomes a powerful marker of identity (like language, nationality, etc.), and a way of organizing people against other people. This is important for us to consider when assessing the cultural values of clients, especially in our initial assessment of their life situation.

Religion is man-made. In order to compete with God for the domination of the world, Satan, whom Christ called "the prince of this world," was forced to go into the "religion" business. True Christianity is not a religion. True believers are those whose sins have been forgiven by God's saving grace and enter into a personal relationship with Jesus Christ. This is what distinguishes a Christian from religion followers. Not only does the Christian faith carry the truth of redemption by the death of our Savior for our sins on the cross, but it carries the fact that Christ rose again. (Billy Graham Evangelistic Association, 2018, para.1)

Spirituality. The term *spirituality* generally lacks a common definition, due to the many perspectives on what this term implies (Greggo, Sizemore, & Johnson, 2012). Nevertheless, Greggo et al. (2012) provide us with a meaningful description of spirituality that was developed from the 1995 Summit on Spirituality:

> Spirituality is the infusion and drawing out of spirit in one's life. It is experienced as an active and passive process. Spirituality is also described as a capacity and tendency that is innate and unique to all persons. This spiritual tendency moves through the individual toward knowledge, love, meaning, hope, transcendence, connectedness, and compassion. Spirituality includes one's capacity for creativity, growth, and the development of a value system. Spirituality encompasses the religious, spiritual and transpersonal. (p. 5)

Spirituality refers to the inner person or spirit and is generally used in the context of nurturing or growing the inner person. While religious people are generally spiritual people, spiritual people do not necessarily have to be religious. This is an important distinction to understand. The Barna Group (2017) has studied spiritual and religious trends in America for years, developing the concept of the "spiritual but not religious" (SBNR) designation (para. 2). The Barna Group describes two different SBNR categories: a) those who consider themselves spiritual, but say that their religious faith is not very important in their life (SBNR #1); and b) those who are part of an organized religion or affiliated in some way, but in reality live an irreligious life, especially when looking at their religious practices (SBNR #2).

Bauman (2019) writes a simple, yet profound way to define the relationship between spirituality and religion: "religion = spirituality + institutions." Bauman (2009, 2019) further says that many young people find the *institution* part of the equation problematic, with an aversion to the dogmatic assertions of truth. However, they like to be known as respectably religious, so they tend to identify themselves as *spiritual*. This trend helps to identify the reason that many people identify as SBNR (Barna Group, 2017).

> **Religion = spirituality + institutions**

WHAT ARE THE TITLES/ROLES OF THE CHRISTIAN COUNSELOR?

What makes a Christian counselor, a pastoral counselor, or a biblical counselor different from a professional counselor operating from a Christian worldview? According to Scott (2018),

> A cohesive or integrated identity must incorporate a comprehensive understanding of the self from a biblical lens, articulating the influence and operation of this worldview upon the counselor's professional identity. These elements necessitate a consideration of the place for faith development and integration along with the process of professional identity for Christian counselors. (p. 305)

It is important to take a closer look at each of these specific titles and roles, noting their similarities and differences as it relates to professional identity. While there are some gray areas between these foci, it is imperative to have a clear definition in order to better serve clients and set clear guidelines.

Christian Counselor

The *Christian counselor* works under the framework of a Christian faith, where the Bible is a key aspect of working through clients' presenting problems. Hawkins and Clinton (2015) aptly define Christian counseling this way:

> In essence, Christian counseling is a form of discipleship designed to help free people to experience God's pardon, purpose, and power so they can become fully devoted followers of Jesus Christ… it involves the process of leading others to experience wholeness, spiritual maturity, relational competency, and stability in intellect and experience. (p. 31)

They further go on to say that:

> Christian counseling is a dynamic, collaborative process involving at least three persons - the counselor, the client, and the triune God of the Bible - aimed at transformational change for the purpose of producing higher levels of emotional, psychological, and spiritual health in persons seeking help. (p. 41)

Christian counselors usually have some theological training along with their counseling credentials, and these fundamental values and beliefs will be present. During the session, the Christian counselor usually uses counseling theories and techniques, along with prayer, scripture, and other forms of Christian discipleship. Christian counselors also generally work in faith-based institutions, churches, or they engage in private practice work. Generally speaking, Christian counselors tend to not pursue professional licensure but instead may pursue credentialing with other organizations such as the American Association of Christian Counselors (AACC).

In an era of increased specialization, regulation, and licensure (National Conference of State Licensing, 2019), those professionals who identify as Christian counselors and engage in a counseling setting will potentially face increasing regulation from state licensing boards related to educational and clinical standards. Often states have a practice law, regulating how counselors can function as a licensed professional in their setting, and these laws differ in interpretation by the state licensing boards. In the state of Pennsylvania, for example, a law was passed in 2018 which ensures that only licensed professional counselors (LPCs) may practice counseling independently in Pennsylvania (PCA, 2019), while unlicensed counselors must be under supervision while pursuing licensure.

Pastoral Counselor

Pastoral counseling is a form of counseling in which professional clergy and other persons of faith provide counseling and therapy services. These professionals often integrate psychological thought with religious training to provide the best care to their parishioners (Benner, 2003). A pastoral counselor is usually a term given to clergy who hold a degree in divinity and have certification/training in counseling or related areas. Having additional training may help the minister in working with members of their congregation. Presenting issues for pastoral counselors tend to focus on marriage issues or stressors within the family unit, as well as some more common counseling issues such as mood disorders, adjustment disorders, or issues related to spirituality. Church members, and even some people in the community, may utilize this usually free and convenient service through their local church congregation and may find it beneficial. Some churches offer programs, groups, or individual counseling run by those who want to serve in this capacity.

Pastoral counselors are often found working in a church setting, or sometimes in private practice. Many of them are either currently employed on the pastoral staff of a church, or they have previously been employed as a clergy. For the pastoral counselor, he or she may operate similarly to a Christian or a biblical counselor, they may interact with people in their church or parish, in a worship service environment, or in a private counseling setting. The focus of a pastoral counselor is often to help people improve their experience of spirituality within a worshipping community, while also working with them individually during the week. This work can be valuable for those receiving care, but the work often comes with dual relationship issues, which can be common and challenging to work through for the pastoral counselor (Zur, 2019). For these reasons, organizations such as the Christian Association for Psychological Studies (CAPS) that focus on the integration of Christian faith and psychological principles are committed to helping their members navigate dual relationships ethically and responsibly (CAPS, 2005).

In 1963, the American Association of Pastoral Counselors was founded to provide Clinical Pastoral Education (CPE) for pastoral counselors and pastoral counseling centers. In 2004, this group expanded by joining five other pastoral groups, and in 2019, the Association for Clinical Pastoral Education (ACPE) became the accrediting body for CPE distinction (ACPE, 2019). Pastoral counselors are generally not able to accept insurance for their services, and their fees are either met through private pay or provided through their church.

Lay/Biblical Counselor in a Religious Setting

In many churches, there are individuals who naturally gravitate to working with people in a non-professional setting. In response, churches may equip people to care for those in their parish or congregation, gaining specific training from a pastor, a local seminary program, or a non-profit organization. A lay counselor is someone who feels they have skills to help "counsel" others and may be empathetic, a good listener, genuine, and wanting to help out a local organization. They also may have additional training through an educational institution such as a certificate program, rather than an actual degree. An example of this is an organization called HCM International, based out of Ashland, Ohio (HCM, 2019). Led by Dr. Terry Wardle, "HCM International, or Healing Care *Mandate* International is a non-profit ministry dedicated to supporting and resourcing men and women around the globe that are using formational prayer as a means of bringing the healing presence of Jesus Christ to emotionally broken people" (HCM, 2019, para.1).

Some counseling professionals prefer to use the term *biblical counselor*. Biblical counselors are often similar to Christian counselors. Generally, the primary difference between biblical and Christian counselors is their view on whether or not the Bible is a sufficient counseling resource for counselors and their clients, with biblical counselors most often preferring to use the Bible as their sole resource (Zondervan Academic, 2017). For biblical counselors, the Bible is viewed as prescriptive to offer assistance with interpersonal struggles; for example, when working a crisis call-in service, they can provide scripture references to assist with concerns. Because scripture is the primary therapeutic tool offered, biblical counselors are sometimes opposed to an *integrative* approach to counseling that employs secular theory or empirical research in the application of counseling techniques (Entwhistle, 2015; Jones & Butman, 2011). Another difference between Christian counseling and biblical counseling as professions is that biblical counselors are not typically licensed as professional counselors in their state. Many will pursue certificates in biblical counseling to assist with additional knowledge and training. The biblical counselor may have life experience in service as a lay counselor in their own church congregation or may look to this role as a ministry alongside a career.

Professional Counselor (Operating from a Christian Worldview)

Many of you reading this are studying to be a professional counselor and are actively pursuing a graduate degree in counseling that will enable you to pursue professional licensure in your state. Professional counselor licensure will open up many more vocational opportunities and the potential to make a larger salary, as well as the ability to receive third-party payment for counseling services for increased income potential.

A professional counselor operating from a Christian worldview is submitted to the requirements and ethics of their licensing bodies (ie. ACA, CACREP). Depending on their professional setting, it may or may not be appropriate for counselors to include an explicit statement of their faith or worldview in the informed consent offered to clients. In a more secular counseling environment, for example, it would be inappropriate for professional counselors to freely divulge their faith commitments and risk imposing their values, attitudes, beliefs, and behaviors on their clients, violating the *ACA Code of Ethics* (2014, A.4.b). However, there are also counseling practices, churches, and other organizations that freely share about their Christian worldview through their advertising and in their counselor disclosure statements. This would be expressed openly and clearly in the informed consent and discussed collaboratively with each client.

© Sue Pearson

Sue Pearson, M.Ed.
Licensed Professional Counselor

In nearly every Counseling session I've conducted over the past 26 years, one of the first things I have communicated to my clients is that I want to meet them where they are. I want them to feel completely free to share anything that is on their mind. I want them to know there are no expectations or prerequisites in our therapeutic relationship.

As Carl Rogers would suggest, I must ask myself the question, "how can I provide a relationship which this person may use for his own personal growth."

Each client I encounter presents with many layers of needs. All come with emotional and spiritual needs. However, not all recognize or even desire to address their spiritual needs. I believe my job is to create an atmosphere of empathy and understanding that will allow healing and growth to take place, regardless of my clients' belief system.

My intent is to always give the kind of compassion and understanding that Jesus modeled. I think of Matthew 9:36, "When He saw the crowds, He had compassion for them, because they were harassed and helpless, like sheep without a shepherd."

The Gospels are full of stories of Jesus' empathy, compassion and non-judgmental posture. I believe, as a therapist, this is the model I am to follow. I am like a shepherd for my clients.

It can be an overwhelming task, to be sure. Thankfully, as a believer, the indwelling of the Holy Spirit— guides me in truth (John 16:13) and tells me what to say (Luke 12:11-12). In this way, I am bringing the message of the Gospel to each session.

What does counseling from a Christian worldview look like? Instead of a series of counseling tools and techniques, Jones and Butman (2011) suggest a concept that they call "imaging the character of God" (p. 470). They offer the important point that while counseling techniques are important in counseling, the relationship that counselors have with their clients is most important (Jones & Butman, 2011). In other words, our presence with others as we imitate Christ's character is very important in our work with others. Jones and Butman (2011) point to a passage that describes having the character of God, where Paul tells the church in Colossi:

> Therefore, as God's chosen people, holy and dearly loved, clothe yourselves with compassion, kindness, humility, gentleness, and patience. Bear with each other and forgive one another if any of you has a grievance against someone. Forgive as the Lord forgave you. And over all these virtues put on love, which binds them all together in perfect unity. (Colossians 3:12-14, NIV)

This idea of clothing oneself with character is important, and it involves taking on salient personal qualities such as compassion, servanthood, community, accountability, transparency, love, stewardship, holiness, wisdom, and integrity (Jones & Butman, 2011, pp. 471-474). These essential qualities of the Christian life call counselors operating from a Christian worldview to not only to abide by the *ACA Code of Ethics* (2014) but to live all of life with integrity, not merely following a set of rules.

Some faith-related questions to ask your clients as you begin the counseling process:
- What are your spiritual beliefs?
- Do you have a particular faith tradition with which you identify?
- On a scale of 1 to 10, how important does spirituality play in your life?
- On a scale of 1 to 10, how much would you like to include practices of spirituality (prayer, meditation, journaling, etc…) in your counseling experience?

WHAT ARE THE MODELS OF CHRISTIAN INTEGRATION IN COUNSELING?

When looking at the relationship between counseling and the Christian faith, it is helpful to search for a model within the field of Christian counseling to better understand this relationship. There are several models for integrating the practice of counseling (and/or psychology) and a Christian worldview. One well-respected model is "The Model of the Disciplinary Relationship" (Entwistle, 2015). David Entwistle's (2015) model of this relationship consists of three primary categories: antagonistic, intermediate and integrative/allied models.

According to Entwistle, proponents of the "Antagonistic Models of Disciplinary Relationship" model view psychology and Christianity as enemies (2015, p. 191), treating the other view with suspicion and distrust. Generally speaking, there are two different directions for this relationship. On one side are the secular combatants, who see "religion as the enemy of psychology" (p. 192). Then the opposing view are the Christian combatants, who see "psychology as the enemy of Christianity" (p. 200). By way of example, Albert Ellis, an American psychologist, viewed religion as an element that seriously sabotaged mental health for many people. However, Jay Adams, a Christian theologian, believed that clinical psychology was the enemy of Christianity (Entwistle, 2015). Similarly, noted pastor John MacArthur believed that psychology was the enemy of Christianity, further asserting that Scripture was sufficient to solve any counseling or psychological problem (Entwistle, 2015).

The second classification Entwistle describes is the "Intermediate Models of Disciplinary Relationship: Spies, Colonialists, Rebuilders, and Neutral Parties" (2015, p. 216). In this model, spies from either side, according to Entwistle (2015), may steal ideas and information from the other. For example, a psychologist or counselor may adopt religious jargon or ideas from a religious group and take advantage of those ideas for their own advancement. Conversely, a Christian, more than likely someone who is more theologically liberal, may choose to reject supernatural elements of Christian faith and appropriate more humanistic ideas into their faith and theology. Colonialists, in this model, may see the other side as a foreign territory where they can understand some value, but they are deeply committed to their own theological presuppositions. Consequently, as long as psychological principles do not threaten certain theological beliefs, then they may be used and incorporated into the other system, and vice versa. They would then reject anything that would necessitate a change in their theological worldview. Rebuilders, in this model, would subscribe to the idea of Christian psychology (Entwistle, 2015), arguing that "Christianity contains an implicit psychology that is found in Christian tradition and Scripture" (p. 227) and presenting Scripture that supports this distinction. Lastly, the neutral parties in this model encourage the exploration and the uniqueness of both Christianity and psychology. They may run parallel to one another and may provide answers to the same questions, but in the end, they are distinct from one another, and they do not significantly interact with one another. Finally, Entwistle describes the "Allies Model of Disciplinary Relationship" as "the belief that all God's truths are revealed in the book of God's Word (Scripture) and the book of God's works (creation)" (2015, p. 247; see Chart 4.1). Proponents of this model hold that all truth is God's truth, and as such, the two disciplines of psychology and theology can shed light on the truth. Simply put, one discipline does not need to be subservient to the other; both can exist and inform the other (Entwistle, 2015). Many professional counselors operating from a Christian worldview would subscribe to this relationship between psychology and Christian theology. They would assert that all truth is God's truth, contending that psychology, theology, or both can provide answers to a client's problems. In addition to studying models that explain the views and various complexities of integration, it is also important to look at ethical considerations when integrating counseling and a Christian worldview.

Antagonistic models	Intermediate models	Allies model
• Religion as the enemy of psychology • Psychology as the enemy of Christianity	• Spies • Colonialists • Rebuilders • Neutral Parties	• All truth is God's truth • Psychology and Christian theology can exist and inform the other

Courtesy of Stacey Lilley

CHART 4.1

Entwistle's Model of the Disciplinary Relationship

WHAT ARE THE ETHICAL CONSIDERATIONS FOR INTEGRATION?

It is imperative that professional counselors with a Christian worldview have an ethical decision-making model from which to operate. An ethical decision-making model is a method for making sound choices that is consistent with ethical principles. In making ethical decisions, it is necessary for counselors to perceive and eliminate unethical options and choose the best ethical alternative (UC San Diego, 2019). This is especially important when faced with multiple conflicting values. Often, counselors will find themselves involved in ethical dilemmas where they need to make a sound decision based on two or more alternative options. In these situations, it is best to have an ethical decision-making model from which to operate. You will learn more about ethical decision making in Chapter 6.

To operate ethically as a professional counselor, and especially as a counselor with Christian ethics, we must consider these six ethical principles (Kitchener, 1984) as we work with all of our clients, regardless of religious beliefs. These six principles are the foundation for ethical behavior as counselors. They also reflect Christian values and will be discussed in further detail in Chapter 6. These fundamental principles are:

> *autonomy*, or fostering the right to control the direction of one's life;
> *nonmaleficence*, or avoiding actions that cause harm;
> *beneficence*, or working for the good of the individual and society by promoting mental health and well-being;
> *justice*, or treating individuals equitably and fostering fairness and equality;
> *fidelity*, or honoring commitments and keeping promises, including fulfilling one's responsibilities of trust in professional relationships; and
> *veracity*, or dealing truthfully with individuals with whom counselors come into professional contact. (ACA, 2014, p.3)

The principle of *autonomy* is embedded throughout the Old and New Testaments. For example, in his ministry on Earth, Jesus honored each individual's choice, demonstrating the principle of autonomy. Jesus invited people to follow him, but there were times where people chose not to (Matthew 19:21-24; John 6:60-70). The principle of *nonmaleficence* also lines up with principles found in Scripture. In the New Testament, the writers encourage people to stay away from sin because of the harm it would do not only to the person but to others. For example, the Apostle Paul writes about how sin results in death (Romans 6:16, 6:23, & 7:11), and he calls the Church to live according to the Spirit of God instead (Romans 8:2). The principle of **beneficence** is embodied in the life and ministry of Jesus found in the gospels. There are times where Jesus works for the good of the individual by healing and restoring sight (Mark 10:46-52), by healing the lame (John 5:1-8), and by caring for people on the fringes of society such as widows (Luke 7:11-17). The principle of **justice** is found in both the Old and New Testaments, and it involves "treating equals equally and unequals unequally but in proportion to their relevant differences" (Kitchener, 1984, p. 49). Jesus embodied this so well when he brought those in socially low positions (shepherds, tax collectors, women, etc.) to places of authority in the Kingdom of God. **Fidelity** is also found throughout Scripture, and it is most significantly identified in the covenant that God made with his people, starting with Abraham and ultimately the people of Israel (Genesis 17:3-7). It is also found in The Great Commission (Matthew 28:18-20) where Jesus tells his disciples, "and surely I am with you always, to the very end of the age" (Matthew 28:20b). **Veracity** is also a principle reflected in Scripture, with one of the most prominent examples being where Jesus is described in John's gospel as coming from the Father, full of grace and truth (John 1:14). Throughout the gospels, we read how Jesus dealt directly and truthfully with religious leaders, political leaders, the rich and the poor, and the marginalized in society.

Association of Spiritual and Religious Values in Counseling (ASERVIC)

After discussing considerations on integration from a professional in the field, the role of the counselor, and the principles of ethical conduct as counselors, it is important to review a professional association that serves to promote awareness of this topic among counselors. As you learned in Chapter 2, the Association of Spiritual and Religious Values in Counseling (ASERVIC) is a division of the American Counseling Association (ACA). ASERVIC has developed a set of spiritual competencies that all counselors should possess, especially those involved in working with spiritual issues in counseling. There are 14 spiritual competencies that are divided into six categories: culture and worldview, counselor self-awareness, human and spiritual development, communication, assessment, and diagnosis and treatment. See the textbox below for a discussion on the 14 competencies.

Culture and Worldview

1. The professional counselor can describe the similarities and differences between spirituality and religion, including the basic beliefs of various spiritual systems, major world religions, agnosticism, and atheism.
2. The professional counselor recognizes that the client's beliefs (or absence of beliefs) about spirituality and/or religion are central to his or her worldview and can influence psychosocial functioning.

Counselor Self-Awareness

3. The professional counselor actively explores his or her own attitudes, beliefs, and values about spirituality and/or religion.
4. The professional counselor continuously evaluates the influence of his or her own spiritual and/or religious beliefs and values on the client and the counseling process.
5. The professional counselor can identify the limits of his or her understanding of the client's spiritual and/or religious perspective and is acquainted with religious and spiritual resources, including leaders, who can be avenues for consultation and to whom the counselor can refer.

Human and Spiritual Development

6. The professional counselor can describe and apply various models of spiritual and/or religious development and their relationship to human development.

Communication

7. The professional counselor responds to client communications about spirituality and/or religion with acceptance and sensitivity.
8. The professional counselor uses spiritual and/or religious concepts that are consistent with the client's spiritual and/or religious perspectives and that are acceptable to the client.
9. The professional counselor can recognize spiritual and/or religious themes in client communication and is able to address these with the client when they are therapeutically relevant.

Assessment

10. During the intake and assessment processes, the professional counselor strives to understand a client's spiritual and/or religious perspective by gathering information from the client and/or other sources.

Diagnosis and Treatment

11. When making a diagnosis, the professional counselor recognizes that the

client's spiritual and/or religious perspectives can a) enhance well-being; b) contribute to client problems; and/or c) exacerbate symptoms.

12. The professional counselor sets goals with the client that are consistent with the client's spiritual and/or religious perspectives.

13. The professional counselor is able to a) modify therapeutic techniques to include a client's spiritual and/or religious perspectives, and b) utilize spiritual and/or religious practices as techniques when appropriate and acceptable to a client's viewpoint.

14. The professional counselor can therapeutically apply theory and current research supporting the inclusion of a client's spiritual and/or religious perspectives and practices.

What can you say about your own experience with these spiritual competencies and how can you relate to them professionally? One way to effectively incorporate these spiritual competencies is by having a multicultural approach of *cultural humility* (Hook et al., 2018), which means assuming a posture that seeks to understand and learn from another person's perspective. It stands to reason that understanding a person and their particular belief system is essentially another layer of multicultural awareness. If counselors can combine this understanding of others with good self-awareness and self-understanding, then this posture of cultural humility fits very well with a Christian worldview.

American Association of Christian Counseling (AACC) Code of Ethics

The *AACC Code of Ethics* (2014) was developed over the past 25 years to promote standards of care for Christian counselors, therapists, psychologists and those in helping professions. According to the AACC, their Code operates from four main streams of influence:

1. the Bible (both Old and New Testaments) and historic orthodox Christian theology;

2. accepted standards of counseling and clinical practice for Christian caregiving and the established mental health disciplines;

3. codes of ethics from other Christian and mental health professions; and

4. current and developing standards derived from mental health and ministry-related law. (p. 9)

It seems rather clear that the intent of the AACC Code is to use existing ethical standards from other professional groups and allow Scripture to inform them. Much like the ethical principles established by Kitchener (1984) and the *ACA Code of Ethics* (2014), the AACC also has core principles by which it operates ethically. These principles include:

- Compassion in Christian Counseling - A Call to Servanthood
- Competence in Christian Counseling - A Call to Excellence
- Consent in Christian Counseling - A call to Integrity
- Confidentiality in Christian Counseling - A Call to Trustworthiness
- Cultural Regard in Christian Counseling - A Call to Dignity
- Case Management in Christian Counseling - A Call to Soundness
- Collegiality in Christian Counseling - A Call to Relationship
- Community Presence in Christian Counseling - A Call to Humility (p. 11)

The bottom line for counselors who identify as Christ followers is that our highest ethic is love: love of God, and love of others (1 Corinthians 13:13; Matthew 22:36-40). The ethical principles from Kitchener (1984) that were later embraced by the *ACA Code of Ethics* (2014) are reflective of Scriptural principles on many levels. Though some Christians may encounter challenges in fully embracing the *ACA Code of Ethics*, the ethical principles in the ACA Code, as well as the AACC Code, are considerably aligned with the ethics of Scripture.

Multiple Relationships in the Christian Community

Many counselors who are connected in a church congregation often find themselves in confusing situations due to the ethical codes that set boundaries on dual relationships. Being aware of your role in varying contexts can be tricky. For example, in a given situation, you may need to decide whether you are serving in the role of the counselor, in the role of the pastor, or in the role of a fellow member of the church. Leaders in Christian communities, including counselors, are often in situations that involve multiple relationships and multiple roles. How do we navigate these roles and maintain our ethical responsibility to avoid dual relationships?

As a counselor, it is imperative to know which title you are claiming and to be clear about your role, job description, and relationship boundaries.

In any setting, a counselor will be faced with ethical dilemmas. However, when a counselor is working with clients connected to them in a close-knit faith community, it is important to be aware of situations in which the counselor and client may interact with one another outside the counseling context. Within a religious community, members not only attend church together, but may also attend the same social functions, may have interactions in business, and may even go to the same school. This is particularly true in smaller, rural communities. The topic of multiple relationships and varying roles needs to be openly discussed during intake and requires the informed consent of the client. The pros and cons of entering the counseling relationship must be clearly explained and examined given the potential for outside interactions.

Counselors in contexts that may involve multiple relationships must be aware of the competition between the values of Christian kindness and compassion and the values of their professional expectations and ethics. Without mindful awareness and collaborative dialogue between counselor and client, it can be easy to violate dual relationship principles in church communities, resulting in potential harm for clients. Below, we consider a case example of multiple relationships in a church setting.

The Case of Suzy

© LightField Studios/Shutterstock.com

Suzy is a licensed professional counselor who works in private practice in a secular setting and also attends a local church where she teaches an adult Sunday school class. She was approached one day by a fellow church member asking if she would consider seeing her daughter since she was having anxiety issues. Suzy has extensive experience in working with children and anxiety. This situation creates an ethical dilemma with the potential for multiple relationships. For Suzy, what information does she need to make a sound ethical decision that honors her faith commitments as well as her profession? What will be the personal interaction that she has with this child and/or parent both presently and in the future? How will the child feel and respond to seeing their counselor frequently outside of her sessions?

Sanders (2016) outlined some excellent questions and key points to ponder that counselors in multiple relationship situations in a faith community may need to ask themselves:

- Is engaging in this counseling relationship this the best choice for Suzy's client?
- Will engaging in a counseling relationship harm Suzy's potential client?
- Is her potential client able to maintain healthy boundaries during treatment?
- Will having multiple relationships affect her counseling relationship with the potential client?
- Can Suzy remain objective during this treatment?
- Did Suzy seek out supervision and did she provide a rationale for the multiple relationships in her notes?

Exercise: Application of the ACA Codes to the Case of Suzy

The *ACA Code of Ethics* (2014) has some helpful advice for how Suzy should operate in her role as an LPC. Perhaps it is helpful to ask some questions in how to address the situation with Suzy:

- How do the principles of autonomy, nonmaleficence, beneficence, justice, fidelity, and veracity come into play in her decision making? It would be helpful to look at the preamble of the *ACA Code of Ethics* (2014) and consider which of these ethical principles relate to this situation.
- Could taking on this client create any potential maleficence in the relationship long term? Since as counselors our first duty is to do no harm, it is of utmost importance to make sure that whatever course we choose, we seek to do good to our clients or to potential clients who are seeking help and support (ACA, 2014, A.1.a).
- Would working with this young lady from her church as a client impact the client's mother's sense of autonomy? From Suzy's perspective, she should make sure, particularly if she decides to have the girl as

her client, that the mother does not feel any sense of obligation to relate to Suzy differently in the life of the church. The burden is on Suzy to make sure that the girl and her mother's autonomy is not compromised.

- If the daughter did not see Suzy, would her options of finding mental health care be severely limited? When assessing a client's situation, financial considerations are very important, along with access to counseling services. If they are in a rural setting, sometimes accessing qualified mental health professionals can be difficult. If there is a financial need in the client's family, sometimes churches may be able to provide financial assistance. All of these considerations should be addressed in finding the right counselor for a client.

- Could the mother feel a sense of obligation if the counseling relationship with Suzy and her daughter did not work out? Especially if there is a dual relationship, the counselor must be aware of the potential for the relationship being negatively compromised.

- Could taking this girl on as a paying client create some injustice in their relationship at church? There are two considerations that Suzy must look at when taking on a paying client. The first is addressed in the previous question. The second issue is the potential for a power imbalance if the girl and her mother pay Suzy for these sessions. This must be taken into consideration if Suzy accepts the girl as a paying client.

The *ACA Code of Ethics* (2014) also has many different sections pertaining to ethics. Section A addresses the counseling relationship, and this section may have some good advice for how Suzy might interact in this potential dual relationship. Section A.6, for example, speaks to how Suzy could ethically operate in a way that creates the best outcome for her fellow church member's daughter. Section A.6.b reads as follows:

> Counselors consider the risks and benefits of extending current counseling relationships beyond conventional parameters. Examples include attending a client's formal ceremony (e.g., a wedding/commitment ceremony or graduation), purchasing a service or product provided by a client (excepting unrestricted bartering), and visiting a client's ill family member in the hospital. In extending these boundaries, counselors take appropriate professional precautions such as informed consent, consultation, supervision, and documentation to ensure that judgment is not impaired and no harm occurs. (p. 5)

Based on this particular code, Suzy should consider the risks and benefits of taking on the girl as her client. She should do that by consulting with another counselor, seeking supervision, and documenting her rationale for the decision, especially if she makes the decision to take her as her client. Additionally, should Suzy make the decision, there should be an opportunity for both her new client and her mother to have a clear process of informed consent, making sure that all parties involved understand the parameters of the relationship.

Based on the information given about Suzy and this situation, if you were Suzy, how would you respond to her fellow parishioner asking Suzy to counsel her daughter? What ethical principles, codes of ethics, and state licensing laws would impact your decision to provide counseling services for this girl struggling with anxiety? If you do decide to take the daughter as a client, what are some specific issues you would address in your counseling notes for the client?

The Case of James

Other ethical considerations that require the application of integration may include differences in worldview or value systems. For example, what if a client comes to you as a Christian counselor, but his particular ideas about Christianity are not in line with your own theological ideas? Consider James, a 42 year-old, single male client who presents with depression and anxiety. James reports that he feels like his life is a failure for several reasons: he has a dead-end and low-paying job (pizza delivery driver), he never graduated from college, he is single and not dating anyone, he is overweight and out of shape, and he does not have any friends. He occasionally attends a non-denominational church, but he keeps to himself. He also reported feeling anxious about his faith, stating that he grew up in a Pentecostal church but never had a "conversion experience" to know he has received salvation from God. For people from a Pentecostal background, many believe that when someone is saved and receives the Holy Spirit, they will speak in tongues (Acts 2:1-12). James said that he no longer considers himself

Pentecostal, but he continues to worry about not being saved and that his worry is just another example of being a failure (Brown & King, 2019).

Exercise: Application of the ACA Codes to the Case of James

How might you approach your work with James as a counselor who is Christian? Again, let us take a look at the *ACA Code of Ethics* (2014). What code or codes may come into play? How do our own personal values come into play when working with James? Consider Code A.4.b:

> Counselors are aware of—and avoid imposing—their own values, attitudes, beliefs, and behaviors. Counselors respect the diversity of clients, trainees, and research participants and seek training in areas in which they are at risk of imposing their values onto clients, especially when the counselor's values are inconsistent with the client's goals or are discriminatory in nature. (p. 5)

Here are some other questions to consider in this situation.
- What role do you play in his life? Particularly if you are working in a church-related ministry, James may come seeking his counselor to have a Christian perspective, or at the very least to point him to God in the counseling process.
- Is James coming to you as a spiritual authority in his life? In other words, are you his priest, pastor, elder, or spiritual father/mother? If you are, or if James sees you as more than a professional counselor, he may be asking you to share your views. In these situations, it is important to, again, understand what your role in his life really is.
- Does James' theological worldview line up with your personal Christian values? If they do, then it may be easier for you to navigate your counseling relationship with James while not imposing your attitudes and beliefs in counseling, (ACA, 2014, A.4.b). If his beliefs do not line up with yours, even if both of you are Christian, you will need to understand what your role is with your client.
- James described that he is concerned that he may not be saved. How do you navigate his beliefs if you disagree with his thought process? This goes along with the previous question, but perhaps there are some things that you can do as James' counselor. You can appeal to some

sacred texts like the Bible, or you could connect James to a spiritual authority in the community where you live, like a priest or a pastor.

How might you respond to James in this situation, understanding that we are not to impose our values, attitudes, and beliefs onto our clients (ACA Code, 2014, A.4.b).

Questions to ask of myself as a counselor?
- Am I clear on what I believe theologically?
- It is my job to inform my client about a theological issue?
- How much should I disclose about my theological beliefs as a professional counselor in my particular setting?

The Case of Dmitri

© tommaso79/Shutterstock.com

Often, client backgrounds do not include the same theological training that Christian counselors may have received, resulting in other ethical considerations related to theology. For example, consider Dmitri, a 20-year-old young adult who was adopted from Russia by his parents. He was rescued from an orphanage at 18 months, where his caregivers told Dmitri's adoptive parents that he was abandoned at 2 months of age by his birth parents because they were unable to care for him financially. He was sexually abused by an older foster child in the home when he was 10 years old, and that child was removed. Dmitri began exhibiting some psychiatric symptoms at age 10, and those symptoms dramatically increased at about age 13 when puberty began for him. He would start reacting negatively when his parents would direct him to do something in the house, he started lashing out at his siblings physically, and he would threaten his parents. He was hospitalized at 17 years of age with symptoms of depression and suicidal ideation. Now at age 20, he comes to you at the insistence of his parents, and he confidentially tells you that not only is he experiencing suicidal ideation, but he has the means to carry out his plans. He tells you that he does not want to go back to "that stupid hospital," but he cannot stop thinking about suicide. He also says that suicide is an unpardonable sin and that he will "just go to hell, and that will be that." How do you respond to him ethically?

As we consider the fundamental ethical principles of clients, there may be times that one or more of these principles may need to be lessened, while others may take more precedence. In this case, some of Dmitri's autonomy likely needs to be taken away to allow for nonmaleficence, beneficence, and veracity in his life (ACA, 2014, Preamble). That may mean that the counselor will be acting ethically by removing a lot of his autonomy and involuntarily committing him to an inpatient hospital setting. The issue of his own personal safety is a top priority, but at the same time, as a Christian, does our faith matter in this case? Is there anything that one could say in response to someone who fatalistically says that he is resigning himself to hell? Should we step in and say something? As a Christian, how might you respond to Dmitri upon his insistence that he is resigned to just kill himself and go to hell? Will he go to hell if he kills himself?

The bottom line for counselors is that our primary responsibility is to respect the dignity of clients and promote their welfare (ACA, 2014, A.1.a). Counselors find ways to seek out supervision, consultation, training, and education in situations where we need to make ethical decisions. In essence, counselors very seldom make an ethical decision in isolation. Counselors seek out consultation, education, supervision, and training while protecting our clients' confidentiality. It has been said that the six rules of ethical counseling are: consult, consult, consult, and document, document, document. Each ethical situation we encounter is unique in and of itself, and so we must understand our limitations and seek different angles of solutions to each client we encounter, especially those where there is a potential conflict of values.

WHAT KINDS OF ISSUES MIGHT BE TOUGH TO NAVIGATE?

> "I'm not focusing on your outside. I'm trying to find the masterpiece inside you."
> — Tim Clinton, The Impressionist

Clients come to counseling with a myriad of very complex and difficult struggles. With counseling being a transformative process, how do we encourage clients to open up their lives to us around these tough challenges? As a counselor with a Christian worldview, we are called to help our clients navigate through life challenges. Sometimes counselors-in-training will wonder if they can work with certain groups of people. Perhaps the counselor-in-training is uncertain how to handle client struggling with questions about same sex attraction or questions about reconciling faith and homosexuality, gender identity questions, abortion, pornography, demon possession, or drug usage, particularly marijuana. There is no doubt how we experience the world will shape how we counsel. As a counselor grows, their professional and personal development must include space to look at these questions in his or her life, and to wrestle with how to handle the difficult theological matters. This process is a lifelong journey for counselors operating from a Christian worldview. Perhaps a good question to ask when considering the process of how to care for people who may not agree with you theologically would be: *Is this a concern that can be resolved, or is this an ongoing challenge that needs to be developed and managed differently?* Some follow up questions to consider might be: *Can you live with the possibility that the concern you are addressing has no definitive answer right now? How then shall we live in light of this?*

The bottom line from a Christian worldview, as mentioned previously, is that a Christian clinical mental health counselor's highest ethic is love: love of God and love of others. As Christians, ACA Code A.1.a (2014) comes out of our love for others: "The primary responsibility of counselors is to respect the dignity and promote the welfare of clients." Clients are not "issues"; they are people who are made in the image of God (Genesis 1:27), and should be treated as such. No matter what a client's lifestyle choices are, clinical mental health counselors that identify with a Christian worldview follow God's call to love our neighbor as ourselves (Matthew 22:39) and to do to others as we would want them to do to us (Luke 6:31).

Section A.4.b of the *ACA Code of Ethics* (2014) indicates that it is inappropriate to impose our value system and beliefs onto others, but it is important that we identify the spiritual values of our clients along with their cultural values and that we navigate them well with our clients. Following are a few examples of pressing issues that many counselors who operate from a Christian worldview may find challenging.

Integration as Conversation
Mark R. McMinn, Ph.D.

© Lisa McMinn

The more I study, ponder, read, and write about integration, the more I am drawn to a relational understanding of what it is. Integration models and concepts are important, and many of them help us understand the interaction of Christianity, counseling, and psychology, but what if the relational process of integration is even more important than the best models and paradigms we can build?

The best conversations are curious. We want to know about one another, so we ask questions and consider various perspectives. So, too, with integration, it seems important to enter with curiosity about faith, counseling theory, psychology, and the other people involved in the conversation. For several centuries now, modernity has pushed us toward cinching down certainty, but these days it seems sort of silly to think that with enough study we could somehow discern the exact purpose and meaning of a particular Bible passage or know the precise application of that passage when sitting with a client facing profound depression. One of the gifts of postmodernity is that it elevates the relationship above substance and allows us to try on various ideas and have discussions among those with varying ideas. And this has implications for the clients we sit with because they also are much more interested in conversation than hearing the certainties, we think we possess.

I do a little math exercise with my students where I have them calculate the number of clients per week they may meet with after completing their graduate degree (let us assume 25 clients), then the number of weeks per year they might work (let us assume 50 weeks), and the number of years they might practice before retiring (let us assume 30 years). Based on the math, and these assumptions, a new counselor or psychologist might have 37,500 professional conversations with clients over the course of a career! Many of these conversations will be transformative for clients, and some of them will be life-changing. Clinical conversations change us as counselors and psychotherapists also. Over and over, we touch topics of faith, the deepest meanings, and matters of life, and mental health. How well are we able to host generous, hospitable, empathic, meaningful conversations that allow space for both our similarities and differences?

My daughter, Megan Anna Neff, and I began meeting several years ago for weekly conversations. Megan Anna had a previous seminary degree and was in the process of getting her doctoral degree in psychology, so not surprisingly, we had many conversations about integration topics. Those conversations led to a book where we explore this conversational approach to integration (Neff & McMinn, 2020). I have learned so much in this process, not just from the thought-provoking theological content Megan Anna brings, but also from the chance to consider and ponder ideas together—to be integrators in dialog with one another, and then to invite others into these rich and meaningful conversations in our classrooms, clinical offices, and writing.

Contributed by Mark McMinn. © Kendall Hunt Publishing Company.

Abortion

Out of all the political issues in our culture today, abortion ranks at the top of the list as one of the most divisive issues (Cohn, 2013). The primary question many Christians ask is: "when does human life begin?" If human life begins before birth, then destroying that human life before birth is murder. At the same time, some Christians would support abortion based on their view of a women's autonomy, promoting the freedom to choose. There may be multiple reasons for supporting this view including the mother's health, financial difficulties, and lack of partner assistance. Both parties will find value in their viewpoint; however, it may be a problem when the values of the client clash with our personal views.

Many professional counselors will undoubtedly encounter clients who find themselves in an unplanned pregnancy. If your client chooses an option that you do not agree with, how do you approach this? How do counselors navigate ACA Code A.4.b (2014) and avoid imposing personal values when they do not agree with the decision that someone makes about abortion, adoption, or choosing to parent a child of an unplanned pregnancy? As counselors who are Christians, it may be more helpful to also look at the surrounding issues of each person we encounter, similar to the way Jesus did when he encountered the woman at the well (John 4). Jesus chose not to engage in a long conversation about an issue of the day (where Samaritans and Jews should truly worship), but instead to talk to the woman about her own condition (she had five husbands). The principle here is that if counselors operating from a Christian worldview are going to love their neighbor as themselves, they must choose to look at each individual first, rather than seeing that person as an "issue."

As counselors, we must also be willing to engage the sociological debate surrounding abortion. For example, an abortion activist might offer a challenge: "You Christians care a lot about unborn children, but you don't seem to care about born children." Choosing to carry a child to term, or choosing not to carry a child to term in an unplanned pregnancy carries with it many significant ramifications. An ethical counselor operating from a Christian perspective will always take into account how those impacted by this decision will maintain ongoing support and care through family, friends, and community resources.

As mentioned previously in the preceding section you will want to consider if this an issue that can be resolved, or is this an ongoing challenge that needs to be developed and managed differently. Here are some issues that counselors need to pay attention to as they care for their clients who are facing an unplanned pregnancy:

- The client ultimately needs to come to a decision on their own and feel supported in counseling.
- The client needs to work through their own personal ethics around the issue of abortion, adoption, and choosing to parent their child. If they choose to place their child in an adoptive home or have an abortion, then what feelings to they need to work through regarding this decision?
- During the counseling process, what are the client's mental health concerns that may need to be addressed during and after their pregnancy?
- During this process, your nonverbal language needs to be in check as you work with your client who may choose a different path than the one you would personally choose.
- Depending on their decision, what resources, supports, and referrals are needed to assist them with their decision? Thinking from a holistic perspective, how do counselors find balance in the spiritual, emotional, physical, relational, and financial aspects of their decision?

It is important to look at not only how you counsel this person with a loving heart, but also how you help your client navigate through their decision. Compassionate care is the key. The empathy that a counselor provides a client during this process is so important. For these reasons, you must understand your own feelings as you work with someone. Counselors need to not only be in tune with their client's mental health in the initial decision, but also with possible emotional outcomes that may occur after the decision. Just because your client ends their counseling with you does not necessarily mean that they will not need to readdress thoughts and feelings that spring up a few years or more down the road.

Jill Duba Saueheber, Ph.D.
Western Kentucky University

Every week for as long as I can remember, I attended weekly mass. While I was not engaged in any kind of formal formation during high school, my identity as a Roman Catholic continued to grow roots due to the incredibly faithful Catholic women around me (my mother, both of my grandmothers, and my aunts). I then pursued a degree in biology at Saint Xavier University, a Catholic institution located on the side south of Chicago inspired by the Sisters of Mercy. Often, I would attend daily mass or simply rest in the chapel. After completing my master's in Marriage and Family Counseling at Governors State University in 1999, I began working in a private Christian counseling agency. I felt as if everything fit. It was not until my doctoral program in Counselor Education and Supervision at Kent State University that I was exposed to tenets and cultural norms different from those within my Christian circle. For example, my doctoral program, at least at the time, was heavily focused on social construction and narrative therapy. This was my first exposure to relativism. And this was the first nudge of many to dive more deeply into the teachings of the Catholic Church. As I studied, my roots deepened even more. (How Catholicism is perceived in the secular world is far from its beautiful teachings associated with grace, forgiveness, love, compassion, healing, and acceptance.) Catholicism became who *I am*. It contains my values, my beliefs, how I move through the world and in relationships, what my marriage looks like (or at least strives to look like), and hopefully tells the world that my utmost priority is to be more like Jesus and the Virgin Mary with and among others.

What does all of this mean for me professionally? Everything. I do not believe it is possible to leave a part of yourself outside the counseling room. Secondly, why on earth would we want to do that? Even Alfred Adler emphasized the importance of bringing one's whole self in relationship with others. We are our best counseling-selves when we bring all of us to the room. (Unintentional countertransference occurs when we do not.) And, there is absolutely nothing contradictory about being a Roman Catholic or Christian, and being able to follow the American Counseling Association Code of Ethics. In fact, the teachings of the Church, many found in the Catholic Code of Canon Law and Catechism of the Catholic Church emphasized similar behaviors and dispositions that Catholics are called to emulate hundreds of years before the ACA ethical codes were even created. (Readers are encouraged to study the texts of their specific Christian faith perspectives, specifically as they relate to mercy and compassion.)

My job as a professional, as well as when I am out walking my labrador Gabriel, is to "be the light of Christ." It is that simple, and it is that so greatly profound. When I work with clients, some whom are transgender, some who are cheating on their wives, others who are causing great harm to their bodies on a daily basis, my position is to be there *with them.* It is when our ego dominates our sessions, do we find ourselves pondering whether we are contradicting our values with someone who does not behave according to how we believe they should. The ego believes it knows all and it knows more. The ego wants to make people make the right choices. Jesus, on the other hand, while *he* may know what is truly right and good, would still sit with anyone who approached him. He would listen. He would gaze. He would contain. He would remain compassionate. He would want to know more about the story. If we are truly like the great man we believe in, we too can work with anyone who enters our counseling office.

Contributed by Jill Saueheber. © Kendall Hunt Publishing Company.

Anxiety and Depression

It is a common misconception that spiritual/religious individuals will not suffer from anxiety or depression. A client may feel shame as they question whether their spiritual beliefs are "good enough" to rid them of their struggles. When dealing with concerns like anxiety and depression, spiritual beliefs may help the client to find meaning and purpose in their life which may, in turn, neutralize their negative emotions (Bonelli, Dew, Koenig, Rosmarin, & Vasegh, 2012). While some clients may feel positive emotions, others may feel shame or guilt for going to counseling or dealing with these concerns.

Regardless of our spiritual beliefs, no one is immune to having these issues. Dr. Jeremiah Johnston (2015) feels the church's response to suicide and mental health is the most important apologetics question of today's time. Johnston stated that if the church can answer this question, then it could be the key to unlock a new revival among people, recommending that, as a society, we answer this question intellectually, compassionately and biblically. Johnston asserts that nearly every family is struggling with "invisible diseases" (i.e., anxiety and depression), but that others cannot see the struggle from the outside. As counselors, it is our job to remove the stigma and work to remove the shame. Johnston (2015) is quick to point out that those hurting with mental health issues cannot be "fixed at the altar" with passionate prayers and anointing oil. As counselors you will be working with clients that are where they are due to a myriad of reasons. It is unreasonable to think that our clients would be able to resolve this problem quickly when these issues may have been accumulating for some time. Just as your clients need good social support, Johnston encourages us to be present and to look at mental illness "as a physical dysfunction of the brain that causes a person the inability to think, feel or act in their person's normal manner" (2015, p. 107). Counselors must also encourage their clients who use their spiritual beliefs to gain strength during difficult times that their hurting is not a result of a lack of faith. Their problems are not a result of failure as Christians; however, they do have control over their actions to better their situation. Counselors need to hear their clients, be present, and help them to utilize resources as they work through difficult times.

Demonic Possession

Demonic possession is another area that carries cultural, spiritual, and counseling challenges for counselors. Students may feel conflicted when their culture and counseling world do not agree on the cause of mental health issues. This might be seen in a Haitian community which feels one of their community members is demonically possessed, or in the esoterically spiritual person who has their house anointed to rid their dwelling of evil spirits. According to Dr. Ron Hawkins (personal communication, Jan 29, 2019), Christians believe Satan is a real enemy of God's work in our world. He has a following and we call them, in biblical terminology, demons. These demons follow his bidding and are the arch enemies of all that God seeks to do with His people. In Dr. Hawkins view, it is good counseling practice to stay away from labeling anything as demonic too quickly. For counselors to ascribe to the idea that all schizophrenics are demon possessed would be providing your client a disservice; additionally, it would not be sustainable given what we know about that particular form of mental illness.

As counselors, we must be aware that the challenges people face in the area of mental health have multiple causes. Instead of focusing on whether the demonic position is real or exists, the focus should be on seeing the experience through the client's eyes. Our challenge as a counselor is to identify the source or sources of the issue being faced by this particular client, at this particular time, under these specific circumstances. The goal is to help clients identify the origins of their problems, because they are seeking our help and have entrusted us to help them become healthier on all fronts.

Finally, the issue of demonic possession is similar to other situations where counselors may not have experience in this arena. It is ethically appropriate as counselors to seek supervision, education, and consultation on issues related to demonic possession. Some counselors and other religious figures have done work in these areas and may even specialize in these kinds of situations (Driscoll, 2015). It is very appropriate for counselors to consult with experts outside our area of expertise, much like a counselor might consult with a physician when encountering a client with a physical illness. An additional and important ethical consideration is to not practice outside of the bounds of your competence. Any issue outside of our training and licensure would need to be referred out to another professional.

Infidelity Issues

When working with married couples, infidelity issues can be very challenging for counselors. In these situations, counselors must help their clients work through feelings of hurt, abandonment, mistrust, and fear for the future. Infidelity can have many contributing factors, and the responsibility may be shared by more than just the client. It may be helpful to look at three areas with couples when there is infidelity:
- What dysfunctional behavior led up to this point and is currently occurring?
- What is each individual's contribution to the environment of the marriage/relationship?
- What is the goal of working on the relationship?

© Monkey Business Images/Shutterstock.com

In situations of infidelity, there is usually a myriad of issues to address that brings a couple to counseling. For example, there may be substance abuse or pornography addition in one or both spouses, one or both may be the victim of childhood sexual abuse which significantly affects their sexual relationship together, there could be additional pressures that one spouse may have at work, there may be a significant family history of infidelity, or there may be changes in the spiritual and religious practices of one or both spouses. Therefore, it is important for the counselor to assess each situation individually. As with most issues, there may be internal struggles within yourself or client based on our experiences in this area. It is also a delicate balance in working with two or more individuals as opposed to one. It is imperative that the counselor remain neutral and that neither party feels isolated or unsupported during the counseling sessions. Dr. Talal Alsaleem recommends the counselor hold individual sessions along with the couple sessions to allow each person to react to the story (Speciale, 2019). The couple must be able to discuss the situation and find answers to their questions. If you have one member wanting a divorce and the other to reconcile, you may need to initially work with the couple on what the goal of counseling will be. Sometimes a couple may decide to divorce, and if that is the case you may need to work with the couple to find an amicable way to do that. Regardless Dr. Alsaleem recommends active transparency and looking at the uncomfortable truths in order to work through the untrusting time (Speciale, 2019).

Lesbian, Gay, Bisexual, Transgender, and Questioning

The discussion of LGBTQ+ issues is far beyond the scope of this section, or even this chapter. It is important to note that as counselors operating with a Christian worldview, this issue has impacted the contemporary church on many levels. Many different Christian groups and denominations have changed their historical positions on issues of sexuality in the past 30 years, and many Christian groups have struggled with these issues on a denominational level. For example, in 2019, the United Methodist Church voted to continue to oppose same-sex marriage and not ordain gay clergy (Zauzmer & Bailey, 2019). The Episcopal Church also garnered a lot of national news in 2003 when they ordained their first openly gay bishop. In 2015, "the canons of the church were changed to make the rite of marriage available to all people, regardless of gender" (The Episcopal Church, 2019, para. 2). In 2015, the largest conference of churches in the Mennonite Church USA voted to withdraw from the denomination over LGBTQ+ issues, with the official separation happening in 2018 (Heinze-kehr, 2018). People have left congregations, denominations, or stopped attending church entirely over discussions regarding sexuality. As counselors operating from a Christian worldview, this issue is unlikely to resolve soon, and we must openly address it and be open to other points of view.

It is important to recognize that when we engage this discussion, we are willingly opening ourselves up to the tension that these matters create. As we mentioned previously, perhaps a good consideration is whether this is an issue that can be resolved, or whether it is an ongoing challenge that needs to be developed and managed differently. Can we continue to hold to our own values and beliefs while still honoring the positions and considerations of others?

LGBTQ+ issues are often ones that cannot be resolved, but rather are ongoing challenges that need to be developed and managed differently by a new generation of professional counselors who operate from a Christian worldview. McMinn suggested starting with integration as a conversation (McMinn, 2019), opening a dialogue for ongoing discussion based on a more historically orthodox view of Christian sexuality. The hope is that counselors will use integrative conversations as the beginning of a respectful and generous dialogue on how we care for people while holding on to our theological values as Christians. We do hope that you will engage this challenging area with humility and a deep desire to understand God and other people well, ultimately offering both grace and truth to people who may differ with you theologically.

Counselors who operate from a Christian worldview form their ideas from both their professional ethics foundations and their theological views. The commitment to both as professional counselors may at times create situations where we are personally uncomfortable. As professional counselors, we must be willing to offer emotional and spiritual protection for people who do not agree with our theological views. We must also understand that integrating one's faith in our counseling practice can create confusion or conflict for the LGBTQ+ person, and depending on their interpretation of scripture can place significant stress on the client. Support groups may be helpful to allow clients to work through their confusion and find a safe place to share their feelings (Vespone, 2016), as well as offering support to increase self-esteem, improve mental health, and affirm identity (Kwon, 2013). Counselors are trained to help those experiencing distress, emotional dysregulation, and other concerns, and can serve as a resource for those experiencing internal and external conflict related to sexual identity (Vespone, 2016).

Pornography Use

The use of pornography is a growing issue in our culture, with so many people having significant exposure to graphic images that rewire their cerebral cortex (more about neuroscience will be discussed in Chapter 13). Wilson (2017, 2012) was one of the first researchers to notice that young men were experiencing erectile dysfunction problems due to their pornography use. Further, there are numerous high profile cases where people caught in sex crimes and sex scandals were later found to have been engaged in significant pornography use. Many studies have focused on the impact of pornography use in our culture. A recent Barna (2016a) report notes the following:

> Young adults, ages 18-24 are both more likely to actively seek porn regularly and more likely to come across porn more often. Fifty-seven percent of young adults ages 18 to 24 report seeking out porn at least once or twice a month, compared to 37 percent of teens, 43 percent of older Millennials, 41 percent of Gen-Xers, and just 17 percent of Boomers. (para. 8)

The Barna Group (2016b) also makes the following observations about contemporary pornography use in our culture:

- Most people define pornography upon the function it serves for sexual arousal. There is a wide array of definitions of pornography.
- Pornography is much more of a researchable topic than it was years ago. People generally are much more willing to talk about their pornography use than they were in previous generations.
- Most Americans believe porn is "bad for society," but those attitudes are shifting toward neutrality or "good for society" among younger generations.
- Teens and young adults view "not recycling" as more immoral than viewing porn. 32% say viewing porn is "usually or always wrong" compared to 56% who say not recycling is "usually or always wrong."
- Almost half of the young adults say that they come across unsolicited pornography once a week, even when they are not seeking it.
- Pornography usage among young women seems to have become more common, perhaps due to digital access.
- Most teens are "sexting"—either on the receiving or sending end of sexually explicit images. The Barna group says that 62% of teens and young adults have received a sexually explicit image and 41% have sent one (usually from/to their boy/girlfriend or friend).

With these trends in culture, it is imperative for emerging counselors operating from a Christian worldview to recognize some important truths. First, pornography use is easily accessible, and it impacts many people, both male and female, both directly and indirectly, and both inside and outside the church. Its use among younger people is rapidly growing (The Barna Group, 2016a; The Barna Group, 2016b). Second, shame, shame-proneness, and attachment are contributing factors to heightened internet pornography use (Carboneau, 2018). It will be imperative for counselors and community members to see people in a way that encourages rather than shames them. For example, counselors can take proactive steps both inside and outside the church to offer support groups and safe places where people can find support and encouragement to walk towards healing in this area of their life, rather than simply managing behavior. Third, for counselors working with couples in crisis, pornography use is often a contributing factor to their conflict (Bloom & Hagedorn, 2014). Therefore, assessing pornography use in the initial session is important, especially when there is sexual dysfunction in a marriage. Finally, it is important to understand that pornography use, and especially pornography addiction, is deeply connected to brain chemistry. For the counselor operating from a Christian worldview, how we approach people who are struggling with pornography use/addiction will be important as we consider each client and each couple individually.

As counselors who are Christians, our ultimate authority is to God, loving Him with our heart, mind, soul, body, and spirit, as well as loving our neighbor as ourselves. We must be willing to live in the tension of loving people, living with grace, and holding firm to things that are right and true. Jesus himself gives us examples of how to do this with the woman caught in adultery (John 8:1-11) and when he was anointed by a sinful woman (Luke 7:36-50), but in each of these situations, there was significant tension and struggle. As followers of Jesus Christ in the counseling profession, how do we walk in these difficult places? The answer to that question may not be an easy one for you, but we believe that it is an ongoing issue of "integration as conversation" (McMinn, 2019).

HOW DO COUNSELORS WITH A CHRISTIAN WORLDVIEW COUNSEL DIFFERENTLY?

"Who can listen to a story of loneliness and despair without taking the risk of experiencing similar pains in his own heart and even losing his precious peace of mind? In short: Who can take away suffering without entering it?" Henri J.M. Nouwen (1994)

Many professional counselors and students have a story they have lived through that propelled them to this vocation and calling. For the counselor with a Christian worldview, there is often a sense of calling and a sense of purpose that drives them to seek further training to help others. Much like the Apostle Paul writes about in Galatians 6:2, we seek to "Carry each other's burdens, and in this way you will fulfill the law of Christ." You are reading this book because you likely have a back story of healing and restoration in your own life, or you may be just starting this journey towards healing. Regardless, it is important to recognize this drive, and from this place, we position ourselves to walk with people who are hurting.

Counselors with a Christian worldview counsel people differently. They recognize the importance that spirituality plays in a client's story, their journey, and the process of counseling. They recognize that, as the second step of the 12 Steps of Alcoholics Anonymous says, they "Came to believe that a Power greater than ourselves could restore us to sanity" (Alcoholics Anonymous, 1981). And from that place, they recognize that healing is much more than managing behavior in another person. The Christian counselor must maintain a balance within themselves by utilizing careful insight, seeking to integrate their faith and counseling skills (Scott, 2018).

Restoring Brokenness

As counselors operating from a Christian worldview, we might ask "How do we restore brokenness?" This question may be the wrong one to ask. Perhaps a better question to ask is: *How do we position people in a way that God can ultimately heal them?* This is a question that may never have a complete answer, but as Christians, it is important to make the choice to recognize some important implications of our faith.

First, inherent in any counselor-client relationship, there is a power dynamic happening. When clients come in for help, it is an easy temptation for us to think that we are in a position of power, creating an "us" and "them" between the professionals and the non-professionals. All counselors, but especially those who are followers of Jesus, must resist this temptation and position ourselves in a way that levels the playing field. Christians take their cues from Philippians 2: 3-4: "Do nothing out of selfish ambition or vain conceit. Rather, in humility value others above yourselves, not looking to your own interests but each of you to the interests of the others." The next section of this passage in Philippians 2 speaks to how Jesus willingly left his position of power to help someone else. As counselors, we walk in this same vein, walking with others as fellow human beings in need of God.

Second, and this follows from the first implication, counselors must recognize that we are not the client's Savior, nor their divine Healer. As Christians, we recognize that ultimately Jesus Christ is our Great Physician, and He is the one who heals us through his own suffering and death (Isaiah 53:5). Recognizing that we are not pressured to save anyone is a freeing thought for Christian professional counselors, because our role is to ultimately help someone heal holistically and help them ultimately connect with God for their healing. This enables us not to feel pressure to rescue our clients but rather to attend to our clients, seeing our clients as God sees them. This is a mindset for us to emulate, because it not only allows us to walk in humility as counselors, but it also prevents burnout, where we feel that we must rescue our clients. We will allow Jesus to be our clients' rescuer, and we will walk with someone as that happens.

And finally, as Christians, we must be committed to not only our professional and emotional development but also our ongoing spiritual development. One of the recent trends in the field of professional counseling is a focus on spirituality in counseling. One of the significant ways that professional counselors who integrate faith in their counseling think and operate differently is that we operate from a spiritual base where we connect with God through Jesus Christ and the Holy Spirit. Of course, this is an ongoing journey for all Christians, and, as we work with many broken people throughout our professional life, it will be imperative for us to continue to nurture our spiritual lives as we work with people who are "poor in spirit" (Matthew 5:3).

SUMMARY

This chapter focused on understanding the balance between being a professional counselor and a Christian. It is ethically important for counselors operating from a Christian worldview to "explore their own cultural identities [including spiritual identity] and how these affect their values and beliefs about the counseling process" (ACA, 2014, A. Introduction). Spiritual issues should be openly addressed within the professional realm, and clear definitions and guidelines should be presented to the client. There are many considerations to weigh in on, including defining the role of the counselor, following ethical guidelines, and meeting the needs of your client. It is imperative for counselors with a Christian worldview to hold themselves to a higher standard. Feeling called to serve in this area is a privilege as our clients allow us access into their personal world. As licensed professional counselors and Christians, we must respect our client's position and work with them, meeting them where they are, and showing love and kindness above all other attributes. This is what it means to be a counselor who operates from a Christian worldview.

FOR THE ROAD AHEAD

Check out the Chapter 4 video at this link:

https://www.khpcontent.com/

Reflections on the Journey

- As you begin to think about working as a counselor, what do you personally feel are going to be difficult populations to work with?
- In what setting do you see yourself practicing? Have you spoken to someone who has served or is serving in that setting? What do they see as the pros and cons of their work and some of the ethical considerations within their role?
- In what areas do you need to grow in your theological understanding to be a more effective counselor operating from a Christian worldview?
- How will you further prepare yourself to work with people who do not share the same values as you?
- If the greatest ethic is love and greatest gift is the presence of Christ in your life, what are some tangible ways that you can live these out in your counseling practice?

For Further Exploration

Hawkins, R., & Clinton, T. (2015). *The new Christian counselor: A fresh biblical & transformational approach.* Eugene, OR: Harvest House Publishers.

Johnston J. (2015). *Unanswered: Lasting truth for trending questions.* New Kingston, PA: Whitaker House.

Shook, M. (Producer). (2019, March 27). EP121: Spiritual bypass – Finding ways through instead of around with Craig Cashwell [Audio podcast]. *The Thoughtful Counselor.* Retrieved from https://wp.me/p7R6fn-Gr.

REFERENCES

Alcoholics Anonymous (1981). *The twelve steps of Alcoholics Anonymous.* Alcoholics Anonymous Publishing. Retrieved from https://www.aa.org/assets/en_US/smf-121_en.pdf

American Association of Christian Counseling (2014). *AACC Code of Ethics.* Retrieved from https://www.aacc.net/wp-content/uploads/2017/10/AACC-Code-of-Ethics-Master-Document.pdf

American Counseling Association (2014). *ACA Code of Ethics.* Alexandria, VA: Author

American Counseling Association (2019). *20/20: Consensus definition of counseling.* Retrieved from https://www.counseling.org/about-us/about-aca/20-20-a-vision-for-the-future-of-counseling/consensus-definition-of-counseling

Association for Clinical Pastoral Education (2019). About ACPE. Retrieved from https://www.acpe.edu/ACPE/About_ACPE/ACPE/About_ACPE/About_ACPE.aspx

Barna Group (2017). Meet the "spiritual but not religious" April 6, 2017. Retrieved from https://www.barna.com/research/meet-spiritual-not-religious/

Barna Group (2016a). Teens & young adults use porn more than anyone else. Retrieved from https://www.barna.com/research/teens-young-adults-use-porn-more-than-anyone-else

Bauman, C. (2009). The specter of "spirituality"-On the (in)utility of an analytical category. *Religion & Education, 36*(2), p. 54-67.

Benner, D. G. (2003). *Strategic pastoral counseling: A short-term structured model.* Grand Rapids MI: Baker Academic.

Billy Graham Evangelistic Association (2018). Answers (August 31, 2018). Retrieved from https://billygraham.org/answer/defined-sin-christians-obsess/

Bloom, Z. & Hagedorn, B. (2014). Male adolescents and contemporary pornography: Implications for marriage and family counselors. *The Family Journal, 23*(1), 82-89. doi:10.1177%2F1066480714555672

Bonelli, R., Dew, R., Koenig, H., Rosmarin, D. & Vasegh, S. (2012). Religious and spiritual factors in depression: Review and integration of the research. *Depression Research and Treatment, 2012,* 1–8.

Brown, D. & King, J. A. (February 2019). Incorporating Values vs. Imposing Values: Navigating Religious Beliefs in Counseling. Roundtable Discussion. NBCC Law and Ethics Conference, New Orleans, LA.

Carboneau, R. A. (2018). Religiosity, moral disapproval, shame and pornography use: Assessing the relationship between shame and sexual behaviors (Doctoral dissertation). Retrieved from https://digitalcommons.liberty.edu/cgi/viewcontent.cgi?article=2840&context=doctoral

Christian Association for Psychological Studies (CAPS) (2005). Ethics Statement of the Christian Association for Psychological Studies, Inc. Retrieved from https://caps.net/ethics-statement/

Cohn, B. (2013). The divided states of America, in 25 charts. *The Atlantic*, June 28, 2013.

Corey, G. (n.d.). Integrating spirituality in counseling practice. Vistas online, 25. Retrieved from https://www.counseling.org/docs/default-source/vistas/integrating-spirituality-in-counseling-practice.pdf?sfvrsn=10

Driscoll, M. (2015). *Demons, deliverance and discernment: Separating fact from fiction about the spirit world.* Catholic Answers Press.

Entwistle, D. (2015). *Integrative approaches to psychology and Christianity* (3rd ed.). Eugene, OR: Cascade Books.

Episcopal Church (2019). LGBTQ in the Church. Retrieved from https://www.episcopalchurch.org/lgbtq-church

Geertz, C. (1973). *The interpretation of cultures.* New York: Basic Books.

Garzon, F. L. (2011). Spirituality in counseling. In T. Clinton & R. Hawkins (Eds.), *The popular encyclopedia of Christian counseling* (pp. 22–24). Eugene, OR: Harvest House.

Glover, E (2018). Live like Mother Teresa: Finding your own Calcutta. Franciscan Spirit (3-13-2018). Retrieved from https://blog.franciscanmedia.org/franciscan-spirit/live-like-mother-teresa-finding-your-own-calcutta

Greggo, S. P. (Ed.), Sizemore, T. A. (Ed.) & Johnson, E. L. (2012). *Counseling and christianity: Five approaches.* Batavia, IL: Christian Association for Psychological Studies Books.

Hawkins, R. Knight, A. Sibcy, G., & Warren, S. (2019). *Research based counseling skills: The art and science of therapeutic empathy.* Dubuque, IA: Kendall Hunt.

Hawkins, R., & Clinton, T. (2015). *The new Christian counselor: A fresh biblical and transformational approach.* Eugene, OR: Harvest House Publishers.

HCM International (2019). Retrieved from https://hcminternational.org/

Heinzekehr, H. (2018). Lancaster Mennonite Conference formally exits Mennonite Church USA. *The Mennonite*, January 7, 2018. Retrieved from https://themennonite.org/daily-news/lancaster-mennonite-conference-formally-exits-mennonite-church-usa/

Hook, J. N., Watkins, C. E., Davis, D. E., Owen, J., van Tongeren, D. R., & Marciana, J. R. (2018). Cultural humility in psychotherapy supervision. *American Journal of Psychotherapy, 70*(2), 149-166. doi:10.1176/appi.psychotherapy.2016.70.2.149

Hawkins, R. & Clinton, T. (2015). *The new Christian counselor: A fresh biblical & transformational approach.* Eugene, OR: Harvest House Publishers.

Johnston J. (2015). *Unanswered: Lasting truth for trending questions.* Newkingston, PA: Whitaker House.

Jones, S. & Butman, R. (2011). *Modern psychotherapies: A comprehensive Christian appraisal.* Downers Grove, PA: InterVarsity Press.

Kitchener, K. S. (1984). Intuition, critical evaluation and ethical principles: The foundation for ethical decisions in counseling psychology. *Counseling Psychologist, 12*(3), 43-55.

Kwon, P. (2013). Resilience in lesbian, gay, and bisexual individuals. *Personality and Social Psychology Review, 17*(4), 371–383.

Langberg, D. (20151). Trauma as mission field. World Reformed Fellowship. Retrieved from http://wrfnet.org/resources/2011/06/trauma-mission-field-wrf-board-member-dr-diane-langberg

Merriam-Webster's collegiate dictionary (2017). Springfield, MA: Merriam-Webster Incorporated.

National Conference of State Licensing (2019). *The state of occupational licensing research, state policies and trends.* Retrieved from http://www.ncsl.org/Portals/1/Documents/employ/Licensing/State_Occupational_Licensing.pdf

Neff, M. A., & McMinn, M. R. (2020). *Embodying integration: A fresh look at Christianity in the therapy room.* Downers Grove, IL: IVP Academic.

Nouwen, H. (1994). *The wounded healer: Ministry in contemporary society*. London: Darton, Longman & Todd.

Pennsylvania Counseling Association (PCA), 2019. SB 530 fact sheet. Retrieved from: http://www.pacounsel-ing.org/aws/PACA/pt/sp/advocacy.

Scott, S. (2018). Fractured therapists: The consequences of disintegrated functioning in faith and practice. *Journal of Psychology and Christianity, 37*(4), 305-312.

Speciale, M. (Producer). (2019, May 1). EP125: Counseling Infidelity – A Conversation with Dr. Talal Alsaleem [Audio Podcast]. *The Thoughtful Counselor.* Retrieved from https://wp.me/p7R6fn-Hr.

State Board of Social Workers, Marriage and Family Therapists and Professional Counselors (2019). *Licensure of professional counselors: Code of ethical practice and standards of professional conduct.* § 49.73. Dual or multiple relationships affecting the licensee's judgment. Retrieved from https://www.pacode.com/secure/data/049/chapter49/s49.73.html

Sanders, R. K. (2016) Maintaining a balance: The challenge of multiple relationships for Christian therapists. *Journal of Psychology and Christianity, 35*(4), 320-329.

UC San Diego (2019). Making Ethical Decisions: Process. Retrieved from https://blink.ucsd.edu/finance/ac-countability/ethics/process.html

Vespone, B. (2016). Integrating identities: Facilitating a support group for LGBTQ students on a Christian college campus. *Christian Higher Education, 15*(4), 215-229.

Walker, D., Gorsuch, R., & Tan, S. (2011). Therapists' integration of religion and spirituality in counseling: A meta-analysis. *Counseling & Values.* Retrieved from doi:10.1002/j.2161-007X.2004.tb00254.x

Wampold, B. E. (2015). How important are the common factors in psychotherapy? An update. *World Psychiatry, 14*(3), 270-277.

Wilson, G. (2017). *Your brain on porn: Internet pornography and the emerging science of addiction.* Commonwealth Publishing.

Wilson, G. (2012, May 16). *The great porn experiment. TEDxGlasgow.* [Video File]. Retrieved from https://www.youtube.com/watch?v=wSF82AwSDiU

Zauzmmer, J. & Bailey, S. P. (2019). United Methodist Church votes to maintain its opposition to same-sex marriage, gay clergy. *Washington Post.* February 26. 2019. Retrieved from https://www.washingtonpost.com/religion/2019/02/26/united-methodist-church-votes-maintain-its-opposition-same-sex-mar-riage-gay-clergy/?noredirect=on&utm_term=.b7b05ec890de

Zondervan Academic (2017). Biblical counseling vs. Christian counseling: What's the difference? 30 September 2017. Retrieved from https://zondervanacademic.com/blog/biblical-counseling-vs-christian-coun-seling-whats-the-difference

Zur, O. (2019). Ethics of dual & multiple relationships in pastoral counseling and faith, religious & spiritual communities. Zur Institute. Retrieved from https://www.zurinstitute.com/resources/dual-relationships/dual-relationships-spiritual-communities/

CHAPTER 5
Cultural Diversity and Social Justice

Nivischi N. Edwards, Ph.D., Arleezah Marrah, Ph.D.,
Jennifer Schwirzer, M.A., & Kimberly C. Harris, M.A.

> "He who passively accepts evil is as much involved in it as he who helps to perpetuate it. He who accepts evil without protesting against it is really cooperating with it."
> -Dr. Martin Luther King Jr.

Following Christ: Grace for Our Work

John Chapter 10 talks about living an *abundant* life. John 10:10 (King James Version) specifically speaks the following: "The thief comes not, but to steal, and to kill, and to destroy. I am come that they might have life, and that they might have it more abundantly." Jesus came so *all* of his children may experience the abundant life that he died to provide, so we *all* may live. The description of the thief is in opposition to that of the shepherd. The thief came to steal, kill, and destroy, but the shepherd protects life.

© Arthimedes/Shutterstock.com

After reading this chapter, you will understand more about:

- The meaning of cultural diversity
- The definition of social justice and advocacy
- The process of advocacy and the need to address institutional and social barriers that impede access, equity, and success for clients
- The role and process of the professional counselor advocating on behalf of the profession.
- Cultural humility and how to use it in a counseling setting.

The following CACREP standards are addressed in this chapter:
Professional Counseling Orientation and Ethical Practice:

- The role and process of the professional counselor advocating on behalf of the profession (CACREP, 2016, Standard 2.F.1.d.)
- Advocacy processes needed to address institutional and social barriers that impede access, equity, and success for clients (CACREP, 2016, Standard 2.F.1.e.)

Social and Cultural Diversity:

- Multicultural counseling competencies (CACREP, 2016, Standard 2.F.2.c.)
- The impact of heritage, attitudes, beliefs, understandings, and acculturative experiences on an individual's views of others (CACREP, 2016, Standard 2.F.2.d.)
- The effects of power and privilege for counselors and clients (CACREP, 2016, Standard 2.F.2.e.)
- Strategies for identifying and eliminating barriers, prejudices, and processes of intentional and unintentional oppression and discrimination (CACREP, 2016, Standard 2.F.2.h.)

Looking at social justice and diversity of culture, those groups who oppress other groups (consciously or unconsciously) take on the spirit of the thief as described in John 10:10. They steal the identity, peace, and self-worth of those Jesus came to bless with abundant life. They kill and destroy the abundant life that Christ came to enable them to live. Interestingly, the reason Jesus came, to give life more abundantly, is the direct opposite of that of the thief, who only wants to steal, kill and destroy. The word *more* as it relates to the abundant life exemplifies a supply beyond the immediate need.

As counselors-in-training, you are preparing for a career where you will likely meet people at times in their lives when they feel like things may have died, been stolen, or destroyed. How amazing is it that you will be able to walk alongside them as a journey companion and help them navigate the muck and mire, until they can begin to glimpse the *more* abundance that is rightfully theirs. The life for which Christ died so they may live.

As you navigate justice and injustice within a culture that often lacks fair treatment for many, you will gain enhanced awareness and humility about the best ways to advocate for yourself and others. You can promote a better society where all people will experience the true life of abundance that Jesus intended, so we all may live.

D r. Martin Luther King Jr. stated, "He who passively accepts evil is as much involved in it as he who helps to perpetuate it. He who accepts evil without protesting against it is really cooperating with it" (King Institute, n.d.). In this chapter, the need for social justice and advocacy are addressed. Through this, the principles of social justice and advocacy, especially as they relate to the field of counseling, are defined and discussed, along with the need to incorporate cultural humility. Examples of how Jesus himself was a social justice advocate, citing specific ways that He and others in the Bible fought against societal norms and cultural mores, will be shared. May this chapter inspire you to become an advocate of this profession and work toward greater equity for all people, especially those who walk into your counseling office and those you serve as a counselor.

WHAT IS CULTURAL DIVERSITY?

© paulaphoto/Shutterstock.com

When I (N. N. Edwards) was a Master's student, the first chapter of my textbook on multicultural society described culture as "the totality of learned, socially transmitted behavior of a group that emerges from its members' interpersonal transactions" (Axelson, 1985, p. 3). In successive chapters, as it relates to cultural diversity, Axelson went on to share profiles of American people of different races, socio-political issues, education, work, career, and developmental needs and explored the counselor's role with the client in today's counseling practices. At one time, culture and diversity reflected one's race, ethnicity, gender, socioeconomic status, age, and religion. Today, without revealing how long ago I completed that degree, what stands out to me most is how much our society's definition of cultural diversity has changed. This contrast became more evident when I read the Association of Multicultural Counseling and Development's (AMCD) guidelines for inclusion and accessibility. Specific mention of the use of gender pronouns for self-identification as well as the proper use of said pronouns when responding to others is expressed in the inclusion and access statement. For example, I am encouraged to self-identify as she, her, hers and asked to refer to someone else as a person instead of a specific gender. The definition of diversity and culture has evolved over the decades.

This shift and heightened awareness also reflect today's society and culture as it relates to diversity and social justice. No longer do counselors solely look at one's race, economic status, religion, or perceived gender in order to define a person's culture or diversity characteristics. Clinicians are encouraged to go a step further in assessing a situation and the persons with whom they are connecting in order to perceive truth about their experiences. With issues of cultural diversity and social justice, you are directed to look within, take a deep breath, and approach it from a place of seeming ignorance instead of as an expert (Sue & Sue, 2015). Sue and Sue (2015) defined cultural diversity as "the integration, acceptance, and embracing of cultural differences that include race, gender, sexual orientation, and other sociodemographic identities" (p. 748). At the end of this chapter, cultural humility is defined and discussed, guiding you to a more rounded approach in understanding the importance of your role in social justice. You may choose to approach cultural diversity, social justice, and advocacy from a humble place.

WHAT DO COUNSELORS NEED TO KNOW ABOUT SOCIAL JUSTICE AND ADVOCACY IN COUNSELING?

There has been much discussion in the counseling field about the importance of increased advocacy and social justice (Ratts, Sing, Nassar-McMillan, Butler, & McCullough, 2016). Additionally, Kiselica and Robinson (2001) reported that successful counselors who advocated for the profession and related to the needs of their clients experienced a higher level of personal satisfaction. This occurs as a result of helping those they serve. Think about it, if a client comes into your office and communicates an experience of mistreatment, your initial instinct may be to empower the client to do something about their negative experience or maybe you will work to get the situation corrected. This in part is what we are called to do as a counselor. We advocate for our clients, especially when they are unable to do that for themselves. We are also called to advocate for issues relevant to the counseling field.

Advocacy involves actions aimed at changing the processes by which public decisions are made, thus affecting the sociopolitical and economic contexts that influence people's lives (Cohen, 2001). Kagan, Burton, Duckett, Lawthorn and Siddiquee (2011) defined social justice as rights to self-determination, a fair allocation of resources, freedom from constraints, and the ability to live in peace and to be treated fairly and equitably. Social justice is a way of thinking that promotes fairness and challenges the devaluing of others. It is inclusive and attempts to move away from an individualized model of blame (Tribe & Bell, 2018). As you learned in Chapter 1, social justice is the "fifth force," after the psychodynamic, cognitive behavioral therapy, humanistic and multicultural forces (Ratts, 2009). Social justice counseling "uses social advocacy and activism as a means to address inequitable, social, political, and economic conditions that impede the academic, career, and personal/social development of individuals, families, and communities" (Ratts & Hutchins, 2009, p. 160).

The *ACA Code of Ethics* (American Counseling Association [ACA], 2014) and *2016 CACREP Standards* (CACREP, 2015) speak to the propensity of counselors and counselor educators to be advocates. There is a call to address barriers and obstacles for client growth and development. Evidence of such advocacy is seen as counselors lobby at both the federal and state level for the profession. The *ACA Code of Ethics* (2014), *Ethical Code for Counselors for Social Justice* (Ibrahim, Dinsmore, Estrada, & D'Andrea, 2011), as well as the codes for the Association for Specialists in Group Work (ASGW; Singh, Merchant, Skudrzyk, & Ingene, 2012) were influenced by the multicultural counseling competencies (MCC) developed by Sue, Arredondo, and McDavis (1992). In 2014, however, AMCD appointed a committee to revise the MCC. The updated competencies, titled the *Multicultural and Social Justice Counseling Competencies* (MSJCC; Ratts, Singh, Nassar-McMillan, Butler, & McCullough, 2015), were endorsed by AMCD on June 29, 2015, and by the ACA on July 20, 2016. The conceptual framework of the MSJCC visually depict relationships among the competencies' key constructs: multicultural and social justice praxis, quadrants, domains, and competencies.

The conceptual framework (Figure 5.1) provides a visual map of the relationship between the constructs and competencies being articulated within the MSJCC. The quadrants reflect the intersection of identities and the dynamics of power, privilege, and oppression that influence the counseling relationship. Developmental domains reflect the different layers that lead to multicultural and social justice competence: (1) counselor self-awareness; (2) client worldview; (3) counseling relationship; and (4) counseling and advocacy interventions. Embedded within the first three developmental domains of the MSJCC are the following aspirational competencies: attitudes and beliefs, knowledge, skills, and action (AKSA; Ratts et al., 2015).

FIGURE 5.1

Multicultural and Social
Justice Praxis

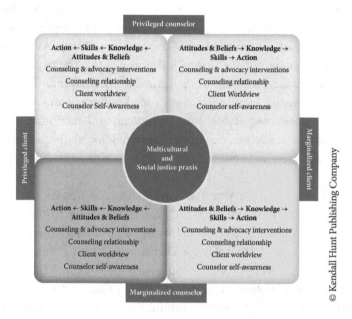

Multicultural and Social Justice Counselor Competencies (MSJCC; Ratts, 2015, pp. 5–11)

- *Counselor Self-Awareness.* Privileged and marginalized counselors develop self-awareness, so that they may explore their attitudes and beliefs, develop knowledge, skills, and action relative to their self-awareness and worldview.
- *Client Worldview.* Privileged and marginalized counselors are aware, knowledgeable, skilled, and action-oriented in understanding clients' worldview.
- *Counseling Relationship.* Privileged and marginalized counselors are aware, knowledgeable, skilled, and action-oriented in understanding how client and counselor privileged and marginalized statuses influence the counseling relationship.
- *Counselor Advocacy and Intervention.* Privileged and marginalized counselors intervene with, and on behalf of clients at the intrapersonal, interpersonal, institutional, community, public policy, and international/global levels.

Counselors as Advocates

The *ACA Code of Ethics* supports counselors and counselor educators becoming change agents of social justice. Section A.7.a states, "when appropriate, counselors advocate at individual, group, institutional, and societal levels to address potential barriers and obstacles that inhibit access and/or the growth and development of clients." (ACA, 2014, p.5). This is imperative and necessary for all involved in the field.

As demonstrated in Figure 5.1, the process of advocacy begins with the counselor and their self-awareness. Assessing biases as well as cultural norms is the first step in the process of becoming more culturally aware and growing the needed muscles for advocacy. Initial questions you may ask yourself as you work on becoming a more justice oriented person overall include: What are my biases? In which areas of my life am I unjust?

Counselor Profile
Samuel T. Gladding, Ph.D.
Professor of Counseling, Wake Forest University

Social justice and advocacy have been a part of counseling ever since the days of the profession's early pioneers such as Frank Parson, Clifford Beers, and Jessie B. Davis. These individuals and others, such as C. Gilbert Wrenn, Carl Rogers, Courtland Lee, Thelma Duffey, and Barbara Herlihy, have been strong in their advocacy for mental health, especially for the downtrodden and underserved. While "social justice" and "advocacy" are modern terms the ideas behind them date back decades.

As professional counselors we are called on to act for the benefit of all in our society and to avoid stereotypes and labels. That means we must stand for policies in government and associations that are truly helpful for those who do not have the resources to help themselves. We must advocate for individuals, groups, and society in promoting social justice and we must promote the profession of counseling too in its developmental, preventative, and therapeutic processes.

Contributed by Samuel Gladding. © Kendall Hunt Publishing Company.

Sue and Sue (2016) posited that counselors can advocate on three levels: advisor, advocate, and consultant. As an *advisor*, the counselor communicates or connects the client with community resources in support of the presenting need. The counselor may also support the clients by offering guidance about the most effective way to navigate different challenges. As an *advocate*, the counselor may lobby for client rights in various areas and about a variety of issues. This may include better client treatment on a personal, local, or national level. In an agency or at a university, this may mean advocating for change in policy for the client's wellbeing. As a *consultant*, the counselor may serve as a guide by providing input to support the needs of the client. A counselor who has certain expertise will serve as an invaluable asset to support the needs of a client. This is one step in the process of becoming more socially aware. There are action steps that can be taken for counselors who want to live a life reflective of social justice.

Action Steps For Becoming an Agent of Social Justice

Lee (2018) outlined personal action steps to help counselors in the process of living a life committed to social justice. These steps are to explore life's meaning and commitment, explore personal privilege, explore the nature of oppression, strive for multicultural competence, work to become globally literate and establish a personal social justice compass.

Explore Life's Meaning and Commitment - This includes asking introspective questions to get to the core of understanding personal thoughts and feelings related to social justice and action. Questions may include: Why am I a counselor? What do I want to get out of my work in this profession? What mark do I want to leave on society? What message will I share with my clients about the importance of this work?

Explore Personal Privilege - This includes an evaluation of the gifts one experiences as a result of their birthright. Lee (2018) encourages counselors to, "challenge yourself to find ways to employ your cultural privilege in a manner that will promote equity, human rights, and a fair allocation of societal resources" (p. 283).

Explore the Nature of Oppression - This includes the assessment of one's participation in oppressive behavior either overtly or covertly. This involves asking questions such as, how have I participated in oppressive behavior, or what can

I do differently in my life to minimize or negate my participation in the oppression of others. When power or authority is used unjustly, oppression is often present.

Strive for Multicultural Competence - This includes a continual assessment of a personal multicultural competence by having a heightened awareness, expanding one's knowledge base and attending to clients in a culturally respectful manner without making assumptions about how they prefer to be treated.

Work to become Globally Literate - This includes an understanding of other cultures, nationalities, and ethnic groups and their contribution to the world at large. An awareness of information to enhance global interaction in today's society that may not have been present in the past is also necessary (Lee, 2013).

Establish a Personal Social Justice Compass - This includes establishing a set of personal ideals and values that will influence how you approach life from a just perspective. Reading literature on the topic, speaking with those who are advocates, and staying current on activities that address these objectives are ways to navigate this most important need.

As a counselor, you may envision your role as a helper and supporter. As a result, the idea of advocacy may be daunting. Lewis, Arnold, House, and Toporek (2002) highlighted the *ACA Advocacy Competencies* (AC). These competencies involve three levels of advocacy which include: a) client/student; b) school/community; and c) public arena. The advocacy components focus on acting with and on behalf of the client or the profession. The ACA outlines specific ways to advocate by sharing tips to navigate the process. These include understanding the issue about which you are advocating and knowing your role in the process. Advocacy also involves acquiring information and staying informed about issues that affect the field of counseling by reading journal articles and books, lobbying, and the ethical use of social media.

© Roman Motizov/Shutterstock.com

In 2018, the AC were updated by Toporek and Daniels. The ACA identified advocacy as a central pillar for its strategic initiative. These competencies are used to address different social justice and human rights issues that impact the counseling profession, clients, and communities that counselors serve. The AC (see Figure 5.2) are organized around client involvement in advocacy and the level of advocacy intervention. Effective advocacy that involves the client will promote greater empowerment. Effective advocacy intervention focuses on where, when, how, and with whom the advocacy is to take place. The ACA advocacy competency domains figure below illustrates the tenets. It is important to note that in order to become an effective advocate for the field or for clients, counselors must be culturally aware and ethically sound in their decision making (Lewis, Arnold, House, & Toperek, 2013).

© Kendall Hunt Publishing Company

FIGURE 5.2

ACA Advocacy Competency Domains.

Multicultural and ethical considerations must be the basis of counselor actions.

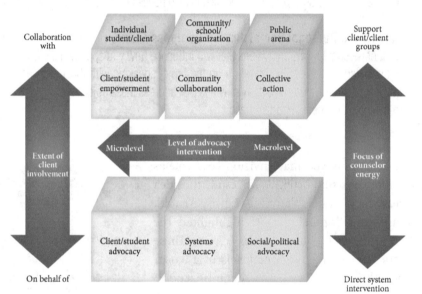

Social Justice and Theology

The Counselor Education and Supervisor Network - Listserv (CESNET-L) is a website for those involved in counselor education and supervision. It has been listed as a professional listserv for counselors, counselor educators, and supervisors that provides an open forum for discussing issues and sharing resources related to the counseling profession. Many who use this forum do so as a means to advocate for the areas about which they are passionate and, at times, as a tool to attempt to discredit those with whom they are not in agreement.

During the Spring of 2019, around Easter, a member of CESNET posted information about the life of Christ. Many members of CESNET are non-religious. As a result of the posting in observation of Christ's death and resurrection, Lile (2019) shared the following framework (see Table 5.1) that looks at the parallel of social justice and religious concepts.

TABLE 5.1

The Religious Nature of Social Justice and it's Intersectional Doctrine

Religious Concepts (from Christianity):	Parallel Social Justice Concepts:
Original Sin	Privilege
Penance	Endlessly attesting to one's privilege in hopes of forgiveness
Conversion/Salvation	Being "woke"
Atonement	Reparations, acceptance of guilt and shame
Heresy	Going against or not conforming to the social justice/intersectional system being asserted
Blasphemy	Directly challenging an intersectional doctrinal tenant
Doctrine	Intersectionality and other supportive writings/concepts
Church	Universities
Pulpit	Classrooms (particularly those within "grievance study" disciplines, the humanities, and ever more in the social sciences)
Preachers	Educators advancing the ideology above objective truth and centering their role around social/political advocacy in line with the doctrine.
Believer	An ally
Faith	Suspension of disbelief in the doctrine. Placing intersectional ideology above objective/scientific reality
Proselytize	Social and political advocacy in keeping with intersectional doctrine
Personal witness	Lived experience
Promised land/ Heaven	Marx's utopian ideal (though expanded by intersectional doctrine beyond class to all other dimensions of privilege/oppression)
Savior	Choose your political figure of the election cycle in whom all hopes lie [better be a Democrat, or even better a democratic socialist… who's not white… or a man (sorry Bernie)]
Satan	Need I clarify this one?
Pharisee	Activists and Social Justice Warriors constantly engaged in virtue signaling to demonstrate their "wokeness," who hold it over everyone else in a legalistic fashion.

Source: J. Lile, personal communication, April 20, 2019

Another member of CSNET commented about the importance of identifying Jesus as a social justice advocate and change agent. J. Richelle Joe stated the following:

> Jesus was a revolutionary and social justice advocate whose very existence challenged the long-standing religious, economic, social, and political systems of oppression that existed at the time. An examination of His recorded acts of protest can give an indication of how we as counselors might operate in society today.

> The miracles recorded in the Gospels shine a critical light on society both then and now. The woman with the issue of blood who was healed by touching the hem of his garment is every woman who does not have access to quality gynecological care for her endometriosis or fibroids. The man with the impure spirit who was left chained in the tombs is every person with a severe and pervasive mental condition that receives inadequate mental health services due to lack of access, stigma within the community, and bias within the mental health profession. The man born blind – the one who was blamed along with his parents for his own blindness – is every person with a disability who has been shamed about their condition and left without accommodations.

> Then there is the man at the pool of Bethesda who can never reach the water when it is stirring in time to receive healing. He has no one to help him and others rush ahead of him for their own benefit. The system is rigged against this man, meaning that he will never experience anything different until the system itself is upended. In how many ways do we allow unjust systems to disadvantage some because they benefit others (sometimes including ourselves)?

> Jesus was so disgusted by such systems and practices that he literally started flipping tables on people taking advantage of others.

> Will we as counselor educators have this same passion for social justice or will we hoard Jesus for ourselves? (J. Joe, personal communication, April 21, 2019)

These examples reflect the importance of social justice and advocacy in the counseling field. As was noted by these present-day counselors, advocacy and social justice are very important to the counseling field.

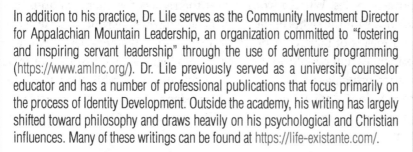

Counselor Profile
Dr. Jesse Lile, LPC, LMFT
Private Practice

A counselor who exemplifies social justice and advocacy from a Christian perspective is Jesse Lile. Dr. Lile is licensed as both a Professional Counselor (LPC) and Marriage and Family Therapist (LMFT) in North Carolina, where he now maintains a part-time private practice focused on marital relationships. In this work, he is largely influenced by Bowen's Family Systems model for *conceptualizing* relational issues while using a modified Emotional Focused approach for navigating the therapy *process*. Dr. Lile is a Christian, and while he works with clients from a range of backgrounds and worldviews, a large portion of his client population are Christians who seek him out because of this shared faith. His work helps these clients navigate relational struggles in a way that both highlights and integrates biblical truths and facilitates spiritual growth for each individual involved in the process.

In addition to his practice, Dr. Lile serves as the Community Investment Director for Appalachian Mountain Leadership, an organization committed to "fostering and inspiring servant leadership" through the use of adventure programming (https://www.amlnc.org/). Dr. Lile previously served as a university counselor educator and has a number of professional publications that focus primarily on the process of Identity Development. Outside the academy, his writing has largely shifted toward philosophy and draws heavily on his psychological and Christian influences. Many of these writings can be found at https://life-existante.com/.

As a Christian, Dr. Lile holds that all people are imbued with inherent value and purpose as image bearers of God. As such, his approach to social justice and advocacy is directly informed by his Christian faith, which is distinct from the social justice movement informed by intersectionality. While the latter social justice approach is concerned with *physical* and *social* well-being alone, the Christian approach to social justice involves a concern with physical, social, and *spiritual* well-being. This additional dimension reflects a valuing of spiritual alignment with God, maximizing the expressions of one's inherent value and purpose, and this necessarily shapes the way he advocates for the physical and social needs of marginalized populations in the world.

Photo and spotlight © Dr. Jesse Lile

Diversity, Social Justice and Advocacy in the Bible

In the Bible, social justice, diversity, and advocacy are discussed. The basic dignity and rights of each person regardless of race, ethnicity, culture, socio-economic status, religion, sex, and sexual preference are affirmed, advocating for the fair and compassionate treatment of all human beings regardless of their choices. Further, the Bible celebrates racial, ethnic, and cultural diversity without celebrating moral and spiritual diversity. A movement today carried by groups such as the AND Campaign advocates a seamless, biblically-informed, culturally-relevant blend of social justice and biblical values. Recently, the AND Campaign (2018) tweeted, "In today's polarized political landscape, many Christians are either all in for social justice at the expense of historic moral convictions or all in for conservative principles at the expense of justice." This movement emphasizes that believers need not feel forced to choose between social justice and biblical morality.

God loves you enough to tell you how to live and then equips you to help others, particularly the marginalized. To truly help the poor, you must advocate for their rights, helping them fight through a system that opposes their advancement, but also helping cease their own contributions to poverty cycles. When advocating for the rights of women, you must also advocate for the rights of the unborn, helping women realize that abortion as a means of birth control leaves a stain upon the conscience. Morality principles in the Bible do not keep it from being a reliable source of social justice principles; rather, its moral principles give biblical social justice tremendous stability, power, and consistency. Inhumanity, injustice, exploitation, marginalization, systematic racism, and poverty are realities that the Bible vigorously decries.

God's heart overflows with this informed, principled compassion. God tells us through the inspired writers that He sees and acknowledges injustice (e.g., Cain and Abel in Genesis 4; Haggar in Genesis 16) and sees all humans as equal (e.g., Jesus' ministry as told in the gospels; Romans 2:11; Galatians 3:28). The moral principles of the Bible should not blind us to the fact that Jesus is the Savior, Friend, and Advocate of all human beings regardless of race, ethnicity, culture, religion, class, or gender. More than this, the principles of justice live in the hearts of His followers, leading us to "learn to do good; seek justice, rebuke the oppressor; defend the fatherless, plead for the widow" (Isaiah 1:17).

SOCIAL JUSTICE IN SCRIPTURE

"Defend the poor and fatherless; do justice to the afflicted and needy" (Psalm 82:3).

"Righteousness and justice are the foundation of Your throne; mercy and truth go before Your face" (Psalm 89:14).

"The Lord executes righteousness and justice for all who are oppressed" (Psalm 103:6).

"Evil men do not understand justice, but those who seek the Lord understand all" (Proverbs 28:5).

"Open your mouth for the speechless, in the cause of all who are appointed to die. Open your mouth, judge righteously, and plead the cause of the poor and needy" (Proverbs 31:8-9).

"Learn to do good; seek justice, rebuke the oppressor; defend the fatherless, plead for the widow" (Isaiah 1:17).

"For You have been a strength to the poor, a strength to the needy in his distress, a refuge from the storm, a shade from the heat; for the blast of the terrible ones is as a storm against the wall" (Isaiah 25:4).

"Thus says the Lord: 'Execute judgment and righteousness, and deliver the plundered out of the hand of the oppressor. Do no wrong and do no violence to the stranger, the fatherless, or the widow, nor shed innocent blood in this place'" (Jeremiah 22:3).

"He has shown you, O man, what is good; and what does the Lord require of you but to do justly, to love mercy, and to walk humbly with your God?" (Micah 6:8).

"But woe to you Pharisees! For you tithe mint and rue and all manner of herbs, and pass by justice and the love of God. These you ought to have done, without leaving the others undone" (Luke 11:42).

Dr. Martin Luther King, Jr. said that for a Christian, the promised land was "the Kingdom of God, a time when the will of God will reign supreme, and brotherhood, love, and right relationships will be the order of society." He said, "We must work with determination to create a society, not where black men are superior and other men are inferior and vice versa, but a society in which all men will live together as brothers and respect the dignity and worth of human personality" (Lynn United for Change (n.d.). Jesus invites every man, woman, and child to be part of His kingdom. Some may wonder why Jesus, someone with such ability to carry out a social justice initiative, did not take up a cause. Clearly, this did not stem from any indifference to fairness and equity on Jesus' part. Jesus wanted to address inequity more effectively by instilling principles that would lead to its ultimate eradication. It's not that He didn't have a heart for social justice. It's that his heart for social justice was so infinitely large that He wouldn't settle for an ineffective, temporary fix. He would overthrow injustice fully and finally by eradicating it first from the human heart. This is why He said, "The kingdom of God is within you" (Luke 17:21). It was heart work with Christ.

Here are a few examples of how Jesus pushed against the social constructs of inequality:

The Woman at the Well (John 4:1-42). Perhaps the tautest racial tension of that day existed between the Jews and the Samaritans. Bitter historic feuds had caused a rift between them, with the Jews abrogating supposed spiritual superiority and the Samaritans lashing back with resentment. As Jesus rested by the well, a Samaritan woman approached. When He asked her for water, she gasped in shock that He, a Jew, would receive water from a woman and a Samaritan.

The Good Samaritan (Luke 10:25-37). As Jesus told the story of the Good Samaritan, His eyes searched the people's faces. Perhaps it was a true story, and the guilty ones were present. A man had been robbed and beaten, left to die on the road from Jerusalem to Jericho. Two religious leaders—a priest and a Levite—saw him, but passed by indifferently. Finally, a Samaritan stumbled upon the man and rushed to his aid, applying first aid, loading him onto his own beast and taking him to an inn where he stayed with him through the night, paid the fees, and left him with some extra cash. In telling this story, Jesus demonstrated how to cross religious and racial divides and help a person in order to carry out God's merciful will.

The Samaritan didn't ask if the man was a Jew or a Gentile. If a Jew, the Samaritan well knew that, were their condition reversed, the man may have spit in his face and passed him by with contempt. Yet before him he saw a fellow human being in need, and this transcended any other concerns.

Zacchaeus (Luke 19:1-10). Tax collectors were a hated class, considered Jewish sells-outs to Rome. Beyond this, Zacchaeus was a short man. Could both the social status and the physical attributes have been issues of prejudice? Possibly. But the deepest lesson in Jesus befriending Zacchaeus may be that Jesus' love and acceptance extended to a man who aligned himself with an oppressive cause. The modern-day equivalent might be a member of a pro-life group working as an accountant for Planned Parenthood. Nonetheless, Jesus loved him and befriended him.

While Jesus didn't lead organized protests against social injustice, His life served as a living rebuke to racial, social, ethnic, and class prejudices. He lived out the principles of His kingdom, a kingdom of the heart.

WHAT IS CULTURAL HUMILITY?

Do nothing from factional motives (through contentiousness, strife, selfishness, or for unworthy ends) or prompted by conceit and empty arrogance. Instead, in the true spirit of humility (lowliness of mind) let each regard the others as better than and superior to himself (thinking more

© Pixelvario/Shutterstock.com

highly of one another than you do of yourselves). Let each of you esteem and look upon and be concerned for not (merely) his interests, but also each for the interests of others (Philippians 2:3-4, Amplified Version, Classic Edition).

Sue and Sue (2015) defined cultural humility as "a complementary component to cultural competence associated with an open attitudinal stance or a multiculturally open orientation to work with diverse clients" (p. 749). The 2000 Census estimated that between the years of 2030 and 2050, visible and racial minorities would become the majority (Greico & Cassidy, 2001). Due to the face of society becoming increasingly diverse, the counseling field responded by making it a priority to train counselors in how to effectively provide counseling services to these populations (Sue, Arredondo, & McDavis, 1992). The AMCD recognized the importance of training and equipping counselors to be multiculturally competent, thus the MSJCCs were developed. As you learned earlier in this chapter, the MSJCCs covered the following areas: (1) counselor self-awareness; (2) client worldview; (3) counseling relationship; and (4) counseling and advocacy interventions. Students in counselor education programs are trained in these three areas which helps them to address their attitudes and beliefs, gain knowledge, and employ skills necessary to be effective when counseling diverse populations (Arredondo et al., 1996).

The outcome of this training is to have counselors who are multiculturally competent and can effectively work with diverse and special populations (Sue & Sue, 2016). Multiculturally competent counselors are aware of their own biases, values, personal convictions, and assumptions about human behavior. They are also actively engaged in learning about their client's cultural worldview. Further, culturally competent counselors are actively practicing and implementing evidence-based interventions while working with diverse populations (Sue & Sue 2016).

Studies have noted that the term *multiculturally competent* has created a narrative that a counselor needs to be fully knowledgeable of their cultural background and biases while also being the expert of their client's cultural worldview in order to be effective in their therapeutic work (Mosher et al., 2017). This is not only overwhelming to a counselor (both novice and seasoned), but it can lead a counselor to perform as an *expert* on their client's cultural worldview which detracts from creating an authentic therapeutic alliance (Mosher et al., 2017; Sue, Zane, Nagayama Hall, & Berger, 2009).

Additionally, this pressure to be an expert can lead to feelings of anxiety and fear in the counselor related to expressing any ignorance about their client's cultural worldview (Hook, 2014; Mosher et al., 2017).

At the other end of the spectrum of this same issue, some counselors believe that they *are* the expert of their client's cultural background due to an assumed cultural competency. This can lead a counselor to hold a narrow view of their client's culture which may develop into stereotyping a client (Hook, Davis, Owen, Worthington, & Utsey, 2013; Mosher et al., 2017). This is harmful to both the client and the therapeutic relationship (i.e., racial microaggressions, empathic failure, etc.; Hook et al., 2013; Mosher et al., 2017).

Hook (2014) expressed these sentiments in an article that discussed his fears and concerns about what it means to be multiculturally competent.

> ...the idea of competence invokes the idea of getting to a certain end point where one if sufficiently proficient. It has the connotation of arriving at a place where one is deemed competent. I do not think that is the best way to think about training in multicultural counseling and diversity. I think it is dangerous to think we have somehow arrived regarding understanding individuals and groups who are different from us. That stance sets many people up to try to hide their limitations instead of owning and learning into them as a regular part of growth. To prop up our sense of competence, we are more likely to make false assumptions about individuals who are different. (p. 278)

Hook et al. (2013) and Hook (2014) further discussed how engaging in humility rather than trying to be the expert in therapy helps a counselor focus more on the client's needs to heal and be heard above the counselor's needs to know and strive for perfection. Also, during this process of engaging in humility, the counselor maintains an openness to learning about the client's worldview (Hook, 2014). This helps to deepen the therapeutic alliance between counselor and client, which leads to improvement in the therapeutic process (Hook et al., 2013; Hook, 2014; Mosher et al., 2017).

> Viewing myself as always in the process of leaning into my areas of discomfort seems to lower my defensiveness and open me up to new learning. I find this focus on an open and humble

stance much more helpful than a focus on how well I am doing, which sirs up perfectionistic striving that tends to interfere with my ability to be present and receptive to client's needs. (Hook, 2014, p. 278)

Additionally, Hook et al. (2013) found that humility, along with the integration of the MCCs, provides a balance for counselors to continue growing in their expertise as multicultural competent counselors while maintaining the awareness of their limitations and putting their client's

needs first. Integrating humility in the counseling process offers the counselor the ability to be transparent and vulnerable which can provide an authentic space for both the counselor and client to successfully grow in their therapeutic relationship.

From their research on the importance and effectiveness of integrating humility in the counseling process, Hook et al. (2013) expressed how humility was essential to being a multiculturally competent counselor. In this study, the term cultural humility was broken down into two components: intrapersonal and interpersonal. Davis, Worthington, and Hook (2010) discussed that intrapersonal humility in individuals includes holding an accurate view of oneself and being aware of your limitations. Interpersonal humility in individuals includes being open to others and their worldview, being other-focused rather than self-focused, and holding others in high regard without feelings of authority.

These components of intrapersonal and interpersonal humility were applied to the lens of multiculturalism (Hook et al., 2013). From this lens, the intrapersonal aspect of cultural humility is being aware and knowledgeable of your cultural background, biases, and your limitations on understanding the cultural background and worldview of your clients (Hook et al., 2013) The interpersonal aspect involves having a genuine interest in your clients and their cultural worldview, being open to learning about their diverse backgrounds, and not assuming the role as an expert of their cultural experiences (Hook et al., 2013). Being a culturally competent counselor who integrates cultural humility means a willingness to be vul-

© Quick Shot/Shutterstock.com

© Lorelyn Medina/Shutterstock.com

nerable with your clients and yourself while continuing to work on your personal growth and discovery.

In a study measuring openness to cultural diversity, researchers looked at how cultural humility played a role in the therapeutic relationship (Hook et al., 2013). The findings from the study showed that the client's perception that their counselor demonstrated cultural humility was positively correlated with both a good working alliance and improvement in therapy (Hook et al., 2013). Another study (Hook et al., 2016) examined the relationship between a counselor's cultural humility and the frequency of racial microaggressions. The study found that counselors who were perceived by their clients to be high in cultural humility were less likely to commit racial microaggressions (Hook et al., 2016). Also, if the counselors who were high on cultural humility did commit a racial microaggression, the impact of the breach in the therapeutic relationship had a lower impact (Hook et al., 2016). The researchers concluded that when a counselor engages in cultural humility, they are more other-oriented, and if they do commit a racial microaggression, then they are more likely to repair the breach in the relationship (Hook et al., 2016).

Cultural Humility in Practice

Now that you have been introduced to cultural humility, how it complements the MCCs, how it assists counselors in being more active as culturally competent counselors, and how cultural humility helps to improve the therapeutic alliance between the counselor and client, you will see how cultural humility can be practically applied in counseling. "Being cultural-ly humble is a lifelong commitment to self-evaluation and self-critique, to redressing the power imbalances…and to developing mutually beneficial and non-paternalistic clinical and advocacy partnerships with communi-ties" (Tervalon & Murray-Garcia, 1998, p. 117). Counselors and counselor educators must demonstrate cultural humility in order to be competent counselors in relationships where worldviews and values will inevitably clash (Davis et al., 2015; Edward, Watkins, Hook, Ramaeker, & Ramos, 2016).

There are four key principles of cultural humility which help to define and establish how it can be integrated into any field of practice (Goforth, 2016). These principles include self-reflection, learning from the client, partnership building, and lifelong learning. Table 5.2 below provides an explanation of how to apply and integrate each of these principles.

TABLE 5.2

Key Principles of Cultural Humility

Principle of Cultural Humility	Application and Integration
Self-reflection	Engaging in an ongoing process of self-reflection and self-critique of my own background, training, and world-view; critiquing skills and knowledge; promoting culturally humble practices
Learning from the client	Learning about my client through their telling of their life story, which illus-trates client worldview, values, and beliefs; counselor is the student and client is the expert
Promotion of partnership building	Moving from being the expert to being an advocate in the local community, which can help empower clients/com-munities
Lifelong learning	Continually reflecting and critiquing my professional journey, allowing for growth and understanding of myself as a cultural being.

Source: Tervalon & Murray-Garcia, 1998

Engaging in critical self-examination and self-awareness. Mosher et al. (2017) discussed how each of these four key principles of cultural humil-ity are demonstrated in the practice of counseling. Engaging in critical self-examination and self-awareness begins with a clinician defining what cultural humility is and how it is practically demonstrated in therapy. As counselors start the exploration process of their own cultural worldview, biases, and values, they can then engage in a deeper reflection on why and how they believe what they believe. For example, if the therapist is an African American male who identifies as a Christian, he must be aware of his privileges (Male, Christian, Middle-class socioeconomic status, advanced degree, etc.) and how these privileges may have oppressed others. He also must be aware of how he is oppressed (African American) and how these oppressed identities may conflict with other identities. Once counselors have insight on their power, privilege, oppressive identities, and worldviews, they can then reflect on the similarities and differences between their client's own privileged and oppressed identities.

When counselors can engage in meaningful reflection of their multiple identities as cultural beings, this process can lead them in becoming aware of how these multiple identities can impact the power differentiation between them and their clients. "When culturally humble therapists more clearly sense their cultural worldviews and perspectives, they commit to intentionally work to reduce their cultural biases and use their power and privilege to work toward justice" (Mosher et al., 2017, p. 226). Such reflection provides a space for counselors and clients to engage in an open and authentic process where they can fully function in their cultural selves. For counselors, this means using cultural humility to understand themselves and their client's worldview and values without having to be the expert of their client's diverse background. Thus, a more in-depth and organic therapeutic process can take place and may lead to a (a) decrease

of cultural biases; (b) opportunities to learn from clients; (c) stronger therapeutic bonds; and (d) opportunities to address power imbalances and work towards justice (Mosher et al., 2017).

Building the therapeutic alliance. A significant finding in research is that the integration of cultural humility in the counseling process is positively correlated to a stronger therapeutic alliance (Hook et al., 2013; Hook et al., 2017; Davis et al., 2014). When a therapist can express to their clients that their

© agsandrew/Shutterstock.com

cultural identities are valued in the therapeutic process, this enables the client to be their authentic selves. "For many clients, their cultural background is an essential aspect of their identities, as well as how they see and move through the world. Communicating to clients, both implicitly and explicitly, that their cultural identities are important and will be respected within the therapy can be a crucial building block of the treatment alliance and set the stage for productive therapeutic work" (Mosher et al., 2017, p. 266).

Cultural humility creates a stronger connection between the therapist and client and can lead to a more collaborative therapeutic process. When the therapist and client collaborate in the work, they can create goals that are in alignment with the needs of the client and implement interventions that are effective in helping the client (Mosher et al., 2017).

Navigating value differences. One of the most challenging issues to manage is value conflicts. Many therapists have found themselves in sessions where their clients have expressed drastically different values and worldviews from their own. Counselors who practice cultural humility are aware of their own cultural biases and worldviews. Counselors who are aware that they are to serve their clients despite vast differences in their worldviews adopt the stance of using their client's cultural lens to direct and guide the therapeutic session. When a therapist is actively other-oriented rather than self-oriented, they can allow the counseling process to move forward smoothly without allowing their values and biases to interfere.

A Biblical Example of Cultural Humility

The ministry of Jesus was marked by serving and laying aside His wants for God's will to be done on the earth. Jesus always put others needs above His own. He washed the feet of His disciples, He fed a crowd of 5,000, and He healed those whom society saw as rejects. He stood up for women in a society that did not allow them to have a voice. In Matthew Chapter 25, Jesus tells us that when we take care of the least of these (i.e., poor, imprisoned, widows, children, etc.), we are also doing it to Him. Jesus and His disciples challenged the religious system by showing compassion for those who were considered outcast, oppressed, and disenfranchised. Acts 17 verse 6 states that His disciples were accused of "turning the world upside down" by the unbelieving Jews. Jesus exposed the hypocrisy and greed of the wealthy religious leaders during His three-year ministry by calling out their legalism and hatred for Him and those who followed His teachings.

The woman who touched Jesus's robe. When considering the interpersonal aspects (i.e., an individual who is willing to meet the needs of another above their own needs and is open to learning about another's cultural experiences and background) of cultural humility (Mosher et al., 2017), it is important to consider the Biblical account of a woman who had an issue of bleeding for 12 years (see Mark 5). Most scholars believed that she was unnamed since she was a woman and the story is being told from a man's perspective (Mowczko, 2013). This lack of identification of her in the Bible is consistent with many stories of women in the Bible and is indicative of the cultural atmosphere towards women at that time (Mowczko, 2013). In today's society, women's access to health services has improved tremendously, but those without health insurance and access to quality doctors continue to report similar issues (Jacobson, 2018). This unnamed woman was out of money and had been taken advantage of by the very doctors who were trained to make her well. She had exhausted all of her financial resources, and yet no one could help her. Further, this woman was not allowed to go to church and fellowship with the saints, because, according to Jewish law, any woman that is bleeding is considered ceremonially unclean. Attending church and engaging in fellowship often provides comfort for those who are experiencing hardships in life. This woman was not allowed to enter the temple for the Jewish religious ceremonies, and anyone who touched her or was associated with her was also considered unclean until evening (Leviticus 15:19). In her desperation, she followed Jesus around in the crowd because she believed that if she could touch the hem of His garment, she would be healed (Mark 5:27-28). When she touched his robe, Jesus immediately noticed power leaving His body. Jesus asked His disciples who touched Him, and in the tradition of the disciples, they stated mockingly that everyone is touching Him as they are in a crowd of people. However, Jesus continues to persist on His conquest to find this person who has pulled on His virtue through their faith. Jesus being all-knowing, knew who touched Him. Likely, He asked His disciples to prove a point about the value of others and their needs being a priority to Him. This woman was not important, had no status, and was considered an outcast. To many, she was just another faceless person in the crowd. However, she was noticed and known by Jesus. Instead of rebuking her, Jesus called her daughter. He claimed this unnamed woman as His own and gave her a name, one of the most endearing names for a woman who had no one.

How Jesus honored and affirmed this woman was an act of cultural humility. Jesus who was on His way to heal an ailing child, stopped what He was doing amidst the chaos of the crowd and acknowledged this nameless woman. Jesus' priority at the time was to heal the child, yet he stopped to meet the needs of this woman who had suffered economically, socially, and spiritually. Jesus could have decided to ignore her and continue towards His destination. Even His disciples were unconcerned with the crowd of people surrounding Him. However, her needs were important to Him. Her healing and well-being was a priority to Him. What is also significant about this story is that Jesus not only redeemed her social status by acknowledging her, but that he also healed her in front of the same people who probably shamed and ignored her due to her illness.

Cultural Humility in Scripture

Each scripture below shows how Jesus humbled Himself to serve the needs of others despite how culture viewed them. He met the needs of others at the detriment of His reputation. He was despised and hated by those in power, and they sought to kill Him for it.

© Paul shuang/Shutterstock.com

- In John 5, Jesus healed a man on the Sabbath which was considered unlawful according to the Jewish laws and customs.
- In Mark 1, Jesus cast out the unclean spirits of a demon-possessed man. This man was considered an outcast by his community and was left tied up with chains.
- In John 11, Jesus raised Lazarus from the dead after he had been dead for four days. In Jewish custom, Jews believed that the soul hovers over the body. However, Jesus purposely waited four days to prove that the religious traditions of the Jews were no longer applicable.

WHAT ARE MICROAGGRESSIONS?

In the previous section, the importance of implementing cultural humility in the counseling relationship as a way to mitigate challenges in the therapeutic relationship was discussed. Specifically, incorporating cultural humility in the therapeutic relationship will aid in the formation of a positive therapeutic alliance and minimize microaggressions. Social scientists Sue, Bucceri, Lin, Nadal, and Torino (2007) declared that microaggressions are the new face of racism, because the nature of racism has shifted over time from overt expressions of racial hatred and hate crimes, toward expressions of subversive racism. Microaggressions are subtle, ambiguous, and often unintentional slights. *Racial microaggressions* refer to brief and commonplace verbal, behavioral, or environmental indignities, whether intentional or unintentional, that communicate hostile, derogatory, or negative prejudicial slights and insults toward racial/ethnic/cultural minority groups (Sue et al., 2007).

Generally perpetrated against people of color (POC; Sue et al., 2007), racial microaggressions are intended to marginalize certain groups, and can be communicated verbally or through actions or inactions. They may be experienced in interpersonal interactions, as well as systemically, institutionally or structurally (Friedlaender, 2018; Sue, et. al., 2007, 2019). Racial microaggressions are characteristically ambiguous and subtle in nature, making them difficult to discern and address (Friedlaender, 2018; Zambrana et al., 2017). As such, they typically are communicated outside of the awareness of the receiver and, at times, internalized, which leads to significant distress (Bryant-Davis & O'Campo, 2005; Wong-Padoongpatt, Zane, Okazaki, & Saw, 2017; Zambrana et al., 2017).

Sue et al. (2007) identifies three types of racial microaggressions. These include: microassaults, microinsults, and microinvalidations. Microassaults are characterized as overt and deliberate messages (Friedlaender, 2018) that may be either spoken or unspoken, as well as actions or inactions which communicate intolerance, hate, or bias towards POC (Berk, 2017). Microinsults are actions or inactions, either verbal, nonverbal or environmental, that include messages that convey insensitivity, rudeness, or are culturally/racially/ethnically demeaning to a person's identity or heritage. These types of racial microaggressions are even more ambiguous than microassaults because they are delivered and often communicated outside of the conscious awareness of both the transmitter and the recipient (Friedlaender, 2018). Microinvalidations are statements that exclude, negate, or nullify the psychological thoughts, feelings, or experiential reality of POC (Berk, 2017).

The metacommunications, or hidden messages, associated with racial microaggressions communicate negative bias and discrimination to POC. Because these hidden messages are communicated and received outside the awareness of the POC, many recipients internalize the negative attributes (Nadal, 2014), which contributes to diminished mental health (Hughes, Kiecolt, Keith, & Demo, 2015) increased anxiety (Soto, Dawson-Andoh, & BeLue, 2011), depressive symptoms (Torres & Taknint, 2015), heightened traumatic stress symptoms (Bryant-Davis, 2007; Bryant-Davis & O'Campo, 2005; Torres & Taknint, 2015), avoidance (Zambrana et al., 2017) and hyperarousal/vigilance (Torres & Taknint, 2015).

For POC, racism is omnipresent, and racial microaggressions are continuous and cumulative (Balogun-Mwangi et al., 2015; Bryant-Davis & Ocampo, 2005; Friedlaender, 2018; Torres & Taknint, 2015). Each sting is remembered, and before the healing is able to begin, another injurious racial microaggression is experienced (Bryant-Davis & Ocampo, 2005). The psychological, physiological and behavioral stress associated with repeatedly experiencing racial microaggressions has been termed *racial battle fatigue* (Smith, Hung, & Franklin, 2011).

The cumulative nature of racial microaggressions and the allostatic load associated with reexperiencing and enduring these psychological injuries time and again (Brody et al., 2014) have been linked with decreased diurnal cortisol levels (Zeiders, Landor, Flores, & Brown, 2017), hypertension, hyperarousal, hypervigilance (Bryant-Davis & Ocampo, 2005), obesity, diabetes, depression (Torres & Taknint, 2015), anxiety (Soto, Dawson-Andoh, & BeLue, 2011; Wong-Padoongpatt, Saw & Zane, 2017), social isolation (Bryant-Davis, 2007) and distrust of health care systems (Nicoladis et al., 2010), which are all associated with poor psychological and physiological (Nadal, 2014) health and decreased overall functioning (Brody et al., 2014).

Addressing racial microaggressions in counseling will require cultural humility. Cultural humility will be born out of genuine intellectual and human curiosity toward the experience others. It will require not only the development of multicultural awareness, but also a measure of comfort with the application of racially/ethnically/culturally appropriate skills, incorporating a humility that both acknowledges and validates the lived experiences of clients of color (Atkins, Fitzpatrick, Poolokasingham, Lebeau, & Spanierman, 2017; Balogun-Mwangi et al., 2015).

Microaggression is a form of social injustice and typically targets a marginalized culture. In the following student spotlight, you will be introduced to a K. C. Harris who experiences racial microaggressions on her job on an almost daily basis.

My Experiences with Racial Microaggressions
K. C. Harris, MA
Graduate Student

One of the worst feelings in the world is to be invisible. It is far worse than being ignored, because at least when you are ignored, there is a sense of acknowledgement. However, to be invisible is to be unacknowledged. To not exist. To not count. To not be worthy. I work in a majority white staffed behavioral health clinic as a psychology technician, and racial microaggressions have been a part of my everyday life working within this clinic.

© K.C. Harris

One example of the racial microaggressions I experience is when my supervisor arrives to the office in the morning. He greets my white colleague in the office next to mine, utters nothing as he passes my office with the open door, and then offers the white colleague in the office on the other side of mine a "good morning". As he continues down the hall until arriving at his office, he greets everyone else. When I shared my concerns with my white colleagues, I was patronized. They desperately sought to assure me that he's like that with everyone; however, he spoke to them. I was also told that I needed a supervisor with a different leadership style to accommodate my needs. Everything was easily explained away. I just needed to "understand how he was," and other responses that were tantamount to "get over it already!"

This has been my experience at work for over a year now. I arrive at work earlier than my colleagues, and for a couple of months, I was the last one in the building, as people left without telling me we had a release. Although experiencing these racial microaggressions on a daily basis is suffocating, I have and continue to engage in research on how to manage and respond to these occurrences. These offenses are on my mind as I enter and exit work and during the workday. I am perpetually waiting for the next shoe to fall. The things that have sustained me throughout this experience include social support, continuously reminding myself of my worth and purpose, and self-efficacy. However, the sting and injury of each and every racial microaggression is still felt. Employing microinterventions to defend myself and others has also been a significant tool in decreasing the impact of racial microaggressions.

I guess, what makes the experience so perplexing for me is that all of my coworkers are licensed clinicians and there is an expectation to operate with a level of cultural humility that works to ameliorate, or at least acknowledge these types of offenses. Clinicians, seasoned or newly licensed, and especially White clinicians, should be aware of their personal biases and privileges, and how that impacts their personal worldviews. They should also be incredibly mindful of how their worldview impacts their interactions with others. It is absolutely imperative for clinicians to assess how their biases will impact their ability to counsel POC and if challenged, see their blindspot, become aware of White fragility and how that can prevent their personal growth and development, as well as the treatment of the clients they serve.

SUMMARY

In this chapter, cultural diversity, social justice, advocacy, and cultural humility have been defined. The process of advocacy and the need to address institutional and social barriers that impede access, equity, and success for clients has been explored. Further, the importance of becoming aware of the role and process the professional counselor plays in advocating on behalf of the profession has been addressed. Additionally, social justice applications in the Bible have been outlined. In exploring these truths, you have the opportunity to introspect and assess your personal values regarding culture, diversity, advocacy, and social justice. Maybe you have connected intimately with the information shared and started to make positive changes in your personal, academic, and professional life by implementing some of these skills. Changes to the counseling field as it relates to culture, diversity, advocacy, and social justice begins with you. As a counselor, you will have the opportunity to positively impact the lives of the clients you serve as well as the counseling field at large. You are encouraged to implement the needed personal work to begin the process of impacting our profession and moving it forward.

FOR THE ROAD AHEAD

Check out the Chapter 5 video at this link:
https://www.khpcontent.com/

Reflections on the Journey

1. What is your personal story about how you may have encountered or engaged in racial microaggressions?
2. Think about what you believe your role/responsibility is as it relates to cultural competence, and what tools you may use to support a client who presents with a need in this area.
3. What are some ways that you can develop cultural humility in your personal and professional life?
4. Think back to a time in your life when you exhibited cultural humility. What areas of your life did this impact the most?

For Further Exploration

Byrd, C. M. (2018). Microaggressions self-defense: A role-playing workshop for responding to microaggressions. *Journal of Social Sciences, 7(96)*, 1–11.

Chavez, V. (2012, August 09). *Cultural humility* [Video file]. Retrieved from https://www.youtube.com/watch?v=SaSHLbS1V4w&t=922s

Cobran, K. (Producer). (2018, December 21). *The space between us* [Audio Podcast]. Retrieved from https://podcasts.apple.com/us/podcast/the-space-between-us/id1411316917?mt=2

Flores, V. (n.d.). *Cultural humility and counseling Hispanic and Latino populations.* Lecture. Retrieved May 10, 2019, fro https://www.naadac.org/cultural-humility-and-counseling-hispanic-and-latino-populations

Hook, J. N., Farrell, J. E., Davis, D. E., DeBlaere, C., Van Tongeren, D. R., & Utsey, S. O. (2016). Cultural humility and racial microaggressions in counseling. *Journal of Counseling Psychology, 63*(3), 269.

Ramsey, F. (2015, July 08). *Was that racist? An inside out parody* [Video file]. Retrieved from https://www.youtube.com/watch?v=Kqs8Ve4_-uA

Ramsey, F. (2015, July 01). *How do you handle a racist joke?* [Video file]. Retrieved from https://www.youtube.com/watch?v=Bg1aTLsS69Y

Shaw, S. (2016, December 27). Practicing cultural humility. Retrieved May 10, 2019, from https://ct.counseling.org/2016/12/practicing-cultural-humility/

Shook, M. (Producer). (2017, April 5). Multicultural Orientation: Cultural Humility and Responding to Cultural Opportunities in Counseling with Sidney Shaw [Audio Podcast]. *The Thoughtful Counselor*. Retrieved from http://wp.me/p7R6fn-9r

Shook, M. (Producer). (2017, October 18). Justice and advocacy in counseling: A conversation with Jonnie Seay Lane [Audio podcast]. *The Thoughtful Counselor*. Retrieved from https://wp.me/p7R6fn-gl

Shook, M. (Producer). (2017, December 1). Recast – Microaggression: Types, dilemmas, and best practices for counselors with Priscilla Wilson [Audio podcast]. *The Thoughtful Counselor*. Retrieved from https://wp.me/p7R6fn-ic

TED. (2017, December). *Juliana Mosely, PhD: Cultural humility* [Video file]. Retrieved from https://www.youtube.com/watch?v=Ww_ml21L7Ns

Foundations for Community Health Workers. (2015, March 5). *Depression, religion and cultural humility: Role play, demo* [Video file]. Retrieved from www.youtube.com/watch?v=Bgr6TXWknQQ

REFERENCES

American Counseling Association (2014). *ACA Code of Ethics*. Alexandria, VA: Author

Anderson, M., Mitchell, A., Koku, L., & Stevenson, H. C. (2018). Embracing racial stress and trauma: Preliminary feasibility and coping responses of a racial socialization intervention. *Journal of Black Psychology, 44*(1), 25-46.

Applebaum, B. (2017). Comforting discomfort as complicity: White fragility and the pursuit of invulnerability. *Hypatia, 32*(4), 862-875.

Arredondo, P., Toporek, R., Brown, S. P., Jones, J., Locke, D. C., Sanchez, J., & Stadler, H (1996). Operationalization of the multicultural counseling competencies. *Journal of Multicultural Counseling and Development, 24*(1), 42-78.

Atkins, S. L., Fitzpatrick, M. R., Poolokasingham, G., Lebeau, M., & Spanierman, L. B. (2017). Make it personal: A qualitative investigation of white counselors' multicultural awareness development. *The Counseling Psychologist, 45*(5), 669–696.

Axelson, J. (1985). *Counseling and development in a multicultural society*. Belmonth, CA: Brooks/Cole.

Berk, R. A. (2017). Microaggressions trilogy: Part 1. Why do microaggressions matter? *Journal of Faculty Development, 31(1)*, 63–73.

Brody, G. H., Lei, M. K., Chae, D. H., Yu, T., Kogan, S. M., & Beach, S. (2014). Perceived discrimination among African American adolescents and allostatic load: A longitudinal analysis with buffering effects. *Child development, 85*(3), 989–1002. doi:10.1111/cdev.12213.

Bryant-Davis, T. (2007). Healing requires recognition: The case for race-based traumatic stress. *The Counseling Psychologist, 35*(1), 135-43.

Bryant-Davis, T., & Ocampo, C. (2005). Racist incident–based trauma. *The Counseling Psychologist, 33*(4), 479–500.

Byrd, C. M. (2018). Microaggressions self-defense: A role-playing workshop for responding to microaggressions. *Journal of Social Sciences, 7*(96), 1-11.

Chao, R. C-L., Meifen, W. Spanierman, L., Longo, J., & Northart, D. (2015). White racial attitudes and white empathy: The moderation of openness to diversity. *The Counseling Psychologist, 43(1)*, 94-120.

Cohen, D. (2001). Advocacy: Its many faces and a common understanding. In Cohen, D., de la Vega, R., Watson, G. (Eds.), *Advocacy for social justice: A global action and reflection guide* (pp. 7–10). Bloomfield, CT: Kumarian Press.

Counsel for Accreditation of Counseling and Related Educational Programs [CACREP] (2015). 2015 standards for accreditation. Alexandria, VA: Author.

Davis, D. E., DeBlaere, C., Brubaker, K., Owen, J., Jordan II, T. A., Hook, J. N., & Van Tongeren, D. R. (2014). Microaggressions and perceptions of cultural humility in counseling. *Journal of Counseling Development, 94,* 483-93.

Davis, D. E., Worthington Jr, E. L., & Hook, J. N. (2010). Humility: Review of measurement strategies and conceptualization as personality judgment. *The Journal of Positive Psychology, 5*(4), 243-252.

Day-Vines, N. L., Wood, S. M., Grothaus, T., Craigen, L., Holman, A., Dotson-Blake, K. M, & Douglass, M.J. (2007). Broaching the subjects of race, ethnicity, and culture during the counseling process. *Journal of Counseling & Development, 85,* 401-09.

DeCarlo, A. (2013). The rise and call of group rap therapy: A critical analysis from its creator. *Group Analysis, 46(2)*, 225-39.

Edward Watkins Jr, C., Hook, J. N., Ramaeker, J., & Ramos, M. J. (2016). Repairing the ruptured supervisory alliance: Humility as a foundational virtue in clinical supervision. *The Clinical Supervisor, 35*(1), 22-41.

Evans, A. M., Hemmings, C., Burkhalter, C., & Lacy, V. (2016). Responding to race related trauma: Counseling and research recommendations to promote post-traumatic growth when counseling African-American males. *Journal of Counselor Preparation and Supervision, 8*(1), 4.

Flynn, J. (2015). White fatigue: Naming the challenge in moving from an individual to a systemic understanding of racism. *Multicultural Perspectives, 17(3)*, 115-124.

Friedlaender, C (2018). On microaggressions: Cumulative harm and individual responsibility. *Hypatia, 33*(1), 5-21.

Goforth, A. N. (2016). A cultural humility model of school psychology training and practice. *Trainer's Forum, 34*(1), 3-24.

Grieco, E. M., & Cassidy, R. C. (2001). *Overview of race and Hispanic origin, 2000* (Vol. 8, No. 2). U.S. Department of Commerce, Economics and Statistics Administration, U.S. Census Bureau.

Heath, T. (2018). Moving beyond multicultural counselling: Narrative therapy, anti-colonialism, cultural democracy and hip-hop. *International Journal of Narrative Therapy and Community Work, 2018*(3), 50-7.

Hemmings, C. & Evans, A. M. (2018). Identifying and treating race-based trauma in counseling. *Journal of Multicultural Counseling and Development, 46*, 20-40.

Hook, J. N. (2014). Engaging clients with cultural humility. *Journal of Psychology and Christianity, 33*(3), 277.

Hook, J. N., Davis, D. E., Owen, J., Worthington, E. L., & Utsey, S. O. (2013). Cultural humility: Measuring openness to culturally diverse clients. *Journal of Counseling Psychology, 60*(3), 353.

Hook, J. N., Farrell, J. E., Davis, D. E., DeBlaere, C., Van Tongeren, D. R., & Utsey, S. O. (2016). Cultural humility and racial microaggressions in counseling. *Journal of Counseling Psychology, 63*(3), 269.

Hughes, M., Kiecolt, J., Keith, V. M., & Demo, D. H. (2015). *Social Psychology Quarterly, 78(1)*, 25-48.

Ibrahim, F. A., Dinsmore, J. A., Estrada, D., & D'Andrea, M. (2011). The counselors for social justice (CSJ) code of ethics. *Journal for Social Action in Counseling and Psychology, 3*, 1–21. Retrieved from http://www.psysr.org/jsacp/Ibrahim-v3n2_1-21.pdf

Jacobson, J. L. (2018). *Women's health: The price of poverty. In the health Of women (pp. 3-32)*. Routledge.

Kagan, C., Burton, M., Duckett, P., Lawthorn, R., & Siddiquee, A. (2011). *Critical community psychology*. Chichester, United Kingdom: BPS Blackwell.

King Institute (n.d.). Retrieved April 12, 2019, from https://kinginstitute.stanford.edu/king-papers/documents/give-us-ballot-address-delivered-prayer-pilgrimage-freedom.

Kiselica, M. S., & Robinson, M. (2001). Bringing advocacy counseling to life: The history, issues, and human dramas of social justice work in counseling. *Journal of Counseling & Development, 79*, 387–397. doi:10.1002/j.1556-6676.2001.tb01985.x

Lee, C. C. (2018). *Counseling for social justice*. Retrieved from https://ebookcentral-proquest-com.ezproxy.liberty.edu.

Lewis, J. A., Arnold, M. S., House, R., & Toporek, R. L. (2002). ACA advocacy competencies.

Lynn United for Change (n.d.). Retrieved May 22, 2019, from http://www.lynnunited.org/mlk.

Malott, K. M. & Schaefle, S. (2015). Addressing clients' experiences of racism: A model for clinical practice. *Journal of Counseling and Development, 93*(3), 361-370.

Miller, M. J., Keum TaeHyuk, B., Thai, C. J., Lu, Y., Truong, N. N., Huh, G. A., Li, X., Yeung, J. G., & HaRim Ahn, R. (2018). Practice recommendations for addressing racism: A content analysis of the counseling psychology literature. *Journal of Counseling Psychology, 65*(6), 669-80.

Mosher, D. K., Hook, J. N., Captari, L. E., Davis, D. E., DeBlaere, C., & Owen, J. (2017). Cultural humility: A therapeutic framework for engaging diverse clients. *Practice Innovations, 2*(4), 221.

Mowczko, M. (2013, September 12). The shame of the unnamed women of the old testament. Retrieved from https://margmowczko.com/the-shame-of-the-unnamed-women-of-the-old-testament/

Nadal, K. (2014). The impact of racial microaggressions on mental health: Counseling implications for clients of color. *Journal of Counseling and Development, 92*, 57-67.

Nicolaidis, C., Timmons, V., Thomas, M. J., Waters, A. S., Wahab, S., Mejia, A., & Mitchell, S. R. (2010). "You don't go tell White people nothing": African American women's perspectives on the influence of violence and race on depression and depression care. *American Journal of Public Health, 100*(8), 1470–1476. doi:10.2105/AJPH.2009.161950

Ratts, M. J. (2009). Social justice counseling: Toward the development of a fifth force among counseling paradigms. *Journal of Humanistic Counseling, 48*(2), 160-172. doi:10.1002/j.2161-1939.2009.tb00076.x

Ratts, M. J., Hutchins, A. M. (2009). ACA advocacy competencies: Social justice advocacy at the client/student level. *Journal of Counseling & Development, 87*, 269–275. doi:10.1002/j.1556-6678.2009.tb00106.x

Ratts, M. J., Singh, A. A., Nassar-McMillan, S., Butler, S. K., & McCullough, J. R. (2015). *Multicultural and Social Justice Counseling Competencies.* Retrieved from http://www.counseling.org/docs/default-source/competencies/multicultural-and-social-justice-counseling-competencies.pdf?sfvrsn=20

Ratts, M. J., Singh, A. A., Nassar-McMillan, S., Butler, S. K., McCullough, J. R. (2016). Multicultural and social justice counseling competencies: Guidelines for the counseling profession. *Journal of Multicultural Counseling and Development, 44*, 28–48. doi:10.1002/jmcd.12035

Roysircar, G., Arredondo, P., Fuertes, J. N., Ponterotto, J. G., & Toporek, R. L. (2003). *Multicultural Counseling Competencies, 2003: Association for Multicultural Counseling and Development.* American Counseling Association, 5999 Stevenson Ave., Alexandria, VA 22304.

Singh, A. A., Merchant, N., Skudrzyk, B., & Ingene, D. (2012). Association for Specialists in Group Work: Multicultural and social justice competence principles for group workers. *The Journal for Specialists in Group Work, 37*, 312–325. doi:10.1080/01933922.2012.721482

Smith, W., Hung, M., & Franklin, J. (2011). Racial battle fatigue and the miseducation of black men: Racial microaggressions, societal problems, & environmental stress. *The Journal of Negro Education. 80*, 63-82.

Soto, J., Dawson-Andoh, N. A., & BeLue, R. (2011). The relationship between perceived discrimination and generalized anxiety disorder among African Americans, Afro Caribbean, and non-Hispanic Whites. *The Journal of Anxiety Disorders, 25*(2), 258-265.

Sue, D. W., Alsaida, S., Awad, M. N., Glaeser, E., Calle, C. Z., & Mendez, N. (2019). Disarming racial microaggressions: Microintervention strategies for targets, white allies, and bystanders. *American Psychologist, 74*(1), 128-42.

Sue, D. W., Arredondo, P., & McDavis, R. J. (1992). Multicultural counseling competencies and standards: A call to the profession. *Journal of Multicultural Counseling and Development, 20*(2), 64-88.

Sue, D. W., Bucceri, J., Lin, A. I., Nadal, K. L., & Torino, G. C. (2007). Racial microaggressions and the Asian American experience. *Cultural Diversity and Ethnic Minority Psychology, 13*(1), 72-81.doi:10.1037/1099-9809.13.1.72

Sue, D. W., Capodilupo, C. M., Torino, G. C., Bucceri, J. M., Holder, A. M. B., Nadal, K. L., & Esquilin, M. (2007). Microaggressions in everyday life. *American Psychologist, 62*(4), 271-286.

Sue, D. W., & Sue, D. (2016). *Counseling the culturally diverse: Theory and practice* (7th ed.). Hoboken, New Jersey: John Wiley & Sons, Inc.

Sue, S., Zane, N., Nagayama Hall, G. C., & Berger, L. K. (2009). The case for cultural competency in psychotherapeutic interventions. *Annual Review of Psychology, 60*, 525–548.

Tervalon, M., & Murray-Garcia, J. (1998). Cultural humility versus cultural competence: A critical distinction in defining physician training outcomes in multicultural education. *Journal of Health Care for the Poor and Underserved, 9*(2), 117-125.

Tribe, R., & Bell, D. (2018). Special thematic section on "social justice issues for counselling psychologist in greece." *The European Journal of Counselling Psychology, 6*(1), doi:10.5964/ejcop.v6i1.145.

Toporek, R. L., & Daniels, J. (2018). 2018 update and expansion of the 2003 ACA Advocacy Competencies: Honoring the work of the past and contextualizing the present. Retrieved from www.counseling.org

Torres, L., & Taknint, J. T. (2015). Ethnic microaggressions, traumatic stress symptoms, and Latino depression: A moderated mediational model. *Journal of Counseling Psychology, 62*(3), 393-401.

Wong-Padoongpatt, G., Zane, N., Okazaki, S., & Saw, A. (2017). Decreases in implicit self-esteem explain the racial impact of microaggressions among asian americans. *Journal of Counseling Psychology, 64*(5), 574–583.

Zambrana, R. E., Harvey Wingfield, A., Lapeyrouse, L. M., Dávila, B. A., Hoagland, T. L., & Valdez, R. B. (2017). Blatant, subtle, and insidious: URM faculty perceptions of discriminatory practices in predominantly White institutions. *Sociological Inquiry, 87*(2), 207-232.

Zeiders, K. H., Landor, A. M., Flores, M., & Brown, A. (2017). Microaggressions and diurnal cortisol: Examining within-person associations among African American and Latino young adults. *Journal of Adolescent Health, 63*, 482–88.

CHAPTER 6
Legal and Ethical Considerations in Professional Counseling

DAVID R. BROWN, PH.D. & APRIL CRABLE, PH.D.

> "A thought transfixed me: for the first time in my life I saw the truth as it is set into song by so many poets, proclaimed as the final wisdom by so many thinkers. The truth—that love is the ultimate and the highest goal to which man can aspire. Then I grasped the meaning of the greatest secret that human poetry and human thought and belief have to impart: The salvation of man is through love and in love."
> — Viktor Frankl

Following Christ: Grace for Our Work

The Bible has much to say about love; it is mentioned 484 times throughout the Old and New Testaments. Perhaps one of the best-known of biblical scriptures, written by the Apostle John, describes the purpose of Jesus' death and resurrection: "For God so loved the world that He gave His only begotten Son, that whoever believes in Him shall not perish, but have eternal life" (John 3:16 New American Standard Bible). Echoing this idea, John later writes, "Greater love has no one than this, that one lay down

© Artit Fongfung AF/Shutterstock.com

- The professional ethics for counselors, including awareness of professional counseling associations
- The *ACA Code of Ethics* (2014) and how it is used to guide professional practice and relationships with clients
- Ethical decision-making models to assist students in navigating ethical dilemmas, values conflicts, and application of ethical and moral principles.
- Differences between law and ethics and associated implications for counseling practice.
- Counselor characteristics and behaviors that influence therapeutic practice and relationships.

The following CACREP standards are addressed in this chapter:
Professional Counseling Orientation and Ethical Practice:
- Ethical standards of professional counseling organizations and credentialing bodies, and applications of ethical and legal considerations in professional counseling (CACREP, 2016, Standard 2.F.1.i.)
- Strategies for personal and professional self-evaluation and implications for practice (CACREP, 2016, Standard 2.F.1.k.)

Counseling and Helping Relationships
- Counselor characteristics and behaviors that influence the counseling process (CACREP, 2016, Standard 2.F.5.f.)

his life for his friends" (John 15:13). In his letter written to the Christians in Rome, the Apostle Paul explains the breadth and depth of God's love for all people: "For I am convinced that neither death, nor life, nor angels, nor principalities, nor things present, nor things to come, nor powers, nor height, nor depth, nor any other created thing, will be able to separate us from the love of God, which is in Christ Jesus our Lord" (Romans 8:38-39).

It is arguable that love defines Christianity and is central to all the teachings of Christ Jesus. Moreover, Jesus stated that the two greatest commandments are to love God and love others as oneself (Mark 12:38-31). Love represents the heart of Christianity, and it also represents the best of the counseling profession: respectful and compassionate care for others. As we consider the role of ethics in counseling practice, Christians are fortunate that the values of our faith prepare us for working and relating with others. A love for others, accompanied by an inherent respect for others because they are made in the image of God, should guide a counselor's professional practice, relationships, and interactions with others.

The aim of this chapter is to familiarize you with key ethical and legal concepts. Because this is a textbook preparing you for the counseling profession, we will invariably discuss ethics, ethical reasoning, and ethical principles from a counseling perspective. However, it is also important to understand that ethics plays a role in almost everything we do. Thus, it is our intent with this chapter to not only emphasize the importance of ethics within the counseling profession, but also to encourage you to be intentional about your decisions and consider the potential ethical implications before you act. Effective professional practice depends upon working with your client's best interests in mind, as well as having "good intentions, or wanting to do the right thing" (Remley & Herlihy, 2016, p. 5). For this reason, ethical considerations are infused into all counselor training and addressed in all aspects of counseling, as well as by other helping professions, because understanding ethics is vital to the way in which we conduct ourselves personally and professionally. As you go through and process this information, remember to take a deep breath and relax: you will see this information again, and it will be reinforced in all counseling coursework. Further, you will learn about ethics in greater detail as you progress through your counselor training, including an in-depth study of legal and ethical considerations within your ethics course.

When thinking of ethics, various dichotomies may come to mind, such as right versus wrong, good versus bad, or maybe moral versus immoral. These are all excellent examples of ethical thought, but they also do not fully describe the intricacies of ethics. From a surface-level perspective, ethics may seem fairly straightforward – after all, professional organizations routinely develop and publish ethical guidelines for their members, and existing legal codes detail permissible behavior, as well as various corrective actions against those who break the law. We engage in ethical decisions every day, often without realizing that we are doing so: whether to eat a couple extra doughnuts at breakfast; if it really is a problem to drive faster than the speed limit; or even, how much is too much to share on social media.

What defines something as an ethical situation is not whether the final decision is good, bad, right, or wrong (although it is arguable that breaking the law is bad); instead, our actions become ethical situations because we have to decide what is the best response for a situation at that specific time. For example, the decision whether to exceed the speed limit when driving falls under the jurisdiction of traffic laws – and from personal experience, we can share that driving faster than the posted speed limit may result in a traffic citation and a fine! However, sometimes your reasoning for exceeding the speed limit is understandable and perhaps deemed acceptable, such as rushing to the emergency room at the local hospital. Other times, while your rationale might seem reasonable to you (*"I need coffee NOW, so I can function this morning"*), a police officer will likely not consider it to be

© LightField Studios/Shutterstock.com

a justifiable excuse to exceed the speed limit. Thus, the same behavior (i.e., driving faster than the speed limit) may sometimes be treated differently, and the difference between these examples is the situation.

Using the previous example, we may not give much thought to decisions about exceeding the speed limit; you may consider a posted speed limit to be more like a guideline rather than an enforceable traffic law. Moreover, at other times, situational differences may present new information that influences your decision to speed: current mood, driving experience, being in a school zone, weather conditions, amount of surrounding traffic, curviness of the road, proximity of a police officer, or any number of other circumstances. By considering these factors, you are determining the most appropriate response to this situation. Further, within this example you are also determining what you consider to be the most important factors and making a decision based upon them (i.e., *"I shouldn't drive very fast when there is a lot of ice on the road"*).

A misconception is that a student's assessment of ethical practice begins during field experience. We would like for you to imagine that the courses, communication, and the ethical and professional presentation are all a part of an audition for a role in a production called Field Experience and Practice. Faculty members are set with the task of ensuring your readiness for practice. Your understanding of ethics will guide your actions, and your counseling faculty are tasked to ensure that you develop a robust knowledge of professional ethical behavior.

WHAT ARE ETHICS?

When we think of ethics, the image that may come into our minds is a set of scales, where we weigh the merits of competing ideas, values, thoughts, behaviors, and such. An iconic image of the legal profession is a blindfolded Lady Justice, holding a set of scales and a sword. The meaning of this image is that justice should be impartial (blindfold), given without fear or favor (sword), by carefully weighing all relevant evidence (balance). This is a fairly accurate concept of ethics, which can be defined as a set of standards that outline what is acceptable and unacceptable human behavior in all situations. Put merely, ethics tells us what is right and wrong (Resnik, 2015). Ethics is determined by the shared beliefs, morals, and values of others.

Counselors share professional values and moral principles. It is logical to question the need for ethical standards if we have laws. Laws and ethics are different but can be closely related. Laws can deviate from ethics. For example, in counseling, it is unethical to be friends with your clients, but this is not against the law. Many laws are created from and based upon ethics (i.e., people's awareness of right and wrong). Laws are created and enforced by the government. Ethics are created by professional boards and organizations and enforced by ethics committees. In the counseling profession, ethics are enforced and governed by state, national, and international licensing and certification boards and counseling associations such as the American Counseling Association (ACA).

© Kaspars Grinvalds/Shutterstock.com

Portrait of a Professional Counselor: La Shanda Sugg

La Shanda Sugg, LPC, is a therapist, consultant, and the founder of Labors of Love Counseling & Consulting, LLC (www.thelaborsoflove. com). With a trauma specialty and a focus on multigenerational families, La Shanda combines emerging neuroscience, EMDR, and Developmental and Relational Trauma Therapy to help people improve their quality of life and relationships. La Shanda believes that by exploring and healing from historical experiences that have left wounds and imprints, clients are able to make cognitive and behavioral changes that positively impact their present and future. In addition to providing therapy for families, couples, and individuals, La Shanda also conducts trauma-specific trainings and consultation for companies, community agencies, schools, and faith-based organizations.

© Nick Asher

La Shanda stated, "Ethics was, honestly, a scary class; I remember feeling anxious over making decisions that could potentially harm clients and experiencing angst about balancing my personal values with my professional obligations. What I find most helpful in navigating both areas is doing my own work." With specific emphasis on self-awareness, self-care, and supervision, La Shanda has prioritized evaluating her desire and drive to help others with her own need to be well during the process. She believes that continuing education is an avenue to continuously explore her personal beliefs and ways of being, which is far more than passively sitting in a training session. La Shanda notes that she uses supervision to not only review her caseload but to also process how she is being impacted by her work, taking every opportunity to participate in learning and development that involves personally experiencing the role of a client and as a healer. She believes that these intentional efforts have helped her feel more confident and competent in her work, as well as not being caught off-guard by triggers and personal wounds that have gone undetected.

Contributed by La Shanda Sugg. © Kendall Hunt Publishing Company.

The American Association of Christian Counselors (AACC, 2014) notes that ethics are "values in action" (p. 8), stating that an ethics code provides practical boundaries to guide professional behavior. We can further separate values into personal values and professional values. Our *personal values* guide us in determining right and wrong conduct in how someone leads their life. *Professional values* are a set of shared values established by organizations to guide the conduct of its members; it is these values that we address in this chapter. *Ethical standards* are derived from professional values, and these define the shared guidelines for professional and organizational conduct.

Code of Ethics and Ethical Principles

Ethical standards are essential to counselors because they provide a set of guidelines that define professional practice, establish safeguards in the field of counseling, and protect clients, communities, and counselors (Super, 1953). Although the American Counseling Association (ACA) is comprised of a large body of professional counselors, it could not identify itself as an association without an established code of ethics (Allen, 1986). The *ACA Code of Ethics* (2014) is the golden standard of counseling clinical practice that informs professional counselors and counselors-in-training of their professional and ethical responsibilities, roles of a counselor, and their responsibilities to clients. Furthermore, it informs the public of practice standards (ACA, 2014; Herlihy & Corey, 2015). The *ACA Code of Ethics* is also a guide to help counselors with decision-making as it relates to counseling-related issues. It is impossible for ethical codes to provide the answer to every ethical or professional decision a counselor may face; however, the ethics code is to be used as a guide to help derive the best course of action.

The American Counseling Association states in the 2014 revision of the *ACA Code of Ethics* that professional values are the basis of ethical principles, which are, in turn, "the foundation for ethical behavior and decision-making" (p. 3). The American Psychological Association (APA; 2017) refers to these principles as "aspirational in nature" (p. 3), noting that the "intent is to guide and inspire psychologists toward the very highest ethical ideals of

the profession" (p. 3). Similarly, the National Association of Social Workers (NASW) claims that ethical principles are "ideals to which all social workers should aspire" (2017, p. 5). AACC (2014) echoes these statements, asserting that ethics "affirmatively educates counselors in the direction of becoming helpers of excellence" (p. 9). These ideals and aspirations provide a conceptual foundation upon which to build ethical standards.

Thus, the ethical codes, as developed and published by various helping professions, articulate several important ethical principles that presuppose the ethical standards. ACA (2014) identifies six underlying principles to their ethical standards: autonomy, nonmaleficence, beneficence, justice, fidelity, and veracity. Similar items from the ethical principles stated within the ethics code of the American Psychological Association (APA; 2017): beneficence and nonmaleficence, fidelity and responsibility, integrity, justice, and respect for people's rights and dignity. While slightly different, NASW's (2017) ethical code identifies six core values that relate well to the ethical principles defined by ACA and APA: service, social justice, dignity and worth of the person, importance of human relationships, integrity, and competence.

Basing their ethical codes upon scripture and general revelation, AACC (2014) identifies seven biblical-ethical foundations, and the Christian Association for Psychological Studies (CAPS; 2005) names seven biblical principles, all demonstrating the significance of Christian values in guiding professional ethical behavior. All of these principles reflect Kitchener's (1984) seminal work in ethical decision-making, exploring the reasons why ethics are important to the decision-making process, and, perhaps even more importantly, to reinforce and respect the inherent value and worth of people and personhood.

Part of our discussion about the role of ethics pertains to the ethical principles noted previously. The primary purpose of ethical standards in the helping professions is to promote and to protect client welfare (AACC, 2014; ACA, 2014; APA, 2017); this purpose demonstrates the prominence of ethics in counseling, as well as the need to further explore foundational ethical principles as these provide an underlying rationale for the ethical standards. Understanding the six ethical principles espoused by the ACA assists counselors in applying ethical standards within the clinical services they provide to clients and determining the best approach to addressing ethical dilemmas; these principles also apply to counseling instruction, supervision, and research.

Further, Kitchener (1984) claimed that these ethical principles are the most critical when evaluating ethical concerns, noting that "they are already implicit in much of what is written about ethical issues in the profession" (p. 46). AACC (2014) and CAPS (2005) also cite biblical authority and general revelation as underlying ethical standards, practicing from the standard of first loving God, then loving others as you love yourself (Mark 12:28-31).

Ethical Principles

As previously noted, ethical standards are based upon underlying ethical principles. In this section, we will explore the six ethical principles as described by the American Counseling Association (2014). This section will also explain the six ethical principles, associated values, and provide relevant examples of how each principle is applied within clinical practice. Within each example, we will also note the values that underlie the ethical principles and how these are often applied to ethical dilemmas.

First, we will discuss *autonomy*, which can be defined as the right to self-control, to self-direct, or to self-govern. As an ethical principle, this means that counselors respect the right of clients to choose their own thoughts, behaviors, and direction in life. With a respect toward client autonomy, counselors are careful not to impose their own thoughts, beliefs, values, and opinions upon the client, nor to overrule the client's right to choose (see §A.4; ACA, 2014). Notably, there are some situations, as defined by legal codes, where the client's autonomy may be restricted; the purpose in doing so is to protect the client or others from harm: lethal self-harm attempts, plans of violence against others, disclosed abuse of children or elderly persons, and so on. Placing value on human life and avoidance of mistreating others echoes the Christian belief that humanity is created in the image of God (Genesis 1:26-27), and, therefore, has inherent value and worth (CAPS, 2005). From this perspective, the value of human life has greater prominence than the client's autonomy. It is also important to note that in such situations, a client's autonomy is not to be disregarded or cast aside as unimportant; instead, the client's autonomy is temporarily set aside to meet a greater obligation of promoting the client's welfare. As you become more familiar with ethics codes, you will find that ethical principles and ethical standards sometimes conflict with one another; this is something we will discuss later in this chapter.

As noted above, sometimes ethical principles do not align. *Nonmaleficence* is an ethical principle that sometimes competes with a client's right to autonomy. Nonmaleficence pertains to a counselor's obligation to avoid harming clients, or inflicting the least harm possible. As a value that is firmly embedded within and well-known from the medical profession, preventing and avoiding harm to others is considered one of the strongest ethical principles (Kaplan et al., 2017; Kitchener, 1984). In situations where the counselor must set aside the client's right to self-determination, it is done with the intention of avoiding harm to the client; in other words, refusing to respond may cause harm to the client. As an ethical principle, nonmaleficence is often combined with *beneficence*, which is working for the good of others, the community, or the profession. A counselor who embodies beneficence aspires to promote health, well-being, and harmony. These ethical principles closely match what many Christians believe defines the Christian faith: Jesus' commandment to love God and love others (Mark 12:28-31). If we follow Jesus' commandment, then we will serve our clients out of love, and interact with them in a manner that places value in their health and well-being. As related to our previous discussion of client autonomy, intervening with a client's plan of violence toward someone else can prevent harm coming to the client, others, their families, and the local community.

The next ethical principle we will discuss is *justice*, which is about interacting with and treating others in an equitable and fair manner. Kitchener

(1984) suggested that an understanding for justice could be "equal persons have the right to be treated equally, and nonequal persons have the right to be treated differently if the inequality is relevant to the issue at hand" (p. 49). In this definition, "equal persons" and "nonequal persons" refers to treating all people the same unless their individual differences require different treatment, or if there is some precluding rationale for different treatment. Indeed, Kitchener (1984) further explained that if the inequality between two individuals is not relevant within a given situation, then they should be treated the same. An example of equal treatment would be collaborating with two different clients to develop counseling plans, which is a standard guideline for clinical practice (see §A.1.c; ACA, 2014). However, within this same example, the counseling interventions provided in each service plan may be different, even if both clients are seeking treatment for the same mental health concern. While the issue is the same (the mental health concern), the treatment modality (the intervention) may not be the same – this represents unequal persons being treated unequally as each client's individual needs and context are considered when developing a service plan. Thus, having a justice orientation toward one's clients may involve treating clients differently when relevant, which also intersects with the ethical principles of beneficence and nonmaleficence. Counselors must consider individual context when evaluating the uses of and the results from a therapeutic intervention. The failure to ascertain a client's individual needs shows a disregard to equitable treatment; in our example, the clients received both equal and unequal treatment because individual circumstances must be considered within therapeutic intervention.

Advocacy efforts toward equality correspond well to the next ethical principle we will discuss: *Fidelity*. As a basic function within all helping professions, fidelity involves a counselor remaining faithful to the commitments made to clients, "including fulfilling one's responsibilities of trust in professional relationships" (ACA, 2014, p. 3). Adherence to fidelity within professional relationships means that a counselor fulfills all professional obligations to their clients, including following contracts, avoiding lying, not misrepresenting any information given to clients, providing accurate reporting, etc. Failure to remain trustworthy and reliable not only has implications for the individual counselor, but it also provides a reason for the public to mistrust the counseling profession. Except in situations where the counselor is required by legal code to do so, violations of fidelity can cause harm to the client and do not promote the client's welfare, both of which run afoul of the ethical principles of nonmaleficence and beneficence.

The final ethical principle that we will discuss is *veracity*; this principle relates to being truthful, accurate, and consistent with others (ACA, 2014). Veracity is closely related to fidelity, as both involve honesty and truthfulness; these are qualities that counselors nurture and encourage in professional counseling relationships. Just as counselors desire clients to honestly share their concerns and challenges and disclose relevant sensitive information within their counseling sessions, clients have a right to expect that counselors will respond to and interact with them in an authentic and genuine manner. Counselors must also be careful to honestly represent themselves, their training, and their professional expertise. With a genuine desire to help others and to appear proficient in providing services to clients, counselors may be tempted to either dismiss or overstate their level of competence. It is an admirable quality to comfort a client and express hope that the client will achieve their goals; however, this should not come at the expense of misrepresenting oneself. Being dishonest may eventually cause problems for both the counselor and the client if the counselor is not sufficiently skilled to provide a requested service or a necessary level of care. Further, if helping professionals misrepresent their training, education, and credentialing, they may be violating both ethical and legal codes.

The *ACA Code of Ethics* (2014) are not the only guidelines you need to follow in practice. There are state and federal laws and regulations that you must adhere to as a counselor. It is essential that you are aware of the state and federal guidelines you must abide. Due to situational variances in ethical conduct, there will be occurrences in clinical practice when the law and ethical standards are in direct conflict with one another, or the law does not align well with ethical standards. In these cases, you will adhere to the code of ethics if it establishes a higher standard than the law. In doing so, we strongly recommend that you review research and best practices, consult with other mental health colleagues, and apply ethical decision-making to determine the best course of action. These methods for ethical decision-making will be addressed throughout the remainder of this chapter.

WHAT ARE VALUES AND VALUE CONFLICTS?

Through our explanation of ethical principles and our discussion of situations where potential ethical dilemmas may arise, we must also consider the implications of conflicts between our personal values and the values espoused by professional organizations. It is likely that you will find much with which you agree in professional ethics codes. Many work within the helping professions because they feel a call to help others; the desire to promote client welfare and taking care to avoid harming others may resonate within you. Being fair, honest, and truthful with others may closely match how you interact with them, as well as how you want others to relate with you. When our personal values align with professional values, we feel congruence with our work. However, just as we previously discussed conflicts among ethical principles, we may also find conflict within ourselves: a contradiction between our personal and professional values. These conflicts are sometimes more difficult to navigate, since the conflicts arise in opposition to something we consider important and valuable. As our values can represent deeply held beliefs, we may struggle to consider other perspectives or have difficulty conceptualizing how to respond. Because these situations will undoubtedly arise, we strongly believe that all helping professionals must become self-aware and explore their values and beliefs in order to anticipate potential values conflicts, as well as how to address the conflicts that do arise. Therefore, it is important for counselors and counselors-in-training to explore personal and professional values conflicts and the appropriate manner in which they should respond.

It is important to note that thoughts and behaviors are based within one's values: an individual's values are demonstrated in their words and actions. Value conflicts are not inherently bad, nor do they necessarily represent negative situations. Further, a counselor does not need to fear or strenuously avoid values conflicts. In fact, occurrences of values conflicts are fairly common and simply display individual differences. Values conflicts may often represent seemingly insignificant differences, such as our opinions regarding fashion, salaries of professional athletes, or what type of vehicle to purchase. However, values conflicts can become significant events when the difference impairs the counselor's ability to work with the client or uphold the ethical principles we previously discussed. Again, counselors need not attempt to actively avoid these situations, but they do need to carefully avoid forcing their beliefs and values on their clients. The *ACA Code of Ethics* (2014) acknowledges that counselors may hold deeply personal values, but the ethics code also states that counselors must be careful not to impose their values on their clients (see §A.4.b). Violations of this ethical standard also represent violations of the ethical principle of autonomy.

Remley and Herlihy (2016) identified and discussed *bracketing* as the preferred method for counselors to avoid imposing values on their clients, noting that one of the most challenging lessons that counselors learn is to "respect values that are different from their own and to avoid imposing their own personal values on their clients" (p. 3). Thus, bracketing can be defined as temporarily setting aside one's personal values when working with clients. Respecting a client's values and beliefs demonstrates the counselor's adherence to the ethical principles of autonomy, nonmaleficence, beneficence, and justice. In our discussion of bracketing, as well as within the greater conversation of value conflicts, it is important to note that counselors are not called to become valueless, nor should they assume that they must accept their clients' values. Instead, counselors maintain a strong self-awareness of their personal beliefs and values and carefully avoid influencing clients with them.

Portrait of Professional Counselor in Private Practice
Tim Barber, LPCC

© Ryan Watters

Tim Barber is a Licensed Professional Clinical Counselor and supervisor in the state of Ohio, is also credentialed as a Certified Sex Addiction Therapist, and has completed advanced training in Psychobiological Approach to Couples Therapy (PACT) and Eye Movement Desensitization and Reprocessing (EMDR). Tim is the principle owner, Executive and Clinical Director of Counseling Alliance, LCC, a faith-based private practice (www.counseling alliance.com). Counseling Alliance serves a variety of client populations, but the majority of their work focuses on relationship issues, various forms of compulsive sexual behaviors, and trauma. Therapists are licensed as counselors by the state of Ohio, most are members of the American Counseling Association, and all have advanced training in multiple areas. The Counseling Alliance approach to therapy considers the whole person with an emphasis on interpersonal neurobiology. Specific approaches include attachment-focused therapies, trauma-based therapies such as psychodrama, EMDR, and a Developmental and Relational Trauma (DART) model based on the work of Pia Mellody. Compulsive sexual behaviors are addressed primarily through a model developed by Dr. Patrick Carnes.

As a licensed counselor, Tim notes that he is bound not only by the laws and ethics of the Ohio Counselor, Social Worker, and Marriage & Family Therapist Board but also the *ACA Code of Ethics.* Tim believes that spirituality should be considered as a multicultural issue to be explored, and differences may present a faith-based practitioner with certain values and ethical concerns to navigate. For Tim, those concerns are deeper than the avoidance of cultural encapsulation; they are matters that deeply impact one's personal identity. Two primary examples of such concerns include working with members of the LGBTQ community and those coming from different faith systems, a non-Christian faith tradition, or professing no faith at all. Obviously avoiding the imposition of his own values is a primary concern. As a professional who identifies as a Christian, Tim works first and foremost to demonstrate unconditional positive regard for each person seeking treatment as a beloved person, created in God's image and dearly loved by God. The challenge is to meet each person where she or he is as a person for whom Christ died, while at the same time communicating about, or around, issues that are inconsistent with Tim's own value system. A primary guide for Tim is to see each person in light of the potential person they can become. Seeing God's potentiality in that person allows Tim to see past the differences they may have. For Tim, this goes beyond bracketing his beliefs and values and meeting the person where he/she is in a manner consistent with the way Jesus met sinners where they were. Seeing God's potentiality in each person frees Tim from the need to "correct" clients' belief system or behaviors. From that place of acceptance, Tim can help clients meet their identified needs in the firm belief that an all-powerful God has the ability to speak to them about what He wants for them.

Is this approach perfect? According to Tim, not by any means! He notes that at times it is inwardly agonizing to see a person make a decision that he personally believes is detrimental to them. However, he believes that his role is not that of a prophet or evangelist; he believes that if he demonstrates grace to his clients, they may be more open to exploring a life of faith on their own (1 Corinthians 3:6). In short, the meeting of each client at their point of need in a spirit of acceptance and support, and in the belief that God is already at work in that person's life at some level, allows Tim to trust God's long-term plan for that person.

Contributed by Tim Barber. © Kendall Hunt Publishing Company.

Counselors should carefully consider what bracketing their values really means, noting that the concept of bracketing represents a value itself as well as reflecting a value of the helping professions, as determined by committees, task forces, and similar groups of individuals. As previously noted, both personal and professional values are developed through a variety of sources and experiences. And, as such, both personal and professional values can change as we discover new information or engage in new experiences; as we synthesize new awareness and knowledge, our beliefs and values may change accordingly. An example of changing values is the introduction of physician-assisted suicide for terminal end-of-life concerns. The helping professions have long valued life, health, and well-being and have appealed to the principles of beneficence and nonmaleficence to instruct clinicians to intercede on behalf of their clients if there is any concern that the client intends to harm him/herself (see §A.1.a; ACA, 2014). However, the ACA Ethics Revision Task Force removed an entire section related to providing end-of-life care in the 2014 edition of the *ACA Code of Ethics* (see §A.9; ACA, 2005). Kaplan and colleagues (2017) noted that this section was removed because "bracketing counselor values with clients who are struggling with significant end-of-life issues is not qualitatively different than other value-related issues that counselors have to struggle with" (p. 117). Ironically, according to current cultural values, suicidal thoughts related to terminal end-of-life concerns are considered personal values, whereas other instances of suicide ideation are not. In our example, a counselor interceding on behalf of a client contemplating suicide related to end-of-life concerns would be imposing his/her values on that client; interceding on behalf of clients considering suicide for other reasons is considered a professional responsibility.

Thus, while counselors may intuitively know not to impose their beliefs and values on their clients, as it is also enumerated in the *ACA Code of Ethics* (§A.4.b; 2014, p.5), it may sometimes be unclear when personal values intersect with or deviate from professional values. It is imperative that counselors remain well-informed of changes within ethical codes, as well as maintain self-awareness of how their beliefs, values, and opinions may influence the clinical services they provide. This influence is not inherently dangerous to professional practice, as counselors are not value-less; however, counselors must be willing to participate in the counseling process with clients as collaborators and colleagues, not as therapists who "know better" and "have all the answers" to the client's concerns.

Spiritual Integration

While discussing moral principles and ethical standards, including how personal and professional values intersect with the professional responsibilities of a mental health counselor, it is also necessary to explore how to manage values differences. Our broad discussion of navigating differences in values, especially those related to spirituality and religious beliefs, will also closely explore ethical considerations when integrating spirituality into counseling. For the purposes of this text, we will discuss different views of Christian integration, understanding that other faith and philosophical traditions can follow a similar format. Further, as we proceed, we want to emphasize that any discussion of counselor training and skills necessary to become skilled in spiritual integration is not complete without also discussing spiritual self-awareness and how one's own faith influences their thoughts and behaviors. Accordingly, Hagedorn and Moorhead (2011) suggested that counselors who do not understand their own spiritual views and the implications of such may not be able to effectively address such topics with clients. We must also remember there are a variety of perspectives on Christian integration, and the major difference among varying Christian perspectives, as well as current secular approaches to counseling and psychology, relates primarily to sources of authority (Johnson, 2010). This means that a strong foundation is necessary to both support and demonstrate the effectiveness and utility of an approach. Authority can come from a variety of sources: knowledge, reason, logic, tradition, and revelation, to name a few. Most secular approaches employ objective means to support their perspectives, such as through research that follows scientific methods. All of these sources of understanding serve as an appropriate foundational and authoritative basis and should not be considered mutually exclusive.

Models of Christian integration differ from secular models through using the Bible as their primary source material (Entwistle, 2015). However, while all Christian integration models support the authority and use of scripture, they differ through the primacy of scripture in clinical intervention. As an example, Johnson (2010) presents five perspectives of Christian integration that display a diversity of Christian thought, from a model where scripture is considered the sole source of authority and the only appropriate resource for clinical intervention, to a model where scripture is considered just one of several equally authoritative sources. Each of these models represents Christian integration, and the counselor must determine which approach best fits his/her conceptualizations of therapy.

Christian Values, Biblical Principles, and Ethical Codes

The values that best define Christianity are arguably found within Mark 12:28-31, where Jesus explains to a young religious leader that the greatest commandment is to love God, and the second greatest commandment is to love others as you love yourself. Thus, the Christian ethic can be defined in a single word: *Love*. The Great Commission (Matthew 28:18-20) echoes these commandments: making disciples means to teach others to love God and love others. This is perhaps a simple concept, but the implementation is challenging. A quick look back through historical Christianity provides numerous examples in which the idea of "loving God and loving others" was not clearly demonstrated. However, the Christian faith has remained throughout the centuries, and the Gospel has not changed: love God and love others.

Love is also a common theme found in literature, music, film, and other media. One example is the song "All You Need is Love" that was released by The Beatles in July 1967; it was immediately embraced as a counter-culture message to protest the on-going Cold War and western nations' involvement in the Vietnam War. This song was released as a part of "Our World," the first international satellite-broadcast television show. Written with simplistic lyrics in order to be more easily understood by an international audience, this song was England's contribution to the television show. A few years later in an interview, John Lennon explained that the song's message was intended to be relevant to everyone: "Love is appreciation of other people and

PF1/WENN.com/Newscom

allowing them to be. Love is allowing somebody to be themselves, and that's what we do need" (Womack, 2017, p. 12). The love that Lennon is describing is about respecting others for who they are, with no expectation of who they should be. In many ways, this is akin to ACA's (2014) ethical requirement for counselors to avoid imposing their beliefs and values on others (see §A.4.b), as well as giving clients the autonomy to choose. However, Lennon's explanation falls short of fully describing what loving others really means; he did not adequately express the breadth of love and how it can benefit oneself and others.

The concept of loving others matches well with the ethical principles embraced by the ACA (2014). These six ethical principles not only guide professional practice, but they describe different facets of treating others with care. Counselors are encouraged to collaborate with clients instead of giving directives; this protects the client's autonomy. Collaborating with a client means to work with them, to join with them. Counselors walk alongside their clients on a therapeutic journey; they do not walk ahead to lead their clients, nor do they walk behind to push their clients. Autonomy requires respect for others, caring for and desiring the best for the client, even when you do not agree with their choices.

Loving others means wanting the best for them, doing what you can to help them. This value is demonstrated within the ethical principle of beneficence (ACA, 2014). In their therapeutic journeys, clients may need help in learning new skills, considering different perspectives, or overcoming imposing challenges. Counselors provide this assistance and guidance, using their knowledge and skills to support clients in achieving their goals. In a similar manner, counselors are careful to limit risks to their clients and avoid harming them (i.e., nonmaleficence). Loving others may also mean taking action to minimize harm. When working with a client to limit harm, counselors may sometimes need to confront their clients about words or behaviors that are impairing progress or are perhaps self-inflicting additional wounds. Failing to act in these situations would not exemplify loving others.

The ethical principles of fidelity, justice, and veracity can also be found in love. Loving others means treating others with honesty and fairness and being dependable to them. If, as a counselor, you want what is best for clients (beneficence) and wish to avoid harming them (nonmaleficence), your actions must match your claims (fidelity). A true partnership with a client requires you to be honest and truthful (veracity) in the information you provide; if you hold back or misrepresent something, not only does it have the potential to harm the client, but it can also impair your relationship with the client. The same applies to treating the client with fairness: an equitable partnership with a client (justice) will not last if you do not deal fairly and honestly with the client, or if you are not faithful when working with the client. A lack of honesty and dependability may also prevent a client from making truly well-informed decisions (autonomy). While Jesus' call to love God and to love others was directed toward the religious leaders who were questioning him, these concepts are applicable in all relationships, both professional and personal. Jesus explains this in greater detail in what is commonly known as the "Sermon on the Mount" (Matthew 5), where he instructs the crowds of people listening to him about different and practical ways in which they can be kind to others, avoid sin, and remain faithful, honest, and dependable. In doing so, Jesus' words countered religious law, revealing how loving God and loving others often extends past what legal codes require, focusing more on the *spirit* of the law rather than stringently following the *code* of the law.

The Bible contains a well-known scripture passage that expresses the meaning of love. This scripture is often used at weddings, as a bride and groom express their feelings of love and commitment to one another. This short passage captures what it means to love God and love others:

> If I speak with the tongues of men and of angels, but do not have love, I have become a noisy gong or a clanging cymbal. If I have the gift of prophecy, and know all mysteries and all knowledge; and if I have all faith, so as to remove mountains, but do not have love, I am nothing. And if I give all my possessions to feed the poor, and if I surrender my body to be burned, but do not have love, it profits me nothing.
>
> Love is patient, love is kind and is not jealous; love does not brag and is not arrogant, does not act unbecomingly; it does not seek its own, is not provoked, does not take into account a wrong suffered, does not rejoice in unrighteousness, but rejoices with the truth; bears all things, believes all things, hopes all things, endures all things. (1 Corinthians 13:1-7)

These words, written by the Apostle Paul as a letter to the church in Corinth, are intended to express that even the greatest of skills and abilities are nothing if love is not a part of them. While affirming the benefits and necessity of the spiritual gifts (e.g., prophecy, speaking in tongues, revelation) that the Christians at Corinth were seeking, Paul explains in this letter that these gifts have no value if they are not used and given with love. The six ethical principles defined within the *ACA Code of Ethics* (2014) are similar: following them is good, but they are hollow values if not adhering to them with love for others.

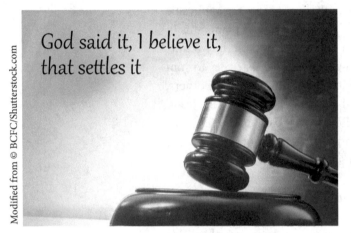

God said it, I believe it, that settles it

Modified from © BCFC/Shutterstock.com

Christian Values and Ethical Value Conflicts

While identifying love as the central Christian value, we have discussed how loving others fits within the ACA's (2014) six ethical principles. However, just as ethical principles may conflict in certain situations, Christian values may sometimes be in conflict with the counseling profession's ethical values. One reason for this is the source of authority for each group of values. Christians generally believe that the values of loving God and loving others are provided in sacred scripture as revealed by God. The sources of authority for the ethical principles of autonomy, beneficence, nonmaleficence, justice, fidelity, and veracity come from human thought, ethical reasoning, and cultural norms (Kitchener, 1984; Remley & Herlihy, 2016). It is important to make this distinction, since the significance we hold for our morals and values is typically based upon a source of authority – this provides a foundation for what we believe.

Knowing these authoritative sources is also importance since we want our values to be based in a foundation that is both reputable and consistent. Authoritative sources can also give prominence to one's views. An unfortunate byproduct of authoritative sources is that they can be used as a battering ram to demonstrate supremacy over competing views and values. The Apostle Paul warns us away from such foolishness (1 Corinthians 3).

All six of these ethical principles combine to provide a moral foundation to ethics codes. According to Remley and Herlihy (2016), additional ethical principles have been suggested as foundational to ethical standard, such as respect for persons, self-care, and reparations. Moreover, CAPS (2005) and AACC (2014) cite scripture and general revelation of God's will as higher sources of authority that underlie ethical standards. Articulating all of these moral foundations gives meaning and authority to professional ethical standards, offering overarching reasons for helping professionals to aspire to follow these principles and permitting these principles to guide their ethical decision-making. And while these ethical principles ideally have equal value, we must also acknowledge that ethical principles may conflict with each other in certain situations; counselors may face a difficult decision to determine which ethical principle takes priority. Urofsky, Engels, and Engebretson (2008) noted that "when principles conflict, the practitioner must carefully weigh, balance, sift, and winnow competing principles to determine which principle has precedence" (p. 68). It is in these situations where counselors may struggle, when circumstances do not align with ethical standards codes, or when experiencing values conflicts, requiring counselors to carefully determine the best way to respond.

WHAT ARE COUNSELORS' ETHICAL RESPONSIBILITIES?

Our primary responsibility as counselors is to practice the moral principle of beneficence. Remember, beneficence is the practice of placing the client's welfare first and our number one priority. Client welfare is the first ethical standard in the *ACA Code of Ethics* (2014). The standard reads, "The primary responsibility of counselors is to respect the dignity and promote the welfare of clients" (§A.1.a; ACA, 2014, p. 4). It is the counselor's job to protect the integrity of the counseling relationship and the counseling profession. By choosing this profession, you are assuming the responsibilities of meeting the ethical and legal standards of the profession, which includes making ethical decisions, protecting the rights of the clients, maintaining competency, fostering social change, establishing healthy boundaries, and understanding counseling legal and ethical issues.

We tend to become much more interested in and aware of ethics when facing a dilemma, or when the best response is not easily determined. Ethical dilemmas develop when events, behaviors, and/or intentions do not

© iQoncept/Shutterstock.com

fit nicely within our "right" and "wrong" categories, and we may struggle to conclude what the best response should be. These ethical challenges may arise from a variety of reasons: values conflicts, miscommunications and misunderstandings, differences in spiritual or religious beliefs, or perhaps even a lack of sensitivity to racial, ethnic, or cultural differences. In any of these situations, we may find it necessary to take a moment to reflect upon the dilemma, how it arose, and the best way to resolve it.

Ethical Decision-Making

Ethical dilemmas become quandaries simply because they represent situations that are not easily answered or when there is a conflict between two or more ethical standards. These dilemmas stretch us and require us to seek out the necessary information to find answers to our questions – all this to eventually discover that there is not necessarily a "correct" answer, but there is, perhaps, a "best" answer. Although some ethical concerns may appear relatively simple to understand, we need to refrain from asking "What's the right thing to do?" or even "What's the best thing to do?" Instead, the question should be "What *should* we do?" This question rightly focuses us on the moral implications that are involved. This brings us back to ethics, which is concerned with all three questions: not just whether to respond or the best way to respond, but how we should respond in order to satisfy the values underlying the ethical standards.

We must also consider the role of our personal values in ethical dilemmas. Accordingly, this demonstrates how ethics play a vital role in the professional preparation and practice of mental health counselors. Due to the ambiguous nature navigating interpersonal needs and differences and providing competent and professional care to others, counselors may often find themselves facing ethical dilemmas.

Profile of a Chemical Dependency Counselor
Michelle Pritchard, LPCC-S

As a Licensed Professional Clinical Counselor and Supervisor and as a Licensed Independent Chemical Dependency Counselor, Michelle Pritchard is the Director of Clinical Services at the Center for Addiction Treatment (https://www. catsober.org/). Michelle notes that when she began her journey as a new counselor, she found blending her Christian beliefs with her professional ethics to be challenging until she began to understand two concepts: 1) The way God works through her isn't always a direct approach, and 2) this work isn't about herself.

© Gary Kessler

Michelle believes that ethical literature, discussions, and boundaries should be focused on how decisions impact the client. Some questions she might ask include "How would the decision to accept a gift from a client affect the relationship dynamics? How would it affect the counselor's ability to remain objective?" Michelle's professional experiences tell her that the challenge with ethics is that the resolution to such a scenario may not be the same for each client. Michelle recalls when she was working with her first client who was a lifetime registered sex offender and who also needed substance abuse counseling. She remembers immediately feeling angry, because the mere thought of his actions were gut wrenching. However, when in supervision, she was asked a simple question: "Can you provide him substance abuse counseling?" The question allowed her to see his humanity and her spiritual purpose in his life: to provide him with the therapeutic services he was desperately seeking.

After having worked at the Center for Addiction Treatment for over six years, and as an independently licensed clinical supervisor and the Director of Clinical Services for the past three years, Michelle believes that ethics is the bedrock of every program developed, every supervision session, every meeting, and every community talk she gives. Further, she believes that it is essential to the functioning of a healthy counseling team and the implementation of quality treatment services.

Contributed by Michelle Pritchard. © Kendall Hunt Publishing Company.

In order to consistently address ethical dilemmas, an established framework or method must be employed to ensure that every ethical concern is reviewed in the same manner, even if it involves different ethical codes, different types of conflicts, and different situations. With these requirements in mind, ethical decision-making models were developed to assist helping professionals to consider all aspects of a given situation in order to make the best decision. Following each step in a defined ethical decision-making process helps counselors make well-informed decisions. As we begin to discuss various ethical decision-making models, including what we intend to accomplish through ethical decision-making, we must consider that most models follow the assumption that "the goal of ethical decision making is to minimize subjectivity" (Remley & Herlihy, 2016, p. 15). While this seems accurate, we must also acknowledge that ethical decision-making is inherently a subjective process, especially because counselors are sometimes called to give priority to one standard or principle over another. Thus, ethical dilemmas should not be determined and resolved in isolation; counselors are encouraged to consult with trusted colleagues and seek supervision. Further, counselors should involve clients in the ethical decision-making process; this empowers client self-determination and also adheres to ethical principles (Remley & Herlihy, 2016).

Ethical Decision-Making Models

As Kitchener (1984) suggested, "the ethical principles of autonomy, beneficence, nonmaleficence, fidelity, and justice constitute the foundation for critical evaluative level of ethical reasoning" (p. 44). These principles are, therefore, fundamental to developing guidelines for ethical decision-making. Employing these ethical principles and the ACA (2014) ethical standards within an established framework can help counselors resolve complex ethical concerns in a consistent manner. As such, a number of ethical decision-making models have been developed to address this need; we will discuss a few of them in this chapter.

While not provided as a model of ethical decision-making, Remley and Herlihy (2016) provide a set of guidelines to help counselors address ethical dilemmas. Similar to other models, these guidelines consist of a series of steps that counselors should follow in order to make well-informed and ethical decisions. Remley and Herlihy's (2016) suggestions consist of nine guidelines that reflect what commonly appears in most ethical decision-making models:

- Identify and define the problem.
- Involve your client in the decision-making process.
- Review relevant codes of ethics and the professional literature.
- Consider the principles and virtues.
- Tune in to your feelings.
- Consult with colleagues or experts.
- Consider the context.
- Identify desired outcomes and consider possible actions to achieve the outcomes.
- Choose and act on your choice. (pp. 16-17)

Even the most experienced counseling professionals may struggle with ethical decision-making. Their struggle is not from a lack of experience; instead, it comes from the challenge of navigating through a complex situation that may involve conflicting and competing standards and values. After making an ethical decision, a counselor may still question if he/she made the right choice. Before second-guessing one's decision, a counselor can also use several self-tests to determine if the best decision has been made before acting upon it.

Stadler (1986) suggested applying three tests to all ethical decisions. If the decision agrees with all three tests, then it should be considered a sound determination. However, if it does not pass one or more of the tests, then the counselor should reconsider the decision prior to acting upon it. The first test is *universality*, where the counselor should consider if he/she recommends the same decision-making process to another helping professional in a similar situation. The second test is *justice*, where the counselor should consider if he/she would treat others the same in a similar situation. The third test is *publicity*; in this test, a counselor should consider if he/she would share a decision with others, or if he/she would be concerned if this decision is widely published. Only when the counselor is satisfied with a decision, should he/she act upon it.

One of the most well-known ethical decision-making models is published by Forester-Miller and Davis (2016); this model consists of seven steps and requires consulting the *ACA Code of Ethics* (2014). You can find this ethical model steps in Figure 6.1. Endorsed by the American Counseling Association, this ethical decision-making model embeds Stadler's (1986) three tests within Step 6, encouraging counselors to consider all aspects of a decision prior to implementing it.

FIGURE 6.1

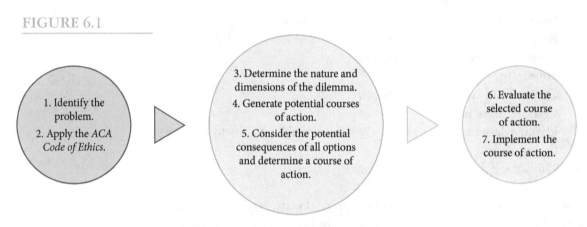

1. Identify the problem.
2. Apply the *ACA Code of Ethics*.

3. Determine the nature and dimensions of the dilemma.
4. Generate potential courses of action.
5. Consider the potential consequences of all options and determine a course of action.

6. Evaluate the selected course of action.
7. Implement the course of action.

Courtesy of Robyn Simmons; source: Forester-Miller & Davis, 2016, p.5

It is important for us to mention that a number of ethical decision-making models have been developed, and it is not our intention to recommend one model over another. Most ethical decision-making models contain similar features; their differences lie in associated details that may split steps in one model to another or include specific items. An example of this is the model proposed by Schmit, Schmit, Henesy, Klassen, and Oliver (2015); their integrative model, shown in Figure 6.2, blends Forester-Miller and Davis' (2016) model with the "Intercultural Model of Ethical Decision Making" developed by Luke, Goodrich, and Gilbride (2013). Schmit et al. (2015) asserted that Forest-Miller and Davis' (2016) model does not adequately address cultural, religious, and worldview factors, and that combining it with a model specifically addressing these factors alleviates this weakness. The blended model consists of eight steps:

FIGURE 6.2

Integrative Ethical Decision-Making Model

1. Awareness of the existence of a problem.
2. Identify the problem and corresponding culture, religious, and worldview factors.

3. Research, identify, and apply pertinent policies, procedures, and codes of ethics.
4. Consider the consequences of all options and determine a course of action.

5. Evaluation and follow through.
6. Examine the cultural, religious, and worldview factors related to each course of action.

7. Consider the consequences of all options and determine a course of action.
8. Evaluation and follow through.

Courtesy of Robyn Simmons; source: Forest-Miller & Davis, 2016

In your work as a counselor, you may find something similar: an existing ethical decision-making model does not fully address the specifics of your situation. New situations, such as the emergence of ever-changing technology, may require a proactive response. Further, as cultural norms change, you may find that shifting values no longer quite match your own. Flexibility when addressing ethical dilemmas, values and legal conflicts is necessary to navigate through complex and challenging situations.

FIGURE 6.3

Comparison of Ethical Decision-Making Models

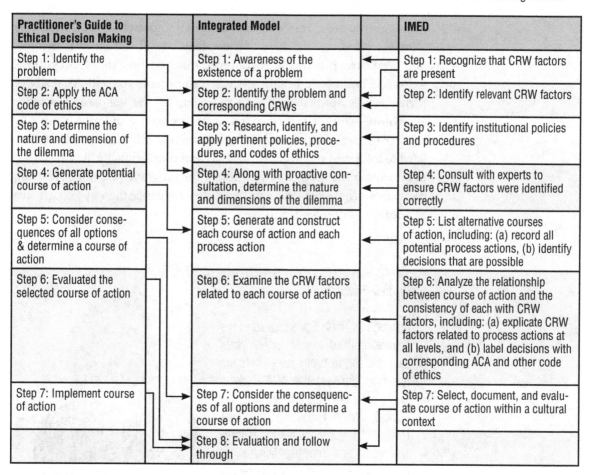

Practitioner's Guide to Ethical Decision Making	Integrated Model	IMED
Step 1: Identify the problem	Step 1: Awareness of the existence of a problem	Step 1: Recognize that CRW factors are present
Step 2: Apply the ACA code of ethics	Step 2: Identify the problem and corresponding CRWs	Step 2: Identify relevant CRW factors
Step 3: Determine the nature and dimension of the dilemma	Step 3: Research, identify, and apply pertinent policies, procedures, and codes of ethics	Step 3: Identify institutional policies and procedures
Step 4: Generate potential course of action	Step 4: Along with proactive consultation, determine the nature and dimensions of the dilemma	Step 4: Consult with experts to ensure CRW factors were identified correctly
Step 5: Consider consequences of all options & determine a course of action	Step 5: Generate and construct each course of action and each process action	Step 5: List alternative courses of action, including: (a) record all potential process actions, (b) identify decisions that are possible
Step 6: Evaluated the selected course of action	Step 6: Examine the CRW factors related to each course of action	Step 6: Analyze the relationship between course of action and the consistency of each with CRW factors, including: (a) explicate CRW factors related to process actions at all levels, and (b) label decisions with corresponding ACA and other code of ethics
Step 7: Implement course of action	Step 7: Consider the consequences of all options and determine a course of action	Step 7: Select, document, and evaluate course of action within a cultural context
	Step 8: Evaluation and follow through	

WHAT ARE COUNSELORS' LEGAL RESPONSIBILITIES?

Counselors are charged with understanding and staying abreast of legal issues that directly impact their work with clients and their legal responsibility to clients as a mental health professional. This is not a responsibility that you can take lightly. There can be serious repercussions for not abiding by the legal responsibilities you have to your client. Laws are often confusing and complicated, making them difficult to understand. Counselors abide by mental health laws passed by federal and state legislatures. The mental health laws passed are to protect the welfare of clients. Laws are a part of all aspects of the mental health field. You will need to learn how to identify and address legal issues in clinical practice.

Although you are required to have a general understanding of these laws, there are resources out there that can help you. If you are ever involved in a legal case, it is highly encouraged that you find an attorney that is well-versed in mental health laws who can provide you with legal advice, review legal cases that have set a precedent on the standard of practice, and consult with colleagues, counseling associations, and your liability insurance carrier. The purpose of this section is to introduce you to laws related to informed consent, malpractice, and confidentiality. It is important to remember that as you move through the program, you will be learning more about these key terms and how they influence the way you practice as a competent professional.

Portrait of a Professional Counselor
Dr. Jodie Edwards

© Jodie Edwards

Although Dr. Jodie Edwards entered the counseling field almost twenty years ago, she still distinctly remembers the first time she read the *ACA Code of Ethics* as a graduate student. She remarked, "When I read the Code line by line, I felt this immense sense of responsibility and some trepidation about the duty I had to uphold the numerous ethical considerations found in the Code. I knew I was a conscientious person, but I wondered if I would be able to adequately apply the guidelines in complicated, real-life situations." Jodie said she initially felt a heavy burden as she began to understand the gravity of the ethical dilemmas she might face.

Dr. Edwards earned her license as a Professional Clinical Counselor and Supervisor, she taught graduate counseling for 11 years, and then opened ThrivePointe, a group private practice (www.thrivepointe.com) in Ohio. Jodie says that a key strategy in becoming a confident, ethical therapist is realizing you can be well-prepared and you don't have to face ethical dilemmas on your own.

First, she focuses on the fact that the Code, along with state laws and rules, provides excellent direction to determine best practices and helps us to know when an ethical dilemma exists. Second, Jodie encourages counselors to utilize a systematic ethical decision-making model to thoroughly consider dilemmas and develop a strong rationale for actions taken. When she's facing a complicated dilemma, Jodie says she finds it helpful to write out all of the information about the ethical issues involved, including the positives and negatives of each possible course of action. Third, Jodie emphasizes seeking support from peers and supervisors throughout the ethical decision-making process; she notes, "None of us should ever feel like we are alone in processing difficult situations. We can turn to trusted colleagues, the American Counseling Association, our licensing board, and our malpractice insurance company for assistance in determining the best way to apply the Code of Ethics."

Contributed by Jodie Edwards. © Kendall Hunt Publishing Company.

Informed Consent

Before entering into any therapeutic relationship with a client, counselors are ethically, and in most states legally required to inform clients of their rights, the counselor's rights and policies, and any state and federal laws the counselors are mandated to follow in a written document. Counselors cannot assume that clients have a working knowledge of how counseling works or the implications of entering into a therapeutic relationship. According to the ACA (2014), the informed consent should include, but not be limited, to the following:

> The purposes, goals, techniques, procedures, limitations, potential risks, and benefits of services; the counselor's qualifications, credentials, relevant experience, and approach to counseling; continuation of services upon the incapacitation or death of the counselor; the role of technology; and other pertinent information. Counselors take steps to ensure that clients understand the implications of diagnosis and the intended use of tests and reports. Additionally, counselors inform clients about fees and billing arrangements, including procedures for

nonpayment of fees. Clients have the right to confidentiality and to be provided with an explanation of its limits (including how supervisors and/or treatment or interdisciplinary team professionals are involved), to obtain clear information about their records, to participate in the ongoing counseling plans, and to refuse any services or modality changes and to be advised of the consequences of such refusal. (§A.2.b; p. 4)

This document is referred to as the "Informed Consent" (ACA, 2014; Anderson, 1992; Welfel, 2013). The informed consent is a legal document; it is a representation and introduction of you and your practice to the client. The client should have the information needed to make an informed decision to consent for treatment. The informed consent is developed to protect you and the client. The informed consent is a working document, and it should remain a part of the therapeutic process. Counselors use the informed consent to hold the client and themselves accountable. It helps to maintain the integrity of the therapeutic relationship. The informed consent should not just be filed away in a client's chart but should be used throughout treatment to ensure that the agreement is upheld by the counselor and the client. For example, if a client repeatedly fails to appropriately cancel appointments, you can refer to the informed consent to remind the client of the cancellation policy.

Informed consents are also used in research as well as supervisory relationships (ACA, 2014). As a student, you will enter in a supervisory relationship with your site supervisor as well as with a faculty member while engaging in field experience. You will continue with supervision after completing the program for post-graduate supervision to obtain hours for licensure. The content of the informed consent for supervision is similar to the informed consent you would provide a client. The supervisory informed consent introduces the supervisor's supervision model, identifies the roles and responsibilities of the supervisee as well as the supervisor, and explains the process of evaluating the supervisee's clinical practice. The informed consent for supervision is also a working document that should be included throughout the supervisory relationship.

Client Confidentiality

Confidentiality is the foundation of the therapeutic relationship. Clients have to trust that counselors will protect their privacy by not sharing what is disclosed in therapy (ACA, 2014). The United States Supreme Court supported confidentiality in counseling, recognizing that it was essential for the success of the therapeutic process and treatment (Jaffee v. Redmond, 1996). Confidentiality is protected by state and federal laws and ethical standards. Counselors are not just protecting information that is shared in session, but also safeguarding against undue disclosure that the client is participating in counseling as well as maintaining the security of the client's records. There are times when you may be forced to break confidentiality. This is referred to as *limits of confidentiality*. Laws also mandate the limits of confidentiality. Counselors must inform and ensure that clients understand the limits of confidentiality (ACA, 2014). Counselors are required to break confidentiality when they become aware of suspected abuse and when a client poses an imminent threat to self or others. A client knowingly exposing people to life-threatening diseases, such as HIV and AIDS, may also be considered an imminent threat to others (VandeCreek, Knapp, & Brace, 1990) based on varying state laws and ethical guidelines.

The most well-known limitation on confidentiality is when clients pose an imminent threat to themselves or to others. The case of Tarasoff vs. Regents of the University of California (1976) set the precedent of legally requiring counselors to warn potential victims once it has been assessed that the client poses an imminent threat to others. It is essential to review your own state's laws regarding the duty to warn because not all states have a Duty to Warn law. Some states have similar laws such as a Duty to Protect or a Duty to Treat or have different standards regarding the duty to warn; therefore, knowledge of your own state's laws is necessary before deciding to break confidentiality. If there is no state law regarding duty to warn, you will rely on ethical codes to help address the dilemma.

Client Privilege

Privileged communication relates to laws that prevent counselors from sharing a client's confidential information in court. Clients have the right to use privilege to prevent counselors from sharing any information obtained in counseling in a court of law (Knapp & VandeCreek, 2012). Although client privilege sounds similar in theory to confidentiality, they are fundamentally different. It is important that you do not confuse the two in practice. Privileged communication is a legal term, whereas confidentiality is an ethical term that describes professional conduct.

Privilege belongs to the client, and the client can waive it at any time by authorizing the counselor to disclose information to the court of law (Hopkins & Anderson, 1990). There are different ways a counselor may have to address privilege: 1) a client or the client's legal representation acting on the behalf of their client may ask the counselor to testify about the client and/ or their participation in services; 2) a client automatically waives privilege if they file a lawsuit or formal board complaint against their counselor; or 3) if a counselor receives a subpoena or a court order to testify about their client.

A *subpoena* is a legal document or order requiring a practitioner to appear or testify in court on a certain day and time and/or to release client documents. This can be issued by the clerk of court and is often signed by an attorney. If the subpoena is not court ordered, practitioners may not be legally required to respond and could simply ignore the request. The state's law may prohibit a practitioner from testifying, but the request informs a practitioner that a party has brought forth a motion to compel that practitioner to release documents and/or to testify. However, if the subpoena is signed by a judge or magistrate, it indicates that the judge or magistrate has considered the motion and is now ordering the counselor to comply (APA, 2011, 2016). Practitioners are legally required to respond to a court order. When faced with the decision to breach privilege, it is still the counselor's responsibility to do what is best for the client to prevent harm to the client.

If you receive a subpoena or a court order, you want to apply these following steps:
1. Know the state's mental health and confidentiality laws.
2. Contact the client to discuss the subpoena or court order.
3. Share potential risks and harm due to complying with client (document any concerns shared).
4. After the concerns are addressed and the client still wants the information released, have the client sign a release of information. Release of information needs to be specific to the subpoena or court order.
5. Out of state court orders or subpoenas may not be valid; seek legal consultation.
6. Refer to ethical and legal obligations of counselors as provided for under ethics codes, professional standards, state, federal, or local laws, or regulatory agencies.
7. Seek legal advice from an attorney well-versed in mental health laws (ACA, 2014; APA, 2011, 2016).

If you breach confidentiality either intentionally or unintentionally, you are putting yourself at risk for a malpractice lawsuit. You also want to make sure you are acting in the best interest of your client and not making a decision without being informed of your rights as a counselor.

Competency

As students, when you take a course, you have faith that your professor is competent to teach that course. If not, would the university allow them to teach it, or how would they have earned a doctorate degree? This faith can be applied to any profession. This is the same for medical doctors, carpenters, dentists, teachers, and caregivers. Clients have that same trust and assumption of competency in counselors. A competent counselor has the skills, training, diligence, abilities, and knowledge to provide effective counseling (ACA, 2014; Spruill et al., 2004; Welfel, 2013). A counselor-in-training shows competency not only by meeting the academic standards, but also by demonstrating maturity and professionalism. Students are also assessed for personal dispositional issues that may become roadblocks to the goal of entering into the counseling profession.

Dispositions are defined as values, moral principles, attitudes, and behaviors needed to become a competent counselor (Spurgeon, Gibbons, & Cochran, 2012). These dispositions are often described as the student's level of maturity, ability to show empathy, respect, and openness towards others, ability to demonstrate self-awareness and accept personal responsibility for behaviors, and evidence of resiliency and humility (Hensley, Smith, & Thompson, 2003). Dispositional concerns are often identified as problematic behaviors. These problematic behaviors may present themselves as areas of concern: mental health impairment, lack of self-awareness, unresolved personal issues, and unethical and/or illegal behaviors (Henderson & Dufrene, 2012).

In your graduate counseling program, faculty, leadership, and your site supervisor will equip you with the tools you need and assess your competence and readiness to work in the field of counseling. Furthermore, their role in your academic journey is referred to as *gatekeepers* of the profession. Simply put, *gatekeeping* is defined as a way for counselor educators to determine if you are a good fit for the profession (Vacha-Haase, Davenport, & Kerewsky, 2004). This assessment begins at the time of admission until the end of your program. If remediation is deemed necessary at any point of a student's program, faculty and university leadership are legally and ethically obligated to provide an opportunity for remediation before making a final recommendation for readiness (ACA, 2014; CACREP, 2016; Lambie & Ascher, 2016).

Working towards competency does not end after the program. The pursuit of competence is ongoing. After program completion, you have a basic counseling competency to practice in the field. If you choose to achieve competency in targeted areas of counseling, you are required to gain additional knowledge, receive training, and practice under supervision (ACA, 2014). It is essential to understand that competency in one area of the counseling profession does not necessarily mean that you are competent in another area. Counseling professionals are ethically responsible for assessing their own level of competency and ensuring that they are not practicing outside their scope of proficiency (ACA, 2014).

Counseling Boundaries

The nature of a counseling relationship can be viewed as an intimate relationship. It is a relationship built on trust, a level of intimacy, and vulnerability. It is challenging to compare mental health relationships to any other professional relationships. Clients share their darkest secrets with counselors weekly behind closed doors or often in the comfort of their own homes. Because of this intimacy, there is also a level of vulnerability shared by both the counselor and the client. Counselors need to recognize and respect the power differential and the vulnerability that exists in the counseling relationship, and, because of the power differential and vulnerability, it is important to establish boundaries (Aravind, Krishnaram, & Thasneem, 2012). Knapp and VandeCreek (2012) define boundaries as the "rules of the professional relationship that set it apart from other relationships" that "clarify which behaviors are appropriate and inappropriate in psychotherapy" (p. 87).

The counselor-client relationship is a professional relationship, and it is the counselor's responsibility to establish and maintain boundaries to protect the welfare of the client, the counselor, and the integrity of the profession (Brennan, 2013). Boundaries are established to define the roles in the therapeutic relationship and reduce the risk of client exploitation, and they also provide an opportunity to model appropriate behaviors for clients. Establishing boundaries educates and empowers the client to know when a counselor is crossing the line; they provide clients with the insight of what is acceptable and unacceptable behavior in a counseling relationship. Boundaries decrease a client's vulnerability and increase the counselor's accountability.

Boundaries are not always clear-cut. Counselors rely upon the *ACA Code of Ethics* (2014) for guidance regarding resolving boundary issues. However, these are only guidelines, and only a very few are black and white. For example, the ethics code makes it clear that counselors do not engage in sexual and/or romantic relationships with clients or their family members (see §A.5.a; ACA, 2014).

On the other hand, there are areas in the code that are not so clear cut, such as whether or not the counselor should engage in non-sexual relationships (see §A.6; ACA, 2014). Dual relationships have been a topic of discussion and debate amongst counselors and other mental health professionals. A *dual relationship* (or multiple relationship) is defined as having interactions or a relationship with a client outside of the therapeutic relationship; this relationship can be personal or professional (Graham & Liddle, 2009; Herlihy & Corey, 2015). Counselors have argued that engaging in a dual relationship with a client can do more good than harm to the client (Remley & Herlihy, 2016; Moleski & Kiselica, 2005; Zur, 2007). Other areas of the code that are not so clear cut include gift giving, receiving gifts, hugging, and attending special events such as graduations (see §§A.10.e-f; ACA, 2014). In all these instances, the benefit should always be for the client and should remain within ethical and legal guidelines. The decision to engage in boundary crossing with a client is usually a professional value or preference that counselors have based on their own training, professional experiences, or theoretical orientation. If a counselor is uncertain regarding if a boundary crossing is ethical or acceptable behavior, the counselor needs to refer to the code of ethics, assess for potential client harm, seek consultation from a colleague, and engage in supervision from a supervisor.

Counselor Burnout and Impairment

The essence of a counselor is to help others in need and to assist clients with their personal problems or challenges. The job of helping others can often be stressful and demanding; it is difficult not to be impacted by the pain of clients (Linton & O'Halloran, 2000). A counselor with self-awareness is clear about their own needs and the needs of their clients, and can separate the personal from the professional; they will find themselves doing what is best for themselves and their clients (Gladding, 2009). Counselors often become so entrenched in their role as a helping professional that they become less aware of their own needs and put themselves at risk for burnout. *Burnout* is defined as "a psychological syndrome of emotional exhaustion, depersonalization, and reduced personal accomplishment that can occur among individuals who work with other people in some capacity" (Maslach, 1993, p. 20).

The therapeutic relationship alone can cause burnout, but there are other contributing factors, such as poor boundaries, poor physical and mental health, interpersonal issues, and poor self-care (Pines & Maslach, 1978). Additionally, unchecked client caseloads, competitive job markets, decreases in funding for mental health, long working hours, and a poor salary may also contribute to counselor burnout (Vilardaga et al., 2011). There are clear signs of burnout that alert a counselor that they are significantly impacted by their job responsibilities. These signs include chronic fatigue, self-criticism, uncontrollable anger, lack of interest in the profession, feelings of helplessness, and missing work. Some counselors can quickly overcome bouts of burnout by addressing their needs through proper self-care, utilizing their support system, and taking care of their mental and physical health needs. However, there are some counselors that have poor self-awareness and fail to act. If counselors are unable to address or prevent burnout, they are at risk of experiencing impairment.

Counselor impairment is described as the inability to manage personal stress, mental health, substance abuse, and medical issues that interfere with professional functioning, posing a threat to client safety (Lamb et al., 1987; Lambie & Young, 2007). According to the *ACA Code of Ethics* (2014), it is the counselor's ethical responsibility to assess and monitor themselves for impairment and stop providing services to clients until they have addressed what is causing the impairment (see §C.2.g.). There are many ways to address impairment. Counselors often will make a decision to engage in counseling. Engaging in counseling allows the impaired counselor an opportunity to address their own mental health issues and needs. State licensing boards offer impaired professional programs for counselors who have been cited by the board for unchecked mental health or substance abuse issues. These programs are meant to help the counselor re-enter the field of practice. In addition, the impaired counselor can make a decision to engage in a wellness program (supervision, seeking a support group, consultation group, exercising, and eating healthy) to combat impairment (Corey, Corey, Corey, & Callanan, 2015; Warren, Morgan, Morris, & Morris, 2010).

As a counselor-in-training, you are learning how to help others. It is imperative that you also start learning how to take care of yourself during this process (Grier, Hanson, & Skovholt, 2001). Developing and adopting a self-care plan early in your training is a way to help minimize burnout and lower your risk of impairment. A self-care plan should not be viewed as a one-time plan to address burnout; instead, it should be viewed as a way of life. It is a lifestyle that you want to adopt so that you can remain healthy while completing this program. Students are encouraged to build a support system of other mental health counseling students, talk to your academic and faculty advisors, and utilize your supports such as the writing center, library resources, and your spiritual family.

A Note from a University Clinical Training Director
Dr. Maranda Griffin
Walden University

© Maranda Griffin

Counseling professionals spend a considerable amount of time delivering direct services; whether it be individual, couples, family, or group counseling. I like to consider this as pouring ourselves out. A quote that speaks to this is, "you can't pour from an empty cup." For me, this means we cannot practice in a competent and ethical manner when we neglect to care for ourselves. Counselors and counselors in training (CIT), have an ethical responsibility to self-care. Inattention to self-care and wellness can result in professional behavior and disposition concerns and compromise our primary responsibility to promote the welfare of those we serve. Dispositional concerns can occur at any point within graduate training and throughout our professional career. Therefore, attention to professional behavior and dispositions is important.

Our accreditation standards and professional codes of ethics require assessment and evaluation of dispositions. Multiple tools exist to assess problematic behavior. As a counselor or CIT, we are to self-assess for dispositional concerns by monitoring for signs of impairment. Self-assessment for impairment can be challenging when our capacity to do so is diminished. Once identified, whether that be based on self-assessment, peer identification, faculty or counseling supervisor evaluation, support and remediation are available. If left unaddressed, dispositional concerns threaten academic progress, degree completion, impact client care, and place student, university, and agencies at risk for legal consequences. Given this potential, to keep our cup at an optimal level, we must be intentional and consciously commit to self-care, daily.

Counselor Malpractice

It is not unthinkable that counselors could be fearful of receiving a malpractice lawsuit or malpractice complaints to the licensing board from a client. Counseling faculty are frequently asked by students and both novice and seasoned professionals about lawsuits. It is a valid concern based on the nature of our profession. The response is always the same: the lawsuit or the complaint should not be the cause of the worry, but rather the concern should be about your actions while counseling the client. The reality is that clients can file a lawsuit or a complaint against you at any time; this is their right. It does not mean the client has a legal case or a valid reason to sue or file a lawsuit against you. It also does not mean you did anything wrong. Sometimes, clients threaten to file a lawsuit or a complaint out of anger.

Counselors are ethically and sometimes legally required to provide clients with the steps they need to follow to file a complaint against you in the informed consent. The focus should be on the counselor's actions. Did they practice without an informed consent? Did they apply the six moral principles? Did they maintain boundaries? Did they breach confidentiality or privilege? Because of the nature of the therapeutic relationship, there are so many potential areas for counselors to fall short. The key is to ensure that counselors are practicing within ethical and legal guidelines.

Here are some suggestions to minimize the risk of malpractice:
- Maintain appropriate boundaries.
- Follow the guidelines and expectations defined in the informed consent.
- Practice Self-care.
- Do not practice as a lone wolf (consult and seek supervision) when faced with an ethical decision.
- Solicit and provide opportunity for client feedback.
- Do not practice beyond the scope of practice.
- Document and Maintain accurate and timely records. If it is not documented, it did not happen.
- Continue with training and education.

Malpractice (or professional liability) is when a professional's actions or lack thereof have caused harm to a client. A malpractice lawsuit or claim is a civil lawsuit filed by a client who believes a professional has harmed them by offering incorrect or negligent advice, or by breaching the professional standard of care (Remley & Herlihy, 2016). Counselors protect themselves by purchasing malpractice or professional liability insurance. As students, you are required to maintain malpractice to begin field experiences.

Case Study

Jonas is a mental health counselor-in-training (CT) who is completing an internship experience at a university counseling center, located on the campus where he is a student. When assisting with client intakes, Jonas meets Heidi, an undergraduate student who is seeking counseling to complete a personality assessment that is required for an elementary education course in which she is enrolled. In the intake, Heidi reports no mental health concerns; she only wants to complete the personality assessment for her class. Jonas quickly completes the intake with Heidi and promises her that a counselor will contact her soon. After she leaves, Jonas processes the intake and assigns her case to Jennifer, another CT working at the counseling center; within a few days, Jennifer sets an appointment with Heidi. Knowing this, and finding Heidi extremely attractive, Jonas retrieves her contact information from Heidi's case file and calls her to ask for a date. On their first date,

Jonas tells Heidi how he obtained her phone number and explains he would never again look in her file. Heidi says she is not concerned, since she is only completing an assessment for a class assignment. A couple weeks later, Jennifer spots Jonas and Heidi having a lunch date at a local sandwich shop and confronts him about it in the office. Jonas states that he is not dating a client, so nothing is wrong; Jennifer disagrees since Jonas completed the intake and reports this to Jonas' supervisor.

Exploring the Case Study
Some ethical dilemmas may appear not to have a solution. If we consider a case study as though it were a static situation, we may struggle to discover a resolution or determine a course of action. Fortunately, a counselor's work with their clients rarely prevents attempting intervention; the counseling process presents ongoing opportunities to continue discussions of an ethical concern, present alternative perspectives, and challenge the client. So, do not consider this case study as occurring within a vacuum; consider what you know from the case study and what else you would like to know. Consider what additional questions you might like to ask this client. Consider possible reasons the client may be struggling in this situation. List out the next steps, what you might do if you are working with this client.

This case study is a good example of a situation where someone is grappling with competing values: 1) trying to balance romantic interests with professional ethical obligations; 2) having an interest in dating someone who is a client where you work; 3) wondering whether completing an intake makes someone your client; 4) debating if someone seeking counseling for a class assignment really makes them a client; and 5) using clinical resources to obtain confidential client information for personal reasons. There may also be additional concerns that Jonas does not know how to articulate. In this situation, the supervisor must attend to all of these values and concerns, assisting Jonas to resolve these inner conflicts, as well as upholding any applicable legal and ethical obligations of the counseling profession – namely, the ethical obligation to avoid romantic relationships with clients.

First, we recommend selecting an ethical decision-making model to follow. Most ethical decision-making models are comparable and follow similar steps; the most important consideration is to carefully follow the model to ensure you are making a well-informed decision. We also recommend that you do not make such ethical decisions by yourself: consult with your supervisor and/or some trusted colleagues. In this case study, Jonas may have avoided potential ethics violations by immediately speaking to his supervisor prior to acting upon his attraction to Heidi. So, we encourage proceeding cautiously when you encounter ethical dilemmas. Further, when working through such dilemmas, we do not recommend one ethical decision-making model over another; for the purposes of this case study, we will use the Practitioner's Guide to Ethical Decision-Making (Forester-Miller & Davis, 2016), which is also endorsed by the American Counseling Association. As we go through this model, consider what information you would like to know, or how you might envision working with this client.

1. Identify the Problem

The first step is to identify all the problems and concerns in the case study. We recommend creating a list of these concerns, which will be helpful as you work through the following steps. As we review the case study, it is important not to confuse attraction with behavior – or in the case of a client's situation, not confusing the presenting problem(s) with the ethical dilemma. While these may be (or become) the same thing, we need to be careful not to make this assumption. Going back to the case study, we note that Jonas' attraction to Heidi is not an ethical violation, but it does present an ethical dilemma. The potential for an ethical violation comes from acting upon something; carefully considering the ethical dilemma is what we recommend – this helps us determine the best course of action. In this case study, Jonas acted before fully considering the potential ethical concerns.

Going back to the case study, we can identify several ethical concerns. First, Jonas' intentionally assigned Heidi to another counselor so she would not be officially assigned to him as a client. Other ethical concerns involve: a) accessing a client file that is not assigned to him, thereby disregarding client privacy; b) retrieving confidential client information for personal use; c) developing a romantic relationship with someone he knows within the context of a client; and d) failure to consult with a supervisor regarding a potential ethical dilemma. Do you believe any other ethical concerns are present? If so, be sure to include them in your list. Now that we have identified the ethical concerns, we can move to the next step in this decision-making model.

2. Apply the *ACA Code of Ethics*

With our list of potential ethical concerns, we can match these concerns with current ethical codes. In this example, and since this text is designed for counselors, we will use the *ACA Code of Ethics* (2014) – just note that other ethical codes can be applied as well. To ease our discussion, we will list the ethical concerns alongside a list of application ethical codes. Another important note is that ethical codes will not always provide sufficient assistance in resolving an ethical dilemma; some situations are just too complex. In these types of situations, the counselor should obtain what information they can from the ethics codes and then proceed into the subsequent steps of the decision-making process presented in this model.

a. Intentionally assigning an intake to another counselor so the client would not be officially assigned to Jonas as a client.

§A.6.d – Role Changes in the Professional Relationship

While Heidi was not assigned to Jonas as a client, he served in the capacity of completing an intake with her. There is a reasonable expectation that Jonas may serve as her counselor. This ethical guideline might be of concern if it is determined that Jonas deliberately withheld information from the client with the intention to seek out a romantic relationship with her.

§D.1.f – Personnel Selection and Assignment

Jonas does not appear to be in a supervisory position over Jennifer; however, it seems that he is able to assign clients to other therapists. There is a potential ethical dilemma if Jonas is able to assign clients in a manner that specifically benefits himself.

§F.5.a – Ethical Responsibilities

This ethical standard indicates that all items contained within the *ACA Code of Ethics* (2014) apply to students and supervisees, just as they apply to licensed counselors. Therefore, Jonas has an obligation to determine if his actions adhere to these ethical guidelines. Being a student and counselor-in-training does not mean the *ACA Code of Ethics* (2014) does not apply.

b. Accessing a client file that is assigned to a different counselor, which disregards client privacy.

§B.1.b – Respect for Privacy

According to the *ACA Code of Ethics* (2014), counselors must "respect the privacy of prospective and current clients" (p. 6). As counselors should only seek private information that is deemed helpful to counseling, there could be an ethical dilemma if Jonas sought information having more to do with his attraction to Heidi rather than her reasons for seeking counseling.

§B.3.a – Subordinates

All employees of a counseling agency must adhere to confidentiality and privacy policies. While it does not appear that Jonas is in a supervisory position over other counselors or staff, he must still follow these policies as an employee. By accessing the client file of another counselor, he may have violated the client's privacy and confidentiality rights. There are certainly valid reasons for accessing another counselor's client files, but doing so for personal benefit would likely not be a justifiable reason.

§B.6.b – Confidentiality of Records and Documentation

According to this ethical standard, all client information should remain confidential, and only authorized persons should be able to access this information. While it appears that Jonas is one such authorized person, which is likely necessary for him to fulfill his work responsibilities, it is also probable that he is not authorized to access information about clients assigned to other counselors, unless specific criteria are met (e.g., client or counselor emergency, etc.). By accessing Heidi's information, Jonas likely violated a workplace policy, as well as violated the "spirit" of this ethical standard.

§D.1.e – Confidentiality

Since it appears that Jonas serves in more than one role at his internship placement site (e.g., intake worker, counselor), this should be clarified with Heidi at the time of her intake interview. It does not appear that Jonas provided this information to Heidi, and it presents a potential ethical dilemma.

§F.5.a – Ethical Responsibilities

Related to our discussion of Jonas' actions, we must revisit this ethical standard, since it states that all items contained within the *ACA Code of Ethics* (2014) apply to students and supervisees, not just licensed counselors. Therefore, as previously stated, Jonas has an obligation to determine if his actions adhere to this ethical guideline: as a counselor-in-training working at an internship placement site, the *ACA Code of Ethics* (2014) fully apply to Jonas and this situation.

c. Obtaining confidential client information for personal use.

§B.1.c – Respect for Confidentiality

According to the *ACA Code of Ethics* (2014), counselors must "protect the confidential information of prospective and current clients" (p. 7). It is arguable that Jonas maintained confidentiality by not revealing any of Heidi's information. However, because he obtained this information for personal benefit, and for a reason that is a potential ethical violation, his actions present an ethical dilemma regarding maintaining confidentiality with Heidi's private information.

§B.3.a – Subordinates

All employees of a counseling agency must adhere to confidentiality and privacy policies. While it does not appear that Jonas is in a supervisory position over other counselors or staff, he must still follow these policies as an employee. By accessing the client file of another counselor, he may have violated the client's privacy and confidentiality rights. There are certainly valid reasons for accessing another counselor's client files, but doing so for personal benefit would likely not be a justifiable reason.

§B.6.b – Confidentiality of Records and Documentation

This ethical standard also applies to this potential ethical dilemma, since Jonas specifically sought Heidi's confidential information for personal use. As previously stated, it does not appear that Jonas has revealed Heidi's contact information (the information he obtained) to anyone else. So, while Jonas' actions present a possible ethical violation, Heidi's confidentiality seems to remain. There is still justifiable concern if client information is obtained and used for personal benefit.

§D.1.e – Confidentiality

Because Jonas appears to serve in more than one role at his internship placement site (e.g., intake worker, counselor), he is obligated to explain to Heidi during the intake about his multiple roles. If this information was not provided to Heidi, then it presents a potential ethical dilemma.

§F.5.a – Ethical Responsibilities

A rationale for this ethical standard was previously addressed and is applicable for this potential ethical dilemma.

d. Developing a romantic relationship with someone Jonas knows within the context of a client.

§A.5.a – Sexual and/or Romantic Relationships Prohibited

Jonas states that because Heidi is not assigned to him as a client, then he is not forbidden from having a romantic relationship with her. Still, there is potential ethical dilemma, since Jonas works at the site where Heidi is receiving services, he completed Heidi's intake information, and he has access to Heidi's confidential information. An ethical dilemma exists because there are several noted potential ethical concerns.

§F.5.a – Ethical Responsibilities

A rationale for this ethical standard was previously addressed and is applicable for this potential ethical dilemma.

e. Failing to consult with a supervisor regarding a potential ethical dilemma.

§C.1 – Knowledge of and Compliance with Standards

This standard notes that counselors are responsible to know and comply with the *ACA Code of Ethics* (2014). While this standard does not imply an ethical violation, it does indicate that Jonas has an obligation to determine and demonstrate that his actions are ethically sound.

§C.2.e – Consultations on Ethical Obligations

Building upon §C.1, this ethical standard notes that counselors should seek consultation regarding any potential ethical dilemmas. Due to the nature of this situation, it would be best for Jonas to consult with his supervisor prior to acting upon his attraction to Heidi. So, while it is possible that Jonas' action may be determined as ethically sound, he did not consult with his supervisor before acting.

§F.1.a – Client Welfare

Because supervisors have an obligation to ensure their supervisees are in compliance with ethical standards, Jonas' supervisor may be justifiably concerned that Jonas' actions are a possible risk to client welfare. Building upon §C.2.e, consultation with his supervisor before acting could avoid a possible ethical violation.

§F.4.c – Standards for Supervisees

Just as Jonas has an ethical obligation to follow applicable standards in the *ACA Code of Ethics* (2014), his supervisor has an ethical obligation to explain the ethical code to Jonas. While we do not know if Jonas' supervisor has addressed the *ACA Code of Ethics* (2014) with him, by not consulting first with his supervisor, Jonas has prevented his supervisor from discussing his ethical dilemma and discussing application standards with him.

§F.5.a – Ethical Responsibilities
A rationale for this ethical standard was previously addressed and is applicable for this potential ethical dilemma.

Did you identify any other ethical standards that apply to this case study? If so, include them in your list and provide a rationale. It is best to take a conservative approach to identifying applicable ethical standards. Subsequent steps in this decision-making model will continue to address the ethical standards, so any standards that are later determined as non-applicable can be removed. With our list of ethical standards, we can apply them to the ethical dilemmas.

3. Determine the Nature and Dimensions of the Dilemma

As we go through applicable ethical standards, we can determine if they provide an appropriate answer to the ethical dilemma(s). If not, then we should proceed to this step to further evaluate the dilemma, apply relevant ethical codes, and review the associated ethical principles. Forester-Miller and Davis (2016, p. 3) provide four items to consider at this point, if the ethical dilemma is not resolved:

· * Examine the ethical dilemmas implications for each of the ethical principles: autonomy, beneficence, nonmaleficence, justice, fidelity, and veracity.

 * Review relevant professional literature to ensure that you are using current professional thinking and are aware of any diversity issues involved in this situation.

· * Consult with experienced counselors or supervisors who follow the *ACA Code of Ethics* (2014).

· * Consult with your state or national professional associations to see if they can provide any additional assistance with the dilemma.

The purpose of considering these four items is to gather additional information that may help us resolve these concerns. The first item asks us to refer to the six ethical principles that form the foundational values underlying the *ACA Code of Ethics* (2014). Remember that the ethical principles are aspirational in nature and may not directly fit our ethical dilemmas; however, it may be helpful to consider these principles within the context of Heidi's situation. Although she is not seeking services for a mental health concern, she is seeking a legitimate counseling service that defines her as a client at a university counseling center.

Searching through current, related professional publications may also provide insight into these ethical dilemmas. In doing so, we must ensure that we are seeking information from legitimate, professional, and preferably peer-reviewed resources. With a wide variety of information that is readily available, we must only utilize resources that represent "best practices" from the counseling profession. Further, as previously noted within our review of applicable ethical standards, we noted the importance of consulting with one's supervisor or a trusted and experienced counselor. Forester-Miller and Davis' (2016) third suggestion is to consult with more experienced counselors. Due to their greater experiences and training, they may be able to provide a proper resolution for one's ethical dilemma. Finally, Forester-Miller and Davis (2016) suggest contacting professional organization for assistance. One such option is consulting with the ACA Center for Policy, Practice, and Research (https://www.counseling.org/knowledge-center/ethics#consult). This service is designed to assist ACA members in ethical dilemmas related to counseling practice. Note that this service does not provide legal counsel, nor should it be used as a hotline; instead, it is designed to provide additional assistance to counselors in resolving ethical dilemmas.

4. Generate Potential Courses of Action

As we reach this step in the ethical decision-making model, we may develop potential courses of action. By reaching this step, we are likely considering a complex ethical dilemma that may have several possible resolutions. For example, a potential resolution to our case study is for Jonas to end his relationship with Heidi. It is unlikely that Jonas (and maybe Heidi) would be happy with this solution – however, it arguably would resolve almost all of the identified ethical dilemmas (inappropriate access of confidential information is likely to be addressed in a different manner). As we brainstorm different courses of action, we should develop a list of all possibilities, no matter how we may feel about them. The purpose of this step in this decision-making model is to create a list of all options; we will evaluate the appropriateness and practicality of each course of action in the upcoming steps.

5. Consider the Potential Consequences of All Options and Determine a Course of Action

After completing a list of possible courses of action, we can also list out potential consequences for each option. As we review all our options, we may find that some are not practical, lead to undesirable consequences, or may even violate additional ethical standards. As we noted in Step 4, one course of action is for Jonas to end his relationship with Heidi. Potential consequences of this action include resolving several ethical concerns, avoiding disciplinary actions for ethical violations, hurt feelings, loss of relationships, termination of services, and anger over ignoring ethical standards that could prevent this situation. Do you have additional consequences to add to this list? If so, be sure to include them.

Once we have considered the potential consequences of each course of action, we can remove the ones that do not fit, or are incomplete, or may result in undesirable consequences. We certainly do not want to employ a course of action that will lead to additional problems! From the options that remain, we may select Plan A, Plan B, and so on. Further, it is important to note that resolving an ethical dilemma may not prevent other consequences from occurring. In our case study example, if it is determined that Jonas has violated professional ethical standards, he may be disciplined by his internship placement site, as well as by the counseling program in which he is enrolled, regardless if he ends his relationship with Heidi. Once we are satisfied with our options, we can move into the next step to further evaluate what is the best course of action.

6. Evaluate the Selected Course of Action

As we move into Step 6 of this decision-making model, we are now ready to evaluate the potential courses of action we generated in Step 5. While we have removed the options that are clearly undesirable, we may still need to narrow our options. Forest-Miller and Davis (2016) encourage us to use an additional method to determine if our plans are sufficient. The final method is Stadler's (1986) three tests: justice, publicity, and universality. The first test (justice) helps us determine if we would be willing to treat others in a similar manner. Further, is this course of action something that seems fair? The second test (publicity) asks us to consider if we would have any concerns about others knowing about the selected course of action? For example, if the plan was reported in the local news, would we have any concerns with the greater scrutiny given to this plan? The third test (universality) asks if we would recommend this course of action for a similar situation. This final test ensures that we are being impartial with the plans we develop, that we did not create a plan that is only applicable to one situation or individual.

If we believe that our course of action sufficiently passes all three tests, then we are ready to move to Step 7. If we determine that the plan does not meet one or more of these tests, or, perhaps, leads into different ethical concerns, then we will need to re-evaluate the plan. If a "back-up" plan is in place, we can run it through the same three tests. Either way, once we are satisfied with the plan, we can proceed to the next step.

7. Implement the Course of Action

In this final step of this ethical decision-making model, we are now ready to implement a course of action. However, even after the plan is implemented, we are not yet done! We still need to evaluate how the plan is proceeding. It is possible some unforeseen circumstances may arise that requires us to adjust, terminate, and/or re-evaluate the plan. As Forester-Miller and Davis (2016) note, although we may develop what we believe to be the best course of action, it still may be challenging to implement the plan. In our previous example of Jonas ending his relationship with Heidi, we may determine this as the best option; however, it will likely be difficult and painful for Jonas to end this relationship. Still, in order to meet our ethical obligations to our clients (e.g., promote client well-being) and to the counseling profession, we must follow the best course of action to resolve ethical dilemmas.

Summary

It is our desire that you understand the importance of following ethical guidelines. These standards are set in place to protect both the client and the counselor. We understand that it is sometimes challenging and even frustrating to follow the *ACA Code of Ethics* (2014). In the case study example, Jonas' attraction to Heidi caused him to make questionable decisions that led him into several ethical dilemmas. From an outsider's perspective, it is easy to judge Jonas' actions and question his ability to think through potential ethical concerns. However, ethical dilemmas often involve complex situations – which explains the difficult in determining the best course of action. So, we encourage you to become familiar with the *ACA Code of Ethics* (2014) and consult with a trusted, experienced colleague or supervisor when any potential ethical concerns rise. Ethical dilemmas are almost always easier to resolve with a group than when alone.

SUMMARY

FOR THE ROAD AHEAD

Check out the Chapter 6 video at this link:

https://www.khpcontent.com/

In this chapter, you were introduced to some important concepts related to ethical, professional, and legal issues in counseling. The impact of ethical principles and the ethics of the counseling profession were explained. An overview of the role of personal, professional, and Christian values as they relate to ethical decision-making have been highlighted in this chapter. Additionally, you were provided with a framework of how to apply an ethical decision-making model when faced with an ethical dilemma. The authors discussed how you would ethically integrate spirituality into counseling.

Later in the chapter, you learned the significance of the counselor's legal and ethical responsibilities to clients and the role the law has in the governance of counselors. The authors also emphasized the need for self-care, boundaries, and maintaining competency for the protection of the client's welfare and also for the welfare of the counselor. After reading this chapter, we hope that you are more comfortable with understanding key ethical concepts and have gained an awareness of the role of ethics and the law have over our profession; it is a part of everything we do as counselors.

Reflections on the Journey

1. As a counselor in training, what self-care strategies are you using to prevent burnout? Identify one strategy and implement this week.
2. Can you identify one dispositional issue, you need to work on while you are enrolled in the program?
3. Which of the faculty profiles, you found the most interesting? If you had an opportunity to share a comment or ask a question, what would it be?
4. What is a possible value conflict you might encounter when working with clients?
5. Some counselors in training and seasoned counselors find that ethics evoke some feelings of anxiety. Did you experience any anxiety or concern related to the profession after reading this chapter?

For Further Exploration

AllCEUs Counseling Education. (2016, December 26). *Common ethical violations | Counselor toolbox episode 88* [Video file]. Retrieved from https://www.youtube.com/watch?v=XY2aCCZ0tMY

AllCEUs Counseling Education. (2013, November 11). *Ethics and boundary issues in counseling* [Video file]. Retrieved from https://youtu.be/lxp7YqJ7n5Q

Apple (Producer). (2014-2016). *Ethics and psychology* [Audio podcast]. Retrieved from https://podcasts.apple.com/us/podcast/ethics-psychology/id809007108

Barnett J. E., & Johnson, W. B. (2015). *Ethics desk reference for counselors* (2nd ed.). Alexandria, VA: American Counseling Association.

Clinton, T., & Ohlschlager, G. (Eds.). (2002). *Competent Christian counseling: Foundations and practice of compassionate soul care* (Vol. 1). Colorado Springs, CO: WaterBrook Press.

Clinton, T., & Hawkins, R. (Eds.). (2011). *The popular encyclopedia of Christian counseling.* Eugene, OR: Harvest House Publishers.

Mental Health Roundup. (Producer) (n.d.). *Counselor toolbox podcast-addiction, counseling, and mental health continuing education | Recovery |Relationships | Clinical | Psychology | Family | Social Work | Mindfulness | CEUs | AllCEUs* [Audio podcast]. Ethics, Self Care, Counseling Skills and Ongoing Supervision. Retrieved from https://player.fm/series/counselor-toolbox-podcast-addiction-counseling-and-mental-health-continuing-education-recovery-relationships-clinical-psychology-family-social-work-mindfulness-ceus-allceus-by-dr-dawn-elise-s

Holeman, V. T. (2012). *Theology for better counseling: Trinitarian reflections for healing and formation.* Downers Grove, IL: IVP Academic.

Hopkins, B. R., & Anderson, B. S. & American Association for Counseling and Development. (1990). *The Counselor and the Law.* (3rd ed.). [Washington, D.C.] Distributed by ERIC Clearinghouse, https://eric.ed.gov/?id=ED324607

Shook, M. (Producer). (2018, July 11). Spirituality, Ethics, and Church-Based Counseling: Navigating the Territory with Jane Joyce [Audio podcast]. *The Thoughtful Counselor.* Retrieved from https://wp.me/p7R6fn-r2.

Thompson, C. (2010). *Anatomy of the soul.* Carol Stream, IL: Tyndale Momentum.

Wheeler, A. M., & Bertram, B. (2015). *The counselor and the law: A guide to legal and ethical practice* (7th ed.). Alexandria, VA: American Counseling Association.

REFERENCES

Allen, V. B. (1986). A historical perspective of the AACD ethics committee. *Journal of Counseling and Development, 64,* 293.

American Association of Christian Counselors. (2014). *AACC Code of Ethics.* Retrieved from: https://www.aacc.net/wp-content/uploads/2017/10/AACC-Code-of-Ethics-Master-Document.pdf

American Counseling Association (2005). *ACA Code of Ethics.* Alexandria, VA: Author

American Counseling Association (2014). *ACA code of ethics.* Alexandria, VA: Author

American Psychological Association. (2011, November 17). Providing information in a patient's lawsuit: FAQs on subpoenas and depositions. *Practice Update.* Retrieved from https://www.apaservices.org/practice/update/2011/11-17/subpoenas-depositions

American Psychological Association, Committee on Legal Issues. (2016). Strategies for private practitioners coping with subpoenas or compelled testimony for client/patient records or test data or test materials. *Professional Psychology: Research and Practice, 47,* 1–11. Retrieved from: https://www.apa.org/about/offices/ogc/private-practitioners.pdf

American Psychological Association. (2017). *APA ethical principles of psychologists and code of conduct.* Washington, DC: Author.

Anderson, D. (1992). A case for standards of counseling practice. *Journal of Counseling and Development, 71,* 22-26.

Aravind, V. K., Krishnaram, V. D., & Thasneem, Z. (2012). Boundary crossings and violations in clinical settings. *Indian Journal of Psychology, 34,* 21-24. doi:10.4103/0253-7176.96151

Brennan, C. (2013). Ensuring ethical practice: guidelines for mental health counselors in private practice. *Journal of Mental Health Counseling, 35*(3), 245+. Retrieved from http://link.galegroup.com.ezproxy.liberty.edu/apps/doc/A337368923/HRCA?u=vic_liberty&sid=HRCA&xid=9170c3f3

Christian Association of Psychological Studies. (2005). *Ethics statement.* Retrieved from: https://caps.net/ethics-statement/

Corey, G., Corey, M. S., Corey, C., & Callanan, P. (2015). *Issues and ethics in the helping professions* (9th ed.). Pacific Grove, CA: Brooks/Cole.

Entwistle, D. N. (2015). *Integrative approaches to psychology and Christianity: An introduction to worldview issues, philosophical foundations, and models of integration* (3rd ed.). Eugene, OR: Cascade Books.

Forester-Miller, H., & Davis, T. E. (2016). *Practitioner's guide to ethical decision making* (Rev. ed.). Retrieved from: http://www.counseling.org/docs/default-source/ethics/practioner's-guide-toethical-decision-making.pdf

Gladding, S. (2009). *Counseling: A comprehensive profession* (6th ed.). Upper Saddle River, NJ: Pearson Education.

Graham, S. R., & Liddle, B. J. (2009). Multiple relationships encountered by lesbian and bisexual psychotherapists: How close is too close? *Professional Psychology: Research and Practice, 40,* 15-21. doi:10.1037/a0013904

Grier, T. L., Hanson, M. R., & Skovholt, T. M. (2001). Career counseling for longevity: Self-care and burnout prevention strategies for counselor resilience. *Journal of Career Development, 27*(3), 167-176.

Hagedorn, W. B., & Moorhead, H. J. H. (2011). Counselor self-awareness: Exploring attitudes, beliefs, and values. In C. S. Cashwell & J. S. Young (Eds.), *Integrating spirituality and religion into counseling: A guide to competent practice* (2nd ed.) (pp. 71-95). Alexandria, VA: American Counseling Association.

Henderson, K. L., & Dufrene, R. L. (2012). Student behaviors associated with remediation: A content analysis. *Counseling Outcome Research and Evaluation, 3,* 48-60. doi:10.1177/2150137812437364

Hensley, L., Smith, S., & Thompson, W. (2003). Assessing competencies of counselors-in-training: Complexities in evaluating personal and professional development. *Counselor Education and Supervision, 42*, 219–231. doi:10.1002/j.1556-6978.2003.tb01813.x

Herlihy, B., & Corey, G. (2015). *Boundary issues in counseling: Multiple roles and responsibilities* (3rd ed.). Alexandria, VA: American Counseling Association.

Jaffee v. Redmond et al., 1996 WL 315841 (U.S. June 13, 1996).

Johnson, E. L. (Ed.). (2010). *Psychology and Christianity: Five views* (2nd ed.). Downers Grove, IL: InterVarsity Press.

Kaplan, D. M., Francis, P. C., Hermann, M. A., Baca, J. V., Goodnough, G. E., Hodges, S., … Wade, M. E. (2017). New concepts in the 2014 *ACA Code of Ethics*. *Journal of Counseling and Development, 95*, 110-120.

Kitchener, K. S. (1984). Intuition, critical evaluation and ethical principles: The foundation for ethical decisions in counseling psychology. *The Counseling Psychologist, 12*(3), 43-55.

Knapp, S. J., & VandeCreek, L. D. (2012). *Practical ethics for psychologists: A positive approach* (2nd ed.). Washington, DC: American Psychological Association.

Lamb, D. H., Presser, N. R., Pfost, K. S., Baum, M. C., Jackson, V. R., & Jarvis P. A. (1987). Confronting professional impairment during the internship: Identification, due process, and remediation. *Professional Psychology: Research & Practice, 18*(6), 597-603. doi:10.1037/0735-7028.18.6.597

Lambie, G. W., & Ascher, D. L. (2016). A qualitative evaluation of the Counseling Competencies Scale with clinical supervisors and their supervisees. *The Clinical Supervisor, 35*, 98-116.

Lambie, G. W., & Young, M. E. (2007). Wellness in school and mental health systems: Organizational influences. *Journal of Humanistic Counseling, Education, and Development, 46*, 98-113.

Linton, J. M., & O'Halloran, T. M. (2000). Stress on the job: Self-care resources for counselors. *Journal of Mental Health Counseling, 22*(4), 354-364.

Luke, M., Goodrich, K. M., & Gilbride, D. D. (2013). Intercultural model of ethical decision making: Address worldview dilemmas in school counseling. *Counseling and Values, 58*, 177-194. doi:10.1002/j.2161-007X.2013.00032.x

Maslach, C. (1993). Burnout: A multi-dimensional perspective. In W. B. Schaufeli, C. Maslach, & T. Marek (Eds.), *Professional burnout: Recent developments in theory and research* (pp. 19-32). New York, NY: Taylor & Francis.

Moleski, S. M., & Kiselica, M. S. (2005). Dual relationships: A continuum ranging from the destructive to the therapeutic. *Journal of Counseling & Development, 83*, 3-11. doi:10.1002/j.1556-6678.2005.tb00574.x

Pines, A., & Maslach, C. (1978). Characteristics of staff burnout in mental health settings. *Hospital and Community Psychiatry, 29*(4), 233-237

National Association of Social Workers. (2017). *Code of Ethics of the National Association of Social Workers*. Washington, DC: Author.

Remley, Jr., T. P., & Herlihy, B. (2016). *Ethical, legal, and professional issues in counseling* (5th ed.). Boston, MA: Pearson.

Resnik, D. B. (2015, December 1). *What is ethics in research and why is it important?* Retrieved from National Institute of Environmental Health Sciences website: https://www.niehs.nih.gov/research/resources/bioethics/whatis/index.cfm

Schmit, M. K., Schmit, E. L., Henesy, R. K., Klassen, S. L., & Oliver, M. (2015). Constructing an integrated model of ethical decision making in counselor education and supervision: A case conceptualization. *VISTAS 2015: Ideas and Research You Can Use*. Retrieved from https://www.counseling.org/knowledge-center/vistas/by-year2/vistas-2015/docs/default-source/vistas/constructing-an-integrated-model-of-ethical-decision-making

Spruill, J., Rozensky, R. H., Stigall, T. T., Vasquez, M., Bingham, R. P., & Olvey, C. D. V. (2004). Becoming a competent clinician: Basic competencies in intervention. *Journal of Clinical Psychology, 60*, 741-754.

Spurgeon, S. L., Gibbons, M. M., & Cochran, J. L. (2012). Creating personal dispositions for a professional counseling program. *Counseling & Values, 57*, 96-108.

Stadler, H. A. (1986). Making hard choices: Clarifying controversial ethical issues. *Counseling and Human Development, 19*, 1-10.

Super, D. (1953). APGA: Power and performance. *The Personnel and Guidance Journal, 31*, 496-499.

Tarasoff v. Regents of University of California, 17 Cal. 3d 425 (Cal. 1976).

Urofsky, R. I., Engels, D. W., & Engebretson, K. (2008). Kitchener's principle ethics: Implications for counseling practice and research. *Counseling and Values, 53*, 67-78.

VandeCreek, L., Knapp, S., & Brace, K. (1990). Mandatory continuing education for licensed psychologists: Its rationale and current implementation. *Professional Psychology: Research and Practice, 21*(2), 135-140.

Vacha-Haase, T., Davenport, D. S., & Kerewsky, S. D. (2004). Problematic students: Gatekeeping practices of academic professional psychology programs. *Professional Psychology: Research and Practice, 35*, 115-122. doi:10.1037/0735-7028.35.2.115

Vilardaga, R., Luoma, J. B., Hayes, S. C., Pistorello, J., Levin, M. E., Hildebrandt, M. J., ... Bond, F. (2011). Burnout among the addiction counseling workforce: The differential roles of mindfulness and values-based processes and work-site factors. *Journal of Substance Abuse Treatment, 40*(4), 323-335.

Warren, J., Morgan, M. M., Morris, L. N. B., & Morris, T. M. (2010). Breathing words slowly: Creative writing and counselor self-care—the writing workout. *Journal of Creativity in Mental Health, 5*(2), 109-124.

Welfel, E. R. (2013). *Ethics in counseling and psychotherapy: Standards, research, and emerging issues* (5th ed.). Belmont, CA: Brooks/Cole.

Womack, K. (2017). *The Beatles encyclopedia: Everything Fab Four*. Santa Barbara, CA: ABC-CLIO/Greenwood.

Zur, O. (2007). *Boundaries in psychotherapy: Ethical and clinical explorations*. Washington, DC: American Psychological Association.

CHAPTER 7
Counselor Wellness, Impairment, and Self-Care

YULANDA TYRE, PH.D., STACEY C. LILLEY, PH.D., & KRISTY FORD, PH.D.

> "If we don't change, we don't grow. If we don't grow,
> we aren't really living."
> —Anatole France

Following Christ: Grace for Our Work

The term endurance is generally associated with words like challenge, obstacles, strife, the tolerance of pain or harm. Because of this, the act of endurance is considered a unique quality as it requires the completion of a possibly uncomfortable process without giving in. Endurance requires commitment and possibly a willingness to serve and complete a task, characteristics that not all possess. Through-

© PopTika/Shutterstock.com

out the book of Jeremiah, he is called to depend upon God's love to promote his endurance during some very difficult and uncomfortable situations. He was a prophet called to deliver some sad and devastating

CHAPTER OBJECTIVES

After reading this chapter, you will understand more about:

- Key terms in counselors personal, holistic wellness
- The need to continually challenge and improve personal self-care
- Concepts in understanding how counselor wellness enhances client outcome
- Tools to reduce burnout, compassion fatigue, and vicarious trauma in order to keep counselors serving in the field

The following CACREP standards are addressed in this chapter:

Professional Counseling Orientation and Ethical Practice:

- Professional counseling organizations, including membership benefits, activities, services to members, and current issues (CACREP, 2016, Standard 2.F.1.f.)
- Strategies for personal and professional self-evaluation and implications for practice (CACREP, 2016, Standard 2.F.1.k.)
- Self-care strategies appropriate to the counselor role (CACREP, 2016, Standard 2.F.1.l.)

news regarding the destruction of Judah and it's people. Some feel he was a pessimist but I'm sure if Jeremiah was asked, he would label himself a realist. Jeremiah might also see himself as a protector of the truth in many ways. It was God's will that the people be aware of the truth and at times reminded of it.

The reality is that the world is filled with strife, hardship, illness, sickness and at times it can just seem unfair and out of the plan of God. Being Christian does not exclude us from the realities of the world, nor will this be the case for our clients. Today's counselors are faced with difficult situations, in which they must meet their client's needs as well as their own. At times the day to day weight and consistency of issues can take a toll on personal wellness and long term effects. Counselors who pursue their passion to help others must endure the professional race and be equally committed to taking care of themselves while balancing other things such as work, and family. This can be a daunting task for anyone, however, the Christian counselor may feel additional pressure. For the Christian counselor, it may seem hypocritical to help clients work through problems and issues that they too struggle with. While counselors are not perfect, we must diligently and consistently work toward wellness to daily maintenance. Then when needed exercise improvement in our current state of well-being to prevent future burnout from the field. This can be done with some awareness and dependence on God. During Jeremiah's journey God reminded him, "but I will restore you to health and heal your wounds, declares the Lord" (Jeremiah 30:17, NIV). Restoration comes in many different forms and is good for us all. This is a beautiful reminder that in all things God's enduring grace is enough to accomplish all that is set before us to do.

Over the last two decades, increasing attention has been devoted to wellness and counselor resilience. This topic is important on many levels: our own personal wellness, our daily work with clients, and the future of our profession. Contrary to what many counselors think, we are not immune to personal stressors and the effect our work can have on us (Cummings, Massey, & Jones, 2007). For years, a myth in our field was that since counselors are educated in mental health, counselors should know better than to be impaired (Remley & Herlihy, 2016). If only it were that easy to conceive and manage. As counselors, if we do not manage our own wellness, we run the risk for professional burnout and causing harm to our clients. Furthermore, as a Christian who is a counselor, we have a higher calling to be well. Our spiritual framework from which we live and model our life calls us to be well as we honor God (I Cor 16:19-20). This chapter will help provide some guidance as we look at our personal wellness and seek to improve our well-being.

WHAT IS WELLNESS?

Hippocrates, influential in Greek medicine, was one of the first philosophers to connect the body and healthy living. More recently, other fields (e.g., medicine, business, among others) have had a surge of publications regarding wellness and the work environment. Employers are realizing the importance of taking care of their employees as on-the-job functioning is enhanced when they are mentally and physically well.

In 1988, the first publication on impairment was included in a professional counseling journal, ACA's *Journal of Counseling and Development* (Stadler, Willing, Eberhage, & Ward, 1988). Gladding (2006) defined impairment as being "unable to function adequately or at the level of one's potential or ability" (p. 72). In response to the growing concern regarding counselor impairment, ACA created a task force to address this concern among counselors. At that time, they estimated around 600 of their members were experiencing some form of impairment (Stadler et al., 1988). The committee was tasked with presenting an action plan to address the many reasons that counselors suffer from an impairment, in addition to providing suggestions for further research areas (Lawson, Venart, Hazel, & Kottler, 2011). Because the counseling profession was still developing a strong research base, counselors lacked the knowledge regarding specific causes of impairment to be able to move toward remedies (Kottler & Hazler, 1996). It was years later that the profession was able to pull together reasons for impairment and how to improve counselor wellness. In 2003,

ACA formally created the Task Force on Counselor Impairment, leading the way for researchers to shift from looking at illness to being proactive in wellness and prevention.

If intrapersonal functioning is viewed on a continuum, then wellness would be located on one end and impairment on the other end. This same continuum delineates the view of therapeutic impairment for professional counselors. When counselors lack wellness (or are impaired), this affects their professional ability. If a counselor has issues with their own mental health, physical problems, or trauma then the counselor may cause harm to their client. Thus, as a future counselor, attending to your level of wellness is imperative.

Many researchers have devoted their professional work to study and improve wellness for counselors. Dr. J. Melvin Witmer was one of the early pioneers who defined and assessed wellness in practitioners. He offered a wellness class at the University of Ohio in the 1970s and wrote the first book on the topic of wellness in counseling in 1985. His *Wellness Evaluation Lifestyle* instrument measures 19 traits to help counselors develop a plan and improve their wellness. Later, he collaborated with Dr. Jane Myers and Dr. Tom Sweeny to create the *Wellness Wheel*, which is born out of Adlerian theory and will be discussed later in this chapter. This wheel progressed beyond the concept of wellness to include diversity and self-direction (Myers, Sweeney & Witmer, 2000). The wellness wheel is divided into higher-order wellness factors, five second-order factors, and 17 sub-factors that make up The Indivisible Self model. This theory has been pivotal not only in addressing counselor wellness but also as a multidimensional model (Myers, Sweeney & Witmer, 2000). Myers and Sweeney have pioneered the issue of wellness by addressing counselors individually as well as within their context of living (culture, environment, etc.). A well-known instrument, the *5 Factor Wellness inventory*, is a valuable assessment tool for counselors to assess their own wellness or to use with clients (available at www.mindgarden.com). This instrument has been used in countless studies and has a large cross-cultural database with thousands of subjects (Myers & Sweeney, 2005).

In 1994, CACREP published the *1994 Model Legislation* which was designed to encourage remediation of impaired counselors (Glosoff, Benshoff, Hosie, & Maki, 1995). For years, research suggested that counselor wellness would also affect the counseling services provided to clients

(Witmer & Young, 1996). One of the most comprehensive definitions of wellness indicates that wellness is a way of life oriented toward optimal health and well being, in which body, mind, and spirit are integrated by the individual to live life more fully within the human and natural community (Myers et al., 2000). Ideally, each individual is capable of achieving an optimum state of health and well-being.

As a new student, you are most likely entering your program studies with a passion and focus to help others. Many of you may already have a specific practice setting in mind where you might like to work. You may feel passionate about helping a certain population or diagnostic category. These ideas may stem from your past relationships with family or friends, your engagement or service to others prior to reaching this point, or perhaps you feel a calling from the Lord to work in an identified area. On the journey to accomplish the goal of becoming a counselor, you will be met with academic demands, emotional and psychological stress, and personal, family and employment concerns. Financial concerns may crop up, time may be limited, and even technology may seem to work against you at times. As you move into preparation for clinical practice during the practicum and internship stage of the program, you will be met with performance demands related to your demonstration of knowledge and skills, possibly leading to thoughts of self-doubt, anxiety, worry, and shame. These negative life circumstances and self-assessments can be a hindrance to your wellness. Because of this potential, it is important that you are aware of the importance of self-care practices, have the ability to identify symptoms, and are knowledgeable about the best practices on the topic.

As we continue to explore more about wellness, it is important to note that the definition of wellness is more than a simple concept involving the lack of illness or sickness. The World Health Organization (2018) defines wellness as a state of complete physical, mental and social well being. This perspective is consistent with how God desires for us to live in service to Him. When we review the scriptures it is clear that He has a desire for us to live with good physical, mental and spiritual health. Christ has set us free in all areas of our lives. Galatians 5:1 reads, "Stand firm, then, do not let yourselves be burdened again by the yoke of slavery."

There are many contributors to depletions in wellness for today's counselors. Many experience a work setting that includes expectations of 24-hour access, larger caseloads, more pervasive issues, escalating crisis, and decreases in resources (Lindo et. al, 2015; Lawson, 2007). Social challenges, such as school shootings, natural disasters, election stress, police shootings, police brutality, angry drivers, and magnified financial concerns can shift the needs of clients and levels of duress that they experience impacting the wellness of counselors. Counseling, in and of itself, is an emotionally demanding profession as it is established and maintained on the foundation of compassion and empathic engagement with clients. Moreover, individuals may pursue a counseling degree as a result of their own experiences with loss, grief, trauma or crisis. These combined factors can make counselors more susceptible to depletion, impairment, and possible harm to clients (Lawson & Venart, 2005). As you begin your journey as a counselor, it is important that are aware of the various negative impeding factors that can accompany your work in serving clients (Lindo et al., 2015; Mullen, Morris, & Lord, 2017).

Aspirational Wellness

Perceived wellness is the process of looking inward and assessing personal wellness. Aspirational wellness is the degree to which we hope, or aspire, to have wellness. An issue arises when the counselor sees who they are (perception) and it differs from who they want to be (aspiration). This discrepancy can not only be stressful for the counselor personally, but it can affect them clinically. Remley and Herlihy (2016) reported that 86% of clinicians will have at least one episode of distress in their career.

> A new counselor has not been sleeping lately and is worried about paying the bills, her clients, and not having time for relationships in her life. She is taking on more clients to increase her finances but this adding to her stress. Although she may not be impaired at this point she is showing signs of distress. What should the counselor do to monitor herself to ensure that this does not negatively escalate?

Achieving optimal wellness is a process that takes reflection, time, dedication to change, and the ability to balance multiple and changing roles. There is not always a clear and obvious line between impairment and wellness. In these instances, the impairment usually develops over time: it is more like a slow fade than a sudden drop. As you become involved in learning the standards of the field, sharpening a clinical skill set, and developing a professional identity, you may tempted to omit self-care. This omission can start the slide toward physical and emotional depletion, and you may soon discover that there are unmet needs that require attention.

WHAT IS THE ETHICAL RESPONSIBILITY REGARDING WELLNESS?

Personal responsibility. One of the purposes of The *ACA Code of Ethics* (2014) is to "serve as an ethical guide" for its members and "establish expectations of conduct" (p. 3). The code specifically speaks to expectations and standards related to counselor wellness and self-care. In 2014 section C.2.g the code was updated to include verbiage that counselors "monitor themselves" for signs of impairment in their own physical, mental, and emotional health and to refrain from offering or providing professional services when such impairment is likely to harm a client or others. The code advises that counselors seek assistance as needed and to refrain from clinical services when impaired (p. 9).

© Sampien/Shutterstock.com

Gatekeeping responsibility. The code expands on the concept of individual awareness of wellness and goes on to speak about a counselor's responsibility to others in the profession who may be showing signs of impairment. This concept is commonly noted under the definition of *gatekeeping* in counselor education programs (Bodner, 2012). Counselors in training may be made aware of this term initially during their course of study, as it relates to the assessment process of professional disposition or fit for professional practice. During clinical training, it is the responsibility of professional administration and faculty to act as the clinical gatekeeper for counselors in training. In this role, they will act to protect the integrity of the counseling profession and to prevent harm from being inflicted upon future clients receiving services (Homrich, DeLorenzi, Bloom, & Godbee, 2014).

Another layer of the gatekeeping process involves *site supervisors*. This title represents the person providing clinical oversight to counselors in training during practicum and internship experiences. Site supervisors have an ethical responsibility to provide support, guidance, and assessment to counselors in training on skill development and disposition along in conjunction with the university administration and clinical faculty members. This support serves to create a collaborative front to aid in resolving any issues seen during the clinical experience, thus protecting the profession and clients.

WHAT ARE THE DIMENSIONS OF WELLNESS?

For counselors-in-training, an important part of wellness is identifying symptoms of impairment, mitigating issues, and developing a well lifestyle (Lindo, et.al, 2015; Remley & Herlihy, 2016) and includes the identification of the domains of wellness. Myers, Sweeney and Witmer (2000) identified areas of self-directed life tasks or domains (e.g.., sense of control, stress management, emotional control, gender and cultural identity, etc.) and ecological elements (e.g.. media, government) in the development of the Wheel of Wellness (see Figure 7.1 below).

FIGURE 7.1

The Wheel of Wellness

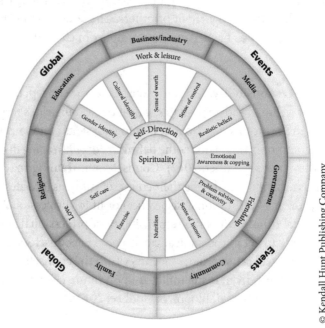

The initial research of these wellness leaders has evolved over time leading to additional domains of counselor wellness. These additional categories include considerations of social, emotional, physical, intellectual, spiritual, psychological, occupational, and environmental. Each of the dimensions will be defined below.

Social Wellness

Social wellness is commonly defined in terms of healthy social and environmental engagement, which may include personal, intimate, social, and professional relationships, etc. Related to this is your relationship styles, which includes your engagement approach, attachment style, level of assertiveness, conflict resolution ability, and communication approaches. Additionally, social wellness includes your ability to work toward common and community goals or ideas toward nature. This area of wellness includes the overall balance of self and your connection to others (Beaumont, 2016; Coasten, 2017; Lawson & Myers, 2011).

Emotional Wellness

Emotional wellness is defined as one's ability to identify, assess, articulate and regulate emotions and behaviors connected to those emotions. This concept is commonly connected to beliefs about self-esteem, self-perception, and self-confidence. The National Institute of Health (NIH; 2018) defines emotional wellness as a positive outlook on life, feelings of joy toward life, as well as a person's emotional ability to handle stress, difficulty, or challenging situations as they occur. The NIH emphasizes the importance of a person's ability to hold on to positive perceptions of life longer and recall good times when needed.

Psychological Wellness

Psychological wellness is closely related to this emotional wellness with similarities in the definition, such as optimism, positive views of self, our environment and the world (Figley, 2002; Cummings et al., 2007; Beaumont et. al., 2016). Psychological wellness involves life satisfaction, happiness, sense of control over destiny, purpose, and belonging. This component of wellness further comprises considerations of cultural beliefs, customs and theoretical concepts of self-actualization, making it an evolving process.

Physical Wellness

Physical wellness was once commonly solely defined by the outward appearance of the body. This definition has expanded over time to include considerations of diet, exercise, sleep, and leisure activity (Beaumont, et. al., 2016; Lawson and Myers, 2011; Hunter, 2016). Physical wellness in many ways is key to all the other forms of wellness as it impacts each area and can be impacted by each of the other areas. For example, a decline in physical wellness can impact mental health, while issues in mental health can impact physical health (i.e. depression). This connection can be seen across all other forms of wellness, making it a vital area of care and maintenance (Hunter, 2016; Lawson, 2017).

Intellectual Wellness

Intellectual wellness can be defined by a person's cognitive ability to engage in learning, critical thinking, and decision making that enhances your life and the lives of others. This area of wellness includes openness to new ideas, experiences, and the development of skills that include a willingness to share with others. A creative and curious nature, a desire to grow and enhance your social environment are also involved in intellectual wellness. There is a connection between intellectual wellness and self-worth, self-determination, tolerance, concepts of lifelong learning and the overall betterment of self for others (Maslach, Schaufeli, & Leiter, 2001; McCaughan & Hill, 2015).

Case Example

Charles has been working at his internship site for the past 6 months. During this time he has had the opportunity to work with clients in need of time management, decision making, anxiety and mild symptoms of depression. Recently one of his clients lost their sibling in a fatal car accident. The client is struggling with unexpected and traumatic loss. Charles has been using theories and techniques that he commonly uses to support his clients, however after working with this client in trying to cope with the grief of this significant and loss, he notices that he is starting to feel lost in session regarding the next steps and in understanding how to support the client in this process outside of showing empathy. He does not feel that his current tools are relevant to the needs of the client and he is noticing a decline in the client's improvement and satisfaction with services. Charles noticed himself feeling agitated when he sees the name of this client on his calendar. He is unsure of how to develop an edited treatment plan or adjust an approach for this client at this time. What can Charles do to enhance his knowledge and understanding of grief and loss to help this client? What is his responsibility in this area? What questions can he ask his supervisor to tap into his wellness and self-efficacy?

Spiritual Wellness

God made us not only to live in this world but to enjoy a personal relationship with Him, starting in this life and continuing on into eternity (Acts 17:27). Spiritual wellness, or spirituality, provides you with a sense of self-awareness and faith in who you are, where you came from, why you are here in the world, what you need, how you live, and where you're going, along with your connection to others and the world (Hotchkiss & Lesher, 2018). In a review of the *Wellness Wheel*, note that spirituality is at the center connecting all of the areas of wellness. Even if a person does not specifically believe in God, as may be the case for your future clients, spirituality helps to support the meaning of life, beliefs, faith, hope, values, peace, worship, prayer, meditation attitudes, purposes, and love toward life, world, or divinity. Spiritual wellness is an evolving process of discovering harmony, meaning, and purpose in life (Myers et al., 2000; Kottler & Hazler, 1996; Lawson & Myers, 2011; Pardess, Mikulincer, Dekel, & Shaver, 2014). It is often used when seeking the truth, in understanding death, forgiveness, self-acceptance, and in building or maintaining relationships with others (Pardess, et. al., 2014).

© Roman Samborskyi/Shutterstock.com

Occupational Wellness

Occupational wellness is defined and measured by your ability to engage in meaningful work practices that bring gratification (Witmer & Young, 1996). When work stress is managed, there is a balance occurring between work, life, leisure, and self. The ACA notes that this definition is important for counselors as they spend most of their time and effort working in service to others. Work allows people the opportunity to pursue economic security and financial well-being, the opportunity to become productive in their industry, utilize talents, develop skills, pursue interests, connect and network with colleagues, and develop an identity in their field of work, among others (Myers & Sweeney, 2005).

Environmental Wellness

Environmental wellness can be seen as an extension of occupational wellness as it involves external factors and space where many of the other forms of wellness are personal and internal (Coaston, 2017). Environmental wellness encompasses living in a way that promotes harmony with nature, community, and balance between home and workspaces. It entails living a lifestyle and maintaining ideas that include respect and stewardship for the earth (i.e. minimizing pollution, recycling, conserving energy). Environmental wellness can also include considerations for safety, health, and disease prevention (biological, physical, chemical, social, etc.). This form of wellness requires an awareness of your relationship and responsibility to both the earth and community (Coaston, 2017).

A Balancing Act

Maintaining balance in each section of the wheel of life can appear to be a daunting task. In many ways, this balance is like riding a bike. When you

get onto a bicycle, you steady yourself and allow the bike to lean toward
you, as you throw your leg across.
After your leg crosses the frame of
the bike you balance the bike and
center yourself on the seat, steady
the handlebars and frame in a way
that allows you to gain your footing,
while simultaneously allowing you
to push off. Once pushed off you will
initially use the handlebars to steer,
while at various intervals peddling.
Managing the Wellness Wheel will

require similar skills. At times you will need to give a great deal of attention to one or more parts of the wheel and, at times, you might not need
to give total attention to one section, allowing for intermittent peddling.
Balance, in this case, involves giving the area/s of the wheel the attention it
needs when needed. This will allow for the ebb and flow of your life and its
circumstances to determine the spin, speed, path, and turns of your wheel.
After some practice, confidence and rhythm will surface allowing a foundation for maintenance. The key to the wellness wheel is in implementing
behaviors and a routine that will help you in sustained wellness, long term
professional satisfaction, and maintenance of client care in the field.

Patricia Wade: Graduate Student

As I sat in my car and gripped the steering wheel, I let out a
long, audible sigh as I looked at the clock on the dashboard.
In less than one hour I would be back at the university counseling center where I was considered a graduate therapist
during my first semester of internship. I would sit across
from a college freshman who was a long way from home
and completely overwhelmed with new responsibilities and
newly found freedom. How was I supposed to help her navigate college life when I was barely making my way through
the maze of becoming a counselor? Who was I kidding? Not
one ounce of me was convinced I had what it would take to
help others. Before pulling out of my garage, I decided to
reach out to a former professor and ask if she had time to talk

later that afternoon. "HELP" was the only word in the subject line. She responded before I even left my driveway.

There are pros and cons to doing an internship at a university counseling center. The pro—you're constantly observed and provided with real-time feedback. The con? You're constantly observed and provided with real-time feedback. "So, let me get this straight," my former professor said in her matter-of-fact, straight up tone, "You feel naked, afraid, and critiqued all day?" I laughed and silently nodded my head even though she couldn't see me through the phone. She went on to add, "So what you're saying is that you feel uncomfortable, incompetent, and incapable." Finally, someone understood. "Yes," I added, "and I feel like a poser."

I quietly waited for a comforting response, convinced it would be something along the lines of, "It takes time to become a truly great counselor who is a master at developing the therapeutic alliance, fostering hope, and facilitating change." Laughingly she replied, "Well, get used to it. You're going to feel uncomfortable, incompetent, and incapable the rest of your career, even as an effective counselor." What? I wanted to laugh and cry at the same time. "But, what does it mean to be an effective counselor?" Now, it was her turn to sigh. "Girlfriend," she said before ending the call, "I have an 80-year-old friend with a very large counseling practice, and she's still asking the same question. You'll figure it out, but there are no short cuts. Stay with it. You have what it takes. People need you."

But, in what way did people need me? This one particular question would be the catalyst of my understanding of what it means to be a counselor. Humbly, I have come to understand that people need me to show up with my whole self—my whole imperfect self. People need me to be fully present to their stories, captivated by their emotions, courage, and resilience. Those who suffer need me to bear witness to their truth, their pain and sorrow, and their triumph and joy. People need to be reminded to breathe. They need to know they have the capacity to heal and grow. So, when I want to grip the wheel and white knuckle it out of fear and discomfort, I'm learning to relax and trust the process. Being a counselor is an extraordinary gift, both sacred and challenging. Thanks to my colleagues and clients, I learn something new every day about myself and the world around me.

Contributed by Patricia Wade. © Kendall Hunt Publishing Company.

WHAT IS IMPAIRMENT?

Counselor impairment can be defined simply as a lack of wellness, or a condition in which the counselor is no longer functioning at their optimal capacity. Impairment has the potential to arise from difficulties in any of the domains on the Wheel of Wellness (Whitmer et al., 1996), but varying states of impairment often enter awareness as counselors experience feelings of burnout, compassion fatigue, or vicarious trauma. Counselors seek to identify these feelings early and assess the difficulties to begin the remediation process and move back toward wellness in every domain.

Burnout

In early stages, impairment may be recognized as feelings of burnout. *Burnout* is a term commonly associated with workplace exhaustion. It identifies a lack of personal wellness experienced in the professional context and can be applied to most any job or career (Maslach et al., 2001). The term is commonly used to define dissatisfaction related to the occupational environment, stemming from stressors such as management demands, a lack of necessary resources, or an inability to navigate office politics. These tensions can lead to undue stress, emotional ambivalence, and psychological exhaustion, developing gradually over an extended

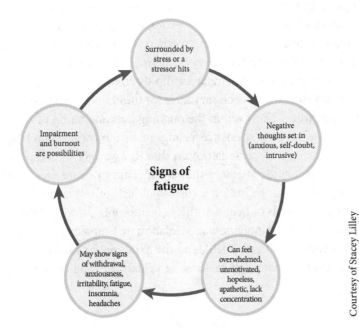

FIGURE 7.2

Signs of Fatigue

Courtesy of Stacey Lilley

period of time into the experience of burnout. The experience may include feelings of emotional, physical, and spiritual exhaustion as well as a reduced sense of personal accomplishment (Maslach et al., 2001).

While the term *burnout* can be related to various contexts, it is often associated with helping professions (Hotchkiss & Lecher, 2018) such as chaplains, clergy, social workers, and counselors. Counselors may be more prone to burnout when they are also experiencing personal concerns such as major life stress, eustress, or medical concerns. Heavy client caseloads, limited resources, limited or inadequate training, limited support, demanding supervisors, office politics, and low job satisfaction are contributors to burnout cited as specific to the counseling profession (Lawson, 2006). When present in the context of the counseling profession, burnout may be seen alongside other wellness identifiers, but can also be the primary symptom, unrelated to other expressions of impairment such as *compassion fatigue* or *secondary trauma* which are discussed more fully in the next sections.

Compassion Fatigue

Another indicator of impairment is the experience of compassion fatigue. Compassion fatigue, like burnout, is often associated with various human service professions (Casey, 2013). It is defined by Figley (2002) to include feelings of burnout but expanded to encompass negative mental health symptoms such as anxiety and depression as well as a reduced sense of satisfaction that once followed helping others. Counselors, by profession, care for and empathize with the heavy burdens of others. Chapter 8 of this text on the authentic counseling relationship discusses the importance of compassion and empathy as necessary tools for the effective treatment of mental health symptoms. However, in the ongoing demonstration of clinical care, many counselors can experience feelings related to compassion fatigue, empathy fatigue, and depersonalization due to a variety of complex factors. These factors include stressors that are specific to counseling and similar helping professions, including a consistent lack of self-care while meeting the critical demands of helping others (Beaumont, Durkin, Hollins-Martin & Carson, 2016), the loneliness and isolation that can accompany leadership positions (Scott & Lovell, 2015), and the experience of secondary or vicarious trauma (Trippany, White-Kress & Wilcoxon, 2004) which will be discussed more extensively in the next section. Fatigue syndrome, as defined by Figley (1995) in his discussion on compassion fatigue, may have a rapid onset due to the daily nature of counselor's work. Figley's (2001) Compassion Fatigue Process chart (see Figure 7.3 below) provides a visual depiction of the mechanisms of compassion fatigue.

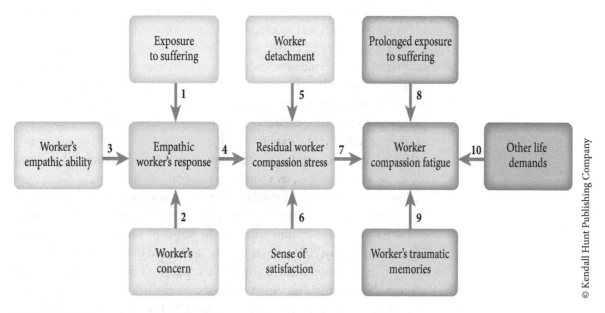

FIGURE 7.3

Model of Compassion Stress and Fatigue

Research Note: A study by Pardess et al. (2014) found that *attachment anxiety* correlated with *burnout* and *vicarious trauma*, while *attachment avoidance* correlated with *lowered compassion satisfaction*. Implications of this study include a personal responsibility for both developing and established counselors to seek ongoing wellness activities that support increases in earned secure attachment.

"What we do as clinicians impact others," says ACA member Robert J. Wicks, an expert on secondary stress in clinicians and the author of books such as *The Resilient Clinician, Bounce: Living the Resilient Life* and *Night Call: Embracing Compassion and Hope in a Troubled World.*

Secondary and Vicarious Trauma

Impairment may also be noted in the experience of secondary and/or vicarious trauma. Secondary trauma is defined as the emotional duress that occurs from hearing first-hand accounts of traumatic experience. For counselors, these experiences arise regularly out of the professional responsibility for empathizing and sharing in the emotional pain of others. This can become a great source of stress for counselors, as high levels of psychological energy are expended with little to no reciprocity expected in return. Over time, secondary trauma can give rise to vicarious trauma, defined as the gradual building of emotional residue due to ongoing exposure to accounts of traumatic experience (Trippany et al., 2004). For counselors, vicarious trauma is the experience of a type of emotional trauma resulting from caring. Vicarious trauma often coincides with feelings of burnout and compassion fatigue, as energy, motivation, compassion, and empathy are lessened over time. The terms *burnout, compassion fatigue*, and *vicarious trauma* are often used interchangeably but are generally viewed on a continuum of low, medium and high in terms of progression in severity (Remley & Herlihy, 2006). On the more severe end of the spectrum is traumatic countertransference, in which the counselor's own trauma history is triggered by traumatic incidents processed by clients, creating the potential for a sense of revictimization for the counselor (Trippany et al., 2004). But while individual experiences and exact definitions may vary, the consistent outcome of the struggle is counselor impairment, with personal results that can include negative physical, mental, emotional, and spiritual symptoms, as well as professional results that include the potential for harm within the therapeutic relationship (Neswald-Potter & Simmons, 2016).

DEFINITIONS:
Burnout: Occupational dissatisfaction due to stressors
Compassion Fatigue: Gradual lessening of compassion over time due to trauma exposure
Empathy fatigue: Emotional exhaustion that occurs as the counselors' own wounds are continually revisited by their client's trauma
Depersonalization: Emotional disconnection of the counselor from the therapeutic process
Secondary Trauma: Emotional duress that occurs from hearing first-hand traumatic experiences
Vicarious Trauma: Gradual building of emotional residue through hearing traumatic experiences
Traumatic countertransference: Triggering of the counselor's trauma by traumatic client incidents

Despite the common language and terminology around fatigue syndromes and impairment, counselors continue to struggle. Counselors often lack the consistency needed to maintain overall wellness through self-assessment and self-care (Figley, 2002; Lawson & Myers, 2011). While counselors are valued for taking care of others, they often allow themselves to be distracted with this care and experience guilt and shame in taking care of themselves. Several factors are noted for the disparity in counselor self-care (Thompson, Amatea, & Thompson, 2014):

1. Inability to recognize personal levels of self-distress
2. Inability to carve out time to engage in self-care
3. Inability to identify and mitigate negative thoughts and beliefs on self-care
4. Lack of willingness to seek support when needed (i.e. supervision, peer support or professional help)
5. Inability to recognize psychological, physical or medical signs of distress, as manifestation may not meet perceived expectations.

Self-care is a critical skill that requires conscious development. In the best case scenario, counselors-in-training seek to establish these habits while still in graduate school and make wellness a priority. The next section reviews recommended tools for success in the area of counselor wellness and self-care.

WHAT ARE BEST PRACTICES FOR COUNSELOR WELLNESS?

As noted previously, *wellness* is the conscious awareness of daily decisions that either contribute to continued wellness or increase the potential for impairment (Mullen et al., 2017; Lindo et al., 2015). Optimal wellness is a lifestyle that spans across several areas of life, actively seeking balance, assessment, and adjustment. You may have an idea of why wellness is important and what areas are necessary for assessment, but it is critical to ask yourself, *"how will I practice wellness?"*. To begin the journey in ongoing wellness it is important to have an idea of the best practices that can help you succeed. Witmer and Young (1996) suggest a model for self-assessment and the establishment of continuing wellness practices, advocating for the development of counselor education programs that encourage comprehensive wellness encompassing intellectual, emotional, physical, occupational, social, and spiritual components

Intellectual Wellness Practices

© bleakstar/Shutterstock.com

Intellectual wellness includes being open to new ideas and enhancing critical thinking, opening a path to insights, resources, knowledge, and skills that can enhance the quality of life and satisfaction with self and the environment (i.e., community, social relationships; Wolf, Thompson, Thompson, & Smith-Adcock, 2014). One method of expanding intellectual development for counselors is through professional development. Professional development can involve attendance at state, regional or national conference, workshops, seminars, observations of groups, reading, listening to podcasts or viewing webinars. The options are endless as professional development can include time sitting with a mentor or expert in a specific area of the profession. As a counselor, this area of wellness can be a challenge due to long work days, time away from client care, and lack of financial support. It is necessary, nonetheless. Imagine how your trust might be diminished in your medical doctor, dentist, financial manager, hair stylist or car mechanic were not remaining up to date in their areas of expertise. Not doing so can be seen as a liability to the clients, the profession, and the counselor. Most states require continuing education credit (i.e., required professional development) in order to maintain licensure.

Emotional Wellness Practices

Emotional wellness involves the capacity for self-regulation, or the awareness and management of the full range of emotions, both positive and negative (Witmer & Young, 1996). Continuous self-assessment of emotion regulation skills is critical for counselors, as we are often engaged in challenging clients to express and manage emotions appropriately. Emotional wellness also includes self-awareness and maintenance of positive self-talk. Again, just as counselors challenge clients to monitor their internal dialogue, it is important that we do the same. Self-compassion is a critical component of self-care, as the way we care for our own mind and heart will ultimately impact how we view and care for others (Beaumont et al., 2016).

Physical Wellness Practices

Physical wellness requires attention to the needs of our body (Witmer & Young, 1996). Nutritious food, adequate sleep, and regular exercise provide the fuel needed to support physical functions. Unfortunately, physical needs are often the first area to be neglected with the onset of busyness or stress. Establishing a time to plan meals and snacks, map out times for sleep and full days of rest, and engage in a regular exercise routine requires intentionality. Creative ideas such as finding a workout buddy, swapping dinner ideas with friends, finding meal ideas on social apps like Pinterest, or joining pre-planned dinner subscriptions can also be useful to help with planning in this area.

Occupational Wellness Practices

Occupational wellness is supported through work, recreation, and leisure activities that lend to a sense of life-purpose and provide benefits such as economic compensation, psychological stimulation, and social networking (Witmer & Young, 1996). While the counselor identity offers a career abounding in meaningful work, it is also important to seek balance through recreation and leisure. Engaging in a hobby or leisure activity can provide an outlet for stress reduction, increase coping skills, and boost innovative ideas. These types of activities enhance a sense of "living-life" beyond work, promoting personal satisfaction and joy and expanding interactions with people, places, and things. Similar to leisure, *creativity* is an outlet for stress reduction, providing a platform to try new things, develop new ways of thinking, engage with diversity, and highlight the uniqueness of artistic expressions. Creative activities can promote self-awareness and provide an avenue for personal expression. Recreation or leisure activities can also complement your clinical work, as creative outlets enhance the ability to connect, communicate, and share ideas.

Social Wellness Practices

Social wellness practices focus on developing and maintaining healthy relational networks, such as in families, friendships, and intimate relationships. Social wellness further involves the capacity to hold on to personal belief systems while maintaining an open and welcoming attitude to interact with others who may be culturally different (Witmer & Young, 1996). Research consistently supports the importance of staying connected to others as a protective factor that boosts resiliency (Beaumont, 2016) to guard against negative mental health symptoms as well as counselor impairment. Connections with friends will be especially important throughout the internship phase as you are transitioning into the field of counseling. While personal time may feel limited, it will be important that you develop and maintain close relationships. Consider meeting with friends to talk about life, rather than work. Join your local counseling association to build a network of professional friends and colleagues. Additionally, be sure to maintain loving and intimate relationships. Research supports that people involved in long-term and loving relationships live longer and have more satisfying lives (Beaumont, 2016).

Spiritual Wellness Practices

Spiritual wellness includes a recognition of the higher power that connects humanity to creation and honor for the resulting value system that flows from individual beliefs about God (Witmer & Young, 1996). Spiritual practices enhance a sense of meaning in life, safeguarding against the cynicism and hopelessness that can accompany client narratives. For many, including Christian counselors, involvement in organized religion offers a theological grounding for making sense out of the senseless, with the added benefit of a community network for protection against isolation and loneliness. While some may not want to participate in regular church life, other regular spiritual practices may serve to enhance wellness in this area. Volunteer service, spiritual retreats, meditation, and nature walks are just a few examples of practices that support ongoing spiritual wellness.

Mindfulness practice is an evidence-based strategy for supporting wellness across multiple domains, including spiritual, physical, and emotional wellness. Mindfulness may be defined as compassionate, purposeful awareness and non-judgmental acceptance of personal experience in the present moment (Shapiro, Carlson, Astin, & Freedman, 2006). The goal of mindfulness practice is to become increasingly adept at maintaining a compassionate awareness of the varying personal thoughts, feelings, sensations, behaviors, or impulses experienced at any given moment in time. While mindfulness has multiple benefits as a clinical strategy for increasing emotion regulation (Menezes, Pereira, & Bizarro, 2012) and decreasing negative mental health symptoms (Chiesa & Serreti, 2009; Hofmann, Sawyer, Witt, & Oh, 2010), it is also useful for supporting ongoing wellness. As a self-care strategy, this practice aims to slow down the stress-filled, hurried pace of life, and has been shown to reduce stress and enhance overall well-being (Goyal et al., 2014). Some view mindfulness as a spiritual or religious practice, emphasizing the connection between the sense of self and awareness of God or creation that often arise. When applied with cultural sensitivity, numerous client populations may benefit from mindfulness strategies. However, because mindfulness claims origins in Zen Buddhism, some religious groups, such as conservative Christians, may be resistant toward the practice (Garzon & Ford, 2016). Initial research supports the importance of religious sensitivity in mindfulness practice, indicating that adapting mindfulness to align with personal belief systems may increase both effectiveness and treatment compliance (Ford & Garzon, 2017).

Self-Stewardship using The Creative Balancing Activity

Dr. Lisa Sosin, Program Director, Ph.D. in Counselor Education, Liberty University

In addition to learning best practice-based knowledge and skills in ethical and effective counseling (ACA, 2014; CACREP, 2016), counselors in training need to recognize the importance of wise and responsible "self-stewardship," a term that I, like Canning (2011), prefer to "self-care." For, like our clients, we are impacted by the ravages of the

© Lisa Sosin

fall of man and bear the scars of the fall's bio-psycho-social-spiritual devastation. Researchers in the area of counselor wellness emphasizes the importance of a healthy life balance. According to Siegel (2012), engaging in certain essential activities helps establish such balance. These activities include sleep, exercise, focused goal orientation, close relationships, quiet reflection, relaxation, and spontaneous play/creativity. Such "essential mental activities strengthen your brain's internal connections and your connections with other people and the world around you" (Rock & Siegel, 2011, Online).

To help counselors in training increase their awareness and balance of these essential activities, I developed a creative activity called The Creative Balance Activity (CBA; Sosin, 2016). Studies indicate that creative activities enrich the psychological states of adults, which in turn improves quality of life and well-being (Simonton, 2000). The ability to be creative in the work environment is associated with general health (Mirowsky & Ross, 2007). Creativity in adult learners is also associated with intrinsic motivation, enterprise, persistence, resilience, curiosity, assessing and testing, problem-solving, and imagination (Tsai, 2012). Moreover, creativity supports adaptability and problem-solving and has been found to enhance the well-being of counselors in training (Lawrence, Foster, & Tieso, 2015).

The Creative Balancing Activity (CBA). The CBA is an artistic assessment related to The Creative Exposure Intervention, an arts-based technique for regulating anxiety (Sosin & Szapkiw, 2016). The supplies needed for the CBA are simply drawing paper and colored pencils, crayons, or markers. There are five steps to the CBA. These are anchoring, depicting the safe place at the center of the drawing paper using the art supplies, depicting and assessing the seven essential activities (sleep, exercise, focused goal-directed activity (i.e., studying, reading, writing), close relationships, quiet reflection,relax ation, and spontaneous play/creativity), developing action points for increasing balance, and sharing with others.

Anchoring includes taking a few minutes to breathe deeply, systematically relax the body, and imagine being in a safe and peaceful place (for Christians this may include imagining being embraced by God and feeling His compassion, grace, and truth [i.e., Matt 11:28-30; NIV]). Depicting the safe place entails drawing a circle at the center of the drawing paper, leaving room around it for the next step, and using art supplies to depict what it feels like in the safe place. It does not matter what the depiction looks like, the CBA is about process, not product. The goal is feeling the safety of being in such a place, and capturing it with an image, colors, and/or phrases. Depicting the seven essential activities involves drawing seven smaller circles around the safe place image each with a depiction (colors, images, words) of one of the seven activities in them. Assessing the seven essential activities entails mindfully considering if and how one is taking time to engage in the activity. Developing action points includes self-compassionately considering how one can increase these activities daily. Finally, sharing is communicating about the experience of using the CBA with a caring family member, friend, or classmate.

To summarize, the CBA is a creative and meaningful way for counselors in training to monitor and modify balance in their lives. Maintaining a balance of these essential activities is a form of self-compassion and self-stewardship. Counselors who take care of themselves are more likely to respond ethically and effectively to their clients and enjoy their vocation throughout their professional lives (Henderson & Montplaisir, 2013).

Contributed by Lisa Sosin. © Kendall Hunt Publishing Company.

HOW CAN I ENGAGE IN WELLNESS SUPERVISION AND PROFESSIONAL DEVELOPMENT?

Engagement in peer consultation can help in identifying wellness issues. Consultants and supervisors can serve to support you and hold you accountable during the inevitable challenges of your career development. As a counselor-in-training, you will have the opportunity and responsibility to engage in various forms of supervision. A strong supervision relationship should not be limited to discussing client issues, challenging cas-

© Monkey Business Images/Shutterstock.com

es, or effective techniques. Your supervisor will act as a teacher, coach, consultant, mentor, evaluator, and an encourager. By staying open to the mentoring process even when feeling challenged or vulnerable, counselors-in-training can maximize the opportunities that supervision offers for personal and professional growth. Even after graduation when entering the early stages of your career and licensure internship, make supervision and peer consultation a part of your ongoing wellness plan. This relational network provides accountability, strengthens emotional support, increases access to resources, and provides a different perspective for case conceptualization (Sperry, 2010).

Furthermore, involvement in professional development activities outside of the classroom can enhance your overall learning experience and help you to establish habits that support ongoing learning and competence in your area of practice. In Chapter 14 you will review information on the future of the profession, future shifts in client needs, and how the counseling profession can adjust to support these needs. For this to happen, it is important to understand your responsibility in the profession. Involvement in the ongoing development of our field will require a continuing personal evolution in training, skills, and understanding of the community. Moreover, we have the collective responsibility for an ongoing emphasis on supporting one another toward a counselor community of wellness, providing any supervision, education, and training needed, particularly for counselors who may have an increased vulnerability for impairment experiences (Trippany, Kress, & Wilcoxon, 2004).

> Good supervision can be difficult to find. You want someone who is competent, will stretch you but will also focus on your self-care. It is imperative to find a supervisor who will challenge and move you clinically but also towards wellness.

Setting Goals for Self-Care

Counselors experiencing stress and burnout will need a plan tailored toward self-care that extends beyond eating healthy and exercising (Coaston, 2017). This plan should be intentional and proactive and needs to include realistic goals. For example, it might be unrealistic to set a goal of exercising for a full hour each day while putting in long hours at an internship. While in graduate school and working towards licensure, put a plan in place to be well. By being intentional and having a plan that is well thought out and detailed, you are more likely to make real changes. Taking these initial steps will place you ahead of the stress curve, being proactive and

© Andrey_Popov/Shutterstock.com

that is tailored your way. A well-established tool commonly used to set, plan and accomplish goals is the use of the S.M.A.R.T. acronym. SMART goal planning statements are designed to foster clear and articulable action steps that can enhance motivation, identify performance goals, objectives and support successful completion (see Table 7.1 below).

S	Specific	What will be accomplished? What actions will you take?
M	Measurable	What data will measure the goal? (How much? How well?)
A	Achievable	Is the goal doable? Do you have the necessary skills and resources?
R	Relevant	How does the goal align with broader goals? Why is the result important?
T	Time-Bound	What is the time frame for accomplishing the goal?

TABLE 7.1

SMART Goals

SMART example to support your use of this time management tool:

S: I would like to enhance my content knowledge on topics related to anxiety during the second quarter of this year. I plan to accomplish this goal by listening to a series of podcast and reading one book on the topic.

M: I will listen to a weekly podcast (Fridays, The Thoughtful Counselor) as I drive back and forth to work. I will additionally listen to an audible book on my 20-minute daily drive into work (ie. *Overcoming Panic Attacks: Strategies to Free Yourself from the Anxiety Trap*) to support the completion of this goal.

A: I believe that this goal is attainable as I have the resources needed to complete the goal. I have loaded both the podcast and book to my phone for immediate access.

R: This goal is important and relevant to me as I plan to begin a new job in the fall, 3rd quarter of this year that will require me to have a strong base of knowledge in this area.

T: I will complete this goal in 90 days.

Tracy Gibson, *MS, ACGC-III, ALC*

© Tracy Gibson

I found the most challenging part of engaging in the master level counseling program was maintaining self-care. As a student, I neglected self-care to complete assignments and tasks related to the program. I worked hard to submit everything on time. As I progressed through the program, I found it emotionally draining, reading course material, evaluating how it would apply to clients and at times myself, while simultaneously keeping up with assignments proved to be a lot at times. Physically, I lost sleep as I worked a full-time job, interned, and attended classes. Mentally, I became drained, eventually, I came to depend on sticky notes and highlighters to help me remember what I was supposed to be doing.

I soon realized that there is no way that I could make it through my program if I continued to neglect my self-care. I put two significant things into place, time management and establishing a time for myself to do things that were not school related. Taking time to do things for myself that did not include school proved to be difficult, however, I noticed that the time I set aside to do things like go to the beach or get dinner with friends, decreased the stress from the program.

As a new full-time counselor, I still sometimes find it difficult to maintain self-care. I now set a strict work/school/personal time schedule. I continue to use a detailed planner, to schedule business and pleasure. Doing this helps me to establish and maintain space for disconnecting from task or people as needed. At times I simply just sleep. Although it can be hard, I also try not to bring work home with me. I've learned that using several methods of self-care has been essential for me to maintain my life and counseling career.

Contributed by Tracy Gibson. © Kendall Hunt Publishing Company.

"A day without laughter is a day wasted." Charlie Chaplin
Then our mouths were filled with laughter and our tongues with joyful songs... Psalm: 126

SUMMARY

FOR THE ROAD AHEAD

Check out the Chapter 7 video at this link:

https://www.khpcontent.com/

Counseling is a unique profession as it challenges you to work on yourself as you gain new knowledge in working with others. This is an evolving process as we are living beings who change and grow. As counselors in training, it is imperative to maintain awareness of the ethical, professional, and spiritual responsibility of self-care. Caring for yourself is not selfish but is essential to being the best counselor you can be. Even Jesus took time away to rejuvenate and make decisions about how to best help others. Also, it is also important to develop an understanding of the history of wellness in the counseling profession, learn to recognize impairment, and engage in active steps to resolve and maintain wellness.

Reflections on the Journey

1. Why are wellness and self-care an important topic for counselors and training?
2. Reflecting on what you have read in this chapter, what might be three barriers to you maintain your wellness and self in the program or as a new professional in the field? After you reflect on these barriers, provide a resolution for each by noting a specific technique or tool to address each concern.
3. Gatekeeping is an important tool for counselors as we often can not see what we are not aware of. Should you notice that a colleague is bordering on impairment what would you say or do to promote awareness and help them? List two clear steps that you would take.

For Further Exploration

Corey, G., Muratori, M. Austin, J.T., & Austin, J.A. (2018). Counselor self-care. Alexandria, VA: American Counseling Association.

For New Counselors, What Are the Benefits of Counseling Supervision? (2013, November 25). ACA Member Blog. Retrieved from https://www.counseling.org/news/aca-blogs/aca-member-blogs/aca-member-blogs/2013/11/25/for-new-counselors-what-are-the-benefits-of-counseling-supervision-

Kiyosak, R. [FreedomKingdom]. (2017, August 8). How to set smart goals [Video File]. Retrieved from https://www.youtube.com/watch?v=wGbmAH4mBPA

Myers, J.E., & Sweeney, T.J. (2005) Counseling for wellness: Theory, research and practice. Alexandria, VA: American Counseling Association.

Myers, J.E., Sweeney, T.J., & Melvin Witmer (2001). Wellness Evaluation of Lifestyle [WEL]. Mindgarden. Retreived from https://www.mind-garden.com/159-wellness-evaluation-of-lifestyle#horizontalTab4

Myers, L. (2018, December 26). Building client and counselor resilience. Counseling Today, Cover Story. Retreived from https://ct.counseling.org/2018/12/building-client-and-counselor-resilience/

Saakvitne, K.W. & Pearlman, L.A. (1996). Transforming the pain: A workbook on vicarious traumatization. New York, NY: Norton Professional Books.

REFERENCES

American Counseling Association (2014). *ACA Code of Ethics.* Alexandria, VA: Author

American Counseling Association (2011). *ACA's task force on counselor wellness and impairment.* Retrieved from <http://www.counseling.org/wellness_taskforce/index.htm>

American Association for Marriage and Family Therapy. (2001). *AAMFT Code of Ethics.* Retrieved from <http://www.aamft.org/resources/lrm_plan/ethics/ethicscode2001.asp>

American Mental Health Association. (2015). *AMHCA Code of Ethics.* Retrieved from http://www.amhca.org/HigherLogic/System/DownloadDocumentFile.ashx?DocumentFileKey=5ff5bc94-e534-091e-c7c1-e3e-a45cf943e&forceDialog=0

Beaumont, E. (2016). Building resilience by cultivating compassion. *Healthcare Counseling and Psychotherapy Journal,* 22–27.

Beaumont, E., Durkin, M., Hollins-Martin, C. J., & Carson, J. (2016). Measuring relationships between self-compassion, compassion fatigue, burnout and well-being in student counsellors and student cognitive behavioral psychotherapists: A quantitative survey. *Counseling and Psychotherapy Research, 16*(1), 15-23.

Bodner, K. E. (2012). Ethical principles and standards that inform educational gatekeeping practices in psychology. *Ethics & Behavior, 22,* 60–74.

CACREP. (2016). CACREP Standards. Retrieved from: https://www.cacrep.org/for-programs/2016-cacrep-standards/

Canning, S. (2011). Out of balance: Why I hesitate to practice and teach "self-care". *Journal of Psychology and Christianity, 30*(1). Retrieved from http://link.galegroup.com/apps/doc/A342175880/AONE?u=vic_liberty&sid=AONE&xid=9ac48fa2.

Casey, D. (2013). Compassion fatigue. *Minnesota Fire Chief, 49*(5), 18-19.

Chart: The Compassion Fatigue Process. Adapted from C.R. Figley (2012), AMEDD Workbook. San Antonio. Figley Institute.

Coaston, S. (2017). Self-Care through self-compassion: A balm for burnout. *The Professional Counselor, 7*(3), 285-297.

Chiesa, A., & Serretti, S. (2009). Mindfulness-based stress reduction for stress management in healthy people: A review and meta-analysis. *The Journal of Alternative and Complementary Medicine, 15*, 593-600. doi:10.1089=acm.2008.0495

Cummings, P. N., Massey, L., & Jones, A. (2007). Keeping ourselves well: Strategies for promoting and maintaining counselor wellness. *Journal of Humanistic Counseling, Education and Development, 46*, 35-49.

Figley, C. R. (1995). *Compassion fatigue: Coping with secondary traumatic stress disorder in those who treat the traumatized.* New York, NY: Routledge.

Figley, C. R. (2002). Compassion fatigue: Psychotherapists' chronic lack of self-care. *Journal of Clinical Psychology, 58*, 1433–1441. doi:10.1002/jclp.10090

Ford, K. & Garzon, F. (2017). Research note: A randomized investigation of evangelical Christian accommodative mindfulness. *Spirituality in Clinical Practice, 4*(2), 92-99.

Frederick, T. V., Dunbar, S., & Thai, Y. (2018). Burnout in Christian perspective. *Pastoral Psychology, 67*, 267-276.

Garzon, F. & Ford, K. (2016). Adapting mindfulness for conservative Christians. *Journal of Psychology and Theology, 35*(3), 263-268.

Gladding, S. T. (2006). *The counseling dictionary* (2nd ed).Upper Saddle River, NJ: Prentice Hall.

Glosoff, H., Bernshoff, J., Hosie, H., & Maki, D. (1994). The 1994 ACA Model Legislation for licensed professional counselors .*Journal of Counseling and Development, 74*(2) 209-220.

Glosoff, H. L., Benshoff, J. M., Hosie, T. W., & Maki, D. R. (1995). The 1994 ACA model legislation for licensed professional counselors. *Journal of Counseling & Development, 74*(2), 209-220.

Goyal, M., Singh, S., Sibinga, E. M. S., Gould, N. F., Rowland-Seymour, A., Sharma, R., … Haythornthwaite, J. A. (2014). Meditation programs for psychological stress and well-being: A systematic review and meta-analysis. *JAMA Internal Medicine, 174*(3), 357-368. doi:10.1001/jamainternmed.2013.13018

Henderson, D. A., & Montplaisir, B. M. (2013). From good to great: Examining exemplary counselor development. *Journal of Counseling and Development, 91*(3), 336-342. doi: 101002/j.1556-6676.2013.00102.x

Hofmann, S. G., Sawyer, A. T., Witt, A. A., & Oh, D. (2010). The effect of mindfulness-based therapy on anxiety and depression: A meta-analytic review. *Journal of Consulting and Clinical Psychology, 78*(2), 169-183. doi:10.1037/a0018555

Homrich, A. M., DeLorenzi, L. D., Bloom, Z., & Godbee, B. D. (2014). Making the Case for Standards of Conduct in Clinical Training. *Counselor Education & Supervision, 53*, 2.

Hotchkiss, J. T., & Lesher, R. (2018). Factors predicting burnout among chaplains: Compassion satisfaction, organizational factors, and the mediators of mindful self-care and secondary traumatic stress. *Journal of Pastoral Care & Counseling, 72*(2), 86-98.

Kottler, J. & Hazler, R. J. (1996). Impaired counselors: The dark side brought into light. *The Journal of Humanistic Education and Development, 34*, 98-107.

Lawrence, C., Foster, V., & Tieso, C. (2015). Creating creative clinicians: Incorporating creativity into counselor education. *Journal of Creativity in Mental Health, 10*, 166–180. doi:10.1080/15401383.2014.963188

Lawson, G. & Myers, J. E. (2011). Wellness, professional quality of life, and career-sustaining behaviors: What keeps us well? *Journal of Counseling & Development, 89*, 163–171.

Lawson, G. (2007). Counselor wellness and impairment: A national survey. *Journal of Humanistic Counseling, Education & Development, 46*, 21-34.

Lawson, G., & Venart, B. (2005). Preventing counselor impairment: Vulnerability, wellness, and resilience. In G. R. Walz & R. K. Yep (Eds.), *VISTAS: Compelling perspectives on counseling, 2005* (pp. 243–246). Alexandria, VA: American Counseling Association.

Lawson, G., Venart, E., Hazler, E. & Kottler, J.A. (2011). Toward a Culture of Counselor Wellness *The Journal of Humanistic Counseling, Education and Development, 46*(1), 5-19.

Lindo, N., Walen, K., Ceballo, P., Ohrt, J., Prosek, D., Blalock, S. (2015) Wellness and burnout prevention: Perceptions of a group supervision intervention. *Wellness and Burnout Prevention, 42*(2), 28-42.

Maslach, C., Schaufeli, W., & Leiter, M. (2001). Job burnout. *Annual Review of Psychology, 52,* 397-422.

McCaughan, A., & Hill, N. (2015). The gatekeeping imperative in counselor education admission protocols: The criticality of personal qualities. *International Journal of Advance Counselling, 37,* 28-40.

Menezes, C. B., Pereira, M. G., & Bizarro, L. (2012). Sitting and silent meditation as a strategy to study emotion regulation. *Psychology & Neuroscience, 5*(1), 27-36.

Mirowsky, J., & Ross, C. E. (2007). Creative work and health. *Journal of Health and Social Behavior, 48*(4), 385-403. doi:http://dx.doi.org.ezproxy.liberty.edu/10.1177/002214650704800404

Mullen, P., Morris, C. & Lord, M. (2017). The experience of ethical dilemmas, burnout, and stress among practicing counselors. *Counseling and Values, 62,* 37-56.

Myers, J. E., & Sweeney, T. J. (2005). *Counseling for wellness: Theory, research, and practice.* American Counseling Association.

Myers, J. E., & Sweeney, T. J. (Eds.). (2005). *Counseling for wellness: Theory, research, and practice.* Alexandria, VA: American Counseling Association.

Myers, J. E., Sweeney, T J. & Witmer, J. (2000). The wheel of wellness counseling for wellness: A holistic model for treatment planning. *Journal of Counseling and Development, 78*(3), 251-266.

Neswald-Potter, R., & Simmons, R. T. (2016). Regenerative supervision: A restorative approach for counsellors impacted by vicarious trauma. *Canadian Journal of Counselling and Psychotherapy, 50*(1), 75-90.

Pardess, E., Mikulincer, M., Dekel, R., & Shaver, P. R. (2014). Dispositional attachment orientations, contextual variations in attachment security, and compassion fatigue among volunteers working with traumatized individuals. *Journal of Personality, 82*(5), 355-366.

Remley, T. P., & Herlihy, B. P. (2016). *Ethical, legal, and professional issues in counseling* (5th ed.). Pearson.

National Institute for Mental Health. (2018). *Emotional wellness toolkit.* Retrieved from <https://www.nih.gov/health-information/emotional-wellness-toolkit>

Rock, D., & Siegel, D. (2011). The healthy mind platter for optimal brain matter. Retrieved from http://www.healthymindplatter.com

Scott, G., & Lovell, R. (2015). The rural pastors initiative: Addressing isolation and burnout in rural ministry. *Pastoral Psychology, 64*(1), 71-97.

Shapiro, S. L., Carlson, L. E., Astin, J. A., & Freedman, B. (2006). Mechanisms of mindfulness. *Journal of Clinical Psychology, 62*(3), 373-386.

Siegel, D. J. (2012). *The developing mind: How relationships and the brain interact to shape who we are.* NY: Guilford Press.

Siegel, D. (2010). The healthy mind platter. Mind your brain website. Retrieved from http://www.drdansiegel.com/resources/healthy_mind_platter/

Simonton, D. K. (2000). Creativity: Cognitive, personal, developmental, and social aspects. *American Psychologist, 55*(1), 151-158. doi:10.1037/0003-066X.55.1.151

Sosin, L. S., & Rockinson-Szapkiw, A. J. (2016). Creative Exposure Intervention as part of clinical treatment for adolescents exposed to bullying and experiencing posttraumatic stress disorder symptoms. *Journal of Creativity in Mental Health, 11*(3-4), 391-408. doi:10.1080/15401383.2016.1251370

Sosin, L. (2016). The Creative Balance Tool: Teaching students how to maintain a healthy mind for optimal academic performance and overall well-being. Center for Teaching Excellence, Liberty University Faculty Orientation Workshop. Retrieved from http://works.bepress.com/lisa_sosin/19/

Sperry, L. (2010). *Highly effective therapy: Developing essential clinical competencies in counseling and psychotherapy*. New York, NY: Routledge.

Stadler, H. A., Willing, K. L., Eberhage, M. G. & Ward, W. H. (1988). Impairment: Implications for the counseling profession. *Journal of Counseling and Development, 66*(6), 258-260.

The World Health Organization. (2018). Wellness. Retrieved from https://www.who.int/healthpromotion/about/HPR%20Glossary_New%20Terms.pdf

Thompson, I. E., Amatea, E. S., & Thompson, E. S. (2014). Personal and Contextual Predictors of Mental Health Counselors' Compassion Fatigue and Burnout. J*ournal of Mental Health Counseling, 36*, 58-77.

Trippany, R. L., Kress, V. E. W., & Wilcoxon, S. A. (2004). Preventing vicarious trauma: What counselors should know when working with trauma survivors. *Journal of Counseling & Development, 82*, 31-37.

Tsai, K. C. (2012). Creative leadership for directing changes. *Business Management and Strategy, 3*(2), 76-84.

Witmer, J. M., Sweeney, T. J., & Myers, J. E. (1998). The wheel of wellness. Greensboro, NC: Authors.

Witmer, J .M., & Young, M. E. (1996). Preventing counselor impairment: A wellness approach. *The Journal of Humanistic Education and Development, 34*(3), 141-155.

Wolf, C. P., Thompson, I. A., Thompson, E.S., & Smith-Adcock, S. (2014). Refresh your mind, rejuvenate your body, renew your spirit: A pilot wellness program for counselor education. *Journal of Individual Psychology, 70*(1), 57-75.

CHAPTER 8

The Authentic Counseling Relationship: Client and Holistic Considerations

KRISTY FORD, PH.D. & CAPRI BROOKS, PH.D.

> The degree to which I can create relationships, which facilitate the growth of others as separate persons, is a measure of the growth I have achieved in myself.
> —Carl Rogers

Following Christ: Grace for Our Work

One of the best examples of an authentic relationship in Scripture is that of Paul and Timothy. The book of Acts highlights Paul and Timothy's first meeting and early beginnings of their relationship on Paul's second missionary journey. In Philippians 2:22 New International Version), Paul testifies to the depth of their relationship, comparing it to family when he says, "But you know that Timothy has proved himself, because as a son with his father he has served with me in the work of the gospel." Second Timothy

© Lightspring/Shutterstock.com

CHAPTER OBJECTIVES

After reading this chapter, you will understand more about:

- Identifying and explaining counselor characteristics and behaviors that influence the counseling process.
- Presenting a holistic systems approach to conceptualizing clients
- Introducing evidence-based counseling strategies and techniques for prevention and intervention.

The following CACREP standards are addressed in this chapter:

Counseling and Helping Relationships:

- A systems approach to conceptualizing clients (CACREP, 2016, Standard 2.F.5.b.)
- Counselor characteristics and behaviors that influence the counseling process (CACREP, 2016, Standard 2.F.5.f.)
- Evidence-based counseling strategies and techniques for prevention and intervention (CACREP, 2016, Standard 2.F.5.j.)

1:2-4 provides further evidence both of their bond and of the respect Paul had for Timothy. Paul again refers to him as a son but adds tender expressions of longing for their continued relationship as he writes, "To Timothy, my dear son: Grace, mercy and peace from God the Father and Christ Jesus our Lord. I thank God, whom I serve, as my ancestors did, with a clear conscience, as night and day I constantly remember you in my prayers. Recalling your tears, I long to see you, so that I may be filled with joy." Paul also offers words of encouragement to Timothy to persevere in his challenging ministry journey in 1 Timothy 1:18 writing, "Timothy, my son, I am giving you this command in keeping with the prophecies once made about you, so that by recalling them you may fight the battle well." An authentic relationship was critically important to completing the work that Paul and Timothy endeavored to accomplish. The job would have been difficult had there been no bond or respect for one another, and throughout their writings, the trust and attachment are evident. In the same way, relationships are vital to the counseling process. The work that the client and counselor undertake together cannot be accomplished without an authentic counseling relationship.

For better or for worse, relationships impact every area of life. For many clients, their personal rrelationships have not been the most positive experiences, and broken or hurtful relationships may have even served as the catalyst for many who are seeking therapy services. Everyone has a natural craving to experience love and understanding within the context of a meaningful relationship. Mental health research cites a prolific amount of evidence related to the necessity of relationships for survival (Johnson et al., 2013; Cozolino, 2010). From a Christian viewpoint, loving interpersonal relationships are not only required for well-being and survival, but are also one of the principal reasons for which mankind was created. Scripture indicates that humanity was created for relationship both with God and with others. As Christians, then, it is not surprising to recognize the attacks of the enemy on this very basic human need. According to the Genesis account of creation, God designed humanity with a need to fulfill two primary motivations, which Jones and Butman (2011) describe as "responsible dominion" and "loving relatedness" (p. 75). These writers assert that while the theme of responsible dominion relates to God's mandate to maintain excellence in

© fizkes/Shutterstock.com

stewardship over creation, the theme of loving relatedness describes God's instruction in Genesis 1:28 for humanity to perpetuate family relationships through childbearing. The dominating force behind the human motivation to seek attachments through interpersonal relationships might be attributed to this specific instruction communicated by God at humanity's creation. Furthermore, Christian theology teaches that humanity bears the image of God, Himself a relational being. Ultimately, Jesus reaffirms the importance of an intentional focus on developing relationships as He outlines the greatest commands to love both God and one another in Matthew 22:36-40.

This chapter focuses on three areas that counselors should consider as they seek to offer an authentic therapeutic relationship.

1. By first giving attention to the self, counselors consider personal characteristics that may be hindering or helping the treatment process.
2. Next, counselors consider personal characteristics of their clients from a systemic perspective, considering holistic and contextual variables that may impact the therapeutic relationship.
3. Lastly, the nature of the relational dynamic itself is considered, as counselors seek to employ evidence-based strategies and techniques related to the therapeutic relationship that support the client toward increased growth and wellness throughout the process.

WHAT ARE THE CRITICAL PERSONAL CHARACTERISTICS FOR THE COUNSELOR?

Everett Collection/Newscom

CARL R. ROGERS

What kind of person do I need to be in order to be an effective counselor? It is a great question! Carl Rogers is honored for his groundbreaking work in the field of mental health, setting the foundation of what is known today as the *Therapeutic Triad*: warmth, genuineness, and empathy. In 1957, he suggested that these three counselor traits were both necessary and sufficient for positive outcomes in therapy. In 1967, Rogers, Gendlin, Kiesler, and Traux found that clients' perceptions of these traits had a significant impact on the reduction of mental health symptoms. Research continues to support this initial finding that positive therapist traits are correlated with positive therapeutic outcomes. When counselors show higher levels of these traits, clients show better progress. While most researchers would disagree that these traits alone are sufficient, they do agree that they are necessary in both the establishment of rapport and the maintenance of a healthy therapeutic relationship (Norcross & Wampold, 2011).

A Warm Attitude

The first characteristic of the therapeutic triad is known as warmth or unconditional positive regard. This is the communication to the client that the therapist genuinely cares for them, respects them, and likes them. This approach is not dependent on what the client says or does, but rather is unconditional, allowing the ability to talk and feel freely without fear of being judged by the therapist. While clients exhibit both positive and negative behaviors, they need to feel completely accepted by the counselor for who they are, not who they are supposed to be (Young, 2017). As a warm attitude is fostered, the client will be reinforced in their feelings of importance and value as a person.

Exhibiting warmth in a session does not mean the therapist condones everything the client says or does. Rather, it means that the therapist sees the client as doing his or her best at this moment, coping with their difficulties in the best way they know how. A counselor occasionally expresses concerns about a behavior but can use a warm attitude to approach the subject in a non-judgmental manner that focuses on the potentially adverse outcomes of the client's behavior rather than on the worth or value of the client as a person. Warmth communicates to the client that they are worthy of love and acceptance, regardless of their current thoughts, feelings, and behavioral choices. This gives the client hope and confidence that change is possible. The client will be more open and honest with the therapist as they know they are accepted unconditionally. This creates a "safe zone" that provides clients with the opportunity to share their most painful experiences, including those that may be shameful, embarrassing, or frightening (Seligman & Reichenberg, 2014).

© Lurin/Shutterstock.com

Galatians 6:2 (NIV) says, "Carry each other's burdens, and in this way you will fulfill the law of Christ." The concept of warmth is woven throughout this verse. Clients who seek out counseling do so because they are carrying a heavy burden of their troubles that is causing them great discomfort or distress. Clients often grieve, worry, and struggle to get through their daily lives. Paul instructs Christian believers in this scripture to help each other by carrying each other's burdens. This is a beautiful word picture of reaching out to take hold of whatever baggage our clients are carrying and to help with bearing the weight. His words guide therapists to be a help for their clients, to help them carry their burdens as we come alongside them to face their struggles together.

© Alberto Andrei Rosu/Shutterstock.com

A Genuine Self

The second characteristic of the therapeutic triad is genuineness. Genuineness is the characteristic of being ourselves. It is the opposite of being phony, fake, and defensive, where what we truly feel on the inside matches what we show on the outside (Stoker, 2013). Genuineness means the therapist is authentic and real during therapy without putting on a façade. Well-trained therapists are self-aware and have a sense of the way their words and actions are perceived by the client. When a therapist is honest, open, and genuine in the therapeutic relationship, the client will be more likely to experience positive change in return (Young, 2017), and demonstrating genuineness may also predict a stronger therapeutic alliance (Jung, Weisjahn, Rief, & Lincoln, 2015).

When genuineness is exhibited by the counselor, it serves as a positive model for the client to express their authentic self as well, and the therapeutic relationship is then free from unnecessary hidden motives or deceptions. Although clients may struggle with honesty and openness in relationships, the counselor should strive to model transparency and encourage the client to do the same. In some circumstances, displaying genuineness might require a therapist to communicate frustration or disappointment to the client. However, Corey (2012) encourages caution on the part of the counselor in this area. This is particularly true when self-disclosure begins to place the focus of the session on the counselor's personal experience, pulling attention away from the client's needs. Good boundaries and a secure sense of self are required in order to maintain balance between helpful sharing and oversharing. Self-disclosure needs to be well-planned, well-timed, and determined to be of benefit to the client. If presented appropriately, self-disclosure can enhance the therapeutic relationship and support positive treatment outcomes (Seligman & Reichenberg, 2014).

The apostle Paul writes, "Love must be *sincere*. Hate what is evil; cling to what is good. Be devoted to one another in love. Honor one another above yourselves" (Romans 12:9-10, NIV). According to Webster's dictionary (2019), the word *sincere* means "free of dissimulation: honest." In this passage, Christian believers are instructed to be honest and genuine in their love and care for one another. Our sinful nature often makes this type of genuine and honest love difficult to extend, but it remains the goal. The characteristic of genuineness in a therapeutic relationship parallels the mandate to demonstrate love in sincerity.

An Empathetic Understanding

The third characteristic in the triad is empathy. No matter the approach to counseling, empathy is a necessary characteristic in a healthy therapeutic relationship (Kottler & Balkin, 2017). Empathy assists the therapist in truly connecting with the client and understanding his or her perspective and experiences (Hook & Ohlschlager, 2002).

Empathy is defined by Rogers (1980) as "entering the private perceptual world of the other and becoming thoroughly at home in it" (p. 142). Empathy in the therapeutic relationship allows the therapist to feel the client's feelings while keeping appropriate boundaries. It is one of the main avenues in which a therapist can connect with a client (Kottler & Balkin, 2017). This type of empathy requires a deep level of understanding as to the client's feelings (Haw-

"Rejoice with those who rejoice; mourn with those who mourn." Romans 12:15

Photo © Christin Lola/Shutterstock.com

kins, Knight, Sibcy, & Warren, 2019). By utilizing empathy, a counselor can, as the saying goes, "walk a mile in the client's shoes", allowing for a deeper relational connection and better understanding of the client's unique background and perspective that fosters positive change. For this to occur, empathy must be communicated to the client using empathetic reflections that are based on respect for the other person and an awareness of the person's worldview (Young, 2017).

The following example illustrates an **empathic reflection** by the counselor:
Client: I can't understand why he broke up with me. I am so upset.
Counselor: I can hear the sadness in your voice about the loss of your relationship.

Empathy is often confused with sympathy. Empathy does not mean the therapist feels exactly what the client feels. Each situation and person are different, and the therapist cannot experience things exactly the way the client does (Hook & Ohlschlager, 2002). Additionally, sympathy may reinforce a client's personal perception as victim and create a barrier between the client and the therapist. Empathy does the opposite; it enhances the relationship between client and therapist (Hawkins et al., 2019).

A Spirit-Filled Character

In addition to the development of the characteristics related to The Therapeutic Triad, Christian counselors have the empowering presence of the indwelling Holy Spirit, whose work in our lives results in an overflow of positive personal characteristics known as the fruits of the Spirit (Moon & Crews, 2002). The characteristics of love, joy, peace, patience, kindness, goodness, faithfulness, gentleness, and self-control are available through submission to the work of God in the process of *sanctification*. The Holy Spirit provides supernatural enabling for demonstrating these characteristics in the counseling relationship, as the mature Christian who is rooted in Christ allows the nature of Christ to be revealed in their character in the same way that fruit grows naturally on a vine (John 15:5). Tan and Scalise (2016) encourage Christians to allow the demonstration of these characteristics in the context of the counseling relationship by submitting to the leadership of the Holy Spirit so that the fruits can overflow. The fruits of the Spirit can be grouped into three categories: Love, joy, and peace; Patience, kindness, goodness; Faithfulness, gentleness, and self-control.

Love, joy, and peace. Love, joy and peace are blessings given by God. They grow and become qualities of character so that they can foster healing in other people through us (Hestenes, 1986). Love, in this passage, is Agape love, which is an unconditional, deliberate love. Agape love seeks only the best for those encountered, regardless of what they may do or say (Barclay, 1976). Agape love is especially important in the counseling setting. Clients may present a variety of past mistakes and information with which a therapist might disagree, yet love is key. To be able to love the client regardless of the past or present is essential to the relationship. Furthermore, joy is also an important part of the fruit. Joy, in this passage, is not joy from things on earth but rather joy that comes from God. Simply put, joy is happiness. God wants believers to experience life abundantly through the joy that He provides. This attitude will be evident to clients in the therapeutic relationship. Finally, peace is foundational to the Christian experience. It is a state of tranquility or quietness. God is the sole provider of deep, lasting peace. Many clients enter therapy feeling the opposite of peace, so the therapist must intentionally model peace for them.

Love is "incomparably the greatest psychotherapeutic agent… something that professional psychiatry cannot of itself create, focus, or release." Gordon Allport (1950, p. 90).

Patience, kindness, and goodness. Patience, kindness, and goodness are qualities that are important in maintaining healthy relationships (Hestenes, 1986). Patience in the counseling setting can be particularly important when working with difficult clients. Kindness is intuitively foundational for all relational development, as children are encouraged to be kind as they learn to form friendships. It is a quality that is needed in all avenues of life and in all relationships. Goodness generally refers to a firm, honest kindness. Firm kindness is necessary in therapeutic relationships where communicating difficult things to clients in a firm tone may be beneficial.

Faithfulness, gentleness, and self-control. Faithfulness, gentleness, and self-control are qualities of character that encourage personal stability and security (Hestenes, 1986). Being faithful means to be reliable or dependable. For example, clients need to know that a therapist will be there for sessions, will not leave them, and can be trusted. Gentleness should not be confused with mildness or weakness. Rather, it means that a believer is willing to submit  to the way and the will of God above his or her own will. Self-control "is the virtue which makes man so master of himself that he is fit to be the servant of others" (Barclay, 1976, p. 52). There is freedom in Christ, and self-control is the act of managing this freedom.

In your professional development as a counselor, it is important to consider both your personal character development and your inner spiritual development. Below, the case study of Sarah illustrates how the skills developed and implemented by her counselor helped her to feel safe enough to open up in her counseling session.

Case Study: Sarah

Sarah walked into the counseling office that day on time. She was rarely on time for a session, but that day she seemed a little more anxious than usual to see the counselor. She began visiting the counselor a few weeks ago after being suspended from school. During a meeting with her mom and the principal, she was told she had to start seeing the counselor weekly. She was frustrated by this and was always very reluctant to open up. This day seemed different.

As she walked into the room, she began talking before she even sat down. In an anxious voice she said, "Okay, I need to tell you something. I'm not sure what to do but my dad called last night." This was significant because Sarah had not spoken to her father in 5 years. Sarah had previously shared some resentment towards him for walking out on her mom. The counselor leaned in and made eye contact with Sarah. The counselor, in a soft and caring voice said, "so your dad called last night. Tell me more about that." Sarah took a deep breath and said, "should I talk to him or not?" The counselor looked at Sarah and said "I wish I could tell you what to do." Sarah responded, "ugh, I was afraid you were going to say that." The counselor responded in a caring voice., "because what you really want is an answer."

This conversation went on for some time. Sarah shared her feelings about the contact with her father. The counselor continued to speak in a soft, caring voice. She continued eye contact and posture of leaning in slightly.

This session was the beginning of a strong counseling relationship. Sarah began to open up and trust the counselor. She felt very connected to her and felt like the counselor truly cared what happened in her life. This is just one case example of how a counselor can connect with a client using empathy, unconditional positive regard, and by developing an alliance with the client. Adolescents often times comes into counseling due to parents or school administration mandate. It takes time and energy to develop a strong trusting relationship. The struggles that adolescents face vary and they come into counseling for a variety of issues. Developing a good relationship is vital to the success of counseling. This may be one of the most difficult things to accomplish when working with teens. Using these basic counseling skills can foster a good counselor/client relationship that can change the outcome of therapy.

It takes time and attention to develop the counseling skills needed to support strong therapeutic alliances. Supervisors and other counselors in the field who are further along in their professional development can serve as examples to follow. Christian counselors have the benefit of studying the life of Jesus, who serves as an example of the perfect counselor for those He came into contact with throughout his ministry. Below is a story from Scripture that illustrates Jesus' skill in offering relational safety. In this case, He reaches out to a woman who would have likely been a difficult client for establishing rapport.

Christ as the Perfect Example

John 8:3-11 says, "The teachers of the law and the Pharisees brought in a woman caught in adultery. They made her stand before the group and said to Jesus, 'Teacher, this woman was caught in the act of adultery. In the Law Moses commanded us to stone such women. Now what do you say?' They were using this question as a trap, in order to have a basis for accusing him.

But Jesus bent down and started to write on the ground with his finger. When they kept on questioning him, he straightened up and said to them,

'Let any one of you who is without sin be the first to throw a stone at her.' Again, he stooped down and wrote on the ground. At this, those who heard began to go away one at a time, the older ones first, until only Jesus was left, with the woman still standing there. Jesus straightened up and asked her, 'Woman, where are they? Has no one condemned you?' 'No one, sir,' she said. 'Then neither do I condemn you,' Jesus declared. 'Go now and leave your life of sin.'"

In this passage, Jesus demonstrates the three characteristics discussed in this chapter: warmth, genuineness, and empathy. It is evident that Jesus cared for the woman unconditionally. He knew she was living a sinful life, yet there is no condemnation in His words. It would have been easy for Him to point out her faults and even cast the first stone, but He did not. Jesus accepted her as she was, unconditionally and without judgment. Jesus extends grace to her, giving instructions in an open and honest manner and encouraging her to leave her life of sin. This encounter reveals the genuine character of Jesus. Lastly, Jesus displays empathy in this passage, as He had compassion on her. He defended her and spoke words that saved her life as the Pharisees were trying to kill her. Thus, Christ is the perfect example of an effective counselor, displaying warmth, genuineness, and empathy.

This devotional illustrates Christ as the perfect example of a counselor who demonstrated the characteristics needed to make others feel safe and accepted. While we will never be perfect, counselors strive to develop the professional skills and personal characteristics that support therapeutic rapport. Next, a counseling student intern on this learning journey discusses her experiences building rapport with her clients:

Clara Soles, Counselor in Training, Liberty University

Clara Soles is a masters level student in the Clinical Mental Health Program at Liberty University. She is currently completing her university sponsored internship at a private counseling practice,

© Clara Soles

with a goal of becoming a Licensed Mental Health Counselor in the state of Florida. She sees a variety of clients but enjoys working with women of all ages. Her favorite thing about working in the mental health field is helping clients find healing and claim freedom over obstacles and limitations in their lives. When interviewed about her experience during practicum and internship, she described her learning process for building rapport and developing the therapeutic relationship:

Working as a master's level student intern the last nine months has taught me that establishing rapport can be a deciding factor for a client. I have heard stories from clients about their previous therapist, and some have felt their therapist was rude, angry, inattentive, or passive. Some clients come into therapy with clear expectations, but some are hesitant because they fear the unknown. Building rapport has helped me to get to know my client, assess their expectations, and communicate my intentions for therapy. I strive to be transparent in communicating what the therapeutic process will look like starting with the intake and assessment phase. I have found that discussing the process of formulating therapeutic goals is beneficial in building rapport. I tell every client that we work as a team to identify goals, and I try to make the client feel empowered in the goal setting phase by discussing what aspects of counseling they control, and where they want to be at the end of therapy.

One interesting challenge to building rapport that I have encountered during my internship has been the fact that I am still an "intern". I had a client who was living with her mother and father and having difficulty transitioning into adulthood because of anger and resentment she had from previous family trauma. She came into the initial session wanting to let go of her bitterness but unsure about counseling. I could sense her hesitation and was able to explore with her why she was uncomfortable. I could tell she desired a change, and I was able to use reflection to clarify and demonstrate active listening to open up a conversation on my role in the therapeutic process. The client's body language started to relax, and I could tell the hard exterior was starting to disappear. She told her parents she had found a therapist to work on her anger, but was met with hostility on their part over choosing an intern. After a few weeks of tension, my client was able to convince her mother to come to a session with her. Her mother came to therapy prepared to defend why she believed her daughter required a more experienced therapist. I worked together with my client to facilitate healthy communication with her mother about why she was attending counseling and what she aimed to get out of counseling. Additionally, I was transparent when answering the concerns over my competency and discussed my therapeutic approach to the presenting problems as well as the process of clinical supervision. I believe demonstrating the benefits of psychoeducation, working through a difficult conversation between the client and her mother, and genuinely discussing the concerns the mother had about my counseling abilities provided an opportunity to strengthen the therapeutic relationship and enabled me to build rapport with my client and her mother.

Cultivating a good reputation is crucial when working in a small town like mine. I made it my goal to create an environment that provides a safe space for the client to be vulnerable and to meet them where they are. I aim to be transparent and approachable with every client. When clients ask me questions about who I am and how I approach counseling, I know they are probably not looking for a wordy theoretical approach. Clients are searching for a genuine connection with who I am in order to feel safe and comfortable to allow me to enter into their pain alongside them.

WHAT IS CASE CONCEPTUALIZATION?

A person is a fluid process, not a fixed and static entity; a flowing river of change, not a block of solid material; a continually changing constellation of potentialities, not a fixed quantity of traits (Rogers, 1961).

General Systems Theory

General systems theory describes processes that have interdependent parts that interact and influence one another (von Bertalanffy, 1969). Systems are evidenced throughout creation such as in the predictability of our own solar system, and systems such as computer systems and heating/cooling systems are developed purposefully to meet various needs. The physical body, as illustrated in the previous scripture passage, serves as an example of systemic interdependency.

Beyond just the physical, the *self* is also comprised of systemic psychological interactions (see Figure 8.1). Thoughts, feelings, and behaviors become even more complex with the addition of social systems including the contexts of family, school, occupation, and the broader culture (Bronfenbrenner, 2005). In other words, human beings are themselves made up of complex

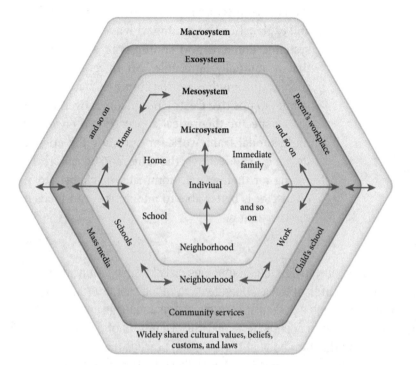

© Kendall Hunt Publishing Company

FIGURE 8.1

Psychosocial Systems

biological and psychological systems. These systems are interdependent on other systemic human beings within the social systemic context and swirl and move in an expanding system of their surrounding cultural contexts in an ever-changing continuum of time.

A Systemic Approach to Conceptualization

Case conceptualization. In the pursuit of an authentic therapeutic relationship, counselors view their clients from both a systemic and a holistic perspective. Various factors should be considered that may contribute to the ease or difficulty of establishing rapport as well as to the overall dynamics of the ongoing relationship. Case conceptualization is a process in which the counselor seeks a "bird's eye view" of each individual client and the unique factors that may contribute to the presenting problem(s). By considering the client using a holistic and systemic approach, the counselor attempts to make sense of the symptoms in order to apply the most

© studioarz/Shutterstock.com

ethical and effective treatment possible (Sperry, 2010). This is an ongoing collaborative process that, following the development of a strong therapeutic alliance, allows the counselor and client to safely explore theories and explanations beginning with assessment in various systemic domains and ending with a treatment plan that is mutually agreeable. An integrative approach such as this emphasizes the common factors that contribute to positive treatment outcomes over adherence to any specific theoretical approach and encourages a multi-modal framework for outlining the etiology of dysfunctional feelings, thoughts, and behaviors. By listening for themes that dominate the client's story, the counselor is better able to understand and focus in on the core issues.

> Case conceptualization (sometimes called a case formulation is the clinician's collective understanding of the client's problems as viewed through a particular theoretical orientation; as defined by the biological, psychochological, and social contexts of the client; and as supported by a body of research and practice that links a set of co-occurring symptoms to a diagnosis and, ultimately, a treatment plan. A strong case conceptualization is guided by the utilization of a theoretical orientation that provides a framework for the clinician from which to condense and synthesize multiple pieces of information into a coherent and well-developed narrative (John & Segal, 2015, p. 1).

The Bio-Psycho-Social-Spiritual approach. This approach to case conceptualization is often referred to as the bio-psycho-social approach, referencing the three critical domains of biological, psychological, and social functioning. Other important domains for assessment can include spiritual functioning, multi-cultural considerations, school and/or career functioning, and significant events across the life-span continuum. Each of these domains represent an area of potential dysfunction as well as a possible resource for resiliency and support. By viewing the client holistically in terms of both strengths and weaknesses, the counselor is better able to conceptualize areas where growth is needed while encouraging their client toward an increased awareness of personal competencies. Moreover, they

330

support the resiliency needed to understand the past in a way that facilitates their future goals. These goals then become the focus of treatment planning by assimilating the initial themes presented in the client's story. Consideration of the holistic person of the client requires conceptualization of the potential impact of each of these domains.

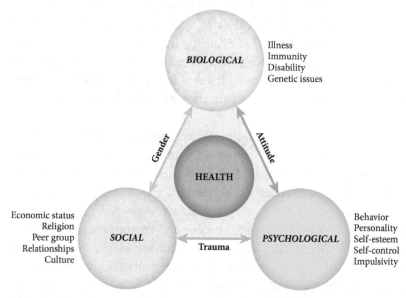

Biological functioning. In order to conceptualize the possible impact of biological functioning on the client's presenting problem, a treatment team approach may be needed to ensure that the client's physical health has been evaluated by a medical professional. Treatment teams include all of the professionals required to assess the various domains of functioning. A medical evaluation may already be complete for many clients, but if not, it is an opportunity to connect the client to a trusted physician by way of referral. The evaluation could include specialty areas of medical practice such as psychiatry, gynecology, or neurology, but at a minimum should include an overall health assessment by a general medical practitioner. Clients can often provide an overview of their physical health, including their medical history, past hospitalizations, chronic illnesses, and current medications. However, it may also be advisable to obtain a release of information to view the client's medical file, particularly in a situation where the client is unable to verbalize their medical history or fully understand the systemic implications of their physical issues. Also, treatment team collaboration may be necessary in cases such as substance abuse treatment when it is suspected that the client may not be disclosing all of the critical information for effective treatment.

Neuroscience principles also inform the conceptualization of biological functioning. Advances in neurobiological science inform psychotherapy by providing an understanding of brain processes and the resulting implications for positive therapeutic outcomes (Siegel, 2010). While many abnormal biological processes, such as disease, chemical imbalance, or brain injury may influence psychological conditions, normal processes within the brain also affect psychological states. Specifically, interactions between primary regions of the brain that shape the transformation of trauma into emotional memories can result in dysfunctional responses such as an overactive flight or fight response, the development of negative schemas, or disruptions in secure relational attachments (Cozolino, 2010).

Psychological functioning. Psychological functioning is generally assessed by first conducting an intake interview for an overview of the client's presenting symptoms. The initial interview is then followed by the administration of empirically-validated psychometric tests to assist the counselor in linking client symptoms to the diagnostic process within case conceptualization in a professionally accountable and responsible manner. Critical dysfunction in thinking, feeling, and behaving are the initial focus of the clinical mental health professional and concentrates on assessment in areas such as suicidal ideation, negative mental health symptoms, poor coping strategies, and abnormal personality. However, identifying resiliency factors is equally important in the assessment of psychological functioning. This identification initiates the exploration of the whole self in terms of both strengths and weaknesses by focusing on areas such as personal values and belief systems, self-esteem, identity constructs, intelligence, and positive personality traits.

Alongside the assessment and conceptualization of presenting symptoms, counselors assess the client's readiness for change (see Figure 8.2). Researchers Prochaska and DiClemente (1982) outlined various levels of motivation toward behavioral change presented by clients, particularly low motivation for discontinuing adverse behaviors. They emphasized the importance of counselor awareness of the stages of change in fostering increased client motivation by addressing ambivalence. Ambivalence, defined as feeling two ways about behavior change, is seen as a natural part of the change process, and further research (Miller & Rollnick, 2004) emphasizes the importance of working with the client at their current level of motivation in order to decrease resistance to therapy. By approaching the therapeutic relationship with respect toward a client's readiness for

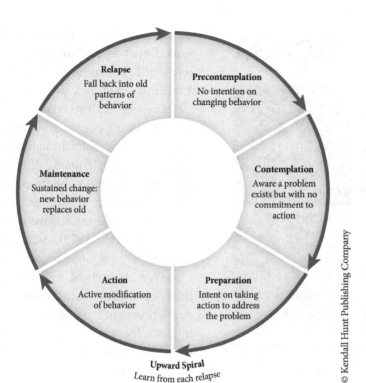

FIGURE 8.2

Stages of Change Model

Relapse
Fall back into old patterns of behavior

Precontemplation
No intention on changing behavior

Maintenance
Sustained change: new behavior replaces old

Contemplation
Aware a problem exists but with no commitment to action

Action
Active modification of behavior

Preparation
Intent on taking action to address the problem

Upward Spiral
Learn from each relapse

© Kendall Hunt Publishing Company

change, resistance can be avoided and a safe environment can be encouraged for the incorporation of new, more adaptive behaviors (Prochaska & Prochaska, 2016).

Social functioning. The health of our social relationships is considerably linked to overall health, both physically and psychologically (Johnson et al., 2013). In order to conceptualize the impact of social functioning, the counselor and client collaborate to explore family history and dynamics as well as broader relationships within the client's community context. Genograms (McGoldrick, Gerson, & Petry, 2008) are a common method of social assessment that provide both a collaborative and a dynamic therapeutic exercise for exploring the family system. The resulting pictorial example of relational function and dysfunction surrounding the client can be used throughout the therapy process to track changes in dynamics. Family relationships, along with the client's broader context relationships, are systemic in nature, meaning the relationships impact the client which impacts the relationships. Additionally, the client's social functioning interacts with the presenting problem in a systematic way, requiring conceptualization of how the client's relationships may be impacting the issue and subsequent relationships.

THEORY OF ATTACHMENT

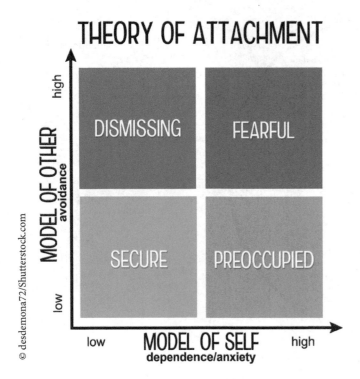

© desdemona72/Shutterstock.com

Attachment theory provides a framework for conceptualizing dysfunction in relationships stemming from insecure attachment patterns, as well as a prescription for healthy relating based on securely developed attachment bonds (Bowlby, 1969). Attachment styles are categories of relational schemas that are shaped by early childhood interactions that predict subsequent reactions in social situations (Ainsworth, Blehar, Waters, & Wall, 1978). Schore (2002) emphasizes that interactions in early caregiver attachment relationships influence personality organization and the development of self-regulation and coping skills for dealing with overwhelming emotion. While a secure attachment schema enhances brain development, insecure and disorganized schemas intensify physical and emotional illness (Schore, 2002). Assessing attachment style is critical for conceptualizing overall social functioning and its systemic impact on other areas of functioning (Schore & Schore, 2008).

Spiritual functioning. Spirituality is often viewed as a multi-cultural consideration with an attitude of religious sensitivity for the client's personal belief systems. It is important for counselor education programs to include competency training in the area of spiritual assessment in order to support the overall conceptualization of a client's presenting concerns (Bohecker, Schellenberg, & Silvey, 2017). For a client who considers themselves to be open to spirituality or identifies with a particular religious orientation such as the Christian faith, spiritual functioning may be conceptualized as an equally important domain alongside biological, psychological, and social functioning. For some clients, religiosity or spirituality may be a sensitive topic, providing an area for cautious and collaborative exploration. Other clients may prefer to avoid this domain altogether and may even indicate that pursuing conversations related to faith could serve as a barrier to the development of therapeutic rapport. By addressing spiritual and/or religious orientation at intake from a stance of religious sensitivity, counselors can evaluate the influence of this domain on other areas and assess the client's openness to further exploration.

Multi-cultural considerations. Multicultural awareness is a core competency expectation of counselor education programs. Developing and deepening the skill is imperative for students as they move forward in the journey to becoming an effective counselor. Adherence to the American Counseling Association (ACA) ethics code includes actively engaging in multicultural sensitivity in order to communicate in ways that are "culturally appropriate" (ACA, 2014, A.2.c.). Multi-cultural considerations include areas where counselor and client may have differing backgrounds, worldviews, values, or belief systems that have the potential to negatively impact the development of the therapeutic relationship due to misunderstanding, unintentional insensitivity, or even blatant bias. Sometimes multi-cultural awareness is best approached by stating the obvious and encouraging a conversation on ways that differing backgrounds may influence the relationship, such as differences in ethnicity and gender. Other times, multi-cultural considerations may require the counselor to maintain an awareness of the subtle ways in which differing perspectives may be influencing the relational dynamic, such as in the case of religious worldviews, political leanings, or gender role expectations.

Activating Multicultural Sensitivity to Develop Rapport
Tonya Gardner, School Counselor

Tonya Gardner serves as a school counselor in the panhandle of Florida. She was presented with the challenge of developing a strong therapeutic alliance with a student, and was encouraged by her unique situation to consider multi-cultural sensitivity factors alongside other client characteristics. She decided to go the extra mile to navigate language barriers in order to help a student. In the following case study, Tonya shares her story on how she activated multicultural sensitivity in order to develop rapport with a client.

It was the second semester during the month of January when I met Dao. She arrived that morning with a nervous smile on her face, repeating the word "yes" while nodding her head in agreement to every question I posed. In that moment, both of our lives changed as apprehension and anxiety filled the space between us. She had just arrived from Vietnam the week before as an honors student with wide eyes full of hope and excitement about a new life in America. In her home country she was in an accelerated program, earning many awards for her academic achievement, embarking on her senior year. However, sitting in the small high school lobby waiting for word from the rural school district office about grade level placement slowly dimmed the sparkle in her eyes as she tried to remain positive, speaking to her relatives in a language I could not understand. I had heard the language before, as her aunt was well-known in our small town for her full-service nail salon, which I happily visited on several occasions. On this day, I did not have to understand the language because I could intuit from her body language that Dao was scared, nervous, and frustrated. Truthfully, so was I.

After what seemed hours, I received the message that Dao would be placed in eleventh grade; a crushing blow to her and the family. I did my best to be positive and I assured her family I would do everything I could to help her graduate sooner. After they left, I began to research state educational laws regarding accommodations for speakers of other languages. The law was very clear that the receiving school district is responsible for finding a way to provide instruction in the student's native language while assisting the student in learning English. The problem for everyone involved was the language barrier. Our community is a small, rural community without the necessary resources for issues such as this one. Even if the district could find the money to hire an interpreter, finding someone who understood the language well enough to help Dao with her schoolwork and help the teachers with instruction would be next to impossible. On Monday, Dao returned to our school. The district director instructed me to "immerse her in the language" by placing her in honors courses and letting her participate if she felt that she could. I checked on her every class period throughout the day for a week. Each day, I received a report from every teacher. I was not surprised to hear that her teachers were struggling. They loved her, thought she was very sweet, but could not communicate with her.

The following Monday, as I passed Dao in the hall, she grabbed me and would not let go. I asked her if she would like to come to my office for a few minutes and she was more than happy to oblige. While we were in my office, she took her cell phone out and began to show me pictures. It was in that moment that I realized she and I were bonding over this small piece of technology to which we both had access, and I decided to try an experiment. I downloaded the Google translate application and I spoke English into my phone, which in turn spoke Vietnamese to Dao. She was so excited to have a conversation with me and I was so happy to bond with her, we lost track of time and she stayed in my office for over an hour. By lunchtime that day, I was able to meet with all of Dao's teachers and explain that they would be needing their cell phones during class in order to communi-

cate with her. After receiving permission from her guardian, I also downloaded the translator application on her phone. By Friday, Dao was making friends and seemed happier.

Although the cell phone application provided a wonderful resource for everyone involved, we still needed other ways to assist Dao in learning the language as well as assist the teachers in finding ways in which to scaffold the language acquisition process. After some research, I discovered that I could borrow a program called Rosetta Stone from our local library and download it on our computers in the library at our school. After installing Rosetta Stone, I changed Dao's schedule so that for one class period each day she would be able to go to the library, utilize the language program, and learn conversational English. I also met with her teachers and requested that they attempt to find time to utilize the Rosetta Stone program in order to understand Vietnamese. In doing this, we were able to break through some of the language barriers.

Once the teachers were better able to understand Dao's needs, they began to find other ways in which to differentiate instruction so that Dao could participate in class. Several of them even translated power points and converted them to Dao's native language so she could understand the coursework. This was no easy task, but our teachers were willing to go the extra mile because they cared about Dao. Additionally, Dao's family was elated that she was happy and was learning. The relationship between the school and the family changed dramatically as a result. By the end of the semester, Dao was speaking some English and was well on her way to understanding written English. She continued to utilize the Rosetta Stone program and was able to graduate after attending summer school rather than having to start her senior year over again. She is now a college student and is very happy to be living in America with her relatives.

Significant life events. Significant events have the power to change the trajectory of life's journey, for better or worse. Negative events produce strong negative emotions that can be quite experientially painful. These events are often powerful enough for the client to create emotional avoidance, meaning that the one thing they need to talk about most is the one thing they avoid discussing at all costs. The result is the build-up of emotional toxicity, as the body struggles with the lack of integration of the event in the overall narrative. In 1967, Holmes and Rahe investigated patient medical records to search for a link between critical life events and the likelihood of developing physical illness. Ultimately, 43 stressful life events were identified and ranked in what is now known as the Holmes-Rahe

Stress Scale, in which higher scores predict a greater likelihood of future illness (Noone, 2017). Effective counselors know that the therapeutic relationship is a critical component for establishing the safety needed to help clients feel supported as they navigate the painful journey of processing through their most significant life events.

TABLE 8.1

Domains of Conceptual-
ization in the Bio-
Psycho-Social-Spiritual
Approach

Domains	Potential Areas for Conceptualization
Biological Functioning	Medical history, Current medications, Substance use and/or abuse, Genetic risk factors
Psychological Functioning	Suicidal ideation, Mental health symptoms, Positive and negative Coping strategies, Self-efficacy and Resiliency
Social Functioning	Attachment style, Family dynamics, Peer and romantic relationships, Communication style, Support system
Spiritual Functioning	Spiritual identity, Religious belief systems, Value systems, Church involvement, Religious coping strategies
Multi-Cultural Factors	Cultural and Ethnic identity, Unique cultural and familial norms, Cross-cultural or acculturation challenges, Language barriers, Sexual orientation, Gender issues and Role expectations
Significant Life Events	Trauma events, Relational ruptures, Grief symptoms, Hospitalizations or other Major health events, Births, Career Changes, Home Relocations

WHAT IS THE THERAPEUTIC ALLIANCE?

Finally all of you should be of one mind. Sympathize with each other. Love each other as brothers and sisters. Be tenderhearted and keep a humble attitude. -1 Peter 3:8

Understanding the therapeutic alliance. The therapeutic alliance is formed as the relationship between the client and counselor deepens and trust is established, thus allowing for increasingly intense levels of therapeutic intervention (Sperry, 2010). Modeling active attention to the dynamics of the relationship is a priority in the counseling process as the therapeutic relationship accounts for a large percentage of the factors that contribute to positive outcomes in therapy (Kottler & Balkin, 2017). In fact, a recent study by Luedke, Peluso, Diaz, Freund, and Baker (2017) observed the affective counselor-client exchanges during the first session of counseling and found that affective counselor-client exchanges were significant in discriminating between clients who dropped out of counseling and clients who remained in counseling. Chapter 9 of this text will discuss more on developing the skills related to these particular counselor-client exchanges.

In addition to guarding against client dropout (Luedke et al., 2017; Sharf, Primavera, & Diener, 2010), research indicates that the therapeutic alliance is more predictive of positive client outcomes, even over adherence to any particular theoretical stance (Wampold, 2015). An integrative psychotherapy approach identifies common outcome variables, such as the therapeutic relationship and patient variables (eg. client motivation to change), as superior predictors of positive outcomes (Beitman & Manring, 2009). While each school of therapy is driven to seek empirical evidence of its superior outcome efficacy as compared to other schools, the integrative psychotherapeutic approach has several advantages over other schools of thought (Norcross & Wampold, 2011). For example, integrationists emphasize the common constructs inherent to every psychological approach such as overlapping strategies and principles. Also, integrationists recognize the continuity of psychotherapy as a whole, stressing each approach to treatment as being more alike than different and identifying core processes, such as the therapeutic alliance, that are common to all psychotherapies.

> "As I look at current research in this area, I find there are a number of elements a counselor simply may have limited to no influence [on], such as past history, the presence of immediate support and family history. However, one element that counselors can direct is the working alliance, which is perhaps the most essential component of the factors that counselors can influence" (Balkin, 2015).

The goal of the therapeutic alliance. The counselor-client relationship is unique among relationships in that the goal is to support the health and growth of the client rather than having the goal of being mutually beneficial. All relationships require focused attention in order to maintain a positive experience for both people involved. Research by Gottman (1999) suggests that a ratio of five positive interactions for every one negative interaction is required in the ongoing maintenance of a successful relationship. The counselor, then, has the critical responsibility to maintain focused attention to the well-being of the relational dynamic, knowing that the therapeutic relationship is a tool that has both the power both to heal and to harm if not given the appropriate attention. The goal of the therapeutic alliance is to build trust so that wounds originating from formative relationships can be addressed. Within the safe context of an authentic therapy relationship, relational tensions and dysfunctional interpersonal dynamics can be recreated and processed with a goal of increasing the ability to engage in deeper levels of relational intimacy while developing a solid sense of self through the establishment of healthy boundaries (McMinn & Campbell, 2007). The incarnational engagement of the Holy Spirit alongside the therapeutic alliance has the potential to initiate the experience of healing in relationships, both with God and with significant others.

> "I think there is way too much attention on the techniques, intervention and skills without exploring more deeply what empowers them. There has always been a disconnect between what counselors think makes the most difference in their sessions and what clients report was most helpful to them" (Kottler, 2015, p. 1)

Evidence-Based Techniques: Communicating Empathy

Empathy. Empathy may be best understood as an ongoing character trait that supports the development and maintenance of a strong therapeutic alliance while increasing the likelihood for positive outcomes in treatment (Nienhuis et al., 2018). Empathy has sometimes been defined as feeling *with* the client, and contrasted with sympathy as opposed to sympathy which is feeling *for* the client (Brown, 2013). Empathy is the ability to experience and understand the feelings of the other person and is associated with a set of therapist's behaviors such as unconditional acceptance of the client's experi-

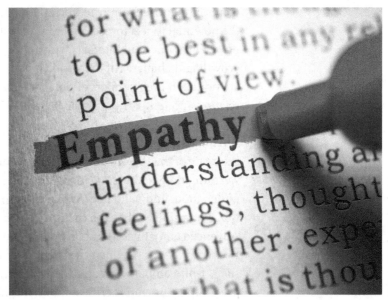

© Feng Yu/Shutterstock.com

ence, active listening, and nonjudgmental communication (Horvath & Bedi, 2002). Empathy allows the client to feel secure in the relationship, scaffolding the development of the trust needed for them to open up and share their thoughts, feelings, and experiences. The communication of empathy within the therapeutic relationship is considered a foundational skill for effective counselors (Sommers-Flanagan, 2015), and research indicates that counselor education programs that include training toward increased empathy are effective in developing the skill (Teding van Berkhout & Malouff, 2015). In fact, empathy is considered an "umbrella skill" for all other counseling skills, meaning it is given priority even while focusing on the practice of other skills (Hawkins et al., 2019). Empathy can be communicated verbally by demonstrating skills such as reflecting the content of the client's narrative and using minimal encouragers. Empathy can also be communicated nonverbally by demonstrating skills such as positive facial expressions and the S.O.L.E.R. active listening technique (see chart). With empathy firmly in place, the basic skills of effective

The S.O.L.E.R. Active Listening Model (Egan, 1998)
Sit up straight (conveying "I am here with you.")
Open posture (indicating openness to listening)
Lean forward (indicating interest in client's words)
Eye contact (expressing interest and reassurance of connection)
Relax (putting the client at ease)

counseling move from rote to real. Empathy takes a relationship that has the potential to feel forced or fake and, instead, makes it feel authentic and powerful as one soul interacts with another and creates an opportunity for growth and change. All the various models and approaches to counseling are united in their support of the most essential component of any helping relationship- empathy (Kottler & Balkin, 2017).

Advanced Empathy. Empathy is arguably the most critical personal characteristic of the therapeutic triad, and when presented in conjunction with warmth and genuineness, it creates a context in which clients feel heard, understood, and validated. While empathy reflects the content and emotion communicated by the client, *advanced empathy* goes one step further. Advanced empathy is the ability of the counselor to understand and reflect feelings or issues of which the client is unaware (Hawkins et al., 2019). As such, while empathy creates the experience of validation for the client's presenting pain and is critical for establishing rapport, advanced empathy helps bring long-buried thoughts and emotions to the surface where they can be effectively processed in the context of the ongoing therapeutic relationship.

Dr. Joshua Watson
Professor and Chair, Department of Counseling and Educational Psychology
Texas A&M University-Corpus Christi

I believe counselors are uniquely positioned to help others on a variety of levels. In addition to the individual clients, couples, and families we serve, professional counselors also provide voice to the unheard and advocate for their communities and the rights of others. Supported by nearly two decades of experience working with clients and training future counselors, I have an idea what leads to counseling success. I often share with my students that they will complete hours of coursework, in many cases across multiple years, to gain the basic knowledge and skills counselors apply. However, the individuals with whom they work receive no training to be a counseling client. In most cases, clients will never know if you apply a technique incorrectly or misappropriate a theory or technique. No, for our clients, what is most important is feeling like they have a genuine, authentic rela-

© Edgar De La Garza

tionship with their counselor. Decades of research support the impact these core conditions have on the counseling relationship and ultimately treatment success. Picture the clients you serve. They likely come to counseling scared, confused, sad, or feeling alone. When we as professionals reach out, as humans first and foremost, and empathize with our clients, we provide a sense of safety and security that is invaluable. In fact, sometimes just being there to listen and support can be the best counseling interventions. As you continue building your skill set through coursework and professional development opportunities, always keep in mind that these skills are only effective when delivered by an individual the client trusts and feels safe around. Build the relationship first, be empathic, and you will find everything else then falls into place.

KEY TERMS

The Therapeutic Triad: Warmth, Genuineness, Empathy

Sanctification: Becoming more and more like Christ in a process of developmental spiritual maturity

Case Conceptualization: An assessment of the client and the presenting problem that views the client from a holistic perspective using the bio-psycho-social-spiritual approach.

Attachment Styles: Categories of relational schemas that are shaped by early childhood interactions and that predict subsequent reactions in social situations.

Stages of Change: The various levels of motivation toward behavioral change presented by clients as presented by Prochaska and DiClemente (1982)

The Therapeutic Alliance: A positive working relationship between a counselor and a client for the purpose of benefiting the client.

Empathy: The ability to experience and understand the feelings of another person.

Advanced Empathy: The ability to understand and reflect the experience of another person that they are not yet aware of themselves.

SUMMARY

FOR THE ROAD AHEAD

Check out the Chapter 8 video at this link:
https://www.khpcontent.com/

The therapeutic relationship is first established by developing rapport with the client and then maintained by giving focused attention to the quality of the relational alliance as therapy continues. Personal counselor characteristics (warmth, genuineness, and empathy), client systemic variables, and ongoing relational dynamics can all play a role in impacting the quality of the alliance. Empathy, or the ability to understand and reflect the client's experience, begins as a critical counselor characteristic and is a focal point of development in counselor training programs due to its role in predicting positive outcomes in therapy. Both empathy and advanced empathy (the ability to reflect client experience that lies outside conscious awareness) are skills that developing counselors can utilize with increasing maturity to support a positive and effective therapeutic relationship.

Reflections on the Journey

- Regardless of your theoretical approach to counseling, the authentic counseling relationship emphasized in this chapter serves as the foundation of counseling. What are some basic concepts from this chapter that you plan to incorporate into your personal theory of counseling?
- The therapeutic triad includes warmth, genuineness, and empathy. How do you see these characteristics as being important to the counseling relationship?
- What factors could interfere with you demonstrating warmth/unconditional positive regard to a client? What if your client is involved with something that you consider to be morally wrong? How would you handle that?
- Can you think of a scenario where being genuine with a client may be difficult? What would you do if you found yourself being phony, fake, or defensive in a counseling session?
- The fruits of the spirit are cultivated in a believer's life through sanctification. How is personal sanctification important to your work as a counselor?
- Viewing the client from both a systemic and a holistic perspective assists in the pursuit of an authentic therapeutic relationship. How do you think this perspective could assist in your case conceptualization?

- Spiritual functioning is important to the overall health of the client. How would you handle a client who has spiritual beliefs that are vastly different from yours?
- Multi-cultural considerations should be accounted for with each client. What types of potential multi-cultural issues do you think will be a challenge for you?
- The therapeutic alliance is important to the counseling process. What are some ways you can work to strengthen this concept in your counseling approach?
- Although the counselor can never fully relate to every experience their client discloses, they can demonstrate empathy in each counseling relationship. How can you show empathy in situations in which it is difficult to relate to the client?

For Further Exploration

Allport, G. W. (1950). *The individual and his religion.* New York: Macmillan.

John, S. & Segal, D. L. (2015). Case conceptualization. In R. L. Cautin & S. O. Lilienfeld (Eds.), *The encyclopedia of clinical psychology.* Hoboken, NJ: John Wiley & Sons. doi:10.1002/9781118625392.wbecp106

Kottler, J. A., & Balkin, R. (2017). *Relationships in counseling and the counselor's life.* Alexandria, VA: American Counseling Association.

Rogers, C. R. (1961). *On becoming a person.* New York: Houghton Mifflin.

REFERENCES

Ainsworth, M. D. S., Blehar, M. C., Waters, E., & Wall, S. (1978). *Patterns of attachment: A psychological study of the strange situation.* Hillsdale, NJ: Erlbaum.

American Counseling Association (2014). *ACA Code of Ethics.* Alexandria, VA: Author

Allport, G. W. (1950). *The individual and his religion.* New York: Macmillan.

Barclay, W. (1976). *The letters to the Galatians and Ephesians: Revised.* Philadelphia:Westminster.

Beitman, B. D., & Manring, J. (2009). Theory and practice of psychotherapy integration. In G. O. Gabbard (Ed.), *Textbook of psychotherapeutic treatments.* Arlington, VA: American Psychiatric Publishing.

Bohecker, L., Schellenberg, R., & Silvey, J. (2017). Spirituality and religion: The ninth CACREP common core curricula area. *Counseling and Values, 62*(2), 128–143.

Bowlby, J. (1969). *Attachment and loss, Vol 1: Attachment.* New York, NY: Basic Books.

Bronfenbrenner, U. (2005). *Making human beings human: Bioecological perspectives on human development.* Thousand Oaks, CA: Sage Publications.

Brown, B. [The RSA]. (2013, December). *Breneé Brown on empathy* [Video File]. Retrieved from https://www.youtube.com/watch?v=1Evwgu369Jw

CACREP. (2016). *2016 CACREP standards.* Retrieved from http://www.cacrep.org/wp-content/uploads/2017/08/2016-Standards-with-citations.pdf

Corey (2012). *Theory and practice of counseling and psychotherapy* (9th ed.) Boston: Brooks/Cole, Cengage Learning.

Cozolino, L. (2010). *The neuroscience of psychotherapy: Healing the social brain* (2nd ed.). New York: W.W. Norton & Company.

Egan, G. (1998). *The skilled helper* (6th ed.). Pacific Grove, CA: Brooks/Cole.

Gottman, J. M. (1999). *The marriage clinic : A scientifically-based marital therapy.* New York, NY: W. W. Norton.

Hawkins, R., Knight, A., Sibcy, G. & Warren, S. (2019). *Research based counseling skills: The art and science of therapeutic empathy.* Dubuque, IA: Kendall Hunt.

Hestenes, R. (1986). *Discovering II Corinthians/Galatians: The guideposts home bible study program.* New York: Guideposts.

Holmes, T. H., & Rahe, R. H. (1967). The Social Readjustment Rating Scale. *Journal of Psychosomatic Research, 11*, 213–218.

Hook, J., & Ohlschlager, G. (2002). The empathic Christian counselor: Skilled helpers influencing client action. In. T. Clinton & G. Ohlschlager (Eds.), *Competent Christian counseling: Foundations and practice of compassionate soul care* (pp. 181–202). Colorado Springs, CO: Waterbrook.

Horvath, A. O., & Bedi, R. P. (2002). The alliance. In J. C. Norcross (Ed.), *Psychotherapy relationships that work: Therapist contributions and responsiveness to patients* (pp. 37–69). New York, NY: Oxford University Press.

John, S. & Segal, D. L. (2015). Case conceptualization. In R. L. Cautin & S. O. Lilienfeld (Eds.), *The encyclopedia of clinical psychology.* Hoboken, NJ: John Wiley & Sons. doi:10.1002/9781118625392.wbecp106

Johnson, S. M., Moser, M. B., Beckes, L., Smith, A., Dalgleish, T., Halchuk, R., … Coan, J. A. (2013). Soothing the threatened brain: Leveraging contact comfort with emotionally focused therapy. *PLoS ONE 8*(11), e79314. doi:10.1371/journal.pone.0079314

Jones, S. L., & Butman, R. E. (2011). *Modern psychotherapies: A comprehensive Christian appraisal* (2nd ed.). Downers Grove, IL: Intervarsity Press.

Jung, E., Weisjahn, M., Rief, W., & Lincoln, T. M. (2015). Perceived therapist genuineness predicts therapeutic alliance in cognitive behavioural therapy for psychosis. *British Journal of Clinical Psychology, 54*(1), 34-48. doi: 10.1111/bjc.12059.

Kottler, J. A., & Balkin, R. (2017). *Relationships in counseling and the counselor's life.* Alexandria, VA: American Counseling Association.

Kottler, J. A. (2015). *Counseling Today Online interview with Richard Balkin.* Retrieved from https://ct.counseling.org/2015/01/its-all-about-the-relationship-qa-with-richard-balkin-and-jeffrey-kottler/

Kottler, J. A. (2015). *The therapist in the real world: What you never learn in graduate school (but really need to know).* New York: W. W. Norton.

Luedke, A. J., Peluso, P. R., Diaz, P., Freund, R., & Baker, A. (2017). Predicting dropout in counseling using affect coding of the therapeutic relationship: An empirical analysis. *Journal of Counseling & Development, 95*(2), 125–134. doi:10.1002/jcad.12125

McGoldrick, M., Gerson, R., & Petry, S. (2008). *Genograms: Assessment and intervention* (3rd ed.). New York: W. W. Norton & Company.

McMinn, M. R., & Campbell, C. D. (2007). *Integrative psychotherapy: Toward a comprehensive Christian approach*. Downers Grove, IL: Intervarsity Press.

Moon, G. W., & Crews, F. (2002). The essential helping relationship: Secrets to counselor character and competence. In. T. Clinton & G. Ohlschlager (Eds.), *Competent Christian counseling: Foundations and practice of compassionate soul care* (pp. 181-202). Colorado Springs, CO: Waterbrook.

Miller, W. R., & Rollnick, S. (2004). Talking oneself into change: Motivational interviewing, stages of change, and therapeutic process. *Journal of Cognitive Psychotherapy, 18*(4), 299-308.

Nienhuis, J. B., Owen, J., Valentine, J. C., Winkeljohn Black, S., Halford, T. C., Parazak, S. E., Budge, S., & Hilsenroth, M. (2018). Therapeutic alliance, empathy, and genuineness in individual adult psychotherapy: A meta-analytic review. *Society for Psychotherapy Research, 28*(4), 593-605. doi: 10.1080/10503307.2016.1204023.

Noone, P. A. (2017). The Holmes-Rahe Stress Inventory. *Occupational Medicine, 67*(7), 581–582.

Norcross, J. C., & Wampold, B. E. (2011). Evidence-based therapy relationships: Research conclusions and clinical practices. *Psychotherapy, 48*(1), 98–102. doi:10.1037/a0022161

Prochaska, J. O., & DiClemente, C. C. (1982). Transtheoretical therapy: Toward a more integrative model of change. *Psychotherapy: Theory, Research & Practice, 19*(3), 276–288. doi:10.1037/h0088437

Prochaska, J. O., & Prochaska, J. M. (2016). *Changing to thrive: Using the stages of change to overcome the top threats to your health and happiness*. Center City, MN: Hazelden Publishing.

Rogers, C. R. (1957). The necessary and sufficient conditions of therapeutic personality change. *Journal of Consulting Psychology, 21*(2), 95–103. doi:10.1037/h0045357

Rogers, C. R. (1961). *On becoming a person*. New York: Houghton Mifflin.

Rogers, C. R. (1980). *A way of being*. New York: Houghton Mifflin.

Rogers, C. R., Gendlin, E. T., Kiesler, D. J., & Truax, G. B. (1967). *The therapeutic relationship and its impact: A study of psychotherapy with schizophrenics*. Madison, Wisc.: University of Wisconsin Press.

Schore, A. N. (2002). The neurobiology of attachment and early personality organization. *Journal of Prenatal and Perinatal Psychology and Health, 16*(3), 249-263.

Schore, J. R., & Schore, A. N. (2008). Modern attachment theory: The central role of affect regulation in development and treatment. *Clinical Social Work Journal, 36*, 9-20.

Sharf, J., Primavera, L. H., & Diener, M. J. (2010). Dropout and therapeutic alliance: A meta-analysis of adult individual psychotherapy. *Psychotherapy (Chic), 47*(4), 637-45. doi:10.1037/a0021175.

Seligman, L., & Reichenberg, L. W. (2014). *Theories of counseling and psychotherapy: Systems, strategies, and skills* (4th ed.). Boston: Pearson.

Siegel, D. J. (2010). *The mindful therapist: A clinician's guide to mindsight and neural integration*. New York, NY: W. W. Norton & Company, Inc.

Sincere. (2019). In *Merriam-Webster.com*. Retrieved May 1, 2019, from https://www.merriam-webster.com/dictionary/sincere

Sperry, L. (2010). *Highly effective therapy: Developing essential clinical competences in counseling and psychotherapy*. New York, NY: Routledge/Taylor and Francis Group.

Sommers-Flanagan, J. (2015). Evidence-based relationship practice: Enhancing counselor competence. *Journal of Mental Health Counseling, 37*(2), 95–108. doi:10.17744/mehc.37.2.g13472044600588r.

Stoker, J. (2013). *Overcoming fake talk: How to hold real conversations that create respect, build relationships, and get results*. New York, NY: McGraw Hill.

Tan, S-Y, & Scalise, E. (2016). *Lay counseling, revised and updated: Equipping Christians for a counseling ministry*. Grand Rapids, MI: Zondervan.

Teding van Berkhout, E., & Malouff, J. M. (2015). The efficacy of empathy training: A meta-analysis of randomized controlled trials. *Journal of Counseling Psychology, 63*(1), 32.

Von Bertalanffy, L. (1969). *General system theory: Foundations, development, applications.* New York: George Braziller, Inc.

Wampold, B. E. (2015). How important are the common factors in psychotherapy? An update. *World Psychiatry, 14*(3), 270–277. doi:10.1002/wps.20238

Young, M. E. (2017). *Learning the art of helping: Building blocks and technique* (6th ed.). New York: Pearson.

CHAPTER 9
Introduction to Counseling Skills

ANITA KUHNLEY, PH.D., ROBYN SIMMONS, ED.D., & GARY ALLEN SIBCY, PH.D.

> "There is no greater agony than bearing an untold story inside you."
> —Maya Angelou

Following Christ: Grace for Our Work

Throughout the scriptures, a theme that emerges is the importance of having a teachable spirit and being open to correction. This has important relevance to learning and developing a solid foundation of counseling skills. Mark 4:25 (Amplified Bible) puts it this way, "For whoever has [a teachable heart], to him *more* [understanding] will be given; and whoever does not have [a yearning for truth], even what he has will be taken away from him." In counseling skills training, counseling students who are open to feedback have an advantage; since they are teachable, they can grow and improve their skills throughout the course of training and beyond.

CHAPTER OBJECTIVES

After reading this chapter, you will understand more about:

- Counseling skills and counseling skill models
- The role and importance of empathy
- A skill set (called EAR) used for working with so called "difficult clients"
- Reasons for client dropout
- Counselor and counseling skill development

The following CACREP standards are addressed in this chapter:

Counseling and Helping Relationships:

- To identify counselor characteristics and behaviors that influence the counseling process such as empathy, cognitive flexibility, and desire to develop clinical expertise (CACREP, 2016, Standard 2.F.5.f)
- To identify essential interviewing counseling, and case conceptualization skills such as paraphrases and minimal encouragers (CACREP, 2016, Standard 2.F.5.g)

The theme of having a teachable spirit is a concept we also see illustrated in the book of Proverbs. For example, consider Proverbs 10:8 (Contemporary English Version) which states, "If you have good sense, you will listen and obey; if all you do is talk foolishly, you will destroy yourself." Another verse that relays this message is Proverbs 9:9 (New International Version), "Instruct the wise and they will be wiser still; teach the righteous and they will add to their learning." It is helpful to remember the spiritual laws or blessings that may be associated with having a teachable spirit. For example, during supervision sometimes counselors in training (CITs) receive feedback, and the corrective feedback may feel like criticism. However, when CITs are able to lean into the discomfort of the feedback and integrate the feedback into their skills and practice, both they and their clients are blessed and can grow as a function of this process.

Counseling skills communicate that you are listening and seeking to understand the concerns of your client. When your client has a sense that you care, this helps to build rapport and allows for greater progress in the therapeutic relationship. As you read this chapter and think about the foundational counseling skills and techniques, it is important to remember these concepts and exhibit excellence in your work as a clinician. Counseling skills communicate respect, care, concern, and an effort to understand, which in turn are associated with a safe space and client disclosure.

Many students enter a counselor training program because they have been told "you give wonderful advice" or "I can tell you anything—you are so easy to talk to." As you can imagine, someone who takes great pride in their advice giving skills may be very disappointed to hear the truth about counseling. Counseling skills are quite distinct from advice giving and they may feel like a new language at times.

Introductory counseling skills textbooks often emphasize the importance of *being with* a client rather than *fixing* a client. One of the primary roles of the counselor is to walk alongside the client, helping the client make sense of his or her story. In order to help the client with this task, you will need to develop competency with counseling skills. Counseling skills are an important component of counselor training and comprise much of the procedural knowledge (how-to knowledge) needed to develop expertise as a counselor. These skills include both basic skills (e.g., attending, summarizing, open-ended questioning, reflecting feeling) and advanced skills (e.g., immediacy, challenging, goal-setting, and advanced empathy). Counseling skills are designed to help the client feel understood while gaining insight and understanding. The first law of counseling skills is to "seek first to understand" (Covey, 2004). As the counselor seeks to understand the client, he or she can do so in a way that helps the client to extend his or her understanding of himself. It has been said that feeling *heard* and feeling *loved* are very similar feelings, and to many people the distinction between the two goes unnoticed (Augsburger, 1982). When a counselor gives his or her full undivided attention to a client, listening with great interest and intent to their story, seeking to understand (rather than to be understood), clients can face their story knowing that they are not alone.

What's Your Story?

"If you just learn a single trick, Scout, you'll get along a lot better with all kinds of folks. You never really understand a person until you consider things from his point of view . . . until you climb inside of his skin and walk around in it."
–Atticus Finch–*To Kill A Mockingbird*

WHAT ARE THE COUNSELING SKILL DEVELOPMENT MODELS?

In order to develop counseling skills and transfer these skills from training to clinical practice, you will undergo a structured training program which includes the core counseling skills (some authors call them *basic* counseling skills). For the purposes of this chapter, we use the terms *core* or *foundational*, as these skills provide a foundation for the other skills. The trifecta of standard counseling skills training models used historically in counselor education and described by a CACREP board member (Dr. Kenyon Knapp, personal communication June 11, 2019) include Ivey (1971), Carkhuff (1969), and Egan (1975). Additional models have developed which suggest varying protocols or combine aspects of previous protocols such as Smaby and Maddux (2010) and Hawkins, Knight, Sibcy, and Warren (2019), among other approaches.

The Ivey Model

Initially, Ivey (1971), and most recently Ivey, Ivey and Zalaquett (2018), developed a model of intentional interviewing techniques known as microskills. This approach to counseling was the first systematic model to focus on observable skills. As this model developed alongside the counseling profession, it was also the first counseling skills model to incorporate a multicultural focus. In this model, counselors develop their counseling skills on the groundwork of ethics, multicultural competence, neuroscience, and resilience. From there, counselors use the basic skills of attending and empathy, observation of body language and facial expression, questioning, encouraging, paraphrasing, summarizing, and reflecting feelings. Imbedded in the hierarchy, after the foundational foci and basic skills, is the understanding of the five stages of the counseling relationship defined by the model. These stages include: 1. building rapport with the client and demonstrating empathic understanding (Empathic Relationship); 2. hearing the client's story and assessing for strengths and skills (Story & Strength); 3. engaging in mutual goal setting for the client (Goal Setting); 4. reframing perspective and identifying alternatives (Restory); and 5. applying concepts from previous stages to life situation (Action). In the initial stages, the counselor uses basic skills; however, as the relationship progresses the counselor will use the more advanced skills of stress management, counselor self-disclosure, feedback, natural and logical consequences, directives, psychoeducation, reflection of meaning, interpretation, reframing, empathic confrontation, and focusing. These skills are further defined in Table 9.1.

Ivey, Ivey, and Zalaquett's (2018) model also incorporates the integration of theory into counseling skills. Further, this model recognizes the importance of counselor authenticity with regard to navigating skill and theory through the filter of individual style. You can find a graphic outlining the microskills and the hierarchical process for the Ivey model in Figure 9.1.

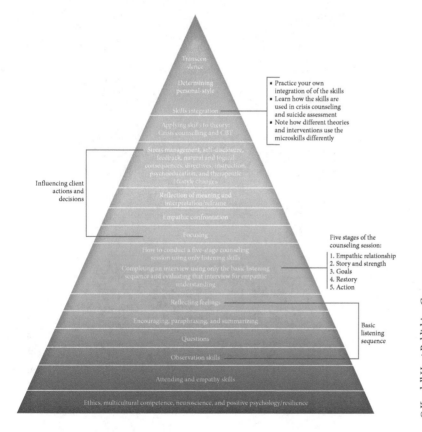

FIGURE 9.1

The Microskills Hierarchy

© Kendall Hunt Publishing Company

The Egan Model

In 1975, Egan presented the Skilled Helper Model which is now in its eleventh edition (Egan & Reese, 2019). This model is a three stage model for client intervention that responds to the following questions: a) what is going on?; b) what do I need/want?; and c) how do I get what I need/want? With each stage, the counselor uses a variety of skills, including active listening, empathy, checking understanding, probing, summarizing, and negotiating (see Table 9.1 for an overview of these skills). Egan also coined the profession-wide accepted acronym for the posturing skill of the counselor called *SOLER,* which stands for **s**it squarely, **o**pen posture, **l**ean in, **e**ye contact, and **r**elax (Egan & Reese, 2019). Figure 9.2 provides a sketch of how counselor skills help clients progress through each stage of this model. In each stage, there is a vertical flow of client awareness and understanding and resulting insight. Further, the flow of client change is also horizontal, with newly identified perspectives leading to increased understanding, needed changes, and the best strategies to make those changes.

FIGURE 9.2

The Skilled Helper Model

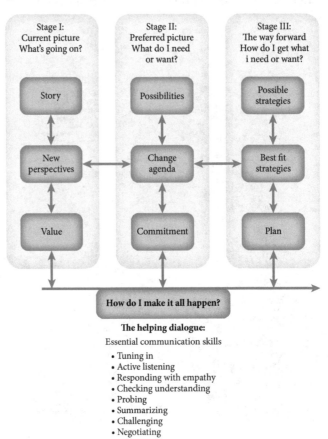

The Carkhuff Model

The Carkhuff (1969; 2008) model of helping is built on four phases: Pre Phase, Phase I, Phase II, and Phase III. In each of these phases, counselor skills correspond with client movement. In the Pre Phase, the counselor uses attending skills to help the client prepare for sharing and for becoming invested and involved in the counseling process. In Phase I, the counselor response skills of reflecting content, feelings, and meaning allow the client to explore the counseling concern. The personalizing skills in Phase II of goal identification and internalization move the client toward greater understanding. Phase III is marked by the initiating skills of goal setting and implementation, moving the client into action. Figure 9.3 provides a graphic representation of this process.

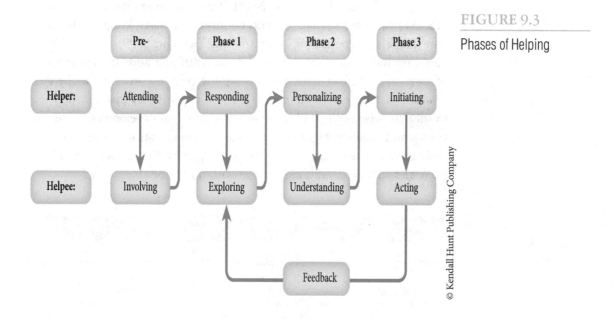

FIGURE 9.3

Phases of Helping

The Smaby and Maddux Model

Smaby and Maddux (2010) developed a counselor training approach called The Skilled Counselor Training Model (SCTM). The primary focus of this model is to help counselors develop and refine counseling skills, both basic and advanced, in order to work with clients from diverse backgrounds. The SCTM breaks down the skills into two categories: Exploring and Understanding and Advanced Skills. The first category, Exploring and Understanding Skills, includes nine basic counseling skills: 1) eye contact; 2) body language; 3) verbal tracking; 4) open ended questioning; 5) paraphrasing; 6) summarizing; 7) stating feelings and content; 8) self-disclosure; and 9) asking for both concrete and specific expressions (Smaby & Maddux 2010, p. xiii). The second category, Advanced Skills, includes: 1) immediacy; 2) identification of specific problem situations, identifying actions taken, and identifying feelings; 3) confronting in a caring manner; 4) deciding; 5) choosing; 6) identifying; 7) consequences; 8) reaching agreements; and 9) reaching deadlines, reviewing goals and actions to determine outcomes. These skills are further defined in Table 9.1.

Smaby and Maddux (2010) developed a psychometrically sound assessment called "The Skilled Counselor Scale" to accompany their skills training model (Smaby & Maddux, 2010). This assessment has been used in pre-test post-test research, to assess counseling skills training and to compare models of counseling skills training (Knight, 2009). The SCTM is based on the work of both Ivey and Carkhuff and adds the component of assessment before, after, and during the training process. Smaby and Maddux (2010) also developed a series of assessments that can be used to measure counselor skill development, personal development, and the therapeutic alliance. Figure 9.4 provides a representation of their conceptualization of the three stages of counseling, with the breakdown of how basic and advanced skills are utilized with these stages.

FIGURE 9.4

The Three Stages of Counseling

I. EXPLORING	II. UNDERSTANDING	III. ACTING
Attending	**Interchangeable empathy**	**Decision-Making**
Eye contact	Stating feelings and content	Deciding
Body language	Self-disclosure	Choosing
Verbal tracking	Asking for concrete and specific expressions	Identifying consequences
Questioning and reflecting	**Additive empathy**	**Contracting**
Open-ended questioning	Immediacy	Reaching agreements
Paraphrasing	Identifying general problem situation, action taken, and feelings	Setting deadlines
Summarizing	Confronting in a caring way	Reviewing goals and actions to determine outcome

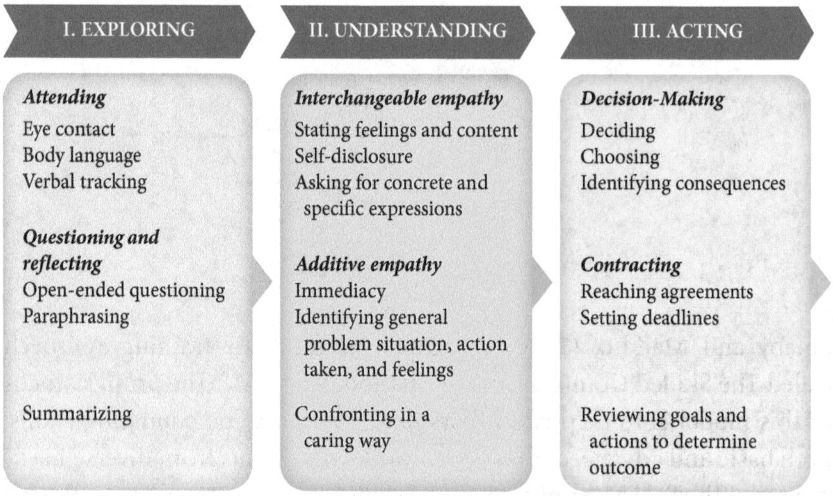

© Kendall Hunt Publishing Company

The Hawkins Model

Hawkins et al. (2019) proposed a counselor training model that offers a strategy for integrating faith into counselor training. This model draws upon the professional literature of Greggo and Becker (2010) who suggested that faith-based CACREP-accredited Counselor Education programs utilize attachment theory for a framework to communicate the safe haven that supervision provides for CITs. Further, in this model, God is conceptualized as the ultimate attachment figure (Greggo & Becker, 2010; Hawkins et al., 2019; Sibcy & Knight, 2018), providing a safe haven and source of emotion regulation and security for the CIT throughout the training process. Attachment theory, due to the copious number of studies performed and literature generated (Greggo & Becker, 2010; Knight, Sibcy, Gantt, Macon, & Carapezza, 2018; Trusty, Ng, & Watts, 2007) provides counselor educators with a conceptual model for discussing faith implications that is readily understood by other counselor educators and CITs regardless of faith background. Researchers have also extended attachment theory to investigate the connection between the counseling skill of empathy and the attachment style of the counselor (Trusty et al., 2007; Attachment concepts will be explored further in Chapter 10).

The implementation of empathy in both foundational and advanced counseling skills is also emphasized in the Hawkins model (Hawkins et al., 2019). Current research demonstrates that empathy is a moderately strong predictor of counseling outcomes; this was generally true regardless of client presenting problem and therapist theoretical orientation (Elliott, Bohart, Watson, & Murphy, 2018). Distinguishing features of the Hawkins et al. (2019) approach include the focus on the therapeutic alliance as a holding environment, as described in attachment theory, with considerations on the movement toward attachment security within the counseling relationship discussed throughout the text. Additionally, spiritual integration contextualized as attachment to God and the discussion of research to support the efficacy and importance of the foundational counseling skills are features that distinguish this approach from other approaches. Some features overlap, however, with many of the skills discussed in Ivey's model and Smaby's model, in addition to the nonverbal approach discussed in Egan's model included in Hawkin's model. Like Smaby and Maddux (2018), the skills content is also divided into foundational and advanced skills. Foundational skills include seven core skills: Informed disclosure of limits of confidentiality or informed consent (starting the session with a script for limits of confidentiality), door openers, minimal encouragers (both verbal and nonverbal), keyword encouragers, paraphrasing, reflecting feelings, and summarizing. The advanced skills in the Hawkins model include: intentional questioning, reflecting meaning, challenging while supporting, reframing, immediacy, and scaling.

© Kendall Hunt Publishing Company

FIGURE 9.5

Developing Core and Advanced Counseling Skills: The Hawkins Model

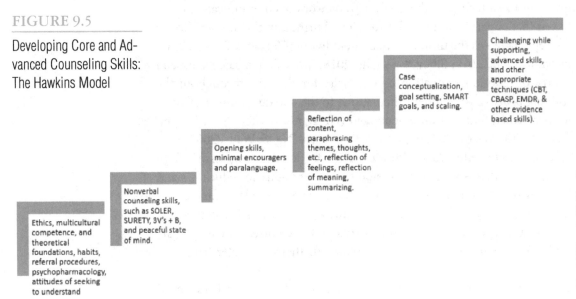

Ethics, multicultural competence, and theoretical foundations, habits, referral procedures, psychopharmacology, attitudes of seeking to understand

Nonverbal counseling skills, such as SOLER, SURETY, 3V's + B, and peaceful state of mind.

Opening skills, minimal encouragers and paralanguage.

Reflection of content, paraphrasing themes, thoughts, etc., reflection of feelings, reflection of meaning, summarizing.

Case conceptualization, goal setting, SMART goals, and scaling.

Challenging while supporting, advanced skills, and other appropriate techniques (CBT, CBASP, EMDR, & other evidence based skills).

WHAT ARE THE COUNSELING SKILLS?

As noted, the specific skills in the previously discussed models are quite similar. Table 9.1 and 9.2 summarize the core and advanced counseling skills described in the previous models, including a definition of the skill and an example of how they are used in counseling.

TABLE 9.1

Core Counseling Skills Defined

Name of Skill	Definition of Skill	Example of Skill
CORE COUNSELING SKILLS (CO = counselor and CL = client)		
Basic Attending Skills (Carkhuff, 2008; Ivey, Ivey, & Zalaquett, 2018; Smaby & Maddux, 2018) *-Minimal Encouragers* (Egan & Reese, 2019) *-SOLER* (Egan & Reese, 2019)	These skills are about the physical presence of the counselor being in tune with and demonstrating connection to the client(s). The skill of minimal encouragers is about encouraging the client to further tell his or her story, as well as to indicate listening and connection to the client. SOLER stands for: **S**it squarely **O**pen posture **L**ean in **E**ye contact **R**elax SOLAR has also been adapted to those that are visually impaired as follows: **S**quarely facing **O**pen posture **L**ean in **A**im (body voice toward client) **R**elax	Being relaxed Demonstrating openness (e.g., no barrier between client and counselor, arms to side rather than crossed in front) Maintaining eye contact Minimal encourages include short spoken utterances and body language, such as: CO: "Mmm hmmm" CO: "Yes, go on..." CO: Head nodding
Door Opener and ***Keyword Encouragers*** (Hawkins, et al, 2019)	The door opener is an open ended question or a statement that invites the client to share what brought them to the session. After opening the door to begin exploring the client's presenting concerns, the counselor listens for key words that he or she may then reflect back to the client. These are often feeling words, or words that may seem significant to the client.	Examples of door openers include: CO: "What would you like to accomplish during our time together in counseling?" Or CO: "Tell me about what brought you in today at this particular time in your journey." An example of using a keyword encourager is if the client states, "I am feeling really frustrated with my life right now" the counselor may respond with "frustrated" as an invitation to encourage further discussion.

TABLE 9.1

(continued)

Open Questions (Carkhuff, 2008; Ivey, Ivey, & Zalaquett, 2018; Smaby & Maddux, 2018) **Open Statements/Probes** (Egan & Reese, 2019)	These skills are designed to facilitate the client articulating struggles into words. Two categories have been noted: open and closed. Open questions begins with how, what, when, and where and invite further exploration. Closed questions begin with do, have, could/ would/should, etc... and can be answered with a limiting "yes/no."	Open question: CO: "What is it like for you to be both parent and child to your aging mother?" Open statement/probe: CO: "Tell me more about being both parent and child." or "I am wondering about your relationship with your mom."
Paraphrase (Egan & Reese, 2019; Hawkins, et al, 2019; Ivey, Ivey, & Zalaquett, 2018; Smaby & Maddux, 2018)	Paraphrasing content involves restating the essence of a client's narrative in the counselor's own words.	CL: "I am always doing something for someone else. If it isn't my family, it's my friends. If it isn't work, it is cleaning the house when I get home. I am tired and I feel invisible to everyone who benefits from my hard work." CO: "What I am hearing you say is that you are exhausted from working all day, taking care of your family, taking care of your home, and taking care of your friends. You would like someone to recognize the sacrifices you make every day."
Reflection of Feeling (Egan & Reese, 2019; Hawkins, et al, 2019; Ivey, Ivey, & Zalaquett, 2018; Smaby & Maddux, 2018)	This involves paying attention to feeling words or indicators of feelings and validating these feelings and naming or labeling emotions as they arise. Reflection skills are critical to demonstrating empathy.	CL: ""I am always doing something for someone else. If it isn't my family, it's my friends. If it isn't work, it is cleaning the house when I get home. I am tired and I feel invisible to everyone who benefits from my hard work." CO: "You are exhausted physically and emotionally and you feel like no one is there to meet your needs."

TABLE 9.1

(continued)

| Summarization (Egan & Reese, 2019; Hawkins, et al, 2019; Ivey, Ivey, & Zalaquett, 2018; Smaby & Maddux, 2018) | This is a skill that the counselor uses in facilitating structure to the sequencing of the client's "story." Summarizing is useful at the end of a session, the beginning of a subsequent session, or to help a client refocus. | CL: ""I am feeling really frustrated with my life right now."

CO: "Tell me more about that."

CL:"I am always doing something for someone else. If it isn't my family, it's my friends. If it isn't work, it is cleaning the house when I get home. I am tired and I feel invisible to everyone who benefits from my hard work."

CO: "You are exhausted physically and emotionally and you feel like no one is there to meet your needs."

CL: "Exactly! I just never have time for me or anyone who cares about taking care of me! I want everyone to go away so that I can just rest."

CO: "If everyone would leave you alone, you could replenish."

CL: "Right! I don't want them to go away - I love my family, my friends, and my work. I just need a break."

CO: "I am wondering what that would look like for you."

CL: "A break? Well, a night by myself in a hotel, a night when I can sleep uninterrupted; oh, and a massage! And a pedicure! I want to be pampered! I would also like a thank you from the people in my life. I don't need any grand gesture… just a simple 'I see what all you are doing and I appreciate it.'"

CO: "That would refresh and encourage you. We are nearing the end of our time today. We have covered a lot - your experience being in the "sandwich generation," your desire to care well for people and your exhaustion in doing so, your wish to be appreciated. You identified what it would look like to take a break. I think that is something for you to keep considering over this next week… see if there is an opportunity to make that, or something like that, happen. We can pick up from here when we meet next week." |

The core counseling skills help counselors build a solid foundation of listening and attending skills. However once these are established it is important to go beyond those core counseling skills to the more advanced skills. This includes skills like advanced empathy and challenging while supporting.

TABLE 9.2

Advanced Counseling Skills Defined

ADVANCED COUNSELING SKILLS (CO = counselor and CL = client)		
Name of Skill	**Definition of Skill**	**Example of Skill**
Advanced Empathy (Egan & Reese, 2019; Ivey, Ivey, & Zalaquett, 2018) **Additive Empathy** (Smaby & Maddux, 2018)	The counselor provides an interpretation of the client's story, using reflection of content, feeling, and meaning.	CL: "I don't know why everyone is ready to see me fail. It's like no one is there to support me; they just want to tear me down all the time." CO: "I hear you say that *you can't really count on anyone in your life and **you feel discouraged and disappointed." (reflection of *content and **feeling) CL: "Yeah, I am discouraged because it does not matter what I do, I can't seem to make any progress. If my family would recognize my struggle, I think I could make more strides toward improvement." CO: "I think I hear you say that ***you are not able to fight this battle on your own and that you need someone to believe in you to be successful, is that accurate?" (reflection of ***meaning)
Challenging/Confrontation (Egan & Reese, 2019; Hawkins, et al, 2019; Ivey, Ivey, & Zalaquett, 2018; Smaby & Maddux, 2018)	Counselors use this skill to provide a view point on a client's struggle or experience that differs significantly from the client's perspective. This skill is used when you recognize discrepancies in what the client is saying and what the client is doing, what the client has said previously and what is being said now, or when client non verbals and verbals do not match up.	CO: "On the one hand, you are feeling defeated because you don't have the support you want, but on the other hand, you are still attending counseling which means you still feel hope."

362

TABLE 9.2

(continued)

Counselor Self-Disclosure (Ivey, Ivey, & Zalaquett, 2018; Smaby & Maddux, 2018)	Self disclosure must be appropriate and purposeful and not adding emotional burden to the client or the session. Before disclosing, counselors need to assess for appropriateness of only share minimally, then the counselor needs to return the focus to the client.	CO: "I can recall a time when I was struggling and I felt like no one understood and no one was there for me. It was hard to stay motivated to change. What is this like for you?"
Goal Setting (Carkhuff, 2008; Ivey, Ivey, & Zalaquett, 2018; Smaby & Maddux, 2018)	It is an ethical imperative that counselors work with clients to identify goals to work toward in counseling, identifying an individualized treatment plan. In addition, counselors work with clients to set smaller, concrete goals as they relate to content the client brings into session.	CO: "Tell me two things you would like to work on in here to help during the other 23 hours of the day that you are not here." CL: "I would like to not take the anxiety medications any more, I would like to tell my family that I need their support." CO: "Ok, let's look at what you can do this week with these goals. First, you want to stop taking the medication. Let's see if working on the second and third goal helps with that. For now, maybe we can put that one on the backburner?" CL: "Ok." CO: "Ok. So, the second goal is about telling your family you need their support. What is something you can do this week to let them know? We can role play it. I will be a family member and you be you." [Counselor and Client role play] CO: "Ok, from what we just role-played, what are you willing to do this week?" (Counselor follows this up with when, how, etc…).

TABLE 9.2

(continued)

Immediacy (Egan & Reese, 2019; Hawkins, et al, 2019; Ivey, Ivey, & Zalaquett, 2018; Smaby & Maddux, 2018)	Using the here and now of the counseling session to address issues of tension, trust, dependency, counter-dependency, diversity, lack of direction, etc...	CO: "I noticed that you shifted suddenly and had a look of disagreement on our face when I pointed out that you feel hope. Tell me more about what your thoughts are." CL: "I don't feel hope. I don't see hope. And, frankly, I feel offended that you don't see how important family support is for me." CO: "I see. You are feeling like I don't quite understand you and that I was insensitive in noting hope was there. If hope is not there, share with me what keeps you coming to session."
Influencing Skills (Ivey, Ivey, & Zalaquett, 2018) **Negotiating** (Egan & Reese, 2019)	The influencing skills, including directives, suggestions, and information, are used to introduce clients to new alternatives and to inspire new ways of thinking about old problems. Directives, suggestions, and information invite clients to make changes in thoughts/actions. This can also summarize what Egan and Reese describe as negotiating, in which counselor and client work together to determine what the client is willing to do to make needed changes.	CO: "I would like to suggest that you engage in at least one of the following changes this next week: 1) talking to at least one person in your family to share your feelings, 2) spend 5 minutes a day doing deep breathing, or 3) start a gratitude journal, writing 3 things each day for which you are thankful. Which of these feels like something you can accomplish - and you can do more than one?
Reframing/Interpretation (Ivey, Ivey, & Zalaquett, 2018) **Positive Relabeling** (Hawkins, et al, 2019)	This skill involves providing an alternate more adaptive perspective on a client's presenting problem.	CL: "I hear you say that you don't have the support and encouragement of your family, however you have made so much progress in the short time we have been together. Not feeling supported by family is hurtful, but at the same time it has given you the opportunity to demonstrate your true grit. I believe you have been shortchanging your own strength and determination."

TABLE 9.2

(continued)

Scaling (Hawkins, et al, 2019)	This skill allows clients to see nuances of experiences, potentially helping them to not feel completely over-whelmed with an experience/ feeling. Additionally, scaling over several sessions can help identify progress.	CO: "I hear you say that you are still feeling discouraged, on a scale of 1 to 10 where 1 is totally encouraged and 10 is completely discouraged, where would you fall?" CL: "I guess I am about a 7." CO: "The last time we discussed this, you rated yourself at an 11 on this 1 to 10 scale. It sounds like things are not significantly better, but there has been improvement." CL: "Yeah, I guess so. I didn't remember saying 11, but I completely remember feeling 11. I do see the light at the end of the tunnel - it's just a very long tunnel."
Silence (Ivey, Ivey, & Zalaquett, 2018)	Being silent is not nec-essarily a skill; however, sitting in the silence with a client takes self-control and awareness. Counselors must learn when to allow the silence to happen and when to break the silence. Silence allows counselors to gather thoughts, clients to take a break, clients to process what was just stated, and space for insight to occur.	Counselors need to attend to client's body language to determine if they are uncom-fortable with silence. This will be a cue for the counselor to break the silence. Clients will often break the silence when they have processed their thoughts.

Please note, this is similar to a preview you would see for a movie; you are given a sneak peek of what is to come. You will have coursework which focuses on counseling skill development. It is beyond the scope of this chapter to provide a comprehensive definition and application of each of the core and advanced counseling skills. For more resources on this topic, please see the recommended reading.

Chuck Rodgers on the value of counseling skills in private practice

Chuck Rodgers, is an LPC and LMFT and owner of a Private Practice Counseling Center called "Wyndhurst Counseling" in Lynchburg, VA. In his practice he provides individual, couples, and marriage and family services. He also does intensive counseling. In addition, he has served in a variety of roles throughout the course of his profession, including one who supervises and trains rising counselors. His students and trainees report that they have learned much from him in the way of strong counseling skills. In reflecting on his use of the basic counseling skills (i.e., reflecting content, feeling, meaning, minimal encouragers, open questions, etc…), Rodgers shared, *"They (the core skills) mean everything. They are air to the counseling relationship, and they are air to our clients."*

Rodgers further shared about advanced skills and techniques he has built upon his solid foundation of core skills, *"I rely heavily upon the skills that I've learned from the Gottmans and Michelle Weiner Davis to be able to help struggling couples. I rely heavily upon the skills from David Burns about how to aggressively use Cognitive Therapy with individuals to combat the negative thinking I do. However, without the ability to connect, it matters little how well I know my craft and it matters little the length of my experience. If I cannot be present for my client by the use of these wonderful, wonderful tools, I am nothing.*

However, when I am able to carefully reflect each piece of cognitive content, when I am able to accurately reflect emotion, when I am able to say back to them what I heard them just say to me, something healing, something almost magical happens. All of a sudden they realize that they matter to me…all of a sudden they realize that they matter. That's what it's about. That's why they came and that's why they'll come back."

Rodgers reminds students that it is so important to learn the core skills because in the process of being present with the client, other things are indeed accomplished. When asked what encouragement Rodgers has for counseling students seeking to learn counseling skills, Rodgers noted, *"Master these basic skills and you will master your craft. I used to tell my students, 'Stop trying to fix people…be present for them. When you do that, you'll fix a lot of things…'"*

WHAT IS EMPATHY?

Empathy Defined

You will learn the previously identified counseling skills in your counselor training program, employed as a method of strengthening the *therapeutic alliance*. A strong alliance in the therapeutic relationship is closely tied with the use of skills, especially empathy. It is important to have a practical, working definition of *empathy* in order to use it effectively. For the purposes of this chapter, empathy is defined as *the acknowledgement of what a person is experiencing and/or feeling and the foundational reasons for that experience and/or feeling, such that the person feels deeply understood.* It is crucial to note that empathy is not the same as compassion, which is a feeling of sympathy or sadness for another person's situation or misfortune. Merriam-Webster's dictionary defines *compassion* as "a sympathetic consciousness of others' distress together with a desire to alleviate it" (https://www.merriam-webster.com/dictionary/compassion). While empathy may involve some degree of compassion, it encompasses much more than that. Empathy, as defined by Alfred Adler (1929), is seeing with the eyes of another, hearing with the ears of another, and understanding with the heart of another.

Clinical Empathy

Clinical empathy involves three key components that build upon this more general definition of empathy. The first component is that in order to express empathy, you have to do more than understand; you have to acknowledge (or verbally say) what it is you understand. As a second component of clinical empathy, you will also reflect the underlying reasons for the identified feelings. To do this, you will initially reflect content and feeling, then add reflection of meaning and reframing to indicate the *why* behind the *what*. The third component involves confirmation from the client that understanding has, in fact, been successfully achieved. Clinical empathy has also been extended to include agreed upon goals and agreed upon methods for accomplishing those goals (Platt, 1992; Kiosses, Karathanos, & Tatsioni, 2016; Sibcy, Knight & Gantt, 2019). In a study using randomized controlled trials, Kiosses, Karathanos, and Tatsioni noted, "Clinical empathy includes understanding the patient's situation, perspective and feelings as well as their attached meanings; communicating understanding and checking its accuracy; and acting on that understanding with the patient in a therapeutic way (2016, p.2)."

For example, you, as the counselor, will need to communicate to your client that you understand his or her story. More specifically, rather than simply saying "I understand what you are saying," you will reflect content, feeling, and/or meaning to indicate the key themes heard. This translates to a statement like, "It sounds like you are feeling rejected by your adult children and this both hurts and angers you, given that you devoted your life to raising them" or "I hear that you feel frustrated that things have not been progressing as quickly as you would like in our sessions and that you have invested a great deal of your time, money, and energy in the process." Empathic statements, represented by these examples, indicate to the client exactly what it is you understand from their words. They may say, "yes, exactly!" Or, they may begin elaborating and building upon the content. If they do not have a sense of being understood, they may provide clarification. If they indicate that you still do not understand, then you have attempted empathy, but have not yet achieved it. If they say you "basically" get it, or that you "mostly" understand, you have not fully achieved empathy. In both cases, you will need to continue in a back-and-forth process until they indicate that they are fully understood.

Practically, empathy is manifested through the use of core counseling skills such as reflecting content, reflecting feelings, and reflecting meaning. The basic counseling skills of SOLER, utilization of minimal encouragers, among other skills work in concert with empathy. Empathy mediates the necessary trust in the counseling relationship to allow for the use of more advanced skill sets, such as immediacy, confrontation, and reframing. Counselor skill competence creates a safe space for clients to discuss their story and to work toward transition, acceptance, and/or resolution.

> Love is behind everything. Love or the lack of it. - Fred Rogers

It is important to note that empathy is an umbrella skill. This means that the skill of empathy transcends all of the other skills. Empathy is the foundational counseling skill needed for all of the other skills to operate successfully. As discussed in 1 Corinthians 13, without love, everything else is like the sound of a gonging symbol. Similarly, without empathy, which Carl Rogers has called "a non-possessive love" (Duncan, 2013), counseling skills fall flat. Counseling skills, and in particular the skill or experience of empathic engagement, serve to help the clients sense that they are safe, heard, and understood.

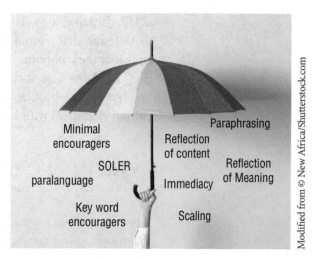

Minimal encouragers

SOLER paralanguage

Key word encouragers

Reflection of content

Immediacy

Scaling

Paraphrasing

Reflection of Meaning

Modified from © New Africa/Shutterstock.com

When people experience negative emotions (anger, sadness, anxiety, worry, loneliness, etc), there is a story behind their feelings. In one sense, counselors like to think of empathy as a tool for helping another person tell this story. As clients make sense of their story, they can also move toward a more coherent narrative of their story (Knight & Sibcy, 2017).

An additional therapeutic benefit of empathic engagement within the counseling relationship is that it fosters a more secure attachment style. We know that clients are able to move away from a less healthy attachment style and move toward a more secure style, not only in their relationships with people, but also with God, the Divine Attachment Figure (DAF; Knight et al., 2018). A secure attachment style allows the client to make sense of and come face to face with the truths embedded in his or her story, decreasing emotional hiding and feelings of shame (Sibcy & Knight, 2019; Siegel, 2003; Thompson, 2010; Sibcy & Knight, 2011; Neborksy, 2006). Not feeling empathized with, along with the pain of attachment injuries, leads to defensiveness. Neborsky (2006) indicated "attachment failures lead to unprocessed feelings of unregulated grief, which, without the empathic other, create unbearable states of aloneness that can only be regulated with defenses" (p. 527). Empathy is also associated with more prosocial behavior, generosity, and other benefits (Rumble, Van Lange, & Parks, 2009).

Further, empathy is a very powerful tool for assisting clients with improving basic brain based skills needed for regulating emotions. The prefrontal cortex (PFC) is the logic area of the brain and is activated by empathy and associated with self-regulation and goal oriented behavior (Amen,

2017; Jankowiak-Siuda, Rymarczyk, & Grabowska, 2011). Researchers have found that regions of the PFC are active when people are invited to consider the emotional states of others (Jankowiak-Siuda et al., 2011). The PFC has been described by neuroscientist, Dr. Daniel Amen, as the boss in your brain who, like your boss at work, may work to keep you on task and in alignment with the company mission.

WHAT IF I CANNOT HELP MY CLIENTS?

Most counselors are adept at using reflecting skills, paraphrasing, asking questions, using clarification, and effective empathy to help clients tell their stories. Counselors can also work at helping clients deal with problems and challenging them while supporting them to find ways to handle their emotions effectively. However, all counselors, no matter how experienced and skilled, find it challenging to deal with therapeutic impasses. A special kind of impasse is when a client expresses negative feelings about you, the therapist. Counselors may refer to these clients as *difficult clients* (i.e., those who show up late, make same day cancellations, or just fail to show up to appointments, without calling or sending an email.) Others vent and complain about their problems but refuse to focus in on a specific problem or to work collaboratively toward concrete solutions. Irving Yalom called these clients in group counseling settings "the help rejecting complainer." (Yalom, 1995, p. 11). In his text on group psychotherapy, Yalom further describes difficult clients this way:

> Advice-giving or advice-seeking behavior is often an important clue in the elucidation of interpersonal pathology. The patient who, for example, continuously pulls advice and suggestions from others, ultimately only to reject them and frustrate others, is well known to group therapists as the "help-rejecting complainer" or the "yes ... but" patient... Some patients may bid for attention and nurturance by asking for suggestions about a problem that either is insoluble or has already been solved. Other patients soak up advice with an unquenchable thirst, yet never reciprocate to others who are equally needy. Some group members are so intent on preserving a high-status role in the group or a facade of cool self-sufficiency that they never ask directly for help; some are so anxious to please that they never

ask for anything for themselves; some are excessively effusive in their gratitude; others never acknowledge the gift but take it home, like a bone, to gnaw on privately. (p.11)

Some clients may complain that counseling is not effective but refuse to follow through with any tasks or outside work assigned by the counselor. The list of behaviors could go on for pages, but what do these difficult clients all have in common? You might expect to see a list of associated personality traits, such as borderline, narcissistic, or passive-aggressive. While these may be challenging personality traits, the real problem is that therapeutic impasses are a function of a rupture in the therapeutic relationship. In other words, there is no such thing as a truly difficult client in this sense. In fact, the client is not the problem at all; but rather, the counselor is the problem.

Now, this may sound offensive, and I (G. Sibcy) had the exact same reaction when I was a doctoral student. During my doctoral program, I attended a workshop conducted by Dr. Kottler, a renowned therapist and prolific writer during the 1990s. The workshop was titled *How to Effectively Deal with Your Most Difficult Clients* (Kottler, circa 1990). At that time, I had a caseload of difficult clients, and I was looking for a magical elixir. The workshop began with Kottler asking each participant to write down a situation involving a difficult client. He then asked for volunteers to come up front with him and role play the situation we had written down: he would play the therapist and we would role play our difficult client. Through a series of artful maneuvers, he was able to transform our client's difficult behaviors into cooperation and collaboration. Dr. Kottler worked with each of the volunteers and helped us see that the real problem was how the counselor was relating to the client. I was both amazed and outraged, asking "How did he turn this whole thing back on me. I am the expert here. How can this be my problem? Why do I have to change the way I relate when my client is the one with the problem." But it was precisely that kind of hubris that was really the heart of the matter.

Around the same time, Kottler (1992) emphasized the importance of taking responsibility for being congruent in and out of counseling settings, sharing from his own experience about a time when a student approached him wanting to find out why he was given a C on a paper. Kottler noted that he responded defensively and became aware of the lack of congruence. I (A.K. Kuhnley) can think of times when I, too, have been incongruent, encouraging empathy among my students, but then struggling to be empathic when I heard complaints from students regarding assignments. Kottler challenges counselors and counselor educators to evaluate their own congruence and incongruence. It can be difficult to have these honest self-assessments, but this process is very important on the route to becoming more congruent. Kottler acknowledges the *imposter syndrome* that can emerge as counselors interact with clients; furthermore, as counselor educators interact with students. We struggle through the tendency to fein perfectionism and clinical prowess rather than owning the challenges inherent to living in a fallen and imperfect world, and striving to be therapeutic despite being imperfect and fallen therapists (Kottler, 1992).

As the title of this section denotes, counselors will likely feel at some point in time that they cannot help their client(s). Students have sometimes asked questions such as, "I have experienced so much trauma, will I really be able to help anyone?" or "I have not gone through any significant loss or trauma, will I really be able to help anyone?" These and similar questions have been identified as a part of the imposter syndrome. Though frequently observed among counseling students, imposter syndrome maybe even more pronounced within counselors and counselor educators in underrepresented ethnic backgrounds (Avent Harris, Trepal, Prado, Robinson, 2019). Examining areas of counselor congruence and incongruence, as well as expressions of counselor empathy and lack of empathy, may help us to develop a new perspective on difficult clients.

The lesson on evaluating the counselor role in problematic client interactions is not something that you visit only once, but rather should be a continuously emerging theme. To help make sense of this, start by noticing that these clients have a negative effect on you to become more aware of the dilemma. Clients are often experts at pulling others (including their counselor) into a relational pattern that mirrors the same problems they have in other relationships. Unless you have developed your counseling skills, you will likely become overwhelmed, frustrated, and helpless to do anything to make a meaningful impact on this person's life. The next section briefly outlines the Empathy, Assertiveness, and Respect (EAR) Model which includes the skills you will need to develop in order to effectively help difficult clients.

Difficult Clients: Using the Empathy, Assertiveness, and Respect (EAR) Model

Begin to work on this now, in your day-to-day life as you progress through your training, instead of waiting until you get into your practicum and internship. These skills will help equip you to handle difficult people in your life and transform the way you engage in conflict. You may even find these skills especially helpful when you encounter unfair criticism and blame from others. EAR skills are broken into 4 sets: 1) willingness skills; 2) empathy skills; 3) assertiveness skills; and 4) respect skills. Each set of skills is broken into two sub-sections: the "what skills" and the "how skills".

Willingness skills. What is willingness? To improve or change a behavior, you need to be willing to commit yourself to making that change. You must be open to the fact that changing behavior is a difficult task. Thus, you need to have a clear sense that the behavioral change is worth it for you. Essentially, there are three mindsets or assumptions you must be willing to make.

> "Intimacy requires humility and your willingness to examine your own failures in a relationship."- Dr. David Burns
> (2008, location 449, Chapter 3, P.3).

First, you need to update your definition of what it means to be in a close relationship. Dr. David Burns, (2008) defines intimacy as your willingness to endure the negative feelings you get when you get close to another person, including examining your own failures. Some will say that their relationship with a certain person is so close they never experience negative feelings toward him or her. However, if that person has not yet experienced negative feelings toward the other, then they really are not as close to them as they think. Whenever you get close to another person, because you both share a human nature, you will experience conflict. It is not uncommon in the early stages of a relationship for people to feel closer than they really are. Robert Firestone (2014; 1987) refers to this as the *fantasy bond*. During this stage of a relationship, people tend to be on their best behavior. Also during this stage people tend to be much more forgiving of foibles and shortcomings than they are as the relationship progresses. It is an illusion to think that the other person is flawless and perfect. At the same time, if you are in a close but conflicted relationship, you have to decide the degree of intensity of negative feelings you are willing to endure. You have to decide how much challenge you are willing to deal with in order to maintain this relationship. If you believe the relationship is worth the effort, then you may proceed to the next level of commitment.

Second, when you are in a challenging relationship with plenty of conflict, you have one of three choices you can make (Burns, 2008):

> 1) You can continue doing what you are doing, namely, trying to change the other person's behavior. Predictably, you will continue to get the same outcome. Remember from the psychology of behaviorism we know that the best predictor of future behavior is past behavior.
> 2) You can decide to leave the relationship because the other person refuses to change or the investment required by you is to great.
> 3) You can decide to take 100% responsibility for changing the only person you can change: namely, yourself. Choice #3 is the only choice that will ultimately work if you plan on transforming your relationships, and yet it is very painful to take responsibility for our actions, especially our mistakes. Yet, it is among the most powerful decisions we can make.

If you decide to pursue choice number 3, you will need to accept the fact that you are fully responsible for your own behavior. You will need to surrender your demand that the other person makes changes and focus specifically on changing your own interpersonal interactions with the other person. This is a difficult challenge, no doubt, because a natural human tendency is to assign blame to the other person for the problems in the relationship. This is just as true for personal relationships as it for therapeutic relationships. As David Burns (2008) points out, we must accept that the vast majority of the problems in our interpersonal relationships are due to our own hang-ups, and we are responsible for changing those. To the extent that you assign the responsibility to the other person, you will continue to experience yourself as a helpless victim to the behaviors and attitudes of others. We realize this might involve a radical change in the perception of personal responsibility responsibility. Interestingly, however, it is exactly what most relationship experts assert; and, not surprisingly, it is very much in alignment with scriptural principles.

We want you to understand and appreciate that relationships are a two-way interaction: what the other person does affects you but also what you do affects them. As you will learn, if you change the way you interact, it will have a powerful effect on how others interact with you. This is also consistent with what you will learn in your family systems theories classes: that one change in the system may have an impact on the whole system, because in a system, each member is connected. According to Bowen's (1978) theories on therapeutic systems, particularly in a family system, the individual members of the system are connected to one another, and when one person changes, it can provide an impetus for a change in others.

It does require energy to make shifts in the self and take personal responsibility. We are not suggesting that you are obligated to invest this much energy in every person you encounter. While these skills can eliminate conflict in nearly every relationship you encounter, it does not mean that you should be willing to invest in every relationship as if it were a close relationship. Toxic people do exist —some are family members, others may be acquaintances, fellow church goers, or co-workers. Some people are burdensome, critical, or downright mean-spirited, and you always reserve the right to end the relationship. This is always a choice you have, as part of the process of deciding how much you are willing to invest in the relationship.

You may be wondering if it is worth the effort? Only you can answer that question. If, after repeated attempts to change your behavior in relation to the other person, you continue to observe that they have not made any meaningful changes in their behavior, you may decide to end the relationship. If, for some reason, you cannot end the relationship (e.g., you cannot fire your siblings or your boss), you will find these skills can go a long way in diminishing the conflict and anger, but they will not necessarily transform a toxic person into a warm, sensitive, caring individual.

In a counseling relationship, however, these skills, if administered in a disciplined and sensitive manner, can in fact promote transformation of the most difficult and toxic individuals. Clients can learn to become more sensitive, warm, empathic people if they are committed to change. At the core of all effective counseling and psychotherapy is the therapeutic relationship. The question is whether we, as counselors and psychotherapists, are willing to endure the negative feelings required to maintain such a relationship, without losing our own sense of self or sacrificing our happiness. It can be done. The question whether or not you are willing to begin

the journey, learn and master the necessary skills, and challenge yourself to become a disciplined, relational agent of change.

Third, in addition to learning new relational behaviors, you will need to be willing to give up certain behaviors that are completely incompatible with a close relationship. As we will see, there are certain behaviors, woven into our very constitutional structure, that are naturally reinforced at the brain level and that cause us to engage in intimacy defeating patterns. While there are many dozens of behaviors that fit these criteria, to simplify they are broken down into two categories: 1) blame and 2) being right.

Blame is defined as your desire to get even with another person who hurts you. Think about it. When a driver cuts you off in traffic, when someone makes a disparaging comment about your looks or your personality, or when someone is disloyal or talks badly about you behind your back, your most basic instinct is to get even. Fundamentally, we want justice; we want to get even. Why? Scripture talks about this as an "eye for and eye." When someone smacks us on the cheek, our basic urge is to smack them back (a little harder than they smacked us, just so they learn a lesson). Neuroscience confirms this. The brain literally reinforces retribution by delivering a shot of dopamine (the feel-good chemical) to a special reward center in the brain called the nucleus accumbens (see more about the dopamine reward center in Chapter 10). Hollywood capitalizes on this. For example, characters such as James Bond or various superheroes offer a central storyline that revolves around the defeat of a nefarious villain. This villain is often someone who deserves justice: not just getting caught, handcuffed and hauled off to prison. That would be too anticlimactic. The bad guy has to die a horrible death. Remember the scene from xyz where person x falls backward off a skyscraper, his eyes bulging as he plummets to his death on the concrete below. Perhaps you can distinctly remember the feelings and sensations associated with a story like this—walking out of the theater with a sense of satisfaction and a feeling of warmth (dopamine!), knowing justice had been served. Maybe you even replayed that scene over in your mind. Why? Because we crave justice.

Similarly, some engage in the role of the martyr. The martyr role involves an intimacy defeating relational pattern in which the person receives a dopamine rush from sacrificing their needs, wants, and desires to others, creating an attraction to the role of the victim. In this position, the martyr basks in the experience of being the victim with negative self-talk such as, "Whatever, what's the use? Why try to get what I want? No one cares about me and my needs. I'm just a worthless, bag of bones." This position is reinforced not only by the dopamine surge released when one retreats into this relational space, but it is also reinforced by escaping the disappointment they have come to expect from others letting them down. For such individuals, escaping disappointment is more important than feeling happy. The avoidance of pain can be a powerful motivator, sometimes even more powerful than the pursuit of pleasure. For the martyr, the cost of happiness seems too high because feeling good may be hindered by let downs and disappointments.

A clinical example. Jack is a 35-year male who is divorced, lives alone, and works as a sales manager at a department store. He came to counseling for treating his depression, which involves chronic feelings of loneliness, intense sadness combined with intense self-criticism. You've decided to use cognitive behavior counseling with Jack and so explain the basics of cognitive counseling and assigned him the Feeling Good Handbook. In the initial sessions, Jack seemed motivated to change and he seemed to 'buy-in' to the basic rationale for using cognitive counseling. However, as treatment progresses, Jack starts missing appointments, showing up late, and not completing any of the assigned tasks outside of counseling (e.g., mood logs, behavior activation assignments, etc). You also notice that Jack has not been staying current with his bill, often failing to pay co-pays at the beginning of session and not paying missed appointment charges.

Imagine Jack shows up to today's session and announces, "Today is my last day of counseling." You inquire about his reasons and he says, "I just don't feel like counseling is helping me. I've been coming for the last couple of months, paying a ton of money but getting no results. I'm still just as depressed, if not more, than when I first started." Consider how would you respond to this situation.

Empathy skills. In order to achieve empathy, you need some basic tools and concepts. These are broken down into the *What Skills* and the *How Skills*. The What Skills are the actual tools and concepts you will need to help the person tell the whole story. The How Skills are tips about how to use the skills effectively.

The What Skills:

- Feeling Empathy—acknowledging what the other person is feeling, this involves reflecting feeling, and may require the use of tools such as the feeling wheel. This involves you helping them label their feelings using feeling words (see Figure 9.6 for a list of basic emotions on a feeling wheel). This is not as easy as it sounds because many people tend to confuse what they feel with why they feel that way. Also, keep in mind that people can have multiple feelings at the same time about the same situation. For example, if a client says, "You don't care about how I feel. You just want to teach me facts and information. You're always trying to explain things to me." This statement does not have any labeled feelings. But you should be able to infer that the person is feeling frustrated and possibly disappointed. Looking back at Jack's statement, consider what feelings you imagine he is experiencing?

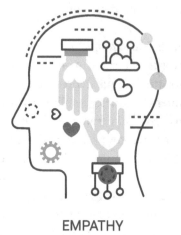

EMPATHY

- Thought Empathy- Helping the person verbalize the reasons or perceptions behind their feelings. (Please see Table 9.3.) Just like emotions, people may have mul-

© Lemberg Vector studio/Shutterstock.com

tiple reasons for the same emotion. So, if a client says, "I'm feeling frustrated." You will need to help them explore the reasons they are feeling frustrated. If they go on to say, "I'm frustrated because you don't seem to care about how I feel but you just want to teach me facts and information," you might say, "Okay, so when I start trying to teach you things, you get frustrated because I'm not really tuning into how you feel." If your client agrees, then you've achieved empathy. Keep in mind that it's possible to have more than just one emotion at the same time. Understanding the connection between thoughts, feelings, and behaviors can promote thought empathy (See Table 9.3).

Thoughts/Automatic Appraisals	Feelings	Behaviors
• Perception of Danger or Threat—real, imagined or symbolic • Perception of Threat that is overwhelming and inescapable	Anxiety/fear	Avoidance Escape Safety Freeze-shut down/disconnection Can motivate problem solving
Perception of injustice or being blocked from something desires	Anger	Agression-physical or verbal Defensiveness Assertiveness Can motivate problem solving
Perception of Loss— real, imagined, or symbolic	Sadness, Grief	Energy Depletion; Lack of Exploration, curiosity, interest
Perception of Safety	Interest, curiosity, intimacy	Exploration, creativity, social engagement

TABLE 9.3

The Connection between Thoughts, Feelings, and Behaviors

• Inquiry: This skill is essential for helping your client explore, elaborate, and link their concerns, thoughts, feelings and perceptions together. Keep in mind, many people have great difficulty distinguishing their thoughts (their perceptions and interpretations of events) from their feelings. As we will discuss in the How Skills, this skill must be done in a warm, sensitive, and curious manner. If you come across in a critical, judgemental manner, it will shut down the process of exploration as your client will likely become defensive. If someone is feeling frustrated and annoyed with you, inquire about what it is that you are doing that is frustrating them. You will use inquiry to get both sides of the story: what they are feeling and the reasons they are feeling that way. This is relatively easy if the person is complaining about a situation that doesn't involve you. For example, Jenny, a seasoned professional counselor, says to Loyd, her client, "When you wife starts complaining about all the things you don't do around the house, how do you feel?" He replies, "I really get angry." The counselor continues, "Okay, you get angry because…?" The client finishes the sentence, "Because nothing is ever good enough for her. All the time I spend at work supporting our family goes completely unnoticed. She doesn't appreciate all I do." The counselor summarizes, "So when you wife complains about you not doing different things around the house, you feel angry because nothing is good enough for her; she does not take into account all the hard work you do. All of that goes unnoticed and unappreciated." He agrees, "Yes, that's exactly right." In this instance, Jenny achieved perfect empathy by using inquiry to flesh out the differences between the event (wife complaining), the thoughts and interpretations (she does not appreciate all the work I do to support the family), and the feeling (anger).

- Disarming Acceptance. This principle is illustrated in Jesus' statement about turning the other cheek. He is not advocating a martyrdom complex. He is not suggesting you become a masochist, someone how takes pleasure in other's abusive behavior. Instead he is describing a basic law of relationships, built into the nature of the universe. We call it the acceptance paradox: If you accept a person's criticism (turn the other cheek) the other person will very likely not hit you again. However, if you resist the criticism with blame and defense of the truth, they will whack you again, and again, and again. You may have noticed that in the above example, the counselor did not challenge her client's perspective. This can be challenging because our most basic impulse is to challenge distortions and defend the truth. But the goal of empathy is understanding, not correction. Acceptance is about trying to look at the world through your client's eyes and understanding how they feel, based on their perception of reality. When you do this, it helps your client feel understood and accepted. In the example of Loyd and his wife, this task was not too difficult for Jenny because her client was complaining about someone else. The real challenge comes when the client's anger and frustration is directed at you, as in the case of Jack. This requires a great deal of discipline on the counselor's part to not retreat into a defense mode, challenging the client's perceptions and expectations. Instead, the counselor needs to do something that is entirely unnatural: see the truth—even if it is just a grain of truth—in the client's criticism. When this happens, often the client's anger melts away.

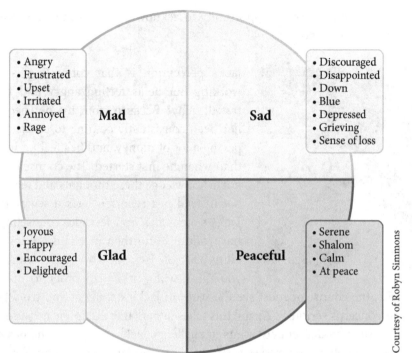

FIGURE 9.6

The Feeling Wheel

Courtesy of Robyn Simmons

Looking back to Jack's case. He announces that today is his last day of counseling because he doesn't feel like counseling (that is, you) is helping. In his mind, he believes he's been a compliant client, one who shows up to all of his appointments, completes out of session assignments, and pays his bill in a timely manner. The counselor says, "You don't feel counseling is helping. What do you think will help you?" Jack replies, "I don't know. If I knew, I wouldn't be here right now, would I? That's what I'm paying you for."

Obviously, this backfired. Why? For several reasons, but most importantly the counselor did not really acknowledge and accept Jack's feelings. When Jack expressed his discontent with the counseling process, it would be important for the counselor to use reflecting skills including both reflecting feeling and content. You might object, because the counselor did say, "You feel like counseling is not working." But keep in mind, even though Jack used the phrase, "I feel" does not mean he's actually labeling a feeling. "counseling is not working" is a thought not a feeling. As you review the feeling wheel above in Figure 9.6, what is the underlying feeling? It is important to use empathy, and even advanced empathy to seek to understand what a client is both thinking and feeling and to reflect it back to the client so they have an opportunity to acknowledge that they are feeling understood or not.

Jack's perception is that counseling is not working but he is feeling angry and frustrated. Why? Because from his perspective, he's been consistently coming to counseling, paying a lot of money, and he's feeling worse than when he first started. The counselor did not acknowledge these thoughts and feelings, but instead just repeated back a segment of Jack's statement, "You feel like counseling is not working," and then placed the responsibility back on Jack (i.e., by asking 'what do you think will work?'). In order to disarm Jack, the counselor must see the truth in Jack's statement and truly take his concerns seriously. Again, this takes remarkable discipline because the counselor so desperately wants to challenge Jack's distortions, he has not been compliant, he misses sessions, shows up late, doesn't complete assignments, and he doesn't pay his bill.

With this in mind, let's rewind the tape and try a new tactic. The counselor says, "Jack, this is really important. You've spent a lot of time and money on counseling but it's just not working and you seem pretty frustrated and disappointed." He responds, "Yep, that's right. I don't think it's worth my time to continue. I guess counseling just isn't for me."

This is an improvement. The counselor took Jack's concerns seriously ("this is really important") and acknowledged his thoughts and feelings. But, in order to have any real chance of salvaging this case, the counselor will need two additional skills:

Assertiveness skills. Developing the skill of assertiveness involves you acknowledging your own thoughts and feelings about how the other person's behavior affects you. To do this effectively, you will need to keep two things in mind. First, you must be specific about the other person's behavior. You can do this be stating your complaint in this form, "When you do _____, I feel _____. " For example, instead of saying, "You never appreciate anything I do to help you. I feel like nothing ever makes you happy," you might say, "When you say I never do anything to help you, I feel frustrated and confused. I definitely want to help you as much as I can but I'm not sure the things I do are what you want or need from me." Second, be careful about not making critical judgements about the other person's intentions and motivations. We use the healthy-intention-unhealthy-method distinction. For example, if a client misses a counseling session because they did not like how they felt after their previous session, you might say, "I can totally understand why you missed the last session; you didn't like how the session before ended. You felt badly and you didn't want to go through that again (healthy intention). However, if you miss the following session (unhealthy-method), I have no way of knowing. I really want you to let me know if something I say or do upsets you so I can revise what I'm doing. Your feedback, even if its critical, is super important to me. I want to hear it, even if its painful (modeling acceptance of criticism)."

Another important aspect of assertiveness is expressing your own feelings about how your behavior affects the client. This is a natural extension of the acceptance-based empathy, discussed earlier. The counselor might say, "I'm glad you told me about how poorly the last session went for you. I feel badly because I totally missed it. I had no idea I had upset you and I never checked-in with you to find out before you left. That is a huge mistake on my part." Notice how the counselor acknowledges feeling badly about his lack of sensitivity to the client's negative emotional reaction to the session and his failure to check-in with the client before ending the session. Note that it is important to consider how your verbal and nonverbal interactions impact the client. The counselor acknowledging feeling badly about the lack of sensitivity and failure to check in goes a long way in repairing a ruptured relationship and models for the client how to use assertiveness not just to express feelings about how other people affect them but also about how open expressions of acceptance of responsibility for their own mistakes look.

Respect skills. Without respect, no matter how skillfully you use the other skills, your efforts will not be received. Respect has two levels. First, you avoid being critical and judgmental about the other person's intentions, as noted above. You also avoid blaming the client or trying to prove the other person wrong. You also avoid retreating into the martyr position (e.g., "I guess I just can't do anything right"). These maneuvers are the intimacy defeaters discussed earlier. Second, you clearly state how much you value the other person and your relationship with them. So in the example of the client who was upset at the end of a session and consequently missed the next one, the counselor may have added, "I'm glad you told me about how poorly the last session went for you. I feel badly because I totally missed it. I had no idea I had upset you and I never checked-in with you to find out before you left. That is a huge mistake on my part. I really value our relationship and want to make sure you always feel safe and respected."

Respect is woven into the fabric of all the other skills. For example, a counselor was running late for an appointment because she was dealing with a crisis situation from the previous session for which the client needed to be hospitalized. Her next client was clearly upset about having to wait 30-minutes. The counselor responded, "I'm really glad you told me how upset you are about this (respect and acceptance empathy). I really feel badly about how long you had to wait (assertiveness). I know your time is very valuable and it's frustrating to just sit in the waiting room (thought and feeling empathy). If I could have changed the situation, I would have. The last thing I want to do is give you the impression I don't take your time seriously (respect)." In this case, the counselor had no other option but to deal with the previous client's crisis. But instead of trying to defend her actions or reveal anything about the previous client's situation (a potential privacy violation), she focused on using effective empathy, assertiveness, and respect. The client may respond by saying, "I know, things happen that are out of your control. Can we just use our time to talk about a situation I had last week with my boss and we can reschedule for next week?" Once a client believes a counselor values his or her feelings, the client is ready to move on. However, had the counselor ignored the feelings and tried to defend her actions, the client would most likely have remained angry and uncooperative. The combination of empathy, assertiveness, and respect melted away the defenses and turned the situation into a productive session.

The How Skills:
The How Skills of empathy, assertiveness, and respect have to do with the way you use them. There are several important principles involved.

1. **Pay attention.** Attend to eye contact, your tone of voice, your body language, and your gestures. These are the nonverbal counseling skills. Be sure you are always warm, accepting, and sensitive. Carl Rogers often referred to this as unconditional positive regard (see "Research Based

counseling skills: The art and science of therapeutic empathy for more on this, by Hawkins et al., 2019). You may need to watch yourself on film and get critical, corrective feedback from your supervisors, and others, about how well your body language matches your words.

2. **Be genuine.** This is no small task. You have to mean what you say, but do so in a disciplined way.

3. **Be humble.** Humility is the key to being genuine. This is especially so in acceptance empathy. Jesus' reminds us of this when he says that in order to save yourself you must lose yourself. Again, this is a basic principle in the relational universe. Others have referred to this as the "death of the ego." You have to lay your pride aside and be willing to accept that you are a flawed individual and you sometimes act in ways that are destructive, even when it is not your intention. This does not mean you have to accept things that untrue about yourself or your intentions. But it means you accept responsibility for your behavior and its effects. For example, if a client says, "You don't care about my time. I waited 20-minutes for you out in the waiting room." You don't have to say, "Yes, you're right. I don't really care about your time and I feel badly about that." But you can say, "I know your angry about having to wait so long. I feel badly about running late and I can understand why you would think I don't care about your time. But I really do; and I need to be more disciplined in how I manage my time so that I don't give you that impression."

There are two keys to effectively using this skill. The first is learning how to be specific about what it is the person is doing. For example, instead of Loyd saying to his wife, "All you do is complain about what I don't do, you never appreciate all the work I do to support this family" he might say, "When you complain about me not doing things around the house…" This keeps it specific. The second key is to express your feelings in a way that doesn't judge the other person's motives or intentions.

So, if someone says, "I'm frustrated because you are so concerned about trying to teach me facts and information, but you don't care about my feelings" to simply say, "I understand what you are feeling," is not sufficient. They will likely feel misunderstood even though you said you understand. If you say, "It sounds like you're frustrated" or "You feeling frustrated with me," you would be getting closer, since you are reflecting the feelings back. However, if you can reflect feelings along with content and meaning that would be most effective.

Another possible benefit of refining and developing the counseling skills, especially those that may communicate a positive effect, is the prevention of dropout. Researchers have confirmed the importance of the therapeutic relationship (which you read about in Chapter 8) in determining success (or failure) in counseling (Horvath, Del Re, Fluckiger, & Symonds, 2011; Luedke, Peluso, Diaz, Freund, & Baker, 2017; Norcross & Wampold, 2011). Luedke et al (2017) indicated that a staggering 15-70% of clients either drop out or do not attain a satisfactory outcome. Research suggests that in order to achieve clinically significant change, this requires 12 sessions of psychotherapy (Anderson & Lambert, 2001; Luedke et al., 2017). However, if clients are dropping out prior to this 12 session threshold, they are not able to experience the benefits of counseling, nor the empathy of the core skills and the benefits of advanced evidence based technique (Norcross & Wampold, n.d.; See Figure 9.7).

FIGURE 9.7

Evidence-based Practice: The Intersection of Clinical Expertise, Patient Characteristics, and Research

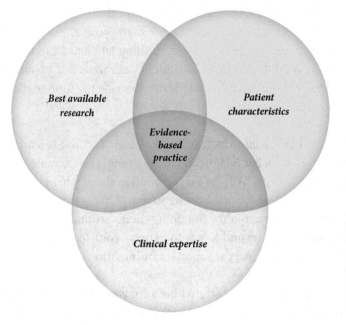

© Kendall Hunt Publishing Company

Predictors of Client Dropout. Using the Specific Affective Coding System (SPAFF; Coan & Gottman, 1989), Luedke et al (2017) applied this system of behavioral interaction coding to the dyadic interactions between counselor and client. Examples of both positive and negative interactions include, but are not limited to:

Positive Interactions:
- high validation (includes some counseling skills such as paraphrasing)
- low validation (communication of acceptance through gestures such as head nods
- interest (genuine interest in the other's feelings or thoughts)
- humor (shared laughter, with feelings of happiness, private jokes, or good natured teasing)

Negative interactions:
- contempt (may include sarcasm or hostile humor and indicates a lack of respect)
- criticism (blaming or character attacks)
- defensiveness (one will use excuses and/or counter criticism)
- tension (can be manifested through nervous laughter)
- tense humor (mutual uncomfortable nervous laughter)

The results of the Luedke et al. (2017) study illustrated that defensiveness and low validation were significantly varied between the two groups of clients (clients who continued returning to counseling and clients that dropped out of treatment). Clients who discontinued treatment had higher average displays of low validation themselves. The researchers indicated that low validation was demonstrated by the client nodding and providing what is referred to as *back channeling* verbal or nonverbal responses.

© pio3/Shutterstock.com

The term *back channel* came from Yngve in 1970. Yngve used the term *channel* to reflect the two channels of conversation. The main channel describes the channel used by the speaker to provide information, and the back channel is the channel used by the listener to provide information back to the speaker, without claiming the floor (White, 1989). It seems that when the counselor is doing most of the talking and the client is doing most of the listening/backchanneling, it is as if the wires are crossed. Back channeling is a term that comes from the linguistics and pragmatics literature (Tolins & Tree, 2014) and includes responses such as "mm hmm," "uh huh," and "ok." Back channeling interjections are considered reactive and thought to influence the direction of narration. Linguistics researchers have found that backchanneling responses are both proactive and reactive and serve to shape narrative. Back channeling responses have also been described in the linguistics literature by a number of other names including reactive tokens, response tokens, and accompaniment signals (Tolins & Tree, 2014). Collaborative speakers are speakers that maintain awareness of the listener and monitor their speech to ensure they are answering questions appropriately and also monitor for logical contradictions (Grice, 1975). One theory on back channelling suggests that the speaker's responsibility includes monitoring back channeling in order to monitor his or her own discourse (Clark & Murphy, 1982; Clark & Krych, 2004).

Interestingly, in the counseling literature, these back channeling verbals and nonverbals are called by different terms (Hawkins et al., 2019; Ivey, Ivey, & Zalaquett, 2018). Collaborative communication involves both a speaker and a listener working together in sync (Grice, 1975). In collaborative communication, the speaker is aware of the other speaker and monitors his or her communication in order to ensure that it stays collaborative. A speaker's task is not only to share, but to be aware of the listener's back channeling responses; a collaborative speaker is aware of the listener. A speaker's task is also to be aware of the back channeling, and monitor the conversation in response.

Luedke et al (2017) found that early dropout from counseling was correlated with client demonstrations of more back channeling. In the counseling literature, back channeling responses are often described by specific terms noting each category of back channeling. For example, utterances such as "mm hmm," and "uh huh" are referred to as *paralanguage* (Hawkins et al., 2019; Ivey & Ivey, Zalaquett, 2018)). *Nonverbal encouragers* is the term often used to describe nonverbal gestures such as nodding. Although nonverbal, these are still considered skills to be developed for counselors. When the client is using a larger number of back channeling responses, including nonverbal encouragers, it is a reflection that the counselor is talking beyond what may be considered his or her conversational turn within the counseling context. So, in light of a counselor employing high levels of low validation responses, it makes sense that clients might drop out of counseling.

Predictors of Client Retention. Additionally, the Luedke et al (2017) study found that counselors who were identified as providing higher levels of validation, communicated through counseling skills such as the reflecting skills of paraphrasing, and had lower levels of tension and were more likely to have clients who return to counseling. Given that retention is of critical importance in counseling, demonstrating the skills, maintaining a sense of comfort and safety, and providing the client with the conversational floor may be important strategies for retaining clients. This provides clear research support for the importance of the use of reflecting skills by counselors. Good reflecting skills such as paraphrasing are highly validating to clients, and predict that clients will return to counseling. Luedke and her colleagues indicated, "Unsurprisingly, counselors who provided higher levels of validation and were more comfortable in the room (e.g., fewer displays of tension) were more likely to see clients return to therapy (Luedke et al., 2017, p. 131). The science of counseling involves integrating research content including work like Luedke, where the art involves a masterful execution of the core skills (see Figure 9.8 below).

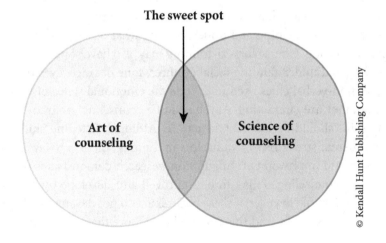

The sweet spot

Art of counseling

Science of counseling

© Kendall Hunt Publishing Company

FIGURE 9.8

The Overlap of the Art and Science of Counseling

Dr. Ashley J. Luedke, has lead research in this area and has collaborated with several colleagues. Dr. Leudke is a counselor educator who works at St. Bonaventure University in New York. She earned her Ph.D. at Florida Atlantic University in Boca Raton, Florida. She has worked with a team of researchers there including Dr. Peluso, Dr. Diaz, Dr. Freund, & Dr. Baker, (2017) and they conduct research on the therapeutic relationship including the nonverbal and verbal components of counseling in order to understand what leads to retention in counseling. When asked what one thing she would like to share with counselors in training, Dr. Luedke stated:

"If beginning students could have one takeaway from my research it would be to never underestimate how much information you can get from your client/student based on their nonverbal communication, but also more importantly how much your client/student is getting from your nonverbal communication. The way we say things and the expressions used are sometimes more impactful (for better or worse) than our actual words are. It isn't about being neutral all the time, that doesn't work. Be human and connect and be aware of how your presence/tone/body language may impact those you are trying to help." (Luedke, 2019, personal communication).

WHAT IF I CAN'T DEVELOP COUNSELING SKILLS?

A foundational skill set for professional counselors involves expertise in communication skills. Some who decided to pursue a career in the helping professions already have a solid skill base. Beginning counselors may be fairly adept at listening and understanding what other people are thinking and feeling. Counselors-in-training may also have some basic skills at reading and understanding facial gestures, tone of voice, eye contact and other non-verbal clues used to decode the emotional states of those with whom they are interacting. At the end of a counseling program, counseling skills should be like second nature. Although listening skills are often inherent strengths for counselors in training, there is always room for growth and improvement. In addition, research demonstrates that foundational counseling skills can be improved and developed with practice (Knight, 2009). However, if these basic skills do not develop during training, students might find this career choice more than a little challenging and may really want to reflect more about what factors have influenced the choice to pursue counseling as a career path.

The Emergent Model of Clinical Expertise (See Figure 9.9; Sibcy, 2017; Sibcy & Knight, 2019) postulates that it requires 10,000 hours of practice to develop expertise that includes factual knowledge, procedural knowledge (i.e. "how-to" knowledge, such as conducting an intake and identifying a presenting problem), contingent knowledge (i.e. if-then knowledge, such as if a client is depressed, counselor does sucide risk assessment), and reflective knowledge (i.e. knowledge so automatic it works like a reflex). Thus, in order to develop these foundational skills such as paraphrasing, reflecting feelings, using paralanguage, and identifying keywords, it will take much practice and intentionality. Even still, after these 10K hours of practice, there is not a point of arrival. If you have driven with a GPS, you may be familiar with your digital assistant announcing, "you have arrived!" when you reach your destination. However, in counseling expertise, there is not a designated point where an announcer comes over the loudspeaker and says, "You have arrived at clinical expertise! Congratulations!"

© Kendall Hunt Publishing Company

FIGURE 9.9

The Emergent Model of Clinical Expertise

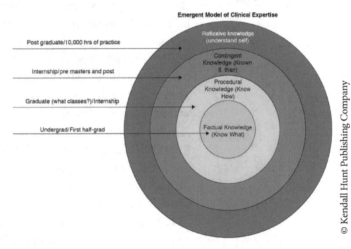

Those training to become counselors with a history as athletes or performers may struggle, because often after a productive session, there is no external affirmation or acknowledgment such as exists in sports or entertainment. After a counseling session, there is no roaring applause from an audience. One of the important lessons learned on the journey of becoming a counselor is to develop a sense of internal satisfaction after the process of walking alongside a client and helping them sort through and organize their thoughts and feelings (Silvey & Knight, 2019).

Studies have indicated that more time spent training and practicing the skills leads to greater gains and refinements in several skill areas, as well as in other areas of the counselor's personal development including self-efficacy (Knight, 2009; Schaefle, Smaby, Maddux, & Cates, 2005; Fox, 1982). You are more likely to increase your benefits the more time you spend on skills training and practice. Often, students feel anxious when they go into their skills training courses because they are asked to perform live or to video the interaction. This is different from other coursework they may be more familiar with that involves reading, remembering, and sharing information on a test or quiz. However, it is important to remember that this training is instrumental in ensuring that students master the skills for creating a safe place for clients to do meaningful work.

© Nataliya Sdobnikova/Shutterstock.com

It is critical, as noted in the devotional at the beginning of this chapter, to have a teachable spirit while learning counseling skills. If you, as a CIT, take feedback personally and respond in a defensive manner, then you may lose valuable growth time defending an action, or worse launching a counter criticism. This pattern can be a manifestation of what Dr. John Gottman calls Negative Sentiment Override (Gottman & Silver, 1999) This may make things more difficult interpersonally. The paradox is that if you take your criticizer seriously and use the skill set of EAR, you may find that your relationship and sense of connection is actually made stronger. Proverbs 15:1 (NIV) says, "A soft answer turns away wrath but a harsh word stirs up strife." One way you demonstrate respect to your clients is by respecting the growth process. Ultimately, the teachable spirit is a model of relating characterized by empathy and respect. In some ways, it also requires a sacrificing of the self. This sacrificing of self has sometimes been referred to as the death of the ego. The scriptures provide good imagery in the kernel of wheat that must fall to the ground and die in order to grow. The scripture says, "I tell you the truth, unless a kernel of wheat is planted in the soil and dies, it remains alone. But its death will produce many new kernels—a plentiful harvest of new lives," (John 12:24, NLT). Here are some examples: There is a paradoxical principle at work here in this first one, if you truly want to find yourself, then you have to first lose yourself. Another important principle is to remember that you reap what you sow. This reaping is not only for the negative, but also for the positive. If you want to be able to impact the lives of others, you must also be willing to be impacted.

If you feel like you are questioning your fit within the profession and the counselor skill set, below are some suggested courses of actions:

- Evaluate your current skill set, including strengths and areas for development
- Know which area of counseling/context is a fit with your strengths. If empathy is difficult, perhaps you would prefer to focus on assessment, intake, or screening and evaluation work.

- Consult with a trusted mentor in the field and analyze the pros and cons of continuing pursuing this degree
- Assess your expectations and create a realistic and detailed growth plan
- Consider sitting in the other chair and talking with a professional counselor about your goals, strengths, and areas of needed development

Ongoing Development

Becoming an expert in foundational and advanced counseling skills may involve some natural inclination, along with much hard work, dedication, and practice. This is not meant to be discouraging, but counselor trainees are encouraged to evaluate their inclinations, abilities, and the work required to refine them. Learning to be a professional counselor is more than knowing a great deal of book knowledge, but also requires continuous honing of the skills to become a skilled and disciplined relational agent—one who not only facilitates deep, trusting, empathic relationships with others, but who has the ability and motivation to understand themselves and has the courage to continuously challenge themselves to see their own blind spots. Even more, you have to be open and willing to work on these blind spots in the same way you challenge your clients to do so.

© ESB Professional/Shutterstock.com

Notice the theme throughout this text on the journey of becoming. Since this is a lifelong journey, we are always in the process of growing. To some, this prospect is too overwhelming and they often burn out or change professions altogether. To others, this call to continuous growth and transformation is exciting. Reflecting on this process of refinement and growth, the authors would like to share words of wisdom:

- I (G. Sibcy) often tell my students that I'm much like a highway: always under construction. Just as soon as I fix one pothole, another one crops up. Lines need to be repainted, signs need to be updated, and sometimes the road is reduced to one lane while the other lane is being repaved.
- I (A. Kuhnley) often share with students that I am on the journey to becoming, that there is still more growth and development occurring each day.
- I (R. Simmons) encourage my students to live in the "ing" rather than the "ed." I never want to be finished with developing who I am as an individual or as a counselor.

SUMMARY

FOR THE ROAD AHEAD

Check out the Chapter 9 videos at this link:

https://www.khpcontent.com/

Counseling skills and techniques are a critical component of counselor training. The listening skills should become like second nature as a counselor prepares to be a "Sunday player" (Jacobs, 2013). In the sport of football, the pros play on Sundays. College football games are scheduled on Saturday, and highschool games may be scheduled for Thursday or Friday nights. Becoming a Sunday Player, requires much dedication, practice and hard work. In the Emergent Model of Clinical Expertise, it is clear that it may require more than 10,000 hours of practice to obtain mastery/expert level in the field. Mastering core skills such as reflecting content, reflecting feeling, reflecting meaning, paraphrasing, and minimal encouragers will help to develop a secure foundation. In addition, advanced skills such as those designed to deal with so called "difficult clients," such as empathy, assertiveness, and respect will help the counselor to develop as a strong therapeutic rapport even in more challenging situations. As you advance in your counselor training program, you will learn to provide comprehensive case conceptualizations, offer diagnostic impressions, and construct treatment plans. However, you must first learn to effectively listen to the client in order to accurately identify a diagnosis, which then informs an appropriate treatment plan.

Reflections on the Journey

Reflecting back to Table 9.1 and Table 9.2, which counseling skills do you think will be the:

- Most challenging
- Least challenging
- Most beneficial

Consider that with the information in this chapter and the additional video sources, you already have enough to start practicing some of the basic skills (e.g., attending, minimal encouragers, identifying and reflecting feelings). Think of two friends or family members who will allow you to practice these skills with them.

For Further Exploration

Burns, D. D. (1999). *The feeling good handbook*. New York, NY: Penguin.

Burns, D. (2008). *Feeling Good Together: The Secret to Making Troubled Relationships Work*. New York: Broadway Books.

Luedke, A. J., Peluso, P. R., Diaz, P., Freund, R., & Baker, A. (2017). Predicting dropout in counseling using affect coding of the therapeutic relationship: An empirical analysis. *Journal of Counseling and Development, 95*(2), 125+. Retrieved from http://link.galegroup.com. ezproxy.liberty.edu/apps/doc/A491138089/AONE?u=vic_liberty&sid=AONE&xid=32795ca5 Retrieved from:

Seigel, D. J. (2010). *Mindsight: The new science of personal transformation*. New York, NY: Bantam.

REFERENCES

American Counseling Association (2014). *ACA Code of Ethics*. Alexandria, VA: Author

Adler, A. (1929). *Practice and theory of individual psychology*. London: Lund Humphries.

Amen, D. (2017). What is the executive center of the brain? Retrieved from: https://www.amenclinics.com/blog/what-is-the-executive-center-of-the-brain/

Anderson, E. M., & Lambert, M. J. (2001). A survival analysis of clinically significant change in outpatient psychotherapy. *Journal of Clinical Psychology, 57*, 875-888.

Aspy, D. N., Aspy, C. B., Russel, G., & Wedel, M. (2000). Carkhuff's human technology: A verification and extension of Kelly's (1997) suggestion to integrate the humanistic and technical components of counseling. *Journal of Counseling and Development, 78*(1), 29-37.

Augsburger, D. (1982). *Caring enough to hear and be heard*. Ada, MI: Baker Publishing Group.

Avent Harris, J. R., Trepal, H., Prado, A., & Robinson, J. (2019). Women Counselor Educators' Experiences of Microaggressions. *TheJournal of Counselor Preparation and Supervision, 12*(2). Retrieved from https://repository.wcsu.edu/jcps/vol12/iss2/2

Bernard, J. M., & Goodyear, R. K. (2019). *Fundamentals of clinical supervision* (6th ed.). New York, NY: Pearson

Brown, D. P., & Elliott, D. S. (2016). *Attachment disturbances in adults: Treatment for comprehensive repair*. New York, NY: Norton & Company.

Bowen, M. (1978). *Family therapy in clinical practice*. New York: Jason Aron-son, Inc.

Burns, D. (2012). *The Feeling Good Handbook: The new mood therapy*. New York: Harper Collins.

Burns, D. (2008). *Feeling Good Together: The Secret to Making Troubled Relationships Work*. New York: Broadway Books.

Carkhuff, R. (1969). *Helping and human relations* (Vols. I & 2) . New York: Holt, Rinehart and Winston.

Carkhuff, R. (2008). *The art of helping* (9th ed.). Amherst, MA: Possibilities Publishing, Inc.

Clark, H. & Murphy, A. (1982). Herbert H. Clark, Gregory L. Murphy Audience design in meaning and reference. *Adv. Psychol. 9,* 287–299.

Clark, H. H. & Krych, M. A. (2004). Speaking while monitoring addressees for understanding. *Journal of Memory and Language, 50*(2004), 62-81. doi:10.1016/j.jml.2003.08.004

Clinton, T. & Sibcy, G. (2012). *Attachments: Why you love, feel and act the way you do.* Brentwood, TN: Integrity Publishers.

Coan, J. & Gottman, J. M. (2007). The Specific Affect Coding System (SPAFF). *Handbook of Emotion Elicitation and Assessment* (pp. 267-285). Oxford University Press.

Covey, S. R. (2004). *The seven habits of highly effective people: Restoring the character ethic.* New York, NY: Free Press.

Duncan, S. (2013, May 14). *Carl Rogers and Gloria – counseling (1965) full session* [Video File]. Retrieved from https://www.youtube.com/watch?v=24d-FEptYj8

Egan, G. (1975). *The skilled helper: A systematic approach to effective helping.* Pacific Grove CA, Brooks/Cole.

Egan, G. E. & Reese, R. J. (2019). *The skilled helper: A problem-management and opportunity-development approach to helping.* Boston, MA: Cengage.

Elliott, R., Bohart, A. C., Watson, J. C., & Murphy, D. (2018). Therapist empathy and client outcome: An updated meta-analysis. *Psychotherapy, 55*(4), 399-410. doi:10.1037/pst0000175

Firestone, R. W. (1987). Destructive effects of the fantasy bond in couple and family relationships. Psychotherapy: Theory, Research, Practice, Training, 24(2), 233-239. http://dx.doi.org.ezproxy.liberty.edu/10.1037/h0085709.

Firestone, R. W. (2014). The Fantasy Bond: The Structure of Psychological Defenses. Santa Barbara, CA: The Glendon Association.

Fox, R. W. (1982). The effects of a residential basic counseling skills training program (Doctoral dissertation). Retrieved from http://ezproxy.liberty.edu/login?url=https://search-proquest-com.ezproxy.liberty.edu/docview/303260708?accountid=12085

Gottman, J.M. & Silver, N. (1999). *The seven principles for making marriage work.* New York, NY: Three Rivers Press.

Gottman, J. M., Woodin, E. M., & Coan, J. A. (1998). *Specific affect coding system manual: 20-code version* (4.0). Seattle, WA: NCAST-AVENUW Publications.

Greggo, S. & Becker, S. P. (2010). The attachment paradigm: A secure base for counselor education? *Journal of Psychology and Christianity, 29*(1), 46-56.

Grice, H. P. (1975). Logic and Conversation. In H. Cole and J. L. Morgan (Eds.), *Syntax and Semantics* (Vol 3, pp. 41-58). New York, NY: Academic Press.

Hagimoto, A., Nakamura, M., Masui, S., Bai, Y., & Oshima, A. (2018). Effects of trained health professionals' behavioral counseling skills on smoking cessation outcomes. *Annals of Behavioral Medicine, 52*(9), 752–761. doi:10.1093/abm/kax049

Hawkins, R., Knight, A., Sibcy, G., & Warren, S. (2019). *Research based counseling skills: The art and science of therapeutic empathy.* Dubuque, IA: Kendall Hunt.

Hill, C. E., Roffman, M., Stahl, J., Friedman, S., Hummel, A., & Wallace, C. (2008). Helping skills training for undergraduates: Outcomes and prediction of outcomes. *Journal of Counseling Psychology, 55,* 359–370. doi:10.1037/0022-0167.55.3.359

Horvath, A. O., Del Re, A. C., Fluckiger, C., & Symonds, D. (2011). Alliance in individual psychotherapy. *Psychotherapy, 48,* 9-16. doi:10.1037/a0022186

Ivey, A. E. (1971). *Microcounseling: Innovations in interview training.* Springfield, IL: Thomas.

Ivey, A. E., Ivey, M. B., & Zalaquett, C. (2018). *Intentional interviewing and counseling: Facilitating client development in a multicultural society* (9th ed.). Boston, MA: Cengage.

Jankowiak-Siuda, K., Rymarczyk, K., & Grabowska, A. (2011). How we empathize with others: A neurobiological perspective. *Medical Science Monitor, 17*(1), 18–24.

Jacobs, E. & Schimmel, C. (2013). *Impact therapy: The courage to counsel.* Star City, West Virginia: Impact Therapy Associates.

Knight, A. M. (2009). *Effective practices in teaching counseling skills and its relationship with emotional intelligence.* VIrginia Beach, Virginia. ProQuest Digital Dissertations.

Knight, A. M., & Sibcy, G. A. (2017). *Redeeming attachment: A counselor's guide to facilitating attachment to God and earned security.* Dubuque, IA: Kendall Hunt.

Knight, A., Sibcy, G., Gantt, A., Macon, K., & Carapezza, K. M. (2018). The impact of brief God attachment workshop attendance on God attachment. *The Virginia Counselors Journal, 36*, 48-55.

Knowles, M. (1988). *The modern practice of adult education: From pedagogy to andragogy.* Englewood Cliffs, NJ: Cambridge.

Kottler, J. A. (1992). Confronting our own hypocrisy: Being a model for our students and clients *Journal of Counseling and Development, 70*(4), 475. doi:10.1002/j.1556-6676.1992.tb01641.x

Kottler, J. (circa 1990), "How to effectively deal with your most difficult clients." CA: Workshop.

Kuhnley, A. K., Shaler, L. S., & Silvey, R. J. (2019). *Fostering a community of inquiry through creative teaching practices in counselor education.* Clearwater, FL: Association of Creativity in Counseling.

Lekka, F., Efstathiou, G., & Kalantzi-Azizi, A. (2014). The effect of counselling-based training on online peer support. *British Journal of Guidance & Counselling, 43*(1), 156-170.

Luedke, A. J., Peluso, P. R., Diaz, P., Freund, R., & Baker, A. (2017). Predicting dropout in counseling using affect coding of the therapeutic relationship: An empirical analysis. *Journal of Counseling and Development, 95*(2), 125+. Retrieved from http://link.galegroup.com.ezproxy.liberty.edu/apps/doc/A491138089/AONE?u=vic_liberty&sid=AONE&xid=32795ca5 Retrieved from:

Keller, M. B., M. D., McCullough, J. P., Klein, D. N., Arnow, B., Dunner, D. L., Gelenberg, A. J., . . . Zajecka, J. (2000). A comparison of nefazodone, the cognitive behavioral-analysis system of psychotherapy, and their combination for the treatment of chronic depression. *The New England Journal of Medicine, 342*(20), 1462-70. Retrieved from http://ezproxy.liberty.edu/login?url=https://search-proquest-com.ezproxy.liberty.edu/docview/223932925?accountid=12085

Neborsky, R. J. (2006). Brain, mind, and dyadic change processes. *Journal of Clinical Psychology: In Session. 62*(5), 523–538.

Norcross, J. C., & Wampold, B. E. (2011). Evidence-based therapy relationships: Research conclusions and clinical practices. *Psychotherapy, 48*, 98-102. doi:10.1037/a0022161

Norcross, J. C. & Wampold, B. E. (n.d.). Adapting the relationship to the individual patient. Retrieved from: http://citeseerx.ist.psu.edu/viewdoc/download?doi=10.1.1.463.7645&rep=rep1&type=pdf

Platt, F. W. (1992). Empathy: Can it be taught? *Annals of Internal Medicine.* 117(8):700–701, OCT 1992. doi:10.1059/0003-4819-117-8-700_2

Rumble, A. C., Van Lange, P. A. M., & Parks, C. D. (2010). The benefits of empathy: When empathy may sustain cooperation in social dilemmas. *European Journal of Social Psychology, 40*(5), 856-866.

Siegel, D. (2003). Toward an interpersonal neurobiology of the developing mind: Attachment relationships, mindsight, and neural integration. *Infant Mental Health Journal, 22*(102), 67-94.

Sibcy, G. A. & Knight, A. M. (2011). *Emotional intelligence, attachment theory, and neuroscience: Implications for counselors.* American Association of Christian Counselors World Conference, Nashville, TN, September.

Kiosses, V. N. Vassilios, K. T., & Tatsioni, A. (2016). Empathy promoting interventions for health professionals: A systematic review of RCTs. *Journal of Compassionate Health Care, 3*(7), doi:10.1186/s40639-016-0024-

Sibcy, G., Knight, A. & Gantt, A. (2019). Intentional and advanced empathy. In R. Hawkins, A. Knight, G. Sibcy, & S. Warren, *Research based counseling skills: The art and science of therapeutic empathy*. Dubuque, IA: Kendall Hunt.

Schaefle, S. (2005). Counseling skills attainment, retention, and transfer as measured by the skilled counseling scale. *Counselor Education and Supervision, 44*(4), 280.

Sibcy, G. A. & Knight, A. M. (2019). *Theoretical foundations*. In Hawkins, R., Knight, A.M., Sibcy, G.A., & Warren, S. (Eds.), *Research-based counseling skills: The art and science of therapeutic empathy*. Dubuque, IA: Kendall Hunt.

Siegel, D. (2010). *Mindsight: The new science of personal transformation*. New York, NY: Bantam.

Silvey, R. J. & Knight, A. M. (2019). The journey of becoming. In R. Hawkins, A. Knight, G. Sibcy, & S. Warren (Eds.), *Research based counseling skills: The art and science of therapeutic empathy*. Dubuque, IA: Kendall Hunt.

Smaby, M. & Maddux, C.D. (2010). Basic and Advanced Counseling Skills: The Skilled Counselor Training Model. Belmont, CA: Brooks/Cole.

Smith, K. (2016). Learning from triads: training undergraduates in counselling skills. *Counselling & Psychotherapy Research, 16*(2), 123–131. doi:10.1002/capr.12056

Thompson, C. (2010). *Anatomy of the soul: Surprising connections between neuroscience and spiritual practices that can transform your life and relationships*. Carol Stream, IL: Tyndale Momentum.

Trusty, J., Ng, K., & Watts, R. (2011). Model of effects of adult attachment on emotional empathy of counseling students. *Journal of Counseling and Development, 83*(1), 66-77.

Tolins, J. & Tree, E. J. (2014). Addressee backchannels steer narrative development. *Journal of Pragmatics, 70*, 152-164. doi:10.1016/j.pragma.2014.06.006

White, S. (1989). Backchannels across cultures: A study of Americans and Japanese. *Language in Society, 18*(1), 59-76. Retrieved from http://www.jstor.org/stable/4168001

Yalom, I. (1995). *The theory and practice of group psychotherapy*. New York, New York: Basic Books.

CHAPTER 10
Counseling Theories

PATTI HINKLEY, ED.D. & CHRISTINA VILLARREAL-DAVIS, PH.D.

> "Theory is fun. You probably think I am exaggerating a little in this statement, but really, for me, theory is fun. Looking at all of the different ways to understand human activity is entertaining to those of us who are people watchers or, even worse, nosy busybodies who are always asking, 'Now why did he or she do that?'"
> —Nancy L. Murdock (2017, p. 3)

Following Christ: Grace for Our Work

Proverbs 29:18 (King James Version) reveals "Where there is no vision, the people perish; but he that keepeth the law, happy is he." The Message (MSG) version provides us a more contemporary translation, "If people can't see what God is doing, they stumble all over themselves; but when they attend to what he reveals, they are most blessed."

For Christians, this scripture reminds us not to lose sight of our creator and His will for our lives. Having a vision to see and follow His will keeps us on the right path; however, without it, we can get lost and head in

the wrong direction that can lead us to stumble, or worse, destruction. For counselors, understanding the myriad theories of counseling and identifying with a theory (or theories) of how people heal and change, can provide you with a vision and plan that will guide you in all aspects of the counseling process. The beginning counselor can feel overwhelmed at times when a client is facing severe emotional and psychological turmoil; by having a foundation in a theoretical model the counselor has a plan. This vision will assist the counselor in understanding their client better, addressing their needs and goals, establishing their treatment plan, and progressing through the phases of treatment. The counselor will also feel these theories will provide a myriad of tools to use in addressing a variety of their client's issues. This is an excellent time for new counselors to branch out and decide what theories hold meaning and purpose for them and ultimately create a vision in working with their client.

CHAPTER OBJECTIVES

After reading this chapter, you will understand more about:

- The core counseling theories, including basic philosophy, assumptions and key concepts, and therapeutic relationship and goals.
- The rationale for choosing a counseling theory and how that plays a role in the counseling process.
- The systems approach to conceptualizing clients.
- A brief critique of the core theories through the lens of Christianity.

The following CACREP standards are addressed in this chapter:
Professional Counseling Orientation and Ethical Practice:
- Theories and models of counseling (CACREP, 2016, Standard 2.F.5.a

Have you ever wondered how counseling actually works? Are there guiding principles used in counseling? To answer this question, you would first want to ask yourself, "What is my belief on how people change and feel better?" or "What is my approach in counseling?", meaning what is my *counseling theory*? A counseling theory is a theoretical framework used in counseling to help counselors better understand their client's thoughts, behaviors/actions, and feelings, which will guide treatment planning, therapy goals, and therapeutic outcomes. Theories relate to a personal beliefs on how people reach optimal mental wellbeing. There are multiple theories in practice today; however, due to the brevity of this chapter, a succinct overview of a few major counseling theories will be provided. This chapter will briefly focus on: psychodynamic theories, humanistic theories, cognitive and behavioral theories, and a few other popular theories. An additional purpose of this chapter is to provide a critique and an explanation of how these theoretical approaches are viewed through the lens of Christianity. Lastly, a case study is provided so you can review an application of a few theories as well as test your own understanding. Recommended readings are provided to encourage you to further explore and study counseling theories from both secular (see Murdock, 2017) and Christian (see Jones & Butman, 2011) perspectives. Hopefully, as you gain a better understanding of the theories you will find yourself gravitating toward one or a few theories that fit your belief system and personality style.

DOES HAVING A COUNSELING THEORY REALLY MATTER?

As a brand-new graduate counseling student, it is normal to question your theoretical orientation. When the topic comes up, what will your answer be? Freudian? Rogerian? CBT? Postmodern? You probably are undecided at this point. In fact, you might even ask yourself if identifying with a theory really matters, especially when researchers (Lambert & Barley, 2001; Lambert & Cattani-Thompson, 1996) and experts (see Kottler, 2018) in the field have noted that the client-counselor relationship is more significant than the counselor's theoretical orientation. For example, Lambert and colleagues (1996, 2001) have investigated client outcomes in counseling and have found common factors in therapeutic change, with the therapeutic relationship being the most important. However, do not use this as an excuse not to choose a theory, because these same researchers and experts will also encourage you to work from a theoretical approach that fits you best!

© Anton Watman/Shutterstock.com

Being grounded in theory will provide you, the counselor in training, a foundation, and frame of reference to work from so you do not get lost. In other words, theory is just like your GPS system on your smartphone, it will provide you with directions on where you need to go. According to Murdock (2017), "theory is practical and important. Theory is fun. Theory works. Theory is essential to human life. Counselors who don't have theory are likely to get lost in their genuine efforts to help their clients" (p. 3). Additionally, Halbur and Halbur (2019) deliver some challenging words, "A theoretical orientation provides helpers with a framework for therapy that sets the foundation for intentional counseling. For the counselor, being intentional is a prerequisite to ethical and effective helping" (p. 4).

Lastly, you might be wondering how to choose a theory and how to pick one that fits you best. Murdock (2017) recommends you select a theory that is consistent with your beliefs about people, your personal values, and your preferred method of connecting with others. Halbur and Halbur (2019) agree, providing an entire chapter on various strategies that can help to find your preferred theory. It is filled with questions, the *Selective Theory Sorter-Revised* (STS-R) survey that helps identify your theory preference, information on counseling theory and personality type via the *Myers-Briggs Type Indicator* (MBTI), and other activities to honestly assess your personal values, beliefs, and worldview. Overall, these ideas will help you choose a theory, but that decision does not need to happen today. You need additional time and exposure to the diversity of theories prior to making a realistic and honest choice (Granello & Young, 2019).

PSYCHOLOGICAL SCHOOLS
THIN LINE ICONS

The Major Counseling Theories

The current major theories described in this chapter will be divided into schools of thought in psychology and counseling. They include psychodynamic theories (psychoanalytic theory, Jungian theory, and Adlerian theory), humanistic/existential theories (existential theory, person-centered theory, and Gestalt theory), and behavioral and cognitive theories (behavioral theory, cognitive theory, and cognitive-behavioral theory). Other major theories, including family systems theory, solution-focused brief therapy, and narrative therapy will also be discussed. A brief case study for applying each school of thought is provided for you at the end of the chapter. Lastly, a timeline of the counseling theories presented in this chapter can be found below.

Orientation	Clinical Psychologists	Counseling Psychologists	Social Workers	Counselors
Behavioral	15%	2%	11%	8%
Cognitive	31%	19%	19%	29%
Constructivist	1%	1%	2%	2%
Existential/ Humanistic	1%	7%	4%	5%
Gestalt/Experiential	1%	1%	1%	2%
Integrative/Eclectic	22%	31%	26%	23%
Multicultural	1%	2%	1%	1%
Psychoanalytic	3%	1%	5%	2%
Psychodynamic	15%	9%	9%	5%
Rogerian/PC	2%	3%	1%	10%
Systems	2%	4%	14%	7%
Other	2%	12%	4%	3%

TABLE 10.1

Theoretical Orientations of Psychotherapists in the U.S.

Source: Prochaska & Norcross, 2018

HISTORICAL TIMELINE OF THE EARLY THEORIES

1886 – Sigmund Freud began therapeutic practice and research in Vienna.
1900 – Sigmund Freud published "Interpretation of Dreams" – beginning of psychoanalytic thought
1911 – Alfred Adler left Freud's Psychoanalytic Group to form his school of Individual Psychology
1913 – Carl Jung also departed from Freudian views and developed his own school of Analytical Psychology
1936 – Karen Horney published Feminine Psychology as she critiqued Freudian psychoanalytic theory
1951 – Carl Rogers published Client-Centered Therapy
1951 – Gestalt Therapy is published by Fritz Perls, Paul Goodman, & Ralph Hefferline.
1953 – B.F. Skinner outlined Behavioral Therapy
1954 – Abraham Maslow helped found Humanistic Psychology
1955 – Albert Ellis began teaching methods of Rational Emotive Therapy – beginning of cognitive psychology
1959 – Victor Frankl published an overview of Existential Analysis
1965 – William Glasser published Reality Therapy
1967 – Aaron Beck published a Cognitive Model of depression

WHAT ARE THE PSYCHODYNAMIC THEORIES?

Psychodynamic theories include psychoanalytic theory, Jungian theory, and Adlerian theory. These theories have a shared belief that people are influenced by unconscious motivations and use different approaches to bring the unconscious to conscious awareness. The traditional psychoanalytic theory does not emphasize the therapeutic relationship when compared to Jungian, Adlerian, and modern psychodynamic approaches.

Psychoanalytic Theory

© Everett Historical/Shutterstock.com

Sigmund Freud (1856-1939) is known as the key creator in psychoanalytic theory, terming it *psychoanalysis*, which is defined as a theoretical system which aims to bring the repressed unconscious conflicts to the conscious awareness by means of dream interpretation and free association. His early interest in the work of Josef Breuer and Jean-Martin Charcot on hysteria led to the development of this theory (Johnson, 2016). The well-known case study of "Anna O" (later identified as Bertha Pappenheim), who suffered from severe hysteria, was treated with daily hypnosis sessions by Breuer that significantly reduced her symptoms, leading to the revelation of repressed traumatic memories (Johnson, 2016).

Assumptions and Key Concepts

Constructs of psychoanalytic theory have become evident in today's American culture and everyday language with the frequent use of psychoanalytic terms, such as *denial*, *repression*, and *Freudian slip* (Johnson, 2016). The most basic assumption of psychoanalytic theory is that early life experiences shape an individual's social relationships into adulthood (Freud, 1920, 1952; Johnson, 2016). This deterministic view of human behavior is led by irrational energies, unconscious motivations, and instinctual drives (Freud, 1920, 1952). Freud, later in his career, identified instinctual drives as *life instincts* (sexual energies and later expanded to all self-preserving energies) and *death instincts* (aggressive and destructive energies; Freud, 1940/1949). Several other theories have been birthed from this one, including ego psychology, object-relations theory, self-psychology, and relational psychoanalysis.

Personality structure. Freud (1940, 1949) also identified three systems of the personality structure that operated as one, the *id*, *ego*, and *superego*. The id is ruled by the *pleasure principle*, which seeks immediate gratification and avoids pain. The ego is ruled by the *reality principle*, which understands the reality in the external world, regulates the impulses of the id, and formulates a plan to satisfy those desires. Lastly, the superego is shaped by parental figures and society, based on adopted morals and ethics, and influenced by psychological rewards and punishments.

Psychosexual development. Pertinent to psychoanalytic theory is understanding how personality is formed in early childhood through a series of pleasure-seeking, *psychosexual stages* (oral, anal, phallic, latency, and genital). Freud (1940/1949) used the term *libido* to describe the psychosexual energy, which was the chief motivator behind human behavior, and too much or too little satisfaction can lead to a fixation, which can hinder subsequent stages.

Defense mechanisms. The notion of anxiety is essential in psychoanalytic theory and is a result of the unconscious surfacing to conscious awareness (Freud, 1920/1952). In order to better cope with anxiety and not overwhelm the ego, various defense mechanisms help protect the individual from unwanted feelings. According to Corey (2017), defense mechanisms reject or warp reality and operate on an unconscious level.

Transference and countertransference. One of Freud's (1920, 1952) most fundamental concepts

FIGURE 10.1

Freud's Iceberg Metaphor Structural Model of the Psyche

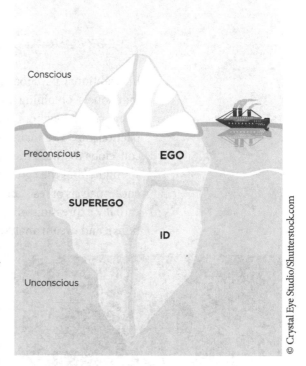

© Crystal Eye Studio/Shutterstock.com

© arka38/Shutterstock.com

CHAPTER 10: *Counseling Theories*

of psychoanalytic theory is *transference*, which refers to projecting one's emotional reactions to another. *Countertransference*, the counselor's emotional reaction to their client based on their own unconscious struggles, can be useful in providing insight into the client's world when the counselor is aware of the process and effects on treatment (Johnson, 2017).

Therapeutic Relationship and Goals

In traditional psychoanalysis, the psychoanalyst is more concerned with individuals obtaining insight as well as experiencing the emotions and memories throughout counseling (Freud, 1920, 1952), than the therapeutic relationship. The main goal in psychoanalytic therapy is bringing the unconscious to awareness, whereby addressing the unconscious conflicts and strengthening the ego through techniques such as the analysis of transference, analysis of resistance, *free association* interpretation (i.e., the process of verbally expressing what is on the mind without any restrictions or hesitations), and dream analysis (Freud, 1920, 1952; Freud, 1940, 1949).

© Yuri Turkov/Shutterstock.com

Are you familiar with Freud's famous couch? He adopted the couch from his earlier hypnosis training and believed that lying down was conducive for free association, the process of verbally expressing what is on the mind without any restrictions or hesitations. However, it has been frequently noted that Freud's main purpose in using the couch is that he did not like his patients staring at him all day.

Jungian Theory

Carl Jung (1875-1961), a Swiss psychiatrist, is the creator of Jungian analytical theory. He was a close friend and colleague of Freud until their relationship ended over theoretical differences, mainly Freud's deterministic views of human nature. Jung took a more holistic and culturally diverse perspective of human behavior, which he obtained from his travels and studies on religions, myths, folklore, mysticism, and the occult (Nelson &

Finn, 2016). He placed great importance on midlife and encouraged the confrontation of the unconscious through creative activities, such as painting and writing (Jung, 192). In fact, Jung learned a lot from his own personal midlife experiences, or what we would call in today's age a "midlife crisis," and recounted those events in his autobiography *Memories, Dreams, Reflections* (1961).

© rook76/Shutterstock.com

Assumptions and Key Concepts

The most basic assumption of the Jungian analytic theory is that each person is in the process of becoming oneself, finding meaning in life, and deepening spiritually, which he referred to as *individuation* (when the conscious and unconscious are fully and beautifully integrated, when one has found the meaning of life; Jung, 1928/1954; Jung, 1936/1959). Jung emphasized that this did not occur until after midlife (Jung, 1928, 1954; Jung, 1936, 1959).

Human development. Jung (1928) focused on the development throughout the lifespan and identified four developmental stages: childhood (ruled by primal desires, influenced by experiences but not necessarily shaped personality), adolescence (a time of biological changes and focus on education, career, and intimate relationships), middle age (a time of deeper self-reflection and finding meaning in life), and old age (a continuation of reflection on life and mortality) (Nelson & Finn, 2016). In Jungian theory and during the *second half of life*, the aging process is an opportunity for the continuation of personality development (Corbett, 2013).

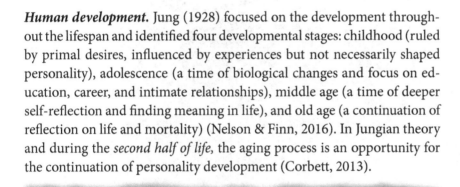

Did you know that Jung described the perfect balance of the self as syzygy, as astronomical term used to describe the equal gravitational pull of our perfectly aligned planets? Nelson and Finn (2016) reveal that syzygy not only exists in a single person, but it can also be seen in a well-balanced team or couple. From a Christian perspective, the perfectly balanced team is seen in the Holy Trinity: God the Father, God the Son, and God the Holy Spirit.

Personality structure. Jung's (1936, 1959) view of personality structure includes the *personal conscious* (what is known to the person), the *personal unconscious* (what is unknown and/or not yet known to the person), the *ego* (what lies within the personal conscious to determine which emotions, memories, and thoughts are remembered), and the *collective unconscious* (the deepest level of the unconscious). The collective unconscious is portrayed in images experienced in dreams that Jung referred to as *archetypes*, and he believed these images were universal experiences tied to the person's ancestral past (Jung, 1911, 1956, Jung, 1936, 1959; Jung, 1923, 1971). Figure 10.2 reveals personality types based on Jung's work on archetypes.

© moibalkon/Shutterstock.com

FIGURE 10.2

12 Major Personality Types based on Jung's Archetypes

Therapeutic Relationship and Goals

The client-therapist relationship is vital during the therapy process and necessary for change to occur. The primary goals are individuation and fully integrating the personal conscious and personal unconscious, which leads to finding meaning in life (Jung, 1928). Techniques and methods to meet goals included the experience of *catharsis* (i.e, the letting go and releasing of pent-up emotions during the process of counseling, which usually occurs through a therapeutic activity/experience/and/or verbalization), dream analysis, analysis of transference and countertransference, assessments (word association tests, projective tests, and type indicators), bringing the unconscious to the conscious, and using insight to reach full integration and meaning in life (Nelson & Finn, 2016).

The Myers-Briggs Type Indicator (MBTI), developed by Katharine Cook Briggs and her daughter Isabel Briggs Myers, is a personality self-assessment based on Jung's psychological types. The personality differences are sorted into four opposing pairs with the possibility of 16 psychological types. The theory behind these opposing pairs is all about preferences, how people get their energy, how people view the world around them, and how people make decisions. Those dichotomous pairs are Extroversion (E) / Introversion (I) , Sensing (S) / Intuition (N), Thinking (T) / Feeling (F), and Judging (J) / Perceiving (P). For further exploration, students are encouraged to review , *Gifts Differing: Understanding Personality Type* by Isabel Briggs Myers and Peter B. Myers (1995).

© Amir Ridhwan/Shutterstock.com

Adlerian Theory

The key creator of Adlerian theory is *Alfred Adler* (1870-1937), who was an Austrian physician and psychiatrist. Never a student of Freud's or a believer in psychoanalysis, he joined Freud's weekly discussion group, the Viennese Psychoanalytic Society, until their theoretical differences led to a split and Adler formed his own group, the Society for Individual Psychology (Dufrene, Henderson, & Eckart, 2016). Rudolf Dreikurs helped popularize Adlerian theory in the United States and continued Adler's work of child guidance clinics by establishing them in America (Murdock, 2017).

Album / Fine Art Images/Newscom

Assumptions and Key Concepts

The basic philosophy of Adlerian theory centers on *social theory*, which looks at a person within the context of their environment and connectedness to their social environment (Dufrene et al., 2016). Through *social learning*, Adler (1927, 1946) believed people had the power to change themselves. Adler (1924, 1959) termed his approach *Individual Psychology* to emphasize the whole person and indivisible makeup of personalities, which meant the person could not be divided up into parts as Freud believed. Individual Psychology is grounded on three main constructs: all human behavior is goal-directed and purposeful, people have within themselves a drive toward living harmoniously and contributing to *social interest*, and choices are influenced by the person's social world and seen through the context of the whole person (holistic view) (Adler, 1927, 1946; Adler, 1924/1959). Adler (1927, 1946; 1924, 1959) also believed that a person must be understood in relation to and in connection with all their social systems emphasizing that a person was *socially embedded*, which is the Adlerian belief that people do not develop in isolation.

"Meanings are not determined by situations. We determine ourselves by the meanings we ascribe to situations."
–Alfred Adler

Head © grmarc/Shutterstock.com

Human development. Adler (1924, 1959) viewed human development through the configuration of an individual's *lifestyle*, which was established early in life around the age of 5 or 6. A lifestyle is "composed of a person's relationship with the self, others, and the universe" (Dufrene et al., 2016, p. 140) and "includes the convictions, choices, and values people develop that influence their decisions and behaviors" (Carlson & Johnson, 2015, p. 226). Since the development of the individual and their lifestyle starts in early childhood, Adler (1927, 1946; 1924, 1959) placed emphasis on exploring lifestyle, *birth order, family constellation,* and *early recollections.* Other key concepts in Adlerian philosophy include *encouragement, private logic, basic mistakes, basic tasks,* and *inferiority complex* (Adler, 1912, 1926; Adler, 1927, 1946; Adler, 1924, 1959).

Encouragement: people seeking counseling are not seen as mentally ill, but discouraged

Private Logic: each person's subjective creation of their own reality

Basic Mistakes: the self-defeating thoughts and behaviors

Basic Tasks: work, friendship, and love/intimacy; recreational, spiritual, and parenting/family were later added by other notable Adlerians

Inferiority Complex: feelings of inferiority that are a normal part of life and begin in childhood

Therapeutic Relationship and Goals

A collaborative and egalitarian relationship is essential in Adlerian therapy. Watts (2017) emphasizes that a strong therapeutic relationship is developed when counselors demonstrate social interest and refer to this approach as "relational psychotherapy" (p. 146). The overall goal is to encourage the client to develop more social interest (Adler, 1927, 1946; Adler, 1924, 1959). Other goals include helping the client recognize and comprehend mistaken beliefs about self, others, and the world; making changes in those mistaken beliefs; and connecting in more meaningful ways in the social world (Adler, 1927, 1946; Adler, 1924, 1959). Adlerian techniques used to meet these goals include lifestyle analysis, examining the family constellation, questioning, interpretation, encouragement, natural and logical consequences, acting "as if," pushing the button, catching oneself, creating images, pleasing someone, and paradoxical intention. A brief case study explaining the Adlerian approach is provided at the end of the chapter.

Looking Through the Lens of Christianity at Psychodynamic Theories

One of the major critiques of classic psychoanalysis is Freud's strong deterministic view of human nature, which is in direct contrast with Christian beliefs. Jones and Butman (2011) contend that psychoanalytic philosophy "allows no room for anything supernatural, for the kind of general or

special revelation so central to the Christian faith, nor for a more constructive perspective about our spiritual urgings for deeper meaning and significance in life" (p. 118). It is also no secret that Freud attacked religion. According to Jones and Butman, from the psychoanalytic perspective, religion "is seen as a kind of universal neurosis that civilization substitutes for a more authentic personal reality based on scientific (objective) knowledge" (p. 116). As such, the Christian counselor is cautioned when using classic psychoanalysis and contemporary psychodynamic models (i.e., ego psychology, object-relations theory, and self-psychology) are favored because of their focus on human relationships, which is similar to the Christian belief of being created for relationship with God and others (Jones & Butman, 2011).

The Christian integration of Jung's psychoanalytic theory is more evident in the literature. In Kam's (2018) literature review, he noted the linkage of Jung's view of the unconscious and the Christian concept of the soul, particularly how dreams derive from the soul. He noted many religious authors, including Christian psychiatrist Paul Meier who wrote on dreams, stating they arise from the unconscious and are windows to the soul. Kam also proposed the integration of Christian theology with Jungian psychoanalysis to overcome the *shadow* of self-deception and feelings of inferiority. Kam's integration includes psychoanalytic psychoeducation and bringing the unconscious to the conscious through dream analysis or guided imagery exercises on unconscious metaphors with Christian integration, which includes renouncing distorted beliefs about self and God and replacing them with a Biblical perspective, using prayer, and inviting Jesus to intervene when re-scripting painful memories.

Adlerian therapy is one of the simplest theories to integrate with Christianity. According to Watts (2000), the common ground between Adler's Individual Psychology and Christian beliefs is of great significance. Adler's view of human nature, including that people can determine their future, they are goal-oriented and striving for perfection, viewed holistically, and relational (social interest) are all compatible with the Christian faith (Johansen, 2010). Watts (2000) emphasizes the greatest commonality is the shared perspective on social relationships. Watts (2000) states, "The Bible affirms that humans have a three-fold relationship responsibility: to God, to others, and to themselves" (p. 320). Johansen (2010) added that Adler's less deterministic viewpoint aligns with the Christian's view that people have the freedom to choose noting the Christian term *free will* and scripture found in Deuteronomy 30:19 (King James Version) where God says, ". . . I have set before you life and death, blessing and cursing: therefore choose life, that both thou and thy seed may live."

WHAT ARE THE HUMANISTIC/ EXPERIENTIAL THEORIES?

The humanistic theories include Gestalt, Person-Centered, and Existential therapies. Humanistic counselors believe that each individual has an inclination toward being authentic or fully functioning. A focus is placed on the therapeutic relationship and in-session techniques or experience in order to influence change in the client.

Existential Theory

The key contributors to Existential therapy are philosophers in the 1800s who questioned human existence. *Soren Kierkegaard, Friedrich Nietzche, Martin Heidegger,* and *Martin Buber* were the initial founders of the humanistic movement. *Victor Frankl, Rollo May, Irvin Yalom,* and *James Bu-*

gental developed the theory to lead the movement into what we see today which is more of an existential approach (Corey, 2017; Murdock, 2017).

Existential therapy places a focus on exploring the meaning of life. Irvin Yalom, is a renowned existential therapist, though he is a psychiatrist by training, his theoretical approach has influenced the work of many counselors. He is a prolific author and has written more than a dozen books and been involved with several films. Yalom (1980) defines existential therapy as an approach to counseling which focuses on concerns about one's existence. It does not have a clearly defined model and set of techniques, but rather is an attitude toward human suffering which primarily deals with questions surrounding meaning. The overall goal is to help clients to experience the reality of their existence and find personal meaning in their actions, their lives, and their suffering (May, 1983; Corey, 2017).

Assumptions and Key Concepts

An Existential therapist focuses on exploring themes such as meaning, freedom, responsibility, anxiety, aloneness, and mortality as these relate to a person's current struggle (Corey, 2017). A central theme to Existential therapy is that all humans struggle with questions around what it means to be human and how to make life meaningful through choices that are made (Neukrug, 2018). *Existential therapy operates on the assumption that clients are free and, therefore, are responsible for their choices and actions.* Clients are the authors of their own lives and when they are thrust into a meaningless and lonely world, it then becomes a catalyst to drive them to find meaning in life (May, 1961). Emotional and psychological problems are viewed as an inner conflict which is caused by the individual's view of his own existence. Viktor Frankl's approach, termed *Logo Therapy* (1963), is a great example of this. In the preface of Frankl's famous text, *Man's Search for Meaning*, Allport (1963) writes about Frankl's approach. Allport shares that his approach was birthed out of his experience in a concentration camp, where he lost his father, mother, brother, and wife. They either died in the concentration camps or were sent to the gas oven. Allport emphasized that a psychiatrist with these experiences who writes about meaning is certainly one worth listening to.

Therapeutic Relationship and Goals

The goal for the existential counselor is to enter into their client's world to truly understand them and, by remaining in the present, use the therapeutic alliance to facilitate change (May, Angel, & Ellenberger, 1958; Kottler & Shepard, 2015; Corey, 2017). Through a caring relationship, the counselor intervenes in their client's crises and tries to stimulate new ways for them to embrace and live their lives (May, 1961). Rollo May (1958) wrote about the importance of grasping the *being* of clients, which is a deeper level from just having knowledge of specific things about clients. Attention is given to the immediate experience with the aim to help them develop a greater sense of meaning and purpose. The therapist also invites clients to recognize factors that block freedom and to recognize that life is not just happening to them, but that they have the freedom to take responsibility and action to make life meaningful (Corey, 2017).

Person-Centered Theory

The key player in person-centered therapy is *Carl Rogers*, who is known as the most influential theorist for counselors and psychotherapists due to his focus on building a warm therapeutic relationship (Grenello & Young, 2019). *Unconditional positive regard, empathy,* and *genuineness* are key terms of person-centered therapy that describe the therapeutic relationship. When these conditions exist the client then feels comfortable enough to make real change. Rogers believed that if he could provide a certain type of relationship that the client will then discover the "capacity to use that relationship for growth, and change and personal development will occur" (Rogers, 1961, pg. 33).

CARL R. ROGERS

Everett Collection/Newscom

Unconditional positive regard: sense of total acceptance
Empathy: deep understanding of the client
Genuineness: being real within the context of the therapeutic relationship
Actualizing Tendency: an innate tendency toward fulfilling one's potential

Assumptions and Key Concepts

Rogers believed that people have an *actualizing tendency,* or the potential for understanding themselves and for resolving their own problems. In person-centered therapy, empathy is the first step in therapy rather than assessment and diagnosis. The therapeutic relationship between the counselor and the client is seen as sufficient for change and no other intervention or techniques are necessary (Rogers, 1957[1]; 1961). Therefore, this approach is more a *way of being* with the client rather than a *way of doing* (Kottler & Shepard, 2015). Even though person-centered therapy has declined in popularity over the years (Granello & Young, 2019), the basic skills in building an empathic relationship are taught to all who enter the counseling profession. The presence of the fundamental conditions of empathy, positive regard, and genuineness in the therapeutic relationship has been tested throughout the years. It is supported in literature that these elements reliably predict improvement over the course of psychotherapy (Norcross & Wampold, 2011).

© ibreakstock/Shutterstock.com

Therapeutic Relationship and Goals

Person-centered counseling is *non-directive,* allowing clients to talk about the issues that are important to them in the moment. The counselor is nonjudgmental and assists the client in both the cognitive and emotional experience of the problem (Rogers, 1957). While this takes place, the counselor is warm and expresses unconditional positive regard which allows the client to feel safe, connected and understood. The primary goal of the counselor is to tune into the client's story and reflect the client's feelings and overall experience. This, in turn, helps the client to feel accepted leading to awareness, autonomy, and self-empowerment. This will help the client to gain a greater ability to manage life and resolve concerns. The end goal of therapy is to help the client become fully functioning and more capable of dealing with life's problems (Rogers, 1951[1]; 1957; Seligman & Reichenberg, 2014). A brief case study explaining the Person-Centered approach is provided for you at the end of the chapter.

Working from a Person-Centered Orientation
Peggy Ceballos, Ph.D., NCC, RPT-S

Dr. Peggy Ceballos is an Assistant Professor at the Department of Counseling and Higher Education at the University of North Texas. With certifications in Child-Centered Play Therapy (CCPT; a Person-Centered orientation and play therapy approach in working with children) and Child Parent Relationship Therapy (CPRT; training parents to be therapeutic agents of change in their child's life by teaching them child-centered play therapy skills), Dr. Ceballos has vast experience in working with Latino children and families and has published numerous journal articles and book chapters on the topics of play therapy, CCPT, CPRT, immigrant Latino families, and social justice advocacy. Dr. Ceballos' greatest scholarly accomplishments include the following articles she co-authored with her colleagues: *Factors Related to Play Therapists' Social Justice Advocacy Attitudes* (2013) and *Empowering Latino Families: Effects of a Culturally Response Intervention for Low-Income Immigrant Latino Parents on Children's Behaviors and Parental Stress* (2010) (study on CPRT with immigrant Latino parents).

Dr. Ceballos' Theoretical Approach: During graduate school, Dr. Ceballos found herself drawn to humanistic theories, but it wasn't until the end of her Master's program that she realized the person-centered philosophy really coincided with her own personal beliefs and philosophy of human nature. While working as an elementary school counselor, Dr. Ceballos vividly recalls working with a young boy who had been a victim of sexual abuse and allowing him to lead the play, which is central to CCPT. During this self-directed play, the young boy was able to play out his past sexual trauma in the sandbox and begin working out the effects of sexual abuse that had plague him. Dr. Ceballos also recounted the other instances when she directed the boy's play and the outcome was not as effective. This was a turning point for her, and she sought out additional training and supervision in CCPT to grow in knowledge and experience. Additionally, while completing her Ph.D. at the University of North Texas, which houses the largest play therapy training institute in the world (The Center for Play Therapy in Denton, TX), she realized how empowering this theoretical approach can be for families through CPRT. Dr. Ceballos stated that in CPRT, "Parents are the agents of change in their child's life and this is so empowering for them." Dr. Ceballos also described how the person-centered philosophy aligns with her beliefs and personality asserting that she is a very relational person, believes in the self-actualizing tendencies of person-centered theory, and feels very natural allowing the child to take the lead in play therapy sessions. She finds this theory very effective with the population she works with, immigrants and Latino children and families, who are faced with poverty and societal stereotypes. It helps them feel empowered as they are fully accepted for who they are, which also facilitates self-actualization. Dr. Ceballos expressed that in her work with children, "kids get the message [the core beliefs of person-centered philosophy] that contradicts the stereotypes" and it is the healing relationship that leads to improved wellbeing. If you are interested in learning more about person-centered theory or CCPT, Dr. Ceballos recommends taking a graduate level course that will allow in-depth exploration, attending workshops at state and national conferences, and getting supervision from someone who is well versed and experienced in the theory.

Gestalt Theory

The Gestalt approach to therapy is also an experiential approach and focuses more on the process of therapy rather than the content. It is a way of seeing and knowing that emphasizes action and dynamic awareness rather than introspection (Perls, Hefferline, & Goodman, 1951). *Fritz Perls* is considered the founder of Gestalt therapy and he believed humans are oriented toward growth and are viewed as functioning holistically while striving to meet needs through contact with their environment. However, this environmental contact can produce anxiety as it can be painful or uncomfortable. The result may be avoidance which leads to unmet needs and even dysfunctional behavior (Passons, 1975). To assist with change the therapists place themselves as fully as possible into the experience of the client while withholding analysis, judgment or interpretation (Perls et al., 1951). At the same time, they look for ways to increase the client's awareness of what they are doing in the present moment. Another aspect of therapy is to look at the role of unfinished business from the past that may be impacting dysfunctional behavior in the present.

Assumptions and Key Concepts

The main premise of Gestalt therapy is moving toward who we *are* rather than who we *should be*. Fritz Perls (1969) believed that awareness by itself can be curative. In therapy, clients are expected to be active and become aware of their own feelings, sensations, and perceptions rather than looking to the therapist to provide them with interpretations or insights. Some of the key concepts include being in the *here-and-now*, direct experiencing, self-awareness, along with working on unfinished business (Perls, 1969; Corey, 2017). If a client becomes aware of the situation he is in and lets the situation control his actions, he then learns how to cope with life (Perls, 1969). Becoming aware of blocks to energy and resistance is also important to Gestalt therapy. Arnie Yontef and Schulz (2013) indicate that Gestalt therapists believe people change and grow when they experience who they really are in the world. The term *creative adjustment* is used by Gestalt counselors to explain the balance of changing the environment to meet the needs or changing the person to fit the environment (Yontef & Jacobs, 2014). The *empty chair* is also a technique that became the prominent icon for classical Gestalt therapy in the 1960s and early 1970s (Konopka, Hermans, & Goncalves, 2019).

Therapeutic Relationship and Goals

In Gestalt therapy, the therapist typically will start out by building empathy in order to enrich the therapeutic alliance. However, as therapy continues the therapist will become more active and directive. A focus is placed on the present situation and is a place to experiment and also encourage creativity (Seligman & Reichenberg, 2014). The therapeutic goals are to assist the client in attaining awareness and through that awareness have greater choices. Awareness takes place between the *I-thou* context of the therapeutic relationship which helps the client to become aware so authentic choices can be made. This awareness includes knowing one's environment, knowing oneself, as well as accepting oneself (Perls, 1969; Corey, 2017). When a difficulty or painful event is brought into awareness the therapist invites the client to explore this issue (Wheeler & Axelsson, 2015). This can allow the client to bring closure to unfinished business while developing skills to manage life successfully.

Looking Through the Lens of Christianity at Humanistic Therapy

As a Christian counselor, there are aspects of humanistic therapy that can be helpful if they are considered within the authority of God's truth. Person-centered therapy focuses on a warm empathic relationship which clearly exemplifies the love of Christ. Jones and Butman (2011) suggest

that there is no approach to psychology that mirrors the concerns of the faith as well as does existential therapy. It is good for an individual to reflect on their actions and take responsibility for their choices. However, Olson (2002) suggests that the goal for the Christian is a *reconciled life* rather than an *actualized life*. As a Christian, one should seek to emulate the life of Christ and be guided by the Holy Spirit (Olson, 2002). Jones and Butman also point out that the existential understanding of psychopathology is incomplete as it sees guilt as a manifestation of inauthenticity, rather than a result of sinful choices. The Christian faith teaches a moral responsibility for our actions and we are held responsible by God for our choices. In humanistic psychology, the self is held accountable, while in the Christian faith humans are accountable to God. The Christian is instructed to submit to God and his commands, seeking to please God rather than himself.

> "What does the Lord require of you, but to fear the Lord your God, to walk in all his ways, to love him, to serve the Lord your God with all your heart and with all your soul, and to keep the statutes of the Lord." (Deut. 10:12-13, ESV).

WHAT ARE THE BEHAVIORAL AND COGNITIVE THEORIES?

According to behavioral and cognitive therapists, behavioral change takes place by changing self-defeating thoughts, assumptions, and perceptions. Cognitive and behavioral therapies are often combined as both believe that thoughts precede actions and emotions. Therefore, intervention at both levels is needed to resolve many problems. Both therapies also follow a psychoeducational model which views therapy as a learning process in acquiring new skills, learning new ways of thinking as well as new ways to cope with problems.

> "People are disturbed not by events,
> but by the views which they take of them."
> —Epictetus

Behavioral Therapy

B.F. Skinner, Albert Bandura, Ivan Pavlov, and *Joseph Wolpe* were a few of the major contributors to Behavioral Therapy. The behavioral approach is an action-oriented therapy that places a focus on directly observable behavior while viewing an individual as both the producer of and a product of his own environment. It was originally viewed as a counterpoint to the humanistic theories of Carl Rogers and Abraham Maslow (Corey, 2017; Kottler & Shepard, 2015). One contribution to behavioral therapy is explained in *Beyond Freedom and Dignity* (1971), in which B.F. Skinner discusses how the environment plays a vital role in determining an individual's behavior. One of his key terms is *operant conditioning* which refers to teaching voluntary behaviors that interact with the environment in order to meet needs (Skinner, 1971). Ivan Pavlov, a Russian contributor, is known for the phenomenon of classical conditioning as illustrated in the following diagram. He received the Nobel Prize in 1904 while experimenting with dogs using classical conditioning in relation to the physiology of digestion (Clark, 2004). Another contribution is social learning theory, in which Albert Bandura posits that behaviors that are detrimental to individuals may have been learned in order to cope with environmental and even self-imposed demands (Bandura, 1969). As a brief summary, behavioral therapy has a strong reliance on the principles of the *scientific method* where concepts and procedures are tested and then revised depending on the results of empirical studies. The central characteristics include a focus on *observable behavior*, the *current determinants of behavior*, *learning experiences* to promote change, and *assessment and evaluation* (Skinner, 1971; Corey 2017).

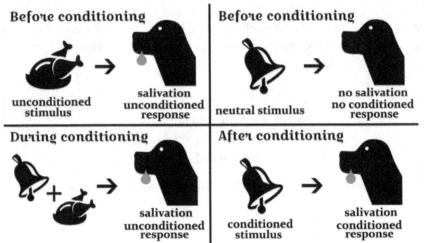

Before conditioning

unconditioned stimulus → salivation unconditioned response

Before conditioning

neutral stimulus → no salivation no conditioned response

During conditioning

+ → salivation unconditioned response

After conditioning

conditioned stimulus → salivation conditioned response

Assumptions and Key Concepts

Behaviorists believe humans are naturally motivated to adapt to their environment. The contemporary behavioral movement includes four major areas of development: *classical conditioning* (learning that takes place through pairing, see example above), *operant conditioning*, (change that takes place from a learned consequence), and *social-cognitive theory* (learning that takes place from observation of other people and events), along with more attention in recent years to *cognitive factors* influencing behavior (Corey, 2017; Murdock, 2017). In addition, the most recent behavioral developments include mindfulness and acceptance-based therapies. Behaviorists believe that dysfunctional behavior was learned, so treatment involves learning new ways to behave that are more adaptive to the environment. There can be diverse therapeutic strategies to promote behavioral change. The treatment will be followed by an objective evaluation of the outcome with a focus on behavioral change. The primary goal of therapy is to increase personal choice and provide new conditions for learning. A good therapeutic relationship is necessary as the relationship is used to bring about behavior change along with behavioral techniques (Corey, 2017; Spiegler, 2016). The therapist takes on an active and directive role as he teaches skills, models for the client, as well as provides performance feedback. More current research on the application of behavioral treatments in counseling includes motivational interviewing which attends to a client's resistance through a form of asking questions which increase motivations for change. This behavioral strategy has significant empirical support, especially in counseling addictions (Miller & Rollnick, 2013).

Therapeutic Relationship and Goals

An emphasis on current behavior is key with a focus on precise treatment goals. Therapy is directive and consists primarily of assessment and intervention (Antony, 2014; Murdock, 2017) A behavioral therapist will begin counseling with assessment, which is the process of collecting information needed for treatment. Functional analysis is often used in behavioral therapy, which is a way of understanding a problem by looking at what happens before and after the problem takes place. It, in turn, provides a means to optimize clinical decision-making (Virues-Ortega & Haynes, 2005; Grenello & Young, 2012;). For example, functional analysis could be used to examine a young lady with an addiction to shopping. The counselor would assess what happens prior to her felt need to shop, such as a conflict at work. Next, the counselor would analyze the client's response by asking questions about how much she buys, where she goes shopping, how much money she spends. Lastly, the counselor would analyze the aspects that are rewarding to her shopping behavior. These rewards could be a reduction in her anxiety, increased happiness, and approval from her peers. By obtaining this information, the counselor will help the client review the current level of shopping and then set goals for reducing the shopping behavior. The counselor will then incorporate behavioral techniques to learn new coping behaviors as well as weaken the shopping behavior. The client typically will determine what behavior to change, the therapist then determines how the behavior can best be modified. Behavioral therapists also tend to focus on evidence-based strategies that have research support for specific client problems (Corey, 2017).

Clem Murray/MCT/Newscom

Aaron Beck is a key contributor who initially developed cognitive therapy in the 1960s to provide a structured approach to treating depression. It has grown since then to become one of the leading approaches in counseling today (Seligman & Reichenberg, 2014). Beck's model of *cognitive therapy*, is used synonymously with *cognitive behavioral therapy* (CBT) due to the theory's utilization of behavioral interventions to assist in modifying thinking patterns (Beck, 2011). Albert Ellis' rational emotive behavior therapy (REBT), as well as Donald Meichenbaum's cognitive behavioral therapy, developed out of Beck's basic assumptions. Recent *third wave* therapies, such as mindfulness-based cognitive therapy (MBCT), dialectical behavior therapy (DBT), and acceptance and commitment therapy (ACT) have also evolved from CBT (Gill & Freund, 2018).

Cognitive counselors posit that abnormal or disruptive emotions and behaviors are manifested from faulty *cognitions* and *beliefs*. These distorted cognitions then take shape in childhood leading to irrational beliefs causing individuals to be more susceptible to developing emotional disorders in life (Beck, 1976). Therefore, the focus of therapy is to help clients to evaluate and challenge their thinking patterns while teaching them how to modify their own dysfunctional thoughts and beliefs. As clients begin thinking more rationally and realistically, they will then feel better and act in a more productive manner (Beck, 2011).

Assumptions and Key Concepts

The cognitive model of therapy implies that our emotions and behaviors are a product of the way we think (Beck, 1976; Beck, 2011). *Schemas* are cognitive structures that organize incoming information that is received and help us create meaning. Cognitive therapist emphasizes that content derived from schemas then contributes to *core beliefs,* or primary, underlying, root, beliefs, which in turn lead to the interpretation of events, leading to how we think, act and feel. These are formed early in life and are developed through personal experiences or through watching others

(Neukrug, 2018; Murdock, 2017; Kazantzis, Dattilio, Dobson, & Beck, 2017). For instance, think about the word *moviestar*. You likely instantly came up with words or images that you would associate with a moviestar (For example: beautiful/handsome, rich, sports car, fashionable). If I then told you that you looked like a moviestar, your schema of a moviestar would activate the way you think and further influence how you would respond. *Automatic thoughts*, or swift evaluative thoughts that go through a person's mind, are another key concept in cognitive therapy which can be helpful in identifying beliefs. They are specific to a situation and are considered to be the most superficial level of cognition (Beck, 2011). Cognitive therapists then conceptualize each client's situation by evaluating the schemas, core beliefs, and automatic thoughts.

Three General Types of Automatic Thoughts (Beck, 2011):
1) Distorted thoughts that are contrary to the evidence (e.g., "I never receive compliments.")
2) Accurate thoughts, but the conclusion drawn is distorted (e.g., "I failed the test, I know I will fail out of the program.")
3) Accurate thoughts, but dysfunctional (e.g., "It is going to take me forever to receive my counseling license!")

Cognitive behavioral therapy is a psychoeducational model that teaches clients to identify, evaluate, and modify their cognitions and behaviors. The basic premise is that changes in thinking will lead to changes in feeling and acting. The *A-B-C framework* is central to cognitive behavioral therapy: A stands for activating event or adversity, B stands for the client's belief about A, and C stands for the consequence or reaction (Beck, 1976; Dryden, 2012). For example, in viewing the following picture, there is a negative event that took place in not getting selected for choir. The belief or cognition is "I have a terrible voice. I'm never going to be any good at singing." This leads to feelings of sadness, and potentially the action of giving up on singing. In therapy the belief or cognition would be explored for accuracy and a new more rational cognition would be introduced, such as "many people have told me I have a good voice, therefore, I will try again with a different choir in the future". This then changes the feeling to hope and the action of trying again. In most cases, the treatment is short term, problem-focused, and goal oriented. While some attention is given to the past, it primarily focuses on the present.

Cognitive (ABC) Model
(Beck, 1976; Ellis, 1962; Seligman, 1991)

A - Adversity
(Negative Event/Circumstance)
I didn't get selected for choir

B - Beliefs

I have a terrible voice. I'm never going to be any good at singing.

C - Consequences
(Feelings/Behaviors)
Feel sad, give up on practicing singing

RESEARCH NOTE:
The A-B-C framework of cognitive therapy is consistent with current research on growth mindset versus a fixed mindset. People with a fixed mindset believe that intellectual abilities are permanent and unchangeable and are extrinsically motivated. Recent studies have shown that having a growth mindset can improve performance in school settings (Yeager & Dweck, 2012; Brougham & Kashubeck-West, 2017).

Therapeutic Relationship and Goals

Cognitive counselors seek to create a sound non-judgmental therapeutic relationship which provides the foundation to help clients to develop the skills needed to evaluate their thinking and make decisions for change. *Collaboration* (i.e, the role the therapist takes to facilitate the client toward a desired goal), *empiricism* (how the therapist helps the client to evaluate his experience based on a scientific method), and *Socratic dialogue* (i.e., a series of questions that assist the client in exploring their thoughts, beliefs, and overall perceptions of their world) are the three major elements of the cognitive behavioral therapy relationship (Kazantizis, et al., 2017).

While asking questions surrounding the presenting problem, the counselor will actively listen for inconsistencies as well as emotional discrepancies (Seligman, 2014). The counselor will then develop a case formulation to assist with treatment planning. Treatment focuses on challenging faulty cognitions that are related to the problems being presented. Often both cognitive and behavioral interventions are used to help with this change process (Beck, 2011; Kazantizis, et al., 2017). Some useful behavioral activities that often are incorporated include physical exercise, social skills training, relaxation techniques, role plays, and assertiveness training. A brief case study explaining the Cognitive-Behavioral approach is provided for you at the end of the chapter.

Looking Through the Lens of Christianity at Behavioral and Cognitive Therapies

When viewing behavioral therapy through a Christian lens, it is important to note that behaviorism developed under the view of logical positivism and inductive empiricism which basically believes that all meaningful assertions must be analytically or empirically verified or falsified. Therefore, statements such as "God exists" are false and meaningless because they are unverifiable and cannot be determined as truth (Jones & Butman, 2011). Obviously, this is not in agreement with the Christian faith where God exists and is above nature and the creator of nature. Also, the Bible encourages us to act out of a motive to serve God and we are not reduced to a drive for tangible reinforcement. We are taught that "whether you eat or drink, or whatever you do, do all to the glory of God" (I Cor. 10:31, English Standard Version). On the other hand, Christians are also taught to act on the Word of God. Behaviorism is a goal and action-oriented therapy. Setting goals and utilizing "actions" in therapy can be effective in changing unbiblical thoughts to godly thoughts. James 1:22 (English Standard Version) states that we are to "be doers of the Word, and not hearers only, deceiving yourselves". He goes on further in 1:24 (English Standard Version) to state that "one who looks into the perfect law, the law of liberty, and perseveres, being no hearer who forgets but a doer who acts, he will be blessed in his doing".

Cognitive therapy is one of the more fruitful models for Christians to incorporate due to several of its premises supported through Scripture

(Jones & Butman, 2011; Carlson & Gonzalez-Prendes, 2016). We are instructed as Christians to transform our identities by renewing the mind (Rom 12:12) and form a new identity in Christ (Rom 6:1-14). However, in cognitive therapy people are helped to feel and function better on their own terms rather than to form an identity in Christ. God teaches in the Bible that through our struggles we learn and grow in holiness manifesting Christlikeness (Jones & Butman, 2011). So rather than seeking to get better for our own satisfaction, the goal should be ultimately to grow in Christlike character qualities. Another aspect of cognitive therapy that is supported by biblical principles is the belief that what we believe has implications for our well-being. This is supported in Scripture found in Philippians 4:8-9, where we are taught to think on true, noble, right, pure, and lovely thoughts.

WHAT ARE THE FAMILY SYSTEMS AND CONSTRUCTIVIST THEORIES?

Up until now, we've focused solely on theoretical approaches in counseling individuals, but what about the family? In this section, *family systems theory*, which views the client as part of a multifaceted family system, will be explored. This section will also review *constructivist theories*, based on social constructivism, which views reality subjectively and from a social and collaborative process. Constructivist theories include solution-focused brief therapy (SFBT) and narrative therapy (NT), which views the client, not the counselor, as the expert.

Family Systems Theory

The foundation of all family theories is the conceptualization of the family as a network, or as seen in the literature, a system. According to Goldenberg, Stanton, and Goldenberg (2017), *family systems theory* "emphasizes the family as an emotional unit or network of interlocking relationships best understood from a historical or transgenerational perspective" (p. 470). From this perspective, individuals are viewed and examined on how they influence and interact with one another, and at the same time, when change occurs within a person it has a rippling effect on the entire family

system (Lambert, Carmichael, & Williams, 2015). Key creators that developed approaches birthed from family systems theory include *Virginia Satir* (Satir Transformational Systemic Therapy), *Salvador Minuchin* (Structural Family Therapy), *Jay Haley* and *Cloe Madanes* (Strategic Therapy), *Murray Bowen* (Bowen's Family Systems Theory), and *Susan Johnson* and *Lee Greenberg* (Emotionally Focused Therapy).

Assumptions and Key Concepts

Since this theory views the individual within the context of their family system, basic assumptions of family systems theory center on identifying and better understanding systemic patterns and behaviors when conducting family therapy. Identifying the stage of the *family life cycle* (a set of stages that a family experiences over time (from the emerging young adult leaving home to the family approaching the end of their days); each stage produces an emotional challenge for family members that if successful, leads to family development and growth) can help provide a developmental perspective of the family system as developmental tasks must be met to successfully move to the next developmental stage (Haley, 1973; McGoldrick, Carter, & Garcia-Preto, 2011).

Some key concepts in family systems theory include the concepts of *organization* and *wholeness* (Goldenberg et al., 2017), *family rules and patterns* (Jackson, 1965; Satir, 1972), *homeostasis* (Jackson, 1957), *subsystems*

(Minuchin, 1974), and *boundaries* (Minuchin, 1974). When family boundaries become too close, they have become *enmeshed*; and if they become too distant, then they have become *disengaged* (Minuchin, Montalvo, Guerney, Rosman, & Shumer, 1967). Lastly, *triangulation* is a key concept of dysfunctional families that refers to the process when a parent pressures the child to ally with him or her in contradiction with the other parent (Minuchin, 1974).

Organization: the system and its parts are predictable and organized

Wholeness: the organized parts are one and are greater than the sum of its parts

Family rules and patterns: spoken and unspoken rules and patterns that help understand the family system

Homeostasis: the family's attempt to self-regulate to maintain stability and balance, as well as resist change

Subsystems: parts of the overall system that have identified functions to be carried out

Boundaries: metaphoric lines that help separate and differentiate the roles and functions of family members

Enmeshed: when family boundaries become too close

Disengaged: when family boundaries become too distant

Triangulation: the process when one family member pressures another to ally with him or her in contradiction to a third family member

Therapeutic Relationship and Goals

Humanistic elements are crucial in building the therapeutic relationship with all family members and creating a safe environment conducive for exploration of family behaviors and patterns. "Family counselors must address both the process (how something is being communicated) and content (what is being communicated)" (Lambert et al., 2015, p. 352). Common goals across various theoretical approaches in family therapy include helping the family improve communication styles, change dysfunctional family patterns, restructure family organizations, establish healthy boundaries, and differentiation from family members (Murdock, 2017). Techniques used in family therapy include family sculpting (Duhl, Kantor, & Duhl, 1973), enactment (Minuchin & Fishman, 1981), achieving intensity (Minuchin & Fishman, 1981), directives (Haley, 1987; Papp, 1981), reframing (Minuchin, Colpinto, & Minuchin, 2007), process questioning (Goldenberg et al., 2017), and family genograms (Bowen, 1978).

> A family genogram is a pictorial description about family members that includes details about family relationships and family/generational patterns. Genograms typically include at least three generations and provide information about what has occurred over time. For a thorough review on genograms, the text Genograms: Assessment and Interventions (3rd ed.) by McGoldrick, Gerson, and Petry (2008) is recommended.

A brief case study explaining the family systems approach is provided for you at the end of the chapter.

Solution-Focused Brief Therapy

Solution-focused brief therapy (SFBT) is considered a postmodern, constructivist approach because it focuses on the client's own ability to create their reality, believing that the client knows exactly where they need to go as well as self-determined to get there (de Shazer, 1982). SFBT was developed in the late 1970s by *Steven De Shazer* and his wife *Insoo Kim Berg* at the Brief Family Therapy Center in Milwaukee, Wisconsin (Miller & Marini, 2015).

© pixinoo/Shutterstock.com

Assumptions and Key Concepts

SFBT is considered a highly optimistic approach to counseling. O'Hanlon and Weiner-Davis (2003) identified basic assumptions of SFBT to include the following: clients have the ability and resources to solve their concerns, change is inevitable and the problem won't always seem as severe or always be present, the therapist does not need a lot of information about the problem to resolve it, it is not necessary to understand the reasoning behind the problem, a small change can kickstart the process of resolution, clients are in charge of defining their goals, quick resolution is possible, and there is not one correct way to view a situation. SFBT also has roots in family systems theory and the counselor's knowledge of unhealthy family patterns can help facilitate problem-solving by encouraging clients to utilize a new and healthier solution (West-Olatunji & Rush-Ossenbeck, 2016). Key concepts in SFBT include *exceptions* (times when the problem does not exist despite the severity of the client's reported concern), *change talk* (the positive language used in session when discussing change, such as saying *when* as opposed to *if*), *solutions* (the perceived solution to the concern that is acceptable to the client) and *strengths and resources,* or the viewpoint that the client already has the strengths and resources to solve their problem (de Shazer, 1982, 1985, 1991).

Therapeutic Relationship and Goals

In SFBT, the relationship is seen as a collaborative process in which the therapist is respectful of the client's worldview and nonjudgmental (de Shazer, 1988). Concerning goals, SFBT counselor should focus on small, practical, attainable changes that will lead to further changes (de Shazer, 1982). Furthermore, the goals should accomplish three things: change the *viewing* of the problematic situation, change the *doing* of the problematic situation, and bring forth the client's *strengths* and *resources* that solve the problematic situation (O'Hanlon & Weiner-Davis, 2003). Goals are met through techniques including the pretherapy question, miracle question, exception question, scaling questions, and formula first session task (de Shazer, 1982, 1985, 1991). Corey (2017) also noted that providing feedback to clients at the end of each session as well as being mindful of working towards termination are vital aspects of SFBT.

Narrative Therapy

Like SFBT, Narrative Therapy (NT) is also rooted in social constructivism and the subjective belief of the client's truth and reality through social interactions. *Michael White* and *David Epston* are considered the key contributors in NT. The basic philosophy of NT is that people create their meaning of life through subjective narratives influenced by social interactions, and these stories become the client's truth and reality (White, 1992).

Assumptions and Key Concepts

In addition to social constructivism, another vital assumption in NT is understanding social power. According to Murdock (2017), "power is seen as determining the truths by which society operates, which in turn strongly influence the stories individual create and tell about their lives" (p. 481). A central concept in NT is the client's *stories*, which is also grounded in the client's cultural and use of language (White & Epston, 1990). The client's perception of the world around them is what determines how they tell their story, and the past stories they've told speak to what they will tell themselves in present and future stories (Westerhof & Bohlmeijer, 2012). The types of stories people tell include the *dominant story*, or the most pressing events that are consistent with the storyline which, if problematic, lead to emotional pain; the *alternate story*, or other aspects of the story that are known but are often pushed aside by the dominant stories and that often beneficial in helping clients; and the *problem-saturated story*, or the very problematic stories that clients usually bring to counseling (White & Epston, 1990).

Therapeutic Relationship and Goals

Continuing with the social constructivist philosophy, the therapeutic relationship is seen as a collaborative process where the therapist plays the role of the investigator (White, 2007). In NT, the client is the expert in changing their story and the counselor plays the role of the investigator (White, 2007; White & Epston, 1990). Ultimately, the goal in NT is for the client to develop new, more enjoyable stories, which in turn become a part of their *preferred story* (White & Epston, 1990). The narrative therapist meets this goal through various techniques, which include asking lots of questions, externalizing and deconstructing the problem, searching for unique outcomes, looking for alternative stories, reauthoring narratives, and documenting the evidence (White, 1992, 2007: White & Epston, 1990).

Looking Through the Lens of Christianity at Family Systems and Constructivist Theories

Many of the theoretical beliefs and techniques of family therapy approaches are consistent with Christian principles (Jones & Butman, 2011). Specifically, "family therapy reinforces the Christian values of principled interpersonal relationships, concerns for social justice for the marginalized, resources found in community, and support for families to help them accomplish their functions and purposes" (Jones & Butman, 2011, p. 392). A noteworthy critique of family systems theory is its postmodern, constructivist view on reality and truth, and how multiple perspectives of the individuals within a family system can exist, which has the potential to conflict with Christianity's position on truth. "Christians hold to the core assumption that 'God is truth' and that objective truth exists and matters" (p. 377).

Since SFBT and NT are rooted in social constructivism and the subjective belief of the client's reality and truth based on social interactions, it can also conflict with the Christian's position on truth as stated above. Another critique of SFBT is the Christian concept of an individual's sinful nature, which goes against the core assumption that people will choose to do moral good (Bidwell, as cited in Frederick, 2008). However, Frederick (2008) provides some implications for Christian integration. First, he related the present focused approach of SFBT to the Kingdom of God, which can be lived in the present. He proclaims, "The Kingdom of God is a future that one can experience now" (p. 418). He also emphasizes that when a client's solutions lead to experiencing life, restoration, peace, and happiness, they are in essence experiencing the redemptive power found in the Kingdom of God.

In addition to the social constructivist critique, another criticism of NT is the *hyper-individualism* and *problem-saturated* descriptions during the deconstruction process of the client's narrative (Kwok, 2016). However, "with God's narrative, Christian narratives can be stories of liberation, restoration, reconciliation, and recreation. In this way, Christians can practice narrative therapy without becoming hyper-individualistic" (Kwok, 2016, pp. 209-210). As such, for the Christian client, God's story for their life becomes their *preferred story*.

An Integrative Theoretical Approach
Gary Sibcy, Ph.D., LPC, LMFT

© Wolf Creek Photography

Dr. Gary Sibcy is a Professor in the School of Behavioral Sciences and a counselor educator. He has a unique identity in that he has been trained as a counselor and licensed, and additionally pursued a Ph.D. in Clinical Psychology and licensed as a psychologist as well. He currently serves as a Clinical Psychologist at Piedmont Psychiatric Center in Lynchburg, Virginia in addition to teaching in the Professional Counseling Program at Liberty University. Dr. Sibcy has authored numerous book chapters, journal articles, and dozens of professional training videos, and co-authored several books. Gary has been counseling for over 25 years and began by specializing with children and families with a focus on anxiety and depression. Over the years he has seen the whole spectrum of childhood disorders with complex cases of ADHD, Oppositional Defiant Disorder along with disorders involving severe mood dysregulation. He has now further specialized in treating families with children and adolescents diagnosed with the new DSM-5 diagnosis, Disruptive Mood Dysregulation Disorder.

Dr. Sibcy's Theoretical Approach: The foundation for his theoretical approach is based on an integrative theory of personality that includes attachment theory and interpersonal neurobiology. Attachment theory is concerned with how children develop their sense of identity and achievement from their interactions with primary caregivers. Children either develop a secure attachment or insecure attachment based on whether their primary caregivers provide a safe haven (or safe base) for them (Bowlby, 1988). This safe haven allows them to freely explore as well as provides safety for them when they feel threatened, hence helping them to manage emotions and return to a regulated state. So, in the assessment stage of therapy, Dr. Sibcy explores attachment experiences by 1) looking at the client's current interpersonal world, 2) assessing the quality of secure base relationships, and 3) also looking at what types of skills the client has for engaging effectively. He calls himself a "**Rational Eclectic**" as he rationally pulls from empirically supported treatment options to meet specific needs/goals. *The goal is to help the client uses the therapist as a secure base and then transfer this learning to others while discovering the ultimate security in their personal relationship with God.*

Dr. Sibcy's Thoughts on the Future of Counseling Theories: The days of schoolism are dead (counseling from just one type of theory). He related it to the medical field, where a cardiologist would not say the heart is the only important part of our bodies that contributes to it being healthy. Medical doctors know that all areas of the body are interconnected to make everything work well. In the old days, each theorist thought he/she had the "right way" to function in therapy. In our present age counselors are recognizing the need to form an approach that includes aspects from many theories.

In addition, Dr. Sibcy spoke about the move toward using empirically supported treatment and "building therapies to fit disorders, instead of taking one theory and stuffing the disorder into that theory". He mentioned the Trans-Diagnostic Movement where there is a unified protocol of using empirically supported treatment packages that can be delivered individually to address different areas of problems. For more information about this movement or work by Dr. Sibcy, see the additional reading list at the end of the chapter.

Contributed by Gary Sibcy. © Kendall Hunt Publishing Company.

HOW DO YOU APPLY THEORY TO COUNSELING CLIENTS?

Case Study: Ashley

Ashley is a 25-year-old single female whose chief complaint is that she feels depressed. She seems to have no energy nor finds much pleasure in life. She tends to oversleep, up to 12 hours a day. Lately, she's had a decrease in appetite, eating just one time a day. She isn't close to her family and has a distant relationship with her parents and siblings. She doesn't have any close friends at the present time and dislikes her current job as a sales clerk.

Psychodynamic Theories (Adlerian Approach). During the initial phase of therapy, the Adlerian therapist focuses on establishing an egalitarian relationship and views Ashley from a holistic and social perspective recognizing her lack of social connectedness to family members and friends. Next, through encouraging and collaborative efforts, the therapist explores Ashley's lifestyle, basic mistakes, and feelings of inferiority that are leading to her depression. During the third phase, the Adlerian therapist focuses more on social interest, recognizing what lifestyle patterns have and have not helped. Lastly, the therapist reorients Ashley to social interest encouraging her to connect and contribute to others and society, which can help her overcome feelings of interiority and fulfill basic life tasks. Additionally, since Ashley has expressed dissatisfaction with her current job, the therapist administers the Myers-Briggs Type Indicator to assess what careers best fit her personality type.

Humanistic/Existential Theories (Person-Centered Approach). In the initial phase of therapy and throughout, the counselor shows empathy and unconditional positive regard as the client tells her story. Feelings will be encouraged as Ashley begins to feel safe within the therapeutic relationship. The therapist will use reflection and personal relationship skills to encourage continued exploration. This in turn leads Ashley to a greater understanding and acceptance of herself along with increased insight. As this process of reflection continues it hopefully will lead Ashely to determine possible courses of action to help alleviate the depression. Ashley eventually gains greater self-acceptance and begins to self-direct her life in making better choices that will lead to more effective behaviors and positive feelings.

Behavioral and Cognitive Theories (CBT Approach). In the initial assessment phase, the CBT counselor would explore Ashley's thinking patterns and underlying beliefs that may be contributing to her depression. As Ashley tells her story, the counselor will be listening for themes in her schemas and automatic thoughts as well as look for unhealthy behaviors that might be contributing to her depression. The counselor will conceptualize the case while determining a treatment plan. Most likely the treatment plan for ongoing therapy would include both cognitive and behavioral interventions, which lead to changes in her beliefs. This then lends to healthier thoughts and actions which will eradicate the depressive symptoms.

Family Systems and Constructivist Theories (SFBT Approach). During the first session, the SFBT therapist listens empathically and adopts

Ashley's language to build the therapeutic relationship asking her, "What do you mean by you feel 'depressed'?" To help identify the solutions she already possesses the therapist asks, "What is it like when you are not depressed?" and "If a miracle happened and your problem was solved during the night, how would you know it was solved and what would be different?" Towards the end of the first session, the therapist provides a summary of the session and assigns the first session formula task as homework telling Ashley, "Between now and the next time we meet, I would like you to observe, so that you can describe to me next time, what happens in your life that you want to continue to have happen." During the remaining 5-6 sessions, the therapist continues to work with Ashley on reconstruction the problem, exploring solutions, evaluating the progress of solutions using scaling questions, and addressing what needs to be done to have the problem solved.

Reflection on Theory Development
Joslynn McNeish-Edgerton, Counseling Student

© Joslynn McNeish-Edgerton

It's difficult to pinpoint precisely when my professional identity first arose since it is undeniably a process with no due dates or time-lines. It took several years for my identity to mature, and it involved several key clinical administrators who were dedicated to investing their endless efforts and time not only in providing supervision but also in guidance; I was concurrently privileged and challenged.

Above everything else, authenticity is key to me. I believe that I did myself an injustice spending countless hours attempting to mimics counseling sessions from YouTube and shaping myself into the next Carl Rogers. It wasn't until I became comfortable in my own skin, experiences, and therapeutic orientation that I truly unlocked my confidence. It was as if my confidence was locked behind limiting beliefs that I had told myself. "You'll never be like B. F. Skinner, Alfred Adler, or Albert Ellis." The truth is, I won't, and neither will you.

Our beliefs, motives, experiences, attributes, and values differ greatly from these honorable psychotherapists. Nevertheless, our worldview will enable us to reach and relate to populations that they perhaps could not. Recognizing and taking ownership of my story has shaped the development of my skill level and my understanding of theories. To me, this is the definition of professional identity.

Contributed by Joslynn McNeish-Edgerton. © Kendall Hunt Publishing Company.

SUMMARY

In this chapter, we have provided a brief snapshot of a few core counseling theories including psychodynamic theories, humanistic theories, cognitive and behavioral theories along with a few others that are popular among counselors today. The purpose was to provide a small glimpse into the world of counseling theories to whet your appetite. Theories play an important role as they are used by counselors to help understand how psychopathology develops as well as to provide an understanding of how people change. As you counsel, you will conceptualize each client's story through your theoretical approach. This then becomes your roadmap for determining treatment. As you continue in the program, you will slowly develop your theory as you gain knowledge and experience as well as become aware of your own philosophy in approaching life's problems. Throughout your classes, you will have many opportunities to study theoretical concepts in much more detail as well as test many skills and techniques. Throughout this process, you will begin to form your own personal approach to counseling. You probably noticed that all the theories discussed have both compatibilities and incompatibilities with the Christian faith. We have just touched the surface when looking at a few theories through the lens of Christianity, however, your Christian faith should deeply inform your overall understanding of mental health and happiness, as well as psychopathology and how people change.

FOR THE ROAD AHEAD

Check out the Chapter 10 video at this link:
https://www.khpcontent.com/

Reflections on the Journey

Jerome is a 65-year-old African American male who has been working as a journeyman electrician for 30 years and is about to retire. Although he reports that he was feeling very excited about retiring from the physical demands of his job, he has recently started to experience excessive worries about retiring, possible finances strains, and getting quality medical care. Lately, he has had difficulties controlling his worries, feels restless and on edge, has difficulties concentrating at work, difficulties falling and staying asleep due to racing thoughts, and has been more irritable with his family at home. Physically, Jerome reports tension in his muscles and feelings of fatigue. He has tried coping with his anxieties by focusing on the benefits of retirement, but the worries "consume" him even when his wife assures him that even though they are not rich, they are financially stable.

- How would Sigmund Freud, Carl Jung, and Alfred Adler view Jerome? How would their views be similar and different? What approaches and techniques would they use to bring about therapeutic change and what would that look like? How would these psychodynamic approaches be much different from other theoretical viewpoints?
- How would Victor Frankl/Irvin Yalom, Carl Rogers, and Fritz Perl view Jerome? How would their views be similar and different? What approaches and techniques would they use to bring about therapeutic change and what would that look like? How would these humanistic approaches be much different from other theoretical viewpoints?
- How would B. F. Skinner, Albert Ellis, and Aaron Beck view Jerome? How would their views be similar and different? What approaches and techniques would they use to bring about therapeutic change and what would that look like? How would these behavioral and cognitive approaches be much different from other theoretical viewpoints?
- How would a family systems therapist, solution-focused therapist, and narrative therapist view Jerome? How would their views be similar and different? What approaches and techniques would they use to bring about therapeutic change and what would that look like? How would these approaches be much different from other theoretical viewpoints?
- As you worked through these questions and contemplated this case, what theory or theories did you see yourself aligning most with and why? How did the theory or theories align with your Christian worldview?

For Further Exploration

Carlson, K. M., & Gonzalez-Prendes, A. (2016). Cognitive behavioral therapy with religious and spiritual clients: A critical perspective. *Journal of Spirituality in Mental Health, 18*(4), 253-282.

Clinton, T. & Sibcy, G. (2006). *Why you do the things you do: The secret to healthy relationships.* Nashville, TN: Thomas Nelson.

Clinton, T. & Sibcy, G. (2009). *Attachments: Why you love, feel and act the way you do.* Brentwood, TN: Integrity Publishers.

Clinton, T. & Sibcy, G. (2011). *Loving your child too much.* Nashville, TN: Thomas Nelson.

Gill, C. S., & Freund, R. R. (2018). *Spirituality and religion in counseling: Competency-based strategies for ethical practice.* New York, NY: Routledge.

Halbur, D. A., & Halbur, K. V. (2019). *Developing your theoretical orientation in counseling and psychotherapy* (4th ed.). New York, NY: Pearson.

Jones, S. L., & Butman, R. E. (2011). *Modern psychotherapies: A comprehensive Christian appraisal* (2nd ed.). Downers Grove, IL: InterVarsity Press.

Knight, A., & Sibcy, G. (2017). *Redeeming attachment: A counselor's guide to facilitating attachment to God and earned security.* Dubuque, IA: Kendall-Hunt.

Pearce, M. (2016). *Cognitive behavioral therapy for Christian clients with depression: A practical, tool-based primer.* West Conshohocken, PA: Templeton Press.

Robbins, C. (2018). *Unified protocol for transdiagnostic treatment of emotional disorders.* New York, NY: Oxford University Press.

Rogers, C. R. (1961). *On becoming a person: A therapist's view of psychotherapy.* New York, NY: Houghton Mifflin.

REFERENCES

Adler, A. (1926). *The neurotic constitution* (B. Glueck & J. Lind, Trans.). New York, NY: Dodd Mead. (Original work published 1912)

Adler, A. (1946). *Understanding human nature* (W. B. Wolfe, Trans.). New York, NY: Greenberg. (Original work published 1927)

Adler, A. (1959). *The practice and theory of individual psychology* (P. Radin, Trans.). Patterson, NJ: Littlefield, Adams. (Original work published 1924)

Allport, G. (1963). Preface. In: Frankl, V. *Man's search for meaning.* New York, NY: Washington Square Press.

Bandura, A. (1969). *Principles of behavior modification.* New York, NY: Holt, Rinehart, and Winston.

Beck, A. (1976). *Cognitive therapy and the emotional disorders.* New York, NY: Penguin Books.

Beck, J. S. (2011). *Cognitive therapy: Basics and beyond.* New York, NY: Guildford Press.

Bowen, M. (1978). *Family therapy in clinical practice.* New York, NY: Aronson.

Brougham, L., & Kashubeck-West, S. (2017, September-August). Impact of a growth mindset intervention on academic performance of students at two urban high schools. *Professional School Counseling, 21*(1). Retrieved from http://link.galegroup.com/apps/doc/A549159567/AONE?u=vic_liberty&sid=AONE&xid=2ed4080c

Carlson, K. M., & Gonzalez-Prendes, A. (2016). Cognitive behavioral therapy with religious and spiritual clients: A critical perspective. *Journal of Spirituality in Mental Health, 18*(4), 253-282.

Carlson, J., & Johnson, J. (2015). Adlerian therapy. In I. Marini & M. A. Stebnicki (Eds.), *The professional counselor's desk reference* (2nd ed., pp. 225-228). New York, NY: Springer Publishing Company.

Ceballos, P. L., & Bratton, S. C. (2010). Empowering Latino families: Effects of a culturally responsive intervention for low-income immigrant Latino parents on children's behaviors and parental stress. *Psychology in the Schools, 47*(8), 761-775. doi: 10.1002/pits.20502

Clark, R. E. (2004). The classical origins of Pavlov's conditioning. *Integrative Physiological and Behavioral Science: The Official Journal of the Pavlovian Society, 39*(4), 279-94.

Corey, G. (2017). *Theory and practice of counseling and psychotherapy* (10th ed.). Boston, MA: Cengage Learning.

Corbett, L. (2013). Successful aging: Jungian contributions to development in later life. *Psychological Perspectives, 56*, 149-167. doi:10.1080/00332925.2013.786932

de Shazer, S. (1982). *Patterns of brief therapy*. New York, NY: Guilford Press.

de Shazer, S. (1985). *Keys to solutions in brief therapy*. New York, NY: Norton.

de Shazer, S. (1988). *Clues: Investigating solutions in brief therapy*. New York, NY: Norton.

de Shazer, S. (1991). *Putting differences to work*. New York, NY: Norton.

Dufrene, R. L., Henderson, K. L., & Eckart, E. C. (2016). Adlerian theory. In D. Capuzzi & M. D. Stauffer (Eds.), *Counseling and psychotherapy: Theories and techniques* (6th ed., pp. 138-167). Alexandria, VA: American Counseling Association.

Duhl, F. J., Kantor, D., & Duhl, B. S. (1973). Learning, space, and action in family therapy: A primer of sculpture. In D. A. Bloch (Ed.), *Techniques of family psychotherapy: A primer* (pp. 47-64). Oxford, England: Gruen & Stratton.

Dryden, W. (2012). The "ABCs" of REBT III: A study of errors and confusions made by Ellis and Joffe Ellis (2011). *Journal of Rational-Emotive & Cognitive - Behavior Therapy, 30*(3), 188-201. doi:10.1007/s10942-011-0140-6

Frederick, T. V. (2008). Solution-focused brief therapy and the kingdom of God: A cosmological integration. *Pastoral Psychology, 56*, 413-419. doi:10.1007/s11089-008-0123-4

Freud, S. (1949). *An outline of psycho-analysis*. New York, NY: Norton. (Original work published 1940)

Freud, S. (1952). *A general introduction to psycho-analysis*. (J. Riviere, Trans.). New York, NY: Washington Square. (Original work published 1920)

Gill, C. S., & Freund, R. R. (2018). *Spirituality and religion in counseling: Competency-based strategies for ethical practice*. New York, NY: Routledge.

Goldenberg, I., Stanton, M., & Goldenberg, H. (2017). *Family therapy: An overview* (9th ed.). Boston, MA: Cengage Learning.

Granello, D. H., & Young, M. E. (2019). *Counseling today: Foundations of professional identity* (2nd ed.). New York, NY: Person.

Halbur, D. A., & Halbur, K. V. (2019). *Developing your theoretical orientation in counseling and psychotherapy* (4th ed.). New York, NY: Pearson.

Haley, J. (1973). *Uncommon therapy: The psychiatric techniques of Milton H. Erickson, M.D.* New York, NY: Norton.

Haley, J. (1987). *Problem-solving therapy* (2nd ed.). San Francisco, CA: Jossey-Bass.

Jackson, D. D. (1957). The question of family homeostasis. *Psychiatric Quarterly Supplement, 31*, 79-90.

Jackson, D. D. (1965). Family rules: Marital quid pro quo. *Archives of General Psychiatry, 12*(6), 589-594. doi:10.1001/archpsyc.1965.01720360061010

Johansen, T. (2010). *Religion and spirituality in psychotherapy: An individual psychology perspective*. New York, NY: Springer Publishing Company.

Johnson, A. L. (2016). Psychoanalytic theory. In D. Capuzzi & M. D. Stauffer (Eds.), *Counseling and psychotherapy: Theories and techniques* (6th ed., pp. 80-108). Alexandria, VA: American Counseling Association.

Jones, S. L., & Butman, R. E. (2011). *Modern psychotherapies: A comprehensive Christian appraisal* (2nd ed.). Downers Grove, IL: InterVarsity Press.

Jung, C. G. (1928). Psychoanalysis and the cure of souls. In *Collected works* (2nd ed., Vol. 11, pp. 348-354). Princeton, NJ: Princeton University Press.

Jung, C. G. (1954). Child development and education. In *Collected works: The development of personality* (Vol. 17, pp. 47-62). Princeton, NJ: Princeton University Press. (Original work published 1928)

Jung, C. G. (1956). *Collected works: Symbols of transformation* (2nd ed., Vol. 5). Princeton, NJ: Princeton University Press. (Original work published 1911)

Jung, C. G. (1959). Conscious, unconscious, and individuation. In *Collected works: The archetypes of the collective unconscious* (Vol. 9, Part 1, pp. 42-53). Princeton, NJ: Princeton University Press. (Original work published 1936)

Jung, C. G. (1961). *Memories, dreams, reflections.* New York, NY: Random House, Inc.

Jung, C. G. (1971). *Collected works: Psychological types* (Vol. 6). Princeton, NJ: Princeton University Press. (Original work published 1923)

Kam, C. (2018). Overcoming self-deception: Integrating Christian theology with Jungian psychoanalysis. *Journal of Psychology and Christianity, 37*(2), 137-152.

Kazantzis, N., Dattilio, F., & Dobson, K. (2017). *The therapeutic relationship in cognitive-behavioral therapy.* New York, NY: Guilford Press.

Konopka, A., Hermans, H., & Goncalves, M. (2019). *Handbook of dialogical self-theory and psychotherapy: Bridging psychotherapeutic and cultural traditions.* London: Routledge.

Kottler, J. A. (2018). *The secrets of exceptional counselors.* Alexandria, VA: American Counseling Association.

Kottler, J. A., & Shepard, D. S. (2015). *Introduction to counseling: Voices from the field* (8thed.). Stamford, CT: Cengage Learning.

Kwok, W. (2016). Narrative therapy, theology, and relational openness: Reconstructing the connection between postmodern therapy and traditional theology. *Journal of Psychology & Theology, 44*(3), 201-212.

Lambert, M. J., & Barley, D. E. (2001). Research summary on the therapeutic relationship and psychotherapy outcome. *Psychotherapy, 38*(4), 357-361.

Lambert, S. F., Carmichael, A. R., & Williams, L. (2015). Guidelines in counseling families. In I. Marini & M. A. Stebnicki (Eds.), *The professional counselor's desk reference* (2nd ed., pp. 351-356). New York, NY: Springer Publishing Company.

Lambert, M. J., & Cattani-Thompson, K. (1996). Current findings regarding the effectiveness of counseling: Implications for practice. *Journal of Counseling and Development, 74,* 601-608.

May, R., Angel, E., & Ellenberger, H. F. (Eds.). (1958). *Existence: A new dimension in psychiatry and psychology.* New York, NY: Basic Books. doi:10.1037/11321-000

May, R. (Ed.). (1961). *Existential psychology.* New York, NY: Crown Publishing Group/Random House.

May, R. (1983). *The discovery of being: Writings in existential psychology.* New York, NY: W. W. Norton.

McGoldrick, M., Carter, B. A., & Garcia-Preto, N. (2011). Overview: The life cycle in its changing context: Individual, family, and social perspectives. In M. McGoldrick, B. A. Carter, & N. Garcia-Preto (Eds.), *The expanded family life cycle: Individual, family, and social perspectives* (4th ed., pp. 1-19). Boston, MA: Allyn & Bacon.

McGoldrick, M., Gerson, R., & Petry, S. (2008). *Genograms: Assessment and intervention* (3rd ed.). New York, NY: W. W. Norton & Company.

Miller, E., & Marini, I. (2015). Solution-focused brief psychotherapy. In I. Marini & M. A. Stebnicki (Eds.), *The professional counselor's desk reference* (2nd ed., pp. 229-234). New York, NY: Springer Publishing Company.

Miller, W. R., & Rollnick, S. (2013). *Motivational interviewing: Helping people change* (3rd ed.). New York, NY: Guilford Press.

Minuchin, P., Colapinto, J., & Minuchin, S. (2007). *Working with families of the poor* (2nd ed.). New York, NY: Guilford Press.

Minuchin, S. (1974). *Families and family therapy*. Cambridge, MA: Harvard University Press.

Minuchin, S., & Fishman, H. D. (1981). *Family therapy techniques*. Cambridge, MA: Harvard University Press.

Minuchin, S., Montalvo, B., Guerney, B. G., Rosman, B. L., & Shumer, F. (1967). *Families of the slums: An exploration of their structure and treatment*. New York, NY: Basic Books.

Murdock, N. L. (2017). *Theories of counseling and psychotherapy: A case approach* (4th ed.). New York, NY: Pearson.

Myers, I. B., & Myers, P. B. (1995). *Gifts differing: Understanding personality type* (2nd ed.). Palo Alto, CA: Consulting Psychologists Press.

Nelson, K., & Finn, A. (2016). Jungian analytical theory. In D. Capuzzi & M. D. Stauffer (Eds.), *Counseling and psychotherapy: Theories and techniques* (6th ed., pp. 109-137). Alexandria, VA: American Counseling Association.

Neukrug, E. (2018). *Counseling theory and practice* (2nd ed.). San Diego, CA: Cognella Academic Publishing.

Norcross, J. C., & Wampold, B. E. (2011). Evidence-based therapy relationships: Research conclusions and clinical practices. *Psychotherapy, 48*(1), 98-102. doi:10.1037/10022161.

O'Hanlon, B., & Weiner-Davis, M. (2003). *In search of solutions* (Rev. ed.). New York, NY: Norton.

Olson, R. P. (2002). Christian humanism. In R. P. Olson (Ed.), *Religious theories of personality and psychotherapy: East meets west* (pp. 247-323). New York, NY: Hawthorn Press.

Papp, P. (1981). Paradoxes. In S. Minuchin & H. C. Fishman (Eds.), *Family therapy techniques*. Cambridge, MA: Harvard University Press.

Parikh, S. B., Ceballos, P., & Post, P. (2013). Factors related to play therapists' social justice advocacy attitudes. *Journal of Multicultural Counseling & Development, 41*(4), 240-253. doi: 10.1002/j.2161-1912.2013.00039.x

Passons, W. R. (1975). *Gestalt approaches in counseling*. New York, NY: Holt, Rinehart & Winston.

Perls, F., Hefferline, R., & Goodman, R. (1951). *Gestalt therapy: Excitement and growth in the human personality*. New York: Dell.

Perls, F. (1969). *Gestalt therapy verbatim*. Lafayette, CA: Real People Press.

Prochaska, J. O., & Norcross, J. C. (2018). *Systems of psychotherapy: A transtheoretical analysis* (9th ed.). New York, NY: Oxford University Press.

Redekop, R., Luke, C., & Malone, F. (2017). From the couch to the chair: Applying psychoanalytic theory and practice to counseling. *Journal of Counseling & Development, 95*(1), 100-109. doi:110.1002/jcad.12121

Rogers, C. (1961). *On becoming a person: A therapist's view of psychotherapy*. Boston, MA: Houghton Mifflin Company.

Rogers, C. R. (1957). The necessary and sufficient conditions of therapeutic personality change. *Journal of Consulting Psychology, 12*(2), 95-103.

Satir, V. (1972). *Peoplemaking*. Palo Alto, CA: Science and Behavior Books.

Seligman, L., & Reichenberg, L. (2014). *Theories of counseling and psychotherapy* (4th ed.). Upper Saddle River, NJ: Pearson Education.

Sibcy, G., & Knight, A. (2019). Case conceptualization, scaling, and preliminary goal setting. In R. Hawkins, S. Warren, A. Knight, & G. Sibcy (Eds.), *Research-based counseling skills: The art and science of therapeutic empathy*. Dubuque, IA: Kendall Hunt Publishing Company.

Skinner, B. F. (1971). *Beyond freedom and dignity*. New York, NY: Alfred A Knopf, Inc.

Spiegler, M. D. (2016). *Contemporary behavior therapy* (6th ed.). Boston, MA: Cengage Learning

Watts, R. E. (2000). Biblically based Christian spirituality and Adlerian psychotherapy. *The Journal of Individual Psychology, 56*(3), 316-328.

Watts, R. E. (2017). Adlerian and constructivist therapist: A neo-Adlerian perspective. *The Journal of Individual Psychology, 73*(2), 139-155. doi:10.1353/jip.2017.0012

West-Olatunji, C. A., & Rush-Ossenbeck, M. (2016). Constructivist theories: Solution-focused and narrative therapist. In D. Capuzzi & M. D. Stauffer (Eds.), *Counseling and psychotherapy: Theories and techniques* (6th ed., pp. 493-523). Alexandria, VA: American Counseling Association.

Westerhof, G. J., & Bohlmeijer, E. T. (2012). Life stories and mental health: The role of identification processes in theory and interventions. *Narrative Work: Issues, Investigations, & Interventions, 2*(1), 106-128.

Wheeler, G., & Axelsson, L. S. (2015). *Gestalt therapy.* Washington, DC: American Psychological Association.

White, M. (1992). Deconstruction and therapy. In *Experience, contradiction, narrative, and imagination: Selected papers of David Epston & Michael White, 1989-1991* (pp. 109-151). Adelaide, South Australia: Dulwich Centre.

White, M. (2007). *Maps of narrative practice.* New York, NY: Norton.

White, M., & Epston, D. (1990). *Narrative means to therapeutic ends.* New York, NY: Norton.

Virués-Ortega, J., & Haynes, S. N. (2005). Functional analysis in behavior therapy: Behavioral foundations and clinical application. *International Journal of Clinical and Health Psychology, 5*(3), 567-587.

Yalom, I. D. (1980). *Existential psychotherapy.* New York, NY: Basic Books.

Yeager, D. S., & Dweck, C. S. (2012). Mindsets that promote resilience: When students believe that personal characteristics can be developed. *Educational Psychologist, 47*, 302-314. doi:10.1080/00461520.2012.722 805.

Yontef, G., & Jacobs, L. (2005). Gestalt therapy. In D. Wedding & R. J. Corsini (Eds.), *Current psychotherapies* (10th ed., pp. 299-338). Belmont, CA: Brooks-Cole.

Yontef, G., & Schulz, F. (2013). *Dialogic relationship and creative techniques: Are they on the same team?* Los Angeles, CA: Pacific Gestalt Institute.

CHAPTER 11
Assessment and Diagnosis

VASTI HOLSTUN, PH.D. & SUMMER KUBA, PH.D.

> "Measure what you value instead of valuing only what you can measure."
> —Andy Hargreaves

Following Christ: Grace for Our Work

When the Bible talks about *assessment*, the connotation is often judgment or evaluation. In Daniel 5 we read about King Belteshazzar being "measured and found wanting" (Daniel 5:27, New International Version). In Matthew 25 we read about God separating the *goats* from the *sheep* based on their deeds. And there are of course other biblical references that support the fact that God both notices and evaluates people (1 Corinthians 4:5; Acts 17:31; 2 Corinthians 5:10).

After reading this chapter, you will understand more about:

- The historical perspectives of assessment and testing in the counseling profession.
- The nature and meaning of assessment and testing as it relates to the multiple roles of counselors across disciplines.
- The importance of test worthiness, scoring and interpreting procedures, different types of assessments, as well as report writing.
- The diagnostic process, including differential diagnosis and the use of current diagnostic classification systems (Diagnostic and Statistical Manual of Mental Disorders (DSM) and the International Classification of Diseases (ICD).
- The legal, ethical, and professional issues as they relate to assessment, testing, and diagnosis.

The following CACREP standards are addressed in this chapter:
Assessment and Testing:

- Historical perspectives concerning the nature and meaning of assessment and testing in counseling (CACREP, 2016, Standard 2.F.7.a.)
- Use of assessments for diagnostic and intervention planning purposes (CACREP, 2016, Standard 2.F.7.e.)
- Ethical and culturally relevant strategies for selecting, administering, and interpreting assessment and test results (CACREP, 2016, Standard 2.F.7.m.)

However, the Bible also refers to another aspect related to *assessment*: a use that is more closely aligned to the content of this chapter. In Luke 12:7, Jesus says, "Indeed, the very hairs of your head are all numbered. Don't be afraid; you are worth more than many sparrows." This verse tells us that God knows us so deeply and intimately that nothing about us is trivial, not even the hairs on our head. He is interested in every detail about us, and nothing can deter his attention away from our needs. Other biblical passages emphasize similar themes: God keeps track of our sorrows and tears (Psalm 56:8, NLT), and He numbers our days (Job 14:5). One of the most beautiful passages in the Bible (Psalm 139) also talks about God's profound interest in us and how much He knows about us — even things of which we are not aware. At the end of the chapter, the psalmist asks God for a thorough assessment (v. 23-24 ESV) that will help him stay on a godly path. As much as biblical assessment can be about judgment and evaluation, it is also about how well God knows us and how He hopes that we will also take the time to know Him, even as we work toward a better knowing of ourselves.

Assessment in counseling is commonly used to evaluate. However, for the most part, assessment in counseling is used to help us get to know our clients better. While we may never know everything there is to know about a client, understanding as much as possible about their struggles and their strengths comes in handy when we establish counseling goals. Assessment is also part of the diagnosis process. In counseling, diagnosis is a complex process and is often viewed from controversial standpoints in our profession. All counselors are required to understand the process of assessment and diagnosis, even if their particular specialty or place of work does not require its use regularly.

WHAT IS THE HISTORY OF ASSESSMENT?

Political events and cultural influences impacted assessment history and assessment development in social sciences. While various forms of assessment have been around for hundreds of years, dating back to antiquity, formal assessment as we know it today started at the end of the 19th century and early 20th century (Drummond, Sheperis, & Jones, 2016). We offer a few important highlights here. You will learn more about these historical aspects when you take your *Assessment in Counseling* course.

World History Archive/Newscom

One of the most notable events in the assessment history happened in Europe, at the end of the 19th century. The French government passed a law that mandated schooling for all children, and psychologist Alfred Binet (1857-1911) was hired to help identify children with low cognitive abilities so that they could be placed in remedial classes. In the 1890s Binet developed the first version of an IQ test. This is significant because after over 100 years and several revisions, we now have the Stanford-Binet IQ test, known as one of the most reliable and commonly used intelligence tests available today (Neukrug & Fawcett, 2014).

The first two decades of the 20th century have seen the development of several types of tests, including projective tests (*Rorschach Inkblot Test, Jung Word Association Test; Goodenough Draw-a-Man Test*), achievement tests (*Thorndike Handwriting, Language, Spelling, and Arithmetic Tests; Terman, Kelley, and Ruch's Stanford Achievement Test*), and vocational interest inventories (*Strong Vocational Interest Blank, Clark's Aptitude Testing*). Additionally, Binet's initial IQ test was revised and renamed to *Binet and Simon Intelligence Scale* and was later translated into English (Drummond et al., 2016). The translation of Binet's test, however, was somewhat misused in the United States. While the test was normed in France by Binet, it was used in English and then translated into other languages to test immigrants from all over the world. Needless to say, the majority of those who were tested scored in the low intelligence functioning range (Gregory, 2007).

World War I marked another important milestone in test development. The US armed services developed a group intelligence test with two versions:

Army Alpha and Army Beta (Hood & Johnson, 2007). The military used these tests to screen cognitive ability and assign personnel to various jobs. This marked the beginning of utilizing tests in other areas such as education and industry.

An important scientific influence at the beginning of the 20th century also impacted test development. New statistical concepts started to emerge – such as Pearson's theory of correlation and Spearman's measurement theory. These new scientific aspects helped with measuring the validity and reliability of test constructs and scores (Neukrug & Fawcett, 2014).

Another historical aspect that supported test development was the emergence of vocational guidance in education (Sweeney, 2012). School counseling, as we know it today, was born from this particular development. Because of its close ties with education, formal testing and evaluation have always been part of the counseling profession. As a matter of fact, during this time in history, counseling was practically synonymous with testing (Hood & Johnson, 2007). Over the years, the profession of counseling evolved to include much more than testing. However, testing and assessment remained an integral component of the profession.

The following two decades (the 1930s and 1940s) saw the development of additional types of tests. After undergoing revisions, many of these tests are still used today. Some examples are the *Graduate Record Examinations* (GRE), still required by many graduate programs for admissions, and intelligence tests, such as *Wechsler Bellevue Intelligence Scale* and *Wechsler's*

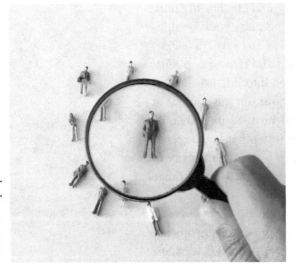

Intelligence Scale for Children (WISC), now in its 5th edition. During this time, the *Stanford – Binet Scale* underwent its first revision. Another projective test still used today, was developed in the 1930's: *Murray's Thematic Apperception Test* (TAT). In the 1940s, personality tests emerged with the development of the *Minnesota Multiphasic Personality Inventory* (MMPI), now in its 2nd edition. Today the MMPI is the most widely used psychometric test for measuring adult psychopathology in the world (Drummond et al., 2016). Burros' first *Mental Measurements Yearbook* was also published in the 1930s. This is a database that catalogs most or all tests that are available for purchase in the fields of psychology, education, business, and leadership.

The following two decades – 50's and 60's – saw an influx of more educational testing as a result of the *National Defense Education Act*. Because of the political context following World War II and the launch of Sputnik, the demand for mathematicians, particularly individuals skilled in applied mathematics, made such an impact on our culture that the government pushed for education reform and included funding for new vocational initiatives (Drummond et al., 2016). As such, we now have the *National Assessment of Educational Progress*, the *Kuder Occupational Interest Survey*, and also scales of intelligence and development that are geared towards infants and preschoolers (ie. *Wechsler Preschool and Primary Scale of Intelligence; Bayley Scales of Infant Development*). In 1960, the *Stanford -Binet Intelligence Scale* was revised again. Lindquist's electronic test scoring, as well as new norms in developing achievement tests and theories about the nature of human intelligence also marked this decade (Drummond et al., 2016). Additionally, *Bloom's Taxonomy of Educational Objectives* redefined how tests were constructed and utilized in social sciences.

The 1970s and 1980s saw new developments in testing and regulations. The *Family Educational Rights and Privacy Act* (FERPA) passed in 1974. This added a layer of protection to how tests were used, and it regulated the privacy of the individuals. Also, the first version of the *Individuals with Disabilities Education Act* (IDEA) was developed, which created the need to evaluate children with disabilities. The use of computers in testing increased, and by the 1980's we had computer-adaptive and computer-assisted tests. The *Wechsler Intelligence Scale for Children* was revised, and Thorndike, Hagen, and Stattler's revision of the *Stanford-Binet Intelligence Scale* was published. Additionally, the *Revision of the Standards for Educational and Psychological Testing* took place at that time. Several new tests were developed and published: *Peabody Picture Vocabulary Test*, a test for verbal ability, still used today; *Millon Clinical Multiaxial Inventory* (MCMI),a psychological test that identifies personality traits and psychopathology, still used today in its 4th edition; and the *Kaufman Assessment Battery for Children* (KABC), another IQ test still used today.

The last decade of the 20th century saw the implementation of the *Americans with Disabilities Act* (ADA), which, as with IDEA, created the need for assessments that help identify individuals with disabilities in order to

provide benefits and services. Another important milestone in the '90s was the creation of the *Health Insurance Portability and Accountability Act* (HIPAA), which regulates how personal health information is to be used and protected. Other tests were revised, and new tests developed, which are still in use today:the *Sixteen Personality Factor Questionnaire, Fifth Edition*; the *Wechsler Adult Intelligence Scale, Third Edition*; the *Wechsler Individual Achievement Test*; and the *Stanford-Binet Intelligence Scale, Fifth Edition*. The *Standards for Educational and Psychological Testing* underwent a new revision. The MMPI authors published a test version for adolescents – the MMPI - A. Finally, with the arrival of the internet, internet-based tests started to expand and become more readily available.

In the first two decades of the 21st century, several political developments have influenced testing. The *No Child Left Behind Act* of 2001, as well as the *Individuals with Disabilities Education Improvement Act* of 2004, have had a significant impact on testing in education. Schools and school districts are held accountable to show that their students are making adequate progress every year through state testing. Even today, there are strong opinions about the benefits and drawbacks of each of these legislations.

The *Every Student Succeeds Act* (ESSA) was passed in 2015 to replace the *No Child Left Behind* (NCLB) law. While the standardized testing provision remains, the federal government has given state governments more autonomy in how they measure student achievement. The States are still required to submit their goals and standards to the US Department of Education; however, the states' departments of education hold the final responsibility on what standards are implemented and measured. Students in grades third through eighth are tested yearly, and then again in their Junior year in high school. The states also decide the consequences or supports that are given to low performing schools.

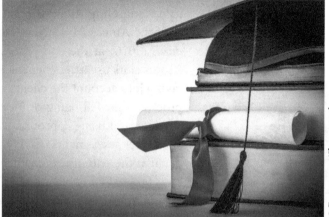

Several tests were revised at the beginning of the new millennium. Here are some of the most current editions at the time of this writing: *Strong Interest Inventory*; *Wechsler Intelligence Scale for Children, Fifth Edition*; *Wechsler Preschool and Primary Scale of Intelligence, Third Edition*; *Kaufman Brief Intelligence Test, Second Edition*. Also, the *Standards for Educational and Psychological Testing* (2014) were revised again, and the *International Test Commission Standards* were created.

In looking at this brief history, tests and assessments were created to fulfill a recurring need to analyze and categorize certain human abilities and traits. Testing and assessment categorize these abilities according to norms and also try to identify abilities, behaviors, and other human characteristics that deviate from the norm. While we can see the usefulness of such measurements, we can also surmise that because of the complexity of the human mind, assessments and tests can present with limitations and subjectivity.

WHAT DO COUNSELORS NEED TO KNOW ABOUT ASSESSMENT IN COUNSELING?

Now that you have the historical perspective of assessments and the assessment process, we can dive into choosing the most effective assessment(s) for your clients. In this section, you will learn how to identify the most effective assessments, begin to understand the administration, scoring, and interpretation process as well as how to utilize this valuable information to write the most detailed assessment report. You will also be provided with an overview of a variety of assessments that are relevant to the clinical and school counseling setting today.

Before we move on, stop for a minute and review Section E of the American Counseling Association's (ACA) *Code of Ethics* (2014) and Section A of the American School Counselor Association (ASCA) *Ethical Standards* (2016) at the end of this chapter. According to the ACA (2014), "Counselors use assessment as one component of the counseling process, taking into account the clients' personal and cultural context. Counselors promote the well-being of individual clients or groups of clients by developing and using appropriate educational, mental health, psychological and career assessments" (p. 11). Although we will discuss ethics in greater detail at the end of this chapter, these codes will help you to understand your professional obligation, will guide you through the critical elements related to the assessment selection process, and will set the groundwork for the rest of this chapter.

Choosing the Most Effective Assessment

So, which assessment(s) should counselors choose? As we ponder this question, we must first understand the *why* behind administering an assessment in the counseling setting. Think about the information that can be gathered from assessments as an overall picture - a picture of how your client may think, feel, behave, or even reason. This picture provides information about clients' strengths and weaknesses as well as insight into the dynamics of their personality.

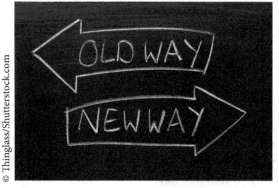

Counselors administer assessments in order to gain a more thorough view into who the client is and what needs they currently have (Aiken & Groth-Marnat, 2006; Hays, 2013; Neukrug & Fawcett, 2015; Young, 2017). Assessments allow the counselor and client to partner together to make the most informed decisions regarding the treatment process, which ultimately becomes the roadmap in facilitating client change.

The purpose of assessment and testing in counseling is to help clinicians and their clients develop goals for their work (Young, 2017). This is important to note because counselors never rely solely on tests or formal assessments in order to formulate these goals. Identifying the purpose behind the selection of each assessment will not only allow for the development of more focused counseling goals but will also strengthen client trust and ultimately enhance the counselor-client relationship (ACA, 2014; ASCA, 2016; Tymofievich & Leroux, 2000). A comprehensive assessment of a client for the purposes of diagnosis and establishing treatment goals will always include a clinical interview, in addition to inventories and tests. Many clinicians base their goals and assessment solely on the clinical interview and only use formal assessment when the clinical interview doesn't provide a clear picture of the client's needs. This is not always an effective practice because, at times, it does not provide enough detailed information to create an effective treatment plan.

Counselors also choose to use assessments to aide in problem identification and goal setting (Hays, 2013). In other words, asking "what is it that brings this individual to counseling?" Sometimes clients enter our office and know exactly what they want to work on and are ready to set goals and develop an action plan. If this is the case, wonderful! Move forward with choosing an assessment that will help the client reach his/her identified goals (Neukrug & Fawcett, 2015). Other times, clients are not sure where or how to even begin. What they believe the problem to be may not actually be the real problem at all. If this is the case, assessments can be used to help both the counselor and the client identify the problem or concern at hand. Assessments will guide the treatment process and provide goal-setting opportunities.

Now that we understand the *why*, we must answer the question of *how*. How do we ensure that we are choosing the most effective and appropriate assessment(s) for our clients? The next step is to analyze test *worthiness*, or how good an assessment is based on research (Corcoran & Fischer, 2013; Hays, 2013; Neukrug & Fawcett, 2015). In other words, is this assessment *valid* and *reliable*? Does it take into account *cultural fairness*? Is it *biased*? Does it make sense to use this assessment in this particular situation with this particular client based on the presenting problem and/or the client's goals? Let's take a deeper look at these four measures (validity, reliability, cultural fairness, practicality) of test worthiness.

© Castleski/Shutterstock.com

Validity. *Validity* is a critical element in selecting the most effective assessment (Corcoran & Fischer, 2013; Heppner & Heppner, 2004; Sperry, 2012). Validity is defined as "the degree to which all of the accumulated evidence supports that intended interpretation of test scores for the intended purpose" (Neukrug & Fawcett, 2015, p. 339). If an instrument is valid, then it measures what it is designed to measure (Hays, 2013). For example, if you step on a bathroom scale and the scale gives you your current body temperature, then it does not measure what it was designed to measure, which is your weight. In terms of the counseling profession, if you are in need of an assessment to measure the degree of anxiety your client is experiencing, you must choose an assessment that has been proven, through research, to specifically measure anxiety.

Reliability. Another critical element to consider when selecting the most effective assessment is reliability (Corcoran & Fischer, 2013; Sperry, 2012). *Reliability* is defined as, "the degree to which test scores are free from errors of measurement, also, the capacity of an instrument to provide consistent results" (Neukrug & Fawcett, 2015, p. 337). If an assessment is reliable, it produces consistent or similar results when it is repeated (Hays, 2013; Heppner & Heppner, 2004). For example, think back to our bathroom scale. If you step on the scale and every morning it gives you a significantly different reading, then the scale is not reliable. It is not producing consistent or similar results. In terms of the counseling profession, if given a clinical assessment twice, the client should get the same or very similar results.

© SNeG17/Shutterstock.com

As a point of clarification, an instrument cannot be valid without being reliable. In other words, the bathroom scale should always measure your weight and give consistent results every time it is used in order to be valid. An instrument that measures anxiety cannot be valid unless it gives consistent results on the client's anxiety. However, a reliable instrument isn't always valid. The bathroom scale could give you consistent results, but if it measures your body temperature, it's still not a valid measurement for your body weight. By the same token, an instrument that gives consistent results (so it's reliable), but measures IQ is not a valid instrument for measuring anxiety.

Cross-cultural fairness. It is also important to consider *cross-cultural fairness.* As counselors, we must consider the diversity (culture, disability, ethnicity, gender, age, race, language, religion, spirituality, sexual orientation, and socioeconomic status) of our clients (ACA, 2014; Hays & Mcleod, 2018). We must take into account the equitability of the assessment prior to administering it to our clients and consider how each of the diverse variables is relevant to the client (Lee, Blando, Mizelle, Orozco, 2007). If diversity is not considered in the development of the assessment, then we are looking at issues of *bias.* Bias refers to any factor that could potentially cause the assessment scores to be higher or lower than they would be if the assessment considered individual diversity (Aiken & Groth-Marnat, 2006; Lee et al., 2007). In other words, the scores are distorted in some way. Recall the paragraph at the beginning of the chapter about the Binet's

IQ test translated from French into English, and then subsequently translated through interpreters to measure the IQ of new immigrants. You can see the potential for misunderstandings and misinterpretation of cultural norms in just this one instance. This can happen with many assessments. If this is the case, we could be looking at consequences for the client which include misdiagnosis, implementation of inappropriate interventions, and ultimately negative consequences for the client, leading to ineffective clinical decisions (Aiken & Groth-Marnat, 2006; Hays, 2013). However, if there is an absence of bias, then we can postulate that an assessment score would have the same meaning no matter the diversity of the client (Hays, 2013).

Finally, the assessment must be practical. When deciding on the best assessment for your client, there are several elements to consider to avoid possible setbacks. In determining *practicality*, we should consider each of the four elements: cost, time, formatting, and readability (see below) and then ask ourselves if it makes sense to administer this assessment (Neukrug & Fawcett, 2015).

1. Cost - Insurance reimbursements and financial cutbacks are common in public and private counseling agencies as well as educational settings. You not only have to look at what the client can afford but in a school setting, you must consider the cost per student.

2. Time - This includes the time it takes to administer the assessment as well as the time it takes to score and interpret the assessment. You should ask yourself if the length of time to administer the assessment is appropriate for that particular client in that specific setting. Remember that time is money!

3. Formatting - There is a wide-range of formatting options when it comes to assessment. Assessments may be multiple choice, essay, paper-pencil, computer-based, and short response. Other formatting issues may be the size of the print, sequencing of questions, or type of question (Neukrug & Fawcett, 2015). It is important to consider the individual needs of your client in order to choose the best fit in regards to formatting.

4. Readability - This is important because it relates to your client's ability to comprehend what is being asked. We need to consider the developmental and educational level of our clients to ensure our client clearly understands the test. If the assessment questions are beyond their level of understanding, we will be looking at skewed results which will

lend itself to inappropriate interventions which may lead to very little positive change.

If, after considering the practicality of the assessment, you determine the assessment to be appropriate for your particular client in your specific counseling setting, you must then reflect on your professional competence (ACA, 2014; Meier, 2015). Take a minute to think back to the *ACA Code of Ethics* (2014). What does it say about counselor competence in regards to assessments? The question you should ask yourself is, "Am I qualified to administer, score, and interpret the results of this particular assessment?"

Counselor Competence

Counselor competence, as it relates to the administration, scoring, and interpretation of assessments, is heavily stressed in the *ACA Code of Ethics* (2014). Qualification guidelines were established by the ACA and are listed in the 2014 *Code of Ethics* to ensure high professional standards in the use of assessments with clients and to ensure counselors have the knowledge, skills, training, and experience to administer and score assessments and to interpret the results (ACA, 2014; Turner, DeMers, Fox, & Reed, 2001). Because of the significant effect assessments can have on our client's lives, we must be cognizant of this three-tiered system (Levels A, B, and C) developed by the American Psychological Association (APA, 1954; Turner et al., 2001).

Level A. Level A includes tests that can be administered, scored, and interpreted by responsible non-psychologists who have carefully read the test manual and are familiar with the overall purpose of testing (Amer-

ican Psychological Association, 1954, p. 146-148). To clarify, in individual qualified to administer Level A assessments are those with at least a bachelor's degree who have a general knowledge of the assessment process and have reviewed the testing manual and feel confident in their ability to administer the assessment (Neukrug & Fawcett, 2015)

Level B. Level B includes tests that require technical knowledge of test construction and use and appropriate advanced coursework in psychology and related courses (American Psychological Association, 1954, p. 146-148). Those qualified to administer Level B assessments are those with a master's degree who have taken a specific course in assessment and evaluation but have not received additional training on specific assessment protocol (Neukrug & Fawcett, 2015).

Level C. Level C includes tests that require an advanced degree in psychology or licensure as a psychologist and advanced training/supervised experience in the particular test (American Psychological Association, 1954, p. 146-148). To be qualified to administer a Level C assessment, one must have a minimum of a master's degree, have taken a course in assessment and evaluation, and have advanced training in the specialized assessment (ACA, 2003). According to the ACA (2003), this has been broken down even further to include:

- Skill in practice and knowledge of theory relevant to the testing context and type of counseling specialty.
- A thorough understanding of testing theory, techniques of test construction, and test reliability and validity.
- A working knowledge of sampling techniques, norms, and descriptive, correlational, and predictive statistics.
- Ability to review, select, and administer tests appropriate for clients or students and the context of the counseling practice.
- Skill in the administration of tests and interpretation of test scores.
- Knowledge of the impact of diversity on testing accuracy, including age, gender, ethnicity, race, disability, and linguistic differences.
- Knowledge and skill in the professionally responsible use of assessment and evaluation practice.

As you move on through this chapter, you will find examples of assessments at each competence level in Tables 11.1-11.5.

As you can see, there is a lot that goes into the assessment process and ensuring the well-being of our clients. As professionals, we must take this process seriously and only utilize assessments that we are competent to administer. We asked a professional in the field, Dr. Hass, about her thoughts on the importance of counselor competence when administering assessments, and she shared a few important thoughts below.

Dr. Jessica Haas
Assistant Professor, Nova Southeastern University

© Jessica Haas

Jessica Haas, LGPC, NCC, Ph.D., is a researcher, psychotherapist, and counselor educator based in Ft. Lauderdale, FL. She is an Assistant Professor in the Department of Counseling at Nova Southeastern University, where she instructs courses in testing and assessment and has extensively training in the *Neuroticism-Extroversion-Openness Personality Inventory-Revised* (NEO-PI-R). Her research focuses on understanding the effects of racism-trauma on individuals, communities, and organizations. Other areas of specialty include non-racist white identity, resilience leadership, and contemplative practices. She has shared her expertise as an invited speaker, professional guest, workshop facilitator, at refereed counseling conferences, and in scientific publications. A central focus of her work is to inspire and equip the scientific community with empirical findings to influence the social and political policies that govern American society.

Contributed by Jessica Haas. © Kendall Hunt Publishing Company.

Following the Standards for Educational and Psychological Testing, many psychological tests and materials are available for purchase only to those professionals who are competent to administer and interpret psychological tests. This is because assessment administrators assume the onus of protecting the welfare of examinees, complying with relevant laws, and maintaining competence. They also ensure performing duties with fairness, honesty, integrity, and care to avoid any testing conditions that might invalidate the results (Nitko, 2004).

The professional responsibilities for the selection, administration, interpretation, and use of psychological tests and results fall to the test administrator, or test user (AERA et al., 2014). To meet the provisions of competence, the test user must know the psychometric test, possess administrative skills, and have ethical training on the responsible use of measures. Proper selection and use of psychological tests require knowledge of descriptive statistics, measurement error, the meaning of scores, and normative interpretation of test scores. To adequately meet concerns for reliability and validity during the test administration, the test user must consider the context of reliable scores. Inferences made from estimates of reliability in one context are not interchangeable in other settings (Geisinger, 2013). Any modification of standardized procedures may introduce systematic error into the testing process. Test users must consider these unique challenges when utilizing translation services or altering assessment procedures for examinee abilities in sensory, perceptual, or motor capacity (Institute of Medicine, 2015). Test users must understand the sociocultural contexts of test takers, including the effects of ethnicity, race, gender, age, and education level on the test results (Turner et al., 2001). It is also the administrator's professional responsibility to determine "the degree to which evidence and theory support the interpretations of test scores for proposed uses of tests" (AERA et al., 2014, p 11). So, the test user must be grounded in psychological theory and use empirical evidence to show a relationship between the test and what it is measuring (Furr & Bacharach, 2013; Sireci & Sukin, 2013).

TERMS TO KNOW

Validity: The degree to which all of the accumulated evidence supports that intended interpretation of test scores for the intended purpose

Reliability: The degree to which test scores are free from errors of measurement, also, the capacity of an instrument to provide consistent results

Cross-Cultural Fairness: Degree to which cultural background, class, disability, and gender do not affect test results

Bias: Factors that cause scores on assessment instruments to be consistently higher or lower than they would be if the measurement were accurate

Practicality: Feasibility considerations in test selection and administration

Commonly Used Assessments

Now that we understand the *why* (why we use assessments) and the *how* (how we choose the most effective assessment) of assessment in the counseling profession, we must choose *which* assessment(s) will help us to better understand our clients and their individual needs. In a sense, we are using these assessments to help unlock the door to the most intimate parts of our clients' lives.

> "Ask, and it will be given to you; seek, and you will find; knock, and the door will be opened to you." (Matthew 7:7, NIV)

Counseling assessment encompasses both informal and formal procedures (Neukrug & Fawcett, 2014). Informal procedures include observations, rating scales, classification methods, records and personal documents, performance-based assessment, and environmental assessment. Formal procedures include actual testing, such as personality testing (objective tests, projective tests, and interest inventories), and ability testing, or achievement/aptitude testing (readiness, diagnostic, intellectual and cognitive functioning, cognitive ability, special aptitude, and multiple aptitudes). See Tables 11.1-11.5 for examples of both formal and informal assessments.

© frankie's/Shutterstock.com

IQ TEST   **Practical Questions**

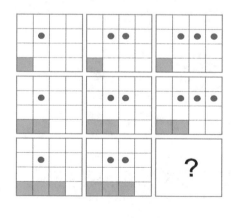

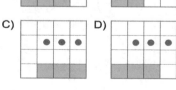

© Emir Kaan/Shutterstock.com

TABLE 11.1

Intelligence/Aptitude Tests
(Assessments used to
measure what an individual is capable of doing)

Assessment	Description	Setting	Counselor Competence
Stanford-Binet Intelligence Scale	Verbal & nonverbal intelligence -knowledge -fluid reasoning -quantitative reasoning -working memory -visual-spatial processing Ages 2-85+	Clinical School	Level C
Wechsler Scale (WAIS)	General cognitive functioning to determines disabilities/giftedness 3 Scales -Preschool/Primary Scale (ages 2-7) -Scale for Children (ages 6-16) -Adult Scale (ages 16-90)	Clinical School	Level C
Kaufman Assessment Battery for Children (KABC-II)	Cognitive ability -visual processing -short/long term memory -fluid reasoning Ages 3-18	Clinical School	Level C

Source: Hays, 2013; Aiken & Groth-Marnat, 2006; Neukrug & Fawcett, 2014

© garagestock/Shutterstock.com

TABLE 11.2

Career/Occupational
Assessments
(Tests that allow for
exploration of possible
occupations or careers)

Assessment	Description	Setting	Counselor Competence
Occupational Information Network Interest Profiler (O*NET)	Career exploration tool-6 domains -Worker: characteristics, worker requirements, worker experience -Job-Oriented: occupational requirements, workforce characteristics, occupation-specific experience Free online database https://www.onetonline.org/	Clinical School	Level A
Strong Interest Inventory (SII)	Identifies strengths/weaknesses -occupational themes -occupational scales -personal style scales -basic interest scales -response summary Ages 16+	Clinical School	Level B
COPSystem	3 Career Measurement Instruments -COPS: Career Occupational Preference System Interest Inventory Ages 7th grade-adult -CAPS: Career Ability Placement Survey Ages middle school-adult -COPES: Career Orientation Placement & Evaluation Survey Ages middle school-adult	Clinical School	Level B

Source: Aiken & Groth-Marnat, 2006; Brown, 2012; Hays, 2013; Neukrug & Fawcett, 2014; Niles & Harris-Bowlsbey, 2017

TABLE 11.3

Personality Tests
(Assessments used to
identify different personality types)
*Objective Personality
Test-Used to assess areas
of personality (paper/
pencil test)
*Projective Personality
Test-Used to interpret personality factors (response
to stimuli)

Assessment	Type	Description	Setting	Counselor Competence
Myers-Briggs Type Indicator (MBTI)	Objective Person- ality	Measures personality based on how clients make judgments and perceive the world. Includes 4 Dimensions -Extraversion/Introversion -Sensing/Intuition -Thinking/Feeling -Judging/Perceiving Ages 14+	Clinical	Level C
Minnesota Multiphasic Personality Inventory- (MMPI-A) (MMPI-2)	Objective Person- ality	Measures psychopathology and assists in the diagnosis of emotional disorders. Commonly Used Scales -Depression -Lie -Paranoia -Masculinity-Femininity -Schizophrenia -Social Introversion Adolescent version (MMPI-A) ages 14-18 Adult version (MMPI-2) ages 18+	Clinical	Level C
Beck Depres- sion Invento- ry-II (BDI-II)	Objective Person- ality	Measures severity of depression Ages 13+	Clinical School	Level B
Beck Anxiety Inventory (BAI)	Objective Person- ality	Measures severity of anxiety Ages 17+	Clinical School	Level B

TABLE 11.3

(continued)

Neuroticism-Extroversion-Openness Personality Inventory-Revised (NEO-PI-R)	Objective Personality	Measures 5 factors of personality -Openness -Conscientiousness -Extraversion -Agreeableness -Neuroticism Ages 12+	Clinical	Level C
Rorschach Inkblot Test	Projective Personality	Examines personality characteristics and emotional functioning	Clinical	Level C
Kinetic Family Drawing (KFD)	Projective Personality	Assess the perspective of children on their families	Clinical School	Level A

Source: Aiken & Groth-Marnat, 2006; Hays, 2013; Neukrug & Fawcett, 2014

Assessment	Description	Setting	Counselor Competence
Stanford Achievement Test (Stanford 10)	Assesses subject areas and academic progress in school. Type of survey battery test Grades K-12	School	Level B
Iowa Test of Basic Skills (ITBS)	Determines the basic skills needed to make progress through school. Type of survey battery test Grades K-8	School	Level B

TABLE 11.4

(continued)

Wechsler Individual Achievement Test (WIAT-III)	Screens broad areas of ability. Type of diagnostic test Grades PreK-12	School	Level B
Kindergarten Readiness Test (KRT) (Larson & Vitali)	Assesses maturity and developmental areas. -awareness/understanding/interactions in the environment -judgment and reasoning -numerical awareness -visual/fine-motor coordination -auditory attention span/concentration Type of readiness test Ages 4-6	School	Level A
SAT	Assessment of reading, writing, and math Type of cognitive ability test Undergraduate college exam	School	Level A
GRE General Test	Assesses quantitative and verbal reasoning as well as analytical writing Used to predict graduate school success Type of cognitive ability test Graduate college exam	School	Level A
Conners 3rd Edition (CRS-R)	Helps diagnosis attention-deficit/hyperactivity disorder (ADHD), Oppositional defiant disorder (ODD), Conduct disorder Completed by teacher, parent, and/or self-report Ages 6-18	School	Level B

Source: Aiken & Groth-Marnat, 2006; Hays, 2013; Neukrug & Fawcett, 2014

TERMS TO KNOW

Survey Battery Test: Paper/ pencil test measuring broad knowledge

Diagnostic Test: Test used to assess learning disabilities or learning difficulties

Readiness Test: Test used to assess readiness for kindergarten.

Cognitive Ability Test: Test used to measure what an individual is capable of doing

© Rawpixel.com/Shutterstock.com

TABLE 11.5

Informal Assessments (Assessments that are subjective in nature and developed to address a specific need or area)

Assessment	Description	Setting	Counselor Competence
Rating Scales	Assesses quantity or preferences of a characteristic or attribute. Quick/easy to develop but objective in nature. -Rank-order scales -Likert-type scales -Numerical scale	Clinical School	Level A
Checklists	Identifies if the client has or does not have specific characteristics or attributes. -Behavior checklist -Feeling checklist	Clinical School	Level A
Genograms	Picture representation of a family tree. Analyzes relationships and patterns.	Clinical	Level B
Observations	Observations conducted as a means to target specific behavior.	Clinical School	Level A

Source: Aiken & Groth-Marnat, 2006; Corcoran & Fischer, 2013; Hays, 2013; Neukrug & Fawcett, 2014

© Stephanie Hunter-Brown

Stephanie Hunter-Brown
Counselor-in-Training

As a future school counselor, I believe that these assessments are of great importance in helping the interdisciplinary team at the school to determine the best way to address the needs of students who have demonstrated difficulty in accessing the general curriculum. For example, when the MTSS and/or Child Study team convenes, a social developmental history is completed by the parents and behavioral scales may also be utilized. The Conners Comprehensive Behavior Rating Scale is used to better understand certain behavioral, social, and academic issues in children between 6 and 18 years old. It is often used to help diagnose attention deficit hyperactivity disorder, or ADHD. Finally, classroom observations of students can be conducted by the school counselor to gain more insights on the student's academic and social behaviors.

In addition to this, the WISC-IV, which measures intellectual ability of children from 6 to 16 years was developed to provide an overall measure of general cognitive ability, and also measures of intellectual functioning in Verbal Comprehension (VC), Perceptual Reasoning (PR), Working Memory (WM) and Processing Speed (PS). The scores of these assessments are used during our child study team meetings to guide us in the decision-making process. This assessment is a major component in the team's decision on whether or not a child is eligible for special education services. It also supports the team in deciding which category best fits a student's learning disability. The Woodcock Johnson IV is another assessment that might be used in order to determine the student's cognitive ability and detect any possible learning disabilities.

Through a balanced approach of a variety of assessments as well as the input of every team member, we can be assured that the student will receive the proper support to succeed not only academically, but socially and emotionally as well.

Contributed by Stephanie Hunter-Brown. © Kendall Hunt Publishing Company.

Now that you've heard from a student just like you, let's take a look at the following case example. As you read, consider how you might utilize assessments with this client.

Case Example

Samantha is a 15-year-old high school sophomore who recently saw her medical doctor due to daily headaches. Samantha's parents made a referral to your counseling office when no medical reason was found for the headaches. Samantha currently holds a 4.0 GPA; she is on the varsity cheerleading team, works at a local grocery store 8-10 hours a week, takes private singing lessons once a week, and is the vice-president of the National Honor Society where she organizes volunteer opportunities for her peers. She reports daily headaches, lack of appetite, and difficulty sleeping. Samantha indicated that she worries about her future and filling out college applications because she doesn't know what career she wants to pursue. She reports being irritable at home and breaking down if she earns anything lower than a 95% on her school work. Samantha indicated that sometimes she feels her heart race and even gets angry at her parents for no reason. Based on parental input, Samantha has always been a high achieving student who tends to seek constant validation from the adults in her life, including her parents, teachers, and coaches. Her parents reported this emotional change started about 9 months ago, mid-way through her freshman year. When asked what she would like to work on in counseling, Samantha indicated that she would like help narrowing down a college major because she doesn't even know where to start.

Case Application: Based on the information in this case, what two assessments from Tables 11.1-11.5 do you feel would be most beneficial in working with Samantha? Explain your rationale for choosing these assessments and how you plan to use them to guide your counseling sessions.

HOW DO WE SCORE AND INTERPRET ASSESSMENTS?

As discussed previously, we must consider counselor competence when it comes to administering assessments (ACA, 2014; Turner et al., 2001). This also comes into play when scoring and interpreting the results. Depending on the specific assessment, scoring and interpreting can be an extremely complex process. In order to provide you with an overview of how scoring and interpretation work, there are a few terms you must

© chase4concept/Shutterstock.com

become familiar with. First you must understand a raw score. A *raw score* is a value given before the interpretation process (Hays, 2013; Neukrug & Fawcett, 2015). For example, if you were to earn a score of 67 on a test, how have you done? Well, we can't really answer that question… yet. We have to consider some important questions. How many questions were there? What were others' scores? Are we looking for a high or low score? In order to answer these questions, we need to look at the established norms for that particular assessment. In other words, based on the assessment, what is normally predicted for a similar client or group? *Norms* allow us to compare individual scores with comparison samples (Hays, 2013; Neukrug & Fawcett, 2015). Norms are established by comparing the individual score to a similar group to ensure cross-cultural fairness. In other words, we are manipulating the raw score to create a derived score.

Let's look now at mean, median, and mode. The *mean* is the average of a set of scores, the *median* is the middle value, and the *mode* is the score that occurs most frequently (Pituch & Stevens, 2016). These terms are referred to as a measure of central tendency and tell us how close our score is to the middle of the distribution (Neukrug & Fawcett, 2015). This information is important when interpreting scores and determining where a client falls when compared to others.

As you can see, scoring and interpretation can be an intricate process which clearly supports the idea that counselor competence must be considered prior to choosing, scoring, and interpreting an assessment (ACA, 2014; Turner et al., 2001). However, no matter what the score is, it is important for us to provide feedback and clarification on results so our client does not misunderstand the meaning of the results.

HOW DOES ASSESSMENT RELATE TO THE DIAGNOSTIC PROCESS?

The idea of diagnosis and treatment in counseling comes from the medical model (Hansen, 2016). At its core, the medical model states that finding the cause or origin of a disease or condition, or clearly identifying the condition, will help with treating it. While physical conditions are the same across cultures (i.e., a broken arm looks the same and gets treated similarly in the US, Japan, or Germany), mental health issues are heavily impacted by the culture of the individual (Hansen, 2016). Additionally, mental health diagnoses are defined based on certain symptoms that cannot always be judged objectively. So you can see how mental health diagnoses present with a certain level of interpretation on the clinician's part.

© Chinnapong/Shutterstock.com

Generally, counselors agree that an important part of their role is understanding client struggles and the impact these struggles have on the client's well-being. In this process, the counselor helps clients make meaning out of their experiences and gain insight. Through this process of meaning-making, clients work with the counselor to find their way to wellness. However, when the diagnosis process is simplified to just figuring out a cluster of symptoms and the attributions connected to them, the client's process of meaning-making can be confusing and delayed (Hansen, 2016). This, in turn, can hinder the therapeutic progress for the client. Therefore a counselor's understanding of the complexity of the diagnosis process can, in itself, support client progress.

There are two specific classifications that are currently used for mental health diagnoses. The most common system used by all mental health professionals is the *Diagnostic and Statistical Manual – Fifth Edition* (DSM-5). The other system is the *The International Classification of Disease – Tenth Edition* (ICD-10). While most mental health professionals learn about diagnosing by using the DSM-5, insurance companies require practitioners to use the ICD-10 codes when they bill for reimbursement. Each of these systems record diagnoses based on diagnostic criteria such as symptoms, time frames, and impairments (Wiger, 2012). However, these diagnoses are not always clear cut, and interpretations can be very subjective in nature. There is also an issue of periodic revisions of the DSM and the drastic changes that happen during these revisions. For example, for about 50 years, individuals with a certain cluster of symptoms have received the diagnosis of Asperger's syndrome. At the last (5th) revision of the DSM in 2013, this diagnosis was eliminated and is now part of the autism spectrum disorders (ASD). People with this diagnosis received many types of supports, as it was considered a disabling condition for some individuals. What happens now for those individuals who used to carry this diagnosis? Are they no longer impacted? Do they still get their supports?

Case Study: The Case of Tony

Consider the following situation. Tony was diagnosed as a child with Asperger's syndrome. Because this condition impacted his learning and social development, Tony had an IEP (Individual Education Plan) in school with accommodations, modifications, and supports. The support provided in this plan helped him throughout his school career. However, Tony entered High School in 2013 when the DSM 5 revised this diagnosis. As a result, he had to be reevaluated and diagnosed with autism spectrum disorder in order to benefit from the protection of his IEP. While this extra evaluation was a bit of an inconvenience, what impacted Tony most was how he should identify himself. Up until 2013, Tony had very strong feelings about "being Asperger's". He and his family were very connected with a support group for "Aspies" and active in the "Aspie" community. The change in the DSM-5 impacted Tony's identity development, as the "Aspie" community struggled to understand what that meant for them and their own personal identity. A healthy orientation to a disability identity involves a significant amount of normalization (Darling, 2003). In Tony's case, it seemed that his diagnosis was "upgraded" to a disability that suggested that he was impacted a lot in certain areas with which he didn't struggle. This made "normalization" more difficult for him. At the same time, he felt marginalized by the elimination of the Asperger's syndrome diagnosis because this meant that Tony's personal struggles were not understood. For Tony and his parents, it seemed that their choices were to either have Tony lumped in with a group of individuals (autism spectrum disorder) with whom he felt he had little in common or to accept that he was neurotypical. Neither one of these *labels* applied to him. As you can see, a diagnosis label can have a very strong impact not only on treatment but on the individual's personal and emotional development.

Additionally, the diagnostic process presents with several conundrums in the mental health profession. For example, school counselors do not diagnose in their setting. However, school counselors often use assessments and testing to help formulate goals and select interventions for students. These goals are mostly connected with academic and career goals, but also with behavioral and emotional goals. Marriage and family therapists (MFT's) do not typically diagnose when they work with the family system because that would imply that one of the family members bears the sole responsibility for the family issues (i.e., dad has major depressive disorder, and that's why everyone needs family therapy). For an MFT, the whole family system is the client, and the goals are directed to the entire system as a whole. These systemic goals often clash with the individualized perspective that diagnoses take in the DSM-5 (Wilcoxon, Remley, & Gladding, 2013). Licensed professional counselors typically utilize the diagnostic process; however, in many cases, it is only for insurance reimbursement purposes. This can also present some ethical conundrums (Welfel, 2016). We will discuss these in detail in the Ethics Section at the end of the chapter.

Diagnosis, Psychopathology, and the Christian Counselor

As Christian counselors, when we consider psychopathology and diagnosis, we also need to consider the origin of mental health issues. Are mental health issues part of the "sin problem" as defined by Christian theology, or is there more to it? Can mental health issues be viewed outside spirituality? How do we integrate spirituality when we discuss diagnosis in mental health? These questions can be difficult to answer for many Christian counselors.

© fizkes/Shutterstock.com

Historically, the Christian church has viewed some mental health pathologies as belonging in the spiritual realm. Many of the primary pastoral figures attributed mental health issues to some sort of spiritual conflict. While mental health professions have gradually included spirituality and religion as part of the general human experience and as significant in promoting mental health well-being, it is not always easy to integrate a spiritual worldview in counseling (McRay, Yarhouse, & Butman, 2016).

We already know that healthy spirituality and religion have a positive impact on one's mental health (Diener, Tay, & Myers, 2011; Plante, 2014). But there is also ample evidence to suggest that certain spiritual and religious beliefs can have a negative impact on mental health (Magyar-Russel & Griffith, 2016; Vieten & Scammell, 2015). Additionally, psychology and counseling, in general, have recorded religious views on normal and abnormal behavior from a negative perspective (McRay et al., 2016). While historically, pastoral writers have attributed certain aspects of psychopathology to demonic forces as the origin of pathological behavior, today most Christian counselors distinguish between mental health illness and sin or spiritual influences. The arrival of the field of mental health starting with Freud appeared to shift even Christians from seeing behaviors as *sin* to seeing behaviors from either a mental health perspective or a criminal perspective (McRay et al., 2016). Christian counselors also have the added burden of being concerned with how the field looks with regards to their professional stance – not wanting to be identified as biased, unscientific, or complete "quacks".

© Jarretera/Shutterstock.com

However, Christian counselors need to make sense of their personal worldview and its integration within the counseling profession (Thomas & Sosin, 2011). We are urged to not allow our worldview to color the way we see our clients, but how can we set aside (or *bracket*) our views if we have not given any thought to how diagnosis and psychopathology integrate within our personal worldview? Each of us individually have to take that journey toward integrating our personal and professional views and sorting out our values as they relate to mental health issues. Of course, as counselors, we should always consider the client's worldview and attempt to connect with the client even when they don't share our beliefs. Although this can present challenges, all counselors need to understand their own beliefs and strive to not impose them on their clients (Welfel, 2016). We present some general principles in this chapter, however, your task throughout this program is to reflect on your own religious and spiritual worldview, and integrate them into a harmonious context within your professional orientation as a counselor.

Recall that earlier in the chapter, we discussed that one of the most important roles of the counselor is to help clients make meaning out of their struggles. Meaning-making in the context of spirituality and religion impacts both the counselor and the client. Johnson (1987) suggests an important distinction between psychopathology and sin. He argues that there is a difference between *sin* (living independent of God, or in disobedience to God) and *weakness* (living within less than ideal parameters, but without committing moral offenses). God looks at sin with judgment (Romans 2:12-15), but at weakness with compassion (Romans 8:26). From this perspective, the Christian counselor needs to distinguish between consequences of moral choices and individual weaknesses that are determined by socio-economic factors or physiological factors. This distinction should happen without forgetting that there is often an interplay between responsibility for choices and weaknesses within one's environmental context.

McRay and colleagues (2016) recommend that Christian counselors ask themselves the following question: "In what ways does sin affect mental health and well-being?" (p. 85). Other good questions to ask ourselves include, "What is God's view/position/role in remedying issues of mental health?" and "How does salvation impact one's remedy of mental health issues?" The answer to the initial question is that of course, sin affects mental health in many different ways. Regardless of whether a person meets criteria for a specific diagnosis, many people commonly struggle with having meaningful, nurturing relationships and managing anger, or feelings of hopelessness and anxiety. The answer to the other questions is that we as Christians believe that God is directly involved in restoring mankind through salvation, and He does that by influencing our client's stories and circumstances. The mere fact that a client is now with a Christian counselor (whether they explicitly sought them out or not) is proof enough that God is interested in this client's well-being and is providing the best opportunities for them to grow and change. Finally, God's work of salvation also involves restoration and renewal of the mind (Romans 12:2, NIV). In the New Testament, the Greek word for "salvation" (σώζω - pronounced "sōzō") is also translated with "healing", or "being made

whole" (Mark 5:34; 6:56; Romans 8:24, NKJV). Part of becoming saved also includes physical and emotional healing. Counselors work towards supporting clients to find their own way to wellness, renewal, and healing, which comes from the therapeutic relationship.

> "But I will restore you to health and heal your wounds, declares the Lord." (Jeremiah 30:17, NIV)

Christians also believe that people are responsible for their own actions and that we all have choices. These are also basic tenets of the changes promoted in counseling. When considering the origins of psychopathology and the impact of sin, we should also pay attention to our view of human nature. Christians believe that humans are created for relationships with God and fellow humans. Our own wishes, desires, and longings can better be explained through a Christian perspective (McRay et al., 2016). In this context, helping clients integrate their spiritual values with the counseling techniques we present will strengthen clients' motivation to change. As a matter of fact, several counseling theories have as basic premises individual choice and restoring relationships. Choice theory/reality therapy and cognitive behavior therapy are two examples of counseling orientations that utilize these principles on a regular basis.

As far as viewing diagnosis from a Christian perspective, we can look at mental health conditions, not as expressions of sin, but as the consequences of sin (McRay et al., 2016). When we understand that mental health issues have their origin in a combination of sources and are the result of generational sin, societal sin, individual sin, and the impact that sin has on our physical nature, we can formulate a complex understanding of the origin of client issues. Moreover, our views on this matter will also shape the way we treat our clients and support restoration, healing, and justice (see Isaiah 58:6-12).

Jewish tradition embraces a similar view of spirituality and restoration from the Tikkun Olam perspective (Schlosser, Foley, Stein, & Holmwood, 2010). This perspective (Hebrew for "heal" or "repair" the world) emphasizes the restorative and collaborative role of counseling and spirituality in a client's life. While this particular expression is found in the Jewish tradition, Christians embrace a similar stance of taking responsibility for the well-being of their neighbor (Mark 12:31). It is perhaps no coincidence that a large number of professionals who shaped the field of counseling and psychology have predominantly Jewish and Christian roots (Schlosser et al., 2010).

Dr. Gregory Elliott
Assistant Professor, Colorado Christian University

Dr. Gregg Elliott has been a Licensed Professional Counselor since 2003 and has been licensed in the State of Colorado since 2006. He has a Ph.D. in Counselor Education and Supervision from Adams State University and is an Assistant Professor at Colorado Christian University's Master of Arts in Counseling program. Dr. Elliott practices part-time in a Denver-area inpatient hospital, and his clinical expertise and research interests are in working with suicidal clients and in training mental health clinicians to work with suicidal clients. Dr. Elliott is the president-elect of the Colorado Counseling Association (2019-2020), the third largest state association of the American Counseling Association. He has served as the President of the Collegiate Career Services Association of Colorado and Wyoming (CCSA) from 2008 - 2009 and was a Rocky Mountain Association for Counselor Education and Supervision (RMACES) Emerging Leaders award winner in 2016. He is a member of the American Counseling Association (ACA), the Colorado Counseling Association (CCA), the Association for Counselor Education and Supervision (ACES), RMACES, Chi Sigma Iota (CSI), and the American Association of Suicidology (AAS). Dr. Elliott has recent publications on the topics of the development of self-efficacy to work with suicidal clients and the impact of program modality on counseling student CPCE subscale scores.

As a licensed professional counselor, I operate with a holistic view of people and wellness and recognize that we all have physical, social, emotional, spiritual, intellectual, and occupational components to our being. One of the philosophical and educational perspectives that set licensed professional counselors apart from the other mental health professions is the incorporation of the wellness model where the therapeutic goal is for each client to achieve positive health in each of these areas to the degree possible (Remley & Herlihy, 2016). Similarly, we are strengths-

based and we incorporate a developmental perspective. To best conceptualize and assist our clients, we have to acknowledge and consider our clients' functioning in each of these areas, the interaction between levels of wellness in each area on the other areas, and what strengths the client possesses that can be encouraged and fortified. The American Counseling Association (ACA), Council for the Accreditation of Counseling and Related Educational Programs (CACREP), and the Association of Spiritual, Ethical, and Religious Values in Counseling (ASERVIC) all recognize that counselors must be able to assess and meet clients' spiritual and religious needs (Schweiger, Muse-Burke, & Sallavanti, 2017).

From a Christian perspective, scripture tells us that "We are his workmanship, created in Christ Jesus for good works, which God prepared beforehand, that we should walk in them" (Ephesians 2:10, ESV). Matthew 9:35-37 illustrates Jesus' response to the oppressed and hurting when it tells us that "Jesus went throughout all the cities and villages, teaching in their synagogues and proclaiming the gospel of the kingdom and healing every disease and every affliction. When he saw the crowds, he had compassion for them, because they were harassed and helpless, like sheep without a shepherd" (ESV). As followers of Christ who are counselors, we are similarly called to go out amongst God's creation with compassion and participate in God's mission of healing and restoration. God doesn't make mistakes, but God does allow challenges and obstacles in our lives in order to shape us; "Behold, I have refined you, but not as silver; I have tried you in the furnace of affliction. For my own sake, for my own sake, I do it" (Isaiah 48:10, ESV), and Proverbs 27:17, "Iron sharpens iron, and one man sharpens another" (ESV).

Diagnosis and psychopathology is one of the areas of clinical mental health in which we participate in order to communicate with other mental health professionals and to allow clients to have our services paid for by third-party payors. However, diagnosis is rarely a cut-and-dry process (Yalom, 2002) that can accurately be accomplished in a single intake session. The DSM-5 itself has been often criticized for its circular reasoning and stringent adherence to the disease model, and diagnoses often are misunderstood and misapplied by our clients to their detriment. Some mental health disorders appear to be biological in nature, while others with identical symptoms have their etiology in trauma. To operate in today's mental health professions, clinical mental health counselors do need to be able to recognize symptoms, diagnose per the DSM-5, develop a treatment plan, and document treatment accordingly. But we also do well to remember our roots in holism and the wellness model and that sometimes the best treatment comes from empathy and unconditional positive regard and not from a plastic pill bottle.

Contributed by Gregory Elliot. © Kendall Hunt Publishing Company.

The Importance of Diagnosis

As you can see, your background and your counseling specialty can influence the way you view the diagnosis process. While there are many voices that speak against the medical model of diagnosis (Hansen, 2016), it is important to note that counselors of all specialties need to have at least a basic understanding of diagnosis (see Dr. Elliott's statements in the previous Spotlight). Understanding diagnosis gives all mental health professionals a common framework when communicating within their field and with those in related professions. For counselors who work with insurance companies, understanding diagnosis has bearing in the reimbursement process. Some practitioners feel strongly against diagnosis, and believe that they will always be in private practice, only accepting private pay, and therefore they won't diagnose. While that is certainly a possibility, remember that counseling is a profession focused on service. Accepting insurance makes your services available to a larger segment of the population who might not be able to access mental health services otherwise.

Beyond applying a diagnostic label, the diagnosis process should generally be about meaning making (Hansen, 2016). As counselors, our job is to help clients make meaning out of their suffering and gain insight into what would alleviate it. Diagnosing strictly from a medical model paradigm might misattribute one's symptoms and prevent the client from making

meaning out of their life circumstances. Paradoxically, the more you get to know someone, the harder it is to diagnose them (Yalom, 2002). Think of your own personal struggles. Since you know yourself best, how would you diagnose yourself? When taking a Psychopathology course, many counseling students feel like they have at least half a dozen of the disorders described in the textbook. This emphasizes the fact that when you get to know someone better, it is difficult to put on a single label that describes them. Instead of trying to diagnose yourself, it would be more helpful to you to identify what your struggles are, understand where your struggles come from, what they mean for you, and how you can make changes in your life to alleviate these struggles. This process can be facilitated really well through a counseling relationship.

HOW DOES ASSESSMENT RELATE TO TREATMENT PLANNING?

As mentioned before, most counselors agree that the main purpose of a counseling relationship is to help clients make meaning out of their suffering and their life circumstances (Hansen, 2016). However, many counselors also find that the purpose of treatment is to alleviate symptoms that are disruptive and negatively impact one's life. Furthermore, it's important for counselors to differentiate when medication should be involved. Even critics of the medical model acknowledge the fact that certain mental health issues have their roots in neurobiological problems and thus need to be addressed with medication (Hansen, 2016). Such diagnoses would include schizophrenia, severe bipolar disorder, or debilitating major depression. While counselors are not prescribers and often believe that medication is a last resort, there is enough research to support the idea that many mental health issues are best treated with both counseling and medication (Cuijpers, Reynolds, Donker, Anderson, & Beeman, 2012). Understanding the intricacies of diagnosis can help counselors support their clients through the process of deciding the best course for their treatment.

© dizain/Shutterstock.com

As mentioned previously, treatment planning can look differently depending on your specialty. While school counselors never assign a diagnosis, and marriage and family therapists hardly ever do so, all counselors should establish treatment goals with their students or clients. Based on theoretical orientations, there are several ways to look at establishing goals, however we will focus on some basic principles to follow.

First, you and your client need to have a general understanding of how you will know the counseling is working, and how you will know when you are done. Developing a treatment plan will provide clarity of purpose, clear communication, accountability, and even compensation for the provider (Wiger, 2012). All mental health practitioners should identify a problem and establish therapeutic goals, including those practitioners who are reluctant to rely on the diagnosis. Secondly, even when using diagnosis solely for reimbursement purposes, treatment planning should go beyond diagnosis, symptoms, and impairments (Wiger, 2012). It needs to focus on the client's strengths, limitations, personal resources, and their level of functioning. A good way to think about these areas is to use the acronym SNAPs: strengths, needs, abilities, and preferences (Wiger, 2012). Finally, when agreeing on treatment goals, it is very important that these goals be established in collaboration with the client and reviewed periodically. Goals should be measurable and realistic for the client's situation. Here is how this may look for different counselors:

Let's take the case of a 12-year-old girl with Generalized Anxiety Disorder (F41.1 in ICD-10 and 300.02 in the DSM-5). Her symptoms include excessive worry about bad things that might happen at night, so she has difficulty going to sleep. She sometimes worries about her parents getting sick or losing their jobs. At school, she has trouble starting and completing school work because she worries that she can't do a good enough job. In working individually with this child, a licensed professional counselor may choose as a goal to enhance her ability to effectively cope with a full variety of life's anxieties (Jongsma, Peterson, McInnis, & Bruce, 2014). She is in 6th grade, and her anxiety is also impacting school work. She either cannot start on an assignment until she figured every possible angle, or she never finishes classroom work on time. A school counselor may choose to set a goal of "Consistently completing daily assignments". The school counselor will then work with her classroom teachers to support this goal, and help the student learn some good strategies of alleviating anxiety and staying on task. Let's also assume that her anxiety is impacting the entire family because she has difficulty going to sleep at night. A family therapist may focus on the family conflict that is the potential source of anxiety, and work with the entire family towards this goal. Perhaps during the course of treatment, the marriage and family therapist will notice that the girl's parents tend to be angry with each other and fight at dinner time, creating an environment in which it is difficult for her to relax. As you can see, your professional specialty can impact the way you establish counseling goals.

© iQoncept/Shutterstock.com

Concepts to Consider Regarding the Case

As mentioned before, counselors should help their clients make meaning out of their circumstances. The client identified above, and her family would have a difficult time making changes unless they attempt to give some meaning to these struggles. Given the details above, what do you think is the meaning of this girl's anxiety? What does it mean for her and for her family? Jot down a few thoughts about how you might help her and her family find meaning through this struggle. Consider looking at this from the three counseling specialties mentioned above (professional counselor, school counselor, or marriage and family therapist).

Developing Goals and Objectives in Counseling

While goals are the desired outcomes of counseling to improve functional impairment, objectives are the incremental steps that lead to achieving these goals (Wiger, 2012). For example, in the case above, the licensed professional counselor will probably have an objective to help the child verbalize how thoughts, feelings, and behaviors contribute to anxiety and its treatment (Jongsma et al., 2014). Alternatively, the school counselor may involve accommodations that are set in place by the teacher, such as giving the student a quiet place to work and allowing for extra time to finish assignments. The school counselor could also provide her with some breathing techniques that will allow the student to lower her heart rate and focus on the assignments at hand. The family therapist might work with the family to identify that the frequent conflict between parents, and between parents and the older sibling (who is "in trouble" all the time) is impacting this child's ability to handle her anxiety. In this case, the objective would be to provide the family with conflict resolution techniques that will be conducive to a more peaceful home environment.

Using Assessment to Track Treatment Progress

According to Wiger (2012, p. 121), an effective treatment plan will answer the following questions: "Why am I in therapy/counseling? What will we talk about and do? How do I know how well therapy/counseling is working? How will we know when therapy/counseling should terminate?" To answer these questions, the counselor will need to use various types of assessments. These can be formal or informal. Informal measures can be as simple as checking in with the client on a regular basis on how the process of therapy is working for them (Yalom, 2002). As far as progressing towards the termination of treatment, some counselors find the following informal principles helpful: when the therapeutic goals are met when the client distress is very much diminished, and when the client seems not to have a lot to talk about in a session and appears somewhat disengaged. It's important to note that these three aspects work together, and we must never use one single aspect of the three mentioned above as a sole indicator for termination.

Using formal assessment at the beginning of therapy to establish a diagnosis or identify a problem helps with the focus of treatment and establishing goals. Progress can also be measured formally throughout treatment. One example of effective formal measurements for progress in counseling was developed by Scott Miller (2012): *The Outcome Rating Scale* (ORS) and *The Session Rating Scale* (SRS). These scales help practitioners gage the progress of the client towards their goals in general, and also how they feel about each session after they attend. There are several formats and versions for these scales and they can be used by both children and adults, in a clinical setting or a school setting. Having a way to assess progress in treatment on a regular and consistent basis will help both the client and the counselor ensure that the goals are being reached. It will also give an indication of whether they need to be changed.

Writing an Individual Case Report

Once all of the assessment information has been gathered, it is time to write the individual case report. Often, reports will include some or all of the information below (Thomas & Sosin, 2011; Neukrug & Fawcett, 2015).

1. **Demographic/Identifying Information:** This may include; first and last name, address, phone number, email address, age and date of birth, sex, and ethnicity.
2. **Presenting Problem/Reason for Referral:** Typically the referral source is given and a description as to why the individual is seeking counseling.
3. **Family Background:** This section may include significant information related to the client's family dynamics and upbringing as well as current marital status and children.
4. **Religious Background/Affiliation:** An evaluation of past and present religious experiences is included, as well as how they influence daily living, values, and impact decision-making. Does the client have a personal relationship with God?
5. **Counseling and/or Medical History:** Physical as well as mental health issues will be documented in this section. Medications will be listed here as well as anything impacting the client's current mental state.
6. **Substance Use:** This may include the use or abuse of any legal or illegal substances. This is not limited to alcohol or drugs but also included food, prescription medication, and/or cigarettes.
7. **Educational History:** Educational/vocational information, including the level of education, career paths, and overall job satisfaction, is included in this section.
8. **Mental Status Exam**

This is an assessment of the client's appearance, behavior, emotional state, thoughts, and cognitive function.

1. **Strengths and Weaknesses:** This section is based specifically on the client's perception. What do they see as their strengths and weaknesses?

2. **Assessment Results:** This section includes not only raw scores but also standardized scores which help make meaning out of the data. It is important for this section to be objective and to include results so they can be understood by others outside the counseling profession (clients, parents, teachers).

3. **Diagnosis:** As previously discussed a diagnosis is based on client's symptoms and is obtained from the DSM-5 (Diagnostic and Statistical Manual – 5th Edition) or the ICD-10 (The International Classification of Disease – 10th edition).

4. **Case Formulation/Summary:** In this section, you will include a summary of the case. This is your opportunity to cover the main details in a succinct manner while also including but defending any inferences that are made.

5. **Treatment Recommendations:** This section will come after you have analyzed and synthesized all of the above information. The recommendations should be appropriate, logical, and relate to the individual needs of your client.

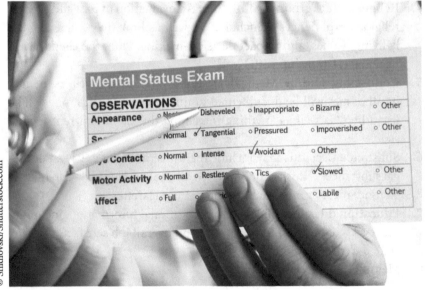

As you finalize the written report, including all areas mentioned previously, remember that each client you come in contact with is created in the image of God. Your clients are all part of God's unique design. Therefore, they deserve to have an individualized approach to the counseling process, free from judgement and protected by sanctity of life as well as the professional organizations that provide guidelines to protect the well-being of our clients.

> "For you created my inmost being; you knit me together in my mother's womb. I praise you because I am fearfully and wonderfully made; your works are wonderful, I know that full well."
> (Psalm 139:13-14, NIV)

WHAT ARE THE LEGAL, ETHICAL, AND PROFESSIONAL ISSUES IN DIAGNOSIS AND TESTING?

Clinicians exercise one of their most influential activities when engaging in the diagnostic process (Behnke, 2004). Receiving a diagnostic label can impact clients in powerful ways; from influencing self-esteem and personal relationships to career choices; increasing opportunities for advancement, as well as financial well-being. Certain diagnoses will impact an individual's freedom and choices (such as being able to drive, purchase a firearm, or even obtain medical or life insurance). This is very important to remember because as we have discussed before, the process of utilizing assessment for diagnosis purposes can be very subjective (Welfel, 2016).

© Zurainy Zain/Shutterstock.com

Case Study: The Case of Cora

Let's take the case of Cora. She is an enlisted soldier in the US Air Force. When she was last deployed, she was sexually assaulted by another soldier.

As you may imagine, her mental health was negatively impacted, and she developed symptoms of trauma and anxiety. After she reported the incident, the soldier who attacked her told their superiors that she was planning to vindictively destroy his career by making false accusations about him. As a result, Cora was met with suspicion and distrust. This exacerbated Cora's mental health symptoms, and she started to behave somewhat erratically and became defensive at work. She exhibited several symptoms that are categorized under the Post-traumatic Stress Disorder (PTSD) such as recurrent, intrusive, and distressing memories of the traumatic event, avoidance of distressing memories, persistent and exaggerated negative beliefs about self, irritable behavior and angry outbursts, hypervigilance, and sleep disturbance (APA, 2013). She was ordered to undergo a psychological evaluation. Among other tests, she was administered the MMPI-II and the MCMI-IV (mentioned earlier in the chapter). Based on the test results, and also on the narrative from her commanding officers, she was diagnosed with a personality disorder. Even though these tests are normed to identify PTSD and personality disorders, the MMPI-II did not show any pathology. The MCMI-IV showed slight elevations on two subscales that measure personality disorders. There is ample evidence that PTSD can have common symptoms with personality disorders (Cloitre, Garvert, Weiss, Carlson, & Bryant, 2014). However, Cora was diagnosed with a personality disorder and not PTSD. Now Cora is scheduled for an administrative separation from the military since they have strict policies against employing individuals with personality disorders. Given the history of her sexual assault, it's a lot more likely that her diagnosis is PTSD. However, because of the narratives from her commander, and the slightly elevated scores on a personality test, the suspicion of a personality disorder is going to end her career in the military. Moreover, in conjunction with dealing with a difficult work situation, Cora now struggles to understand what it means to have a personality disorder and how that impacts who she is as an individual, and her relationships with her loved ones.

Using Assessment in Differential Diagnosis

As you can see, the diagnosis of a personality disorder, in this case, is very likely misapplied. The series of situations Cora was exposed to (sexual assault while deployed, followed by the accusations from the perpetrator, and the distrust experienced in her unit) just prior to her mental health evaluation was enough to prevent her from responding truthfully to the

© Rawpixel.com/Shutterstock.com

assessments given to her. There is well-documented evidence that inter-personal/behavioral difficulties that had onset only prior to, or were greatly exacerbated by exposure to traumatic events can look very much like a personality disorder (PD; Cloitre et al., 2014). Cora not only has no prior self-reported or documented history of PD-like symptoms, but she also meets an overwhelming number of criteria for the PTSD diagnosis.

As mentioned before, she was administered two personality tests. The MMPI-II that should have shown personality disorder traits did not display anything clinically significant. Furthermore, the two elevated scales on the MCMI-IV that were called in support of an Unspecified Personality Disorder, while somewhat elevated, were not anywhere near the personality disorder range. Additionally, a PD is, by definition, expected to be persistent. The fact that she did not display these symptoms prior to her first sexual assault, and the consistent improvement that she showed over several months of treatment (excellent work performance, improved social/emotional functioning, receptivity to feedback) are inconsistent with a PD diagnosis and are further evidence that this diagnosis is inaccurate.

This particular case study is also a good example of the need to establish differential diagnosis criteria. Many symptoms look alike in the DSM-5 (or ICD-10), and practitioners need to be well-versed in the understanding of the symptoms, including similarities and differences between different disorders. In the case described, the differential diagnosis process was not followed adequately. The impact for Cora was negative, with permanent consequences for her career and personal life.

Over the years, concerns have been voiced about the imperfections of the diagnostic process in the mental health field (Hansen, 2016; Yalom, 2002). More recently, with the new ICD-10 and the DSM 5 revisions, many professionals and even the public at large have started to understand that diagnosis in the mental health field is far from precise and all-encompassing (like it can be in the medical field). There are several factors that can influence the diagnosis process. One factor relates to how clients pay for services. When insurance reimbursement is involved, practitioners tend to assign diagnosis more readily than when clients pay for services out of pocket (Kielbasa, Pomerantz, Krohn, & Sullivan, 2004; Lowe, Pomerantz, & Pettibone, 2007). There are also instances of mental health professionals favoring diagnostic procedures, even when the diagnosis is not justified (Welfel, 2016). Societal stigmas attached to diagnosis can be a concern, as well as the invasion of privacy that is involved in the process of diagnosis. Furthermore, many clients struggle to understand what the diagnosis means for them. As you may have noticed in the case study, clients often internalize the meaning of their diagnosis and how they view themselves as a person.

© Lightspring/Shutterstock.com

A pitfall that is difficult to avoid by many mental health professionals is the casual diagnosis. You may have noticed that in light of certain developments with public figures, some mental health professionals use diagnostic language about people with whom they don't have a professional relationship (politicians, criminals, people on the news) – giving a false impression that the diagnostic process is simple, magical, or dehumanizing (Welfel, 2016). As Christian practitioners, we should heed the biblical advice for such situations: "Do not let any unwholesome talk come out of your mouths, but only what is helpful for building others up according to their needs, that it may benefit those who listen" (Ephesians 4:29, NIV). Casual diagnosis is unethical and damaging to our professional reputation.

Applying Ethics in Testing and Assessment

Testing and assessment have its own set of ethical considerations. The use of testing continues to grow, and modern technologies make it easier to administer and score. However, there are several ethical considerations to keep in mind. As we mentioned before, in the diagnosis section, testing is an invasion of privacy. In Cora's case, there seems to be too much reliance on test scores for decision making, without enough consideration of an individual's background and history. Additionally, as you noticed earlier in the chapter, tests can be biased and even discriminating against certain cultural groups. Finally, the self-incriminating nature of testing can leave individuals exposed to serious personal and professional consequences without the right to rebuttal (Welfel, 2016). In Cora's case, the interpretation of personality tests and subsequent diagnosis had devastating consequences. If Cora were evaluated through a clinical interview, and given a proper perspective of her test scores, she would have more likely been diagnosed with PTSD and not a personality disorder. Even if PTSD led to her being dismissed from the military, she would have qualified for financial benefits, such as disability benefits and healthcare insurance.

© bearsky23/Shutterstock.com

© smolaw/Shutterstock.com

In the educational realm, there are several conflicting messages when it comes to testing. There is a level of contention about intelligence tests not measuring the right constructs, as intelligence is a very complex concept. Because of the lack of consistency between grading systems across the nation, some argue that one cannot rely on grades or diplomas, but competencies should be demonstrated through a formal test. Others argue that multiple-choice tests should be replaced with actual performance assessments. And finally, as you may have heard before, high-stakes testing puts too much pressure on students, teachers, and parents, and it can be detrimental to learning in general.

According to Welfel (2016), three categories of persons are involved in test taking: the test developer, the test user, and the test taker. When preparing assessment instruments, test developers are supposed to abide by two fundamental ethical principles. First, tests should have sufficient evidence to support their validity and reliability, appropriate test norms, and come with an updated, comprehensive test manual. The second ethical principle is to prioritize the welfare of the consumer above the profit (Welfel, 2016). Tests should have clear directions, describe strengths and weaknesses, as well as diversity information pertaining to groups of diverse racial, ethnic, and linguistic backgrounds.

Test users (counselors and other mental health professionals) need to remember that their main ethical obligation is to the test takers. They also have ethical obligations towards the test developers. Tests are typically copyrighted, and part of the validity of the test includes the test taker's lack of familiarity with the test. As such, test users should protect this assumption by keeping tests secure and not copying or disseminating tests indiscriminately. Sending a test home with a client is inappropriate. As you might imagine, once the tests have left our possession, there is no telling how the client may use them. While we may ask clients to fill them out themselves, we don't know who actually completes the tests once they leave our office.

Currently, the legal information on test security and client rights is conflicting. The *HIPAA Privacy Rule* (HIPAA Rule, U.S. DHHS, 1996) requires that clients be allowed to have access to their treatment records, including test results. However, copyright issues would conflict with clients viewing actual test items. The *ACA Code of Ethics* attempts to clarify the issue by saying that clients can have access to all data about their performance, but cannot access test materials that belong to the publisher of the test (ACA, 2014, Standard 9.07).

Counselors who use copyrighted tests and assessments need to abide by ethical and legal standards. Just for clarification purposes, it is illegal and unethical to use test items from an existing instrument or adapt them for the counselor's use. Practitioners are encouraged to purchase existing tests or go through the appropriate procedures to develop their own (Welfel, 2016).

As mentioned earlier in the chapter, test users (professional counselors and other mental health professionals) need to possess certain qualifications in order to administer and interpret tests. Recall the categorizations of tests (Levels A, B, or C) described earlier in the chapter. Most professional counselors meet the criteria for levels A and B tests. Here are some general requirements that are necessary for developing adequate competencies in administering and interpreting tests (Welfel, 2016):

- Coursework in statistics and measurement that will help the user understand basic concepts, such as reliability, validity, norms, and data provided by test publishers.
- Coursework in assessments and measurements, including the use of test manuals and review of research
- Training for understanding specific tests, including strengths, limitations, and application for diverse populations
- Supervision in administering and interpreting specific tests.

As Christian counselors, abiding by ethical and legal principles goes beyond our professional obligations. Justice and honesty are biblical principles that should always be followed. Furthermore, when using assessment and diagnosis, we need to remember the incredible responsibility given to us because of the power and authority our profession gives us. Leviticus 19:15 admonishes us to "judge our neighbor fairly". This doesn't only apply

© Gustavo Frazao/Shutterstock.com

to the courtroom, but also the therapy office when we evaluate and diagnose. Moreover, we are admonished to not judge at all (Matthew 7:1). This is an important application for us as counselors. We need to lead with empathy and unconditional positive regard, not with judgment. While it's important to learn about our clients, we need to refrain from judging them unfairly and harshly. The Bible tells us that even the "Father doesn't judge, but gave the judgment to the Son" (John 5:22). Why would the Father appoint the Son as judge? Because the Son has compassion on us, having lived as one of us (Hebrews 4:15). As counselors, we need to learn from the Son and ensure that our assessment of our clients is infused with compassion and care. We know very well what it is like to struggle with many things that our clients go through. Our compassion and unconditional positive regard are the most effective tools we have to support their personal growth. Should you have additional ethical issues or concerns, please see Table 11.6 below for a list of resources.

TABLE 11.6

Counseling & Assessment Resources for Ethical Practice

American Association of Christian Counselors (2014). Christian Counseling Code of Ethics. https://www.aacc.net/code-of-ethics-2/
Association for Assessment and Research in Counseling http://aarc-counseling.org/
American Counseling Association (2014). *ACA Code of Ethics.* Alexandria, VA https://www.counseling.org/
Association for Spiritual, Ethical, and Religious Values in Counseling (ASERVIC). http://www.aservic.org/
American Psychological Association (2017). Ethical Principles of Psychologists and Code of Conduct. Washington, DC https://www.apa.org/
American School Counselor Association (2016). ASCA Ethical Standards for School Counselors. Alexandria, VA https://www.schoolcounselor.org/
American Association of Marriage and Family Therapy (2017) AAMFT Code of Ethics https://www.aamft.org/Legal_Ethics/Code_of_Ethics.aspx

SUMMARY

This chapter introduced two important components of the counseling process: assessment and diagnosis. Both serve as a guide to help ensure that individual client needs are being met while also creating a collaborative relationship between client and counselor.

FOR THE ROAD AHEAD

Check out the Chapter 11 video at this link:
https://www.khpcontent.com/

We started the chapter by looking specifically at the historical timeline of assessments and the impact the past has had on the current assessment and diagnostic process. The chapter then offered a brief introduction to test worthiness and what makes for an appropriate and effective assessment. A variety of assessment types were included (Intelligence/Aptitude, Career/Occupational, Personality, Educational Ability, and informal assessments) as well as examples of each. Emphasis was placed on gathering information from trustworthy assessments, which helps not only the client but the counselor as well. This information creates a picture of client strengths and weaknesses as well as attitudes, values, thinking patterns, and beliefs. All these elements can then be used to determine a diagnosis and develop a treatment plan to facilitate change.

We also discussed the diagnostic process and how a diagnosis can help the client make meaning out of life challenges, while also fostering insight into ways in which to make healthy and appropriate changes. The diagnostic process was examined through a Christian perspective while also taking into consideration the clients' worldviews.

Finally, a brief overview of the report writing process was included, as well as ethical considerations. We focused on the importance of adhering to the ethical standards used to guide the counseling profession with a specific focus on the *ACA Code of Ethics,* Section E (2014).

Reflections on the Journey

- After reading and exploring this chapter; in your own words, define assessment as it relates to the counseling profession.
- What are three ways you can ensure that you are meeting the ethical standards set forth in the ACA Code of Ethics (2014) regarding assessment in counseling?

- Identify the possible pros and cons of using assessments in the counseling process? Be able to support your answer using the ACA Code of Ethics.
- What are the benefits of administering assessments during the counseling process?
- Brainstorm creative ways you might include your client in the assessment selection process.
- Why should counselors consider client diversity when choosing an assessment?

For Further Exploration

Website for the Association for Assessment and Research in Counseling (a subdivision of ACA): https://www.counseling.org/about-us/governance-bylaws/candidate-profiles/divisions-and-regions/association-for-assessment-and-research-in-counseling . Students can explore the website.

Brief article about how school counselors use data in order to conduct a needs assessment for a school counseling program: https://www.school-counselor.org/newsletters/october-2018/upgrading-your-needs-assessment?st=NJ

Podcast on psychological assessment by a psychologist: https://podcasts.apple.com/us/podcast/ttp-68-dr-alex-beaujean-what-are-we-actually-measuring/id1200313948?i=1000420433808

Presentation on the clinical interview: https://www.youtube.com/watch?v=NBtwOnB4HYw

List of movies that depict certain mental health disorders:

Grand Torino - depression, alcoholism, social isolation, cultural issues.

The Fisher King - Red Knight - PTSD/trauma symptoms in a homeless man https://youtu.be/MtqyPFhubVs

As Good As It Gets - Obsessive-compulsive disorder. https://youtu.be/oAK0FmZbsu8

Girl, Interrupted - Antisocial Personality Disorder. https://youtu.be/JT7ItsxgcMw

Good Will Hunting – Attachment Disorder.

Thank You for Your Service – PTSD, working with the military population, suicide.

REFERENCES

AERA (American Educational Research Association), APA (American Psychological Association), and NCME (National Council on Measurement in Education). Standards for educational and psychological testing. Washington, DC: AERA; 2014.

Aiken, L. R. & Groth-Marnat, G. (2006). *Psychological testing and assessment* (12th ed.). Boston, MA: Pearson.

American Counseling Association (2014). *ACA Code of Ethics.* Alexandria, VA: Author

American Counseling Association (2003). Standards for qualifications of test users. Alexandria, VA: Author. Retrieved from http://aarc-counseling.org/resources

American School Counselor Association (2016). ASCA Ethical standards for school counselors. Alexandria, VA: Author. Retrieved from https://www.schoolcounselor.org/asca/media/asca/Ethics/EthicalStandards2016.pdf

American Psychiatric Association. (2013). *Diagnostic and statistical manual of mental disorders*(5th ed.). Arlington, VA: Author.

American Psychological Association. (1954). *Technical recommendations for psychological tests and diagnostic techniques.* Washington, DC: Author.

Behnke, S. H. (2004). Release of test data and the new ethics code. *APA Monitor, 35,* 90-91.

Brown, D. (2012). *Career information, career counseling, and career development* (10th ed.). Boston, MA: Pearson.

Cloitre, M., Garvert, D. W., Weiss, B., Carlson, E. B., & Bryant, R. A. (2014). Distinguishing PTSD, complex PTSD, and borderline personality disorder: A latent class analysis. *European Journal of Psychotraumatology, 5,* 10.3402/ejpt.v5.25097. doi:10.3402/ejpt.v5.25097

Corcoran, K., & Fischer, J. (2013). *Measures for clinical practice and research: A sourcebook* (5th ed.). New York, NY: Oxford University Press.

Cuijpers, P., Reynolds, C. F., Donker, T., Andersson, G., & Beekman, A. (2012). Personalized treatment of adult depression: Medication, psychotherapy, or both? A systematic review. *Depression and Anxiety, 29*(10), 855-864. doi:10.1002/da.21985

Diener, E., Tay, L., & Myers, D. (2011). The Religion Paradox: If religions makes people happy, why are so many dropping out? *Journal of Personality and Social Psychology 101,* 1278-1290.

Drummond, R. J., Sheperis, C. J., & Jones, K. D. (2016). *Assessment procedures for counselors and helping professionals* (8th ed.). Boston, MA: Pearson.

Darling, R. B. (2003). Toward a model of changing disability identities: A proposed typology and research agenda. *Disability & Society, 18,* 881–895. doi:10.1080/0968759032000127308

Furr, R.M., & Bacharach, V.R. (2013) *Psychometrics: An introduction.* Thousand Oaks, CA: Sage Publications, Inc.

Geisinger, K. F. (2013) Reliability. In Geisinger, K. F., Bracken, B. A., Carlson, J. F., Hansen, J. C., Kuncel, N. R., Reise, S. P., Rodriguez, M. C (Eds.), *APA handbook of testing and assessment in psychology.* Washington, DC: APA

Gregory, R. J. (2007). *Psychological testing: History, principles, and applications* (5th ed.). Boston, MA: Allyn & Bacon.

Hansen, J. T. (2016). *Meaning systems and mental health culture: Critical perspectives on contemporary counseling and psychotherapy.* Lanham, MA: Rowman & Littlefield

Hays, D. G. (2013). *Assessment in counseling: A guide to the use of psychological assessment procedures* (5th ed.). Alexandria, VA: American Counseling Association.

Hays, D. G. & Mcleod, A. L. (2018). The culturally competent counselor. In Hays, D. G., & Erford, B. T (Eds.), *Developing multicultural counseling competence: A systems approach* (3rd ed.). New York, NY: Pearson.

Health Insurance Portability and Accountability Act of 1996 (HIPPA). Pub. 1. No. 104-191, 110Stat. 1936 (1996).

Heppner, P., & Heppner, M. (2004). *Writing and publishing your thesis, dissertation & research: A guide for students in the helping profession.* Belmont, CA: Brooks/Cole, Cengage Learning.

Hood, A. B. & Johnson, R. W. (2007). *Assessment in counseling: A guide to the use of psychological assessment procedures* (4th ed.). Alexandria, VA: ACA

Institute of Medicine. (2015). Psychological Testing in the Service of Disability Determination. Washington, DC: The National Academies Press. Retrieved from https://doi.org/10.17226/21704.

Johnson, E. L. (1987). Sin, weakness and psychopathology. *Journal of Psychology and Theology, 15*(3), 218-26.

Jongsma, A. E., Peterson, L. M., McInnis, W. P., & Bruce, T. J. (2014). *The child psychotherapy treatment planner* (5th ed.). Hoboken, NJ: Wiley & Sons, Inc.

Kielbasa, A. M., Pomerantz, A. M., Krohn, E. J., & Sullivan, B. F. (2004). How does clients' method of payment influence psychologists' diagnostic decisions? *Ethics & Behavior, 14*, 187-195.

Lee, W., Blando, J., Mizelle, N., & Orozco, G. (2007). *Introduction to multicultural counseling for helping professionals* (2nd ed.). New York, NY: Routledge Taylor & Francis Group.

Lowe, J., Pomerantz, A. M., & Pettibone, J. C. (2007). The influence of payment method on psychologists' diagnostic decisions. Expanding the range of presenting problems. *Ethics & Behaviors, 17*, 83-93.

Magyar-Russel, G. M. & Griffith, G. L. (2016) Addressing unhealthy and potentially harmful expressions of religiousness and spirituality in clinical practice. *Spirituality in Clinical Practice, 3*(3), 159-162.

McRay, B., Yarhouse, M., & Butman, R. (2016). *Modern psychopathologies: A comprehensive Christian appraisal* (2nd ed.). Downers Grove, IL: InterVarsity Press Academic.

Meier, S. T. (2015). *Incorporating progress monitoring and outcome assessment into counseling and psychotherapy: A primer.* New York, NY: Oxford University Press.

Miller, S. & Bargmann, S. (2012). The Outcome Rating Scale (ORS) and the Session Rating Scale (SRS). *Integrating Science and Practice, 2*(2), 28-31.

Neukrug, E. S., & Fawcett, R. C. (2014). *Essentials of testing and assessment: A practical guide for counselors, social workers, and psychologists* (3rd ed.). Stamford, CT: Cengage Learning.

Niles, S. G., & Harris-Bowlsbey, J. (2017). *Career development interventions* (5th ed.). Boston, MA: Pearson.

Nitko, A. J. (2004). *Educational assessments of students.* Englewood Cliffs, NJ: Prentice Hall.

Pituch, K. A., & Stevens, J. P. (2016). *Applied multivariate statistics for the social sciences* (6th ed). New York, NY: Routledge.

Plante, T. G. (2014). Four steps to improve religious/spiritual cultural competence in professional psychology. *Spirituality in Clinical Practice, 1*(4), 288-292. Retrieved from http://dx.doi.org.ezproxy.liberty.edu/10.1037/scp0000047

Remley, T. P. Jr., & Herlihy, B. (2016). *Ethical, legal, and professional issues in counseling* (5th ed.). Boston, MA: Pearson.

Schlosser, L. Z., Foley, P. F., Stein, E. P., & Holmwood, J. R. (2010). Why does counseling psychology exclude religion? A content analysis and methodological critique. In J.G. Ponterotto, J. M. Casas, L.A. Suzuki, & C. M. Alexander (Eds.), *Handbook of Multicultural Counseling* (3rd ed.). Thousand Oaks, CA: Sage.

Schweiger, E. M., Muse-Burke, J. L., & Sallavanti, M. I. (2017). Developing spiritual competence: A look at a counseling and spirituality course. *Journal of the Pennsylvania Counseling Association, 16*, 23-31.

Sireci, S. G., Sukinm T. (2013) Test validity. In Geisinger, K.F., Bracken, B.A., Carlson, J.F., Hansen, J.C., Kuncel, N.R., Reise, S.P., & Rodriguez, M.C (Eds.), *APA handbook of testing and assessment in psychology.* Washington, DC: APA

Sperry, L. (2012). *Family assessment: Contemporary and cutting-edge strategies* (2nd ed). New York, NW: Routledge Taylor & Francis Group.

Sweeney, T. J. (2012). Leadership for the counseling profession. In C.Y. Chang, C. A. Barrio Minton, A. L. Dixon, J. E. Myers, & T.J. Sweeney (Eds.), *Professional counseling excellence through leadership and advocacy.* New York, NY: Routledge.

Thomas, J. C. & Sosin, L. (2011). *Therapeutic Expedition: Equipping the Christian counselor for the journey.* Nashville, TN: B&H Publishing.

Turner, S. M., DeMers, S. T., Fox, H. R., & Reed, G. M. (2001). APA's guidelines for test user qualifications: An executive summary. *American Psychologist, 56*(12), 1099-1113.

Tymofievich, M., & Leroux, J. A. (2000). Counselors' competencies in using assessments. *Measurement & Evaluation in Counseling & Development, 33*(1), 50. Retrieved from http://search.ebscohost.com.ezproxy.liberty.edu/login.aspx?direct=true&db=f5h&AN=3238329&site=ehost-live&scope=site

Vieten, C. & Scammell, S. (2015). *Spiritual & religious competencies in clinical practice.* Oakland, CA: New Harbinger Publications, Inc.

Welfel, E. R. (2016). *Ethics in counseling and psychotherapy: Standards, research and emerging issues* (6th ed.). Boston, MA: Cengage Learning.

Wilcoxon, S. A., Remley, T. P., & Gladding, S. T. (2013). *Ethical, legal, and professional issues in the practice of marriage and family therapy* (5th ed.). Boston, MA: Pearson

Wiger, D. E. (2012). *The psychotherapy documentation primer* (3rd ed.). Hoboken, NJ: John Wiley & Sons, Inc.

Yalom, I. D. (2002). *The gift of therapy: An open letter to a new generation of therapists and their patients.* New York, NY: HarperCollins.

Young, M. E. (2017). *Learning the art of helping: Building blocks and techniques* (6th ed.). New York, NY: Pearson.

CHAPTER 12
Research, Program Evaluation, and the Counselor

Anita Knight Kuhnley, Ph.D., Kristy Ford, Ph.D., & Gary Allen Sibcy, Ph.D.

> "It's not that I'm so smart, it's just that I stay with problems longer... I have no special talent. I am only passionately curious."
> —Albert Einstein

Following Christ: Grace for Our Work

Mindset has been identified by study skills experts as the starting point for both efficient and effective learning (Chew, 2014). Sometimes, students report having feelings of anxiety when it comes to classes that involve statistics or research. Given that anxiety, it is not surprising that students sometimes report self-defeating thoughts as well. Thoughts such as "I am not good at research," or "I do not know what I am doing when it comes to statistics" can increase anxiety and interfere with mastery of the material, because working memory resources go to fuel the anxiety rather than to increased cognitive effort (Chew, 2014; Knight & West, 2011).

CHAPTER OBJECTIVES

After reading this chapter, you will understand more about:

- The ethical requirements to use research-informed counseling strategies.
- The basic principles and concepts in research.
- How research is used in the counseling profession.

The following CACREP standards are addressed in this chapter:

Research and Program Evaluation:

- The importance of research in advancing the counseling profession, including how to critique research to inform counseling practice (CACREP, 2016, Standard 2.F.8.a.)

Scripture provides reminders about the importance of *thinking about our thinking* (Romans 12:2; Ephesians 4:22–24; Colossians 3:2). This is known as *metacognitive monitoring*. As Christians, we are admonished to "take captive every thought to make it obedient to Christ" (II Corinthians 10:5, New International Version). The visual image in this phrase is a great example of metacognitive monitoring, as we first notice the thoughts that consume us, and then suspend each individual thought in a mental prison until we can make a conscious decision about both the truth and goodness of the thought. What a relief to know that even our thoughts are subject to obedience to Christ! As we walk in close communion with Him, He will help us to discern whether the captive thought should be freed, or whether it should be held in suspicion or perhaps sentenced to death. Aware of the struggles of the human condition, Jesus understands our temptation to worry. He reminded his followers to guard against the habit of worry, saying: "Therefore I tell you, do not worry about your life… Can any one of you, by worrying, add a single hour to your life?" (Matthew 6:25–27).

We can all acknowledge the basic truth that as followers of Christ, we have no need for worry; however, it is important for counselors in training to remember the importance of mindset in managing anxious thoughts. Metacognitive monitoring is the starting point for effective and efficient learning, working toward a continuous renewing of the mind and regulated thought processes. From there, anxiety can turn to excitement, and you just might discover that you begin to identify with Einstein's *passionate curiosity* for research.

HOW IS RESEARCH RELEVANT TO COUNSELING?

Counseling ethics require counselors to use research supported interventions and treatments (American Counseling

Association [ACA], 2014). Reading peer-reviewed journals to seek out appropriate evidence based treatments is important in honoring this ethical guideline. Professional associations, such as the Association for Assessment in Research and Counseling (AARC), exist to help counselors integrate research into practice and use practice to inform research. Counselors can also employ research protocols to evaluate counseling programs and track client progress. An understanding of the basics of research design and the importance of measuring effectiveness in your work as a counselor will create a strong foundation and sense of purpose with which to approach your training in research methods and program evaluation.

This chapter invites you to put on your investigative cap and consider what it means for a research study to be *robust*. You are invited to think critically about the threats that could invalidate the research design. Counseling research must consider two major forms of validity: *internal validity*, related to the capacity for counselors to conclude that research outcomes are linked to treatments, and *external validity*, related to the ability to generalize research outcomes to other contexts. Counselors are important consumers of counseling and psychological research. Research provides important information that informs counseling practice. For example, counselors have an ethical obligation to select appropriate interventions for the appropriate population, and need access to empirical evidence that those interventions are effective. In order to be a good consumer of research literature, it is critical for counselors to understand key concepts in research.

In this chapter, we will explore threats to *internal validity*, such as history and maturation, threats to *statistical validity*, such as low statistical power and violated test assumptions, and threats to *external validity*, including factors that make it difficult to apply study findings to other settings or populations. Counselors can learn to recognize these threats in research literature, making it possible to understand the limitations of research and become more discerning consumers of research.

WHY DO SOME STUDENTS FEEL INTIMIDATED BY RESEARCH?

Research on counseling practices and outcomes has been prioritized within the professional literature (Hays, 2010) and emphasized by professional organizations (ACA, 2014). For example, the *ACA Code of Ethics* dedicates an entire section to research ideals entitled "Research and Publication" (See §G; ACA, 2014, p.15). In addition, research is emphasized by the accrediting agency that guides much of the curriculum in counselor training programs: The Council for Accreditation of Counseling and Related Education-Related Programs (CACREP) devotes one of the eight core program areas to "Research and Program Evaluation" (CACREP, 2016, Section 2.F.8.). As a division of the ACA, the AARC publishes a journal entitled *Counseling Outcome Research and Evaluation*, dedicated to promoting research and assessment in counseling. In this journal's introductory article, Hays (2010) lays the groundwork rationale for continuing to promote research and practice and for implementing the *scientist practitioner model*, which emphasizes using research to inform practice and, in turn, using practice to inform research.

Over time, the trend in the counseling literature has been toward encouraging more scholarly activity among counselors, more robust designs among researchers, and more research involvement overall (Watkins, Lopez, Campbell, & Himmel, 1986; Peterson, Hall, & Busser, 2016; Atieno Okech, Astramovich, Johnson, Hoskins, & Rubel, 2006; Balkin, Gosnell, Holmgren, & Osborne, 2017). Despite the clearly established importance and value of counseling related research, counseling psychology researchers (Watkins et al., 1986) investigating the time spent in various professional activities among counselors found that *less than 8%* of their time was spent on scholarly work, and the most often reported number of publications was *zero*.

Lack of Self-Efficacy in Research Activity

For many counselors, this lack of congruence between the value of research in the field and the actual practice of research has remained. Thus, increasing counselor involvement in scholarship has been a goal of the profession. Kahn (2001) identified a series of factors that may be involved in predicting research interest, and one of those may be identifying with the investigative type, as designated in Holland's (1997) theory of vocational choice. Identification with the investigative type of Holland's Code was a direct predictor of research interest in some studies (Kahn, 2001; Kahn & Scott, 1997). In addition, counseling researchers have found research competency may play an important role in scholarly productivity. If students do not have a sense of competence in research this can impact their *self-efficacy* in scholarly activity. In addition, the role of counselor educators as mentors of counselor trainees is important, as the mentor's involvement in research may influence their student's involvement (Khan, 2001).

> **Research Self-Efficacy** - the belief that one can be successful in research.

Anxiety about Participating in Research Activity

In addition to questions about personal competency, students in the helping professions may experience stress and anxiety about participating, in spite of valuing research. Studies conducted among social work undergraduates indicate this phenomenon, as students reported valuing research, but still reporting feelings of stress and anxiety when engaging in research related activities (Negrea et al., 2018). Researchers further indicated:

> BSW students' feelings toward research are, in fact, quite complex (Secret, Ford, & Rompf, 2003) and can include research-related anxiety and lack of confidence (Unrau & Beck, 2004) Research-related anxiety has been defined as "students' unpleasant emotional state or condition about research, especially research methods, statistics, and mathematics. (Maschi et al., 2013, p. 801)

When a student becomes anxious during his or her studies, cognitive resources move to manage the anxiety, leaving less available energy to manage the cognitive load associated with problem solving tasks, such as statistical analysis or research (Chew, 2012, personal communication; Knight & West, 2012). Dweck (2016) explained the primary distinction between growth mindsets and fixed mindsets, conveying that those with a *growth mindset* believe that their skills can be refined and fine tuned through hard work and other strategies, including but not limited to acquiring input from others. On the other hand, a *fixed mindset* is characterized by a belief that one's talents are innate and unchangeable. Those with a growth mindset tend to accomplish more and be more successful than those with a fixed mindset. "This is because they worry less about looking smart and put more energy into learning" (Dweck, 2016, p. 3).

Growth mindset: "I can learn research and statistics. If I have not been successful in the past, then I can acquire new skills moving forward and experiment with new strategies until I find what works."

Fixed mindset: "I am bad at math. I will never be good at research."

If you are prone to anxiety, it will be important to keep a careful watch on your thoughts and redirect them toward growth oriented positive thoughts about research. In addition, if you have had challenging experiences in the past with research, statistics, or other similar classes, remember that new study strategies can be used, making it possible to have more success in the future. See the recommended readings at the end of this chapter for more resources on overcoming anxiety.

Myths Related to Learning about Research

Chew (2014) identified *myths* that students may believe which can create problematic mindset struggles that interfere with learning. These myths include, but are not limited to, the following (Dweck, 2016; Chew, 2014, p. 216):

- Learning is fast
- Knowledge is composed of isolated facts
- Being good at a subject is a matter of inborn talent rather than hard work
- I'm really good at multitasking, especially during class or studying

These myths have the potential to sabotage student success. Learning often takes time, and it is important to allow ample time to review complex concepts, to avoid unnecessary anxiety and increase self-efficacy. Study strategies (such as note cards and highlighting) can help to connect new learning with previous content (Chew, 2014; Berry & Chew, 2008). Learning is hard work, and the belief that all talent or proficiency in a particular subject matter is inborn is a myth. Despite talent, often times experts have to work diligently to refine their skills. Furthermore, Terry, Mishra, and Roseth (2016) suggested that student technology use in the classroom is not actually a function of multi-tasking, but rather of the anxiety activated when not using technology. Thus, it may be helpful to leave technology out of the classroom to resist the urge to engage in multitasking which can lead to distractions and more challenges with learning.

Lastly, McGuire (2015) identified one clear strategy for helping students learn: *metacognition*. In other words, if students spend time *thinking about their thinking*, they may be more successful. Students who frequently engage in metacognition when studying are aware of whether they are thinking about what standard deviation means, or whether they are thinking "this is so hard" as they study. Increased awareness means the potential for increased redirection toward more positive and constructive thoughts.

WHY DO COUNSELORS NEED TO UNDERSTAND RESEARCH?

The ACA emphasizes the value of research in their calls for presentations, credited as a driving force behind the call for a scientist practitioner model in the training of counselors (Peterson, Hall, & Buser, 2016; Hays, 2010). Participating in the scientist practitioner model, involves, as a CIT, developing a researcher identity, and evaluating the efficacy of interventions in practice which may provide guidance and helpful information for constructing effective treatment plans in counseling (Hays, 2010).

© Thanakorn.P/Shutterstock.com

ACA Code of Ethics

Developing and practicing as an effective and ethical counselor involves being a good consumer of research and evaluating the effectiveness of work with clients. Counselors are required to exhibit a scientific basis for their work, as indicated by the ACA *Code of Ethics* (2014, C.2.d. Monitor Effectiveness). This ethical code requires that counselors continually monitor effectiveness and to take action steps to improve and develop services when necessary. Counselors are also required to take "reasonable steps" to "evaluate their efficacy as counselors" (ACA, 2014, C.2.d.). One ethical code, in particular, is titled, "Scientific Basis for Treatment" (ACA, 2014, C.7.a.), indicating that counselors' techniques or procedures should be "modalities that are grounded in theory and/or have an empirical or scientific foundation" (p. 10).

Why I Research

Donna S. Sheperis, PhD, LPC, NCC, ACS, CCMHC
Associate Professor, Palo Alto University

© Donna Sheperis

As a college student, my perception of research was something people did in labs. With rats. Or with beakers and chemicals. I had no interest in those things and did not consider myself a researcher of any sort. Turns out, I was a researcher and had no idea! You see, I was that kid who always asked "why?" And as I grew older, I learned that being told why was not enough. I needed the backstory. I needed research.

Research fills in the gaps of our knowledge. It is essential in counseling because it helps us understand what types of treatments are most effective. Imagine seeing a physician who didn't base her treatment on research – I don't think I would feel very confident as a patient! Research helps us debunk myths and support truths in the way we work. You may not have thought about it this way, but research and the process of researching are nourishment for our minds and can serve as the catalyst for getting excited about our work as a counselor.

What I have learned along my journey as a researcher is that research is not so much about "knowing" as it is "knowing how to know." The drive that was natural to me as a child was further developed in me by mentors who knew how to cultivate curiosity. My trajectory in research had humble, and humbling, beginnings. I was hired by a social psychologist during my master's program to make calls to patients who had been discharged from a rural, community hospital. My task was to conduct a patient satisfaction survey. I had my script, I had been trained, and I had data to collect! I was fairly successful at getting responses…until I called peo-

INTRODUCTION TO COUNSELING

ple who hadn't exactly been discharged from the hospital. They had passed away at the facility and here I was calling to see how their stay was! It was a lesson in research being imperfect as well as an opportunity to practice the very beginnings of my counseling skills.

I persisted with working with data and looking for answers throughout my master's program and into my clinical career. I routinely conducted client outcome studies as a counselor in practice. I performed program evaluations as an agency supervisor. I discovered that virtually everything I did as a clinician deserved to be enhanced by research through data collection and analysis. Even a simple survey of kids in a group asking "which of these faces do you feel like today?" was a way to research whether what we were doing was working.

My research evolved in my doctoral program and beyond. I have found that the more I read research, the better my clinical work is. I have become comfortable reading the entire article, not just the abstract and discussion. And most importantly, I have learned to say yes. When approached by others looking to engage in research, I make time to help or forge a research team. As such, my research has spanned a lot of different arenas in the profession of counseling. I have performed EEG studies with children who have autism to look at how their brains are different from neurotypical children. I have examined how clinicians explore their own values when faced with ethical dilemmas in counseling. I have developed assessments to determine how comfortable clients are with sharing their stories in counseling. I have discovered through research that clients don't care nearly as much about all of the acronyms that come after my name as they do about knowing I am board certified in certain types of counseling. I have even come to discover that I love research!

A goal of mine is to pass this enthusiasm and love of research along to my students and practicing counselors. I want to demystify research and make it accessible. I strive to help counselors understand that they are likely already conducting research and can certainly augment their practice with some readings. I joined the research and assessment division of the American Counseling Association and was fortunate to serve as its president. I attend conferences and listen to the research of others. I present my research regularly and invite feedback, ideas, and discourse about the work.

The little kid that wanted to know "why" is still asking those questions inside of me and I am having a wonderful time exploring research in counseling. And I have never researched rats or used beakers and chemicals....at least not yet!

Contributed by Donna Sheperis. © Kendall Hunt Publishing Company.

© garagestock/Shutterstock.com

The current ethical counseling codes emphasize the importance of research and of a scientific basis for procedures, even more now than in past renditions. In this way, the ethical codes represent how our profession has developed and adapted over time. The first edition of the code of ethics was published in 1959 and has been revised approximately every seven years to demonstrate the changing priorities of the field (Walden, Herlihy, & Ashton 2003). The adaptations of the code of ethics have been described as a mirror, illustrating how the profession has changed as a whole. Donald Super, often cited for his work in career development, was the founding president of the American Personnel and Guidance Association (APGA; now the American Counseling Association). Super established an Ethical Practices Committee within a year of the organization's beginning, and this emphasis on ethics has continued. Prior to 2005, the language reflected the need to monitor effectiveness, but did not include the more research specific language of the recent ethical codes (2005 and 2014): "Counselors have a responsibility to the public to engage in counseling practices that are based on rigorous research methodologies" (ACA, 2014, Section C. Introduction, p. 8).

"The purpose of research is to reach well-founded (i.e. valid) conclusions about the effects of a given experimental manipulation or intervention." Alan Kazdin

HOW CAN COUNSELORS BECOME DISCERNING CONSUMERS OF RESEARCH?

Counselors have the potential to serve as both producers and consumers of research literature. Consuming research well and using it to guide scientifically supported practice is an important first step. Counselors need to be good consumers of the research, but what is needed for this to happen? There are several knowledge tools to have in your tool kit. This chapter is devoted to exploring these knowledge areas, starting with defining empirically supported treatments used for evidence based practice.

Utilizing Empirically Supported Treatments

Defining ESTs. In this section, we will explore what it means to be a consumer of the research literature by understanding how research supports the development empirically supported treatments. When discussing empirically supported treatments (ESTs), it may be helpful to explore the origins of this terminology. The National Institute of Mental Health (NIMH) compared therapeutic treatments in psychology and counseling to the use of aspirin in medicine, and the APA developed a task force to explore the idea of having designated treatments

© Castleski/Shutterstock.com

supported by research for designated psychological diagnoses (APA Task Force, 2006; Sommers-Flanagan, 2015). Originally, the term *empirically validated treatment* was used to describe treatments that adhered to a strict and controversial protocol. Sommers-Flanagan (2015) reported that in the original definition, the treatment had to meet two primary guidelines: 1) the treatment had to be *manualized* (documented and written up in a manual as a prescribed series of interventions that can be replicated and used by others in a similar manner), and 2) the treatment had to be demonstrated to perform superior to a placebo or alternate treatment in at least two designs by two different research teams *or* demonstrate effectiveness in multiple studies in a series of studies using single case design conducted by at least two different research teams. However, these guidelines were controversial among researchers (Chambless & Hollon, 1998), and the description was altered from *empirically validated treatments* to the current term of *empirically supported treatments* (EST).

Expanding ESTs and broadening to EBP. Thanks to robust research, empirically supported treatments have evolved into over five dozen different therapeutic approaches. Some specific diagnoses have fewer EST's associated with them; For example, dialectical behavior therapy (Shearin & Linehan, 1994; Sommers-Flanagan, 2015) is currently the only recognized EST in the treatment of borderline personality disorder. However, other conditions, such as depression, have multiple ESTs. Some counselors prefer the terms *evidence based treatments* or *evidence based practice* (EBP) over the term *empirically supported treatments*, allowing for a wider inclusion of protocols that do not necessarily adhere to the strict requirements of EST protocols but do have some research support.

FIGURE 12.1

Features of Empirically Supported Treatments

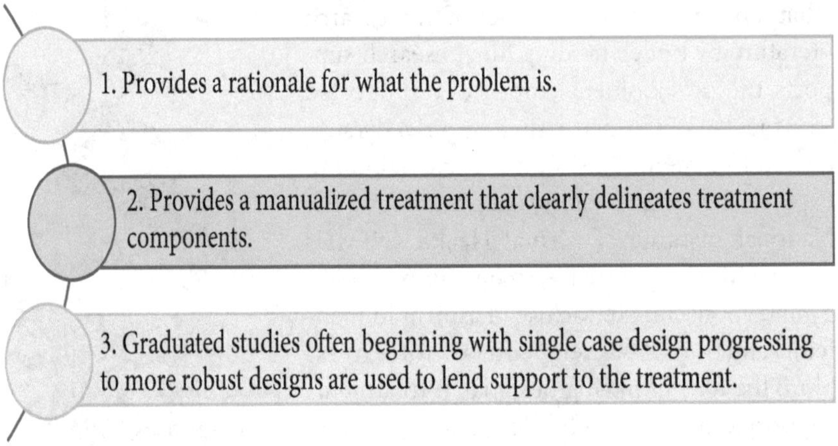

1. Provides a rationale for what the problem is.

2. Provides a manualized treatment that clearly delineates treatment components.

3. Graduated studies often beginning with single case design progressing to more robust designs are used to lend support to the treatment.

Training in ESTs. Clark (2018) highlighted a recent meta analysis conducted by McHugh, Whitton, Peckham, Welge and Otto (2013) which indicated that people prefer therapy three times as much as medication. Clark (2018) further noted that there is a significant need to bridge the gap between research and practice. Thus, a program was developed called The English Improving Access to Psychological Therapies (IAPT) with the aim of training 10,500 therapists in evidence based treatments, in order to offer better care to clients. Table 12.1 includes a selection of evidence based interventions and treatments available for counselor training.

IAPT Evidence Based Training Curriculum Samples (Adapted from Clark, 2018)	
Depression	Minimum of two depression treatments 1) Cognitive Behavioral Therapy & 2) Behavioral Activation
Anxiety	One EBT for each anxiety disorder: **Panic disorder Treatments:** • Barlow and Colleagues CBT program & • Clark and colleagues cognitive therapy program **PTSD Treatments:** • Edna Foa's imaginal reliving • Ehler's and Clark's cognitive therapy

TABLE 12.1

IAPT Evidence Based Training Curriculum Samples

Source: adapted from Clark, 2018

Clark (2018) further noted that the treatments are approved by the National Institute for Health and Clinical Excellence (NICE). NICE (2011) represents integrated care and patient perspectives, with the purpose of providing an objective assessment of treatment interventions and conclusions about effective treatments. In order to identify evidence based treatments, a NICE committee identifies a particular population in need of treatment, then determines the correct intervention (or multiple available options) for that population. Clinicians are then trained in different treatment protocols for comparison, and the clinical outcomes are discussed in an ongoing exploration and identification of alternative treatment options.

Research Designs of ESTs. The final phase for developing an empirically supported treatment (EST) would be a *randomized controlled trial* (RCT). A randomized controlled trial is considered the gold standard in social sciences research, and often includes: random selection, random assignment, pre-test post-test design, and

© Ollyy/Shutterstock.com

a control group for comparison. If a treatment shows promise in early clinical outcomes, then it advances through increasingly rigorous testing designs. ESTs are ranked in the literature with qualifiers such *weak*, *moderate* or *strong* support. Empirical support is initially demonstrated when the treatment is shown to be more effective than the control treatment; however, strong support indicates that the treatment is at least as good as or better than other known effective treatments. In addition, the RCT should ultimately be replicated by two independent research groups to show strong support.

In other words, treatments that have been submitted to this process can be arranged along a continuum of empirical support, with those that are at the lower end including single case designs and at the higher end including RCT designs with a control group or comparison group. The strongest ESTs at the top of the spectrum are those that (1) have shown positive outcomes in a RCT in which the comparison group received an established effective treatment, and (2) have been independently replicated.

Case Conceptualization and ESTs. As the field moves away from schoolism toward empirically supported treatments (Sibcy & Knight, 2019), counselors need to stay informed by research, as an ever-increasing number of treatments are considered empirically supported. Thus, you will need to know how to critically review research. Armed with this understanding, treatments supported by empirical data can then be connected to your clinical case conceptualization of the problem, linking the diagnosis or symptoms to the treatment components you will use in practice. ESTs provide a rationale for the impact of the treatment on the problem, supporting the process of case conceptualization. Furthermore, ESTs include a treatment manual (a *manualized protocol*) which clearly articulates the treatment components, including delivery and sequence.

Counselors become discerning consumers of research by using the research literature to explore ESTs for use in evidence based counseling practice. For example, you may ask, "What evidence is there to support that cognitive behavioral analysis of systems psychotherapy (CBASP) is effective to treat chronic depression?" You would then scour the literature in search of a peer reviewed journal article that provides insight into the outcomes of CBASP treatment. For example, a six month clinical outcome study by Swan et al. (2014) on CBASP for chronic depression

© M-SUR/Shutterstock.com

indicates that CBASP is an acceptable form of treatment for depression with 60% of the patients in the study, who were diagnosed with chronic depression, demonstrating clinically significant change. In order to determine whether this research is helpful, you will need a set of skills to make sense of this article (discussed further in the next section). A thorough understanding of this research assists in determining whether to pursue continuing education training to become a CBASP trained therapist and implement CBASP interventions with clients diagnosed with chronic depression (Swan, et al., 2014).

Movement toward evidence based treatments is an important current and future direction for the field. As a future counselor, if you are using cognitive behavioral therapy (CBT) for panic disorder, you need to be sure that CBT is indicated. You need to know if the research supports this treatment method, and you need to ask the question, "how does CBT as an EST conceptualize panic disorder?" This will help you to better understand the treatment and its application to your case conceptualization.

In order to identify appropriate evidence based treatments, it is important to read peer-reviewed journals and content published by professional organizations such as the ACA. For more information on the role and benefits of joining organizations such as ACA, please review Chapter 2.

Promoting Research in the Field

ACA initiatives. Although, the field of counseling values and emphasizes research, counselors sometimes integrate research done on therapeutic interventions by other helping professions, including psychology. However, ACA leadership has acknowledged the lack of research specific to counseling and developed initiatives such as The Center for Counseling Practice, Policy, and Research (West-Olatunji, 2013). This ACA initiative purposes to promote research among counselors, and to make it more accessible to those practicing counseling. Scholars within the profession of counseling are invited to write briefs that promote best practices in counseling. Counseling scholars are also invited to submit briefs that summarize research based approaches to a diverse number of specified client challenges. These can be accessed in the knowledge center for ACA practice briefs via the following website: https://www.counseling.org/knowledge-center/practice-briefs. The resource includes briefs on evidence based treatments for a range of problems including: PTSD for youth, erectile dysfunction, depression, gambling disorder, and much more. As the counseling research base continue to develop, counselors are encouraged to seek out counseling literature first when it is available, but also use research from other helping disciplines such as psychology as needed.

APA initiatives. The American Psychological Association (APA), has an internet-based collection of scientific articles called *Research in Action*. These sources purpose to share helpful information about the practical relevance of psychological science in daily life. For example, the article entitled, "How to be a Smart Consumer of Psychological Research: Evaluate Research-based Claims to Become a Better Consumer of Products and Services that Shape your Daily Life," (Vivalt, 2019) gives guidelines for cultivating a habit of seeking out evidence, rather than accepting a claim to be true at face value.

Additionally, counselors use a manual of publication guidelines developed by the APA (2010) to guide their writings in professional counseling journals, as well as the presentation of their research findings at professional conferences. The manual reminds social sciences researchers that the most important part of being a wise consumer of psychological research "is looking that, from a scientific perspective, all claims require evidence, not just opinions." (APA, n.d., p. 1). APA compares the discerning consumer of research to the role of a jury member. You may be familiar with the value that all people are *innocent until proven guilty.* Until there is evidence beyond a reasonable doubt against a suspect, he or she is deemed innocent. The jury member is on the lookout for evidence, and approaches the evidence with a healthy degree of skepticism.

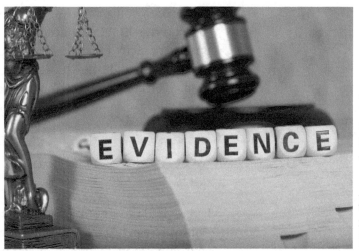

© Tolikoff Photography/Shutterstock.com

Discerning Robustness and Validity in Research

Now, that you have explored research in terms of evidence based treatment, an important next step in becoming a discerning consumer of research is to identify the type of research design utilized in the study in order to evaluate the robustness and validity of the research. Not only does the ideal jury member avoid drawing conclusions without evidence, but he or she also evaluates the validity of the evidence. Thus, the juror is attentive to the methods used to obtain the evidence and make the claim. Robust and valid methods lend themselves to acceptable claims. Likewise, the same is true in research. The results of a research study are only as valid as the study design itself, so understanding validity is a critical step in becoming a discerning consumer. It is also important to avoid relying on the outcome of one study, since various threats to validity can compromise studies in different ways. When assessing clients, we often rely on a battery of assessments rather than just one, as this gives a fuller picture; the same can be helpful in research (Vivalt, 2018).

WHY IS VALIDITY SO IMPORTANT IN RESEARCH?

Counselors may hear claims about effective treatments at conferences, via professional newsletters, and even from peers. How do you know if the information you are hearing, or the study you are reading, is considered robust research? A key concept in evaluating research literature is *validity*. But what exactly is validity? Furthermore, why are there so many different forms of validity, such as statistical validity, internal validity, external validity, or face validity? You will hear this term often, as it is a critical concept for consuming research in a discerning manner.

WHAT IS VALIDITY?

It is beyond the scope of this chapter to provide a comprehensive discussion of research methodologies; however, you will learn more detail in your research methods and program evaluation course, which will cover important concepts to prepare you to review research literature. You will investigate the concept of validity and threats to validity with much more detail on your journey of becoming a competent and ethical counselor, but in this section we will briefly overview four types of validity in research design: measurement validity, experimental validity (internal and external validity), construct validity, and statistical validity.

Measurement Validity

Measurement validity, or test validity, is sometimes described as a measure of truthfulness or reality and, in the case of an assessment, whether the test measures what it claims to measure (Knight & Tetrault, 2017; Jackson, 2016). Truman Lee Kelly was a renowned psychometrician whose work was informed by other key figures such as Thorndike and Pearson. Pearson developed the well-known product moment coefficient (Kelly, 1927, 1904). Kelly (1927) explored measurement challenges involving validity and reliability which go hand in hand. Regarding validity and reliability, he wrote, "The problem of validity is that of *whether a test measures that which it purports to measure. The challenge of reliability is *how well it measures* it" (Kelly, 1927, p. 14).

> **Measurement (Test) Validity:**
> whether a test measures what it sets out to measure.

For example, if a test claims to measure emotional intelligence (such as the Mayer Salovey Caruso Emotional Intelligence Test; MSCEIT) but instead is actually measuring intelligence quotient (IQ) or some component of personality, then it would not be valid. Further, there are different forms of validity of an instrument. *Face validity* indicates that if you take a look at the face value of the instrument it appears to measure what it claims to. This is a necessary but not sufficient form of validity. Another form of validity when evaluating assessments is *construct validity*, with the purpose of identifying whether the test aligns with other tests measuring the same construct. For example, if a clinician wants to measure depression, if an assessment such as the Beck Depression Inventory is correlated with another assessment known to measure depression such as Patient Health Questionnaire-9 (PHQ-9) then it may be said to have construct validity. Psychometrics is a term used to describe the measurement of individual characteristics, such as abilities, knowledge, personality, skills, and so on.

> **Test Construct Validity** - an assessment has construct validity when its scores are correlated with scores on other assessments known to be associated with the same construct.

Experimental Validity

Another use of the word *validity* applies to human subjects research, extending beyond psychometrics to evaluate the validity of a research study. There are two types of experimental validity to consider when evaluating counseling research. These include *internal validity* and *external validity*. Researchers also consider *statistical validity* and *construct validity* within each study (Creswell, 2014). Research in the social sciences often discusses potential threats to validity, with threats to internal validity considered the most severe (Creswell, 2014).

In consideration of the overall experimental validity of a study, it may be helpful to first review some concepts you have likely encountered in your past studies of science. An *independent variable* (IV) is the variable that is manipulated by the researcher(s) in order to impact the dependent variable. In counseling research, the independent variable is often the treatment, and the dependent variable (DV) is often the measure of psychopathology (e.g., Beck Depression Inventory; BDI). Other factors besides the treatment (the IV) that may impact a client's symptoms as reflected in the scores on the measure (the DV) are called *confounding variables*. Ideally, counseling researchers implement strategies to control for any variables that may influence treatment outcomes. Any variable that has the potential to undermine the results a study is referred to a *threat to internal validity*. This concept is central to the quality of social science research.

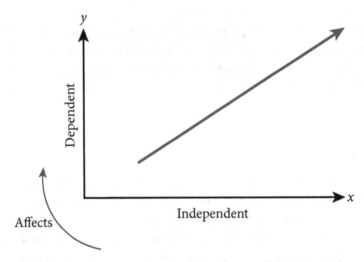

Internal validity. Researchers use strategies such as random sampling, random assignment, and the implementation of a control group to increase the *internal validity* of the study. These practices increase the level of confidence with which the researcher can conclude that any changes in the study participants were due to the experiment rather than outside factors. However, in counseling research, it is often not possible to use strategies such as these. Counselors may be dealing with one client at a time, with no access to large samples, and counselors may not have the opportunity to randomly select participants since clients often self-select into treatment. However, it is important to identify whether the internal procedures and methodologies used to conduct the study are such that the change that clients experience is associated with the treatment rather than being a function of other factors such as the passage of time or other confounding variables. For example, how can you be sure that the progress they made in the study is due to the specified treatment and would not have happened simply as a result of going to counseling (treatment as usual)? Internal validity helps us control for potentially confounding factors and determine whether study outcomes can actually be attributed to the treatment itself.

Threats to internal validity. Internal validity is assessed by the extent to which the intervention (the IV) can be considered to be responsible for the results, changes, or differences among conditions (the DV; e.g., measured symptoms). The more internally valid a study, the more confident we can be that the outcomes of the study can be attributed to the IV, rather than to confounding variables. Counselor trainees will learn much more about specific terms and concepts in a required research methods and program evaluation course within CACREP accredited counselor training programs; however, a key concept to begin to become familiar is *threats to internal validity.* Below, we will consider some of the most powerful threats that have the power to invalidate a study, beginning first with those factors that threaten the internal design of the study.

History. History includes any event (other than the intervention) occurring at the time of the experiment that could influence the results or account for the pattern of data otherwise attributed to the experimental manipulation. Historical events might include family crises; changes in job, teacher, or spouse; power blackouts; or any other events. These are occurrences that relate to the passage of time. One way to control for these occurrences is to have a control group that would be having similar experiences alongside those in the experimental group.

Maturation. Aging is a universal experience. In the Fleetwood Mac song, *Landslide*, Stevie Nicks sings "even children get older, and I'm getting older too." Time passes for all of us, and time does not stop for research; yet, its passage may be a threat to the robustness of a study.

This variable is referred to as *maturation* and may be a threat specifically to the internal validity of a study. Maturation may be defined as any change over time that may result from processes within the subject. Such processes may include growing older, stronger, healthier, smarter, and more tired or bored. Identifying participants that have characteristics or demographics in common that would allow them to develop in similar ways may help control for this threat to internal validity. It is also important to determine whether the problem being treated has developmental implications. Comparison groups receiving a pre-test and a post-test following the same passage of time in the course of treatment may help to control for threats like history and maturation. History and maturation often go hand in hand.

Testing. Testing involves any change that may be attributed to the effects of repeated assessment. Testing constitutes an experience that, depending on the measure, may lead to systematic changes in performance.

Instrumentation. Instrumentation may also threaten internal validity. Instrumentation is any change that takes place in the measuring instrument or assessment procedure over time. Such changes may result from the use of human observers whose judgments about the client or criteria for scoring behavior may change over time. This could also happen if, for example, clients complete a paper and pencil pre-test, but then complete the posttest online after treatment. Seeking to develop methods for standardizing instrumentation may help us reduce variation and instrumentation effects. In addition, participants may become familiar with the nature of an assessment and recall questions, increase self-awareness, or learn and improve in other ways as a function of the test taking itself.

Statistical regression. An additional threat to internal validity is *statistical regression.* This involves any change from one assessment occasion to another that might be due to a regression of scores toward the mean. If clients score at the extremes on one assessment occasion, their scores may change in the direction toward the mean on a second testing.

© Iamnee/Shutterstock.com

Selection bias. Selection biases include any systematic differences between the groups before the experimental manipulation or intervention. Any differences between groups (e.g., experimental and control) may be due to the differences that were already evident before they were exposed to the different conditions of the experiment. This is more likely to occur when the sample of a research study is self-selected. However, random assignment of participants to either the treatment group or the control group can help reduce this problem.

Artic Circle © 2014 Alex Hallatt, Dist. by King Features Syndicate, Inc.

Case Study on Selection Bias

As an example of selection bias, we developed a study that offered an empathy workshop on the use of skills like the EAR technique and other research-based interventions, and assessed empathy before and after participation in the workshop. In process of the study, we found that many more counselors self-selected for an emotional intelligence training workshop rather than for the empathy training. Perhaps counselors see themselves as already empathic and not in need of change? Regardless of the reason, there was apparent selection bias.

Attrition. Some studies are longitudinal or take extended time and sampling. *Attrition* may be defined as the loss of subjects over the course of an experiment, changing the composition of the groups in a way that leads to selection biases. For example, if a counselor wants to conduct a longitudinal study to explore the impact of a treatment, but the study requires six months of treatment to see a clinically significant change, some participants may cease involvement for a variety of reasons, such as disinterest or changes in life circumstances. Attrition affects other types of experimental validity as well.

Diffusion of treatment. In social sciences research, *diffusion of treatment* can also be a concern, and happens when the control group demonstrates changes in response to the intervention. This phenomenon is often attributed to group members sharing treatment information across groups, or to demonstrations of new behaviors by the treatment group observed by members of the control group.

External validity. Furthermore, when making conclusions about a study, it is equally important to know that the results of the study are *clinically relevant*, or applicable to the clients you see in treatment, as opposed to simply reflecting the statistical power of the study (statistical validity). This type of experimental validity is known as *external validity* and is concerned with whether the findings in counseling research can be generalized from one client sample or study to other samples or studies. External validity addresses to what extent the results can be generalized or extended to people, settings, times, measures/ outcomes, and characteristics other than those included in this particular demonstration. For example, a child may believe that what he or she experiences in her family of origin is common, and that all children have similar family experiences. As socialization occurs, children learn that there are many different types of families and that it is not wise to generalize from an experience with one individual to other individuals, such as assuming that one bad babysitter means all babysitters will be bad. Likewise in research, it is typically not advisable to generalize from a sample size of one person to the larger population, or to generalize from a sample group that has notably dissimilar characteristics compared to the general population. While internal validity looks at how much we can attribute the findings of a study to the independent variable, external validity looks beyond the study to where the outcomes will be applied in the real world.

Threats to external validity. Considering external validity helps us to design more robust research, and threats to external validity can interfere with the ability to generalize the results. Establishing external validity involves the exploration of the questions such as: a) Can we assume the treatment protocol, as it was delivered in the study, can be transported into various clinical practice settings?; b) Does the protocol apply to other groups (e.g., diverse, ethnic, racial, socio-economic, or religious) or to other geographical locations, or delivery methods (e.g., in-home, group home, IOP, outpatient)?; and c) What are the boundary conditions of the treatment?

Threats to external validity can be addressed by using the most natural treatment setting possible and by using randomized sampling to select participants. The exclusion criteria of the study lists the decision rules used to differentiate those included in the study from those excluded. In many cases, the exclusion criteria are so rigorous that the average person included in the study does not look anything like the average person seen in clinical practice. For example, Foa et al. (2018) conducted research using exposure therapy to treat post-traumatic stress disorder in a sample of military personnel; however, exclusion criteria included: "current bipolar or psychotic disorders, alcohol dependence, moderate to severe traumatic brain injury, suicidal ideation, or other disorders warranting immediate attention" (p. 355). Alcohol dependence may serve as a coping behavior, and persons in the clinical population may have a co-morbid diagnosis of one of the preceding items. Consequently, these exclusion criteria may apply to many of the traumatized individuals seen in normal clinical contexts.

Construct Validity

Another type of validity, *construct validity*, focuses on the conceptual basis, or construct, that drives the change process. To support construct validity, the researcher begins by describing how and why the treatment should work. Construct validity answers questions related to whether researchers are able to draw conclusions based on research methodologies. Construct validity explores questions including: Given that internal validity was sufficient and the intervention (IV) was determined to be responsible for the outcome (DV), what specific aspect of the treatment was responsible for the change? Is there evidence that the proposed *mechanism of change*, or the core identified change construct, was involved?

For example, cognitive theory suggests that changes in depressive symptoms require that the person first change their negative pattern of thinking and then as a function of the change in thinking the depressive symptoms will decrease. While cognitive therapy may have been effective in alleviating depressive symptoms as demonstrated by a randomized controlled research design, is there evidence that this occurred because participants in the CBT group made changes in their negative thinking? This would require, at the very least, that negative thinking was measured at the beginning of treatment, somewhere in the middle of treatment, and again at the end of treatment. Those practitioners researching the impact of their cognitive treatments would have to show how the cognitive therapy group demonstrated changes in the negative thinking and that these changes would be correlated to the reduction in depression scores on an assessment of depression symptoms.

Statistical Validity

The last type of validity we will discuss in this chapter is *statistical validity*, sometimes referred to as *data-evaluation validity*. Data-evaluation validity reveals the extent of the relationship that is evidenced between the experimental manipulation or intervention and the outcome. The question is whether the data and methods used for evaluation could mislead and demonstrate a relationship that does not exist, or could fail to demonstrate an experimental effect that does exist. You will learn more about these questions and how to address them in your research methods course work.

An important part of evaluating data in research involves understanding *effect size*. While it is beyond the scope of this chapter to provide a full explanatory model of effect size, you will learn much more about effect size in your future readings and study of research. Statistical significance reflects statistical power or sample size, but effect size gives you information about the effect your treatment had (whether, small, moderate, or strong).

Being a good consumer of the research involves learning how to calculate effect size. As you continue on the journey of becoming a counselor and researcher, gaining enhanced understanding of statistical validity, along with internal and external validity, will help you to make sense of a research study and evaluate it as a good consumer.

Identifying Researcher Safeguards against Threats to Validity

In order to be a good consumer of excellent research, counselors need to be able to recognize when a study has specifically identified the safeguards utilized to account for potential threats to internal and external validity. One of the objectives of *robust* research studies is this explicitly stated control for confounding variables. In other words, increased control for threats to validity equals increased robustness of the research. The use of a randomized, controlled, pre-test/post-test design will account for most threats to internal validity, making this design the gold-standard of research investigation.

FIGURE 12.2

Robustness of Research Design

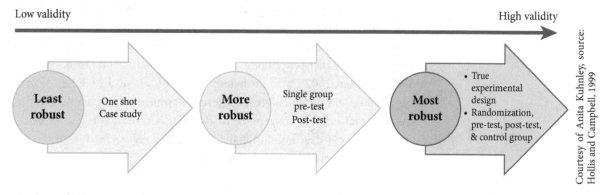

Courtesy of Anita Kuhnley, source: Hollis and Campbell, 1999

However, there are exceptions to the rule that randomization and pre-test/post-test design will control for internal validity. One exception is *attrition*. In many cases, attrition is controlled for by using an intent to treat analysis (Hollis & Campbell, 1999), to preserve the accuracy of randomization and include participants that have dropped out of treatment or not adhered to all treatment outcomes. There is concern that clinical effectiveness may be overestimated if an intention to treat analysis is not completed, and you will learn more about this in your future research methodologies coursework.

Diffusion of treatment is best managed through fidelity of treatment procedures (usually including a treatment fidelity measure) which are thought to enhance both internal and external validity. There are various methods for including treatment fidelity procedures such as training treatment providers in a standardized manner, using a treatment manual in the delivery of treatment, and including a checklist or assessment to ensure that the treatment is being delivered as intended (Borrelli et al., 2005).

HOW DO I MOVE FROM CONSUMING TO PRODUCING RESEARCH?

The Scientist-Practitioner Model

The Association for Assessment and Research in Counseling (AARC) emphasizes and encourages research in counseling. As a future counselor, you may decide to join professional organizations to have access to additional training and development beyond your classroom training, and you may want to consider joining an organization like AARC that facilitates the development of research skills. Consuming and producing research to inform your clinical work and that of the professional community is endorsing a *scientist-practitioner model*. The scientist practitioner (S-P) model (Stricker, 2002), also known as the Boulder Model (Baker & Benjamin, 2000), was named after a conference sponsored in part by the Veterans Association that took place in Boulder, Colorado. The conference established a premise that clinicians should use research to inform their practice and use practice to inform their research.

Although the Boulder Model was first developed by psychologists, counselors and divisions of the American Counseling Association (i.e. AARC) have adopted the model and promoted the use of the model among counselors. The Boulder conference involved an effort to bring together two seemingly distinct paths: academic psychologists conducting research, and psychologists seeking to apply research-based content to practice. Given the differing agendas among psychology practitioners and researchers, it is quite remarkable that the scientist practitioner model found agreement. The process required that 73 people agree on 70 resolutions in just 15 short days (Baker & Benjamin, 2000). The Boulder model was born, and continues to live on in the majority of psychology programs, as well as extending to counseling programs (Baker & Benjamin, 2000; Hays, 2010). For the purposes of this text the *scientist practitioner model* will be defined as *a model used by psychologists and counselors that uses research to inform practice and practice to inform research.*

> **Scientist Practitioner Model** - a model used by psychologists and counselors that uses research to inform practice and practice to inform research.

Employing the Scientist Practitioner Model in Counseling

Hays (2010) indicated a movement in the field of counseling toward evidence-based treatments and advocated for counselors to implement the scientist practitioner model. Stricker (2002) identified the common components among various S-P models and explains the core elements (See Table 12.2 below). The components of a scientist practitioner model, as described by Stricker (2002, p. 1278) and emphasized by Hays (2010) include:

(a) in the process of doing clinical work, they display a questioning attitude and search for confirmatory evidence;
(b) they apply research findings directly to practice;
(c) they undertake an evaluation of their individual practices;
(d) they produce research, either collaboratively or more traditionally. (Stricker, 2002, p. 1278)

Scientist Practitioner Model: Criteria Adapted from Stricker (2002, p 1278) & supported by Hays (2010)	
S-P Practice Requirement 1	The S-P must approach clinical practice with an inquisitive attitude & must search for evidence to confirm conclusions
S-P Practice Requirement 2	The S-P uses research to inform practice. He or she does this by directly applying research findings to clinical practice.
S-P Research Requirement 3	The S-P engages in the process of producing research either collaboratively or otherwise

TABLE 12.2

Scientist Practitioner Model Criteria

Counselors undergo training in diagnosis and treatment planning as a part of their counselor preparation coursework (CACREP, 2016). This lends itself to a questioning, or curious, attitude. The second requirement in this list involves being familiar with the research literature in the field. Recall, as discussed previously in this chapter, the importance of being familiar with ESTs and differentiating the treatment per client needs (i.e.CBT, CBASP, or behavioral activation more appropriate for my client's depression). This process is also supported by the field of counseling, because many state licensing boards require that Licensed Professional Counselors (LPCs) obtain continuing education units (CEUs) in order to renew their licenses and stay current. This is often an opportunity for counselors to attend a conference or a training sponsored by their professional organization. The last requirement, to engage in producing research, may be more challenging for counselors and counselor educators with heavy teaching loads and/or heavy client loads. The next section of this text explores ideas for how counselors and counselor educators can fulfill Stricker's (2002, p. 1278) third requirement, becoming a part of research or research teams who are producing meaningful studies that can provide implications for practicing clinicians. Then that research, when put into practice, can provide meaningful feedback to inform continuing research.

S-Ps and ESTs. Chambless and Hollon (1998) indicated that empirically supported treatments are "clearly specified psychological treatments shown to be efficacious in controlled research with a delineated population" (p. 7). The authors expounded on the work of Kiesler (1966), who emphasized the need for more systematic research evaluating the impact of therapist interventions on client outcomes. Kiesler provided his research conclusions on the use of person-centered psychotherapy with clients diagnosed with schizophrenia as an example, including the idea that "more rigorous experimental control is needed" (p. 94).

Despite the resistance of some counselors to integrate research into their practice, Peterson, Hall, and Buser (2016) surveyed a large group of counselors, finding that school counselors tended to value data on their practice more highly. Meanwhile, counselors in other contexts rated research as the least important of the CACREP core competencies. As the field moves toward evidence based treatment and with managed care's emphasis on accountability, evidenced based treatments are becoming increasingly important. For example, if your field experience site deals with managed care, you may use a software program like TherapyNotes.com where providers include a diagnosis and a treatment plan. When you begin billing insurance, you may be required to sign a waiver that indicates you believe this treatment to be *medically necessary* for your client.

© Pressmaster/Shutterstock.com

Becoming a Producer of Research

While counselors may feel discouraged because they do not have the resources to conduct gold standard, randomized controlled trials, it is important to note that it is still possible to develop an empirically supported treatment with other more feasible methods, such as a series of single case design studies (Tolin, McKay, Forman, Klonsky, & Thombs, 2015). Single case designs only require one client, with the client serving as his or her own control group with baseline data. S-P's such as Dr. James McCullough, who developed cognitive behavioral analysis of systems psychotherapy (CBASP), an evidence based treatment for working with clients with chronic depression, provides recommendations for how clinicians can gather clinically relevant research data when using his approach. For example, CBASP includes a protocol of highly structured interventions, and McCullough provides suggestions on how to assess these practices in treatment and chart the progress in order to evaluate the efficacy of treatment. Counselors, can use protocols like this to get started in evaluating their practice. Tracey (1983) indicated that a feasible area of research for counselors is single case design research, as this model would enable counselors to research effective counseling interventions, evaluate programs, and evaluate supervision. However, he attributes the paucity of this type of research to a lack of awareness by counselors on the topic. While most counselors are aware of case studies, they do not have an understanding of the more rigorous *n of 1* experimental designs (Tracey, 1983).

Honeycutt Hollenbaugh (2011) conducted research on how to promote involvement in research within graduate counseling students. Factors that contributed to greater productivity in research included the following: "research self-efficacy, interest, mentorship, and the research environment"

(p. 1). Yaa Tiwa Offei Darko, was a graduate counseling student that engaged in mentorship, was interested in research, embraced opportunities to engage in the research environment, and developed self-efficacy in the process. As you seek to maximize your research experience, consider Yaa Tiwa's experience and how it impacted her in the student profile below.

Yaa Tiwaa Offei Darko, M.A., QMHP-C
Counselor-In-Training

© Yaa Darko

Research, I have come to understand, has been a part of my journey as a student from the minute I decided to study abroad. My comprehension of this idea commenced during the last year of my undergraduate studies when I took an advanced directive class geared towards collecting data. The preparation to present the analyzed data at my institution's symposium, like any other novel activity, evoked anxiety, confusion, and doubt. The feeling of fear and doubt stemmed from my confusion regarding the types of methods to be utilized in the process and how I would analyze raw data to deduce substantial information. The more I dipped my foot in the process, the more I realized its importance. The answers derived from questions posed, and lessons taught from my research courses became alive to me. I discovered a new found desire, which ignited a yearning to continue this process while joining others who share a similar passion.

Acquiring a master's degree in Clinical Mental Health Counseling at Liberty University opened my eyes to the notion that research begins where one is and goes beyond the classroom. I recall at the beginning of the program when my professor urged a group of us to present our meta-analysis research on bipolar disorder at the Virginia Association for Counselor Education and Supervision (VACES) Graduate Student Conference. Presenting at VACES was the first step I made into the professional world of research, and it certainly was not the last. I was fascinated by all the questions attempted to be answered through evidenced-based techniques and methodologies. Once I had an inquiry, I began to realize that the process of research provided the path to acquire answers. I discovered many opportunities outside the classroom, as I networked with colleagues and professors across the state. I could now grasp the practical results of my research education, which encouraged me to get involved and be a part of the movement to grow the counseling field through evidenced-based research. Becoming a part of the research team spearheaded by my research professor granted me many opportunities to present ongoing qualitative and quantitative research on the topics of empathy, God attachment and habits of an effective counselor at Virginia Counselors Association (VCA) Conventions, Virginia Association for Counselors Education and Supervision (VACES) conferences, Southern Association for Counselors Education and Supervision (SACES) conference, Association of Creativity in Counseling (ACC) conference and the Conference in Higher Education and Pedagogy (CHEP). Moments of growth continued to sprout from co-creating and administering workshops geared towards expanding our research among the student population on our campus and in the online world.

Looking back at the young lady who had anxiety regarding research and the appropriate use of its methodologies, I believe growth spurs from continuous involvement and a passion for discovering more. I remind myself that once answers are sought, research begins. Whether through a simple conversation or the use of the consensual qualitative approach, the process of research has found its way in our everyday life. As I move on to a doctorate program, I know this foundation undergirds the rest of my research journey. In the interactions with my peers, colleagues, community, and the world at large, I hope to continue to ask questions and seek answers, expanding the mental health field as the world continues to evolve.

WHAT ARE THE DIFFERENT TYPES OF RESEARCH COUNSELORS CAN PRODUCE?

Quantitative Research

Quantitative research emphasizes objective measurement and data analysis. Quantitative studies exist on a continuum from descriptive survey research design to a group comparison design called the true experimental design. Recall that an experimental design is more robust and controls for forms of invalidity by implementing strategies such as the use of a control group to compare treatment outcomes, and the use of random selection or random assignment in order to obtain a sample that is representative of the population (Knight & Tetrault, 2017). The true experimental design is the gold standard, and the flowchart in Figure 12.3 illustrates the different research designs.

FIGURE 12.3

Quantitative Research
Designs

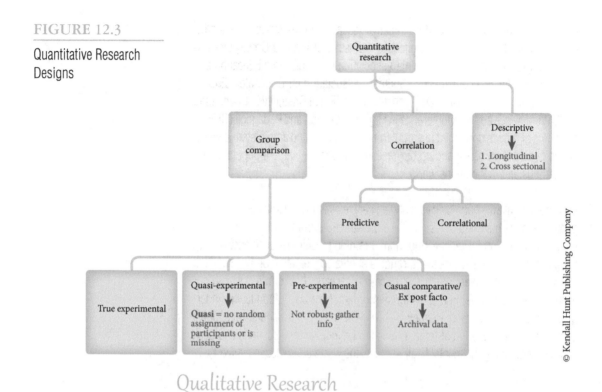

© Kendall Hunt Publishing Company

Qualitative Research

Qualitative research focuses on narrative and themes, and often involves interviews or transcript analysis to search for themes embedded within stories or other content. While quantitative research is associated with numbers and statistics, qualitative research embarks on a search for the narrative behind the numbers. Figure 12.4 provides a listing of some of the key types of qualitative research.

FIGURE 12.4

· Types of Qualitative
Research

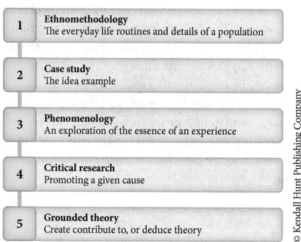

© Kendall Hunt Publishing Company

Counseling students may be most familiar with the type of qualitative research known as *case studies.* In ethics courses, counselor educators often use case studies to evaluate various ethical scenarios. In addition, counselors seeking out continuing education opportunities may find their training involves the application of ethical principles to specific case studies. Qualitative researchers and counselors emphasize hearing people's stories: "The very nature of the guidance and counseling profession makes it suitable for the use of case studies, narratives and life histories" (Berrios, & Lucca, 2006, p. 175).

Mixed Methods

In addition to quantitative and qualitative research designs, yet another design may offer the best of both quantitative and qualitative research. When a researcher includes both a quantitative and a qualitative component to their work, then it is a *mixed methods* design. A researcher may opt to conduct survey research to gain quantitative data and descriptive statistics, in order to describe measures of central tendency (i.e. mean, median, and mode), and then also interview participants to add a qualitative, or narrative, component to the research.

Program Evaluation

Program evaluation strategies support counselors in measuring effectiveness in counseling practice. ESTs have some limitations, despite the rigor of the clinical trials used, and sometimes even very robust studies demonstrate limitations, such as only addressing the internal validity of the study without addressing the external validity needed to generalize to clients. Thus, it is important for counselors to use program evaluation strategies to measure their own effectiveness in practice. *Single case designs* are often used in individual practice evaluation of outcomes. Kazdin (1983) devoted a comprehensive text to the topic of single case design, and indicated that, due to the possibility of conducting experimental research with one subject at a time, this design is more common in psychology and counseling field. Single case design studies have also been referred to as *intensive research design* or *n of 1 studies* (Kazdin, 1983). In a recent example, a study by Furlonger, Kiley, Moore, Busacca and Chittleborough (2018) designed a self-management program that used a single-case experimental design. This research included a baseline measurement, an intervention, and a 6-month follow-up to help older individuals begin and maintain a higher intensity fitness regime.

There are two common methods of program evaluation. In the first method, a valid and reliable instrument, such as the *Beck Depression Inventory-II* (BDI-II; Beck, Steer, & Brown, 1996) can be used to measure change in symptoms of depression following treatment. The assessment phase involves gathering baseline data on how the client is functioning and is accomplished during intake and treatment planning. Then, the treatment phase first involves psychoeducation and case conceptualization to establish a framework for agreed upon goals and methods for treatment (Sibcy & Knight, 2019). Next, treatment is delivered for a specified period of time, with an outcome measurement taken at each session (ie. the BDI-II at each session). Following the period of treatment, the final score on the measure or their average score is compared to the client's baseline score (where they started).

Once this data is collected, you can use different criteria to evaluate the effectiveness of your treatment. For example, if your goal for treatment is remission, then success could be defined as a BDI-II score within the normal range following treatment. Another criteria could be reliable change, meaning that the improvement made is beyond or outside the parameters of normal chance. In this case, treatment success is defined by determining the standard deviation compared to the parameters for reliable change (approximately 1.5 standard deviations). So, if you are using the BDI-II as your measure, and let's say the SD is 6, your client's score would have to change by 9 points in order to determine statistically reliable change, as opposed to the change happening by chance.

In the second method of program evaluation, counseling effectiveness is measured by reliable change represented by what is termed *response rate*. Response rate is reflected when a pretest score drops to half the baseline score. For example, if the client starts treatment with a depression score of 20, and their depression ratings fall to a score of 10, then that would be considered reliable change. Likewise if their baseline score was 30, then they would need to fall to 15, and if their baseline was 40, then they would need to fall to 20, and so on. There are other methods and strategies that you will learn later in your training that will support you in evaluating your counseling outcomes (program evaluation) in terms of reliable changes made.

A Case Study in Program Evaluation

How might a counselor evaluation clinical effectiveness with clients suffering from clinical depression? Imagine that you are working as a counselor in an integrative health care facility, with several physicians, nurse practitioners, and physician assistants. You were hired because the facility wanted to include counseling as a part of their service line for treating a number of different mental health concerns, but specifically they want you to treat clients diagnosed with mild to moderate depression who would rather try counseling before starting antidepressant medication. As part of your initial training, you attended a workshop on how to use Behavioral Activation (BA), an empirically supported treatment for depression. You are working with a clinical supervisor to help you learn how to apply what you learned in the workshop with real clients you see in clinical practice. How could you measure your effectiveness in treating clients with mild to moderate clinical depression using BA?

One of the easiest and best ways to do this is to use a single-case research design, since an RCT would be difficult and costly to apply in this clinical practice setting. Further, since BA has already been established as an EST, you already know it is efficacious as a treatment. What you are hoping to investigate, however, is whether BA is effective in *your specific clinical practice setting*, with a counselor (yourself) who is just beginning to learn how to use this treatment.

Initially, you will need to select a valid and reliable measure of depression, something that is quick and easy to administer to your client prior to beginning of each session while the client is still in the waiting room. A commonly used measure for depression is the *Personal Health Questionnaire-9* (PHQ-9; Spitzer, Williams, & Kronke, et al., 2000). The clients you will see will typically have depression scores on the PHQ-9 that fall between 10–19, indicating moderate to moderately severe depression. Because the clients are wanting to try counseling first, medication will not be added to the treatment plan until the client has completed at least 12 counseling sessions with you or unless the client's depression worsens or their suicide risk increases.

Imagine you have completed the training and will meet with your clinical supervisor for your weekly supervision appointment. You talk with your supervisor about the best way to administer the BA treatment with your client who is struggling with moderate depression. Together you decide on a *session by session protocol* for administering the treatment that spanned the 12 sessions. Then, there are several different criteria you can examine to determine whether your treatment has been effective:

Remission Status. Based on PHQ-9 cut-off scores, if your client's depression score drops to 4 or below, your client has achieved a state of remission. So lets say that your client started with a depression score of 15. At session, 10, their score has dropped to 4 and remains there for the next two sessions. We can say that the treatment was effective in that it helped your client achieve a normal range of depressive symptoms. (Technically, to be in full remission, a client would need to remain in this range for a minimum of 8 weeks, continuously).

Response Status. Treatment response is often defined as a client cutting their depressive score in half. So if your client started at 15 and dropped to 7, they would have "responded to treatment" even though they did not achieve full remission. They would be in partial remission.

Reliable treatment response status. Another method commonly used to determine strength of treatment response is to show that the person's response treatment is beyond what might occur by chance. This is done by identifying the standard deviation of the measurement. Although people use different criteria for assessing reliable change, a common method is to use 1.5 standard deviations of change. So for example, if a scale has a standard deviation of four, it would require a six point reduction to achieve a reliable change status. So, if your client went from a starting score of 15 and dropped to 9, you could say they made a reliable change. In other words, there is only a 10% chance that the client's score dropped due to chance.

In order to measure progress in this program evaluation, you might conduct this type of treatment tracking for ten clients. In the instance, for example, that four of your clients achieved scores of 4 or below on the PHQ-9 and three of your clients reduced their scores by half, you might report that at least 70% of your clients responded to treatment, with 40% achieving remission. That is a great result! Or, if you were using reliable change index, and 80% of your clients reduced their depressive scores by at least 6 points, you could say that 80% of your clients achieved reliable change.

So, as a counselor what kinds of things do you need to learn to evaluate program effectiveness? In order for counselors to measure effectiveness and measure counseling outcomes, counselors need to:

- Be familiar with assessments that measure symptoms for common diagnoses like depression,such as the PHQ-9, along with the statistical specifics such as standard deviations (i.e. PHQ-9; SD= 4)
- Understand ways to establish clinical significance (ie. remission status)
- Understand effect size and key statistical concepts
- Understand the benefits of the S-P model
- Identify key clinical outcomes to measure (ie. diagnoses such as depression or individual characteristics such as attachment security) and their interaction (how do attachment scores on the Experiences in Close Relationship Revised [ECR-R; Fraley, Waller, & Brennan, 2000] change as depression is treated)
- Make a habit of reading research literature regularly, seeking to identify methods of treatment that work for your particular client

Now that you have completed the reading of this chapter, we hope you have a better idea of what it takes to be a discerning consumer of the counseling research, the ethical requirements to use evidence based treatments in practice, some ideas about how to assess the validity or robustness of a study, and feasible ways to measure your own effectiveness in practice. Becoming familiar with the different forms of validity (internal, external, construct, and data evaluation) and the threats to validity will give you a strong foundation to build on as you continue to learn more about how counselors can be both consumers and designers of robust research studies. We hope you will develop the confidence needed to engage in research, and develop a researcher identity as a scientist-practitioner.

HOW CAN I LEARN TO ENJOY RESEARCH ON THE CIT JOURNEY?

"It is the glory of God to conceal a matter; to search out a matter is the glory of kings." Proverbs 25: 2

© Deborah Feingold/Corbis Entertainment/Getty Images

As this chapter comes to a close, and you think about your future research endeavors, it is important to remember to enjoy the learning journey. Enjoying research may sound like an oxymoron to some, but it does not have to be. Research can be an enjoyable and even glorious task. When a counselor or CIT identifies an area of research interest and begins to search out peer-reviewed literature on the topic, perusing counseling and psychology databases for the content, it can be very interesting, satisfying a curiosity and enriching practice. I often encourage students to think about what they would look for if they were going to "surf the web" for fun. Reviewing peer-reviewed literature is not unlike other web surfing; however, the task is to identify evidence based literature, and the search may involve using library databases or Google scholar rather than Google.

When I (A. Knight Kuhnley) teach research, I invite students to select their own mental health counseling research topic that represents a needed gap in the professional literature. I find that they become more interested in research because they are interested in their topic of choice. It may be helpful to think about the populations God has put on your heart or to consider the needs of the clients you serve. I would like to review the closing words of Mister Rogers, to remind you of something he told us all when we were younger when you were much younger, adapting the sentiment to the important role counselor's play as an S-P (Rogers, 1969, https://americanrhetoric.com/speeches/fredrogerssenatetestimonypbs.htm), "You have made today a special day, just by your being you. There is no one else in the whole world like you. [Your research will make a special contribution to counseling, just by your doing it. There is no one else in the world that can do research just like you.] And people can like you just the way you are." Just as Mister Rogers sought to communicate a meaningful expression of care during each program to his young television neighbors, your research can make a difference in identifying effective treatments for your "counseling neighbors" needing that expression of care.

SUMMARY

The purpose of this chapter was to explore the important role of research and program evaluation in the life and work of the counselor. Different types of validity including, internal validity, external validity, construct validity, and statistical validity were discussed. Research methods robustness were examined, discussing threats to validity as well as some controls for creating robust research designs. Trends in research in the field such as the movement from schoolism to evidence based practice were also explored. For you as a CIT, this movement toward the use of empirically supported treatments (ESTs) means that your research coursework training will be priceless in preparing you for the future direction of counseling. Cultivating strategies on becoming a good consumer and producer of the research literature, as well as measuring your counseling effectiveness through program evaluation, is critical. Organizations such as the Association for Assessment and Research in Counseling (AARC) exist as divisions of ACA to promote the role of resources in counseling and encourage the adoption of models such as the scientist practitioner model (S-P) in which research informs practice and practice informs research.

FOR THE ROAD AHEAD

Check out the Chapter 12 video at this link:

https://www.khpcontent.com/

Reflections on the Journey

In the chapter we discussed an overview of the S-P model and requirements for becoming an S-P, that is a counselor who uses research to inform practice and then in turn uses practice to inform research. In addition, a case study was presented applying an S-P mindset to a program evaluation example. As you think about the case, take a moment to consider your own journey and what this will look like. Consider the following: What will it look like for you to integrate research into your practice as a future counselor? What are some variables you may want to measure in your n of 1 studies?

For Further Exploration

This article mentioned frequently throughout the chapter discusses the benefits of evidence based treatments (treatments supported by research):

Clark, D. M. (2018). Realizing the mass public benefit of evidence-based psychological therapies: The IAPT program. *Annual Review of Clinical Psychology, 7*(14), 159-183. doi:10.1146/annurev-clinpsy-050817-084833.

The following text is a study guide that breaks down complex research concepts into understandable terms, it includes illustrations and is user friendly:

Knight & Tetrault (2017). *Research and program evaluation key concepts: A Study Guide.* Charlotte, North Carolina: Kona Media and Publishing Group.

This article by Dr. Danica Hays is cited frequently throughout this chapter as the introductory article for the second CORE journal and discusses the scientist practitioner model:

Hays, D. G. (2010). Introduction to counseling outcome research and evaluation. *Counseling Outcome Research and Evaluation, 1,* 1–7. doi:10.1177/2150137809360006

REFERENCES

American Counseling Association (2014). *ACA Code of Ethics.* Alexandria, VA: Author

American Psychological Association (APA). (n.d.). *How to be a wise consumer of psychological research.* Washington, D. C.: APA.

American Psychological Association (APA) Presidential Task Force on Evidence Based Practice. (2006). Evidence Based Practice in Psychology: Evidence based practice. *American Psychologist,* (61), 261–285.

American Psychological Association (APA). (2019). *How to be a wise consumer of psychological research: Evaluate research-based claims to become a better consumer of products and services that shape your daily life.* APA, Psychological Science, research in Action.

American Psychological Association. (2010). *Publication manual of the American Psychological Association* (6th ed.). Washington, DC: American Psychological Association.

Armento, M., & Hopko, D.(2007). The Environmental Reward Observation Scale (EROS): *Development, Validity, and Reliability. Behavior Therapy, 2*(38), 107–119. doi:10.1016/j.beth.2006.05.003

Atieno Okech, J. E., Astramovich, R. L., Johnson, M. M., Hoskins, W. J., & Rubel, D. J. (2006). Doctoral research training of counselor education faculty. *Counselor Education and Supervision, 46*(2), 131-145. Retrieved from http://ezproxy.liberty.edu/login?url=https://search.proquest.com/docview/201098321?accountid=12085

Baker, D. B., & Benjamin, L. T., (2000). The affirmation of the scientist-practitioner: A look back at Boulder. *American Psychologist, 55*(2), 241–247. doi:10.1037/0003-066X.55.2.241

Balkin, R. S., Gosnell K. M. R., Holmgren, A. & Osborne, J. W. (2017). Nonlinear analysis in counseling research. *Measurement and Evaluation in Counseling Research, 50*(1–2), 109-115.

Beck, A. T., Steer, R. A., & Brown, G. K. (1996). *Manual for the Beck Depression Inventory-II*. San Antonio, TX: Psychological Corporation.

Behenck, A. S., Braga, J. S., Gomes, J. B., & Heldt, E. (2016) Patient rating of therapeutic factors and response to cognitive-behavioral group therapy in patients with obsessive-compulsive disorder. *Issues in Mental Health Nursing, 37*(6), 392-399. doi:10.3109/01612840.2016.1158335.

Berry, J. W., & Chew, S. L., (2008). Improving learning through interventions of student-generated questions and concept maps. *Teaching of Psychology, 35*, 305-312. doi:10.1080/00986280802373841

Berrios, R., & Lucca, N. (2006). Qualitative methodology in counseling research: Recent contributions and challenges for a new century. *Journal of Counseling Development, 84*, 174-186.

Borders, L. D., & Bloss, K. K. (1994). Helping students apply the scientist-practitioner model: A teaching approach. *Counselor Education & Supervision, 34*, 172-179.

Borrelli, B., Sepinwall, D., Ernst, D., Bellg, A. J., Czajkowski, S., Breger, R., … Orwig, D. (2005). A new tool to assess treatment fidelity and evaluation of treatment fidelity across 10 years of health behavior research. *Journal of Consulting and Clinical Psychology, 73*, 852–860. Retrieved from https://psycnet.apa.org/fulltext/2005-13740-008.pdf

Burns, D. (2018). *Five secrets training- "I Feel" statements*. Feeling good website. Retrieved from: https://feelinggood.com/tag/empathy/

Chambless, D. L., Baker, M. J., Baucom, D. H., Beutler, L. E., Calhoun, K. S., Crits-Christoph, P., . . . Woody, S. (1998). Update on empirically validated therapies. II. *The Clinical Psychologist, 51*(1), 3–16. Retrieved from http://www.div12.org/sites/default/files/UpdateOnEmpiricallyValidated Therapies-2.pdf

Chambless, D. L., & Hollon, S. D. (1998). Defining empirically supported therapies. *Journal of Consulting and Clinical Psychology, 66*(1), 7-18.

Chew, S. (2014). Helping students get the most out of learning. In Bennasi, V., Overson, C. & Hakala, C. (Eds.), *Applying the science of learning in education: Infusing psychological science into the curriculum*. Washington, D.C.: Division Two, APA.

Clark, D. M. (2018). Realizing the mass public benefit of evidence-based psychological therapies: The IAPT Program. *Annual Review of Clinical Psychology, 7*(14), 159-183. doi:10.1146/annurev-clinpsy-050817-084833.

Constantin, K., English, M. M., & Mazmanian, D. (2018). Anxiety, depression and procrastination among students: Rumination plays a larger mediating role then worry. *Journal of Rational-Emotive & Cognitive-Behavioral Therapy, 36*(1), 15-27. doi:10.1007/s10942-017-0271-5

Creswell, W. J. (2014). *Research design: Qualitative, quantitative, and mixed methods approaches*. (4th ed.). Thousand Oaks, California: SAGE Publications

Crowl, T. (1993). *Fundamentals of education research*. McGraw Hill.

Dweck, C. (2016). *Managing yourself: What having a growth mindset actually means*. Brighton, MA: Harvard Business Review.

Dweck, C. (2016). *Mindset: The new psychology of success how we can learn to fulfill potential*. New York City, NY: Random House.

Flett, A. L., Haghbin, M., & Pychyl, T. A. (2016). Procrastination and depression from a cognitive perspective: An exploration of the associations among procrastinatory automatic thoughts, rumination, and mindfulness. *Journal of Rational - Emotive & Cognitive - Behavior Therapy, 34*(3), 169-186. doi:10.1007/s10942-016-0235-1

Foa, E. B., McLearn, C. P., Zang, Y., Rosenfield, D., Yadin, E., Yarvis, J., ... Peterson, A. L. (2018). Effect of prolonged exposure therapy delivered over 2 weeks vs 8 weeks present-centered therapy on ptsd symptom severity in military personnel a randomized clinical trial. *Journal of American Medical Association, 319*(4), 354-364. doi:10.1001/jama.2017.21242

Fraley, R. C., Waller, N. G., & Brennan, K. A. (2000). An item-response theory analysis of self-report measures of adult attachment. *Journal of Personality and Social Psychology, 78*, 350-365.

Furlonger, B., Kiley, S., Moore, D., Busacca, M., & Chittleborough, P. (2018). Using a single-case experimental design to evaluate a cognitive-behavioural self-management counselling intervention. *Asia Pacific Journal of Counseling and Psychotherapy, 1*(9), 46-60.

Hays, D. G. (2010). Introduction to Counseling Outcome Research and Evaluation. *Counseling Outcome Research and Evaluation, 1*, 1–7. doi:10.1177/2150137809360006

Holland, J. L. (1997). *Making vocational choices: A theory of vocational personalities and work environments* (3rd ed.). Odessa, FL: Psychological Assessment Resources.

Hollis, S., & Campbell, F. (1999). What is meant by intention to treat analysis? Survey of published randomised controlled trials. *BMJ (Clinical research ed.), 319*(7211), 670–674. doi:10.1136/bmj.319.7211.670.

Honeycutt Hollenbaugh, K. M. (2011). Fostering research in counselor education and Increasing research productivity in doctoral students. American Counseling Association: VISTAS Online. Retrieved from https://www.counseling.org/docs/default-source/vistas/Fostering-research-in-counselor-education-and-increasing-research-productivity-in-docoral-students.pdf?sfvrsn=6

Ivey, A. E., Ivey, M. B., & Zalaquett, C. (2018). Intentional interviewing and counseling: Facilitating client development in a multicultural society (9th ed.). Boston, MA: Cengage.

Jackson, L. S. (2015) *Research methods and statistics: A critical thinking approach.* (5th ed.) Wadsworth: Cengage Learning

Kahn, J. H. (2001). Predicting the scholarly activity of counseling psychology students: A refinement and extension. *Journal of Counseling Psychology, 48*(3), 344-354. doi:10.1037/0022-0167.48.3.344

Kahn, J. H., & Scott, N. A. (1997). Predictors of research productivity and science-related career goals among counseling psychology graduate students. *The Counseling Psychologist, 25*, 38-67.

Kazdin, A. (1983). *Single case research designs.* United States of America: Oxford University Press.

Kazdin, A. (2017). *Research design in clinical psychology.* New York, New York: Pearson.

Kelly, L. T. (1927). *Interpretation of educational measurements.* Yonkers, New York: World Book Company. Retrieved from http://cda.psych.uiuc.edu/kelley_books/kelley_interpretation_1927.pdf

Kiesler, D. J. (1966). Some myths of psychotherapy research and the search for a paradigm. *Psychological Bulletin, 65,* 110-136

Knight, A. M. & West, L. (2011). *School counselor resource series: Mastering test anxiety.* Alexandria, VA: American School Counseling Association.

Knight, A., & Tetrault, D. (2017). *Research and program evaluation key concepts: A study guide.* Kona Publishing & Media Group.

Kroenke, K., Spitzer, R., & Williams W. (2001). The PHQ-9: Validity of a brief depression severity measure. *JGIM, 16,* 606-616.

Lejuez, C. W., Hopko, D. R., & Hopko, S. D. (2001). A brief behavioral activation treatment for depression. Treatment manual. *Behavior Modification, 25*(2), 255-286. Retrieved from https://www.div12.org/wp-content/uploads/2014/11/BATDmanual_2001.pdf

Martell, C. R., Dimidjian, S., & Hermann-Dunn, R. (2010). *Behavioral activation for depression: A clinician's guide.* New York, New York: Guilford Press.

Maschi, T., Wells, M., Yoder Slater, G., MacMillan, T., & Ristow, J. (2013). Social work students' research-related anxiety and self-efficacy: Research instructors' perceptions and teaching innovations. *Social Work Education, 32,* 800–817. doi:10.1080/02615479.2012.695343

Mayer, J., Salovey, P., & Caruso, D. (2002). *Mayer-Salovey-Caruso emotional intelligence test (MSCEIT).* Toronto, Ontario: Multi-Health Systems, Inc.

McCullough, J., Lord, B., Conley, K., & Marin, A. (2018). A method for conducting intensive psychological studies for early-onset chronically depressed patients. *American Journal of Psychotherapy, 4*(64), 317-337.

McGuire, S. Y. (2015). *Teach students how to learn: Strategies you can incorporate into any course to improve student metacognition, study skills, and motivation.* Sterling, VA: Stylus Publishing.

McHugh, R. K., Whitton, S. W., Peckham, A. D., Welge, J. A., & Otto, M. W. (2013). Patient preference for psychological versus pharmacologic treatment of psychiatric disorders: A meta-analytic review. *Journal of Clinical Psychiatry 74,* 595–602.

Negrea, D., Rapp, C., Westbrook, T. M., Lasher, R., Hahn, S. A., Schure, M., & Goins, R. T. (2018). Research attitude and their correlates among undergraduate social work students. *Journal of Social Work Education, 54*(3), 506-516. doi:10.1080/10437797.2018.143443

NICE (2011). *Common mental health disorders: The nice guidelines on identification pathways to care.* London, The British Psychological Society and the Royal College of Psychiatrists.

Pearson, K. (1924). Historical note on the origin of the normal curve of errors. Biometrika, Vol. XVI, Part IV.

Peterson, C. H., Hall, S. B., & Buser, J. K. (2016). Research training needs of scientist-practitioners: Implications for counselor education. *Counselor Education and Supervision, 55*(2), 80-94. doi:10.1002/ceas.12034

Pychyl, T. A. (2013). Depression and procrastination: What might explain this relation? *Psychology Today.* Retrieved from https://www.psychologytoday.com/us/blog/dont-delay/201306/depression-and-procrastination

Rockinson-Szapkiw, A. J., Hillman, E., Wendt, J., & Kuhnley, A. (In Progress). *A guide for students: Strategies for developing a quantitative research proposal.* Charlotte, NC: Kona Publishing and Media Group.

Rogers, F. (1968). American rehetoric speech bank: Mister Fred Rogers makes a statement to the senate on PBS Funding. Retrieved from https://americanrhetoric.com/speeches/fredrogerssenatetestimonypbs.htm

Secret, M., Ford, J., & Rompf, E. L. (2003). Undergraduate research courses: A closer look reveals complex social work student attitudes. *Journal of Social Work Education, 39,* 411–422. doi:10.1080/10437797.200 3.10779146

Shearin, E. N. & Linehan, M. M. (1994). Dialectical behavior therapy for borderline personality disorder: Theoretical and empirical foundations. *Acta Psychiatrica Scandinavica. 89,* 379, 61-68.

Sibcy, G. A. & Knight, A. M. (2019). Theoretical foundations. In R. Hawkins, A. Knight, G. Sibcy, & S. Warren (Eds.), *Research based counseling skills: The art and science of therapeutic empathy.* Dubuque, IA: Kendall Hunt.

Sibcy, G. A. & Knight, A. M. (2019). Case conceptualization, scaling, & preliminary goal setting. In R. Hawkins, A. Knight, G. Sibcy, & S. Warren (Eds.), *Research based counseling skills: The art and science of therapeutic empathy.* Dubuque, IA: Kendall Hunt.

Sommers-Flanagan, J. (2015). Evidence based relationship practice: Enhancing counselor competence. *Journal of Mental Health Counseling, 2*(37), 95-108.

Spitzer, R. L., Williams, J. B. W., & Kroenke, K., Hornyak, R., & McMurray, J. (2000). Validity and utility of the Patient Health Questionnaire in assessment of 3000 obstetric-gynecologic patients: The PRIME-MD Patient Health Questionnaire Obstetrics-Gynecology Study. *American Journal of Obstetrics & Gynecology, 183,* 759–69.

Stricker, G. (2002). What is a scientist-practitioner anyway? *Journal of Clinical Psychology,* 58, 1277-1283.

Swan, J. S., MacVicar, R., Christmas, D., Durham, R., Rauchhaus, P., McCullough, J. P. & Matthews, K. (2014). Cognitive behavioral analysis system of psychotherapy (CBASP) for chronic depression: Clinical characteristics and six month clinical outcomes in an open case series. *Journal of Affective Disorders, 162,* 268-276.

Tracey, T. J. (1983). Single case research: An added tool for counselors and supervisors. *Counselor Education and Supervision, 3*(22), 185-196.

Terry, A. C., Mishra, P., & Roseth, C. J. (2016). Preference for multitasking, technological dependency, student metacognition, & pervasive technology use: An experimental intervention. *Computers in Human Behavior, 65,* 241-251. doi:10.1016/j.chb.2016.08.009

Tolin, D., McKay, D., Forman, E., Konsky, E., & Thombs, B. (2015). Empirically supported treatments: Recommendations for a new model. *Clinical Psychology Science and Practice, 4*(22), 317-338. doi:10.1111/cpsp.12122

Vivalt, E. (2018). *How to be a smart consumer of social science research.* Economics and Society. Harvard Business Review. Retrieved from https://hbr.org/2018/07/how-to-be-a-smart-consumer-of-social-science-research

Walden, S. L., Herlihy, B., & Ashton, L. (2003). The evolution of ethics: Personal perspectives of ACA ethics committee chairs. *Journal of Counseling and Development, 81*(1), 106-110. doi: 10.1002/j.1556-6678.2003.tb00231.x

Watkins, C. E., Lopez, F. G., Campbell, V. L., & Himmell, C. D. (1986). Contemporary counseling psychology: Results of a national survey. *Journal of Counseling Psychology, 33,* 301-309.

Unrau, Y. A., & Beck, A. R. (2004). Increasing research self-efficacy among students in professional academic programs. *Innovative Higher Education, 28,* 187–198. doi:10.1023/B:IHIE.0000015107.51904.95

West-Olatunju, C. (2013). Research in counseling. *Counseling Today.* Alexandria, VA: American Counseling Association.

CHAPTER 13

The Brain: What Counselors Need to Know

JOHN KUHNLEY, M.D., ROBYN SIMMONS, ED.D., & ANITA KNIGHT KUHNLEY, PH.D.

> "Biology gives you a brain. Life turns it into a mind."
> — Jeffrey Eugenides, Middlesex

Following Christ: Grace for Our Work

In 2 Corinthians, Paul tells the church to cast "down arguments and every high thing that exalts itself against the knowledge of God, bringing every thought into captivity to the obedience of Christ" (2 Corinthians 10:5, New King James Version). Paul also writes in Romans 12:2, "Do not conform to the pattern of this world, but be transformed by the renewing of your mind. Then you will be able to test and approve what God's will is—his good, pleasing and perfect will."

These verses provide two critical lessons related to our minds/brains. First, we are not prisoners of our thoughts.

After reading this chapter, you will understand more about:

- The foundational concept of neuroscience
- The physiological properties of the brain and how they impact mental health functioning, including addiction
- The PolyVagal theory and its impact on clients
- Psychotropic medications and their impact on the brain

The following CACREP standards are addressed in this chapter:

Human Growth and Development:

- Biological, neurological, and physiological factors that affect human development, functioning, and behavior (CACREP, 2016, Standard 2.F.3.e.)

Clinical Mental Health Counseling-Foundations and Cultural Dimensions:

- Neurobiological and medical foundation and etiology of addiction and co-occurring disorders (CACREP, 2016, Standard 5.C.1.d.)
- Impact of biological and neurological mechanisms on mental health (CACREP, 2016, Standard 5.C.2.g.)
- Classifications, indications, and contraindications of commonly prescribed psychopharmacological medications for appropriate medical referral and consultation (CACREP, 2016, Standard 5.C.2.h.)

We have a mighty King who can help us fight against negative and destructive thought patterns, no matter how deeply ingrained they are. Second, our minds are capable of transformation and renewal. In these ancient writings, Paul is asserting concepts that today seem to be newfound.

What we know from neuroscience is that the brain is designed for continuous development. Because God is our Redeemer, He created our brains for redemption. Sin is a destroyer and in its arsenal of weapons are things that can negatively impact our minds. But God created a way for our brains to regenerate and renew so that negative neural pathways do not create a prison of emotional and mental unhealthiness.

As you learned in Chapter 1, neuroscience is shaping up to be the next wave of counseling. As understanding and knowledge increase regarding brain functioning and its impact on mental health, you will be better prepared to apply these concepts in your work with clients. Neurocounseling is the integration of neuroscience concepts in work with clients through psychoeducation regarding the physiological basis of mental health issues (Russell-Chapin, 2016). It is important to note that neurocounseling does not solely involve the psychoeducational aspect of brain functioning; rather, neurocounseling provides a filter of brain science over the foundation skills, values, and counseling models adopted by the counseling profession (Luke, Miller, & McAuliffe, 2019). Beeson and Field (2017) further indicated that neurocounseling has become an area of specialization in the field of counseling.

More and more attention is being paid to the integration of neuroscience in the professional literature. In addition to multiple articles educating readers on the structure and function of the brain, there is professional literature regarding the integration of these concepts with existing therapeutic interventions. Mindfulness approaches (Bingaman, 2016; Ludy-Dobson & Perry, 2010; Navalta, McGee, & Underwood, 2018; Wagner, 2017; and multiple others), creative arts interventions (Perryman, Blisard, & Moss, 2019), and yoga practice (Caplan, Portillo, & Seely, 2013) are identified as having positive neurocounseling implications. Further, neuroscience based approaches have been identified as having success with multiple client issues, including depression (Hoffman, Ettinger, Reyes del Paso, & Duschek, 2017), anxiety (Milad, Rosenbaum, & Simon, 2014), trauma (Navalta et al., 2018), relational functioning (Ludy-Dobson & Perry, 2010), and attention-Deficit/hyperactivity disorder (Erk, 2000), among other issues. Neurocounseling, then, can serve as an overlay for existing modalities, allowing for a more holistic approach to helping clients.

Because, as noted previously, neuroscience is a current trend in the field, and will likely continue to gain ground in the future, we wanted to dedicate an entire chapter to the brain and how you will be able to use this information with clients. In this chapter, you will be introduced to brain structures and functions of those structures, neuroscience concepts, polyvagal theory, and psychotropic medications and how they interact with the brain.

The Case of Brooklyn

© Stock-Asso/Shutterstock.com

Brooklyn is a 23-year-old client who has sought treatment for depression. She reports feeling like she has struggled with depression off and on in her life, with her earliest memory of feeling sad at 8 years of age. She indicated that her parents never seemed to be sad, but a paternal aunt had to be hospitalized a few times for depression. She does not recall any significant childhood trauma that resulted in feeling sad at 8. She remembers it being like a "blanket of nothingness." Brooklyn reported that her parents noticed this and were "overly concerned". They took her to a therapist who "always asked me a lot of questions." She said that she did not like going and begged her parents to allow her to discontinue. They agreed but said if she continued to be sad she would need to return.

Brooklyn learned to hide her sadness. She was somewhat active and involved as a teenager, including being on the yearbook staff and graduating in the top 5% of her class. She did not date or go out with friends on weekends. Despite the facade of normalcy, she showed her parents, Brooklyn continued feeling the deep emotional void internally. When she was alone, she would sit and stare for hours. When she went to college, she welcomed the freedom to sit in her depression and not perform for her parents. As a result, she missed a great many classes. However, she was able to pull mostly B grades and her parents just assumed the drop in grades was because college was more rigorous.

Brooklyn has been out of college for a year and has been working in her field, but she reports she does not find any pleasure in her work nor in relationships with colleagues. Because she is in a technical field, she is allowed to work at home most days. As she has learned to do through the years, she pushes through to get her work done, but then she just sits in darkness or sleeps. She does not have much of an appetite so there has not been a noticeable weight gain. She makes it once a week to have dinner with her parents for which she puts on her "happy face." To the rest of the world, Brooklyn looks fine. However, she became alarmed when she began thinking of ways that she might kill herself and decided to give therapy another try.

Brooklyn's health insurance recommended Taylor, a counselor who practices neuro-informed counseling. After completing a psychosocial history and suicide risk assessment and determining that Brooklyn was not at risk, he determined that a neuroscience approach would be beneficial. In order for Taylor (or any counselor) to be able to use a neuroscience approach, he needed to understand the structure and function of the brain. You will learn more about Taylor's work with Brooklyn later in the chapter.

WHAT DO COUNSELORS NEED TO KNOW ABOUT THE BRAIN?

To fully utilize a neuroscience approach to counseling, you will need to understand the physiological properties of the brain. You will find an explanation of each structure as well as graphics to illustrate the concepts. While this information is complex, it is important and critical to your work as a counselor. With neuroscience gaining more attention in the profession, you will need to be familiar with the structure of the brain and how it functions to understand its impact on mental health.

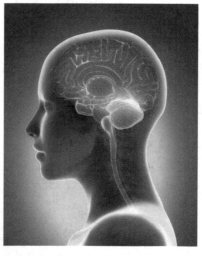

© CLIPAREA l Custom media/Shutterstock.com

The *Nervous System* is a network of nerve cells and fibers interconnected to conduct impulses from sensory input inside and outside the body to processing centers which then convey impulses to direct responses of the body. It includes the brain and spinal cord with connections throughout the body. The *brain* (Figure 13.1) is a powerful 3-pound organ. It is soft and squishy with a gel-like consistency. The brain includes many masses of neurons, or nerve cells, which interconnect with themselves and the body. Historically, science estimated and accepted that the brain contains 100 billion neurons and ten times as many support cells including glial cells. *Glial cells* are non-neuronal cells that have many functions, including provision of structural support and nutrition for nerve cells and synapses. However, advancements in brain cell counting by Azevedo et al. (2009) estimated 86 billion neurons and 85 billion non-neuronal cells. The distribution of these cells creates various parts of the nervous system which have specific and overlapping functions.

Neurons

Neurons (see Figure 13.1), also known as nerve cells, are specialized cells which function for the transmission of electrical or chemical impulses throughout the nervous system. In other words, neurons send information and instruction throughout the body. While most neurons are present at birth, more recently the understanding of neurogenesis in the adult brain has created a paradigm shift in how the "plasticity and stability" of the brain is viewed (Gross, 2000, p. 67). *Neurogenesis* is the formation of new neurons. It occurs in specific brain regions including the hippocampus, which is important in encoding memory. Gonçalves (2016) noted that the "adult-born neurons become functionally active and are thought to contribute to learning and memory, especially during their maturation phase, when they have extraordinary plasticity" (p. 897). What this means is that the part of the brain that is associated with memory (hippocampus), located in the area of the brain known as the *limbic system* (mammalian brain), is continuously generating new neurons.

THE NEURON

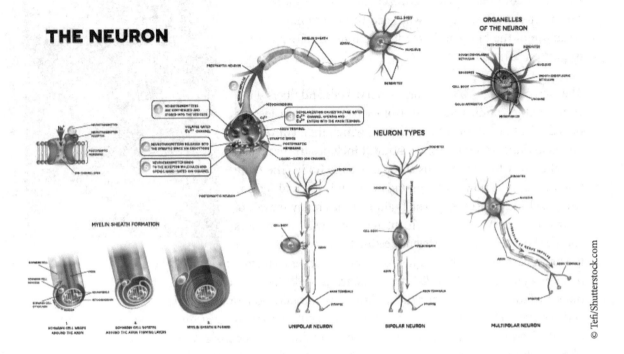

FIGURE 13.1

The Neuron

There are three main types of neurons: sensory, motor and interneuron. *Sensory neurons* have receptors which receive information from inside or outside the body and conduct the messages to the brain and spinal cord. *Motor neurons* receive information from other neurons and produce actions within muscles, organs, and glands. *Interneurons* (found only in the Central Nervous System) receive information from sensory neurons, communicate with other interneurons to integrate the information, and convey information or commands to motor neurons.

A neuron has a cell body (also known as a *soma*) with a nucleus which contains much of the cell's genetic material. It controls gene expression and regulates the activities of the cell. *Dendrites* branch out from the soma to *receive transmissions* from other neurons via synapses (junctions between two nerve cells). An *axon* extends away from the soma and serves to *conduct messages* to other neurons at synapses. The cell's dendrites may receive *excitatory* input that would cause the neuron to fire an impulse and *inhibitory* input which would suppress firing. The neuron receives many inputs simultaneously and the sum of excitatory and inhibitory inputs determines if the neuron will fire an impulse (or action potential) along the axon to transmit to other neurons, organs, or glands. Axons may have myelin sheaths which insulate the axon and speed the transmission of action potentials. Why is this important for you to know as a counselor? Essentially, this is how information is transferred throughout the brain and the body. This transferral of information is foundational to all what makes clients *tick*, so to speak.

Glial cells provide some neurotransmitters, including glutamate and GABA, to neurons. They provide a barrier to block toxic substances and microorganisms from entering the nervous system, and they eliminate dead cells. Examples of *neurotransmitters* include serotonin, norepinephrine, dopamine, acetylcholine, glutamate, endorphins, and gamma-aminobutyric acid (GABA). Table 13.1 provides a functional definition for each of these neurotransmitters. An understanding of the function of neurotransmitters is beneficial in counseling as it helps clients understand the reasoning behind many seemingly unexplainable mental health concerns. For example, if the brain does not produce enough dopamine, clients may feel a sense of anhedonia (inability to feel pleasure or joy). Understanding this as a symptom of depression, that it is a function of brain chemistry, and that there are behavioral changes that can increase the production of dopamine (i.e., exercise, food choices, sleep hygiene, among others) can help clients move beyond feeling the loss of hope that things will get better.

Neurotransmitter	Effects
Acetylcholine	Muscle contraction, activation of pain responses, endocrine regulation, REM sleep functions, learning, and memory.
Adrenaline	Under stress, it stimulates an increase in the heart rate and blood pressure, expands the air passages in the lungs, and redirects blood to the muscles for the "Fight or Flight" response.
Dopamine	Include attention, memory, learning, movement, mood, sleep, and motivation. It is associated with the brain's pleasure and reward system.
GABA	Gamma-Aminobutyric acid is the main inhibitory neurotransmitter. It is the calming neurotransmitter. Low GABA may result in anxiety, sleep problems, muscle pains, headaches, chronic stress. High levels may improve focus.
Glutamate	It is the most abundant excitatory neurotransmitter in the brain. It is involved in learning and memory.

TABLE 13.1

Effects of Common Neurotransmitters

TABLE 13.1

(continued)

Endorphins	Interact with opiate receptors in the brain to reduce the perception of pain. They are released during exercise and provide a sense of well-being and euphoria.
Noradrenaline	Under stress, it stimulates an increase in blood pressure, and participates in the "Fight or Flight" response. It is involved in attention, learning, mood, emotions, sleeping, and dreaming.
Serotonin	Regulation of mood, social behavior, appetite, digestion, sleep, memory, and sexual desire and function.

The Synapse

The synapse (Figure 13.2) is the junction where nerve cells communicate with other nerve cells.

FIGURE 13.2

The Synapse

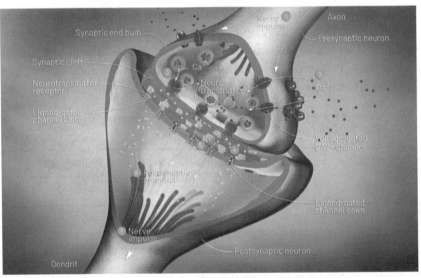

© Christoph Burgstedt/Shutterstock.com

Synaptogenesis is the formation of synapses between neurons. In early childhood, voluminous formation of synapses occurs. While it tapers down, synaptogenesis occurs throughout the person's lifespan. *Synaptic pruning* is a brain process that eliminates the extraneous synapses to increase the efficiency of neural transmission. It has been suggested that autism spectrum disorders, epilepsy, schizophrenia, and other brain disorders are caused by abnormal synaptic pruning (Neniskyte & Gross, 2017).

A number of axons bound together by connective tissue form a *nerve*. Cell bodies produce the gray matter of the brain and spinal cord while myelinated axons, or nerve fibers, produce the white matter. While the brain is a collection of neurons and their axon tracts, neurons exist throughout the body.

Divisions of the Nervous System

The *Spinal Cord* is the main pathway connecting the brain with the *Peripheral Nervous System* or PNS. The PNS includes cranial nerves and spinal nerves with innervation throughout the body. Together the brain and spinal cord comprise the *Central Nervous System* or CNS (Figure 13.3). The brain receives input from organs throughout the body, processes the input, acts upon the input, and stores memories.

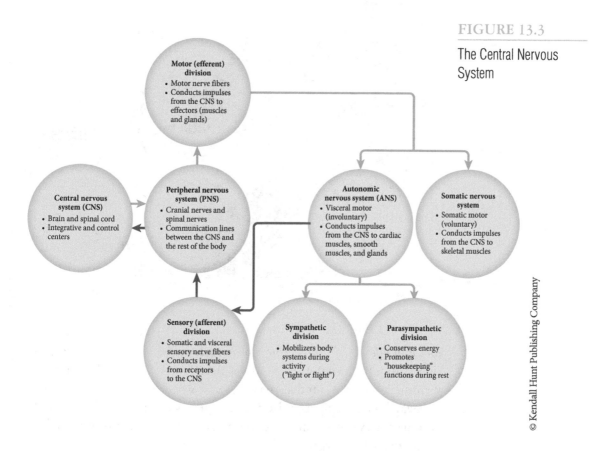

© Kendall Hunt Publishing Company

FIGURE 13.3

The Central Nervous System

The brain and peripheral nervous system work together to produce action and function. The peripheral nervous system has two subdivisions, the *Somatic Nervous System* and the *Autonomic or Visceral Nervous System*. The peripheral nervous system has two types of neurons, the *Sensory or Afferent* neurons and the *Motor or Efferent* neurons.

Sensory or *afferent* neurons (also known as first order neurons) respond to stimuli detected by somatic receptors which perceive external stimuli and visceral sensory nerve fibers (these sense internal conditions and control body homeostasis). These receptors convert the stimuli into electrical impulses for communication within the nervous system. They then conduct the impulses toward the spinal cord and the brain. The cell bodies of sensory neurons cluster in a *Dorsal Root Ganglion* (DRG) of a spinal nerve. Anatomically, dorsum or dorsal refers to the upper side or back of an organism or organ (Figure 13.4).

FIGURE 13.4

Dorsal Root Ganglion

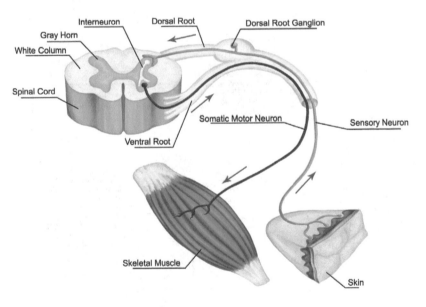

© stihii/Shutterstock.com

Motor or *efferent* neurons project motor nerve fibers (axons) that conduct signals to impact motor or glandular function. The cell bodies of motor neurons are in the ventral horns of the spinal cord grey region. They project away from the spinal cord as the ventral root and join the dorsal root to become a nerve. Ventrum or ventral refers to the lower side or underside of an organism or organ.

Interneurons (also known as *association neurons*) are in the CNS. They create communication circuits with sensory and motor neurons to produce rapid processing of information. They are involved in sensory-motor integration, neural oscillations (repetitive brain wave patterns), and neurogenesis (the growth and development of nervous tissue). In Figure 13.5, the hand touches a cactus and registers pain. The sensory neuron synapses with an interneuron which excites a motor neuron to contract the muscle in the hand to pull the hand away from the cactus. If you have experienced this before, you understand that the synaptic communication feels instantaneous. In the case of a client who is primed for feeling defensive (perhaps as a result of needing to be defensive to self-protect as a child), the emotional reactivity also seems instantaneous. As a counselor approaching clients from a neuro-informed perspective, you can explain this synaptic communication in addition to helping clients understand and learn skills to more effectively cognitively process precipitating events.

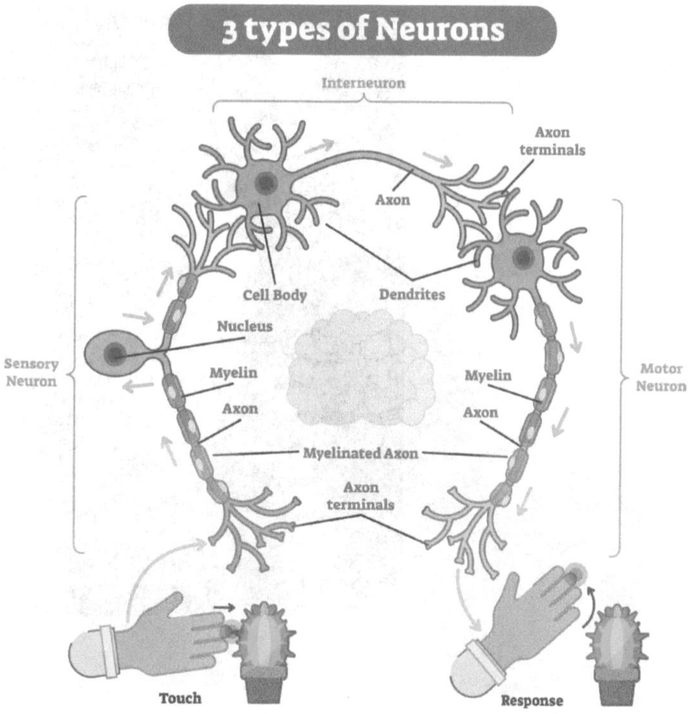

3 types of Neurons

© VectorMine/Shutterstock.com

FIGURE 13.5

Three Types of Neurons

The *Somatic Nervous System* (SNS) controls voluntary body movements performed by the skeletal muscles such as walking, throwing, and lifting. It also controls involuntary muscle responses known as reflexes which involve a neural pathway known as a reflex arc. In the reflex arc, a sensory neuron conducts a signal to the spinal cord and, bypassing the brain, the spinal cord generates a quick reaction in a muscle (such as the knee-jerk reflex). This is spontaneous and subconscious.

There are 31 pairs of *spinal nerves* (Figure 13.6) to conduct sensory information to the spinal cord and commands from the spinal cord to skeletal muscles. Each spinal level has specific areas of innervation for function and correlates with possible symptoms experienced by a client.

FIGURE 13.6

Spinal Nerves

VERTEBRAL LEVEL	NEVER ROOT	INNERVATION	POSSIBLE SYMPTOMS
C 1	C 1	Intracranial Blood Vessels ● Eyes ● Lacrimal Gland ● Parotid Gland ● Scalp ● Base of Skull ● Neck Muscles ● Diaphragm	Headaches ● Migraine Headaches ● Dizziness ● Sinus Problems ● Allergies ● Head Colds ● Fatigue ● Vision Problems ● Runny Nose ● Sore Throat ● Stiff Neck ● Cough ● Croup
C 2	C 2		
C 3	C 3		
C 4	C 4		
C 5	C 5	Neck Muscles ● Shoulders ● Elbows ● Arms ● Wrists ● Hands ● Fingers ● Esophagus ● Heart ● Lungs ● Chest	● Arm Pain ● Hand and Finger Numbness or Tingling ● Asthma ● Heart Conditions ● High Blood Pressure
C 6	C 6		
C 7	C 7		
	C 8		
T 1	T 1	Arms ● Esophagus ● Heart ● Lungs ● Chest ● Larynx ● Trachea	Wrist, Hand and Finger Numbness or Pain ● Middle Back Pain ● Congestion ● Difficulty Breathing ● Asthma ● High Blood Pressure ● Heart Conditions ● Bronchitis ● Pneumonia ● Gallbladder Conditions ● Jaundice ● Liver Conditions ● Stomach Problems ● Ulcers ● Gastritis ● Kidney Problems
T 2	T 2		
T 3	T 3		
T 4	T 4		
T 5	T 5		
T 6	T 6	Gallbladder ● Liver ● Diaphragm ● Stomach ● Pancreas ● Spleen ● Kidneys ● Small Intestine ● Appendix ● Adrenals	
T 7	T 7		
T 8	T 8		
T 9	T 9		
T 10	T 10		
T 11	T 11	Small Intestines ● Colon ● Uterus	
T 12	T 12	Uterus ● Colon ● Buttocks	
L 1	L 1	Large Intestines ● Buttocks ● Groin ● Reproductive Organs ● Colon ● Thighs ● Knees ● Legs ● Feet	Constipation ● Colitis ● Diarrhea ● Gas Pain ● Irritable Bowel ● Bladder Problems ● Menstrual Problems ● Low Back Pain ● Pain or Numbness in Legs
L 2	L 2		
L 3	L 3		
L 4	L 4		
L 5	L 5		
	SACRAL	Buttocks ● Reproductive Organs ● Bladder ● Prostate Gland ● Legs ● Ankles ● Feet ● Toes	Constipation ● Diarrhea ● Bladder Problems ● Menstrual Problems ● Lower Back Pain ● Pain or Numbness in Legs

SPINAL NERVE FUNCTION

YOUR COMPANY NAME

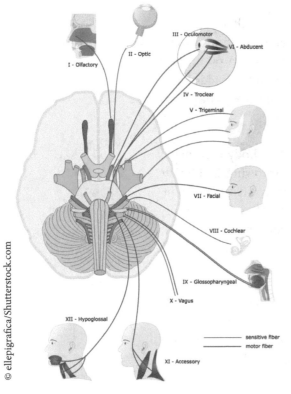

I - Olfactory
II - Optic
III - Oculomotor
VI - Abducent
IV - Troclear
V - Trigeminal
VII - Facial
VIII - Cochlear
IX - Glossopharyngeal
X - Vagus
XII - Hypoglossal
XI - Accessory

sensitive fiber
motor fiber

There are 12 pairs of *cranial nerves* which conduct information to the brain stem and from the brainstem to the periphery. They include the olfactory nerve (I), optic nerve (II), oculomotor nerve (III), trochlear nerve (IV), trigeminal nerve (V), abducens nerve (VI), facial nerve (VII), vestibulocochlear nerve (VIII), glossopharyngeal nerve (IX), vagus nerve (X), accessory nerve (XI), and hypoglossal nerve (XII). Each has a specific function such as smell, seeing, eye movement, hearing, touch, facial movement, and regulation of glands. The optic nerve is the one exception among the cranial nerves as it is part of the CNS (Monro 1895, p. 45) rather than the PNS.

The *Autonomic Nervous System* (ANS) or *Visceral Nervous System* (previously known as the vegetative nervous system) innervates smooth muscle, blood vessels, viscera (internal organs) and glands. It controls bodily functions not consciously directed, such as heart rate, respiration, digestion, and the function of glands. The autonomic nervous system has two divisions: the *Sympathetic Nervous System* (SNS) and the *Parasympathetic Nervous System* (PSNS). These systems have opposite actions.

The sympathetic nervous system mobilizes to prepare for action, especially in the face of danger or intense mental distress. Sympathetic nerve fibers release norepinephrine, a neurotransmitter, which accelerates the heart rate, constricts blood vessels, and raises blood pressure. It prepares the body for the automatic *Fight or Flight* response to fight back against danger or run from it. In addition, there is the *Freeze* option wherein lack of motion may hope the danger will move on. You will learn more about fight, flight, and freeze in the next section. At rest, the sympathetic nervous system is actively contributing to basic homeostasis or balance within the functions of the body.

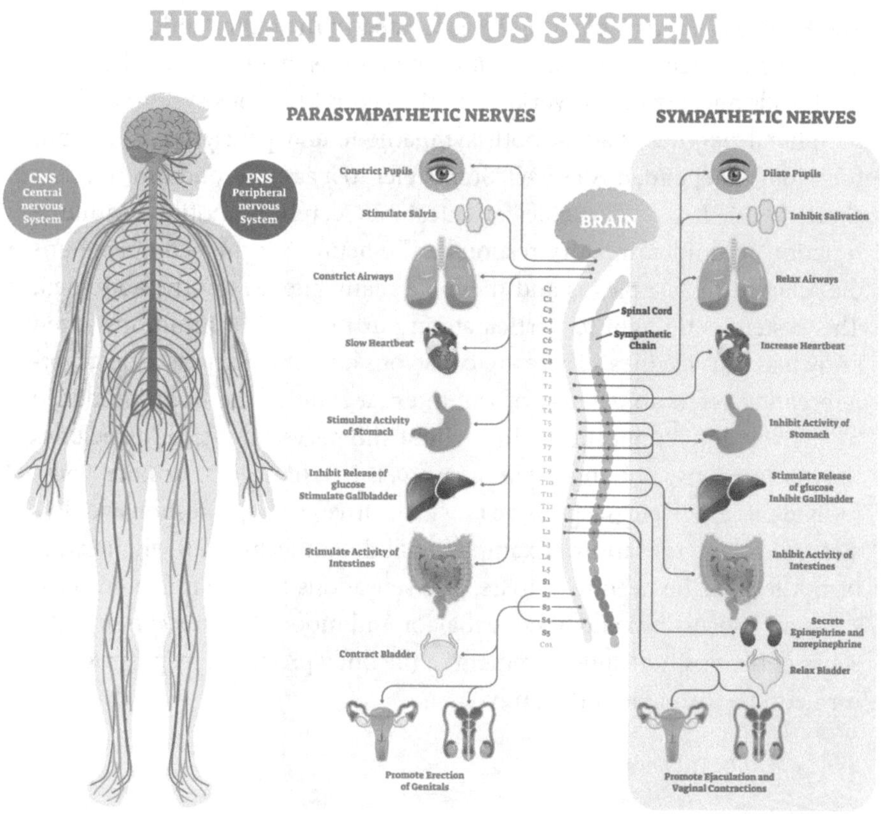

FIGURE 13.7

The Parasympathetic and Sympathetic Nervous System

© VectorMine/Shutterstock.com

The parasympathetic nervous system utilizes acetylcholine as an inhibitory neurotransmitter. It conserves energy. It relaxes sphincter muscles, increases glandular activity, constricts airways and slows the heart rate. It stimulates activity in the stomach and intestines. It stimulates urination, defecation, salivation, lacrimation, digestion, and sexual arousal. It is the *"rest and digest"* system. You may find you have a client who experiences an impact in their gastrointestinal system as a result of a mental health concern. Naturally, you would refer any client with physical symptoms to a medical doctor as the first level of assessment. If there is not a medical reason found for the symptoms, then you can conclude that they are connected to mental health concerns. For example, encopresis and enuresis in children may be tied to anxiety, depression, social problems, and/or academic concerns (Olari et al, 2016). You may never even address the symptoms of enuresis or encopresis, however, those symptoms may resolve as you address the client's anxiety.

The *Enteric Nervous System* (ENS) is located in the gut or abdomen (Figure 13.10). It includes tens of millions of neurons that innervate the intestinal walls and organs. It works with the central nervous system and the peripheral nervous system, both sympathetic and parasympathetic, but functions independently as well. Some refer to it as a "Second Brain" (Gershon, 1999). It is responsible for intestinal secretion, motility, immune function, and inflammatory response. The neurons form a complex bundle referred to as a plexus and there are many plexuses in the abdomen. This system is thought to participate in our instincts or intuitions, often known as "gut feelings". There are conscious and unconscious aspects. *Interoception* refers to a sense of the internal state of the body produced by the vast interconnections throughout the nervous system. It includes the internal sense of hunger, temperature, thirst, or need to urinate. Some individuals are hyper-responsive (very sensitive) or hypo-responsive (less aware) to these sensations. Examples include not feeling full when eating or not feeling the need to urinate. The sensations may be misinterpreted (sensory processing) and affect behavior and mood. *Proprioception* is the sense of the position and movement of the body produced by proprioceptor neurons throughout the body.

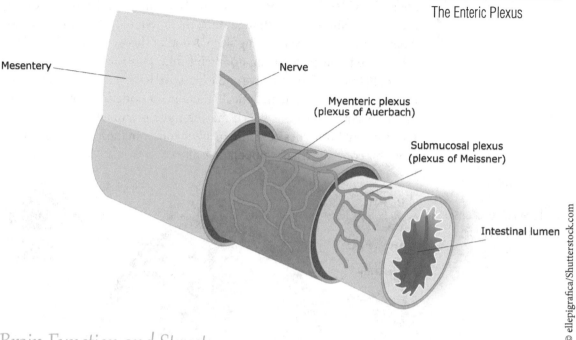

FIGURE 13.8

The Enteric Plexus

Mesentery

Nerve

Myenteric plexus
(plexus of Auerbach)

Submucosal plexus
(plexus of Meissner)

Intestinal lumen

© ellepigrafica/Shutterstock.com

Brain Function and Structure

The brain is responsible for monitoring sensory input; processing, integrating and coordinating input; storing memory; and determining action. It is involved in most of the functions or activities of the body. The three main parts of the brain include the *cerebrum*, the *brainstem*, and the *cerebellum*. The largest part of the human brain is the *cerebrum*. The cell bodies of neurons comprise the grey matter in the outer layer of the brain known as the cerebral cortex. The cerebral cortex has two hemispheres (right and left) and each hemisphere has four lobes (the frontal lobe, temporal lobe, parietal lobe, and occipital lobe). A *gyrus* is a ridge or a fold between two sulci (or anatomical depressions) on the surface in the cerebrum. These gyri or folds increase the surface area of the cerebrum allowing for increased packing of neurons and thus an increased ability for the brain to process information.

The *corpus callosum* provides communication between the hemispheres. Neuronal fibers from the cerebral cortex cross in the corpus callosum creating laterality. The right side of the brain controls the left side of the body and vice versa. There is a myth that humans use only 10% of their brain capacity and could function better if they used more. There is no scientific evidence to support this claim. Neuroimaging demonstrates that the entire brain is active, though different amounts at different times for different functions, even during sleep. Another theory is the right and left side of the brain each having dominant functions such that people who are "right-brained" are creative and expressive while people who are "left-brained" are logical and analytical. There is no evidence supporting this. There are some functions which may be more prominent on one side or the other but both sides of the brain are involved in most functions. However, this concept remains popular despite the lack of evidence base.

FIGURE 13.9

Right Brain Functions and Left Brain Functions

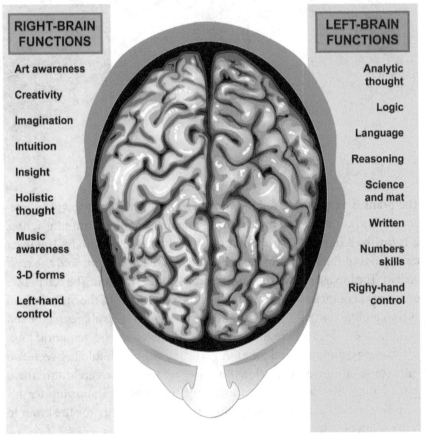

RIGHT-BRAIN FUNCTIONS

Art awareness

Creativity

Imagination

Intuition

Insight

Holistic thought

Music awareness

3-D forms

Left-hand control

LEFT-BRAIN FUNCTIONS

Analytic thought

Logic

Language

Reasoning

Science and mat

Written

Numbers skills

Righy-hand control

© MedusArt/Shutterstock.com

The *frontal lobe* controls cognitive skills. Functions include attention, reasoning, problem-solving, planning, organizing, language and communication, memory, judgment, impulse control, social and sexual behaviors, and personality. The *temporal lobe* is involved in processing sensory input or information. It is the primary auditory cortex. It receives sound input and processes sounds for comprehension including language comprehension. It processes visual input for object recognition and meaning. It interprets the emotions and reactions of others. The *hippocampus* is a small organ located in the middle of the temporal lobe. It is involved in memory, including processing new memory and long-term memory. It is also a major part of the *limbic system*. It plays a role in learning and emotions. The *parietal lobe* processes sensory input for taste, temperature, and touch. It is involved in proprioception (spatial sense and navigation). Input relays through the *thalamus* (a relay center for sensory and motor information involved in consciousness, alertness, and sleep) to the parietal lobe. The *occipital lobe* is the visual processing center. It is involved in color recognition, visuospatial processing, motion perception, and reading. The *cerebellum* is in the back of the brain. It provides for maintaining balance, coordinating eye movements, posture, and smooth body movement.

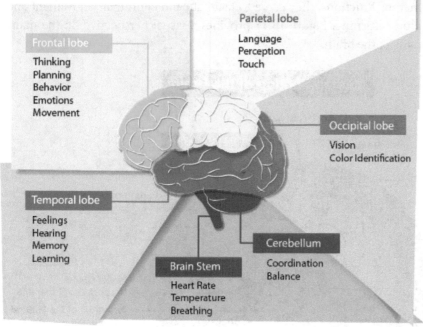

FIGURE 13.10

Regions of the Brain

Modified from © Atthapon Raksthaput/Shutterstock.com

The *diencephalon* is part of the forebrain. It includes the thalamus, hypothalamus, epithalamus, and subthalamus. The *thalamus* is involved in consciousness, sleep and alertness. It is a relay station for all sensory input

CHAPTER 13: *The Brain: What Counselors Need to Know*

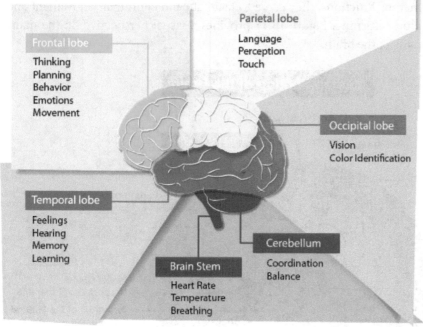

565

except olfaction (smell). The *hypothalamus* contains several nuclei and is part of the limbic system. It regulates certain metabolic processes within the autonomic nervous system. It participates in body temperature regulation, sleep, hunger and circadian rhythms (i.e., a 24-hour cycle of physiological processes). It plays a role in parenting and attachment behaviors (Insel, 1997). It secretes and releases neurohormones involved as releasing factors for stimulation or inhibition of hormones from the pituitary gland for regulating other hormones and their activities. The *brain stem* controls the flow of information between the brain and the rest of the body. It includes the midbrain, the pons, reticular formation, tegmentum, and the medulla oblongata. It regulates basic body functions including breathing, heart rate, blood pressure, swallowing, consciousness and wakefulness. The *limbic system* includes the amygdala, hippocampus, cingulate gyrus, and mammillary bodies. It is involved in memory, learning, and emotions. The *basal ganglia* include the globus pallidus, caudate nucleus, subthalamic nucleus, pallidum, putamen, and substantia nigra. Among the numerous functions, they serve to facilitate and coordinate movement and motor learning. Figure 13.11 provides a visual perspective on the many parts of the brain.

FIGURE 13.11

Structures in the Median Section of the Brain

Median Section of the Brain

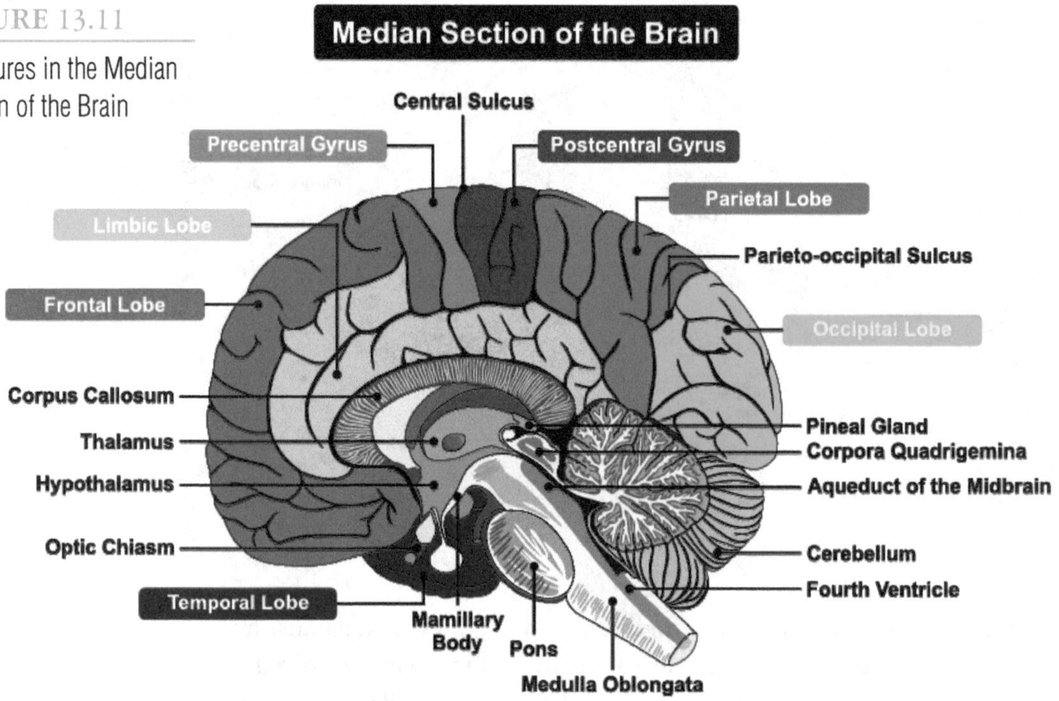

© udaix/Shutterstock.com

Putting It All Together

While there are many parts of the brain, they all function together as a whole. They interact with what is happening in the body and in the world around the body. These parts may have specific functions, but those functions impact other parts and their functions. Impairment in one area may have an impact in many other areas. Understanding this, a counselor may listen to the life experience of a client and detect that emotional difficulties may have a neurological basis with the need for referral to an appropriate professional. There is a myriad of possibilities. Garrard et al, (2002) present seven individual clients with neurological lesions in brain stem structures that exhibited deficits in cognitive function theoretically by lesions to distributed neural circuits. The clinical summary of their Case number one is an excellent example.

> Case 1
> A 43-year-old, right-handed former nursing sister without past history of neurological deficit or headache, who experienced a sudden onset of weakness and sensory disturbance in the right arm, visual blurring, vomiting, and imbalance. Examination revealed a complex ophthalmoplegia, severe cerebellar dysarthria, right-sided sensory disturbance involving the face, and an ataxic quadriparesis. MRI revealed haemorrhage [hemorrhage] into the midbrain and upper pons, and an underlying cavernoma. During rehabilitation, she exhibited marked emotional lability, impulsivity, distractibility, and disinhibition. Formal testing revealed significant deficits in frontal executive function, attention, and word retrieval and a mild weakness of visual memory on a background of a marked decline in intellectual capacity. All deficits were found to be persistent at a follow up assessment five months later. (p. 191)

What this case example demonstrates is that clients can come into counseling for symptoms that look like a particular diagnosis (here, we would want to explore Borderline Personality Disorder and/or Attention Deficit Hyperactivity Disorder), but in fact may be a result of brain trauma. If you were this client's counselor, given the sudden onset of symptoms, you would want to refer to a neurologist for assessment. You would still be able to work with this client on symptom management from a neuro-informed counseling perspective.

WHAT IS NEURO-INFORMED COUNSELING?

Neuroscience Applications for Counseling

As noted previously, neurons serve the function of transmitting impulses, or information, in the brain. Neural connections or pathways determine the destination of that information. In your work as a counselor, you may have a client who suffered emotional rejection from her parents and social rejection from her peers. As a result, a neural connection was made that people do not want to be in a relationship with her. When a new neighbor moves next door, this client may decide to welcome the neighbor by bringing a homemade cake. The neighbor may comment, "Oh, I am diabetic so I can't eat that." The client feels this as a rejection and the neural pathway of "people do not want to be in a relationship with me" thickens and is more deeply embedded.

Neuroplasticity. The brain, however, is capable of *neurogenesis, synaptogenesis*, and *neuroplasticity* (the ability of the brain to create and organize synaptic connections in response to learning, experience, or following injury). Because new neurons are developing and neural connections can be rewired, counselors are able to successfully use neuroscience concepts to assist clients with understanding and altering emotional reactivity. Luke, Miller, and McAuliffe (2019) indicated that this reorganization of the brain, or rewiring, demonstrates how experiences physiologically influence the brain. In the situation with the client who feels rejected by everyone, you could help her understand the concepts of neural pathways and why her immediate experience was rejection. You could explain the brain structures involved and how they may contribute to those negative feelings and that when there is a repeated pairing of experience and thought or feeling, a pathway develops. In *The Organization of Behavior* (1949), D. O. Hebb offered a neurophysiologic postulate:

> Let us assume then that the persistence or repetition of a reverberatory activity (or "trace") tends to induce lasting cellular changes that add to its stability. The assumption' can be precisely stated as follows: When an axon of cell A is near enough to excite a cell B and repeatedly or persistently takes part in

firing It, some growth process or metabolic change takes place in one or both cells such that A's efficiency, as one of the cells firing B, is increased. (p. 62)

Hebbian theory is a neuroscientific theory claiming that an increase in synaptic efficacy arises from the presynaptic cell's repeated and persistent stimulation of the postsynaptic cell. Or, more simplistically, what wires together fires together. You could share with this client that the brain is capable of neurogenesis and neuroplasticity and that she can be released from the strongholds of unhealthy neural pathways. You can then work using a theoretical model discussed in Chapter 9. In particular, CBT and mindfulness techniques pair well with neuroscience applications. However, other theories are also successful (e.g.., Adlerian, REBT, Reality, Solution-Focused, etc...). Approaches which use linguistic devices (e.g., Dialectical Behavior Therapy), such as metaphors, analogies, and similes, are effective (Luke, Miller, & McAuliffe, 2019).

Polyvagal Theory. Stephen Porges' Polyvagal Theory (Porges, 1995) describes the autonomic nervous system's role in affect regulation and social behavior. In this model, the vagus nerve (a set of sensory nerves which connect communication between the brainstem and the heart, lungs, digestive tract, as well as other organs in the abdomen and chest; Seymour, 2017) is directing emotional responses to stimuli. In this model, three response states are identified (see Figure 13.12): social communication (i.e., green zone), mobilization (i.e., yellow zone), and immobilization (i.e., red zone; Porges, 2003). Porges (2003) indicated that social engagement inhibits the sympathetic nervous system, resulting in calm behaviors and a sense of safety. Social engagement involves elements of social communication, such as vocalization, facial expression, and listening. The mobilization state will perceive danger and activate the sympathetic nervous system. The compensatory response is that of fight or flight. With the fight or flight response, individuals will either mobilize into action or flee the negative stimulus. These responses certainly serve a protective purpose. If you are swimming in the ocean and you see a dorsal fin breaking through the water, you will either swim faster to the shore or perhaps develop superhuman strength to fight the shark off. However, these responses are not helpful if you are at work and your boss asks to have a meeting with you. The third state, immobilization, is a response to perceived life-threatening danger that activates the parasympathetic nervous system and results in behavioral shutdown (Roelofs, 2017). Even in this state of immobilization, however, the arousal

FIGURE 13.12

The Polyvagal Chart:
The Nervous System and
Arousal Levels

systems are activated. In a sense, the heightened awareness, increased heart rate, and other symptoms of fight or flight response are imprisoned by the inability to respond (Roelofs, 2017). If you are an opossum, this function serves a significant purpose of protection against predators. However, if you are at a gathering of friends, this would likely invite unwanted attention and concern.

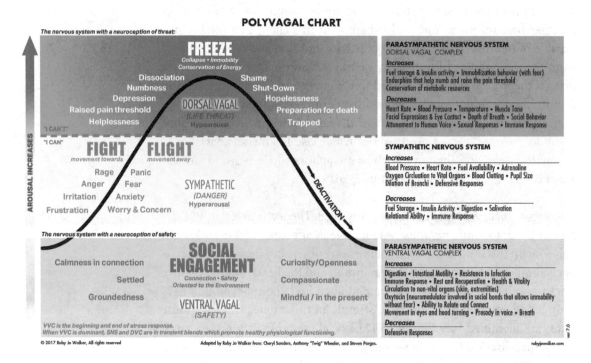

The theory behind the regulation or dysregulation of these physiological/emotional responses is that social interactional behavior plays a role. When a client's historical experience of relationships contains trauma or other negative interactions, the neural pathways that were created contribute to the misreading of threat levels in relationships. However, as noted above, neurogenesis allows for those neural pathways to be rewired. This ability for the brain to heal itself is an example of God's beautiful grace. Further, it has been noted that healing happens in a relationship (Ludy-Dobson & Perry, 2010). Within the counseling relationship, you have a role in ushering your client to this healing. As noted, social communication includes listening, facial expression, and vocalization. The counselor characteristics and skills you will learn about in Chapters 7 and 8 support that you will use authenticity, accurate empathy, and unconditional positive regard (Rogers, 1957) in addition to the skills of mirroring, body language, and tone of voice, in your work with clients. These skills correspond to the green zone social engagement activities that foster a sense of safety.

An understanding of polyvagal theory will be important in much of your work as a clinician, regardless of theoretical approach. As noted previously, some clients will have encountered events that alter their green zone experience of safety. Wagner (2017) discussed the interaction of childhood attachment styles on the polyvagal response system. She noted the following relationships in Table 13.2:

Attachment Style	Polyvagal Zone Response	Social Connection/ Disconnection Response
Secure	Most often, green	Do not feel overwhelmed or distressed
Anxious-Avoidant	Quickly flip to yellow zone	Easily become distressed
Avoidant	Quickly flip to red zone	Appear impervious, but feel very distressed

TABLE 13.2

Polyvagal Response/ Social Engagement Response as a Result of Attachment Style

These responses can impact client functioning relationally, occupationally, and socially. Based on previous negative experiences, existing neural pathways can result in misreading situations and social interactions, resulting in problematic behavioral responses and patterns.

Imagine you are working with a client who has a history of overreacting when someone disagrees. If a neuroscience explanation is not applied, it is possible that the client will be over-pathologized. However, an overlay of polyvagal theory will help you as the counselor conceptualize that this response was a result of an involuntary brain response. You will be able to understand and explain to your client that, after information was sent through the brainstem to the midbrain, the amygdala (which acts as a magnet for negative emotions) hijacked the information so that it would not make its way to the prefrontal cortex where logic could be applied. Rather, the information was sent back to the reptilian brain which caused the "fight" response to deploy. You can then

© Orla/Shutterstock.com

train her how to attend to physiological cues, integrate mindfulness and relaxation techniques, and respond in a less activated state.

As another example, your agency contracts with a local school system and you are placed in an elementary school as a school-based counselor. You have a 2nd-grade client who throws his desk and whatever else he can when he is frustrated over not understanding worksheets or tests. You can explain to him the hand model of the brain (Seigel, 2010). Once your client understands this concept, you can then work with him to help him identify ways to regulate behavior and navigate the frustration tolerance.

Watch this video to learn more about Seigel's hand model of the brain: https://www.youtube.com/watch?v=f-m2YcdMdFw

The Case of Brooklyn (cont.).

Taylor taught Brooklyn about the structures and functions of her brain. He explained that she has a thinking brain (i.e., complex), a feeling brain (i.e., mammalian), and a housekeeping brain (i.e., reptilian). He explained that the reptilian brain is used for primal needs such as body temperature, eating, drinking, protection (i.e., fight or flight), etc… He then explained that the feeling brain was comprised of the limbic system which includes the thalamus, hypothalamus, amygdala, and hippocampus. He explained their role and function with regard to emotions. He also explained about synaptic communication and neurotransmitters. Finally, Taylor explained that the thinking brain involved the neocortex and was in control of logic and reason, which allows for social interaction and planning, among other activities.

As they worked together, Taylor explained how depression interfaces with the brain structures and how those are impacting her emotionally, including the impact of serotonin, dopamine, noradrenaline, and endorphin levels on mood. Along with principles from Cognitive Behavior Therapy (CBT), Taylor helped Brooklyn develop skills to replace negative thoughts with more balanced thinking, specifically as it relates to what is happening in her brain. She was able to embrace that her depression was her experience not her identity. She learned to use combating statements such as "it is not that I cannot enjoy work, it is that my dopamine levels are preventing me from enjoying it right now." She also made behavioral adjustments that aid in healthy brain functioning. She and Taylor created acronyms to help her remember the knowledge and skills she learned.

© fizkes/Shutterstock.com

Brooklyn and Taylor worked together for six months. In this time, Taylor did not only educate. Taylor also empathically engaged with Brooklyn throughout their sessions. The therapeutic relationship itself also had an impact on Brooklyn's brain health, through stress reduction response and neurogenesis (Perry, 2009).

One year later, Brooklyn still feels empowered to fight off her symptoms of depression. She regularly uses the principles of CBT and her understanding of how her brain functions. She is running 3 miles a day and eating only whole foods. Brooklyn has had a short period of time when she felt like the blanket of sadness was coming back and worked with Taylor again for roughly a month. Today, she is living a more full life, enjoying social relationships, is more productive at work, and has a more authentic relationship with her parents.

NeuroSequential Model of Therapeutics

The Neurosequential Model of Therapeutics helps counselors conceptualize clients from a neuroscience perspective. In this model, there are three components: 1) training/capacity building, 2) assessment, and 3) recommendations for the selection and sequencing of therapeutic, educational and enrichment activities that match the needs and strengths of the individual. Perry (2009) indicated that adverse experiences in childhood impact the developing brain. He suggested that the nature of the activity, the quantity of activity, and the pattern of activity each have an impact on the development of the nervous system tissue, in addition to the neurochemistry of the brain. If your client, whether adult or child, indicates there were adverse or traumatic experiences in childhood (i.e., abuse/neglect, natural disasters, poverty, bullying, parental divorce/death/incarceration, etc…), the brain will experience micro changes which can impact the overall structure and functioning of the brain, thus impacting emotions, behaviors, and thoughts.

Perry (2009) indicated:

> This is a significant problem in the conventional mental health approach to maltreated children; many of their problems are related to disorganized or poorly regulated networks (e.g., the monoamines) originating lower in the brain. Yet, our clinical interventions often provide experiences that primarily target the innervated cortical or limbic (i.e., cognitive and relational interactions) regions in the brain and not the innervating source of the dysregulation (lower stress-response networks). Even when targeting the appropriate systems in the brain, we rarely provide the repetitions necessary to modify organized neural networks; 1 hour of therapy a week is insufficient to alter the accumulated impact of years of chaos, threat, loss, and humiliation. Inadequate "targeting" of our therapeutic activities to brain areas that are not the source of the symptoms and insufficient "repetitions" combine to make conventional mental health services for maltreated children ineffective. (p. 243)

Neuro-informed Play Therapy
Christina E. Villarreal-Davis, PhD, LPC-S, RPT-S, NCC

© Toni Arauza

I vividly recall my experiences when I first started to learn about play therapy. The famous quote by the well-known play therapist Garry Landreth made perfect sense to me, "Birds fly. Fish swim. Children play." I thought, "Of course, that's what children do. They play, and they play out their feelings." When I heard Dr. Landreth's other quote, "Toys are children's words and play is their language," it all started to come together even more. From a developmental perspective, children don't have the words, vocabulary, or cognitive skills to say how they feel or verbalize their past experiences, but they can use toys to play out their feelings and retell their story. Better yet, they can take control of their story in play therapy to help overcome their past experiences, hurts, and traumas. Furthermore, after reading about the healing power of the therapeutic relationship in Dibs: In Search of Self (Axline, 1964), I was hooked and passionate about play therapy!

A lot of my play therapy experience has been with children who have experienced some type of trauma, and often multiple traumas, such as neglect, abuse (physical, sexual, emotional), and/or household dysfunction (i.e., witnessed domestic violence, exposed to parental drug abuse, part of a high-conflict parental divorce, witnessed parental substance abuse, or had a parent with a severe mental illness/suicidal). In the literature, this has been referred to as adverse childhood experiences (ACEs; see right) and researchers have found that as an individual's number of ACEs increases, their risk for negative physical and mental health outcomes also increases, including early death (see The Truth About ACEs). This was so influential in my work with children and helped me understand the importance of early intervention. The original study examined ACEs in adults, so it made me wonder about the impact of children in play therapy, the therapeutic healing relationship in play therapy, and how that would impact these children's outcomes in adulthood. My play therapy experiences have revealed that when children are in a safe, non-judg-

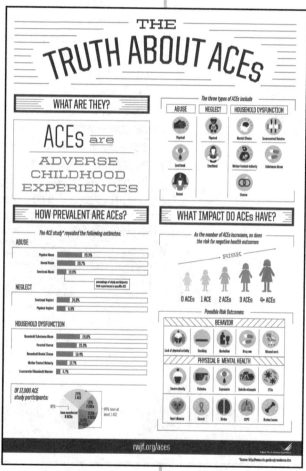

mental environment, they can retell their stories in a way that is meaningful and doable for them. They are now in control of the situation, not the one who inflicted the trauma. They can change the story to regain control when they were in a place of helplessness and hopelessness. Most importantly, they can now feel empowered. The therapeutic alliance and unconditional acceptance gives them the feeling of being loved and relationally connected, perhaps something many of them have never felt before, and they are playing at the heart level, meaning they are not in their heads, which aren't cognitively fully developed yet, but they are carefree and freely playing.

Furthermore, the surge of literature on neurobiology and attachment has provided mental health professional a description of what occurs in the brain when children experience trauma and/or experience situations that lead to attachment disturbances. Severe and/or multiple traumas during the first two years has such a great impact on attachment that even when information is not fully known, which is often the case with foster care and adopted children, I'm almost certain that something has occurred based on the child's behaviors related to trust, boundaries, and lack of attachment with caregivers. Since the human brain forms from the bottom up (see the image below) cerebellum/diencephalon, the limbic, and lastly cortex; see Efferent Distribution of Primary Regulatory Networks), trauma/ACEs will always play a role in the child's developing brain, and children often get stuck at the developmental stage in which the trauma occurred impacting neural systems and integration. When this occurs, children have greater difficulty regulating their emotions and experiences. With these children, I find myself using sensorimotor interventions to engage the body in play therapy, such as child-friendly, therapeutic yoga cards, and mindfulness activities. When I engage the body in play therapy, I'm starting at the brainstem to regulate the body (heart rate, breathing patterns, blood pressure), then the diencephalon can relay this sensory information to the limbic system (the emotional hub of the brain, including the amygdala, the part of the brain that automatically responds emotionally to sensory input, particularly to fear by the fight, flight, or freeze response), and once calmed and regulated, the cortex, where executive function and thinking takes place, can be accessed and utilized in useful ways. For children who have experienced ACEs, their developing brains have been impacted and often have difficulties regulating. Can you imagine how you would respond if your limbic system was always on alert? Always in fight, flight, or freeze mode? Dysregulated. Through a neurobiologically informed play therapy approach, the play therapist can cultivate a climate of relational healing through connection, engaging the body, and attunement, and that's my goal in working with children who have experienced ACEs.

Efferent distribution of primary regulatory networks

Cortex — Abstract & reflective cognition / Concrete cognition / Affiliation / Attachment/Reward / Sexual behavior
Limbic — Emotional reactivity / Motor regulation / Arousal
Diencephalon cerebellum — Appetite/Satiety / Sleep / Blood pressure
Brainstem — Heart rate / Body temperature

DA NE SER

ANS - body

A Neuroscience Explanation of Addictions

It is helpful for you, as a future counselor, to help clients understand addiction by looking at the brain's reward system. (see Figure 13.13)

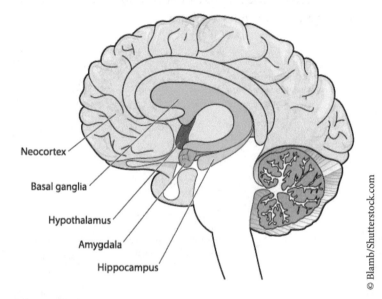

© Blamb/Shutterstock.com

FIGURE 13.13

The Brain's Reward System

The nucleus accumbens, cerebral cortex, amygdala, and hippocampus comprise the brain's reward system. Addictive practices such as using alcohol, marijuana, sex, and gambling flood the brain's nucleus accumbens with dopamine. The hippocampus is associated with memories, and after the nucleus accumbens is flooded with dopamine, the nearby hippocampus stores away the memory of the pleasurable experience, and then the amygdala facilitates the creation of a response that is conditioned (Harvard Medical School, 2011). Think of Pavlov's dogs who began to salivate when he rang a bell, this was a conditioned response. However, how do we determine whether an activity will become addictive? There are three factors which tend to influence whether a substance, experience, or activity will become addictive: 1) how fast dopamine is released during the activity or experience, 2) the level of intensity of the dopamine release, and 3) the consistency and reliability of the dopamine release (Harvard Medical School, 2011). Activities that are required for us to survive and flourish as humans such as eating and sex are associated with this reward system, with those practices being reinforced by a dopamine rush to the nucleus accumbens. This same neural circuitry is overwhelmed with addictive substances. Natural dopamine release that comes with activities such as checking an item off of the to do list comes with time and effort, on the other hand, substances that shortcut this path to dopamine release, over time become less effective. As the brain is not wired for the short cutting of this neurocircuitry. See Figure 13.14 below to review a visual representation of the natural dopamine response.

Clockwise from top left: © Tanya_Knyazeva/Shutterstock.com; © Syda Productions/Shutterstock.com; © Designua/Shutterstock.com; © joshya/Shutterstock.com

FIGURE 13.14

The Natural Dopamine Cycle

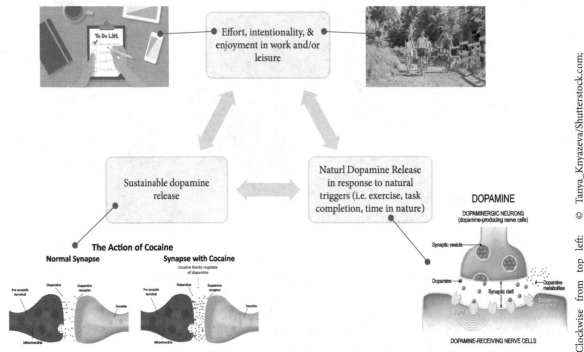

However, when the natural dopamine response is overwhelmed by a dopamine shortcut in the case of substance abuse, over time the brain and synaptic process must adapt. See Figure 13.14 for a comparison.

In treating a client with addiction issues, you may use psycho-educational group and individual interventions to educate that despite the short term gains of the use of pleasurable addictive substances the long term effect is detrimental to their health and capacity to feel pleasure. A phenomenon occurs where it takes greater effort and higher dosages of the addictive substance in order to feel the same level of pleasure over time. In the addictions literature, this is often referred to as tolerance (Harvard Medical

School, 2011). The intensity of some substances may be associated with ten times the amount of dopamine associated with a natural experience, so in order for the brain to cope with this intensity of dopamine, the brain has to make adjustments. In order to dial down the intensity of this over-whelming amount of dopamine the brain eliminates dopamine receptors (down regulation) or produces a smaller amount of dopamine. This phenomenon has been compared to turning down the volume on a speaker (Harvard Medical School, 2011).

Given the intensity of the dopamine release associated with addictive practices, and the strength of memories stored in the hippocampus, recovery from addictive substances can take substantial time and effort, and there is a risk of relapse. Subsequently, counselors may use other treatment intervention strategies such as behavioral interventions or motivational interviewing.

Nervous System Conditions

There are numerous conditions which affect the nervous system and its function. They include traumatic brain injuries, cerebrovascular accidents such as strokes and aneurysms, brain tumors, neurodegenerative disorders (dementia), and mental illnesses. Manifestations vary based on the location of impact. Understanding the nervous system and its function may contribute to differential diagnosis and specific treatment planning. Treatments target various aspects of the nervous system and impact directed at one area may impact function in other areas, that is, they may have side effects. This is particularly true of medications but it applies to other treatments as well.

Neuroscience concepts guide lifestyle intervention measures for general health and well-being and treatments targeting mental health conditions. A foundational concept is that the nervous system, particularly the brain, is plastic (adaptable) and changes based on life experiences. Life experiences can cause changes that may result in improved health or in mental illness. Therapies harness this concept to provide interventions to improve health and overcome or ameliorate mental illness.

WHAT DO COUNSELORS NEED TO KNOW ABOUT PSYCHOPHARMACOLOGY?

"Medication is of course important but do not conclude that a pill dissolving in your stomach is necessarily more powerful than a healing thought dissolving in your mind."
--Norman Vincent Peale (1961) p. 153

Understanding the Basics of Psychotropic Medication

Psychopharmacology is the study of medications (drugs) for the treatment of psychiatric or mental conditions. Any substance that affects the mental function of a person is *psychotropic*, that is it affects mental function, perception, emotions, and behavior. Psychiatric medications such as Prozac (fluoxetine) and Lithium (an element) are psychotropic. Illicit drugs such as cocaine and LSD (lysergic acid diethylamide - a hallucinogenic) are also psychotropic. Although as counselors you do not prescribe medications, you will encounter clients who are taking medications prescribed by various professionals including physicians, nurse practitioners, physician assistants, and (in some states) psychologists. You will also encounter clients who are using illicit drugs. Understanding the nervous system and the indications, effects, and side effects of prescribed medications as well as a basic understanding of illicit substances will assist you in being more effective in helping clients.

Medications alone do not serve as a complete treatment for psychiatric or mental conditions. Counseling is powerful and may assist the client in developing skills to overcome or manage their conditions. Often, a combination approach employing medication and therapy is important. In many cases, counseling and various non-medication interventions are more powerful than medications. In some cases, relief may not occur without medication intervention.

When Counseling Is Not Enough

A case example of the last scenario is an 8-year-old girl with diagnoses of Disruptive Mood Dysregulation Disorder (DMDD), Attention-deficit/hyperactivity disorder (ADHD), combined type, Generalized Anxiety Disorder (GAD), and Oppositional Defiant Disorder (ODD). History revealed she witnessed domestic drug abuse and violence, suffered severe neglect and abuse in her early childhood, experienced DCS removal from her family of origin, and required placement in "specialized foster care" (designed for children with severe medical, emotional and behavioral disorders). She had visitation with her mother and siblings. She struggled at school and at the foster home with outbursts of anger, violence, and destruction. She had an excellent counselor,

an accommodating teacher, and a skilled foster parent. Despite these resources, she could not respond to non-medication measures. The teacher and the parent felt her behaviors were deliberate. The counselor detected something deeper and provided a secure base within which the girl described her experience. When calm she was intelligent and articulate. She revealed ambivalence about both fearing and wanting to return to her family of origin.

Despite counseling, the outbursts continued and safety was a concern. The counselor wondered about her reality testing and self-regulation. The counseling assisted in helping her articulate her distress (with herself and her situation) and her desire to do well. I (John Kuhnley, MD) conducted medication management sessions to monitor progress of non-medication measures while continuing assessment to determine medical necessity for medication. In sessions, I apply counseling techniques to promote exploration, expression, and disclosure while offering coping strategies for improvement of function.

We determined that any experience of emotion by this girl would escalate into anger, violence, and destruction as a repetition experience with her family of origin. Ongoing visitation aggravated the situation. I combined my impressions with the observations of the counselor and considered a neuroscience basis--the psychological processes and neural circuits hypothesized to contribute to pathologic irritability (Leibenluft, 2010). Blocking of goal attainment leads to frustration. Dysregulation of attention-emotion interactions in the amygdala, the anterior cingulate cortex (ACC), the dorsal prefrontal cortex (DPFC), the ventral prefrontal cortex (VPFC), and the parietal cortex coupled with misinterpretation of emotional stimuli by the amygdala, temporal cortex, and medial prefrontal cortex (MPFC) lead to a decreased threshold for amplification of frustration resulting in increased irritability and behavioral dyscontrol. The reaction escalates to dangerous levels and the girl may appear out of touch with reality. An antipsychotic and mood-stabilizing medication is medically necessary to provide a calming effect. Mauri et al (2014) note that "Atypical antipsychotics are reported to induce restructuring of neuronal networks by inducing neuroplastic changes" (p. 1165). There are numerous mechanisms of action involved. In simple terms, I reviewed with the client and the guardian that there was a neurological basis that caused her emotions to go out of control and that it was necessary to calm her brain. I discussed the indications, risks, side effects and precautions of risperidone (Risperdal). They indicated understanding and approval and the guardian signed consent. I started with the lowest dose or 0.25 mg a day with plan to adjust as necessary for response and side effects.

The outpatient nurse conducted a weekly review and they returned to see me in one month. At the first follow-up session, the girl reported, "I'm doing way better with anger issues on the new medicine." The foster mom agreed noting that there was no longer any destructive or dangerous behavior. However, she was "more emotional" at times, but very manageable and learning to use words for expression. She would cry in moments of frustration and would have difficulty with focus. I explained to them that, before the medication, any emotion quickly erupted to anger whereas, after the medication, her brain is calmer and she experiences the real emotion. Her foster mother and her counselor were helping her to identify and express her feelings in words and she was cooperating and responding very well, which the medication cannot make her do, so she gets the credit. She liked that, smiled, and gave her foster mother a hug.

With an understanding of medications and their management, counselors may provide very important assistance to the client in understanding medications, side effects, and treatment expectations. Prescribers have a responsibility to assist clients in this regard but research demonstrates that prescribers have precious little time allotted to address this important task. In addition, clients often have difficulty understanding and/or remembering what they are told by prescribers. A study in the Annals of Internal Medicine by Sinsky et al. (2016) revealed that doctors spend about 8 minutes for evaluation of a client and the rest of the session addressing the medical record while determining a treatment plan.

As a counselor, you have time to establish a collaborative relationship with the client based on empathic listening and your many counseling skills as you develop an understanding of the client and the world of the client. You may be the guiding light for the client who is navigating life challenges and experiencing distress. It is wise for a prescriber to collaborate with a counselor and a client as a team to encourage the client to engage in measures that improve health and well-being. You may provide valuable information and insights with which the prescriber may make more informed decisions regarding the possibilities within medication management. You may facilitate a client's acceptance, understanding, and adherence to a prescribed medication regimen, as well as assist in monitoring for response and adverse effects encountered by the client. Poor adherence to medication may lead to worsening of the target condition, higher cost, an increased utilization of services, an increased burden for the family, lower quality of life, and even premature death.

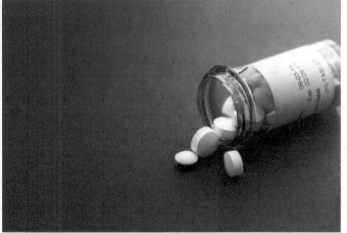

Viswanathan et al. (2012) published a review of interventions to improve adherence to self-administered medications for chronic diseases in the United States in 2012 in the *Annals of Internal Medicine*. The authors reported that "studies have consistently shown that 20% to 30% of medication prescriptions are never filled and that approximately 50% of medications for chronic disease are not taken as prescribed" (p. 785). This includes all medications, not just psychotropic medications. They cited literature estimating that yearly in the United States, nonadherence to medication causes approximately 125,000 deaths, at least 10% of hospitalizations, and a substantial increase in morbidity and mortality with an estimated cost to the U.S. healthcare system of up to $289 billion annually. According to the World Health Organization (WHO), "Accurate assessment of adherence behaviour is necessary for effective and efficient treatment planning, and for ensuring that changes in health outcomes can be attributed to the recommended regimen" (2003, p. 4). Many factors affect a client's adherence to any treatment, including medication. Perhaps the most important factor is effective communication. Ideally, the provider must present the treatment plan in a manner that the client is able to understand and then ask the client to present the information as understood in the client's own words. This does not always happen in clinical practice. Literacy involves reading, writing, and understanding. Health literacy includes the client's ability to understand communication related to health interventions. The Agency for Healthcare Research and Quality defines Health Literacy as "The capacity to: Obtain, process, understand basic health information and services. Make appropriate health care decisions (act on information). Access/navigate health care system" (Health Literacy, 2017). As a counselor, you will want to check in with your clients to make sure they are taking medication as prescribed and refer them back to the provider if there are any concerns.

The ideal client-prescriber engagement includes an empathic interaction and understanding of the prescriber with the client. The prescriber must convey the indications (desired outcomes or benefits to the client) for the medication; the risks of taking and of not taking the medication; and the necessary precautions and potential adverse effects of taking the medication. Since prescribers of medication often have very little time to assess and prescribe a treatment plan, it is no surprise that many clients do not understand the plan. As a counselor, you have the opportunity to develop a secure-base and a therapeutic alliance with the client from which to explore the client's understanding. With basic knowledge of medications and their management, you may assist the client in achieving a better understanding and adherence to the plan. You may interact with the prescriber and/or encourage the client to communicate with the prescriber. Collaborative guidance strives to maintain the safety of the client, to prevent fall into worsening illness, and to promote spiritual, physical, mental, and emotional health and well-being (Kuhnley, 2013).

Counselors may address specific problems through psychotherapeutic interventions specific to those problems. In addition, counselors may assist clients in embracing lifestyle changes and coping skills addressing sleep, nutrition, exercise, stress reduction, and anxiety management. These measures are valuable for everyone, but especially for clients with conditions requiring mental health counseling, medications, and other therapeutic interventions.

Understanding the Function of Psychotropic Medication

The FDA (Food and Drug Administration) reviews medications and approves them for specific indications which a pharmaceutical company has the authorization to include on the medication's "label." However, medications may have benefits for other conditions which are "off-label", that is, for which the FDA did not review for approval. Prescribers may prescribe medications "off-label" if they have an evidence-base or clinical experience to support such prescription.

Pharmacodynamics refers to the effects of a medication within the body. *Pharmacokinetics* refers to how the body processes the medication including absorption, distribution, metabolism, and excretion. Medications have *target symptoms* or desired effects (often based on the pharmacodynamics of the medication). Target symptoms may include depression, anxiety, attention span, and unstable mood which provide the indication for a prescription. However, medications have possible *side effects*, that is, secondary effects, and many of these tend to be undesirable. Occasionally, a side effect may be the desired effect. For example, trazodone is an antidepressant; a side effect is sedation which limits its daytime use but makes it a desirable medication for sleep induction at bedtime. Side effects tend to be most prominent on initiation, dose-increase or discontinuation of a medication. They reflect the body's adjustment to the presence of the medication. Most side effects diminish and disappear with continuation of the medication, so it is best to wait them out as long as they are "manageable". As an example, it is common for a medication to cause nausea initially with resolution in a week or two. However, some side effects cause the client to discontinue medication. An example is the potential sexual dysfunction side effect risk of selective serotonin reuptake inhibitors like fluoxetine (Prozac), which is prescribed to treat depression and anxiety. Another example is potential weight gain associated with many of the antipsychotic medications.

Some clients will have an *allergic reaction* to a medication when their immune system mistakenly identifies the medication as a harmful substance and develops a specific antibody to it. This is different from a medication side effect, though it is very common for clients and providers mistakenly to report an allergy to a medication when in fact the client experienced a

© Antonio Guillem/Shutterstock.com

side effect. An allergic reaction is also different from *medication toxicity* which is the result of excessive dose or overdose of a medication. Manifestations of a drug allergy may include rash, itching, swelling, hives, fever, wheezing, shortness of breath, watery eyes, and runny nose. Allergic reactions may occur with ingestion of prescribed medications, but also with over-the-counter (OTC) medications and herbal preparations. *Anaphylaxis* is a serious and potentially life-threatening allergic reaction causing dysfunction of many body systems with manifestations including trouble breathing because of tightening of the airways and throat; nausea, vomiting, diarrhea and/or abdominal cramping; rapid pulse and reduced blood pressure; and possible progression to seizure and/or loss of consciousness.

A prescriber must conduct an evaluation, consider differential diagnostic possibilities, and select treatments appropriate to the needs of the individual client. Monitoring of response and side effects is necessary during dose adjustments and maintenance to seek optimal response and stabilization of the client. An understanding of the nervous system provides some guidance to the selection of various treatments including medications. The prescriber may match pharmacodynamic effects of medications with symptoms and conditions experienced by the client. The rational and optimal prescription of medication considers an understanding of the biological, medical, psychological, social, and spiritual attributes of the client.

A review of diagnoses and specific medications is beyond the scope of this chapter and text. There are many resources for obtaining this information including Medscape, a valuable online resource at https://reference.medscape.com/. It provides information on drugs, OTCs, and herbals; drug interaction checker; pill identifier; information on diseases and conditions; and much more. Chapter 16 of Hawkins et al (2017) by Kuhnley provides a brief overview of "What Counselors need to know about Psychopharmacology." The *Handbook of Clinical Psychopharmacology for Therapists* by Preston et al. (2017) is a more comprehensive resource. Stahl's Essential *Psychopharmacology: Neuroscientific Basis and Practical Applications 4th Edition* (2013) is an excellent though technical resource.

SUMMARY

While the term *neuroscience* sounds like it may be complex, this chapter illustrates that neuroscience principles can be reduced down to understanding the structures and functions of the brain. With this reductionist perspective, you can start to incorporate brain-based explanations in your understanding of the material you are learning. As you work through the various courses in your counselor training program, you can think about how you might apply neuroscience to the material. When you begin your field experience, you can talk with your supervisor and seek out other practicing clinicians at your site who can offer insights about how they approach neuro-informed counseling. You can also start learning now about the parts and functions of the brain that impact mental health functioning.

FOR THE ROAD AHEAD

Check out the Chapter 13 video at this link:

https://www.khpcontent.com/

Reflections on the Journey

1. Think of three things in your life for which you receive some reward; reflect on how each communicates with the reward system in your brain. Explain this process to a family member or friend.
2. Consider the next time you feel slighted by a friend or a family member. What neural firing may be triggering those feelings/thoughts? Ask yourself whether the slight actually happened or whether it was a neural response.
3. What are your thoughts about psychotropic medication usage for clients? Do you think clients should wait to see how therapeutic intervention works prior to referring them for medication? *or* Do you believe the referral should be in conjunction with a therapeutic intervention?

For Further Exploration

Amen, D.G. (2015). *Change your brain, change your life: The breakthrough program for conquering anxiety, depression, obsessiveness, lack of focus, anger, and memory problems.* Harmony; Revised, Expanded edition (November 3, 2015)

Cozolino, L. J. (2010). *The neuroscience of psychotherapy: Healing the social brain.* New York: W.W. Norton & Co.

Hawkins, R., Knight, A., Sibcy, G., Warren, S. (2018). *Research-based counseling skills: The art and science of therapeutic empathy.* Dubuque, IA: Kendall Hunt Publishing Company.

Korb, A. (2015). *The upward spiral: Using neuroscience to reverse the course of depression one small change at a time.* Oakland, CA: New Harbinger Publications, Inc.

Kuhnley, E. (2018) Chapter 16: What counselors need to know about psychopharmacology: What to listen for in Hawkins, R., Knight, A., Sibcy, G., Warren, S. (2018). *Research-based counseling skills: The art and science of therapeutic empathy.* Dubuque, IA: Kendall Hunt Publishing Company.

Miller, R. (Producer). (2019, February 7). EP114: Reconsidering Chronic Pain – How Understanding the Neuroscience of Pain Can Transform Treatment with Howard Schubiner [Audio podcast]. *The Thoughtful Counselor.* Retrieved from https://wp.me/p7R6fn-Df.

Miller, R. (Producer). (2018, November 14). EP106: Social Baseline Theory – The Primacy of Social Relationships in the Regulation of Emotions [Audio podcast]. *The Thoughtful Counselor.* Retrieved fromhttps://wp.me/p7R6fn-ts.

Miller, R. (Producer). (2018, January 17). Polyvagal Theory Applied: Moving from Fight or Flight to Social Engagement for Sustainable Living [Audio podcast]. *The Thoughtful Counselor.* Retrieved from https://wp.me/p7R6fn-je

Miller, R. (Producer). (2017, November 16). Practical Neuroscience Applications for Understanding and Treating Addiction: A Conversation with Mark Woodford [Audio podcast]. *The Thoughtful Counselor.* Retrieved from https://wp.me/p7R6fn-hf

Miller, R. (Producer). (2017, September 13). Applying Principles of Neuroscience to Support Greater Safety and Co-Regulation in Long Term Committed Relationships: A Psycho-biological Approach to Couples Therapy [Audio podcast]. *The Thoughtful Counselor.* Retrieved from http://wp.me/p7R6fn-e9

Miller, R. (Producer). (2017, May 9). Neuroscience-Informed Cognitive Behavioral Therapy (nCBT): A New Framework for Client Conceptualization and Treatment Planning with Eric Beeson and Thom Field [Audio podcast]. *The Thoughtful Counselor.* Retrieved from http://wp.me/p7R6fn-9N

Perry, B. D., (The ChildTrauma Academy). (2013) 1: The Human Brain [Video webcast]. In *Seven Slide Series.* Retrieved from https://www.youtube.com/watch?v=uOsgDkeH52o

Perry, B. D., (The ChildTrauma Academy). (2013) 2: Sensitization and Tolerance [Video webcast]. In *Seven Slide Series*. Retrieved from https://www.youtube.com/watch?v=qv8dRfgZXV4 Seven Slide Series Video: Threat Response Patterns

Perry, B.D., (The ChildTrauma Academy). (2013) 3: Threat Response Patterns [Video webcast]. In *Seven Slide Series*. Retrieved from https://www.youtube.com/watch?v=sr-OXkk3i8E&feature=youtu.be

Porges, S. (2018, April 23). *What is Polyvagal Theory?* [Video file]. Retrieved from https://www.youtube.com/watch?v=ec3AUMDjtKQ

Preston, J., O'Neal, J. H., & Talaga, M. C. (2017). *Handbook of clinical psychopharmacology for therapists* (8th ed.). Oakland, CA: New Harbinger Publications, Inc.

Shook, M. (Producer). (2017, May 31). Working with Anxiety in School-Aged Youth: Neuroplasticity, Optimizing Stress, and Emotional Freedom Techniques with Amy Gaesser [Audio podcast]. *The Thoughtful Counselor*. Retrieved from http://wp.me/p7R6fn-aK

Stahl, S. M. (2013). *Stahl's essential psychopharmacology: Neuroscientific basis and practical applications* (4th ed.). New York, NY, US: Cambridge University Press.

REFERENCES

Altman J., Carvalho L. R., Grinberg L. T., Farfel J. M., Ferretti R. E., Leite R. E., Jacob Filho W., Lent R., & Herculano-Houzel S. (2009). Equal numbers of neuronal and nonneuronal cells make the human brain an isometrically scaled-up primate brain. *J. Comp. Neurol.* 513, 532–54110.1002/cne.21974

American Psychiatric Association. (2013). *Diagnostic and statistical manual of mental disorders* (5th ed.). Arlington, VA: Author.

Azevedo F. A., Carvalho L. R., Grinberg L. T., Farfel J. M., Ferretti R. E., Leite R. E., Jacob Filho W., Lent R., & Herculano-Houzel S. (2009). Equal numbers of neuronal and nonneuronal cells make the human brain an isometrically scaled-up primate brain. *J. Comp. Neurol.* 513, 532–54110.1002/cne.21974

Beeson, & Field, T. (2017). Neurocounseling: A new section of the journal of mental health counseling. *Journal of Mental Health Counseling, 39*, 71–83.

Benarroch, E. E. (2007). Enteric nervous system: functional organization and neurologic Implications. *Neurology, 69*(20), 1953-1957.

Bingaman, K. A. (2016). Incorporating contemplative neuroscience and mindfulness-based therapies into pastoral care and counseling: A critical correlational method. *Pastoral Psychology, 65*(6), 759-772. doi:10.1007/s11089-016-0719-z

Caplan, M., Portillo, A., & Seely, L. (2013). Yoga psychotherapy: The integration of western psychological theory and ancient yogic wisdom. *Journal of Transpersonal Psychology, 45*(2), 139-158. Retrieved from http://ezproxy.liberty.edu/login?url=https://search-proquest-com.ezproxy.liberty.edu/docview/1519077872?accountid=12085

Clinton, T., & Sibcy, G. (2012). Christian counseling, interpersonal neurobiology, and the future. *Journal of Psychology and Theology, 40*(2), 141-145.

Erk, R. R. (2000). Five frameworks for increasing understanding and effective treatment of attention deficit/hyperactivity disorder: Predominantly inattentive type. *Journal of Counseling and Development, 78,* 389-399.

Garrard, P., Bradshaw, D., Jäger, H., Thompson, A., Losseff, N., & Playford, D. (2002). Cognitive dysfunction after isolated brain stem insult. An underdiagnosed cause of long term morbidity. *Journal of Neurology Neurosurgery & Psychiatry, 73,* 191–194.

Gershon M. D. (1999). The enteric nervous system: A second brain. *Hospital Practice, 34*(7), 31-52, doi:10.3810/hp.1999.07.153

Gonçalves J., Schafer S., & Gage F. (2016). Adult neurogenesis in the hippocampus: From stem cells to behavior. *Cell, 167*(4), 897-914. doi:10.1016/j.cell.2016.10.021

Gross, C. G. (2000). Neurogenesis in the adult brain: Death of a dogma. *Nat Rev Neurosci 1,* 67–73.

Harvard Medical School Mental Health Letter (July 2011). How addiction hijacks the brain. Retrieved from: https://www.health.harvard.edu/newsletter_article/how-addiction-hijacks-the-brain

Health Literacy: Hidden barriers and practical strategies. Content last reviewed December 2017. Agency for Healthcare Research and Quality, Rockville, MD. Retrieved from http://www.ahrq.gov/professionals/quality-patient-safety/quality-resources/tools/literacy-toolkit/tool3a/index.html

Hebb, D. O. (1949). *The organization of behavior: A neuropsychological theory.* New York, NY: Wiley.

Hoffman, A., Ettinger, U., Reyes del Paso, G. A., & Duschek, S. (2017). Executive function and cardiac autonomic regulation in depressive disorders. *Brain and Cognition, 118,* 108-117.

Insel, T. (1997). A neurobiological basis of social attachment. *American Journal of Psychiatry 154,* 6.

Kato, D., Eto, K., Nabekura, J., & Wake, H. (2018). Activity-dependent functions of non-electrical glial cells. *The Journal of Biochemistry, 163,* 457–464.

Kuhnley, J. (2013). When to refer: *Collaborating with a psychiatrist for medication evaluations* [Blog post]. Retrieved from: https://www.aacc.net/2013/11/14when-to-refer-collaborating-with-a-psychiatrist-for-medication-evaluations/

Leibenluft, E. (2010). Severe mood dysregulation, irritability, and the diagnostic boundaries of bipolar disorder in youths. *The American Journal of Psychiatry, 168*(2), 129–142. doi:10.1176/appi.ajp.2010.10050766

Ludy-Dobson, C. R. & Perry, B.D. (2010). The role of healthy relational interactions in buffering the impact of childhood trauma. In E. Gil (Ed.), *Working with children to heal interpersonal trauma: The power of play* (pp. 26-43). New York, NY: Guilford Press.

Luke, C., Miller, R., & McAuliffe, G. (2019). Neuro-informed mental health counseling: A person-first perspective. *Journal of Mental Health Counseling, 41,* 65-79.

Mauri, M. C., Paletta, S., Maffini, M., Colasanti, A., Dragogna, F., Di Pace, C., & Altamura, A. C. (2014). Clinical pharmacology of atypical antipsychotics: an update. *EXCLI Journal, 13,* 1163–1191.

Milad, M. R., Rosenbaum, B. L., & Simon, M. N. (2014). Neuroscience of fear extinction: Implications for assessment and treatment of fear-based and anxiety related disorders. *Behaviour Research and Therapy, 62,* 17-23.

Monro T. K. (1895). Optic nerve as part of the central nervous system. *Journal of Anatomy and Physiology, 30*(1), 45-48.

Navalta, C. P., McGee, L., & Underwood, J. (2018). Adverse childhood experiences, brain development, and mental health: A call for neurocounseling. *Journal of Mental Health Counseling, 40,* 266-278.

Neniskyte, U., & Gross, C. T. (2017). Errant gardeners: Glial-cell-dependent synaptic pruning and neurodevelopmental disorders. *Nature Reviews.Neuroscience, 18*(11), 658-670.

Olaru, C., Diaconescu, S., Trandafir, L., Gimiga, N., Olaru, R. A., Stefanescu, G., Ciubotariu, G.,Burlea, M.

& Iorga, M. (2016). Chronic functional constipation and encopresis in children in relationship with the psychosocial environment. *Gastroenterology Research and Practice, 2016,* 1-7.

Peale, N. (1961). *The tough-minded optimist.* Prentice-Hall.

Perryman, K., Blisard, P., & Moss, R. (2019). Using creative arts in trauma therapy: The neuroscience of healing. *Journal of Mental Health Counseling, 41,* 80-94.

Perry, B. (2009). Examining child maltreatment through a neurodevelopmental lens: Clinical applications of the neurosequential model of therapeutics. *Journal of Loss and Trauma, 14,* 240–255.

Porges S. W. (1995). Orienting in a defensive world: Mammalian modifications of our evolutionary heritage—a polyvagal theory. *Psychophysiology, 32,* 301–318.

Porges S. W. (2003). Social engagement and attachment: A phylogenetic perspective. *Annals of the New York Academy of Sciences, 1008,* 31–47.

Porges S. W. (2009). The polyvagal theory: new insights into adaptive reactions of the autonomic nervous system. *Cleveland Clinic Journal of Medicine, 76,* S86–S90. doi:10.3949/ccjm.76.s2.17

Rogers, C. R. (1957). The necessary and sufficient conditions for therapeutic personality change. *Journal of Counseling Psychology, 21,* 95–103.

Roelofs K. (2017). Freeze for action: Neurobiological mechanisms in animal and human freezing. *Philosophical Transactions of the Royal Society of London. Series B, Biological Sciences, 372*(1718), 20160206. doi:10.1098/rstb.2016.0206

Russell-Chapin, L. (2016). Integrating neurocounseling into the counseling profession: An introduction. *Journal of Mental Health Counseling, 38*(2), 93-102. doi:10.l7744/mehc.38.2.01

Seigel, D. J. (2010). *Mindsight: The new science of personal transformation.* New York, NY: Bantam Books.

Seymour, T. (2017, June 28). "Everything you need to know about the vagus nerve." *Medical News Today.* Retrieved from https://www.medicalnewstoday.com/articles/318128.php.

Sinsky, C., Colligan, L., Li, L., Prgomet, M., Reynolds, S., Goeders, L., … Blike, G. (2016). Allocation of physician time in ambulatory practice: A time and motion study in 4 specialties. *Annals of Internal Medicine, 165*(11), 753. doi:10.7326/M16-0961

Viswanathan M., Golin C., Jones C., Ashok M., Blalock S., Wines R., … Lohr, K. N. (2012). Interventions to improve adherence to self-administered medications for chronic diseases in the United States: A systematic review. *Annals of Internal Medicine, 157,* 785–795. doi:10.7326/0003-4819-157-11-201212040-00538

Wagner, D. (2017). Using new nervous system science to help clients with their digital dating Experience. *Counseling Today.* Retrieved from https://static1.squarespace.com/static/55be7191e4b06da83f-6620d5/t/5a1dd1d40d92971bbc6c4a31/1511903701606/CT_Neurocounseling+Nov_2017.pd

World Health Organization. (2003). Adherence to long-term therapies: Evidence for action. Retrieved from https://www.who.int/chp/knowledge/publications/adherence_full_report.pdf

CHAPTER 14
The Future of Counseling

Andrea Barbian-Shimberg, Ph.D., Kevin B. Hull, Ph.D., Robyn Simmons, Ed.D.,
& April Crable, Ph.D.

> "You've got to be very careful if you don't know where you are going, because you might not get there." –Yogi Berra

Following Christ: Grace for Our Work

"For I am the Lord, I change not..." Malachi 3:6

We live in a rapidly changing culture. Technological advances have expanded the boundaries of industry and science, creating cultural shifts that affect how people think and relate to each other. Rapid cultural change has both positive and negative effects. Equality in the form of increased representation and opportunity in race and gender gives a culture a sense of hope and freedom. However, rapid changes can also create moral dilemmas with no clear solutions. These changes can lead to divisions among leaders, and create insurmountable levels of stress for the members who live in that culture.

© PopTika/Shutterstock.com

CHAPTER OBJECTIVES

After reading this chapter, you will understand more about:

- The expected trends in the profession of counseling and mental health field.
- Job outlook information as it relates to the counseling profession.
- The impact of technology on the counseling profession, mental health and wellness, and client services.
- The impact of the current cultural climate on mental health and wellness.

The following CACREP standards are addressed in this chapter:

Professional Counseling Orientation and Ethical Practice:

- Current labor market information relevant to opportunities for practice within the counseling profession (CACREP, 2016, Standard 2.F.1.h.)
- Technology's impact on the counseling profession (CACREP, 2016, Standard 2.F.1.j.)

594

The Israelites of the Old Testament are an example of a culture that grew and changed rapidly. In a short amount of time, the Israelites became "numerous" (Exodus 1:9, King James Version) and left Egypt, enduring immense challenges and living nomadically until finally claiming the land God had promised to them (Joshua 21:43). Repeatedly in the narrative of Israel's immense growth, the Israelites become restless and impatient, and each time God reminded them of His unchanging nature and everlasting love. He provided constant visible reminders of His presence and told His people "Jerusalem, I can never forget you!" (Isaiah 49:16).

Human beings require a predictable and stable environment in order to feel safe and thrive. Stress occurs when life becomes unpredictable and chaotic, leaving us with no sense of control over circumstances. It is exactly why God repeatedly showed Israel His unchanging nature and that if they trusted Him, all would be well. Similarly, Jesus admonished His disciples to "not worry about tomorrow" because "your Father knows your needs" (Matthew 6:31-32). As Christian counselors, we operate on the foundation of God's unchanging nature, which helps us provide those who seek our help with a sense of comfort and peace. Integrating the foundational principles of God's character with sound counseling theory and techniques equips us and those we counsel with the tools to grow and thrive, no matter how quickly the culture changes around us.

How does the shifting culture impact the future of mental health? Lev Vygostky (1978) said, "A mind cannot be independent of culture" (p. 102). The cultural climate cannot be avoided as television programming, movies, social media, news reports, advertisements, music, merchandising (and the list goes on) are all influences on our lives and are reflective of the current society. With such accessibility to and freedom in media, individuals are able to engage with responses and create cultural shifts. Social media has had a significant impact on how quickly movements grow. Mihailidis and Viotty (2017) suggested that cultural transmission occurs through the insertion of "personal ideas, opinions, and ideologies" (pp. 445-446) by individuals. This influence shapes the cognitive resources, schemas, values, and functioning of those within its cultural sphere. As a counselor, you must accommodate and assimilate to the changing culture around you, as it also impacts the experiences and needs of clients.

© 13_Phunkod/Shutterstock.com

WHAT IS THE IMPACT OF A SHIFTING CULTURE ON CLIENT NEEDS?

The Impact of Climate Change on Mental Health
Debbie Sturm, Ph.D.

I have always been in love with the natural world and, like many others, feel a personal responsibility to make choices to protect it. The benefits of spending time in nature are so immediately palpable: a better mood, less stress, a sense of calm, and even hope. Time away from nature for too long compounds daily stress. As a counselor, I also recognize the benefit for my clients and, as an educator, for my students. So, to me, the connection between nature and our personal well-being is so pro-

© Debbie Sturm

found that I find myself drawn to the wonderings of how to best confront the implications of one of the most pressing nature-related issues of our time, climate change, on mental health and well-being.

For some, it may seem a bit of a stretch to consider climate change a mental health issue worthy of the professional introspection and action within the counseling field. Yet over the past several years, evidence has been mounting with regard to the impact of climate change on human health and well-being.

This evidence ranges from declarations of climate change as a global human rights issue to considerations for migration, disaster response and preparedness, and overall feelings of concern for the future.

The relationship between climate change and the right to health, specifically the "enjoyment of the highest attainable standard of physical and mental health" (A/HRC/32/23) solidified the United Nations Human Rights Council's (HRC) previously held belief that climate change is one of the most significant human rights issues of our times. The United Nations HRC report referenced above provides clarity on the specific conclusions relating to climate change and mental health:

> "Climate impacts on mental health stem from immediate physical effects and more gradual effects on the environment, human systems, and infrastructure. People who experience losses, or are exposed to life-threatening situations, experience higher risks of developing anxiety-related conditions, including PTSD and depression."

Further, the consequences of climate change can have a profound impact on mental health through both its direct impact and its impact on social support systems and cultural traditions. People who experience the loss of homes or loved ones, or are exposed to life-threatening situations, face higher risks of developing stress and anxiety-related mental health issues.

In 2016, the U.S. Global Change Research Program developed a Climate and Health Assessment to serve as both an evidence-based resource and interactive tool detailing the impact of global climate change on human health and well-being. Categories addressed include climate change and human health, temperature-related death and illness, air quality impacts, extreme events, vector-borne diseases, water-related illness, food safety, nutrition, and distribution, mental health and well-being, and populations of concern. Both the American Psychological Association (2011) and the National Association for Social Work, through the work of Task Forces, have adopted platforms, guidelines, and policy recommendations pertaining to climate change and its impact on mental health. In addition, APA, in partnership with ecoAmerica, produced *Mental Health and the Changing Climate: Impacts, Implications, and Guidance*, essentially an overview of the research and toolkit for policymakers, advocates, and practitioners. In 2002, the International Federation of Red Cross and Red Crescent Societies (IFRC) established the Red Cross / Red Crescent Climate Centre. The Climate Centre supports the National Red Cross and Red Crescent Societies in their work to reduce the loss of life and damage to the livelihoods from climate change and extreme weather events.

Economic changes due to climate change (impact on agriculture, migration, ability to afford basic services such as heat, water, and cooling) directly impact the ways in which individuals, families, and communities are impacted. These all align with counselors' beliefs on social justice, vulnerable populations, prevention, and resiliency.

Here is what I believe and what motivates me:
- If counselors truly have an identity inclusive of issues of social justice, then we must be concerned with the human rights issues surrounding the impact of climate change on our communities. Our most vulnerable neighbors will be the hardest hit and will have the most difficult time recovering. Many of them already experience social and environmental justice crises that will only be compounded by increased extreme weather and resource issues.
- As we prepare for disaster response and the emotional aftermath, counselors would benefit from considering a climate-informed pattern of disaster recovery. Rather than disaster-response-recovery, climate-related disasters are now signaling a pattern of disaster-response-recovery-disaster.
- Hundreds of municipalities across the US are engaged in climate mitigation and climate adaptation planning groups. Yet very few have mental health professionals at the table. Knowing that the health, mental health and well-being of our communities are central to this work, counselors have a valuable role to play.
- Those who are paying close attention to or have already been impacted by our changing climate may be experiencing a number of practical and existential concerns, ranging from safety concerns to eco-anxiety to fear for their children's future. If counselors are "informed enough" about climate-related issues, clients will know they have a space to process some of these concerns within session and have them validated.

For me, as a counselor for over 15 years and a counselor educator for more than a decade, I feel a deep commitment and sense of responsibility to our communities to be aware of the impact climate change is currently having and will continue to have. Each community is unique with regard to how that will look. We have a professional vantage point built on our training in trauma, prevention, early intervention and resilience and our ability to empathically absorb the multi-faceted and complex stories of the people we encounter. I believe it is important we lend our voices to the conversations in our communities. To me, being a partner on the front lines of climate response, adaptation, and resilience is part of the future of the counseling profession.

Contributed by Debbie Sturm. © Kendall Hunt Publishing Company.

Anxiety in Children and Adolescents

The incidence of anxiety in children has increased significantly in the last decade. The Center for Disease Control (n.d.) reports that between 2003 and 2012, there was a 1% increase in the diagnosis of childhood anxiety. The research of Ghandour et al. (2018) indicated that 7.4% of children (ages 3-17) struggle with anxiety. By contrast, the prevalence rate for generalized anxiety disorders among adults is 2.9% (American Psychiatric Association, 2013). The prevalence and incidence of anxiety in children and teenagers certainly speak to current trends and future needs for counselors to be able to respond to younger clients. There is a need for evidence-based treatments to be developed. Additionally, as you read in the Research in Counseling chapter, measuring and assessing counselor effectiveness for client interventions is an ethical imperative. As a counselor, you may choose to specialize in treating childhood anxiety. You could then add to the body of research through your work with this population.

Grandparents as Parents

In the United States, there are roughly 2.7 million grandparents raising their grandchildren without the biological parent present in the home (United States Census Bureau, 2014). The reasons vary, but often it is the result of a parent being deemed unable to appropriately care for their children. The current opioid crisis is a frequent cause of parents losing custody. As this continues to be a public health and mental health concern, the numbers of grandchildren being raised by their grandparents will likely increase. Hayslip, Maiden, Page, and Dolbin-MacNab (2015) indicated that there are a number of challenges as a result of being custodial grandparents, including peer isolation, challenges with the physical and emotional aspects of caring for children and adolescents, concern over being judged for their own children's decision making which resulted in the loss of custody, and/or the stigma associated with raising grandchildren. In your work as a counselor, you may find grandchildren are being brought in for counseling; however, the grandparents may also need services. If your focus is not on working with the geriatric population, you will want to find a referral source so that you can assist these grandparents in getting the help they need. Moreover, you could also develop a program that serves the needs of both the grandchildren and their grandparents.

Increased Individualism

Americans, by nature, are individualistic. Unlike collectivistic societies, Americans exercise autonomy and approach decision making from the perspective of how it can be personally beneficial rather than beneficial for the greater good. The preponderance of competition-based reality television, youtube channels that promote the proverbial fifteen seconds of fame, and the popularity of video blogs will likely have an effect on the mental health of the next generation. These activities promote an inflated assessment of power and belief (albeit sometimes true) in being able to influence others' thoughts, feelings, behaviors, and even clothing choices. The striving for purpose and meaning as an individual will likely increase, further fostering the need for external validation and an elevated sense of self-importance. What will this mean for society as a whole? What will this mean for a sense of self-worth when the fifteen seconds of fame is gone? Self-aggrandizement and discontent will likely increase as mental health issues increase. As a future counselor, you may see a need to help clients understand and develop *empathy*. You may also find that being versed in Individual Psychology and being able to apply the Adlerian concepts of social interest (Adler, 1938) will be necessary for this work.

Walk-In Mental Health Clinics

Single Session Therapy (SST) centers, also known as walk-in mental health clinics, have been operating in countries such as Australia (Young, Weir, & Rycroft, 2012), and Canada (Hymmen, Stalker, & Cait, 2013). More recently, these centers are being opened in the United States, including one that opened inside a Texas Walmart in 2019. These clinics operate much like an urgent care clinic for which individuals might seek medical care for a concern that may not require a follow up (e.g., acute bronchitis, flu, etc...). In this manner, clients may only wish to focus on a specific problem rather than a more comprehensive approach to counseling. Some examples may include having feelings of anxiety over a life event, conflict in a relationship, or stress over a decision that needs to be made. Paul and van Ommeran (2013) also indicated that SST is appropriate for the response to a humanitarian crisis, such as natural disasters and man-made crises, such as war.

Young (2018) indicated that SST is not a model, rather it is a method of service delivery. He indicated that counselors need to consider how they would work with clients when they had six sessions and use the same philosophy to work with clients in a single session. In a meta-analysis of reported results from SST treatment centers, Hymmen et al. (2013) found that a large percentage of clients only needed one session, experiencing problem improvement and reporting satisfaction with services provided. In a study of counselors using SST in Australia, Young et al. (2012), found that while service delivery was rated higher and clients felt greater satisfaction, the clinicians felt some stress over the performance aspect of helping clients in one single session. The researchers indicated that this forced counselors to be more flexible and creative in their counseling. However, counselors were able to use the theoretical model of their choice, although Young et al. (2012) did find this approach "is compatible with a client-centered, strength-based approach that is respectful and emphasizes that clients can have control in a self-determining process" (p. 91).

Young (2018) indicated that SST is very much an appropriate method of service delivery because clients often only attend one counseling session, regardless of the clinical concern. 70-80% of clients who attend only one session indicate symptom relief, and it is impossible to predict which clients will return to a subsequent appointment (Young, 2018). Client dropout has historically been a concern for mental health practitioners and much of the reports are anecdotal. Hamilton, Moore, Crane and Payne (2011) found, in a study which investigated client retention based on mental health provider license, client diagnosis, and type of therapy from insurance claim data, that roughly 20% of clients in individual therapy and almost 27% of clients in family therapy will drop out after the first session. Interestingly, clients of marriage and family therapist, psychologists, and psychiatrists had higher drop out rates compared to counselors and social workers. SST centers are likely to be an alternative for clients who have non-crisis needs but do not want to commit to longer-term counseling.

Integrated Behavioral Healthcare

Carl J. Sheperis Ph.D., NCC, CCMHC, MAC, ACS, LPC
Dean, College of Education and Human Development
Texas A&M University San Antonio

Over the next two decades, I anticipate that the counseling profession will move toward a more seamless integration into medical practice. While the concept of integrated behavioral healthcare has been in existence for many years, it has not become a primary practice area for professional counselors. The notion of integrated behavioral healthcare for counselors can raise some questions about professional identity and there are many counselors who entered the counseling profession with a desire to practice outside of a medical model. While there are some valid concerns about the changes in practice that occur through integrated behavioral healthcare, the paradigm surrounding client/patient care is shifting.

© Carl Sheperis

Primary health care has been shifting to a medical home model which is a comprehensive team-based approach that provides patients with coordinated care. This means that both medical doctors and patients are examining ways for one-stop access to quality primary services. In medical home models, there is an opportunity for mental health services to be integrated into the array of accessible services. One of the medical home models of integrated behavioral healthcare that I have used involves a rotation of nurses, PAs, physicians, and counselors for every patient. In other words, when a patient enters a treatment room, the nurse conducts the basic physical assessment functions. Once the nurse has completed the initial evaluation, then the counselor rotates into the treatment room and conducts a mental health assessment including screening for depression, substance abuse, trauma, and overall wellness. After the counselor has finished the assessment, the physician or PA then rotates into the treatment room and completes the medical treatment for the patient. Depending on the findings of all of the assessments, the front desk then schedules follow-up appointments with the appropriate professional (nurse, PA, physician, or counselor). With this model, the patient has very little downtime in the treatment room and leaves with a greater sense of comprehensive care. In addition, the stigma of mental health treatment is reduced because the services are part of the medical process. The patient ends up with a one-stop solution for all of their medical and mental health needs.

The example I provided is only one of many models of integrated behavioral healthcare that are available. The models can range from simple coordinated services to full integration. In 2016 and 2017, I had an opportunity to serve on an advisory board for the federal Health Resources and Services Administration (HRSA) and to help guide the development of integrated behavioral healthcare models that include counselors. We hosted a virtual conference for thousands of multidisciplinary providers and advanced models of practice that were developed by HRSA and the Substance Abuse and Mental Health Services Administration (SAMHSA). The different types of models of integrated behavioral healthcare were well-received and practitioners were excited about the various options available.

There are three primary benefits to integrated behavioral healthcare models that I want to highlight:
1. There is ample evidence that wrap around care for patients improves outcomes
2. Integrating mental health into a medical home reduces stigma and improves receptivity to treatment
3. Integrating mental health counselors into a medical practice has a positive impact on the medical staff.

While there is a movement toward integrated behavioral healthcare, there are still numerous roadblocks that prevent seamless multidisciplinary collaboration. One of the primary problems is related to third-party reimbursement. Many insurance companies maintain outdated models of reimbursement for counselor services with restrictions on provision of co-located services. In other words, there are limitations on the ability of a counselor to provide a billable service in the same office as the medical staff on the same day. There are a few insurance companies who have been evolving their models to fit integrated behavioral healthcare service delivery. However, there will need to be a major overhaul of insurance policies for true integration to occur.

Another roadblock to integration is that counselor training program accreditation standards are not fully aligned with emerging trends in counselor practice. In order for counselors to effectively practice in medical settings, training standards must evolve to include basic medical knowledge. For example, a counselor working in a medical setting needs to be able to engage in common language within the medical practice in order to staff cases and must also be able to understand the interplay of physiological and psychological symptoms in the overall treatment plan.

While roadblocks exist, the federal government is committed to advancing integrated behavioral healthcare models and provides many funding opportunities to community practitioners to launch these services. As medical home models and insurance providers evolve, they are sure to advance the integration of behavioral healthcare more fully. I have seen the benefits of these models and I believe that integrated behavioral healthcare is a major part of the future of counseling.

Contributed by Carl Sheperis. © Kendall Hunt Publishing Company.

"Go into all the world and preach the gospel to all creation"
—Mark 16:15

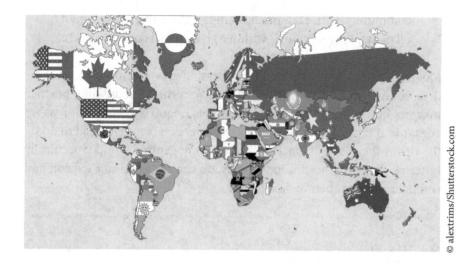

© alextrims/Shutterstock.com

As Christians, we are called to go! As Christian counselors, some of us may also be called to go internationally and minister to others through our clinical work.

Globalization of Counseling

In recent years, much attention has been paid to ensuring the multicultural competence of professional counselors practicing in the United States. Our profession has advocated for added education and training surrounding multicultural awareness, as well as the use of interventions that reach beyond cultural norms and have been proven effective with minorities. While these efforts toward multicultural competence have focused on expanding our practice within the U.S. to meet the needs of minority cultures, globalization focuses on expanding our practice beyond the U.S. borders to meet the needs of the culture being served. Lorelle, Byrd, and Crockett (2012) stated,

> In considering the globalization of counseling, the application of this assumption implies that each local community and individual assigns personal meaning and reacts differently to the experience of counseling. As a result, counseling and the implementation of counseling services in non-U.S. cultures differ significantly from country to country and community to

community, with each model being a valid and effective method of helping individuals within a given social context. (p. 116)

Moving forward, as the counseling profession grows beyond the U.S. borders, counselors must consider that the Westernized counseling practice may not be applicable beyond U.S. borders, requiring redefinition as we engage in international practice. If as a profession counselors fail to do so, the risk is increased of creating a more homogenized world. Specifically in terms of mental health, individuals are subject to greater tension and conflict related to their mental health.

Jerry Vuncannon, Ph.D.
Assistant Professor, Liberty University

© Jerry Vuncannon

When attending graduate school in 2001, my plan was to graduate with a counseling degree, return home to North Carolina, and begin clinical practice. While I did return home and practiced for several years, I never imagined that my clinical training (and eventual Ph.D. in Counselor Education and Supervision in 2006) would lead to several counseling-related endeavors around the world. More specifically, opportunities in Singapore, Malaysia, Cambodia, Mexico, South Africa, and China arose that involved clinical work, teaching, workshop training, supervision, and conference presentations. In addition, another opportunity surfaced where I once served on an international committee comprised of a theologian and mental health professionals representing psychology, psychiatry, social work, and counseling. The committee was formed to address matters of global mental health known as Care and Counsel as Mission, and committee representation included people from the United States, Kenya, Uganda, Australia, Mexico, Czech Republic, Hong Kong, and Wales.

These experiences along with numerous conversations with global colleagues increased my knowledge and understanding of country-specific counseling practices. Space does not allow for full conveyance of these practices, however, some pieces I learned include: there is increased global acceptance and decreased stigma of addressing mental health concerns, especially trauma; some countries have no licensure nor standards regulating counseling practice; countries that do not have a regulatory body may have an established counseling association that helps address standards of practice that include an ethics code; other countries have a national license that may focus on school counseling but not clinical practice; schools that have a counseling program may not be recognized by their government to train counselors (this can be especially true for Christian-based programs); and some counselor-education programs have received non-accredited approval from the International Registry of Counsellor Education Programs (IRCEP; https://www.ircep.org/) which is what I like to call the international arm of CACREP. (IRCEP is similar to CACREP regarding minimum academic standards but for global counseling programs.)

In many respects, my work in other countries parallels works in the US regarding sitting with hurting people, training others in counseling practice, and workshop/conference presentations. However, what is different is the greater awareness for country-specific cultural contexts, adapting to those contexts, need for cultural humility, and excluding what may not be applicable in respective countries. In other words, it is about knowing what training elements are appropriate while including how cultural values, traditions, and perspectives aid in the counseling process. These are some of the things I have learned about counseling worldwide.

There are various constructs to consider in terms of globalization of counseling practice, including global definitions of mental health and wellness, commoditization of the counseling relationship, and access and limitations (Lorelle et al., 2012). Given that mental health services were initially rooted in White middle-class values and traditions, it is fair to acknowledge that the definitions of mental health and wellness must be redefined for the culture in which they are being utilized. For example, symptoms that we may see as being indicative of mental illness in our U.S. culture may not carry the same significance in international cultures. Therefore, it is important to consider that conceptualization, diagnosis, and implementation of counseling models must be specific to the culture being served.

Journalist Ethan Watters (2011) explored the impact of American diagnostic labeling across world cultures in his book, *Crazy Like Us: The Globalization of the American Psyche.* Watters reported that in the last twenty years, eating disorder, mood disorder, psychotic disorder, post-traumatic stress disorder diagnoses have risen on the Asian and African continents.

His contention is not that these issues were not present among the people of these countries before, but rather the westernized influence of the conceptualization of the issues is what has changed (e.g., in Zanzibar, there is a shift from certain behaviors being considered and approached from the lens of spirit possession to a biological explanation and treatment of schizophrenia). Further, Watters noted that westernized approaches to mental health undermine cultural understandings of spirituality, ecology, society, and healing practices. Watters wrote this about the impact this shift has had on the cultural beliefs of these communities:

> The cross-cultural psychiatrists and anthropologists featured in this book have convinced me that we are living at a remarkable moment in human history. At the same time they've been working hard to document the different cultural understandings of mental illness and health, those differences have been disappearing before their eyes. I've come to think of them as psychology's version of botanists in the rainforest, desperate to document the diversity while staying only a few steps ahead of the bulldozers. (p. 7)

CULTURAL DIFFERENCES RELATED TO EATING DISORDERS*

Dr. Sing Lee, an eating disorder researcher in China, commented on how prior to the early 1990s, anorexia nervosa in Hong Kong was not characterized the same as in Westernized cultures. One of the diagnostic criteria for anorexia nervosa is the fear of becoming fat or being overweight. Traditionally, Chinese clients displayed restrictive eating patterns but did not endorse a fear of becoming fat or overweight. However, Dr. Lee noted that between 1998-2007 the clinical presentation of eating disorders changed in Hong Kong, shifting and conforming more toward the Westernized version of anorexia nervosa. Researchers suggest that the influence of the West could have attributed to the shift in symptom presentation.

*(Lorelle, Byrd, & Crockett, 2012)

One of the cornerstones of professional counseling is the therapeutic relationship between the client and the counselor. While individuals can share daily burdens with friends and family, the professional counseling relationship is a fee for service commodity in our Western world. Advocacy efforts have worked to bridge economic gaps and make counseling more affordable and accessible for those of lower socioeconomic status; however, it remains a commodity. It is important to acknowledge that different cultures have different priorities and/or views regarding capitalism and economic exchanges that may impact the accessibility of counseling, as well as the profitability of counseling for the clinician (Lorelle et al., 2012).

Accessibility and physical barriers are also important issues to explore related to the globalization of the counseling profession. Historically, individuals from diverse cultural backgrounds have been less likely to seek mental health treatment. This under-utilization of services could be due to the social stigma related to mental illness and mental health treatment, in addition to, limited access. Limited accessibility to mental health services could be financial in nature, as previously discussed, or structural in nature. Moving forward, as the profession expands internationally, it will be important to assess the structural limitations of communities. These limitations may include, availability of physical office space, transportation to and from treatment locations, and other systemic, social, and socio-economic factors.

Various professional organizations are answering the call to support increased access to counseling worldwide. The ACA has developed a *Strategic Plan and Framework 2018-2021* that addresses various initiatives that align with their mission and vision. One of the initiatives is, "Engaging in proactive leadership demonstrated by supporting human rights and social justice issues by advocating for initiatives that reduce the challenges and barriers faced by clients, students, counselors, and communities" (ACA, 2019, 1.4). Furthermore, on a global level, the International Association for Counselling (IAC) is continuing its efforts to advocate for access to counseling worldwide. Currently, IAC is working on a project entitled *World Mapping of the Counselling Profession,* focused on compiling data and information regarding counseling in 196 countries (IAC, 2019). It is important that as professionals we support these initiatives and engage in opportunities to advocate for the profession worldwide.

Engaging Cultural Humility
Mike Shook, Mental Health Counselor

Mike Shook is a practicing counselor in China, which is a country
that does not have a profession
of counseling as we know it. Of
his experience practicing in China, he says:

© Mike Shook

It has been both a gift and
challenge of learning what cultural humility looks like in action as I collaborate with my
Chinese colleagues. Throughout
Chinese history, there hasn't been the stark distinction between mind and body as
has been in the West since the Enlightenment. I find that my Chinese colleagues
challenge me to take our embodiment seriously and to be open to the idea that not
every person who is experiencing distress needs Western-style counseling such
as talk therapy. My Chinese colleagues have also exposed the rampant individual-
ism weaved into so many of the dominant theories of counseling and have offered
more nuanced and relational approaches to ethical practice that takes community seriously. Yet they have also critically looked at the unique difficulties people
encounter in a collectivistic culture. Their willingness to critically reflect on how
culture and context might contribute to individual or social problems has been a
very formative example of humility that has guided me as I navigate inter-cultural/
multi-cultural practice.

The main challenges I have experienced in my professional identity development
while living abroad are twofold. Firstly, though my online MA program connected
me to wonderful counselor educators as well as classmates who are now colleagues, being abroad has limited my ability to build and maintain professional
relationships with other counselors and mental health professionals. Secondly,
because the helping professions are in their infancy stages here in China, there is
limited access to training and other opportunities to grow as a practitioner. The internet has helped in this regard by democratized many resources for learning and
furthering my professional identity and counseling practice. However, there is no
replacement for the face to face training that allows for both building clinical skills
while creating new professional relationships and friends. Both challenges are the

driver for the creation of The Thoughtful Counselor podcast, which has given me the ability to interact with others in the counseling profession while contributing to the democratization of ideas for other counseling and mental health professionals.

I am also a follower of Jesus. My faith influences every aspect of who I am, including who I am as a counselor. In my practice as a counselor, my faith shows up in a variety of ways. The more obvious ways include how I conceptualize the stories clients bring into counseling, how I understand the process of change and growth, and what my role is in a given conversational moment as someone called to "love my neighbor as myself." The way this looks in practice is different with every person I work with, much like how Jesus specifically attuned to each person he interacted with. I am constantly asking myself "what does it look like in this relationship, this moment, to exemplify God's love and mercy for this person? How do I love this person as I would myself, as God loves them?" These questions bring me to a place of humility and gratitude for the opportunity to walk alongside people from diverse backgrounds and experiences. As a follower of Jesus, I am also called to remember those on the margins of our communities. This call challenges me to actively accommodate people from different socio-economic backgrounds who are often priced out of professional services where I live in Beijing, putting my worth as a counselor not in how much I charge per session but in my identity in Jesus.

Contributed by Mike Shook. © Kendall Hunt Publishing Company.

HOW DOES THE CULTURAL SHIFT OF THE DIGITAL AGE IMPACT COUNSELING?

Technological advances force change at all levels of culture and society. From the wheel to the personal computer to all that we see today, cultures evolve and expand as technology crashes through barriers and spawns new knowledge. The counseling field has evolved as the needs of society have changed due to technological advances. For example, psychological challenges from stress have increased the need for effective counseling techniques to be delivered in an efficient manner, while advances in neuroscience continue to provide a better understanding of the impact of brain development and functioning on human behavior. It is important for the counseling field to be aware of both the benefits stemming from technological advances, as well as the challenges that arise such as shifting moral values and psychological stress.

The digital age has brought many changes to the landscape of modern society and the impact on the counseling profession is profound. The invention of the smartphone brought the power of the personal computer into everyone's hand, complete with limitless information and the ability to connect instantly to people all over the world. Social media, made popular by the smartphone, enables people to be the center of their own digital universe. Social media has changed how people connect and communicate, in addition to shifting cultural values and ideas about relationships and what people think is important. The counseling field accepts the changes that technology and the digital age brings, and understands that simply wishing for a return to the "good old days" is neither realistic nor helpful. People in modern culture require the counseling field to adapt in both understanding technology while using the benefits of technological advances to address psychological needs.

> "Technology is a gift of God. After the gift of life, it is perhaps the greatest of God's gifts. It is the mother of civilizations, of arts and sciences." -Freeman Dyson

Technology and Delivery of Counseling Services

Technology has changed how people receive counseling services. Computer-mediated psychotherapy (CMP) continues to expand in the digital age, providing easy access for consumers of counseling and innovative strategies for practitioners (Baker, 2019). CMP has evolved as technology has pushed the use of computers into mainstream culture and the mental health fields. Smartphones and tablets, laptop computers and VR headsets along with a multitude of software programs and apps are now common in many practitioner's offices. Telemental health, which is comprised of "telephone, mobile devices, interactive video conferencing, email, chat, text, and internet" (Campbell, Millan, & Martin, 2017, p. 169) will continue to be recognized as viable and necessary. Research of telemental health shows it to be as effective as in-person treatment (Hilty, Yellowlees, Myers, Parish, & Rabinowitz, 2016), in addition to providing immediate, cost-effective services to consumers who may not be able to access traditional counseling services. For example, video conferencing is a way to break down socioeconomic and environmental barriers, in addition to providing valuable services to those with chronic illness or victims of natural disasters (Nash, 2019). While video conferencing is as effective as in-person treatment and a vital way to reach underserved populations or those lacking transportation; it also has restrictive components such as financial means or those with technology challenges. With the growing popularity and of video conferencing and CMP's, in addition to favorable outcomes showing the validity and reliability, it is likely that this form of delivery of counseling services will continue far into the future.

App Based Counseling Subscriptions

Dr. Donna Sheperis
Palo Alto University

© Donna Sheperis

App-based counseling is somewhat similar to regular counseling in that you spend time establishing the therapeutic relationship, understanding the client in context, developing trust, and working from a theoretical perspective toward defined goals. The intent is that if we interact 2x day, 5 days per week, that is equivalent to one therapeutic hour. Effectively, the client can have 4 sessions per month within their subscription. Let me set the stage for my work as the distance counseling platforms are all a bit different. I work with a primarily message-based app – meaning we write back and forth to one another in a secure chat room that only the client and I can access. That writing is not in real time. About 20% of my clients also select one or more video sessions per month which are, of course, in real time.

When working on a distance-based platform, all counselors must be licensed and only see clients in the state where they are licensed. They also need to carry their own malpractice insurance. It is not required that we are Board Certified TeleMental Health Providers although that is a credential some have. We go through a lot of training before ever seeing a client.

Most insurances do not cover app-based services. The platform I work with has contracted with industry EAPs to offer the platform as part of their coverage. Even without insurance, an app based platform is often as or more affordable. If the client pays $149 month, for example, and has a $50 copay if they see an in-person therapist, then they can get the equivalent of 4 sessions for less money per month.

Each morning, I log in and respond to any client who has written to me. I also check in on those I haven't heard from or send reminders and encouragers to clients. I do the same in the afternoons, Monday through Friday. If I take time off, I let my clients know and make it up to them with an extra message or, if I take a week or more off, a video session. They can also freeze their account for a week or more and "save" their week for later. Clients typically spend about 3-6 months working with me, but I have had some clients work for a year or longer. I have treated all sorts of counseling concerns in the platform with success – adjustment disorders, mood disorders, complicated grief, relationship concerns, career concerns, sexual identity development – a whole spectrum of presenting problems, diagnoses, ages, and cultures. The vast majority of the people I have seen are happy with the process and find the app-based service to fit their needs.

There are three things I love about this work
a. Clients – they are wonderful. They are truly all trying to be their best selves and I get the awesome honor of helping them. The work of a counselor is always such a privilege!
b. Flexibility – I work from home as a professor. This platform allows me to keep my clinical skills sharp without having to have an office, do my own billing, etc.
c. Breaking barriers – Honestly, I joined the platform because I didn't trust it to be helpful! I wanted to see for myself. The rigorous onboarding coupled with the intense clinical and administrative support offered is impressive. The ethical and legal oversight as well as opportunities to grow as a clinician has been wonderful to my professional identity! I can reach clients that cannot get to a counselor. To me, that is meeting a true social justice aim.

Of course, there are challenges with using texting - as we all know from having a text message or email misinterpreted! If I worry that I cannot convey what I want to say in writing, I can send up to 5 minutes of audio for the client to listen to. In addition, there are some situations that are not a good fit for this platform. Actively suicidal clients, some addictions that would be better suited to inpatient, psychotic symptoms, and clients who may need EMDR are examples of times that I would refer clients to a local provider.

But the advantages far outweigh the challenges! My clients are largely busy, educated, individuals who simply do not have the time to drive 30 minutes across town, have a one-hour therapy appointment, and drive back to work. They are able to work their therapy in and around their lives. In addition, I have the advantage of hearing from clients when they are in distress, or when they have a success, rather than a week or two after the fact. It is a good place to work out "how should I have this conversation with my partner" before having it. It is a good platform for Cognitive Behavioral Therapy work.

Can you tell I really like what I do? The pay is decent, especially when you consider that I have no overhead or billing responsibilities. The clients are awesome and the support staff is well trained. It is like having a private practice with institutional support.

Contributed by Donna Sheperis. © Kendall Hunt Publishing Company.

Mental Health Apps: Tech for Self-Help

Apps make life easier, more enjoyable, and more fun. With just a few swipes, valuable information is available and transactions are possible because of apps. The number of mental health apps (MHapps) designed to track and improve mental health care has increased dramatically, and this trend is likely to continue into the future based on the demand and success of such apps (Bakker, Kazantzis, Rickwood, & Rickard, 2016).

APP OR COMPANY	DESCRIPTION
Crisis Text Line	Counseling for anyone in a crisis
Ginger.Jo	Employer-sponsored mental health coaching
Happify	Activities and games designed to increase happiness
Lantern	Coaching and daily exercises based on cognitive behavioral therapy
MindShift	Guidance for teens and young adults with anxiety, produced by a charity called AnxietyBC
Pacifica	Tools for managing stress, anxiety, and depression
Pear Therapeutics	Plans to roll out "digital therapeutics" that would be prescribed for addiction, schizophrenia, and PTSD
PTSD Coach	Tools for guidance for PTSD from the U.S. Department of Veterans Affairs
7 Cups	Text-based counseling and therapy
Talkspace	Online therapy sessions

TABLE 14.1

Help in Your Pocket

MHapps allow counseling clients to track mood fluctuations, journal about stressors, and implement coping tools, which provides a sense of control. Practitioners find that MHapps are useful tools between sessions to help clients progressing by helping them feel motivated as well as providing a sense of control over the client's emotional and psychological challenges. During sessions, apps provide easily accessible and organized data, and practitioners can easily track their client's progress between sessions. Because technology develops quickly, the scientific examination of approaches that incorporate technology lag behind (Bakker, et al., 2016). A 2019 study examined three MHapps (MoodKit, MoodPrism, and Mood-Mission) to find out the effectiveness of the apps, and what factors were involved if positive changes occurred (Bakker et al., 2019). The researchers discovered that the MHapps are effective, and note that an important factor in the success of the MHapps was the improvement of the client's sense of "competence in their ability to cope with stress and adversity by using specific strategies" (p. 82). The authors call for future research as the use of MHapps continues to grow as modern culture struggles to understand and cope with stress as the result of a fast-paced world.

Tech in Session

Technology has not only changed the delivery of counseling service outside the therapy office but inside it as well. The counselor of today and the future is one that needs qualities of adaptability and being able to change with the technological tides that will continue to bring new tools to better understand clients and help them in their daily lives. Think about how you as a counselor will adapt to a constantly shifting world as technology forces change in the future.

© Veronica Louro/Shutterstock.com

Technology, Play Therapy, and Building Relationships. Technology in the form of video and computer games, along with tablet and smartphone games have infiltrated the counseling field in the last several years. Studies showing the effectiveness of computer/video games as play therapy tools have increased greatly in the literature (Hull, 2009; LaFleur, Hebert, & Dupuy, 2018). Young people use technological devices and spend a great deal of time connecting with others, playing, and being creative through digital media. Tablet and console games have rich themes such as overcoming challenges, pursuing goals, and creating strategies for problem-solving. Two-player games allow the counselor and client to work together or play against each other, which involve the themes of relying on another's help, dealing with losing, or feeling the thrill of victory which can increase the client's sense of self-representation (Hull, 2015). Even a game like Mine-Craft can be used in individual and group counseling sessions to work on social awareness, learning to overcome problems, and practice decision making.

Adolescents spend a great deal of time connecting with the world and expressing themselves through digital media. Including tablet and console games in counseling sessions, as well as music and movie apps like YouTube or Spotify have benefits such as increasing the adolescent's sense of safety through a familiar medium. In addition, the adolescent is allowed to express themselves in an autonomous way. Incorporating the adolescent's social media into the counseling process can be a way to build a relationship, as well as increasing the young person's sense of self-representation to help them feel valued and noticed. The adolescent is more likely to feel comfortable when familiar technological devices and apps are included in the counseling process, and it opens the door for dialogue to occur particularly around difficult topics.

Several video/tablet programs and games exist for counseling young people with special challenges, such as Autism Spectrum Disorder (ASD) and those suffering from trauma. For example, several MHapps for IPad like *Smash Hit, Language Builder,* and *Zones of Regulation* can help counselors who work with young people with ASD find fun, innovative ways to work on social and self-regulation skills. There are even MHapps to help those with ASD navigate the sometimes-confusing world of social media, such as *Social Media Friend, Foe, or Other* (Grant, 2019). The *Virtual Sandtray App* is a digital version of the sand tray (Stone, 2016). This innovative tool for IPad brings all of the therapeutic power of the sand try but delivers it in digital form, making it useful for any setting and without the counselor needing to haul materials. Because it is digital, the *Virtual Sandtray* allows creations to be filed and saved. Goodyear-Brown and Gott (2019) discuss the usefulness of the *Virtual Sandtray* for children who have sensory issues or suffered trauma that makes using an actual sand tray difficult or unpleasant. Known as *titration*, this process is about giving a child many opportunities to practice behaviors that "shape the child in a healthful direction" (p. 109). Allowing a child to become used to the sand tray through digital means first and becoming comfortable with the digital version, can lead to the child engaging with an actual sand tray later.

Virtual Reality. Virtual Reality (VR) is a computer program that creates a simulated, virtual world. A participant is able to enter the virtual world by wearing a headset that creates visual and audio stimuli. Some types of VR allow the participant to move, and the scenes within the environment change as the person moves. VR is portable, relatively inexpensive, and easy to set up. Studies of VR have found it to be useful in many settings and for many types of emotional and psychological challenges. tVR is the name provided when VR is used in a therapeutic context. One of the main areas in which tVR has been used is with post traumatic stress disorder (PTSD) and it has been found to be successful in lessening anxiety and panic attacks, in addition to helping people learn to self-regulate during stressful events (Botella, Serrano, Banos, & Garcia-Palacios, 2015). tVR is valuable in the treatment of PTSD because it can place a person in a stressful situation and monitor the person's reactions to the stress, while at the same time allowing the person to practice tools learned in counseling sessions to regulate emotions.

© TierneyMJ/Shutterstock.com

Another valuable use of tVR is as a distraction tool for use with individuals, particularly children, who are undergoing stressful medical procedures. For children who have suffered traumatic experiences, many medical procedures can trigger images and feelings of being helpless and trapped. Through the use of VR, the child is distracted by being immersed in a completely different environment, along with soothing sights and sounds and thus make the medical procedure more bearable and with less emotional reactions. The focus of current research is on making tVR applicable to all sorts of counseling settings and with various disorders and psychological challenges. tVR offers many benefits through immediate immersion and offering the individual immediate biofeedback which can be tracked as the counselor guides them through the practice of tools to mediate stress responses.

MineCraft in Group Counseling to Improve Social Skills

MineCraft is a game loved by children of all ages. MineCraft has been found to be useful in group counseling with children diagnosed with Autism Spectrum Disorder (ASD). Dr. Kevin Hull conducts groups where MineCraft is played on individual tablets. Each group member creates a character and joins the game. A group member designated as the 'leader' communicates the instructions for their project to the 'workers.' Using a timer, the group works together to work on the project, and the group members switch roles so that each member performs in the role of the leader. Benefits

© Bloomicon/Shutterstock.com

of this approach include practicing communication skills, joint attention, and increased perspective-taking, all done in a fun and familiar way. You can read more about this approach in his book *Group Therapy Techniques with Children, Adolescents, and Adults on the Autism Spectrum* (Jason Aronson, 2014).

Technology has brought many changes to the counseling landscape in recent years. From MHapps to video and computer tablet games, to VR and the many changes that are still to come, technology pushes the boundaries of understanding and working with people. The future of counseling will continue to be shaped by technological advances and it will require us to be diligent in learning and studying new ways to use technology with our counseling clients.

These amazing technological advances also create a shift in communication for which the next generation of adults will likely feel the full impact. Technological communication affords humans to use abbreviated words and acronyms, emojis to express thoughts or feelings, and limitations with fully expressing a thought. Further, the speed of which information is transferred also has an influence on individuals, impacting the ability to patiently wait. For example, words like blog, selfie, vines, gif, and meme were not part of the cultural vernacular 30 years ago. Additionally, words that once meant one thing have taken on a new definition (e.g., "likes" was once a verb and is now also a noun). This development of new terminology will continue as technology continues to advance. The changing language may result in divisions socioeconomically and generationally.

Technology has a significant impact on media images and the transfer of that information. The mental processes related to sharing on social media can distort thinking about what is important and necessary. Much energy is invested in creating the perfect social media post with accompanying the perfect photo. Further, the fear of missing out, often abbreviated FoMO, keeps individuals continuously connected to devices and may speak to interdependency and decreased self-esteem (Dogan, 2019). Researchers have found a connection between extended use (i.e, at bedtime) of devices and decreased sleep and increased depression in adolescents (Lemola, Perkinson-Gloor, Brand, Dewald-Kaufmann, & Grob, 2015). The use of social media also has neuroscience implications for adolescents. A study by Sherman, Payton, Hernandez, Greenfield and Dapretto (2016) found that adolescents experienced increased activity in the brain's reward center when viewing photos which had more social media likes. This reward system is the same reward system that is attributed to addictive behaviors. As noted in a report from Harvard Medical School, this reward system adapts over time and the once pleasure creating event no longer has the same impact (2011). Thus, tolerance to the stimuli is developed. The result is often compulsatory behaviors that serve as an effort to once again receive the same reward. Sherman et al. (2016) also discovered that in viewing photos that receive likes, but are perceived as risky (e.g., alcohol and drug paraphernalia, rude gestures, provocative clothing), resulted in a decrease of activity in the cognitive control areas of the brain suggesting that there is a connection between peer approval and desensitization of risky behaviors.

What will this mean for healthy relationships? What will this mean for professional associations? What will this mean for written communications? What will this mean for self and other expectations and frustration tolerance? Relational and work-place/work-function issues will likely be areas for which clients seek counseling.

HOW DO CULTURAL SHIFTS IMPACT THE PROFESSIONAL LANDSCAPE?

Counselor Education

Changes in client needs, models of therapy, and policies that impact the practice of counseling, in addition to societal and environmental shifts, have an impact on how future counselors are trained. Counselor educators must stay abreast of these trends and adjust accordingly. Without the proverbial crystal ball, it is challenging to see into the future. Thus, predictions about what we may see in the future of counseling is founded in current upswings.

NCE vs. NMHCA. At present, each state uses NCE and/or NCMHCE as the licensure exam. Specifically, 18 states require the NCE, 10 states require the NCMHCE, 13 states plus the District of Columbia allow the choice between the NCE and NCMHCE, and nine states require both exams. As you learned in a previous chapter, the profession was at one time entitled Community Counseling. In 2009, the CACREP standards shifted the language from the former title to Clinical Mental Health Counseling. The last two states that adopted licensure require the NCMHCE. Of the nine states which required both, the NCMHCE is the top tier licensure exam. These trends seem to point toward an increased focus and usage of the word *clinical* in Clinical Mental Health Counseling. Does this mean the NCE has outlived its purpose? Most likely not, however, it's purpose may not carry the same weight it has historically. If there is indeed more of a push to use NCMHCE and less of a push to use NCE, counselor education programs will need to make adjustments in how students are assessed (i.e., more case-based approach rather than traditional multiple-choice exams) across the curriculum.

Implications of state-specific laws. The *Tennessee Law*, signed by Tennessee (TN) Governor Bill Haslam in 2016, made Tennessee the first state to allow mental health counselors and marriage and family therapists to deny services to clients based on their sincerely held beliefs as long as they are not a danger to themselves or others at the time of seeking services. This law is also known as the *Counseling Discrimination Law* (Miller, 2016). The law is controversial because it is in direct conflict with the *ACA Code of Ethics* and was a response to the 2014 revision that ACA made which stated that it is unethical to refer clients solely based on the counselor's personally held beliefs values, behaviors, and attitudes (§A.11.b). People are often confused by this law, assuming it relates to counselor competency. It is essential to understand that this law is not intended to protect clients based on counselor competency; rather, it allows a counselor to not provide or discontinue providing services to someone who does not think, live, or behave the way the counselor believes they should. With the passing of the *Tennessee Law*, concerns have surfaced regarding its implications on the future of clinical practice as well as the way training programs train counselors.

As discussed before, not all clients have an abundance of counselors in their area, and the concern is that there will be clients who may or may not receive services due to this law. Furthermore, will rejection by one counselor send a message to a client that they should not try again? Lastly, does the TN law excuse counselors from working on personal biases or allow them to ignore the importance of increasing self-awareness? Conversely, supporters of the law believe that it protects the counselor as well as the client by preventing the client and counselor from engaging in an unhealthy therapeutic relationship.

Additionally, the TN law does not just impact counseling training programs in TN but also impacts online training programs that enroll TN students and adhere to the *ACA Code of Ethics*. How would the student be assessed in an ethics course if the student indicated s/he would refer based on personal values? What happens if a student refuses to see a client at a practicum or internship site - would the online university be implicated if there were a lawsuit? It is truly difficult to determine how the TN law will change the landscape of the future of counseling; however, it has already made an impact on an awareness of the need to have further discussions regarding how to address not only this law, but also laws from other states that may follow in similar footsteps.

Theoretical Models. As we learn more about human behavior, we also learn more about how to apply the therapeutic intervention to human behavior. While theory textbooks still primarily focus on the same theories introduced to you in Chapter 10, other therapeutic models are gaining in the areas of application, empirical support, and a more holistic understanding of client case conceptualization. While there is great value in the theories outlined in Chapter 10, many of these theories were developed almost 100 years ago and our understanding of human behavior has grown significantly.

In a *Counseling Today* (the magazine of the American Counseling Association) article focused on the future of counseling (Shallcross, 2012), several leaders in the profession were asked what they anticipate for the future of counseling. One counselor educator commented that it is critical to include wellness-based theories in a systemic context. Another counselor educator indicated the need for new theories and models to be developed which speak to evidence-based short term interventions. A third counselor educator noted the need for new theories to develop, including theories which respond to traumatic stress and intergenerational issues. Further, this counselor educator identified the need for "culture-centered counseling theories that come from Eastern Europe, southern Africa, the Pacific Rim or South America" (Shallcross, 2012, para. 88).

Home-Based Counseling. Home -based counseling is a movement that is changing the way counselors provide services by moving the counseling session to meet clients in their homes, rather than in a traditional office or clinical setting (Hammond & Czyszczon, 2014). Home-based counseling is not a new phenomenon. In the past, most home-based services were targeted for families, children with disabilities or children who were on the verge of being removed from their homes. These services were often provided by bachelor and masters level providers with some mental health or human services experiences (Hammond & Czyszczon, 2014). However, the landscape is changing, and an increasing number of master's level and licensed counselors are providing home-based counseling in the community.

Home-based counseling may benefit both clients and counselors. These benefits are similar to the same benefits of teletherapy. It provides an opportunity for clients to receive services who may not have the needed resources (e.g., transportation, child-care, financial, etc...) to receive counseling in a traditional setting. Furthermore, clients also suffer from disabilities, chronic mental health, and medical issues that become a barrier to making their way into an office. Unfortunately, a stigma persists in mental health that prevents people from feeling comfortable to walk into an office or publicly sit in a waiting room until seen by a counselor. Imagine, living in a small town where everyone knows everyone. How long would it be before someone recognized your car parked at the counseling agency or before you would run into someone you knew? Perhaps personally, you are not concerned with someone knowing you and know you are receiving counseling services; but for some, this stigma prevents them from engaging in the services they need to get better. Counselors see home-based counseling as a way to engage in social change (Liu & Estrada-Hernandez, 2010). The ability to engage in a practice that allows counselors to bring needed services to someone's front door is priceless. Counselors may choose home-based counseling, even when access to services is not a challenge, because it provides an opportunity for a bigger picture of what is going on with the client (Cortes, 2004): It broadens the perspective to allow for an assessment of the client that is often limited in a traditional setting. Clients tend to feel more comfortable in their own homes. This increased comfort level can help build a therapeutic bond more quickly with a client as it shows an early level of trust and commitment when you are willing to be in their home instead of being in the comfort of your own office.

The majority of training programs do not train students to engage in home-based counseling (Cortes, 2004; Woodford, Bordeau, & Alderfer, 2006). So, before engaging in home-based counseling, like any other treatment model, it is important to receive training, supervision, and research before deciding whether or not this is the treatment approach for you as a counselor. You will also need to learn how to assess if a client is an appropriate candidate for home-based counseling. Is the client violent or has a history of violence? Who are the people living in the client's home? Is the client actively experiencing psychosis?

Furthermore, ethical considerations are critical for providing home-based services, particularly in the area of maintaining healthy boundaries, as it is easier for lines to get blurred when you are in a client's home versus being in a traditional office. Because you have less control of the environment, there is also a need to be aware of safety concerns (Adams & Maynard, 2000). Safety for you and the client is essential for this to be an effective model of treatment. You also have the responsibility of maintaining all the ethical standards while providing effective treatment. A decision to engage in home-based counseling is not a decision to make lightly.

Licensure Portability

Licensure portability is an essential component of the counseling profession, due to efforts to standardize the education and training of professional counselors. Although Virginia was the first state to implement licensure in 1976, licensure has been an ongoing process and topic of discussion in the counseling profession. In fact, it wasn't until 2009 that licensure was implemented in

© Dontree/Shutterstock.com

all 50 states, with California being the last. Unlike other professions, in professional counseling, licensure occurs on the state level. Thus, there are a host of differences and variations in not only the name of the counseling license (i.e., Licensed Clinical Professional Counselor, Licensed Professional Counselor, Licensed Clinical Mental Health Counselor, etc.) but also the education and training requirements necessary for licensure. Some of the most notable differences in licensure requirements currently seen amongst the 50 states and the District of Columbia (see Figure 14.1) include examination and course requirements, performance of a criminal background check, and inquiries regarding drug and alcohol abuse, mental health concerns and history of unethical practice (Olsen, Brown-Rice, & Gerodias, 2018).

The impact of licensure portability is widespread in that it impacts counselors, their clients, and the profession as a whole. It is estimated that 7.6 million people move from one state to another every year (ACA, 2019). While not all of these individuals are counselors, there are a number of professional counselors who are faced with state to state moves each year. Without licensure portability, these professionals are forced to face a gap in employment as they go through the licensure process in their new residential state. Depending on the state's requirements and application process this could mean months of unemployment and lack of income for counselors. Licensure portability would alleviate many of the pains that are felt with these licensure reciprocity roadblocks. Additionally, the standardization in educational requirements that comes with licensure portability would help counseling students who are pursuing their graduate education and are yet unsure of the state in which they will be working and living. With the number of graduate credit hours ranging from 42-60 and the number of supervision hours ranging from 500-4,500 depending on the state, this process can be extremely overwhelming (ACA, 2019).

Imagine going to your physician for a medical procedure only to learn that a physician practicing one state away is required to undergo more extensive education and training in order to perform the same procedure that your physician is getting ready to perform. How confident would you be in your physician's skills and abilities as compared to the neighboring physician? Given the option, which physician would you choose? Similar to this scenario, from a client's perspective, it is important that they feel confident in their counselor's qualifications. This confidence leads to trust and

FIGURE 14.1

Licensure Variations across States

EXAMINATION REQUIREMENTS

- NCE — 28
- Both NCE and NCMHCE — 10
- NCMHCE — 10
- NEITHER — 3

COURSE REQUIREMENTS

8 CACREP Core Areas*

*Of the 8 CACREP Common Core Areas, there was not a single one that all 50 states required.

DRUG & ALCOHOL ABUSE

22%
- ONLY 11 STATES INQUIRED ABOUT THE APPLICANT'S HISTOR OF DRUG & ALCOHOL ABUSE

HISTORY OF UNETHICAL PRACTICE

6 STATES INQUIRED
- 33 INQUIRED ABOUT PREVIOUS LICENSURE BEING REFUSED
- 29 INQUIRED ABOUT LICENSURE BEING REVOKED OR SUPENDED

PERSONAL MENTAL HEALTH PROBLEMS

54%
- 27 STATES INQUIRED ABOUT THE APPLICANT'S HISTORY OF MENTAL HEALTH PROBLEMS

CRIMINAL BACKGROUND CHECK

14 STATES REQUIRED
- 38 ASKED THE APPLICANT IF THEY HAD BEEN CONVICTED OF A CRIME

a stronger therapeutic rapport. Additionally, licensure portability benefits the public by protecting them from unethical practice by standardizing licensure requirements and providing for more counselors to move and practice in rural and underserved areas (ACA, 2019).

At a professional level, the variances that exist related to counselor education and professional licensure fail to promote both unity within the profession as well as respect from outside of the profession. From the outside looking in, the field may be perceived as disorganized and disheveled, without a united direction. The image of our profession that is portrayed to the public is important in building respect for the profession as a whole. As we advocate for our profession, it is important that we continue to advocate for standardization in licensure requirements and licensure portability.

As previously noted, the continued rise of distance counseling is inevitable. It is important to note the potential impact that distance counseling and licensure portability may have on one another. Current state laws require that counselors be licensed in the state in which the client is physically present during the distance counseling session (Kaplan & Martz, 2014; NBCC, 2016). However, as we have noted in regard to education and licensing requirements, there are variations between states in terms of the training that is needed to provide distance counseling services, whether or not a pre-existing provider-client relationship is necessary, etc. The question becomes whether the rise of distance counseling will influence licensure portability, or whether licensure portability will influence the use of distance counseling. As the profession continues to grow and advocate for both, it will be interesting to see the relationship between the two.

The broad discussion of licensure portability began in 2011, when the 20/20: A Vision for the Future of Counseling initiative advised that licensure portability was essential in advancing the profession of counseling (Kaplan & Gladding, 2011). While attempts by the profession have been limited in their success, professional advocacy efforts continue to head in the right direction. As of June 2016, the Governing Council of the American Counseling Association (ACA) approved the ACA Licensure Portability Model. This model allows for independently licensed counselors without a disciplinary record to be eligible for licensure in any state (ACA, 2019). Current efforts to promote licensure portability are focused on establishing more empirical research to support the proposed need for licensure portability, as well as continued professional advocacy and legislative efforts.

As previously stated, one of the biggest barriers to licensure portability is a lack of standardized educational requirements throughout the profession. Research indicates that there are substantial differences in educational requirements among the 50 states (Figure 14.1; Olsen et al., 2018). While the inception of the National Board for Certified Counselors (NBCC) and the Council for Accreditation of Counseling & Related Educational Programs (CACREP) has been monumental in the growth and development of the counseling profession, we still have a long way to go. To date, more and more counselor education programs are seeking CACREP accreditation, as CACREP's standards have been seen as "the national standard for counseling programs... [which] has set the profession on a path toward a clear counselor identity through its process of preparation program accreditation" (Mascari & Webber, 2013, p. 16). In fact, beginning January 1, 2022, a master's degree or higher from a CACREP accredited counseling program will be required in order to receive National Certified Counselor (NCC) credentials from the NBCC. While a majority of the profession seems to value the standardization that CACREP accreditation provides, others view it as burdensome for educational institutions (Olsen et al., 2018).

Job Market Forecast

In 2019, the United States Health Resources and Services Administration predicted that over the next decade, job opportunities will increase for professional counselors who work with general outpatient client issues, including anxiety, depression, suicidality, grief, stress, and other mental health issues (Bray, 2019). A significant growth margin (21%) has been identified for counselors who work with substance abuse issues. The number of counselors being trained does not match the predicted need; thus, there will likely be a significant deficit of mental health and addictions counselors. A small margin of growth (14%) was predicted for marriage and family counselors. Conversely, it was identified that there will be a surplus of school counselors (Bray, 2019). Perhaps this surplus is related to the increase of mental health counselors who are contracted to work in school systems, as discussed in Chapter 3. With the increase in the number of children seeking school-based mental health services (Bains, Cusson, White-Frese, & Walsh, 2017; Brown, 2006), it is likely that these mental health counselors will be utilized to intervene with behaviors caused by mental health concerns rather than school counselors.

SUMMARY

While the future of the counseling profession may not be crystal clear, it certainly appears to be bright. Key factors influencing the growth and development of the profession include cultural shifts related to (1) changes in the social landscape and climate; (2) the globalization of counseling services; (3) the increased use of technology, not only in session but also as a means of delivering services; (4) the increased need for integrated behavioral healthcare; and (5) the standardization of counselor education and training and licensure portability. As a profession and as individual counselors, it is important that we adapt and grow while maintaining our identity and not straying too far from our roots. Now more than ever, it is important that counselors engage in advocacy efforts, not only advocating for the needs of clients, but also for the profession itself. As Christ followers and counselors in training, it is essential to stay grounded and firmly rooted in the unchanging Lord and Savior Jesus Christ, as He will guide you in your journey of learning how to provide legal, ethical, and Christ-honoring counseling services.

FOR THE ROAD AHEAD

Check out the Chapter 14 video at this link:
https://www.khpcontent.com/

Reflections of the Journey

1. Technology has enabled ease of access for counseling clients and helped to break barriers that previously kept clients from receiving counseling services. How do you plan to incorporate technology into your future work as a counselor in the digital age?
2. Cultural shifts have influenced change in many parts of the counseling field over the past several decades. Which parts of the counseling field do you believe should not change?
3. This chapter highlights counselors who work with different cultures all over the world. How do you see God using you in your future counseling work to expand the boundaries of counseling to other cultures and lands?

For Further Exploration

Gunther, D. (Producer). (2019, February 20). A Breath of Fresh Air: The Ecological Self and Environmental Justice with Dr. Debbie Sturm [Audio podcast]. *The Theory of Change*. Retrieved from http://

theoryofchange.libsyn.com/a-breath-of-fresh-air-the-ecological-self-and-environmental-justice

Shook, M. (Producer). (2018, September 5). The Internationalization of the Counseling Profession: Boundary Issues and Eurocentrism with Barbara Herlihy [Audio podcast]. *The Thoughtful Counselor*. Retrieved from https://wp.me/p7R6fn-rA.

Shook, M. (Producer). (2018, April 10). The Tech-Savvy Counselor: A Conversation with TherapyTech's Rob Reinhardt and Roy Huggins [Audio podcast]. *The Thoughtful Counselor*. Retrieved from https://wp.me/p7R6fn-nR.

REFERENCES

About us: Welcome to IAC. (2019). International Association for Counselling. Retrieved from https://www.iac-irtac.org/?q=node/14

Adams, J., & Maynard, P. (2000). Evaluating training needs for home-based family therapy: A focus group approach. *The American Journal of Family Therapy, 28*, 41–52.

Adler, A. (1938). *Social interest: A challenge to mankind*. London: Faber & Faber.

American Psychiatric Association. (2013). *Diagnostic and statistical manual of mental disorders* (5th ed.). Arlington, VA: Author.

Bains, R. M., Cusson, R., White-Frese, J., & Walsh, S. (2017). Utilization of mental health services in school-based health centers. *Journal of School Health, 87*, 584–592.

Baker, L. (2019). Therapy in the digital age. In J. Stone (Ed.), *Integrating technology in psychotherapy: A clinician's guide to developments and interventions* (pp. 37-47). New York: Routledge/Taylor and Francis.

Bakker, D., Kazantzis, N., Rickwood, D., & Rickard, N. (2019). A randomized controlled trial of three smartphone apps for enhancing public mental health. *Behaviour Research and Therapy, 109*, 75–83.

Bakker, D., Kazantzis, N., Rickwood, D., & Rickard, N. (2016). Mental health smartphone apps: Review and evidence-based recommendations for future developments. *JMIR Mental Health, 3*(1). doi:10.2196/mental.4984

Botella, C., Serrano, B., Banos, R. M., & Garcia-Palacios, A. (2015). Virtual reality exposure-based therapy for the treatment of post-traumatic stress disorder: A review of its efficacy, the adequacy of the treatment protocol, and its acceptability. *Neuropsychiatric Disease and Treatment, 11*, 2533+.

Bray, B. (2019, January). Workforce projections show a coming surplus of school counselors, shortage of addictions counselors. *Counseling Today*. Retrieved from: https://ct.counseling.org/2019/01/workforce-projections-show-a-coming-surplus-of-school-counselors-shortage-of-addictions-counselors/

Brown, M. B. (2006). School-based health centers: Implications for counselors. *Journal of Counseling and Development: JCD, 84*(2), 187-191.

Bucci, S., Schwannauer, M., & Berry, N. (2019). The digital revolution and its impact on mental health care. *Psychology and Psychotherapy: Theory, Research and Practice, 92*(2), 277-297. doi:10.1111/papt.12222

Campbell, L. F., Millan, F. A., & Martin, J. N. (2017). *A telepsychology casebook: Using technology ethically and effectively in your professional practice*. Washington, DC: American Psychological Association.

Center for Disease Control (n.d.). Anxiety and depression in children. Retrieved from: https://www.cdc.gov/childrensmentalhealth/depression.html

Cortes, L. (2004). Home-based family therapy: Misunderstanding of the role and a new challenge for therapists. *The Family Journal, Counseling and Therapy for Couples and Families, 12,* 184–188.

Dogan, V. (2019). Why do people experience the fear of missing out (FoMO)? Exposing the link between the self and the FoMO through self-construal. *Journal of Cross-Cultural Psychology, 50*(4), 524–538.

Ghandour, R. M., Sherman, L. J., Vladutiu, C. J., Ali, M. M., Lynch, S. E., Bitsko, R. H., & Blumberg, S. J. (2018). Prevalence and treatment of depression, anxiety, and conduct problems in U.S. children. *The Journal of Pediatrics, 206,* 256-267.

Goodyear-Brown, P., & Gott, E. (2019). Tech, trauma work, and the power of titration. In J. Stone (Ed.), *Integrating Technology in Psychotherapy: A Clinician's Guide to Developments and Interventions* (pp. 124-136). New York: Routledge/Taylor and Francis.

Grant, R. J. (2019). Utilizing technology interventions with children and adolescents with autism spectrum disorder (ASD). In J. Stone (Ed.), *Integrating technology in psychotherapy: A clinician's guide to developments and interventions* (pp. 124-136). New York: Routledge/Taylor and Francis.

Hamilton, S., Moore, A. M., Crane, D. R., & Payne, S. H. (2011). Psychotherapy dropouts: Differences by modality, license, and dsm-iv diagnosis. *Journal of Marital and Family Therapy, 37*(3), 333-43.

Hammond, C., & Czyszczon, G. (2014). Home-based family counseling: An emerging field in Need of professionalization. *The Family Journal, 22*(1), 56-61.

Harvard Medical School Mental Health Letter (July 2011). How addiction hijacks the brain. Retrieved from https://www.health.harvard.edu/newsletter_article/how-addiction-hijacks-the-brain

Hayslip, B., Jr, Maiden, R., Page, K., & Dolbin-MacNab, M. (2015). Grandparenting. In P. Lichtenberg, B. Mast, B. Carpenter, & J. Wetherell (Eds.), *APA handbook of clinical geropsychology* (pp. 497–512). Washington, DC: American Psychological Association.

Hilty D. M., Yellowlees P. M., Myers K., Parish M. B., & Rabinowitz T. (2016). *The effectiveness of e-mental health: Evidence base, how to choose the model based on ease/cost/strength, and future areas of research.* In D. Mucic & D. Hilty (Eds.), e-Mental Health, Springer.

Hull, K. (2019). Replacing hesitancy and doubt with competence and skill: The technologically minded therapist. In J. Stone (Ed.), *Integrating technology in psychotherapy: A clinician's guide to developments and interventions* (pp. 24-36). New York: Routledge/Taylor and Francis.

Hull, K. (2009). Computer/video games as a play therapy tool in reducing emotional disturbances in children. Dissertation Abstracts International: Section B: *The Sciences and Engineering, 70*(12-B), 2010, 7854.

Hull, K. (2015). Technology in the playroom. In K. J. O'Conner, C. Schaefer & L. D. Braverman (Eds.), *Handbook of play therapy* (2nd Ed.) (pp. 613-627). New Jersey: John Wiley and Sons.

Hymmen, P., Stalker, C. A., & Cait, C. (2013) The case for single-session therapy: Does the empirical evidence support the increased prevalence of this service delivery model? *Journal of Mental Health, 22,* 60-71.

Kaplan, D. M., & Gladding, S. T. (2011). A vision for the future of counseling: The 20/20 principles for unifying and strengthening the profession. *Journal of Counseling & Development, 89,* 367–372.

Kaplan, D. & Martz, E. (2014). Distance counseling, technology and social media. *Counseling Today, 57*(3), 22-24.

LaFleur, L. B., Hebert, Z. J., & Dupuy, A. S. (2018). Leveling up your game: The use of video games as a therapeutic modality, *Journal of Creativity in Mental Health, 13*(1), 58-67.

Lemola, S., Perkinson-GLoor, N., Brand, S., Dewald-Kaufmann, J. F., & Grob, A. (2015). Adolescents' electronic media use at night, sleep disturbance, and depressive symptoms in the smartphone age. *Journal of Youth and Adolescence, 44,* 405-418.

Liu, W. M., & Estrada-Hernandez, N. (2010). Counseling and advocacy for individuals living in poverty. In M. Ratts, R. Toporek & J. Lewis (Eds.), *ACA advocacy competencies: A social justice framework for counselors* (pp. 43–53). Alexandria, VA: American Counseling Association

Lorelle, S., Byrd, R., & Crockett, S. (2012). Globalization and counseling: Professional issues for counselors. *The Professional Counselor, 2*(2), p. 115-123.

Mascari, J. B., & Webber, J. (2013). CACREP accreditation: A solution to license portability and counselor identity problems. *Journal of Counseling & Development, 91*, 15–25.

Miclea, M., Miclea, S., Ciuca, A., & Badua, O. (2010). Computer-mediated psychotherapy: Present and prospects. A developer perspective. *Cognition, Brain, Behavior: An Interdisciplinary Journal, 14*(3), 185-208.

Mihailidis, P. & Viotty, S. (2017). Spreadable spectacle in digital culture: Civic expression, fake news, and the role of media literacies in "post-fact" society. *American Behavioral Scientist, 6*, 441-454.

Miller, H. (2016, April 28). Tennessee Governor signs mean-spirited "Counseling Discrimination Bill" into law. Human Rights Campaign. Retrieved from https://www.hrc.org/blog/tennessee-governor-signs-mean-spirited-counseling-discrimination-bill-int

Hamilton, S., Moore, A.M., Crane, D. R., & Payne, S.H. (2011). Psychotherapy dropouts: Differences by modality license, and DSM-IV diagnosis. *Journal of Marital and Family Therapy, 37*, 333-343.

Nash, J. (2019). Videoconferencing in psychotherapy: Removing barriers to mental health care for vulnerable and underserved populations. In J. Stone (Ed.), *Integrating technology in psychotherapy: A clinician's guide to developments and interventions* (pp. 210-222). New York: Routledge/Taylor and Francis.

National Board for Certified Counselors (NBCC) policy regarding the provision of distance professional services. (2016). National Board of Certified Counselors. Retrieved from https://www.nbcc.org/Assets/Ethics/NBCCPolicyRegardingPracticeofDistanceCounselingBoard.pdf

Olsen, S., Brown-Rice, K., & Gerodias, A. (2018). Professional counselor licensure portability: An examination of state license applications. *The Professional Counselor, 8*(1),88-103.

American Counseling Association. (2019). Our vision and mission: ACA's strategic plan. Retrieved from https://www.counseling.org/about-us/about-aca/our-mission

Paul, K. E. & van Ommeran, M. (2013). A primer on single session therapy and its potential application in humanitarian situations. *Intervention, 11*, 8-23.

Shallcross, L. (2012, March). What the future holds for the counseling profession. *Counseling Today.* Retrieved from https://ct.counseling.org/2012/03/what-the-future-holds-for-the-counseling-profession/

Sherman, L. E., Payton, A. A., Hernandez, L. M., Greenfield, P. M., & Dapretto, M. (2016). The power of the like in adolescence: Effects of peer influence on neural and behavioral responses to social media. *Psychological Science, 27*(7), 1027-1035.

Stone, J. (2016). The virtual sandtray app®. Retrieved from https://www.sandtrayplay.com/Press/Virtual-SandtrayArticle01.pdf.

United States Census Bureau (October 22, 2014). 10 Percent of grandparents live with a grandchild, *Census Bureau Reports.* Retrieved from https://www.census.gov/newsroom/press-releases/2014/cb14-194.html

Vygotsky, L. S. (1978). *Mind in society: The development of higher psychological processes.* Cambridge, MA: Harvard University Press.

Watters, E. (2011). *Crazy like us: The globalization of the american psyche.* New York, NY: Simon and Schuster.

Woodford, M. S., Bordeau, W. C., & Alderfer, C. (2006). Home-based service delivery: Introducing family counselors in training to the home as a therapeutic milieu. *The Family Journal: Counseling and Therapy for Couples and Families, 14*, 240–244.

Young, J., & Dryden, W. (2019). Single-session therapy – past and future: An interview. *British Journal of Guidance & Counselling*, 1-10

Young, J., Weir, S., & Rycroft, P. (2012). Implementing single session therapy. *Australian and New Zealand Journal of Family Therapy, 33*, 84-97.

Young, J. (2018). Single session therapy: The gift that keeps on giving. In M. F. Hoyt, M. Bobele, A. Slive, J.Young, & M. Talmon (Eds.), *Single-session therapy by walk-in or appointment: Clinical, supervisory, and administrative aspects* (pp. 40–58). New York: Routledge.

INDEX

C

May, Rollo, 33, 413, 415
Mayer Salovey Caruso Emotional Intelligence Test
    (MSCEIT), 521
McAuliffe, G., 568
McGuire, S. Y., 509
McHugh, R. K., 514
McMinn, Mark R., 173
McRay, B., 478
Mean, 472–473
Median, 472–473
Medication toxicity, 586
Meichenbaum, Donald, 31, 424
Memories, Dreams, Reflections (1961), 407
Mental health apps, 613–614
Mental health field, 49–53
Metacognition, 509
Microaggressions, 217–220
        microassaults, 217
        microinsults, 217
        microinvalidations, 217
Microassaults, 217
Microinsults, 217
Microinvalidations, 217
Microskills hierarchy, 353
Military and Government Counseling Association
    (MGCA), 65
Miller, J. E., 98
Miller, R., 568
Miller, Scott, 486
Miller, W. R., 128
Millon Clinical Multiaxial Inventory (MCMI), 451
Mindfulness-based cognitive therapy (MBCT), 424
Minnesota Multiphasic Personality Inventory
    (MMPI), 450, 466
Minority counseling, 35
Minuchin, Salvador, 429
Mishra, P., 509
Mixed methods, 537
Mode, 472–473
1994 Model Legislation, 284
Moore, A.M., 600
Moore, D., 537
Moorhead, H. J. H., 242
Morton, Maria, 55–57
Mosher, D. K., 212
Motivational interviewing, 127

Motor neurons, 554, 558
Multicultural and Social Justice Counselor
        Competencies (MSJCC), 196
    client worldview, 196
    counseling relationship, 196
    counselor advocacy and intervention, 196
    counselor self-awareness, 196
Multi-cultural considerations, 335
Multicultural wave (4th wave), 28, 34–35
Multiculturally competent, 208
Multiple relationships in Christian community,
    164–165
Murdock, N. L., 402, 433
Myers, Jane, 284
Myers Briggs Type Indicator (MBTI), 78, 409, 466

N

Nadal, K. L., 217
Narramore, Bruce, 14
Narrative therapy (NT), 428, 432–433
    alternate story, 433
    assumptions, 433
    criticisms, 434–435
        hyper-individualism, 434
        problem-saturated descriptions, 434
    dominant story, 433
    key concepts, 433
    looking through Christianity, 434–436
    preferred story, 433
    problem-saturated story, 433
    stories, 433
    therapeutic relationship and goals, 433–434
National Alliance on Mental Illness (NAMI), 107
National Assessment of Educational Progress, 451
National Association for Alcoholism and Drug
        Abuse Counselors (NAADAC), 70
National Association of Guidance and Counselor
        Trainers (NAGCT), 59
National Association of Social Workers (NASW), 233
National Association of Student Personnel
        Administrators (NASPA), 111
National Board for Certified Counselors (NBCC),
    15, 78, 88
National Career Development Association (NCDA),
    65

National Certified Counselors (NCC), 78
National Certified School Counselors (NCSC), 78
National Clinical Mental Health Counseling
    Examination (NCMHCE), 15, 75
National Counselor Examination (NCE), 15, 75
National Defense Education Act, 451
National Employment Counseling Association
    (NECA), 66
National Vocational Guidance Association (NVGA),
    59
Neborsky, R. J., 369
Nedley, Neil, 103
Nelson, K., 407
Nervous System, 553, 557–562
    autonomic nervous system (ANS), 560
    autonomic or visceral nervous system, 558
    central nervous system (CNS), 557
    divisions, 557–562
    dorsal root Ganglion (DRG), 558
    enteric nervous system (ENS), 562
    interneurons, 559
    motor or efferent neurons, 558
    peripheral nervous system (PNS), 557
    sensory or afferent neurons, 558
    somatic nervous system (SNS), 559
    somatic nervous system, 558
    spinal cord, 557
    visceral nervous system, 560
Neurogenesis, 553, 568
Neuro-informed counseling, 568–579
    neurogenesis, 568
    neuroplasticity, 568
    neurosequential model of therapeutics, 573–576
    polyvagal theory, 569
    synaptogenesis, 568
Neurons, 553–556. *See also* Neurotransmitters
    axon, 554
    dendrites, 554
    interneurons, 554
    motor neurons, 554
    sensory neurons, 554
    soma, 554
Neuroplasticity, 568
Neuroscience wave (6th wave), 36–39
Neuroticism-Extroversion-Openness Personality
    Inventory-Revised (NEO-PI-R), 467

Neurotransmitters, 555
    acetylcholine, 555
    adrenaline, 555
    dopamine, 555
    endorphins, 556
    GABA, 555
    glutamate, 555
    noradrenaline, 556
    serotonin, 556
Nietzche, Friedrich, 413
No Child Left Behind Act of 2001, 452
Non-governmental organizations (NGOs), 118
Nonmaleficence, 160, 235
Nonverbal encouragers, 388
Noradrenaline, 556
Norms, 473

O

Objective personality, 466–468
Occipital lobe, 565
Occupational Information Network Interest Profiler
    (O*NET), 465
Occupational wellness, 292
    practices, 301–302
Offender counseling, 123
O'Hanlon, B., 431
Oliver, M., 252
Olson, R. P, 420
Operant conditioning, 421, 422
Organization of Behavior, The, 568
Organization, 429
Organizational administration, 134
Organizations, counseling, 57–73. *See also individual*
    associations
    getting involved in, 71–73
Ostrowski, J., 109
Otto, M. W., 514
Out of the Shadows: Understanding Sexual Addiction,
    124
Outcome Rating Scale (ORS), 486
Over-the-counter (OTC) medications, 586